T0271081

Regression Analysis

This thoroughly practical and engaging textbook is designed to equip students with the skills needed to undertake sound regression analysis without requiring high-level math.

Regression Analysis covers the concepts needed to design optimal regression models and to properly interpret regressions. It details the most common pitfalls, including three sources of bias not covered in other textbooks. Rather than focusing on equations and proofs, the book develops an understanding of these biases visually and with examples of situations in which such biases could arise. In addition, it describes how 'holding other factors constant' actually works and when it does not work. This second edition features a new chapter on integrity and ethics, and has been updated throughout to include more international examples. Each chapter offers examples, exercises, and clear summaries, all of which are designed to support student learning to help towards producing responsible research.

This is the textbook the author wishes he had learned from, as it would have helped him avoid many research mistakes he made in his career. It is ideal for anyone learning quantitative methods in the social sciences, business, medicine, and data analytics. It will also appeal to researchers and academics looking to better understand regressions. Additional digital supplements are available at: www. youtube.com/channel/UCenm3BWqQyXA2JRKB_QXGyw.

Jeremy Arkes is a retired economics professor from the Graduate School of Business and Public Policy, Naval Postgraduate School, U.S.A. He is currently writing books on economics, nature, and basketball.

Regression Analysis

A Practical Introduction

SECOND EDITION

Jeremy Arkes

LONDON AND NEW YORK

Designed cover image: michal-rojek / Getty Images

Second edition published 2023
by Routledge
4 Park Square, Milton Park, Abingdon, Oxon, OX14 4RN

and by Routledge
605 Third Avenue, New York, NY 10158

Routledge is an imprint of the Taylor & Francis Group, an informa business

First edition published by Routledge 2019

British Library Cataloguing-in-Publication Data
A catalogue record for this book is available from the British Library

Library of Congress Cataloging-in-Publication Data
Names: Arkes, Jeremy, author.
Title: Regression analysis: a practical introduction / Jeremy Arkes.
Description: Second edition. | Milton Park, Abingdon, Oxon; New York, NY:
Routledge, [2023] | "First edition published 2019"—Title page verso. | Includes
bibliographical references and index.
Identifiers: LCCN 2022035701 | ISBN 9781032257846 (hardback) |
ISBN 9781032257839 (paperback) | ISBN 9781003285007 (ebook)
Subjects: LCSH: Regression analysis.
Classification: LCC HA31.3 .A43 2023 | DDC 519.5/36—dc23/eng/20220812
LC record available at https://lccn.loc.gov/2022035701

ISBN: 978-1-032-25784-6 (hbk)
ISBN: 978-1-032-25783-9 (pbk)
ISBN: 978-1-003-28500-7 (ebk)

DOI: 10.4324/9781003285007

Typeset in Bembo
by codeMantra

Access the Support Material: www.routledge.com/9781032257839

To my mother, Judy Arkes (1941–2014). She was always a voice of love, support, and reason.

Contents

Figures

Tables

Author

Jeremy Arkes grew up in Amherst, MA, amidst of the fields of Amherst College. He left this bucolic setting to attend Georgetown University for his undergraduate studies and University of Wisconsin for his Ph.D. in Economics. He spent his first ten years after graduate school working for think tanks: The Center for Naval Analyses (Alexandria, VA) and RAND Corporation (Santa Monica, CA). His main focus was on military-manpower research, but he sprouted out to other fields, such as the areas of substance use and divorce effects on children. From 2007 to 2021, he was an economics professor at the Graduate School of Business and Public Policy at the Naval Postgraduate School in Monterey, California. At NPS, besides continuing to conduct research in military manpower, he added a line of research that uses sports outcomes to make inferences on human behavior.

Dr. Arkes is now retired and writing books on nature, economics, basketball, and politics. He is the author of:

- *Confessions of a Recovering Economist: How Economists Get Most Things Wrong* (2022). This book highlights the mistakes that economists make and how widespread the mistakes are. Most importantly, the book provides a series of recommendations on how improve the field of economics, including his views on how undergraduate and graduate economics curricula should be redesigned.
- *Exploring the Monterey Peninsula and Big Sur: A Nature and Hiking Guide* (2021), which is more than a nature/hiking guide, as it is also a story on the harmony of nature, how that harmony could be disrupted, and connections to human nature.
- *How to Improve the NBA: Sensible and Wacky Ideas to Fix Problems and Add Excitement* (2022).
- *A Year in Nature … A Nation in Chaos* (2022). This has a series of descriptions of and essays on a year in nature in the Monterey (California) area, on the chaotic events in the world and particularly the U.S., and reflections on the connections between nature and the chaos we've experienced.

His websites are:

- www.jeremyarkes.com
- www.montereynature.com
- https://jeremyarkes.medium.com/
- YouTube channel: Just search "Jeremy Arkes".

Preface

I've played a lot of basketball in my life. I was mediocre in high school, being the 6th man (first guy off the bench) on my high-school team. At 5'9", I played all positions other than point guard (even center briefly, as I knew how to box out) ... I could defend, jump, and rebound, but I couldn't dribble or shoot well.

Although I never developed a consistent outside shot until my 30s (and 3-point range in my mid-40s), it was at college (Georgetown University) where I learned to dribble, drive to the basket, and shoot mid-range jumpers – don't mind saying this helped me win a few 1-on-1 and 3-on-3 tournaments. It was in the Georgetown gym where I started to have experiences with the "hot hand," especially on those humid 95-degree summer days. The hot hand is a period of playing at a systematically higher level than what you normally play at, often called "being in the zone" or "*en fuego*." Those of you who play sports may have experienced it in whatever sport you play. My wife says she has experienced it in her dancing career. For me, some days, I just had a better feel for the ball, and I was more likely to make any type of shot I tried.

And it is in one of those hot-hand events for myself that I briefly got the better of 7'2", future NBA-Hall-of-Famer, Dikembe Mutombo. (If you ever meet me and ask, I'll gladly tell you the story.)

So you can imagine my surprise when I read that a bunch of famous economists, statisticians, and psychologists (including some Nobel Prize winners), were arguing, based on several studies that failed to find any evidence for the hot hand, that the hot hand is a figment of our imaginations. Many of them stated things along the lines of "The hot hand in basketball is a myth."

How could they conclude this? I had to investigate it on my own, applying some methods to try to increase the "power" of the test. Sure enough, in 2010, I found some evidence for the existence of the hot hand and published it. But the real breakthroughs came in the next several years, with research by my friends Dan Stone (from Bowdoin College), Josh Miller (University of Melbourne), and Adam Sanjurjo (Universidad de Alicante). They found biases in the original studies (and mine) that would work against being able to detect the hot hand. Josh and Adam's most notable bias is from the Gambler's Fallacy (which I'll discuss briefly in Chapter 6). The bias Dan found (from measurement error) was more intuitive, as measurement error should be on any checklist for potential biases in a study. But no one (including myself) had recognized it.

How could those famous researchers and Nobel Prize winners have made such huge errors? It wasn't just that they missed these sources of bias, but they also used fallacious logic in their interpretations: the lack of evidence for the hot hand was not proof that it did not exist. (I'll discuss this more in Chapter 5).

This was a watershed moment for me that so many established researchers bought into this argument without critically assessing it. While I give myself a pass for missing the large bias that Josh and Adam found, I was guilty of not recognizing the measurement-error bias that Dan had found.

And so this story arc on the hot hand confirmed a pattern I was seeing on other research topics, and it hit me: Yeah, most economists know the lingo and the formulas for why things could go wrong in regression analysis, but many aren't trained well in recognizing these when they occur, and many do not understand the proper way to interpret the results of regressions. I thought that there must be a better way to teach regression analysis.

It was at this point that I realized that I had a story to tell. I have come to understand many concepts of regression analysis that elude many researchers. These concepts came to me, not from my classes, but from my practical experience of estimating thousands of regressions ... and from the many mistakes I have made in my research. The lessons I learned from poring over results helped me connect the dots between several of the essential concepts.

And so, from these experiences with various pitfalls of regression analysis, from mistakes I have made, from what helped me connect the dots between concepts, I have created a story on how to better understand, conduct, and scrutinize regression analysis. I wrote the book that I would have wanted, in my undergraduate or graduate studies, to help me learn regression analysis in an efficient and practical manner and to help me avoid the many research mistakes I made.

Acknowledgments

I would like to thank several of my colleagues/friends. Robert Eger was instrumental to me for his guidance on the process, and his encouragement to take a shot. For technical details, I benefited greatly from discussions with William A. Muir (U.S. Air Force and formerly of the Naval Postgraduate School), John Pepper (University of Virginia), and my hot-hand-in-basketball colleagues, Joshua Miller (Universidad Alicante), Adam Sanjurjo (Universidad Alicante, and also my surf instructor), and Daniel Stone (Bowdoin College). For telling me when some of my attempts at humor worked and when they didn't, I am grateful to my friends at work: Ronda Spelbring, Houda Tarabishi, and Holly Shrewbridge. I also benefited from discussions with several students during my career. I apologize to anyone I have left out, but these students include Jesse Hernandez-Rodriguez, Kevan Mellendick, and Cesar Serna (all from the U.S. Navy), and Vivienne Clark (from the Royal Australian Air Force). Finally, I am grateful for the beautiful hiking trails of the Monterey Peninsula and Big Sur, all of which gave me time to allow some concepts to marinate in my mind so I could sift through them to find the important points.

Abbreviations

2SLS	Two-stage Least Squares
ACF	Autocorrelation function
AFA	Air Force Academy
AFQT	Armed Forces Qualification Test
AIC	Akaike Information Criterion
AICc	Akaike Information Criterion (corrected)
AR	Autoregressive (model)
ARIMA	Autoregressive integrated moving average
ARMA	Autoregressive moving average
ATE	Average Treatment Effect
ATT	Average Treatment effect for the Treated
BIC	Bayesian Information Criterion
BPI	Behavioral Problems Index
CDF	Cumulative distribution function
CEO	Chief Executive Officer
CPS	Current Population Survey
CS	class size
DD	difference-in-difference (model)
d.f.	degrees of freedom
EITC	Earned Income Tax Credit
ExSS	Explained Sum of Squares
FD	first-difference (model)
FTE	full-time-equivalent (worker)
GDP	Gross Domestic Product
GED	General Equivalency Diploma
GPA	Grade point average
HS	High School
IAT	Implicit Association Test
i.i.d.	identically distributed
IQ	Intelligence Quotient
IV	instrumental variable

LATE   Local Average Treatment Effect
LPM   linear probability model
MAPE   mean absolute percent error
MJ   marijuana
MNL   Multinomial Logit (Model)
MSE   Mean Square Error
NBA   National Basketball Association
NCAA   National Collegiate Athletic Association
NFL   National Football League
NIH   National Institute of Health
NLSY   National Longitudinal Survey of Youth
NRA   National Rifle Association
NSDUH   National Survey on Drug Use and Health
OLS   Ordinary Least Squares
PACF   partial autocorrelation function
PDF   probability density function
PI/C   personal income per capita
PTSD   post-traumatic stress disorder
RCT   randomized-control trial
RD   regression discontinuity
RMSE   Root Mean Square Error
RMSFE   root mean square forecast error
RP   relative performance
RR   RESTRICTED regression
RSS   Residual Sum of Squares
SAT   Scholastic Aptitude Test
SE   Standard Error
SETI   Search for Extraterrestrial Intelligence
SUR   Seemingly Unrelated Regression
TS   test score
TSS   Total Sum of Squares
UR   unrestricted regression or unemployment rate
VAR   Vector Autoregression
var ()   Variance

1 Introduction

I'm on a mission, and I need your help. My mission is to make this a better world.

I want society to make better choices and decisions. Sometimes, these decisions should be based on what is morally and ethically the right thing to do. I cannot help much on that front. At other times, decisions need to be based on how they affect people and organizations. In that realm, sometimes statistical analysis can speak to best practices. Statistical analysis sometimes can tell us what health practices and interventions are most beneficial to people, what factors lead to better economic outcomes for people (individually or collectively), what factors contribute to the academic achievement of children, how to make government functions more cost-efficient (which could reduce the tax burden on society), and much more.

All that said, sometimes statistical analysis is unable to speak on many of these issues. This may be because the data are not adequate in terms of having sufficient information and a large enough sample. Or it could be because the statistical analysis was flawed. So we need to be careful in how we interpret and use the results from statistical analyses so that we draw the correct and prudent conclusions, without overreaching or being affected by our pre-conceived notions and hopes for what the analysis would tell us.

My goal with this book is not to answer the important questions on how to make the world better. In fact, I will address some research issues that some of you will care nothing about, such as whether

DOI: 10.4324/9781003285007-1

discrimination is a self-fulfilling prophecy in France and whether the hot hand in basketball is real or just a figment of our imaginations. Despite not being of much world interest, these research issues that I use will serve as useful applications to learn the concepts and tools of regression analysis.

My goal is to teach you the tools needed to address important issues. This book is designed to teach you how to responsibly conduct, scrutinize, and interpret statistical analyses. From this, I hope you will help others make better decisions that will help towards making this world, eventually, a better place.

1.1 The problem

Jay Leno, in one of his *Tonight Show* monologues several years ago, mentioned a study that found that 50% of all academic research is wrong. His punchline: there's a 50% chance this study itself is wrong.

The study Leno referred to may actually *understate* the true percentage of studies that are inaccurate. The major causes of all these errors in research are likely faulty research designs and improper interpretations of the results. These accuracy issues bring into doubt the value of academic research.

Most quantitative academic research, particularly in the social sciences, business, and medicine, rely on regression analyses. The primary objective of regressions is to quantify cause-effect relationships. These cause-effect relationships are part of the knowledge that should guide society to develop good public policies and good strategies for conducting business, educating people, promoting health and general welfare, and more. Such cause-effect issues might include:

- How does some new cancer drug affect the probability of a patient surviving ten years after diagnosis?
- How do parental divorces affect children's test scores?
- What factors make teachers more effective?
- What encourages people to save more for retirement?
- What factors contribute to political extremism and violence?
- How does parental cell phone use affect children's safety?
- How does oatmeal consumption affect bad cholesterol levels?
- Do vaccines affect the probability of a child becoming autistic?
- How much does one more year of schooling increase a person's earnings?
- Does smiling when dropping my shirt off at the cleaners affect the probability that my shirt will be ready by Thursday?

Regressions are useful for estimating such relationships because they are able to adjust for other factors that may confound the cause-effect relationship in question. That is, with adequate data and the right circumstances, regressions can rule out reasons for two variables to be related, other than the causal-effect reason.

A natural human reaction is to be mesmerized by things people do not understand, such as how regressions can produce these numbers. And so, in the roughly ten times that I have used regression results in briefings to somewhat-high-level officials at the Department of Defense (mostly as a junior researcher, with a senior researcher tagging along to make sure I didn't say anything dumb), the people I was briefing never asked me whether there were any empirical issues with the regression analysis I had used or how confident I was with the findings. Most of the time, based on the leading official's response to the research, they would act as if I had just given them the absolute truth on an important problem based on these "magic boxes" called "regressions." Unfortunately, I was caught up in the excitement of the positive response from these officials, and I wasn't as forthright as I should have been about the potential pitfalls (and uncertainty) in my findings. I usually let them believe the magic.

But regressions are not magic boxes. The inaccuracy Leno joked about is real, as there are many pitfalls of regression analysis. From what I have seen in research, at conferences, from journal referees, etc., many researchers (most of whom have Ph.D.s) have a limited understanding of these issues. The result is that published quantitative research is often rife with severely biased estimates and erroneous interpretations and conclusions.

How bad is it? In the medical-research field, where incorrect research has the potential to result in lost lives, John Ioannidis has called out the entire field on its poor research methods and records. The Greek doctor/medical researcher was featured in a 2010 article in *The Atlantic* (Freedman 2010). Ioannidis and his team of researchers have demonstrated that a large portion of the existing medical research is wrong, misleading, or highly exaggerated. He attributes it to several parts of the research process: bias in the way that research questions were being posed, how studies and empirical models were set up (e.g., establishing the proper control group), what patients were recruited for the studies, how results were presented and portrayed, and how journals chose what to publish.

Along these lines, the magazine *The Economist* had a much-needed op-ed and accompanying article in 2013 on how inaccurate research has become (The Economist, 2013). Among the highlights they note are:

- Amgen, a biotech company, could replicate only 6 of 53 "landmark" cancer-research studies
- Bayer, a pharmaceutical company was able to replicate just one-quarter of 67 important health studies
- Studies with "negative results," meaning insignificant estimated effects of the treatment variables, constituted 30% of all studies in 1990 and just 14% today, suggesting that important results showing no evidence that a treatment has an effect are being suppressed – and/or extra efforts are being made to make results statistically significant.

All of this highlights an interesting irony. The potential for valuable research has perhaps never been greater, with more data available on many important outcomes (such as student test scores, human DNA, health, logistics, consumer behavior, and ball and player movements in sports), yet the reputation of academic research has perhaps never been so low.

This is fixable!

This book is meant to effectively train the next generation of quantitative researchers.

1.2 The purpose of research

To understand where research goes wrong, we first have to understand the overall purpose of research. We conduct research to improve knowledge, which often involves trying to get us closer to understanding cause-effect and other empirical relationships. To demonstrate, let's start with the highly contentious issue of global warming. You may have some probability that the following statement is true:

Human activity is contributing to global warming.

Hopefully, that probability of yours lies somewhere between 0.3% and 99.7% – that is, you may have your beliefs, but you recognize that you probably are not an expert on the topic and so there is a possibility that you are wrong. I'm guessing that most people would be below 10% or above 90% (or, even 5% and 95%). But, for the sake of the argument, let's say that you have a subjective probability of the statement being true 45% of the time.

Suppose a study comes out that has new evidence that humans are causing global warming. This may shift your probability upwards. If the new research were reported on the cable news channel MSNBC (which leans toward the liberal side of politics) and you tended to watch MSNBC, then let's say that it would shift your probability up by 7 percentage points (to 52%). If you tended to watch Fox News (a more conservative channel) instead, then the news from MSNBC may shift your probability up by some negligible amount, say 0.2 percentage points (up to 45.2%). Ideally, the amount that your subjective probability of the statement above would shift upwards would depend on:

- How the study contrasts with prior research on the issue
- The validity and extensiveness of the prior research
- The extent to which any viable alternative explanations to the current findings can be ruled out – i.e., how valid the methods of the study are.

With regression analysis, it should be the same thinking of shifting beliefs. People have some prior beliefs about some issue, say in whether the class size is important for student achievement. Suppose that using regression analysis, a new study finds no evidence that class size has an effect on student achievement. This finding should not necessarily be taken as concrete evidence for that side of the issue. Rather, the evidence has to be judged based on the strength of the study relative to the strength of other studies, or the three criteria listed above. People would then shift their subjective probability appropriately. The more convincing the analysis, the more it should swing a person's belief in the direction of the study's conclusions.

This is where it is up to researchers, the media, and the public to properly scrutinize research to assess how convincing it is. As I will describe below, you cannot always rely on the peer-review process that determines what research gets published in journals.

1.3 What causes problems in the research process?

> The only real fiction is non-fiction.
>
> –Mark Totten

Where do I begin? Well, let's discuss some structural issues first, which lead to misguided incentives for researchers.

One major problem in research is **publication bias** (discussed in more detail in Section 13.2), which results from the combination of the pressure among academics to publish and journals seeking articles with interesting results that will sell to readers, get publicity, and get more citations from subsequent research. All of this improves the standing of the journal. But it leads to published research being biased towards results with statistically-significant estimated effects – so studies finding statistically-insignificant effects tend not to be disseminated. Given the greater likelihood of getting published with significant and interesting results, researchers at times will not spend time attempting to publish research that has insignificant results.

In addition, research can be easily finagled. Researchers could add or remove a few semi-consequential variables, re-characterize variables, try different outcomes, and change the sample requirements (or add observations). If they try enough variants, they will likely be able to arrive at a coefficient estimate on a key treatment variable that exceeds the threshold of "significance," which could make the difference between research being publishable or non-publishable or determine whether the research would be publishable in a high-quality journal. The common uncertainty over the optimal model, unfortunately, gives license to researchers to choose the model that has the set of results that are most publishable. Research has no value if its goal is finding significance.

Structural problems in research also result from the influence of sponsors of research. Who are the sponsors of research? Most sponsored research is in the form of contracts and grants from various federal government agencies. Contracts involve a specific research issue that the sponsor would like to be investigated for its purpose; grants are given to investigate specific issues for the general public. Whereas the National Institute of Health (NIH) gives out billions of dollars in grants each year, most other government agencies mostly give contracts. NIH is generally an ideal sponsor of research in that a researcher obtains the funds and is often left alone to do the research and publish what they please from the research, regardless of the results. Still, similar to publication bias, there may be an incentive for the researcher to find something interesting, which would help towards receiving the next round of funding. For contracts, the incentive of researchers is to please the client in order to receive future contracts. Unfortunately, this can lead to conscious and subconscious manipulation of results.

More concerning is research for corporations or foundations with an agenda. Economists are wrong on many things – see Arkes (2022) – but they are correct in their belief that corporations' primary goal is almost always to maximize profits. As a result, pressure for those profits may lead to unethical behavior in research. You probably do not want to trust research that is sponsored by an entity with a financial stake in the results.

This is largely the basis behind the concerns of Dr. Marcia Angell, a long-time Editor (and interim Editor-in-Chief) of the *New England Journal of Medicine*. She wrote an article that all lawmakers and parents should be required to read (Angell 2009). In this article, Dr. Angell states that she does not believe most published clinical research and that she no longer has much faith in the judgment of doctors and medical officials.

The basis of Dr. Angell's realizations is the lack of transparency involved with much medical research, particularly for pharmaceutical drugs. According to Dr. Angell, pharmaceutical companies pay influential academics large amounts of money and/or insert a representative into their sponsored research, usually at medical schools and hospitals. That representative (or the influenced academic) would then have power over the direction of the study and whether the final results can be published – meaning that results showing ineffectiveness or harmfulness of the drug are sometimes suppressed from the public domain.

This is fraud! It can kill people.

Beyond any fraud, pressure for interesting results, and publication bias, perhaps the primary underlying cause of poor research is a fundamental lack of understanding of statistical analysis, particularly regression analysis. Researchers often do not understand how to develop the best model to address a research question, the many things that could go wrong with a model, and the proper interpretation of results. Even research in top academic journals is sometimes based on misguided regression analyses and interpretations. There are certain topics for which almost every article on that topic has poorly executed regression analyses or interpretations … I will get into a few of those later on.

Compounding these problems of poor research, the filtering process is quite weak. The scientific-review process to determine what gets published in academic journals turns out not to be as stringent and as good a quality control as it sounds. The process involves:

- A researcher submits a paper to a journal.
- An editor or associate editor of the journal takes a quick look at the paper to determine if the paper might be of appropriate quality for the journal.
- If so, the editor seeks (typically) up to three referees who should be well-versed on the paper's topic and methods to evaluate the paper.
- The referees produce reports on what is good about the paper and what needs to be addressed. They also often make a recommendation to the editor regarding whether the paper should be rejected, accepted, or be allowed a "revise and resubmit" after addressing the comments.
- The editor (or perhaps higher-up editors) makes the final decision on whether the paper gets published in that journal.

I will speak more on the scientific (peer) review process in Chapter 14, with guidance on how to produce a responsible referee report. But it seems clear that scientific reviews need improving, as evidenced by the somewhat laughable results of a few tests on the quality of peer reviews:

- The *British Medical Journal* sent an article to 200 of its reviewers, in which the journal created eight mistakes in the study design, the analysis, and the interpretation. On average, the reviewers found fewer than two of the eight mistakes (The Economist, 2013).
- Richard Smith (2006), the former editor of the *British Medical Journal* reported that there is evidence showing that referees on the same paper agree on whether a paper should be published just a little more than would be expected if they randomly decided.
- Similar evidence to Smith (2006) was found by Welch (2014) with regard to leading finance and economics journals.

If peer reviewers do not adequately screen research, then we cannot expect much better from the media (who report research results). For example, while the truth on regressions, that they can be rife with empirical problems, is often made loud and clear, it tends to be ignored by the media. An interesting article gets published, and the media report on the research as if it were a certainty, without much consideration of the soundness of the research or of any prior evidence to the contrary. In partial defense of the media, they rely on the (flawed) peer-review process to vet the article.

The fundamental problem comes down to all participants (in the research process and its dissemination) not knowing the right questions to ask to properly scrutinize research. This allows the low-quality research to get through the process.

The *Economist* article mentioned in the opening part of this chapter quoted an academic: "There is no cost [for researchers] to getting things wrong" (p. 26). In fact, there can be rewards for getting things wrong since it is unlikely anyone will ever notice. And the *Economist* article argues that there is a good chance that the results from incorrect research have a disproportionate share of research that gets publicly discussed.

Society needs to address issues of publication bias and the influence of sponsors with a vested interest. Beyond those problems, if the research process can be improved at all levels of the filtering process (by improving how we teach students the fundamentals, interpretations, and pitfalls of regression analysis), then there would be less room for faulty research methods, publication bias, and perhaps fraud. The research process could then be more trusted.

1.4 About this book

I believe that regression analysis is often taught ineffectively and inefficiently. The ineffectiveness is suggested by mounting evidence that much academic research is inaccurate (often due to faulty methods and interpretations). The inefficiency comes from the unnecessary reliance on high-level math, which squanders time on material that 99.3% of students will never use and makes the material inaccessible or unnecessarily difficult for those without strong math skills. I aim to improve how regression analysis is taught with a more logical, practical, and (relatively) low-math approach.

Compared to other books on regressions, this book should better prepare readers for conducting, interpreting, and assessing regression analyses, while simultaneously making the learning of regression analysis simpler, more efficient, and (hopefully) more enjoyable.

1.4.1 The new low-math approach

I was great in math through high school, wasn't so great in college, and struggled mightily in undergraduate and graduate regression classes, given how highly mathematical they were. In college, I would spend way too much of my valuable basketball, socializing, and trying-to-find-a-girlfriend time attempting to decipher equations like this:

$$\hat{\beta}_2 = \frac{\Sigma \left(y_i x_{2i} \right) \left(\lambda^2 \Sigma x_{2i}^2 + \Sigma v_i^2 \right) - \left(\lambda \Sigma y_i x_{2i} + \Sigma y_i v_i \right) \left(\lambda \Sigma x_{2i}^2 \right)}{\Sigma x_{2i}^2 \left(\lambda^2 \Sigma x_{2i}^2 + \Sigma v_i^2 \right) - \left(\lambda \Sigma x_{2i}^2 \right)^2}$$

which comes from the popular *undergraduate* textbook that I had used and is still in use today.

Regression analysis is taught with high-level math, at least in economics curricula, as part of a rite of passage. Professors likely think that getting through these classes separates the real economists from the "partial" economists.

But now, after more than two decades of using regression analysis (as an academic, a consultant, and a think-tanker), I know that high-level math is not necessary for most practitioners. I have a pretty good intuitive feel for regression analysis. This came mostly from performing applications of regression analysis – applications in which I did not use any of the high-level math and proofs that I learned in the regression classes. Rather, I just used intuition and logic, which are largely based on a solid understanding of how regressions "attempt to adjust for other factors" and how different types of relationships between variables can cause problems – neither of which is taught with much detail and enough emphasis in regression classes/books. I believe that a large portion of academics and practitioners lack this level of understanding.

You can develop this understanding and intuition, without the high-level math. Linear Algebra and Calculus, used in most classes on regression analysis, are necessary only for regression theorists, not for practitioners. Teaching regression analysis in the current complex way may prevent some sharp, creative researchers (who may not have such great math skills) from entering the world of research.

I wrote this book, in part, to shift the way that regression analysis is taught so that research can be opened up to creative people, regardless of their higher-math proficiency.

1.4.2 The primary focus is on what could go wrong with regression analysis

Surprisingly, most books on regression analysis give very little emphasis to the pitfalls of regression analysis regarding whether the estimated cause-effect relationships are biased. In fact, they tend to focus more on getting the standard errors correct. Standard errors (covered in Chapter 5) tell you how precise the estimates are, and they are used in the calculations for hypothesis tests. Certain types of regression models or the nature of some data require adjustments to standard errors to ensure that the correct standard errors are used for the hypothesis tests. Corrections are typically on the order of 0%–25%.

But, in my view, it is more important for the hypothesis tests to have accurate coefficient estimates, which indicate the nature of the empirical relationships. The pitfalls of regression analysis generally cause coefficient estimates to be off by a much greater factor than for standard errors, potentially even reversing signs. It is most often errors in coefficient estimates rather than errors in standard errors that are the sources of wrong research. Compared to other regression books, this book pays much more attention and detail to avoiding, acknowledging, and addressing the things that could go wrong in regression analysis with coefficient estimates. It discusses seven main sources of bias (which I call PITFALLS). These include the well-known sources of bias (e.g., reverse causality and omitted-factors bias). In addition, the book introduces two common sources of bias that are not mentioned in any other textbook (to my knowledge): improper reference groups and over-weighting of some groups when controlling for a categorization. Because these sources of bias can rarely be proven to be the case with equations and need to be assessed as to whether they present alternative stories for why two variables are related or not, I focus more on describing the biases in terms of how certain factors are related to each other. I provide the key questions to ask to assess whether there could be a bias, and I give examples of situations in which a given bias could occur.

1.4.3 The ethics of regression analysis

One other important contribution of this book, relative to other books on econometrics/regression analysis, is that there is an ethical component to the book. There are many decisions that go into a study: making proper sample restrictions, choosing what variables to include in a model, and much more. These decisions should be based on minimizing any bias. However, due to incentives to find interesting and convincing results (to get published or please a client or research sponsor), sometimes these modeling decisions are made based on what gives the best result. This is unethical. Furthermore, in an effort to get published or please a research sponsor (who funds research), not being fully forthright about any sources of bias is unethical. This book spells out unethical and ethical practices, as part of an effort to improve the quality of research in the long run. When conducting statistical research, it is important to keep in mind that the livelihood and health of human beings are on the other end of our research, and that gives anyone conducting research the responsibility to pursue the truth on a research topic and report accurately what can be gained from a particular study.

1.4.4 Scope of the book

This book is meant to be a guide for *conducting*, *interpreting*, and *assessing/scrutinizing* regression analysis. It brings a new approach to understanding regressions, replacing the high-level math with more figures demonstrating pathways and more intuition on what is occurring in the regressions.

For students at the undergraduate or graduate level, I give almost all of the basic information needed to conduct valid regression analysis. By avoiding proofs and high-level math, a course using this book could cover more important information, such as giving more detail on how to interpret regressions, what methods to use for different types of outcome variables, what the PITFALLS of regression analysis are (and, there are plenty of them), how to recognize those biases, and how to address some of these PITFALLS. For those who already have a regression/econometrics book, this book will serve as a nice supplement, as it relates many of the key concepts to "everyday" events, such as pouring a glass of beer, having a shooting contest with LeBron James, or searching for intelligent life elsewhere in the universe. Compared to other books on regressions, this book tends to use more stories and simple flow charts than complex mathematical equations to demonstrate the concepts.

Instead of proofs, I will present the details on issues that students are most likely to encounter in their research or others' research and the necessary details students need to develop strategies for their research. This is based on the thousands of regressions I have estimated, coming from several different fields of study. I will describe many of the mistakes I made in my own published research. I have left out of this book minute details that are specific to certain topics. The details that are in most books are often complicated, bog people down, and distract readers from the important intuition and practical aspects of regression models.

There are some more advanced regression methods that are not commonly used, for which I give an introduction without spending too much time on the details.[1] Thus, you will learn most of what you need to know about regression analysis much more efficiently than you would with the existing regression books.

The general game plan of the book is to:

- Describe the nuts and bolts of regression analysis, including the methods for hypothesis testing and its two main inputs (the coefficient estimate and the standard error)
- Briefly discuss problems with standard errors and their corrections (for proper hypothesis testing) … and then tell you why hypothesis tests should not be used, but rather results should be characterized based on the strength of the evidence
- Indicate how coefficient estimates just tell us how variables move together, after attempting to adjust for other factors. It is up to us to objectively assess whether it is causal
- Stress how the coefficient estimate indicates causality only if alternative reasons for the variables moving together (or not) can be effectively ruled out
- Discuss those alternative reasons (to the causality argument) for variables moving together (or not) – these are the main PITFALLS of regression analysis
- Present the PITFALLS for regression analyses that have objectives other than estimating causal effects
- Offer strategies for addressing some of the PITFALLS for coefficient estimates
- Provide alternative regression methods to use when the dependent variable (the outcome) has a non-standard form (such as being dichotomous)

- Provide examples of good research and research that could have been conducted better
- Present how to conduct and write up a research project using regression analysis
- Stress objectiveness, honesty, and other ethical practices for conducting and scrutinizing research.

1.5 Quantitative vs. qualitative research

From graduate school (at the University of Wisconsin), more than 20 years ago, I remember only one research seminar fairly clearly. An economist from Yale, Truman Bewley, talked to us about an investigation into what unemployment does to people, which ended up being part of a larger research project (Bewley 1999). His analysis was not based on formal surveys, but rather Dr. Bewley had conversations with people who had been laid off by plant closings. From what I remember, he asked people about what they had experienced, how the lay-off made them feel physically and emotionally, what they were hoping for, and more.

I did not know it at the time, but what Dr. Bewley did was **qualitative research**, which is explorative research that is meant to describe (in-depth) opinions, attitudes, and behaviors. Qualitative research can be based on many types of data collection, with the more common ones being focus groups, individual interviews, and observations of behaviors. Focus groups and interviews tend to have a minimal basic structure and are designed to allow the responses of the interviewee to direct the flow of the conversation to the thoughts and opinions that are more important to the interviewee. The researcher would then compile the responses from the interviews and try to find commonalities and a story. I don't mean to simplify qualitative research, as there are five main methods of qualitative research (Sauro, 2015).[2] This all stands in contrast to **quantitative research**, in which the variables collected would be the same for everyone.

There are advantages and disadvantages to qualitative relative to quantitative research. I'll briefly describe some. Qualitative research can tell a much more detailed story, and it can speak to underlying motivations for certain behaviors or outcomes. Whereas quantitative research asks "what?", qualitative research asks "how?" and "why?". The main disadvantage of qualitative research is that it is time-consuming, which makes it difficult to generate enough data to make conclusions about a population. In addition, there could be more room for subjectivity to invade the research process with qualitative research.

With quantitative research, it is simple to deal with thousands or millions of observations, and so there could be plenty of power to draw conclusions on a population. Often, however, there are limits to what data can tell us.

This book focuses on quantitative research. But I want to give a shout-out to qualitative research, which can do many things that quantitative research cannot.

1.6 Stata and R code

I conducted numerous regression analyses in this book using the statistical programs Stata and R. On the book's website (www.routledge.com/9781032257839), I have posted the data sets and the Stata and R code used for the analyses in the book. The Stata and R code are in two separate files, and I indicate what section in the book each set of code comes from. The data I posted can be used for other statistical programs besides these. The data are available as a Stata data set (*.dta) and in comma-delimited format (*.csv). If you do not know Stata or R, there are numerous online tutorials for learning them.

1.7 Chapter summary

Regression analysis can address important questions that can help people and organizations make better decisions. Unfortunately, the current state of academic research is marred by a slew of poorly conducted studies, which is giving the whole research community a bad name. This could be largely fixed if researchers were to gain a better understanding of research. Plus, bad research will not be disseminated as widely if the media could better distinguish between strong and questionable research. This book aims to build better researchers by promoting a stronger understanding of how to give proper scrutiny to the research to assess its relevance and contribution to knowledge.

Notes

1 There are many sources on the internet or other textbooks for greater detail on any given regression topic.
2 Sauro, J. (2015). 5 Types of Qualitative Methods. See https://measuringu.com/qual-methods/, accessed July 10, 2018.

References

Angell, M. (2009). Drug companies & doctors: A story of corruption. *The New York Review of Books*, January 15, 2009 issue. (Available at www.nybooks.com/articles/2009/01/15/drug-companies-doctors-story-of-corruption/).

Arkes, J. (2022). *Confessions of a Recovering Economist: How Economists Get Almost Everything Wrong* (self-published), www.amazon.com.

Bewley, T. F. (1999). *Why wages don't fall during a recession*. Cambridge, MA: Harvard University Press.

Freedman, D. H. (2010). Lies, damned lies, and medical science. *The Atlantic*. November 2010 issue. (Available at www.theatlantic.com/magazine/archive/2010/11/lies-damned-lies-and-medical-science/308269/).

Sauro, J. (2015). 5 Types of Qualitative Methods. https://measuringu.com/qual-methods/, accessed July 10, 2018.

Smith, R. (2006). Peer review: A flawed process at the heart of science and journals. *Journal of the Royal Society of Medicine*, 99(4), 178–182.

The Economist (2013). Trouble at the Lab. *The Economist* 409(8858), 26–30.

Welch, I. (2014). Referee recommendations. *Review of Financial Studies*, 27(9), 2773–2804.

2 Regression analysis basics

DOI: 10.4324/9781003285007-2

In this chapter, you will learn:

- The four main objectives of regression analysis, with estimating causal effects being the most prevalent objective
- The various components of regression and what they mean
- The simple version of how regressions are calculated
- How to determine how well a regression explains an outcome
- Why correlation does not mean causation (and why causation does not mean correlation)
- The two main reasons why a regression result could be wrong
- How everyone has their own effect, and what researchers aim to estimate is an average effect
- How to understand regression flowcharts, which will be used throughout the book.

In an end-of-term "reflection" paper I assigned students in my "applied regression analysis" course, a student quoted an old adage (going back at least to the 4th-century B.C.) that most of us know as something Peter Parker (Spiderman's) Uncle Ben told Peter: "With great power comes great responsibility." I almost gave him an "A" just for that one statement.

Knowing how to estimate a regression model, in a sense, gives a person some power. A regression produces numbers representing how two variables are related, with the implication in some cases that this is how one factor affects some outcome, with the many decimal places giving a comically false sense of precision. With almost the entire population not understanding regression analysis, someone who produces numbers can interpret them almost how he/she pleases and rarely would be called out for any mistakes. Those who read about the research often interpret the findings and interpretations as a "fact."

The responsibility that should come with the know-how to estimate a regression model is designing the model well and making responsible conclusions. This means being sure that the conclusions reflect what we can gain from the regression and do not over-reach. In addition, responsibility means that the uncertainties – the imprecision of the estimate and potential alternative explanations or biases – are made loud and clear. Chapter 5 discusses how to make proper interpretations based on the precision/imprecision of estimates. Chapter 6 deals with the potential alternative explanations, or the PITFALLS/biases. Chapter 13 discusses some ethical infractions of researchers and how to be moral and responsible in one's research. Without the lessons of those chapters, there is little value in learning regression analysis, as it has the potential to do more harm than good.

2.1 What is a regression?

I'm pretty middle-of-the-road when it comes to politics – at least, that's what all the political tests I've taken show. These centrist views, along with my knowledge of regression analysis, once got me in trouble at a dinner party with my Aunt Jo's friends in San Francisco.

I merely said that I believe we over-educate people in the United States by sending too many to college – except in educating people on statistical analysis. My aunt's friends took great exception to my statement. They cited stats that say how much more opportunity (i.e., income) people have from obtaining more schooling.

Besides the point that the costs of educating people need to be considered and that many people do not use the skills they learn nor benefit economically from college, I applied what I knew about regression analysis to support my point. Yes, more-educated people make much more money than less-educated people, but it doesn't mean that education *caused* the entire income advantage. There are other differences between more- vs. less-educated people that could contribute to the income differences. So the more-educated people would probably have made more money than the less-educated people even without the differences in education between them.

Regression analysis helps towards eliminating the influence of the other factors to hopefully get closer to the true, average causal effect of something – in this case, a year of schooling. (This is what could inform people on how much education to obtain, given the cost. In addition, it should have bearing on how much governments should subsidize higher education.)

And so I tried making this point about regressions to my aunt's friends. But, among the many limitations of regressions, one of the toughest is slicing through pre-conceived notions.

If I were able to play God for a moment (in geological terms), I would conduct an experiment in which I randomly assigned people to have different levels of schooling and compare their incomes at various points later in their lives. This would tell us, at least for this geological moment of the experiment, how much an extra year of schooling increased people's incomes, on average. From that information, I would have a sense of how much, as God, I should nudge people to obtain more schooling.

Unfortunately, to the best of my knowledge, we do not live in an experimental world. And so we need to devise other methods of examining how much an extra year of school, on average, increases a person's income. We might start with a scatterplot showing years-of-schooling completed and income from wages and salary, as in Figure 2.1. These data come from the National Longitudinal Survey of Youth (NLSY, Bureau of Labor Statistics, 2014), a survey tracking a cohort for over 30 years, starting in 1979.[1] I took a conveniently selected sample of 75 males (aged 39–47) who were still in the survey in 2004, 25 years after the start of the survey. I purposefully made sure that the sample included observations at most levels of schooling, as a random sample would have a large concentration of observations at 12 years (a high-school diploma) and 16 years (a college degree).

A **regression** is an equation that represents how a set of factors explains an outcome and how the outcome moves with each factor. It is pretty clear, from Figure 2.1, that there is a positive correlation

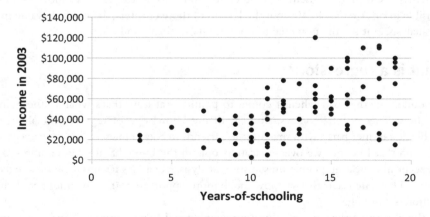

Figure 2.1 Scatterplot of years–of–schooling and income

Source: A random sample from the NLSY of 1979 (Bureau of Labor Statistics, 2014).

between education and income; when education is higher, income tends to be higher. Thus, a regression model would probably show this positive relationship. But the regression model does not indicate why the variables move with each other, and so we have not made the case for there being a causal effect or what the magnitude of any causal effect is because there are alternative explanations to why the variables move together. As mentioned above, before concluding that there is causality, we have to rule out other possible explanations first. This is why researchers use Multiple Regression Models, which attempt to adjust for certain factors in an effort to compare apples to apples when examining the effect of some treatment/factor on an outcome.

We need to start with the Simple Regression Model, which I will do after reviewing the main objectives of regression analysis in the next section.

Before doing so, let me briefly address something you're probably asking yourself: Why is it called a "regression" model or analysis? That's a great question, and I do not know the answer. I searched the internet for a good explanation, but I couldn't find one. After much thought, I came up with a theory. But you will need to wait until Box 2.1 in Section 2.4.2, as you will need some background information for my theory.

2.2 The four main objectives for regression analysis

The most common use of regression analysis is to *quantify how one factor causally affects another*. For example, if a person obtains one additional year of schooling, how much would we expect that person's income to increase? Or, if a child's parents divorce, how much would that affect the child's academic outcomes, on average? When we think of factors that could have causal effects, we normally think of a policy intervention, a behavior, an action, and an event or economic phenomenon. In addition, a characteristic could be a factor that has a causal effect as well, such as race/ethnicity or age having an effect on income.

A second objective of regressions is to *forecast or predict an outcome*. The Army may want to have a good prediction of how many first-year soldiers would attrite (i.e., leave the service for some reason) so that the Army can set optimal recruiting targets for a given year. An insurance company might want to forecast the likelihood that an existing or potential customer would get in an accident. The Army and the insurance company would include in a regression model various factors that may help forecast attrition and the likelihood of an accident.

A third use of regressions is to *determine the predictors of some factor*. For example, parents or school counselors may want to know what factors could predict whether a teenager will drop out of school. In this case, certain factors, such as a parental divorce, may not itself have a causal effect on dropping out, but the divorce may be indicative of other factors (e.g., conflict at home) that could lead to the teenager dropping out. The causal effect of a parental divorce may in fact be zero, but the divorce may still be a strong predictor of dropping out.

A fourth main use of regression analysis is to *adjust an outcome for various factors*. For example, rather than just evaluating a teacher's effectiveness based on his/her students' test scores, we could adjust those scores based on the students' prior scores and perhaps the demographics and English-language status of the students. Or a board of directors for a publicly traded firm, to properly evaluate the performance of a CEO, may want to evaluate quarterly profits after factoring out the industry's influences on the company's quarterly profits. Generally, this objective for regression analysis typically involves trying to gauge "relative performance" or "value-added" by attempting to factor out certain variables that represent environmental and situational factors that are out of the control of the subject being evaluated. This is the concept behind the currently-popular basketball statistic of a player's "real-plus-minus," which calculates how many more points a player's team scores relative to its opponent per 100 possessions, attempting to factor out the influence of the player's teammates and opponents on the court while he plays.

Along the same lines as adjusting outcomes is the goal of detecting anomalies. This involves determining which observations have a much higher or lower outcome than would be expected, given its/his/her contextual factors. For example, outcomes for people with a certain health condition could adjust for certain factors (e.g., year diagnosed and certain health behaviors) to determine who had much better outcomes than would be expected. With that information, further investigation could go into the health practices that might have contributed to the much-better-than-expected outcomes.

Beyond these four main objectives, there is one other objective that is used in many studies: testing the "association" between variables. For example, some studies have examined the association between teenage drug use and early teenage sexual activity. I do not consider testing for "associations" as a "main objective" because these studies typically have the ultimate goal of knowing whether there is a causal effect of one variable on another, which would speak more to the effects of policies than would mere associations. The nature of their data or model makes it difficult to ascertain that any association they find is causal, and so they have to say they are testing for associations. This is not to criticize this type of research, as sometimes this research is meant to demonstrate an association which could suggest causation and which serves as a stepping stone for others to design a study or experiment to test for causality. That said, it typically is not the ultimate objective of regression analysis.

Table 2.1 summarizes the four main objectives of regression analysis and the types of questions they address. The strategies for designing a regression would depend on which of these four purposes the researcher has. Note that the main result from the regression would be different based on the objective.

As mentioned, this book concentrates on the first objective: quantifying cause–effect relationships. To this end, Chapter 6 goes into extensive detail about the main things that could wrong when estimating causal effects and what strategies should be used toward that goal. Chapter 7 describes the strategies to use when estimating regressions for the other objectives.

Table 2.1 The four main objectives of regression analysis and the questions addressed

Regression objective	Generic types of questions addressed
Estimating causal effects	How does a certain factor affect the outcome?
Determining how well certain factors predict the outcome	Does a certain factor predict the outcome? What factors predict the outcome?
Forecasting an outcome	What is the best prediction/forecast of the outcome?
Adjusting outcomes for various factors (to gauge relative performance or to detect anomalies)	How well did a subject perform relative to what we would expect given certain factors?

2.3 The Simple Regression Model

2.3.1 The components and equation of the Simple Regression Model

If you remember 8th-grade Algebra, a straight line is represented by the equation:

$$y = a + bx$$

where:
- x is the horizontal-axis variable
- y is the vertical-axis variable
- a is the y-intercept
- b is the slope of the line.

A Simple Regression is similar in that there is one X and one Y variable, but it differs in that not all points fall on a straight line. Rather, the Simple Regression line indicates the line that best fits the data.

The **Simple Regression Model** (also known as the Bivariate Regression Model) is:

$$Y_i = \beta_0 + \beta_1 \times X_i + \varepsilon_i \tag{2.1a}$$

$(i = 1, 2, 3, \ldots, N)$

This equation describes each of the N data points (observations), not just the line. The five components of the model are:

- The **dependent variable** (Y), which is also called the *outcome, response variable, regressand,* or Y *variable.* (It is the Y-axis variable, or "income" in Figure 2.1.)
- The **explanatory variable** (X), which is also called the *independent variable, explanatory variable, treatment variable, regressor,* or simply X *variable.* Personally, I do not like the term "independent variable" because: (1) it is not descriptive of what the variable does; (2) sometimes, the X variable is "dependent" on the dependent (Y) variable or other factors that are related to the dependent variable; and (3) it is too close to and often gets confused with "dependent variable." I prefer "explanatory variable" or simply "X variable." (It is the X-axis variable, or "years-of-schooling" in Figure 2.1.)
- The **coefficient on the explanatory variable** (β_1), which indicates the slope of the regression line, or how the outcome (Y) is estimated to move, on average, with a one-unit change in the explanatory variable (X).
- The **intercept term** (β_0), which indicates the Y-intercept from the regression line, or what the expected value of Y would be when X = 0. This is sometimes called the "constant" term.
- The **error term** (ε), which indicates how far off an individual data point is, vertically, from the true regression line. This occurs because regressions typically cannot perfectly predict the outcome. (For example, income depends on many things other than years-of-schooling.)

(Note that, following convention, I italicize variable names. But, when I speak generically about an X or Y variable, I do not italicize "X" or "Y.")

The i subscript in the regression line refers to individual i in the sample, so:

- Y_i = income for individual i
- X_i = years-of-schooling for individual i
- ε_i = the error for individual i.

Equation (2.1a) is actually N separate equations, one for each observation:

$$
\begin{aligned}
Y_1 &= \beta_0 + \beta_1 \times X_1 + \varepsilon_1 \\
Y_2 &= \beta_0 + \beta_1 \times X_2 + \varepsilon_2 \\
Y_3 &= \beta_0 + \beta_1 \times X_3 + \varepsilon_3 \\
&\cdots \\
Y_N &= \beta_0 + \beta_1 \times X_N + \varepsilon_N
\end{aligned}
\tag{2.1b}
$$

Note that the coefficients, β_0 and β_1, are the same for each observation.

Sometimes, shorthand is used and the multiplication sign and subject-identifying subscripts are left out, and the equation is just written as:

$$
Y = \beta_0 + \beta_1 X + \varepsilon
\tag{2.2}
$$

2.3.1.1 The X and Y variables

Y is the variable you are trying to explain or predict. Why is Y called the "dependent variable" and X the "independent variable"? Because theoretically (and hopefully) Y depends on what X is and not *vice versa*. Hopefully, X is random with respect to Y, meaning that X changes for reasons that are unrelated to what is happening to Y. If X is affected by Y or if X and Y have common factors, then we have problems, which we will see in Chapter 6.

Sometimes a variable name other than X or Y is used if it is fairly self-explanatory. For example, if "marijuana use" is the X variable, then you could use MJ as the variable name. It gets confusing (and doesn't look good) if you use longer words for variable names. However, I will do so in a few places to keep it simple.

2.3.1.2 The coefficients

The two coefficients are:

- β_0 = the Y-intercept (known as the constant)
- β_1 = the slope of the line (the coefficient on X).

The interpretation would be that, if a person had 0 years-of-schooling ($X = 0$), they would be expected to have an income of β_0, and each extra year of schooling *would be associated with* β_1 higher income, on average. Notice that I say "would be associated with" instead of "causes" or "leads to." I do so because, again, we have not established causality yet.

2.3.1.3 The error term

The **error term** is the difference between the actual Y value and the predicted Y value based on the true population regression equation (as opposed to what is estimated with the sample data). There are three main components of the error term, ε_i:

- The influence of variables is not included in the regression. In the education–income regression, this could include, among numerous other factors: gender, race, and motivation.
- The possibility that the X or Y variable is miscoded. For example, if the person has a college degree (16 years-of-schooling) and is reported to have just two years of college (14), then the model may predict a lower income than the person actually has, which would contribute positively to the error term.
- The effects of random processes affecting the outcome. This could come from a pay raise due to a promotion someone is given because the person who had been in the position unexpectedly quit. Or, in examining students' test scores, a student may guess some answers, and lucky or unlucky guesses will affect the outcome independently of any X variables.

2.3.1.4 The theoretical/true regression equation vs. the estimated regression equation

The equation from above:

$$Y_i = \beta_0 + \beta_1 X_i + \varepsilon \tag{2.1a}$$

is considered the theoretical or true regression equation. But we can never know what the true regression equation is because of the randomness involved with sampling from the population and the random events that influence the outcome. Without knowing the true coefficient, we do not know the true error term. Thus, with data, we produce the estimated regression equation, as follows:

$$Y_i = \hat{\beta}_0 + \hat{\beta}_1 X_i + \hat{\varepsilon}_i \tag{2.3a}$$

$$\hat{Y}_i = \hat{\beta}_0 + \hat{\beta}_1 X_i \tag{2.3b}$$

The "hats" (ˆ) over Y, β_0, β_1, and ε indicate that they are predicted or estimated values. We would say that:

- $\hat{\beta}_0$ is the predicted intercept term.
- $\hat{\beta}_1$ is the predicted coefficient on the variable X.
- $\hat{\varepsilon}_i$ is the predicted error term (known as the **residual**) based on the actual X and Y values and the coefficient estimates.
- $\hat{Y}_i$ is the predicted value of Y based on the estimated coefficient estimates and value of the variable, X. Note that the predicted value of Y does not include the residual because the expected or average residual equals zero with most methods.

2.3.2 *An example with education and income data*

There are various methods for estimating the best-fitting regression line. By far, the most common one is the Ordinary Least Squares (OLS) method. The "Least Squares" part refers to minimizing the sum of the squared residuals across all observations. I will further discuss what this means and the mechanics behind OLS in Section 2.4.

Let's start with a sample on the full set of the 2772 males from the 2004 NLSY who had: (1) positive income from wages and salary reported in the 2004 survey (for 2003 income);[2] (2) a positive number of hours-worked-per-week in 2003; and (3) a non-missing score on the Armed Forces Qualification Test (AFQT), which is a test on aptitude that was taken by 94% of the NLSY respondents in the second year of the survey – we will use the AFQT score later in the chapter (Bureau of Labor Statistics, 2014).

I will just mention it here and not later, but you can follow along with the data set, called **income_ data**, available on the book's website, and the Stata or R code. The two relevant variables for now are:

- $Y = income$ = income of the individual
- $X = educ$ = years-of-schooling.

With the sample indicated above, we obtain the following regression equation (rounding):

$$\hat{Y} = -54,299 + 8121 \times X \tag{2.4a}$$

Or

$$\widehat{income} = -54,299 + 8121 \times (educ) \tag{2.4b}$$

This regression equation says that each year of schooling is associated with an estimated \$8121 higher income in 2003, on average. The \$8121 figure is the coefficient estimate, $\hat{\beta}_1$. We can say that:

$$\hat{\beta}_1 = \frac{\Delta \hat{Y}}{\Delta X} = \$8121 \tag{2.5}$$

Note that equation (2.4a) is the regression equation (i.e., set of coefficient estimates) for the sample I have, which we hope would be representative of the population. If we had a different sample from the population, we would obtain a different set of coefficient estimates. Thus, the estimates will have sampling distributions and, hopefully, will have the desired properties (unbiased and consistent) mentioned in Section A.4 of the Appendix. The way that the uncertainty in the estimates is characterized is with the *standard error*, which will be discussed in Chapter 5 on hypothesis testing. If you are following along with the text data and models, or when you work on the chapter exercises, you will see that the coefficient estimates come with these standard errors and a few other statistics that speak to hypothesis tests, which also will be covered in Chapter 5.

You might wonder how the intercept is negative and of such great magnitude, as it says that someone with 0 years-of-schooling is expected to earn negative \$54,299. The reason for this is that the regression line is mostly derived from where most of the variation in the explanatory variable lies (see Section 2.6). And most of that variation will lie in the 12–16 years-of-schooling range. So the Least Squares regression line is fit in a way that is fairly steep in those years-of-schooling, which results in a negative predicted income for those with very low education. What this suggests is that there may be a better way to fit the data with a non-linear (not straight) relationship ... we'll get into non-linear models in Section 3.2

2.3.3 Calculating individual predicted values and residuals

The **predicted value** indicates what we would expect income to be for a given level of schooling. In our example, there would be a different predicted value of *income* for each level of schooling.

The **residual**, how the actual Y value differs from the predicted value, would be how much more (or less) income is relative to the predicted income, given the level of schooling. With some regression methods, notably the most common one of OLS, the average residual equals 0. Thus, the amount of over-prediction and under-prediction are equal.

To calculate the predicted value and residual, recall from your classes on statistics or probability that: $E[a \mid b]$ = expected value of a, given b. The calculations are:

- Predicted value of $Y = \hat{Y} = E[Y|X] = \hat{\beta}_0 + \hat{\beta}_1 \times X$

  (because $E[\hat{\varepsilon}] = 0$, or the average residual equals 0 in linear regression models)

- Residual $= \hat{\varepsilon} = Y - E[Y|X] = Y - \hat{Y}$.

As an example, one person in the sample has 10 years-of-schooling and \$25,000 of income. His regression statistics would be:

- Predicted value of $Y = \hat{Y} = E[Y|X = 10] = -54,299 + 8121 \times 10 = \$26,911$.

- Residual $= Y - \hat{Y} = Y - E[Y|X] = \$25,000 - \$26,911 = -\$1911$.

The interpretations are that:

- We predict that someone with 10 years-of-schooling would have an income of \$26,911.
- This person with 10 years-of-schooling and an income of \$25,000 has \$1911 lower income than what would be predicted from the regression.

2.4 How are regression lines determined?

2.4.1 Calculating regression equations

Let's do an example with OLS with just four observations I made up to make an easy exercise. This simple exercise will help convey the intuition behind how regression equations are determined when using the most common method, OLS.

Table 2.2 Four-observation example of education and income

Person	Years-of-schooling (X)	Income ($1000s) (Y)	Deviation from mean X	Deviation from mean Y	Numerator for slope $(X_i - \overline{X}) \times (Y_i - \overline{Y})$	Denominator for slope $(X_i - \overline{X})^2$
1	10	40	−3	−5	15	9
2	12	45	−1	0	0	1
3	14	40	+1	−5	−5	1
4	16	55	+3	+10	30	9
	$\overline{X} = 13$	$\overline{Y} = 45$			40	20

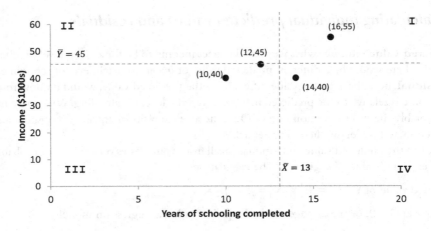

Figure 2.2 Data points for Table 2.2

The four observations from Table 2.2, based on the X and Y values in the second and third columns, are depicted in Figure 2.2, with the mean values (13 years-of-schooling for X and 45 or $45,000 for Y), marked with dashed lines in the figure. The sign of the regression slope will be determined by whether the observations in quadrants I and III dominate those in quadrants II and IV or *vice versa*, based on the product of the deviations from the X and Y means. It looks as though the observations in quadrants I and III dominate, which means that we should have a positive regression slope. Let's do the quick and easy math to check.

When using the OLS method for the Simple Regression Model, the following equation is the estimated slope of the regression line:

$$\hat{\beta}_1 = \frac{\sum_{i=1}^{n}(X_i - \bar{X})(Y_i - \bar{Y})}{\sum_{i=1}^{n}(X_i - \bar{X})^2} \tag{2.6a}$$

or more simply

$$\hat{\beta}_1 = \frac{\sum(X_i - \bar{X})(Y_i - \bar{Y})}{\sum(X_i - \bar{X})^2} \tag{2.6b}$$

Do not be intimidated by this. It is fairly straightforward. The equation represents how X and Y move together (the numerator) relative to how much variation there is in X (the denominator). By moving together, what I mean is that when X has a higher value, then Y has either a higher value (if they move together positively) or a lower value (if they move together negatively). That is, when a given value of X is above its mean (the first quantity in the numerator is positive), does Y tend to be above or below its mean (the second quantity in the numerator)? Let's evaluate each observation.

• Person 1 has below-average years-of-schooling ($X = 10$) and income ($Y = 40$), so his value contributes $+15$ ($= -3 \times -5$) to the numerator, as seen in the second-to-last column of Table 2.2.

- Person 2 has the mean income. Even though the contribution to the numerator is 0, it does not mean that this observation is not contributing to the determination of the slope. The contribution is that Person 2 brings the coefficient more towards 0, as he has below-average years-of-schooling, but average income.
- Person 3 has above-average years-of-schooling and below-average income, so he contributes -5 (= 1×-5) to the numerator.
- Person 4 has above-average years-of-schooling and income, so his value contributes $+30$ (= 3×10) to the numerator.

The sign of the sum in the numerator indicates whether X and Y tend to move together in a positive or negative fashion, and the data indicate they move positively with each other. The sum for the numerator is 40, as shown in Table 2.2, which means that we are estimating that X and Y tend to move positively with each other.

The denominator then scales the numerator based on how much variation there is in X. The denominator equals 20, based on the sum of values in the last column of Table 2.2.

Given these calculations, $\hat{\beta}_1 = 40 / 20 = 2$. This indicates how the two variables tend to move together. That is, when X changes by 1 unit, Y tends to be 2 units higher; or, when years-of-schooling is higher by one year, then income is higher by \$2000, on average.

To then derive the coefficient estimate for β_0, we would use the centroid feature of Ordinary Least Squares:

$$\bar{Y} = \hat{\beta}_0 + \hat{\beta}_1 \bar{X} \tag{2.7}$$

That is, the regression line under OLS goes through the point that has the average X and Y values. This can then be rearranged as follows:

$$\hat{\beta}_0 = \bar{Y} - \hat{\beta}_1 \bar{X} = 45 - 2 \times 13 = 19 \tag{2.8}$$

The two estimates, $\hat{\beta}_0$ and $\hat{\beta}_1$, give the regression equation:

$$\hat{Y}_i = 19 + 2X_i \tag{2.9}$$

2.4.2 Total variation, variation explained, and remaining variation

To give more information on how the regression line is determined and what "Ordinary Least Squares" means, we need to understand the variation in the dependent variable. In Figure 2.3, we see the deviation from the mean $Y = 45$ for each of the four observations.

The **total variation** or **Total Sum of Squares** (*TSS*) of the outcome is the sum of the squared deviations from the mean, or:

$$TSS = \sum_{i-1}^{4} \left(Y_i - \bar{Y}\right)^2 \tag{2.10}$$

In our example, using the deviations from the mean from the 5th column of Table 2.2:

$$TSS = \sum_{i=1}^{4} \left(Y_i - \bar{Y}\right)^2 = (-5)^2 + (0)^2 + (-5)^2 + (10)^2 = 150 \tag{2.11}$$

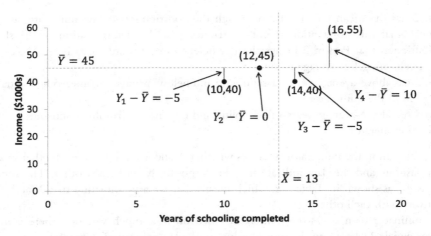

Figure 2.3 The data points relative to mean income for a four-observation regression

Note that this is similar to the variance of a variable except that the "sum of squared deviations from the mean" is not divided by (the number of observations minus one). So var(Y) = $TSS / (n - 1)$. The total variation (TSS) can then be separated into two components:

- $ExSS$ = Explained Sum of Squares = total variation explained by the regression model
- RSS = Residual Sum of Squares = total variation remaining unexplained by the regression model (or the sum of the squared residuals).

The relationship between these different types of variation is:

TSS	=	$ExSS$	+	RSS	(2.12)
total variation	=	variation explained by the regression model	+	variation in the residuals	

or

RSS	=	TSS	−	$ExSS$	(2.13)
variation in the residuals	=	total variation	−	variation explained by the regression model	

Equation (2.13) helps highlight how linear regression models are calculated, when using **Ordinary Least Squares**. The model is estimated by finding the set of coefficients that maximizes $ExSS$ (the amount of variation explained by the model). This, in turn, minimizes RSS (the amount of variation remaining unexplained) since TSS remains constant. Thus, "Least Squares" refers to the minimization of the sum of the squared residuals (RSS).

The regression line that explains most of the variation in Y is our regression equation from above:

$$\bar{Y}_i = 19 + 2X_i \qquad (2.9)$$

Table 2.3 Predicted values and residuals for the four-observation sample

Person	Years-of-schooling completed	Income ($1000s)	Predicted income = 19 + 2X ($1000s)	Residual
1	10	40	39	+1
2	12	45	43	+2
3	14	40	47	−7
4	16	55	51	+4

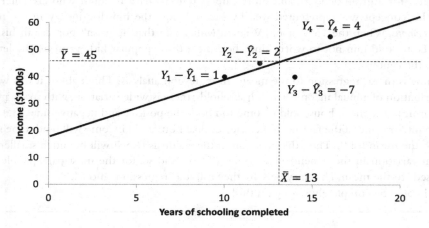

Figure 2.4 The regression line and residuals

With just one explanatory variable, X, no other regression line would explain more variation (i.e., give a higher $ExSS$ and a lower RSS) than this equation for the given four observations. Given this regression line, we can then calculate the predicted value and residual for each person, as shown in Table 2.3 and Figure 2.4.

Person 1, who earns 40, has a predicted income of 39. Thus, his residual is 1. This says that he has a one-unit (i.e., $1000) higher income than we would predict given his education of 10 years-of-schooling. Person 3, on the other hand, earns $7000 less than we would predict or expect, given his 14 years-of-schooling completed. Note that the average residual equals 0.

Figure 2.4 shows the graphical representation of the regression equation, as well as the residuals. In the figure, the predicted value would just be the height of the regression line for a given X value. Thus, the residual is the vertical distance (positive or negative, and not drawn) of the data point to the regression line.

In this model, RSS is calculated as:

$$RSS = \sum_{i=1}^{4} \left(Y_i - \hat{Y}\right)^2 = (1)^2 + (2)^2 + (-7)^2 + (4)^2 = 70$$

This means that:

$$ExSS = TSS - RSS = 150 - 70 = 80.$$

Again, no regression line different from equation (2.9), given these 4 data points, would produce a smaller RSS or a larger $ExSS$.

Box 2.1   Why is it called a "regression" model?

In Section 2.1, I raised this question and said that I did not know the answer, but I developed a theory (building off of a few I have seen). Another use of the word "regression" is in the term "regression to the mean," which means that outlying observations tend to revert towards the mean on the next go-around. For example, tall parents tend to have children who are shorter than them (for a given gender), and short parents tend to have children who are taller than them. This concept was represented well by Lester Bangs, the hip disc-jockey in the movie *Almost Famous*. When the 15-year-old William Miller said that he wasn't popular in his high school, Lester told him not to worry since he'd meet those popular kids again on the lengthy route to the center.

So how is there "regression to the mean" in regression analysis? Think about it this way. In the distribution of annual income across households, there is wide variation, with many people pretty far from the mean household income (on both the positive and negative side). But, after we account for some of the factors of income, residual household income will tend to be much closer to the mean (of 0). Thus, the variation in the residuals (RSS) will be much smaller than the total variation in the dependent variables (TSS). And so, for the most part, people have "regressed" to the mean. That may be why they call it a "regression" model.

But I could be completely wrong on this!

2.5 The explanatory power of the regression

2.5.1 R-squared (R^2)

The discussion of TSS, $ExSS$, and RSS brings us to a relatively important statistic in regression analysis. **R-squared** (or R^2) is the proportion of the variation in the outcome, Y, that is explained by the X variable(s). In other words:

$$R^2 = \frac{ExSS}{TSS} = \frac{TSS - RSS}{TSS} = 1 - \frac{RSS}{TSS} \tag{2.14}$$

In our example in the prior section:

$$R^2 = \frac{TSS - RSS}{TSS} = \frac{150 - 70}{150} = 0.533$$

This says that variation in years-of-schooling explains 53.3% of the variation in income, for this sample of four people. For a Simple Regression Model, R^2 happens to be the square of the sample correlation, $r_{X,Y}$ (see equation A.8 in Section A.1 in the Appendix).

R^2 is one of many "goodness-of-fit" measures in regression analysis. It is the most straightforward of all of them, with a basic interpretation. Unfortunately, it cannot be calculated for certain non-linear models, as will be covered in Chapter 9.

What determines R^2 is how well the regression line explains variation in the dependent variable. The closer the data points are to the regression line: the lower RSS will be, the closer $ExSS$ will be to TSS, and the higher the R^2 will be.

The same formulas for TSS, $ExSS$, RSS, and R^2 are used for Multiple Regression Models, in which there is more than one explanatory variable. The interpretation for R^2 in such models is that it indicates how much of the total variation in the dependent variable (Y) can be explained by all of the explanatory (X) variables.

A high R^2 does not mean that the slope is high. Figure 2.5 shows four cases based on a low-vs.-high R^2 and a low-vs.-high slope. As you can see, there could be a relationship between the X and Y variables that has a steep slope but little explanatory power ("Low R^2, high slope") or *vice versa* ("High R^2, low slope"). Of course, characterizing an R^2 or slope as low vs. high is subjective, so these are just relative R^2's and slopes.

Researchers have different views on the value of the R^2 statistic. For the research objective of forecasting, a higher R^2 is usually the goal. However, for the objective of estimating causal effects, whereas some think it is important to be able to explain a large share of the variation in the outcome, others place less emphasis on R^2. The latter argue that what is important is how Y moves from changes in X, regardless of how much other factors play a role in determining Y. I would agree with this argument. What is most important for a model, when estimating a causal effect, is ruling out explanations for the relationship between X and Y that are alternative to X causing Y. The ability to explain a large portion of the dependent variable (Y) is irrelevant. And, as we will see later, adding more variables to a model, which increases R^2, can sometimes be detrimental to a model by causing a coefficient estimate to move away from the true causal effect.

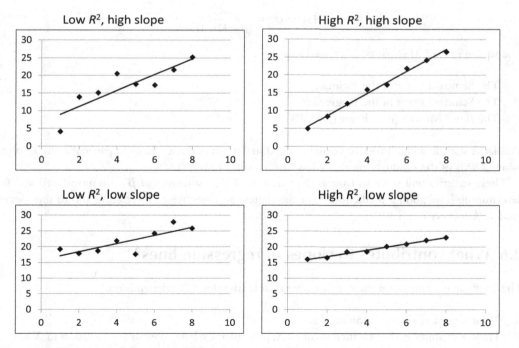

Figure 2.5 Various combinations of R^2 and regression slope

2.5.2 Adjusted R-squared

When a new explanatory variable is added to a model (as in the Multiple Regression Model below), R^2 always increases, even if there is no systematic relationship between the new X variable and the Y variable. This is because there is almost always at least some incidental correlation between two variables. The *Adjusted R^2* corrects for the incidental correlation. The formula is:

$$Adjusted\ R^2 = \bar{R}^2 = 1 - \frac{\Sigma \hat{\varepsilon}^2/(n-K-1)}{TSS\ /\ (n-1)} \qquad (2.15)$$

where n is the sample size, and K is the number of explanatory variables.

When an X variable is added to the model, both the numerator and the denominator of the fraction in equation (2.15) would decrease. The Adjusted R^2 increases only if the new X variable explains more of the outcome, Y, than a randomized variable would be expected to explain variation in Y by chance, thereby reducing the sum of the residuals $\left(\Sigma \hat{\varepsilon}^2\right)$ by a meaningful amount.

What is typically reported for a regression model is R^2. *Adjusted R^2* is mostly used when evaluating whether adding a variable helps the explanatory power of the model.

2.5.3 Mean Square Error and Standard Error of the Regression

An important statistic that will be used later is the estimated variance of the error, or the **Mean Square Error** (*MSE*), calculated as:

$$MSE = \hat{\sigma}^2 = \frac{\Sigma \hat{\varepsilon}^2}{(n-K-1)} \qquad (2.16)$$

The square root of *MSE*, or $\hat{\sigma}$, is referred to as:

- The Standard Error of the Estimate,
- The Standard Error of the Regression,
- The Root Mean Square Error (RMSE).

This latter statistic will tell you the nature of the distribution of the residuals. In particular, the absolute value of 95% of the residuals should be less than roughly 1.96 × RMSE.

These statistics will serve us later as the variance of the estimators of $\hat{\beta}$'s are introduced and for determining how good a prediction is for the regression objective of forecasting and in time-series models (Chapters 7 and 10).

2.6 What contributes to slopes of regression lines?

The coefficient estimate on the explanatory variable (the slope, $\hat{\beta}_1$) depends on:

- Where most of the variation in X lies
- How Y changes with each increment of X, particularly where most of the variation in X lies
- Outliers, as the regression line tries to minimize them.

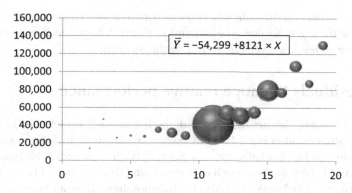

Figure 2.6 Average income by years–of–schooling

Note: Bubble size represents the number of observations at given years–of–schooling
Source: Bureau of Labor Statistics, 2014 ($n = 2772$).

Let's go back to the full-sample regression from Section 2.3.

$$\hat{Y}_i = -54,299 + 8121 \times X_i \tag{2.4b}$$

Figure 2.6 shows the average income for each level of schooling, with the bubble size being representative of the number of observations at each level of schooling – note the small, almost-undetectable bubbles at 3–7 years-of-schooling. We see that most of the variation lies between 12 and 16 years-of-schooling: completion of high school to completion of college. (The bubble is so large for 12 years-of-schooling that it hides the bubbles for 10 and 11 years-of-schooling.) The relationship between years-of-schooling and income in that range appears to be more consistent with the regression line than the observations outside the 12–16 range. Thus, the average change in average income with each year of schooling over this range would, naturally, have greater weight in determining the coefficient estimate than years-of-schooling outside this range. This is why the intercept, $\hat{\beta}_0$, is so largely negative.

Additionally, outliers can have disproportionate effects on a slope. This is the case because of the regression line minimizing the Residual Sum of Squared (*RSS*). Of all the possible regression lines, the regression that keeps the large residuals to a minimum would likely be the one that minimizes *RSS*. Thus, an added large outlier will cause the regression to change to something that minimizes the impact of that new high outlier, while not creating other large outliers.

The effect of an outlier on a coefficient estimate depends on where the outlier occurs:

- A large positive outlier at the average value of X would mostly just contribute to the regression line being higher (a higher constant or Y-intercept).
- A large positive outlier on the left side of the distribution of X would contribute to higher predicted values at that low X value, thus reducing the slope (making it less positive or more negative) and increasing the intercept. This would put an observation, in Figure 2.2, far from the origin in quadrant II, contributing negatively to the coefficient estimate. For example, in Figure 2.2, if an observation with $X = 5$ and $Y = 60$ were added, it would make quadrant II more dominant and perhaps turn the slope negative.

- A large positive outlier on the right side of the distribution of X would contribute to higher predicted values at the given X value (in quadrant I in Figure 2.2), thus increasing the slope (making it more positive or less negative) and decreasing the intercept.

2.7 Using residuals to gauge relative performance

One of my longest-standing debates has been with my friend, Rich, on who the best coach in NBA history is. (Technically, our other big debate, over whether *Shawshank Redemption* should have ended with Red getting on the bus, has lasted longer.) Anyway, Rich argues that Phil Jackson (of the Chicago Bulls and L.A. Lakers) is the best coach ever, even better than my pick of Gregg Popovich (of the San Antonio Spurs), citing Jackson's 11–5 edge in championships. But is it correct to just compare the outcomes (championships) without considering what they had to work with? Put enough talent on a team, and Kim Kardashian could coach an NBA team to a championship.

A proper comparison would consider the quality of their players. Jackson had great talent on his teams, with several all-star players who were high-draft picks. Popovich mostly had just one perennial all-star who was a top pick (and another top pick towards the end of his career), but the rest of his players were low-draft-pick and undrafted players, many of whom were rejects from other teams in whom Popovich found value. Furthermore, whereas Jackson quit and signed on to coach teams with high championship potential, Popovich has stuck with the same team for 26 years and counting. Jackson, one could argue, should have won more championships than Popovich given the talent he had, if he could have just gotten them to like each other and want to win for each other. Popovich figured out how to reinvent his teams based on their skills. Thus, it is arguable that Popovich did more with less. Or we might say that Popovich may have had the higher residual in that, compared to Jackson, he had more championships relative to what would be expected, given his talent – and this may be the better measure of the effectiveness of a coach.[3]

Along similar lines, I have the utmost respect for people who come from difficult backgrounds and end up finding their own way to get a strong education. I think specifically of a friend of mine who never knew her father and had no one in her family get more than an Associate's degree. She earned a Ph.D. and has become a highly successful academic. In a sense, she has a "high residual" in that she advanced in her education and had career success well beyond what would be predicted given her background.

Now, I don't exactly plug my friends' data onto a computer and run a regression, but you can do these basic comparisons. And, if I were to compare my friend above with myself, well I'm not looking so great. My father is a Ph.D. and was a successful Political Science professor, and my mother earned a Master's in Teaching and served as the University Editor (and "safeguard of coherence") at a major university for 37 years until age 73. We were not rich as I grew up, but I certainly was given great models for hard work and academic and professional success. So it certainly isn't as impressive for me to have earned my Ph.D., become an academic, and written this book. My residual isn't nearly as high as my friend's.

From this discussion, you can probably gather that **the residual indicates how well the subject (observation) fared relative to what would be expected given the circumstances the subject had**.

Let's consider a more concrete example with data. One crucial debate in baseball is whether something should be done about the disparity in payrolls, as has been done in other major sports.

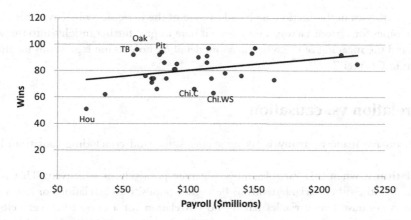

Figure 2.7 Wins and payroll, Major League Baseball, 2013

Big-market teams (the Yankees, Red Sox, and Dodgers, for example) grab players from smaller-market teams during free agency because these big-market teams can pay significantly more. With these teams perennially paying far more than any other team, you would expect them to generally do better than other teams.

A residual analysis could indicate how well certain teams did, given how much they paid in salary. Using data from the 2013 season, regressing wins on payroll gives the following regression line:

$$\widehat{wins} = 71.24 + 0.09 \times (payroll \ in \ \$millions) \tag{2.17}$$

Figure 2.7 shows the graphical representation of the residual analysis. Each data point represents one of the 30 Major League teams. The regression line represents equation (2.17). The vertical distance between each point and the line represents the residual. The teams with the highest residual (most wins relative to what would be expected given their payroll) are:

- Oakland:19.3 (96 wins)
- Pittsburgh:15.6 (94 wins)
- Tampa Bay:15.6 (92 wins).

The teams with the lowest residual are:

- Houston: −22.2 (51 wins)
- Chicago White Sox: −19.0 (63 wins)
- Chicago Cubs: −14.6 (66 wins).

We would say that Houston had 22.2 fewer wins than would be expected, given their salary. The Yankees were not far behind, having 6.8 fewer wins than expected in 2013. The residual speaks to how well the team got value from its players or how well the team saw value in players that other teams did not. Of course, there is always a little (or a lot of) luck represented in the residual. Note that, in 2016 and 2017, two of those low-residual teams (the Chicago Cubs and Houston Astros) won the World Series.

The simple analyses in this section are based on one of the regression objectives from Section 2.2: to adjust outcomes for various factors. I introduce it here to give further insights into the workings of a regression and the meaning of the residual. More detail on how to use regressions for this objective will be given in Chapter 7.

2.8 Correlation vs. causation

A common mistake made by many is taking a correlation and concluding causation. Here is the difference.

A **correlation** is when two variables move together, positively or negatively. That is when one variable is higher, the other variable tends to be higher (a positive correlation) or lower (a negative correlation). In contrast, two variables having no correlation (or a correlation very close to zero) means that when one moves, there is no tendency for the other variable to be higher or lower, on average. Having a positive or negative correlation says nothing about the reason why the two variables move together – whether one of the variables affects the other variable, whether there is a common factor that affects both at the same time, or whether they move together just by coincidence.

Causation is when one variable has an effect on another variable. Causation would mean that, if some randomness or some force were to cause variable X to change, then, on average, variable Y would change as a result.

The important point is this: **a correlation can exist without causation**. Although such a correlation could occur just by chance, a more common cause of a correlation without causation is that some other variable (a "third variable") affects both the X and Y variables. (I will tell you in Section 2.13 below how *a causation can occur without a correlation*.) Here are some examples of relationships that may appear to be causal, but it is also possible that a third variable explains the correlation:

- In education, there is a negative correlation between a student being retained (held back a grade) and their eventual success in school. The potential third variable is the student's general academic aptitude that could affect both whether he is held back and his eventual academic success.
- Many researchers have found a positive correlation between a child experiencing a parental divorce and the child having behavioral problems. While a divorce may have an effect on behavioral problems, the correlation could largely be due to unhealthy family processes having an effect on both the likelihood of a divorce and children's behavior. The divorce itself may have no effect.
- Early studies on coffee drinkers found that they were more likely to die early. However, it turned out that coffee drinkers tended to smoke cigarettes more than non-coffee drinkers. Thus, the positive correlation between coffee drinking and early death was not necessarily due to causation. (Now, most evidence suggests coffee improves health.)

Regression coefficient estimates indicate how two factors move together, which is indicative of the correlation. The regression itself has no say on whether the two factors are correlated due to one causing the other.

Now, let's return to an issue from earlier. From equation (2.4a) in Section 2.3.2, can we conclude that obtaining one more year of schooling would have increased income, on average, by $8121? We cannot because we need to be able to rule out other reasons for why those with more schooling tend to have higher income. Let's consider a few other possible reasons. Those with higher levels of education probably *tend to*:

- Have greater motivation
- Have higher innate (pre-schooling) ability/aptitude
- Have more-educated parents, who could act as role models for aspiring to more highly skilled jobs and could be more likely to help foster the person's learning
- Have grown up in an intact family
- Be less likely to be a racial/ethnic minority
- Have had a higher expected monetary return from schooling – i.e., they believed they had the skills to be handsomely rewarded for their schooling by becoming, say, a high-priced lawyer.

Given all these potential differences, we are comparing apples to oranges when comparing the incomes of more- vs. less-educated people. So, before we conclude that a year of schooling increases income by some amount close to $8121, we need to rule out these other reasons why those with more schooling earn more so that we can compare apples to apples. This would be a very difficult, if not an impossible, task. How would we possibly obtain data on all of these factors?

We will talk about more advanced strategies in Chapter 8, but in the next section, we will turn to simple strategies that likely (but not certainly) help in getting closer to the causal effect – by adding more factors to the model.

2.9 The Multiple Regression Model

Continuing with the example from the prior section, for estimating the effects of schooling on income, we want to remove the influence of the other factors that could contribute to both the amount of schooling a person obtains and his income. That is, we want to hold these other factors constant so that we can compare incomes for people who are observationally similar except for the level of education they have.

One way to eliminate or reduce the influence of some of these other factors may be the **Multiple Regression Model**. There is one primary difference between the Simple and Multiple Regression Models: the Simple model has one explanatory variable; the Multiple model has two or more explanatory variables. The model has the form:

$$Y_i = \beta_0 + \beta_1 X_{1i} + \beta_2 X_{2i} + \cdots + \beta_K X_{Ki} + \varepsilon_i \tag{2.18}$$

where K is the total number of explanatory variables.

Let's extend our model from above that attempts to estimate the causal effects of schooling on income by having two explanatory variables:

- X_1 = years-of-schooling
- X_2 = aptitude score.

The model is:

$$Y_i = \beta_0 + \beta_1 X_{1i} + \beta_2 X_{2i} + \varepsilon_i \tag{2.19}$$

With two explanatory variables, equation (2.19) can be depicted as a plane in a 3-dimensional graph. With three explanatory variables, it becomes 4-dimensional.

The explanatory variables can be classified into two types, characterized here in terms of the objective of identifying causal effects:

- The **key-explanatory (X) variable(s)** is the variable or set of variables for which you are trying to identify the causal effect. This is often called the "treatment." ("Years-of-schooling," X_1, is the key-X variable in our example.) Based on ease of exposition, ease of reading, and what might be more appropriate, I go back and forth between calling this the treatment, the key-X variable, and the key-explanatory variable. For example, sometimes "treatment" does not seem appropriate for describing the key-X variable.
- The **control variables** are the variables included in the model to help identify the causal effects of the key-X variable(s). ("Aptitude score," X_2, is the control variable.)

Distinguishing between the key-explanatory variables and the potential control variables is important for assessing a model and for determining the best set of other control variables to include in a model.

The determination of the coefficient estimates in the Multiple Regression Model is based on the same concept as in the Simple Regression Model in Section 2.4: the estimates are chosen so as to minimize the sum of the squared residuals across the observations. That is, with the actual residual (in contrast to the population error term, ε) being:

$$\begin{aligned}
\hat{\varepsilon}_i &= Y_i - \mathrm{E}[Y_i \mid X_{1i}, X_{2i}] = \left(Y_i - \hat{Y}_i\right) \\
&= Y_i - \left(\hat{\beta}_0 + \hat{\beta}_1 X_{1i} + \hat{\beta}_2 X_{2i}\right),
\end{aligned} \tag{2.20}$$

the estimates, $\hat{\beta}_0$, $\hat{\beta}_1$, and $\hat{\beta}_2$ are chosen to:

$$minimize \sum_{i=1}^{n} \left(\hat{\varepsilon}_i\right)^2 \text{ or } minimize \sum_{i=1}^{n} \left(Y_i - \hat{Y}_i\right)^2.$$

With the NLSY data, I will now estimate equation (2.19), using as a measure of aptitude the percentile score from the Armed Forces Qualification Test (AFQT), which was administered to nearly all NLSY respondents at the time of the second round of interviews in 1980 (Bureau of Labor Statistics, 2014). The score represents a percentile, ranging from 0 to 99, from the distribution of AFQT scores in the U.S. population of 18–23-year-olds.

When we add AFQT percentile (hereafter, called "AFQT" or "AFQT score") to equation (2.4b), the regression equation (using descriptive variable names) is:

$$\left(\widehat{income}\right)_i = -34,027 + 5395 \times (educ)_i + 367 \times (afqt)_i \tag{2.21}$$

Note that I am now using a simpler variable name for years-of-schooling of *educ*. From (2.21), we would say that, *adjusting for the AFQT score*, an extra year-of-schooling is associated with $5395 higher income, on average. To get an initial understanding of how the Multiple Regression Model adjusts for other factors, let's first go back to the original simple model we had:

$$\left(\widehat{income}\right)_i = -54,299 + 8121 \times (educ)_i \tag{2.4b}$$

One reason why those with more schooling may have had higher income was that they tend to have higher aptitude. Thus, part of the estimated $8121 higher income for each year of schooling may be due to the higher aptitude a person with one more year of schooling tends to have – an aptitude that (theoretically) would not depend on their education. But, as researchers, we are interested in how one extra year of schooling would affect a person's income, not the combined effects of an extra year of schooling plus some extra aptitude associated with that extra year of schooling.

To further demonstrate how the Multiple Regression Model works, I will show another way in which the coefficient estimate on years-of-schooling of 5395 in equation (2.21) can be obtained. If we regress years-of-schooling on the AFQT score (equation 2.22a below), calculate the residual or adjusted years-of-schooling from that model (equation 2.22b), and then regress income on adjusted-years-of-schooling (equation 2.22c), we get the same coefficient estimate on adjusted-years-of-schooling as we had on years-of-schooling when the AFQT score was included (equation 2.21). The intercept in (2.22c) is different, but that is inconsequential.

$$\widehat{educ} = 11.036 + 0.053 \times afqt \tag{2.22a}$$

$$(adjusted\ educ) = educ - \widehat{educ} = educ - (11.036 + 0.053 \times afqt) \tag{2.22b}$$

$$\widehat{income} = 54{,}019 + 5395 \times (adjusted\ educ) \tag{2.22c}$$

Thus, controlling for a variable means that we are adjusting the key-explanatory variable for that control variable before determining how it is related to the dependent variable.

Adding the AFQT score into the model helps towards this goal of holding aptitude constant and probably gets us closer to the causal effect of a year of schooling. The variation in income coming from the variation in years-of-schooling is now largely (but not entirely) independent of variation in aptitude. That is, the higher income for those with more schooling can no longer be attributable to higher aptitude, as measured *linearly* by the AFQT score. However, it remains unclear how well the AFQT score captures variation in people's aptitude that contributes to income or whether using a linear effect of the percentile, as opposed to categories of different levels of AFQT scores, is the best method of factoring out "aptitude." That is, perhaps the effect of the AFQT score on income from going from the 80th to 90th percentile is greater than the effect of going from the 10th to 20th percentile, but the model is constraining these effects to be the same. Nevertheless, assuming that the model does a reasonable job in capturing the effects of aptitude, we have just partly addressed one of the reasons why those with more schooling have higher income. Thus, we are likely closer to the true causal effect, even though we may still be a good distance away from that true effect. (I will go into more detail on what "holding other factors constant" means in Chapter 4.)

It would be misguided to make conclusions on the comparison of multiple coefficient estimates without consideration of the scale of the variables. For example, one might examine equation (2.21) and conclude that years-of-schooling is almost 15 times more important than the AFQT score to income. But what would happen if we scaled the AFQT score by dividing it by 100 so that it was on a 0–0.99 scale (instead of 0–99)? The coefficient estimate on *AFQT* would increase by 100 (to roughly, 36,700). It would then appear to be more important than years-of-schooling, but that assessment would be misguided as well. One thing that can be said is that one year of schooling is associated with a greater premium in predicted income than one percentile on the AFQT score.

2.10 Assumptions of regression models

Typical textbooks on regression analysis list several "assumptions" of regression models, often referred to as the "Gauss Markov assumptions" or a similar set called the "Classical Regression Model assumptions." Under these assumptions, OLS coefficient estimates and standard errors are unbiased estimators of the true population parameters – standard errors being the standard deviation in the estimated coefficient estimate.

Personally, I always questioned the use of the term "assumptions." The use of that word makes it seem like we can make the assumption and then we're okay. This is problematic because, as you will see, often many of these assumptions do not hold. I think of them more as *conditions* that are necessary to hold for the researcher to make firm conclusions. And so the researcher needs to assess whether these conditions do in fact hold. Nevertheless, "assumptions" is what they are normally called.

You can give a theory as to why certain assumptions are valid. And, to be balanced and objective, you should mention plausible situations that would result in the assumptions being violated. In Chapter 6, on the things that may go wrong with regression models, I will discuss situations in which some of these assumptions may be violated. Giving an objective assessment of your model would then, ideally, spur you to design an approach that would address any problems and make any corrections necessary. The last thing you want to do is assume that your model answers the research question because all these assumptions are true. Here are the assumptions, described in terms of the true regression equation.

A1. The average error term, ε, equals 0. That is, $E(\varepsilon) = 0$. This can be seen in Table 2.3 in Section 2.4.2. (This is indeed more a property of OLS than an assumption. The intercept automatically adjusts to make this so.)

A2. The error terms are independently and identically distributed (i.i.d.). This means that if one observation has, say, a positive error term, it should have no bearing on whether another observation has a positive or negative error term. That is, a given observation is not correlated with another observation. This could be violated if, for example, there were siblings in a sample. The siblings' incomes (beyond what would be explained by years-of-schooling and aptitude) would probably be correlated with each other, as they have common unobservable determinants. Thus, this would violate the i.i.d. assumption. Violations of this assumption could affect standard errors (measures of uncertainty, covered in Chapter 5), and it could affect coefficient estimates in the case of estimating a time-series model (Chapter 10). There is a correction if there is a correlation between observations.

A3. The error terms are normally distributed. Supposedly, a common mistake is to believe that it is the dependent variable that needs a normal distribution, but it is the error terms that we hope are normally distributed. If error terms were not normal, then it would not mean that the coefficient estimates are biased. Rather, the main problem would be that the tests for significance (Chapter 5) may be off. With the Central Limit Theorem, however, almost any model that has an approximately continuous dependent variable and at least 200 observations should have an approximately normal distribution of error terms – that is, the errors would be asymptotically normal. Others say having 30–40 observations is adequate. Frost (2014) executes some simulations with various non-normal distributions and finds that having 15 observations is adequate, as it results in just as many mistakes (false positives, or incorrectly concluding an empirical relationship when there is not any) as would be expected. Given all this, there should rarely be any concern with this assumption, and the hypothesis tests and confidence intervals for coefficient estimates can be estimated and calculated as they otherwise would be. However, in the case in which the dependent variable is a discrete variable that can only take on a few values (such as a dummy variable, as you will see in the next chapter), then there could be issues with non-normality. (I will discuss this in Sections 5.6 and 12.3.)

A4. The error terms are homoskedastic. This means that the variance of the error term, ε, is uncorrelated with the values of the explanatory variables, or $\text{var}(\varepsilon\,|\,X) = \text{var}(\varepsilon)$ for all values of X. When homoskedasticity does not hold, there is **heteroskedasticity**. The consequence of heteroskedasticity is that the estimated standard errors would be biased and wrong, which would in turn affect the hypothesis tests.

Because the assumption is often violated, it is good practice to always make a simple correction for heteroskedasticity. We will avoid it for now, until the deeper discussion on heteroskedasticity occurs in Section 5.4.2.

A5. The key-explanatory variable(s) are uncorrelated with the error term, ε: If X_1 represents a key-explanatory variable and X_2 the set of control variables, then $E[\varepsilon\,|\,X_1, X_2] = E[\varepsilon\,|\,X_2]$.

Note that the typical corresponding assumption used in most textbooks is that all of the explanatory variables, X, are uncorrelated with the error term. This is often called **conditional mean independence** and can be characterized as, for all X variables:

- $\text{cov}(X, \varepsilon) = 0$
- $\text{corr}(X, \varepsilon) = 0$
- $E[\varepsilon\,|\,X] = E[\varepsilon] = 0$.

But this more stringent assumption is not necessary. Assumption **A5** says that it's okay if the control variables (X_2) are correlated with the error term, but the key-explanatory variable (X_1) cannot be. That is, we want to select the right set of control variables so that the key-explanatory variable is very close to being random and uncorrelated with the error term.

Recall that the error term captures the effects of factors that are not included as explanatory variables. If **A5** were violated, then if the error term were positive, X_1 would tend to be higher or lower than average. The variable, X_1, would no longer be randomly determined with respect to the outcome. Non-randomness of the key-explanatory variable would cause bias if the objective were estimating causal effects.

Consider the issue of how years-of-schooling affects income. If years-of-schooling (the X_1 variable) were correlated with intelligence, and intelligence was part of the error term since it cannot be properly controlled for, then the coefficient estimate on years-of-schooling would be biased because it would reflect the effects of intelligence on income. There are other stories that could cause an X variable to be correlated with the error term. These will be discussed in greater detail in Chapter 6.

Assumption **A5** is one of the key assumptions that is necessary (but very far from sufficient) to determine that a model is validly capturing a causal effect. But I've got some issues with **A5**:

- For two of the regression objectives (forecasting and determining predictors), it is not important that this condition holds. It is only important for estimating causal effects and adjusting outcomes. (I will discuss this more in Chapter 7.)
- This condition is often violated, so technically it might not be such a great idea to make the assumption. Rather, use theory to assess whether it is a good assumption. If there were any possibility of this assumption being violated, then you would need to design a model to address the problem or, at the very least, acknowledge the problem.

Table 2.4 A summary of regression assumptions, how reasonable they are, and what action to take

Assumption	Is it a reasonable assumption?	Action to take if violated
A1. $E(\varepsilon) = 0$	It's an automatic property	N/A
A2. ε is independently and identically distributed	Depends on the situation (see Section 5.4.3)	Easy fix if not so
A3. ε is normally distributed	Yes in most cases, but it most likely won't matter given problems with hypothesis tests (see Chapter 5)	Might need to change the model, or require stronger levels of significance to conclude that the empirical relationship is real
A4. Homoskedasticity $\text{var}(\varepsilon \mid X) = \text{var}(\varepsilon)$	No (see Section 5.4.2)	An easy fix that should almost always be applied
A5. For key-X variable, X_1, $E[\varepsilon \mid X_1, X_2] = E[\varepsilon \mid X_2]$	No (see Chapter 6)	Methods from Chapter 8 (if they can be applied)

When we learn how to assess a model in Chapter 6, the concepts underlying Assumption **A5** will be relevant and will be put in much simpler terms than a conditional expectation of the error term.

Table 2.4 sums up these assumptions and how reasonable they are. The optimal strategy for honest research is to assume nothing. All of the conditions presented in assumptions **A2–A5** pose potential problems. It is the responsibility of the researcher to assess whether it is a problem, make corrections if so, and admit the possibility that there still could be this problem if it is not addressable.

2.11 Everyone has their own effect

When a result from a regression model is relayed to a non-statistical person, sometimes a response will be some anecdote of a case in which a person had the treatment but didn't enjoy/suffer the predicted outcome. For example, someone may say that his son completed four years of college and earns only $30,000, so the monetary benefit of a college education can't be very high. Or one may respond to a study showing that exercise reduces the probability of getting cancer by referring to a friend who exercised vigorously six days per week and still got cancer, so the study can't be true.

Remember that we live in a probabilistic world. To the best of my knowledge, almost nothing is certain, predetermined, or fully explainable by a set of factors. Any regression coefficient estimate is based on how two variables move together, **on average**. It is not an absolute relationship (or effect) for everyone.

In our education-income example, the coefficient estimate indicates how income moves with an extra year of schooling, on average. This will be based on some groups of people for whom income is not much higher with more years-of-schooling and others for whom each year of schooling is associated with much higher income. Furthermore, the average schooling-income relationship will be affected by some levels of years-of-schooling that are associated with fairly low advantages in income and other levels of years-of-schooling (e.g., college years) associated with much greater income advantages.

If a regression were convincing in its ability to isolate the causality of the key-explanatory variable, then the coefficient is an estimate of the **average effect**. If our education-income regression were convincing in this way, then the regression coefficient estimate would indicate how much we believe a year of schooling increases income, on average. Of course, there will be cases such as Bill Gates who became, for a long time, the richest person in the world with just 14 years-of-schooling. And I'm sure there are Ph.D.s out there (with 21+ years-of-schooling) who are waiters making $25,000 or less in Boulder, Colorado. So there are exceptions and outliers.

In the same vein, exercise would probably have varying effects on the probability of cancer for different people. Some people will have a genetic predisposition to get cancer, so exercise may have a smaller effect on their probability of getting cancer. For others, who perhaps have been exposed to environmental toxins or who may not have a healthy diet, exercise may have a larger effect on the probability that they get cancer. Assuming the model is correct and the estimates are unbiased, the coefficient estimate would represent the estimated *average effect* of exercise on the probability of getting cancer, across the population.

In some cases, there may be opposing effects of some treatment on a population. For example, a divorce or separation may have negative effects on some children but positive effects on other children, perhaps those from households having much discord. *The average effect may be estimated to be close to zero, even though many children are truly negatively affected and others are positively affected.*

As another example, let's consider the contribution of teachers to children's achievement. An article about what affects children's academic achievement described what the author considered to be myths on this topic (Phillips, 2014). Myth #1 was that "Teachers Are the Most Important Influence on a Child's Education." To back up the argument that this is a myth, the author said that schools and teachers explain less than 30% of a student's academic success, and socioeconomic status, neighborhood, and the home environment are more important. The blogger and the authors of the book being cited (Berliner and Glass, 2014) were apparently making a common mistake of attributing a general finding to each case. On average, the blogger might be right that these other factors are more important. But my guess is that there are hundreds of thousands of cases per year in which the teacher was indeed the most important factor in a child's educational achievement that year and perhaps in years to come.

Someone I know taught 6th grade in a school largely comprised of first-generation children of Mexican immigrant farm workers. Most of these children had no support from home for their education. They rarely had parents encouraging them to read. This person, a natural in the classroom, was remarkable at generating curiosity in these children. For many of these children, their 6th-grade teacher was the most important influence on their learning in 6th grade (and perhaps beyond).

So the "less-than-30%" figure is an average contribution of teachers. That figure reflects the effects of some teachers who contribute nothing to students' achievement beyond what the children's parents and environment contribute and other teachers who deserve full credit (or blame) for a child's success (or lack thereof).

2.12 Causal effects can change over time

Historically, when the price of oil has increased, profits of U.S. companies tend to decrease, as production and delivery costs are higher. This tended to cause the stock market to decrease. The years 2015 and 2016, however, had a different pattern, as the stock market tended to decrease with *decreases* in oil prices. The difference is likely due to the economy becoming less dependent on oil, delivery of many services being done online, and oil companies becoming a larger share of U.S. companies in the stock market.

The lesson from this is that economic relationships change over time, as the nature of the economy changes. Another good example is that the effects of increases in state tax spending or tax rates could change over time. Perhaps 50 years ago, spending went to, on average, more investments that lowered the cost of conducting business (e.g., building roads and public-transportation systems), whereas today spending may go more towards less productive investments (e.g., bridges to nowhere).

Similarly, relationships between many socio-economic factors can change over time. Parental divorces may have had more harmful effects on children 30 years ago when divorce was less frequent and more of a stigma. Today, the increased prevalence of divorce may help children cope, as they are more likely to have friends having similar experiences.

Thus, it is important to keep in mind that estimated effects from the past may not still be relevant. This is reason #831 for why social science research is less accurate than research in the hard sciences.

2.13 Why regression results might be wrong: inaccuracy and imprecision

It turns out that economists can be wrong in their regression results, even for reasons other than not having read this book. The two main reasons why economists could be wrong are: (1) inaccuracy brought on by a systematic bias; and (2) imprecision or uncertainty.

Let's consider a case of election polling to see the difference. But first, let's consider samples of coin flips. If I were to conduct a series of 100 coin flips and calculate the percent of flips that were "tails," even though the average would be 50% over many series of 100 flips, it will rarely be exactly 50% for a given set of 100 flips. That would be error due to imprecision. The smaller the sample size, the more likely the percentage of flips that are tails would be far from 50%.

It is the same concept with a political poll. Just from sampling error, they might contact or get responses from more of one candidate's supporters than the true representation in the population. This is why polls are always reported with the margin-of-error. For example, if this poll had a margin-of-error of 3 percentage points and had candidate-A receiving 52% of the vote in the poll, it would mean that there is 95% certainty that candidate-A had between 49% and 55% of the vote. Thus, if the true lead for candidate-A were 55%–45%, then 5% of the time a similar poll was conducted, candidate-A would receive under 52% or above 58% of the support in the poll. Lager sample sizes would reduce this imprecision.

Any inaccuracy would come from a problem in methods that would lead to systematically obtaining a non-representative sample of participants. This could occur if they were systematically contacting more people from one party – this could have occurred before pollsters called cell phone numbers, which would bias the samples to those who had a home phone. Alternatively, members of one party could be less likely to answer the phone. If the method were repeated over and over again (reducing the imprecision), the under-representation of one party would tend to remain (meaning, the bias would remain).

A famous example of a systematic inaccuracy/bias occurred in the poll by the *Literary Digest* (later to become *Reader's Digest*) for the 1936 presidential election between Roosevelt and Landon. The poll contacted 2.6 million readers, which approximates infinity, so the margin-of-error would be minimal. They found support for Landon by a 57-43 margin. Roosevelt ended up winning 62-38. The problem was a systematic bias in that the readers of *Literary Digest* tended to be Republicans, and so their poll excessively over-sampled Republicans (and Landon supporters).

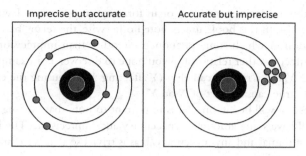

Figure 2.8 Target practice charts to demonstrate imprecision and inaccuracy

This example highlights an important difference between imprecision and inaccuracy. Having a larger sample would reduce imprecision, but it would not reduce any inaccuracy from a systematic bias.

A nice way to see the difference between inaccuracy and imprecision is with target practice, as shown in Figure 2.8 and borrowed from Arkes (2022). On the left target, the six shots are scattered, yet it seems like they are generally centered around the bullseye. In contrast, the six shots on the right target are very close to each other, but they are off-target. The left target demonstrates large imprecision but no apparent inaccuracy or bias. The right target has little imprecision, but a systematic bias of being off-target. The difference is that, if many shots were fired, the central tendency for the average shot would likely be near the center on the left but off-target on the right. If we were just able to see the shots and wanted to predict where the bulls-eye was, it looks like we'd make a good guess (albeit with much uncertainty) on the left, but that we'd be way off-target (but with high certainty) on the right.

In regression analysis, **imprecision** would be represented by a wider range of possible values surrounding the coefficient estimate. The main sources of greater uncertainty are smaller sample sizes, more randomness in the dependent variable (variation unexplained by the explanatory variables), and a narrower range of values for the explanatory variable. As an example of the randomness in the dependent variable, in the issue of how years-of-schooling affects income, income could be affected by many random events, such as luck in getting a certain job or promotion, or a factory closing.

Inaccuracy (or **bias**) in regression analysis would be represented by the coefficient estimate being naturally moved away from its true value for some reason other than imprecision. It mostly would involve a systematic reason why the X and Y variables would be related, other than the reason you are theorizing, such as a causal effect. With regard to the main objective of estimating causal effects, the most common source of inaccuracy is omitted-factors bias, or the influence of a confounding factor. As discussed earlier, we would hope to identify how years-of-schooling affects income, but higher years-of-schooling tends to come with the confounding factors of higher intelligence and motivation, which also affect income. Thus, without fully accounting for intelligence, motivation, and other such confounding factors, we will be systematically off-target in estimating the causal effect of years-of-schooling on income.

The term "bias" has the potential to cause confusion. We often think of "bias" as not being objective or letting personal preferences enter a decision framework rather than objective information. The term "bias" is also used often in terms of "cognitive biases," which involve a systematic error in thinking (such as confirmation bias and anchor-point bias) that causes someone to not be rational in interpreting information, in decision-making, or in forming an opinion – I will discuss some cognitive biases in Chapter 14. In this book, unless noted otherwise, the term "bias" refers to **statistical bias**, which is a situation in which some phenomenon, other than imprecision, moves an estimate away from the causal effect or other relationship you hope to discover. For example, you are hoping to estimate how X affects Y, but a reverse causality (Y affecting X) is causing the estimated relationship to move away from the true causal effect of X on Y.

When I say a regression will be "wrong," it is important to note that "wrong" has many gradients, as every regression will have some amount of inaccuracy and imprecision. The ideal situation would be that imprecision is minimal and any inaccuracy/bias is trivial so that we could accurately obtain a narrow range for a true coefficient.

Let me note that, whereas a bias means that there is an inherent problem with the model, imprecision does not mean there is a problem. However, both bias (inaccuracy) and imprecision could cause an estimated effect to be far off from the true effect.

The dirty little secret is that regressions are not magic boxes that can give an answer to any research question. Rather, many (perhaps most) topics researchers aim to explore have too much imprecision or bias to be able to answer a research question with any degree of statistical and logical certainty. That is part of the value of learning regression analysis: not only learning what can be gained from a study but also what a study cannot determine.

Now, we can understand the statement I made earlier: not only does correlation not mean causation, but also *causation does not mean correlation*. This says there could be a causation (one factor affects an outcome) without there being a correlation. This could occur due to a bias moving the coefficient estimate away from the true effect towards zero.

Chapter 5 will introduce measures of imprecision and convey lessons on how to gauge the strength of evidence of regression results in light of the level of imprecision. Chapter 6 will provide a guide on how to recognize systematic biases that lead to inaccuracy.

2.14 The use of regression flowcharts

Throughout much of the book, I will use what I call regression flowcharts, as depicted in Figure 2.9. The rectangles represent a variable or set of variables, while an oval represents an unobserved factor for which there would not be data due to being unavailable, unobserved, or non-quantifiable. An arrow in the flowchart represents the true effect of a one-unit increase in the pointing variable/factor (even if it were an abstract unobserved factor) on the variable being pointed at. These true effects are unknown to us mortals. The convention I follow is that the main left-to-right arrow would represent

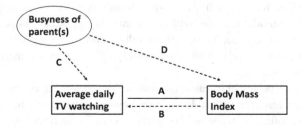

Figure 2.9 A regression flowchart

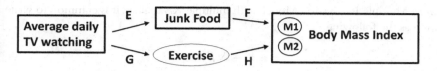

Figure 2.10 A regression flowchart with mediating factors

the causal effect of interest for the model. In this case, we aim to estimate (for children) how the average daily hours of TV watched affect weight, as measured by the Body Mass Index (BMI). That true effect is indicated by the value of **A** in Figure 2.9.

The regression model would hopefully be designed so that it would, as accurately and precisely as possible, produce a coefficient representing the true effect. Yet, as discussed in the prior section, many things might get in the way of that. The flowchart might help us see a few potential problems, such as the outcome affecting the key-X variable (marked as **B**). In addition, the flowchart shows how one possible confounding factor, "busyness of parent(s)" could be in play. I put this confounding factor a bit to the left to highlight that this mostly would occur before the treatment and eventual outcome. (I use the dashed lines to represent potentially-problematic relationships.) If **B** or both **C** and **D** in Figure 2.9 are non-zero, then there would be a bias, as I will describe in Chapter 6.

Figure 2.10 shows another example of a regression flowchart, this time with **mediating factors**. Mediating factors represent factors through which the key-X variable affects the outcome. In our case, I broke down the effect of TV watching on BMI into two mechanisms. Mechanism M1 is that watching more TV affects how much junk food a person eats, which affects BMI. Mechanism M2 has TV watching affecting the amount of exercise a person gets, which in turn affects BMI. I use an oval for "exercise" because it would be difficult to characterize based on the various dimensions of exercise (e.g., duration and intensity). The arrows still represent how a one-unit increase in the pointing variable/factor affects the variable/factor being pointed at. I believe that the values of **E** and **F** are positive, but **G** and **H** would be negative. That is, more TV watching probably reduces the amount of exercise, so **G** < 0. For **H**, we do not want to consider the negative effect of **G** but rather how more exercise would impact BMI, which should be negative (**H** < 0). The value of the mechanism would be the product of the effects along the way. Thus, M1 = **E** × **F**, and M2 = **G** × **H**. Both of these would likely be positive mechanisms (if anything), contributing to a positive effect of TV watching on BMI. Ideally, the sum of M1 and M2 would equal the true effect of **A** (from Figure 2.9), but there would probably be some correlation between M1 and M2 so that their sum is not equal to **A**.

Mechanisms and mediating factors will be important for understanding "holding other factors constant" in Chapter 4 and one of the biases in Chapter 6 (from controlling for a mediating factor).

Figures 2.9 and 2.10 represent the most common types of regression flowcharts that will be used in this book. There will be a few variants of these two that add a few elements.

2.15 The underlying Linear Algebra in regression equations

I propose we leave math to the machines and go play outside.

– Calvin (of Calvin and Hobbes)

When using a Multiple Regression Model, with multiple X variables, it is common to write a regression equation as the following:

$$Y_i = X_i \beta + \varepsilon_i \qquad (2.23)$$

where X_i is, now, a vector for individual i, representing K explanatory variables. The equation can be represented in Linear-Algebra form in the following equation, where each row represents one of the n observations:

$$
\begin{bmatrix} Y_1 \\ Y_2 \\ \cdot \\ \cdot \\ \cdot \\ Y_n \end{bmatrix}
=
\begin{bmatrix} 1X_{11}X_{21}\ldots X_{K1} \\ 1X_{12}X_{22}\ldots X_{K2} \\ \cdot \\ \cdot \\ \cdot \\ 1X_{1n}X_{2n}\ldots X_{Kn} \end{bmatrix}
\times
\begin{bmatrix} \beta_0 \\ \beta_1 \\ \beta_2 \\ \cdot \\ \cdot \\ \beta_k \end{bmatrix}
+
\begin{bmatrix} \varepsilon_1 \\ \varepsilon_2 \\ \cdot \\ \cdot \\ \cdot \\ \varepsilon_n \end{bmatrix}
\qquad (2.24)
$$

$$
\begin{array}{ccccccc}
n\times 1 & & n\times(K+1) & & (K+1)\times 1 & & n\times 1 \\
Y & = & X & \times & \beta & + & \varepsilon
\end{array}
$$

Note that the column of 1's in the first column of matrix X is for the intercept term. In Linear Algebra, the multiplication of two matrices involves transposing each row of the first matrix and multiplying it by the matching entry in the second matrix. Thus, for a product of the two matrices, X and β, the number of columns in the first matrix $(K + 1)$ has to equal the number of rows in the second matrix $(K + 1)$. For observation 1, the equation comes out to:

$$Y_1 = \left(1 \times \beta_0 + X_{11} \times \beta_1 + X_{21} \times \beta_2 + \cdots + X_{K1} \times \beta_K\right) + \varepsilon_1 \qquad (2.25)$$

The product of the $[n \times (K + 1)]$ and $[K \times 1]$ matrix becomes an $[n \times 1]$ matrix, with one entry for each observation. This means that the $[n \times 1]$ matrix on the left-hand side of the equation is the sum of two $[n \times 1]$ matrices on the right-hand side. Note that one could not write $\beta \times X$, as the number of columns in β (1) does not equal the number of rows in X (n). As a result, the notation we would use to represent the product of the X variables and the β coefficients is $X\beta$.

Sometimes, in describing a regression model, a single key-explanatory variable (say, X_1) is separated from the rest, as follows:

$$Y_i = \beta_1 X_{1i} + X_{2i}\beta_2 + \varepsilon_i \qquad (2.26)$$

If it is just a single variable in X_1, then the product of the variable and coefficient is often represented with the coefficient first, as I have had it so far: $\beta_1 \times X_1$ or $\beta_1 X_1$.

What is important is that the proper representation of the product of β_1 and X when X represents a set of variables is: $X_i \beta_1$. I will represent sets of X variables, henceforth, in this fashion. (Note that I do not follow the convention of using bold for vectors, as I do not want to draw extra attention to the vectors, which are typically a minor set of variables in the equations in this book, representing a set of control variables rather than the key-X variable or the treatment.) Other than one brief mention in Section 8.3, *this is the last thing you need to know about Linear Algebra in this book.*

Note that when a generic X is used to represent a set of variables in the Multiple Regression Model, the intercept (β_0) is left out of the equation, just for the sake of brevity or standard practice, even though the intercept is almost always included in regression models (unless specified otherwise). This is because, as in equation (2.24), the constant term (the column of 1s) is typically included.

Hereafter, in Multiple Regression Models in which one component of an equation represents a vector (or set) of several variables, I will assume that the model includes the intercept term and leave the intercept term out of the equations. For equations in which each component of the equation represents just one variable, I will continue to use the intercept term, β_0.

Lastly, note that Linear Algebra is how computers estimate most regressions. This means that the study of theoretical regression analysis and the study of Advanced Econometrics rely more on Linear Algebra. This is where most of the advances in regression analysis come from. For the purposes of almost all of us, we do not need to use it. (I have gone my whole career without any consideration of Linear Algebra or Calculus until I wrote this section.)

2.16 Definitions and key concepts

2.16.1 Different types of data (based on the unit of observation and sample organization)

There are several different ways that data could be organized. This may have implications for the existence of PITFALLS (Chapter 6) and what methods are available for addressing the PITFALLS (Chapter 8).

2.16.1.1 Unit of observation: individual vs. aggregate data

The **unit of observation** indicates what an observation represents, or who/what is the subject. One dimension by which data can be organized is individual entities vs. aggregated data. Individual entities are often an individual or a family, but it could be an organization or business – e.g., a baseball team, with the variables of interest being wins and total payroll. Aggregated data are averaged or summed typically at some geographical or organizational level, such as class-level or school-level data. The data at the aggregate level may be some averaged value for everyone in a classroom (such as a test score) or a state (such as the average years-of-schooling or the proportion of the adult population with a high-school diploma in that state).

2.16.1.2 Sample organization

There are five main types of organization for a sample. They are as follows.

1. **Cross-sectional data.** This is the standard type of data that is used. It involves taking a sample of all subjects (an individual or, say, a state) at a given period of time.
2. **Time-series data.** This is based on one subject over many time periods. An example of this could be quarterly earnings per share for one company over time.
3. **Panel data.** This is a combination of cross-sectional and time-series data. It involves multiple subjects observed at two or more periods each.
4. **Multiple cross-sectional-period data.** This has multiple years (as with panel data), but the subjects are different each year.

5. **Survival data**. This is somewhat similar to panel data in that it involves multiple time periods for each person or subject, but the dependent variable is a variable that turns from 0 to 1 if some event occurs. For example, in an examination of what causes divorces, a couple will be in the data for each year of marriage until a divorce occurs or until the end of observation for the couple. If they get divorced, they are no longer in the sample of couples "at risk" for getting divorced.

A common problem with cross-sectional data is that there are many alternative stories that can contribute to a correlation beyond the causation. For example, if one were to examine how class size affects student achievement in K-12 (which we presume would be negative), then the mechanisms that could contribute to the empirical relationship would include, among others: (1) a true causal effect of class size on student achievement; (2) correlation due to common factors, such as the wealth of a school district; and (3) randomness creating incidental correlation by chance. If there were not adequate data to address the common factors, then the common factors, in this case, would likely contribute negatively to the association between class size and student achievement, perhaps overstating any causal effect. The contribution of incidental correlation towards the estimated effect could be positive or negative.

Having panel data on children or teachers would provide a more accurate estimate of the causal effect of class size. This allows a researcher to hold constant the child's or teacher's average test scores, allowing for an estimate of how children's achievement with a certain class size compares to their achievement with different class sizes. Plus, this often reduces the role of incidental correlation.

A similar problem occurs with time-series data. For example, it would be very difficult to estimate the effects of tax rates on economic growth in a country. If we examined this for the 1990s and 2000s in the United States, we would observe much higher growth rates with higher tax rates, as real GDP growth was higher after the tax rates increased in 1993. In this case, there is likely an incidental correlation: the strong-economic growth generated by the internet boom occurred after President Clinton's tax increases of 1993. It is doubtful that the higher tax rates caused the internet boom.

How can you address this?

You can't … with national data. There is no way to address the incidental correlation!

However, having panel data of state-level tax rates and economic growth *may* provide more accurate estimates. Panel data generally has a major advantage in that it can hold constant the subject (the state in this case) and the time period. It would control for the national effects of the internet boom. Still, there could be problems, as it would not be random what states raised or lowered tax rates. This will be discussed in more detail in Chapters 6 and 8.

2.16.2 A model vs. a method

Mixing up the concept of a model vs. a method is an issue that doesn't bother me much, but it could be an important distinction. A regression model can be distinguished by what variables are in the equation and how the explanatory variables describe the outcome. For example, the explanatory variables could describe the outcome linearly or quadratically. The following are various models:

$$Y_i = \beta_0 + \beta_1 X_{1i} + \varepsilon_i$$
$$Y_i = \beta_0 + \beta_1 X_{1i} + \beta_2 X_{2i} + \varepsilon_i$$
$$Y_i = \beta_0 + \beta_1 X_{1i} + \beta_2 \left(X_{1i} \right)^2 + \varepsilon_i$$

The method is how the equation can be estimated. This could be from regular OLS, or it could be from a Weighted Least Squares method (Chapter 3). There are other possible methods that could be used, as will be covered in Chapters 8 and 9. So a model is characterized by an equation. A method indicates how the model is estimated. And a given model can be estimated with various methods.

2.16.3 How to use subscripts and when they are needed

So far, we have used a single subscript to identify the unit of observation, or what an observation represents (e.g., a single person). In Section 2.3.1, I had equation (2.1a) with subscripts and the equivalent (2.2) without subscripts, as follows:

$$Y_i = \beta_0 + \beta_1 \times X_i + \varepsilon_i \tag{2.1a}$$

$$Y = \beta_0 + \beta_1 \times X + \varepsilon \tag{2.2}$$

There are some situations in which multiple subscripts will be needed (or at least recommended). First, subscripts would be recommended (though not essential) when there are observations over several periods, it would be useful to add a "time" subscript, usually t. (This would be a case in which it would be recommended to make it clear to the reader that the data are not just a snapshot in time.)

Second, subscripts are needed when there is an aggregated variable used in the model that applies to multiple observations. For example, if the annual state unemployment rate (UR) were added to equation (2.1a), it would be:

$$Y_{isy} = \beta_0 + \beta_1 \times X_i + \beta_2 \times UR_{sy} + \varepsilon_{isy} \tag{2.28}$$

This would say that the unemployment rate is measured at the state (s) and year (y) level, meaning that each state has its own value of UR for each year. That UR_{sy} would apply to all observations that were in state s in year y. Having the "i" subscript on Y tells us that that state-year unemployment rate would apply to many subjects being observed in state s and year y. Having the s and y subscripts on variable, X, would be optional if it did not change over time (such as a variable for race/ethnicity).

Third, subscripts are needed when fixed effects are used, but you will not need to worry about this until Chapter 8.

In my view, subscripts are unnecessary if dealing with just a single subscript. However, when multiple subscripts are warranted, then the subscripts become necessary to show in a regression equation.

2.17 Chapter summary

Figure 2.11 demonstrates, through a story, many of the key points of this chapter. More formally, here are descriptions of some of those important points.

* Regressions indicate the statistical relationship between variables. They indicate how some outcome variable moves, on average, when other variables change, attempting to hold other variables in the model constant, or at least adjusting for the other variables.

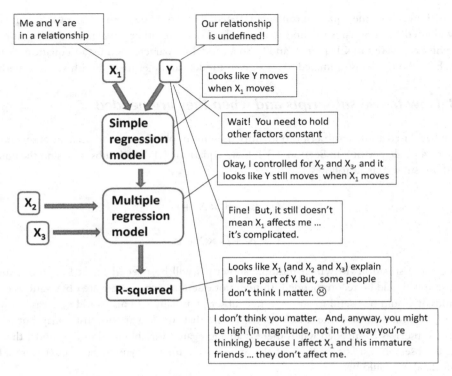

Figure 2.11 Summary of Chapter 2

- The objective of most regression models is to identify causal relationships, in contrast with just correlational relationships. That is, we are often interested in how some treatment variable (*X*) affects an outcome variable (*Y*).
- To conclude causality with any adequate degree of certainty, we need to rule out other causes of two variables having a statistical association.
- The Multiple Regression Model attempts to rule out the influence of other factors by including them in the regression.
- There are two main reasons why regression results can be wrong: imprecision due to not enough observations or randomness in the outcome; and inaccuracy due to a systematic bias.

Exercises

1. Indicate which of the four main regression objectives each of the following research issues would be:
   a. What 4th-grade teacher did best given his/her students' prior achievement?
   b. What is the best guess for how many sailors the Navy will recruit this year?
   c. Do people who swear have higher intelligence?
   d. How much does keeping up with the material affect your eventual grade in the class?
   e. Does keeping up with the material affect your eventual grade in the class?

2. Suppose that, in a particular city, a regression of prices of homes sold in the prior year (*price*) on the number of bedrooms (*bedrooms*) and square feet (*sqft*) yields the following regression model:

$$\widehat{price} = 100,000 + 45,000 \times bedrooms + 10 \times sqft$$

a. Interpret the coefficient estimate on *sqft*.
b. If a home had 2 bedrooms and was 1500 square feet, what would the predicted price be?
c. If that home had a selling price of $170,000, what would be the residual?
d. How would you interpret the residual?
e. What is a possible reason for the residual being what it is?

3. Use the following four observations to estimate how oatmeal consumption explains cholesterol levels:

Oatmeal (ounces per week)	Cholesterol (HDL)
0	130
10	90
10	100
20	100

a. Plot out the data. Based on a quadrant analysis (in Figure 2.2), what sign do you believe the coefficient estimate on oatmeal would be? Justify your answer just from observing the data.
b. Calculate the regression equation: $\widehat{cholesterol} = \hat{\beta}_0 + \hat{\beta}_1 \times oatmeal$.
c. How would you interpret the coefficient estimate on the variable, *oatmeal*?
d. What are the predicted value and residual for the first observation? How would you interpret those?
e. Calculate the R^2 and interpret it.

4. From the book's website, use the data set, **democracy2**. This is a data set of observations by country and year, with measures of democracy, life expectancy, and several other factors and outcomes. (see https://www.v-dem.net/). Use 1985 observations with *condition1*=1 (which is that there are non-missing values for all variables used in this regression).
a. Calculate the means and standard deviations of the following four variables to get a sense of the scales of the variable:
   • *life_exp* (life expectancy)
   • *democracy* (an index of the level of democracy in a county on a 0–1 scale)
   • *avgeduc* (average years of education)
   • *educgini* (inequality Gini coefficient for years of education, on a 0–100 scale).
b. Regress *life_exp* on *democracy*, *avgeduc*, and *educgini*. Interpret the coefficient estimate on *democracy*.
c. For a country with *life-exp* = 60, *democracy* = 0.5, *avgeduc* = 10, and *educgini* = 50, what is the predicted value of the dependent variable and the residual?
d. Interpret the predicted value and the residual.
e. Interpret the R^2.
f. Add *urbanpct* (the percent of the population living in an urban area) as an explanatory variable to the model. Interpret the change in R^2 after adding *urbanpct*.

5. From the book's website, use the data set, **income**. Estimate three separate models, with *income* as the dependent variable. Include just one of the three explanatory variables (*educ, afqt, age*) in each model. Which explanatory variable explains the greatest amount of variation in *income*? How did you arrive at your answer?

Notes

1 The NLSY is provided by the Bureau of Labor Statistics, U.S. Department of Labor. The NLSY started with 12,686 youth in 1979, aged 14–22. It has followed them since, asking questions on labor-market outcomes, demographics (marital history), and many other factors (Bureau of Labor Statistics, 2014).
2 To protect the confidentiality of respondents, the NLSY top-codes income data. Their method is to assign respondents in the top 2% of income values the average for that group. Due to our sample restrictions leaning the sample towards higher-earners (e.g., males and having positive income), 3.9% of the respondents in our sample are in the top-coded group. The cut-off is $145,000, and they are assigned an income of $265,933 (Bureau of Labor Statistics, 2014).
3 You can also examine methods the coaches used: Jackson had his players read about Zen; Popovich taught his players about the background cultures of each of his international players – such as the discrimination experiences of point guard Patty Mills's people from the Torres Strait of Australia – which served towards helping players understand and respect each other. Popovich's players generally liked each other and were objectively unselfish; not so for Jackson's players.

References

Arkes, J. (2022). *Confessions of a Recovering Economist: How Economists Get Almost Everything Wrong* (self-published), https://www.amazon.com/dp/B0BLG2PFHF/.
Berliner, D., & Glass, G. (2014). *50 Myths & lies that threaten America's public schools*. New York: Teachers College Press.
Bureau of Labor Statistics, U.S. Department of Labor. (2014). *National Longitudinal Survey of Youth 1979 cohort, 1979–2012 (rounds 1–25)*. Columbus, OH: Center for Human Resource Research, The Ohio State University.
Frost, J. (2014). How important are normal residuals in regression analysis? *The Minitab Blog*. (Available at http://blog.minitab.com/blog/adventures-in-statistics-2/how-important-are-normal-residuals-in-regression-analysis, accessed December 28, 2017.)
Phillips, M. (2014). 8 Myths That Undermine Educational Effectiveness. *Edutopia*. (Available at https://www.edutopia.org/blog/myths-that-undermine-educational-effectiveness-mark-phillips.)

3 Essential tools for regression analysis

This chapter introduces a few important tools for regression analysis. These tools are important on their own, but some will also help in developing an understanding of essential concepts in the next few chapters. In this chapter, you will learn:

- How to use "dummy variables" to characterize yes/no indicators or qualitative factors
- How to model non-linear relationships between the X variables and the Y variable, which may produce a better fit of the data or better characterize the relationship between an X and Y variable
- How to apply weights in a regression model when certain observations (e.g., larger states, compared to smaller states) should have greater importance in a regression
- How to standardize coefficient estimates to compare those for variables that are on different units of scale.

3.1 Using dummy (binary) variables

3.1.1 The basics of dummy variables

So far, we have dealt with variables that are quantitative in nature: income, years-of-schooling, and AFQT score. For these variables, a higher-vs.-lower value of the variable has meaning in terms of being better or worse or there being more or less of something.

DOI: 10.4324/9781003285007-3

But sometimes there are variables that are qualitative in nature. These variables could be based on categories or based on a yes/no classification. Examples could include:

- Gender
- Race/ethnicity
- Occupation
- Type of college
- Whether a hospital patient receives a certain treatment
- Whether a person used heroin.

To incorporate qualitative factors into a regression, the qualitative variable needs to be converted into one or a series of **dummy variables**, which take on the value of either 0 or 1. Dummy variables are also sometimes referred to as **dichotomous**, **indicator**, and **binary** variables.

When creating the dummy variables, all categories cannot be included in the regression model. Rather, there needs to be a "reference category" (also called "reference group" or "excluded category") so that each group has another group to be compared to. For example, for a yes/no classification (e.g., whether a patient receives a medical treatment), the two categories are boiled down to one variable (say, T, for "treatment") coded as follows:

- $T = 1$ if the person receives the treatment
- $T = 0$ if the person does not receive the treatment (the reference category).

In an example on a categorical variable, if we had a sample of college graduates and were trying to control for the type of college a person graduated from, we may want to use "4-year public university" as the reference category. The college-type variables may then include:

- $C_1 = 1$ if the person graduated from a 4-year private university; $= 0$ otherwise;
- $C_2 = 1$ if the person graduated from a 4-year liberal arts college; $= 0$ otherwise;
- $C_3 = 1$ if the person graduated from a 2-year community college; $= 0$ otherwise;
- $C_4 = 1$ if the person graduated from some other type of college (e.g., music college); $= 0$ otherwise.

Everyone with a college degree would have a value of 1 for exactly one of the variables, C_1 to C_4, with the exception of those who went to a "4-year public university" – the reference group – who have a value of 0 for all four of the variables. *The coefficient estimates on the college-type variables would be how the outcomes for people having graduated from the given type of college compare to the outcomes for people in the reference category, after adjusting for the other factors.*

There is one exception to the rule that there needs to be a reference category. When a model is specified to not have an intercept, then all categories of a qualitative variable could be included in the model. The coefficient estimates on each category would represent what the expected value of Y would be for that category if the other X variables were all 0 – that is, the intercept for each category. But this is a rare type of model, and it can only be used if the categorization is not the key-X set of variables.

To demonstrate how to set up and interpret sets of categorical variables, I took the 2004 NLSY data (on 2003 income), and I added variables for "Black" and "Hispanic" to equation (2.21). This is based on the available classification in the NLSY (Bureau of Labor Statistics, 2014). For simplicity of interpretation, I classified those who are both Black and Hispanic as just Black. Thus, the racial/ethnic categorization would be:

- Black
- Hispanic
- Non-Hispanics of races other than Black (the reference group).

The regression model gives the following equation:

$$\left(\widehat{income}\right)_i = -32,984 + 5704 \times (educ)_i + 304 \times (AFQT)_i$$
$$- 7815 \times (Black)_i - 1642 \times (Hispanic)_i \tag{3.1}$$

The coefficient estimate on *Black* of −7815 indicates that, after adjusting for the other variables included in equation (3.1), Blacks, on average, earn an estimated $7815 less than the reference group of non-Hispanic people of other races. It is not that Blacks earn $7815 less than non-Blacks. Likewise, Hispanics are estimated to earn $1642 less than "non-Hispanic people of races other than Black," on average, after controlling for the other factors.

Whereas the examples here use dummy variables for representing qualitative data, dummy variables can also be used to represent quantitative data. For example, one may want to characterize the AFQT score in categories rather than in linear format. Thus, instead of (or in addition to) using the AFQT score, one could use dummy variables for each AFQT quartile – excluding one quartile as the reference group.

3.1.2 Be mindful of the proper interpretation based on the reference group

As stated above, the coefficient estimate should be interpreted as a comparison to the reference group. You can set up the dummy variables to give the reference group that you want.

Consider an alternative specification for education, using the *highest degree* earned. For the sake of simplicity, let's use some nice easy numbers and a sample of just people who have at least a high-school degree. A "college degree" refers to having a 4-year college degree as one's highest degree, while a "graduate degree" involves having a Master's, Doctoral, or professional degree. Figure 3.1 shows the notional average incomes for each group, plus the average for the first two categories combined, which is weighted towards the "High school" average because a larger share of the sample has just a high-school diploma. ($50,000 would be the average if the sample of high-school-degree people is twice the size of the sample of college-degree people.)

The estimated income premium for a graduate degree depends on what the reference group is. Estimating a model just with a dummy variable for having a graduate degree produces the following equation (with other variables such as the AFQT score excluded for simplicity):

$$\left(\widehat{income}\right)_i = 50,000 + 40,000 \times (graduate\ degree)_i \tag{3.2}$$

Note that the intercept ($50,000) is the average income for the first two groups. The $40,000 estimate is the difference between those with a graduate degree and all others. Thus, without assigning those with just a high-school degree to a separate category, they are counted in the reference group along with

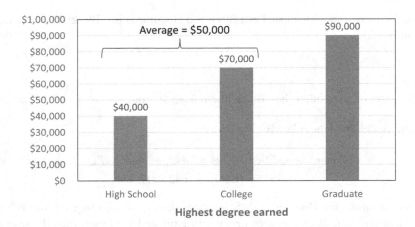

Figure 3.1 Income by highest degree

Source: Bureau of Labor Statistics, 2014 (n = 2363).

those with a college degree. This is an important point: **For a categorization, any group not having a value of one for a dummy variable in the categorization is part of the reference group**.

Adding a variable for "having one's highest degree being a college degree" would make the reference group the one group not part of one of the categories included, which is comprised of those with just a high-school diploma:

$$\left(\widehat{income}\right)_i = 40,000 + 30,000 \times (college\ degree)_i + 50,000 \times (graduate\ degree)_i \tag{3.3}$$

The intercept is now the "High school" average. The $50,000 is the difference, in Figure 3.1, between the $90,000 (for those with a graduate degree) and the $40,000 for those with just a high-school diploma. It follows that the $30,000 coefficient estimate is the difference between the $70,000 (for those with a college degree being the highest degree earned) and the $40,000.

An alternative setup could use "has a college degree" rather than "highest degree is a college degree," which gives the regression equation:

$$\left(\widehat{income}\right)_i = 40,000 + 30,000 \times (college\ degree\ or\ more)_i + 20,000 \times (graduate\ degree)_i \tag{3.4}$$

This is the same as (3.3) except that the coefficient estimate of $20,000 on the graduate degree is now relative to those with a college degree ($90,000 − $70,000). This is because those with a graduate degree (all of whom have a college degree also) have the $30,000 for the college degree contributing to the predicted value, so the coefficient estimate on *graduate degree* is now what is over and above those with a college degree.

3.2 Non-linear functional forms using Ordinary Least Squares

3.2.1 Combining variables for interaction effects

In the research on how divorce affects children, the conventional wisdom is that divorce is harmful to children, but you have a theory that divorce would not be as bad and may actually help children if it gets them away from a dysfunctional situation with high levels of conflict. How can you examine whether divorce effects on children are different for those in such families?

One option is to estimate separate models for families with a high level (H) vs. a low level (L) of conflict. Let's set up the model as follows. Consider a sample of children whose parents were married, as of say, 2010, and we observe them again in 2014, with some of the children having experienced a parental divorce in those four years. The models would be the exact same for the two groups, but with different subscripts for the variable names and coefficient estimates:

$$\text{High-level of conflict families :} \quad Y_{iH} = X_{iH}\beta_{1H} + \beta_{2H}D_{iH} + \varepsilon_{iH} \tag{3.5a}$$

$$\text{Low-level of conflict families :} \quad Y_{iL} = X_{iL}\beta_{1L} + \beta_{2L}D_{iL} + \varepsilon_{iL} \tag{3.5b}$$

where:
- "H" and "L" subscripts refer to the families with "high" and "low" levels of conflict, respectively
- Y is the outcome for child i, measured as the change in test score from 2010 to 2014
- X is a set of control variables
- D is an indicator (dummy variable) for having one's parents divorce between 2010 and 2014.

The test to examine whether children from high-conflict families have different effects of divorce from that for children from low-conflict families would be a comparison of the coefficient estimates, $\hat{\beta}_{2H}$ and $\hat{\beta}_{2L}$. The expectation would be that $\hat{\beta}_{2H}$ would be less negative than $\hat{\beta}_{2L}$ (or even positive) – that is, any adverse effects of the divorce may be lower or non-existent for children from high-conflict families, and the divorce effects may even be positive.

An alternative method is to use **interaction effects**, which would involve combining all children, from both high- and low-conflict families, into one model, as follows:

$$Y_i = X_i\beta_1 + \beta_2 D_i + \beta_3 H_i + \beta_4 \left(D_i \times H_i \right) + \varepsilon_i \tag{3.6}$$

where H is an indicator (dummy variable) for being in a high-conflict family. The interaction term is $D \times H$, which has the "divorce" dummy variable being interacted with the "high-conflict" dummy variable. This variable equals 1 only if the child's parents divorced and the family is "high conflict." The estimated effect of a divorce would be calculated as:

$$\frac{\Delta Y}{\Delta D} = \hat{\beta}_2 + \hat{\beta}_4 \times H \tag{3.7}$$

For children from low-conflict families, the estimated divorce effect would be $\hat{\beta}_2$ (because $H = 0$). For children from high-conflict families, the estimated divorce effect would be $\hat{\beta}_2 + \hat{\beta}_4$ (because $H = 1$).

The test for whether the divorce effects are different for high-conflict vs. low-conflict families would be based on the value of $\hat{\beta}_4$. If there were evidence that the effect of a divorce on children's test scores was different for high-conflict vs. low-conflict families, then the level of conflict would be a **moderating factor** for this effect.

The advantages of using the interaction effect (equation 3.6) instead of separate regression equations (3.5a and 3.5b) are that:

- It is a more direct test of differences in the estimate across the two models rather than comparing two coefficient estimates
- It produces more precise estimates for all variables, as it has a larger sample than separate models.

The disadvantages are that:

- It does not produce a direct estimate of the effect of divorce on children from high-conflict families – rather, you have to add the two estimates ($\hat{\beta}_2 + \hat{\beta}_4$), and the standard error for the hypothesis test may need to be calculated manually
- It is constraining $\hat{\beta}_1$, the estimates on other X variables, to be the same for the two groups – the low-conflict and the high-conflict samples.

These considerations need to be weighed when determining whether to use interaction effects or separate models. The standard in such a situation is to use interaction effects, but of course, both methods could be used.

In sum, interaction variables can inform us on whether one variable moderates the effects of another variable. In the example above, both were dummy variables, but either or both variables in an interaction could be a non-dummy variable. Box 3.1 has an example of this.

Box 3.1 Discrimination as a self-fulfilling prophecy

A great example of interactions comes from Glover et al. (2017), who examine how differently minority cashiers at a grocery-store chain in France perform when they work a shift with a manager who has greater bias against minorities. If minority cashiers did work less productively in the presence of managers with greater bias, then any initial discrimination would tend to be self-fulfilling or self-confirming. This would be an important finding because the normal assumption in studies on discrimination is that any bias by an employer does not affect worker productivity.

The model is the following:

$$Y_{ist} = \beta_0 + \beta_1 \times (minority)_i \times (bias)_{ist} + \beta_2 \times (bias)_{ist} + \delta_i + X_{ist}\beta_3 + \varepsilon_{ist}$$

where:

- Y = one of four dependent variables (for worker i on shift s in time period t):
  - Dummy variable for whether the worker is absent on a given day
  - Minutes worked in excess of schedule
  - Articles scanned per minute
  - Time between customers
- *minority* = dummy variable whether the cashier is a minority
- *bias* = bias measure for the shift manager (based on an "implicit association test") for worker i's shift s in time period t
- *minority* × *bias* = interaction of the two variables

- X = a set of other factors (which are not terribly important)
- δ_i = a set of controls for each cashier.

The coefficient estimate on *bias* will indicate how the level of bias in managers affects the productivity of non-minorities, as it is possible that managers with more bias have other characteristics that motivate performance differently from that of managers with less bias. The coefficient estimate on the interaction (*minority* × *bias*) then estimates how minorities' outcomes respond to greater-bias managers, compared to non-minorities.

There is a little more to the model, but it is not important. I will discuss the results in Section 11.1. But, as a quick preview, there is indeed evidence for, in this setting, discrimination being self-fulfilling.

3.2.2 Logarithmic forms of variables

So far, all of the quantitative variables have been the actual values rather than any transformed value. This means that for any value of X:

$$\beta = \frac{\Delta Y}{\Delta X} \tag{3.8}$$

whether that is after adjusting for other factors or just part of a Simple Regression Model. This indicates how much the variable Y is higher or lower, on average, with a one-unit higher value of the variable X.

In some cases, we may be interested in percent changes in X and/or Y rather than the changes in the actual values. When a variable is transformed to its natural logarithm, it becomes interpreted as a percentage change.

Table 3.1 shows four cases of what are called functional forms, which vary based on whether or not the X and Y variables are transformed to their natural logarithm (ln). In some fields, an elasticity

Table 3.1 Interpretations based on logarithmic forms of the X and Y variables

Functional form	Model	Interpretation	Formula for β_1
Linear	$Y_i = \beta_0 + \beta_1 X_i + \varepsilon_i$	The change in Y associated with a one-unit higher value of X	$\dfrac{\Delta Y}{\Delta X}$
Linear-log	$Y_i = \beta_0 + \beta_1 \ln(X_i) + \varepsilon_i$	The change in Y associated with a one-percent higher value of X.	$\dfrac{\Delta Y}{\%\Delta X}$
Log-linear	$\ln(Y_i) = \beta_0 + \beta_1 X_i + \varepsilon_i$	The percentage change in Y associated with a one-unit higher value of X.	$\dfrac{\%\Delta Y}{\Delta X}$
Log-log	$\ln(Y_i) = \beta_0 + \beta_1 \ln(X_i) + \varepsilon_i$	The percentage change in Y associated with a one-percent higher value of X. (This is also called the **elasticity**.)	$\dfrac{\%\Delta Y}{\%\Delta X}$

While the models here are based on the Simple Regression Model, the same interpretation holds with Multiple Regression Models.

is often calculated, which uses the log-log functional form and is interpreted as the percentage change in Y associated with a one-percentage-point increase in X:

$$\frac{dY}{dX} \times \frac{X}{Y} \text{ or } \frac{\%\Delta Y}{\%\Delta X}$$

Box 3.2 How income regressions are typically estimated

When there are regressions with income, earnings, or the wage rate as the dependent variable, the dependent variable is typically transformed to its natural logarithm. This helps reduce problems of heteroskedasticity (Section 5.4.2), and a percent change is more interpretable across years and different price levels. The coefficient estimate, $\hat{\beta}_1$, from the equation:

$$\ln(income) = \beta_0 + \beta_1 \times (years\text{-}of\text{-}schooling) + \varepsilon$$

represents the estimated percent higher income associated with one extra year-of-schooling. Despite this being the convention, I will continue to use just "income" instead of "ln(income)" for the sake of simplicity in conveying the key concepts.

3.2.3 Quadratic and spline models

There are many situations in which there could be non-linear relationships between the explanatory variable and the outcome. Imagine that you are a professor and you want to examine how much studying affects test scores in your class. Let us assume that, somehow, you are able to randomize how many hours each student studies to avoid any systematic biases of these estimated effects. My guess is that you would probably get a relationship similar to the following in Figure 3.2, which is based on data I made up.

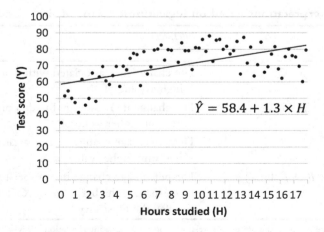

Figure 3.2 Notional example of study hours and test scores

This relationship demonstrates a basic and simple economic concept: diminishing returns. There are likely strong returns to those first few hours of studying, as the students review the core material, but as they study more and more, they are probably being less productive. Maybe they are re-reading things, and maybe they are just losing concentration from too much studying.

Let's say that you use a regression analysis and merely test the linear relationship between hours studied (H) and test score (Y), as follows:

$$Y_i = \beta_0 + \beta_1 H_i + \varepsilon_i \tag{3.9}$$

I inserted the estimated regression line in Figure 3.2. It looks like $\hat{\beta}_1$ would understate the slope for low numbers of hours studied, as seen by the slope of the trend line being lower than the general slope for the data points. And $\hat{\beta}_1$ would overstate the slope for higher values of hours studied. There are two alternative models that could provide for a better fit of the data.

First, there is a **quadratic model** that adds the square of hours studied, as follows:

$$Y_i = \beta_0 + \beta_1 H_i + \beta_2 H_i^2 + \varepsilon_i \tag{3.10}$$

Of course, one could use a higher-order polynomial than a quadratic model (a 2nd-order polynomial). For example, a 3rd-order polynomial would add a cubed-H variable to equation (3.10). This would be more accurate for predicting the test score, but it would make it more difficult to answer the question of whether and how hours studied affects the test score.

Second, one could use what is called a **spline function**, in which you allow H to have a different estimated linear effect at different levels of H. We can see from Figure 3.2 that around 8 hours of studying is when the benefit of studying appears to level off and maybe decrease. Thus, one could estimate the separate marginal effects of "an hour of studying up to 8 hours" and "an hour of studying beyond 8 hours." The model is the following:

$$Y_i = \delta_0 + \delta_1 \times I(H_i \geq 8) + \delta_2 \times (H_i \text{ up to } 8) + \delta_3 \times \left[(H_i \text{ beyond } 8) \times I(H_i \geq 8) \right] + \varepsilon_i \tag{3.11}$$

where $I(\cdot)$ is an indicator function, taking the value of 1 if the expression is true and 0 otherwise. The interpretation of the coefficients would be the following:

- δ_0 would be the intercept, which is the expected score for someone with 0 hours of studying.
- δ_2 measures how much scores move, on average, with a one–unit change in hours studied between 0 and 8 hours of studying; those who studied more than 8 hours would all have a value of 8 for the variable $(H_i \text{ up to } 8)$.
- δ_3 measures how much scores move, on average, with a one–unit change in hours studied of more than 8; those who studied less than 8 hours would have a 0 for the variable $(H_i \text{ beyond } 8)$ and would not contribute to the estimate of δ_3.
- δ_1 would be any difference in the expected score at the spline point, $H = 8$, based on the spline for $(H_i \text{ beyond } 8)$ compared to the spline for $(H_i \text{ up to } 8)$.

The results of the three models are the following:

$$\text{Linear}: \quad \hat{Y}_i = 58.4 + 1.3 \times H_i \quad \left(R^2 = 0.340 \right) \tag{3.12}$$

$$\text{Quadratic}: \quad \hat{Y}_i = 42.3 + 6.6 \times H_i - 0.3 \times H_i^2 \quad \left(R^2 = 0.675 \right) \tag{3.13}$$

$$\text{Spline}: \quad \hat{Y}_i = 44.5 - 0.3 \times I\left(H_i \geq 8\right) + 4.6 \times \left(H_i \text{ up to } 8\right)$$
$$- 0.8 \times \left[\left(H_i \text{ beyond } 8\right) \times I\left(H_i \geq 8\right)\right] \quad \left(R^2 = 0.667\right) \tag{3.14}$$

To demonstrate how the data work for the spline model, a value of $H = 2$ would mean, rounding the coefficient estimates, that:

- (H up to 8) would have a value of 2 and contribute $4.6 \times 2 = 9.2$ to the predicted test score.
- $I(H \geq 8)$ would be 0, so would not contribute to the predicted score.
- (H beyond 8) $\times$ $I(H \geq 8)$ would have a value of 0 and contribute $-0.8 \times 0 = 0$ to the predicted score.
- Combined with the constant of 44.5, the predicted score would be 53.7.

A value of $H = 15$ would produce:

- (H up to 8) would have a value of 8 and contribute $4.6 \times 8 = 36.8$ to the predicted score.
- $I(H \geq 8)$ would be 1, so it would contribute $(-0.3) \times 1 = -0.3$ to the predicted score.
- (H beyond 8) $\times$ $I(H \geq 8)$ would have a value of 7 and contribute $-0.8 \times 7 = -5.6$ to the predicted score.
- Combined with the constant of 44.5, the predicted score would be 75.4.

Figure 3.3 shows the predicted values for the three models of (3.12–3.14). One interesting result is that the slopes for the spline and the quadratic models are greater than that for the linear model up to 8 hours, and the slopes of those two are lower than that for the linear model after about 8 hours. The

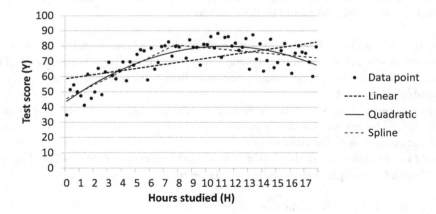

Figure 3.3 Predicted values for the linear, quadratic, and spline models

spline and the quadratic models appear to fit the data better, as can be seen in the R^2's for equations (3.12–3.14). What also is striking is that the linear model will tend to overstate the predicted test score for those on the ends ($H = 2$ or 15) and understate the score around the center of the distribution ($H = 8$).

How do you know if you need to model non-linear effects? You could look at basic plots to observe the nature of the relationship. Alternatively, you could base it on theory. Is there any reason to believe that the effects of the explanatory variable on the outcome would be different for different values of the variable? For example, one would expect different returns to schooling for primary vs. secondary vs. college years-of-schooling. One could imagine that each level of schooling provides different skill sets that are rewarded differently in the workplace. Or, simply, the theory of diminishing returns would suggest a reduced return to greater years-of-schooling.

All of this said, just because the X variable could have varying effects on Y at different levels of the X variable does not mean it needs to be reported this way. Researchers may want to know the average effect of the X variable on Y. They may just want one number, not a series of numbers. In this case, just estimating the average linear effect of the X variable on Y may be all that is needed. Still, it may still be worth mentioning its non-linear effects.

Box 3.3   Does heat bring out voters?

In a thought-provoking article, Van Assche et al. (2017) estimate the effects of temperature on voting participation rates. The idea is that hot temperatures can elicit pro-social behaviors (not just the anti-social behaviors we normally associate with high temperatures). They use aggregated, (U.S.) state-level data for the presidential elections from 1960 to 2016. There were several explanatory variables, but the key-explanatory variable was the average temperature on election day. The results indicated that a 1°C increase in the state's average high temperature on election day was associated with a 0.14% higher voter-participation rate, on average. (This was statistically significant at the 5% level.) This provides some support for their theory for the effects of hot weather.

But might there have been a better way to characterize the temperature data? What is driving the result? Going from normal to hot temperatures? Or maybe going from bone-chilling-freezing temperatures to just cold temperatures? There probably are not many places in the United States that have hot days around election day, in early November. So the effect may have been coming from the lower end of the temperature distribution – comparing the cold election days to the bone-chilling-freezing election days – and not have had anything to do with "heat."

How could the data have been characterized? Perhaps there could have been a spline function, with separate slopes at, say (using Fahrenheit): (1) −50° to 20°, (2) 20° to 70°, and (3) 70° or higher. The slope on the latter group would provide a better test for the authors' theory, and it would rule out the alternative explanation that it could just be people not wanting to vote in freezing weather (which could include snow).

3.3 Weighted regression models

The standard regression model treats each observation the same in terms of its weight (importance) in the calculation of the regression equation. For example, if studying how serving in Iraq affected the likelihood of an Army soldier suffering from post-traumatic stress disorder (PTSD), there is no reason to give any set of soldiers greater weight in the model than a different set of soldiers.

But there are many situations in which each observation should not be counted the same. Some of these reasons include:

- Some surveys, including the NLSY, over-sample from particular sub-populations – e.g., by race or income levels. This means that the data are not going to be nationally representative. The NLSY provides sampling weights to indicate how representative a respondent is of the nation's general population of the same age group.
- The unit of observation, if aggregated, may be based on different-sized populations. For example, if examining how state tax rates affect average state employment growth, one may want to give greater weight to larger states (e.g., California and Texas) than to smaller states (Wyoming and Vermont).
- An analysis of corporations may be more relevant if the larger corporations are given more weight in the model than smaller corporations.

The fix for this is quite simple in most statistical packages and often involves simply indicating the sampling-weight variable one would wish to apply to the observation. Applying weights to OLS would be considered the **Weighted Least Squares** method. But practically any method (some of which you will learn in Chapter 9) can apply different weights to different observations.

As an example, let's consider the relationship between the state unemployment rate and state marijuana use among teenagers (12–17-year-olds), which comes from the National Survey on Drug Use and Health (NSDUH). This is a preview of an issue that will be examined with more detail in Chapters 6 and 8. Let's consider a simple cross-sectional model. The NSDUH provides two-year averages for teenage marijuana use at the state level. Let's take 2009–2010, which had the highest unemployment rates of the Financial Crisis. And let's average the state unemployment rate over those two years. So the dependent variable and explanatory variable are, respectively:

- MJ = Percentage of 12–17-year-olds in the state using marijuana in the past 30 days (2009–2010).
- UR = Average unemployment rate in the state in 2009–2010.

The issue at hand is how states should be weighted. If no sample weights were used, then this analysis would treat Wyoming (with a population of less than 500,000 in 2010) the same as California (with almost 34 million people). However, to weight the sample based on population would make states like Wyoming effectively meaningless for the model. Weighting by the 2010 population would mean that the ten most-populous states would have 54% of the weight in the model, while the ten least-populous states would have 0.3% weight in the model. Alternatively, some use the

Table 3.2 A comparison of models using various weighting schemes (n = 100)

Weight	Regression equation	R^2
None	$\widehat{MJ} = 9.597 + 0.205 \times UR$	0.022
Square root of state's 2010 population	$\widehat{MJ} = 8.971 + 0.244 \times UR$	0.035
State's 2010 population	$\widehat{MJ} = 7.961 + 0.373 \times UR$	0.092

Sources: National Survey of Drug Use and Health (SAMHSA, 2012).

square root of the population, which would produce weights of 38% for the top-10 states and 8% for the bottom-10 states, which seems more reasonable. That said, there is no known optimal weighting scheme.

I estimate the model in all three ways: (1) weight all observations equally (i.e., not indicating any weights); (2) weight observations by the square root of the 2010 population; and (3) weight by the 2010 population.

The results are in Table 3.2. The pattern is that, the more that the state's populations determine the weight of the observations, the coefficient estimate is more positive, and the R^2 increases. The pattern with the R^2 indicates that the population weights help explain more variation in the model, at least for this case. This analysis suggests the possibility that greater unemployment rates lead to greater marijuana use. But there are many potential problems here, which we will learn about in Chapter 6. And, despite the results, it is uncertain which of these three models is optimal, or if there is another weighting scheme better than these.

3.4 Calculating standardized coefficient estimates to allow comparisons

Let's consider an analysis of the Peasant Rebellion in Romania in 1907. Chirot and Ragin (1975) analyzed what factors determined the intensity of the rebellion across counties. The variables were:

- *Intensity* of the rebellion (the dependent variable), which captures the number of deaths, the amount of violence, and the spread of the rebellion
- *Inequality*, measuring a Gini Coefficient for land-owning
- *Commerce*, measuring the percentage of land devoted to the production of wheat, which was the main cash crop
- *Tradition*, measured as the illiteracy rate, signaling the lack of progress and new ideas
- *Midpeasant*, which indicates the percentage of rural households that owned between 7 and 50 hectares.

The model produces the following regression equation:

$$\widehat{intensity} = -12.91 + 1.14 \times inequality + 0.12 \times tradition + 0.09 \times commerce - 0.003 \times midpeasant$$

Table 3.3 Standardized coefficient estimates of determinants of the Romanian Peasant Rebellion

	Standard deviation	Coefficient estimate (dep. var. = intensity)	Standardized coefficient estimate
Intensity	1.77		
Inequality	0.11	1.14	0.07
Tradition	3.86	0.12	0.26
Commerce	11.92	0.09	0.61
Midpeasant	17.38	0.003	0.03

Of course, we need to consider how precise the estimates are and whether they are statistically significant, but that type of exercise will wait until Chapter 5.

Does the regression equation mean that *inequality* has the strongest relationship with the intensity of the rebellion? It does not because we need to take into consideration the amount of variation in each of the X variables, as well as the scale of the variables – note that *inequality* is on a 0–1 scale, whereas the other X variables are on a 0–100 scale.

In particular, what is often estimated or calculated is a **standardized coefficient estimate** – it is often called a *standardized effect*, but I do not like this term, as it is not necessarily an "effect." This statistic removes the units from both the X and Y variables, using the estimated standard deviations of the variables ($\hat{\sigma}_X$ and $\hat{\sigma}_Y$), so that the magnitude of different estimates can be compared.

From the equation from earlier:

$$Y = \beta_0 + \beta_1 X_1 + \beta_2 X_2 + \varepsilon \tag{3.15}$$

the standardized coefficient estimate of a given variable, say X_1, is:

$$\text{Standardized coefficient estimate} = \hat{\beta}_1 \times \left(\frac{\hat{\sigma}_{X_1}}{\hat{\sigma}_Y} \right) \tag{3.16}$$

Simply, a standardized coefficient estimate is the coefficient estimate multiplied by the ratio of the standard deviations of the corresponding variable (X_1) and the outcome (Y).

The last column of Table 3.3 shows the estimated standardized coefficient estimates for the factors determining the intensity of the Romanian Rebellion. The variable with the largest standardized coefficient estimate, *commerce*, has the second-lowest coefficient estimate. The interpretation for *commerce* is that a 1 standard deviation increase in *commerce* is associated with an estimated 0.61 higher standard deviation in *intensity*. In contrast, *inequality*, which has the largest coefficient estimate in the model, has the second-lowest estimated standardized coefficient estimate.

3.5 Chapter summary

This chapter presented some important tools for conducting regression analysis. Dummy variables can be used to represent qualitative factors or different levels of quantitative factors so as not to limit a model to having a linear effect. Further methods for estimating non-linear effects of factors include spline, quadratic, and logarithmic functional forms of models. And interactions of variables allow a variable to have different effects (or contributions) based on the values of other factors. Finally, weighted models can be used when certain observations should have greater importance in a model, such as when using grouped data with different-sized groups. This could produce a better-fitting model.

Exercises

1. Use the **democracy2** data set.
   a. From the regression from Question #4f in Chapter 2 (regressing *life_exp* on *democracy*, *avgeduc*, *educgini*, and *urbanpct*), add in four dummy variables for the region: *africa*, *asia*, *oceania*, and *america* – these four variables, along with *europe*, are mutually exclusive, and all countries fall into one of the groups. Still use the sample restrictions of year = 1985 and *condition1* = 1. Europe is the excluded reference group. How did the coefficient estimate on *democracy* change with the new variables?
   b. Interpret the coefficient estimate on the variable, *asia*.
   c. Interpret the coefficient estimate on the variable, *africa*.
   d. How would the coefficient estimate on *asia* be different *if africa* was the excluded variable and the variable *europe* were included instead?
   e. Estimate the same model but use *america* as the reference category instead of *europe*. How does the coefficient estimate compare to the model in #1a?
2. Repeat the regression from Question #1a, but weight it by *pop1000* (population in 1000s). What are some of the more notable differences in results between this regression and the regression in #1a?
3. From the model in #2, instead of using *democracy*, use interactions to estimate a separate coefficient estimate on *democracy* for each of the five regions. Report the coefficient estimates on the interacted variables and draw a general conclusion.
4. From Question #2, estimate a spline for how *life-exp* moves with *democracy*, both below and above values of 0.5 for *democracy*. Interpret the coefficient estimates on the democracy variables.
5. From the model in #1, calculate the standardized coefficient estimates for *democracy*, *avgeduc*, *educgini*, and *urbanpct*. In magnitude, meaning absolute value, which variables have the smallest and largest standardized coefficient estimates?
6. From the same data, **democracy2**, switch *life-exp* and *democracy*, so you are now regressing *democracy* on *life-exp*, *avgeduc*, *educgini*, and *urbanpct*, along with the region variables. Which variables have the smallest and largest standardized coefficient estimates?
7. Use the data set **oecd_gas_demand**, which comes from Baltagi and Griffin (1983).[1] Regress the (natural) logarithm of gas consumption per car (*lgaspcar*) on the logarithms of income per capita (*lincomep*), the logarithm of real motor gasoline price (*lrpmg*), and the stock of cars per capita (*lcarpcap*) and dummy variables for years 1961 to 1978 (using 1960 as the reference year).
   a. Interpret the coefficient estimate on the variable, *lrpmg*.
   b. Interpret the coefficient estimate on the variable for the year 1975.
8. Consider the average health-index measures for adults based on how much wine they drink and assume there is an equal share (25%) of people in each category, as depicted in the following chart.

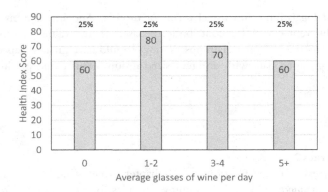

There are five variables:

- o   H = Average health index score
- o W_0 = dummy variable for having 0 glasses of wine per day
- o W_1 = dummy variable for having 1–2 glasses of wine per day
- o W_2 = dummy variable for having 3–4 glasses of wine per day
- o W_3 = dummy variable for having 5-or-more glasses of wine per day

a. What would the coefficient estimates be for the regression equation of
$H = \beta_0 + \beta_1 W_1 + \beta_2 W_2 + \beta_3 W_3 + \varepsilon$?

b. What would the coefficient estimates be for the regression equation of
$H = \beta_0 + \beta_1 W_0 + \beta_2 W_2 + \beta_3 W_3 + \varepsilon$? (Now, 1–2 glasses-per-day is the reference group.)

c. What would the coefficient estimates be for the regression equation of
$H = \beta_0 + \beta_3 W_3 + \varepsilon$?

d. What would the coefficient estimates be for the regression equation of
$H = \beta_0 + \beta_1 W_1 + \beta_2 W_2 + \beta_3 W_3 + \varepsilon$, if W_1 = at-least-1-glass, W_2 = at-least-3-glasses, and W_3 = at-least-5-glasses?

Note

1   The data source is: https://vincentarelbundock.github.io/Rdata sets/data sets.html, accessed July 10, 2018.

References

Baltagi, B. H., & Griffin, J. M. (1983). Gasoline demand in the OECD: An application of pooling and testing procedures. *European Economic Review, 22*(2), 117–137.

Bureau of Labor Statistics, U.S. Department of Labor. (2014). *National Longitudinal Survey of Youth 1979 cohort, 1979–2012 (rounds 1–25)*. Columbus, OH: Center for Human Resource Research, The Ohio State University.

Glover, D., Pallais, A., & Pariente, W. (2017). Discrimination as a self-fulfilling prophecy: Evidence from French grocery stores. *The Quarterly Journal of Economics, 132*(3), 1219–1260.

Substance Abuse and Mental Health Services Administration (SAMHSA), (2012). State Estimates of Substance Use and Mental Disorders from the 2009-2010 National Surveys on Drug Use and Health. NSDUH Series H-43, HHS Publication No. (SMA) 12-4703. Rockville, MD: Substance Abuse and Mental Health Services Administration, 2012.

Van Assche, J., Van Hiel, A., Stadeus, J., Bushman, B. J., De Cremer, D., & Roets, A. (2017). When the heat is on: The effect of temperature on voter behavior in presidential elections. *Frontiers in Psychology, 8*, 929. (Available at www.frontiersin.org/articles/10.3389/fpsyg.2017.00929/full, accessed July 10, 2018.)

4

What does "holding other factors constant" mean?

The primary reason why economists and other researchers use regression analysis, as opposed to just comparing means, is that regressions can theoretically *hold other factors constant*. This concept is the basis for proper modeling and choosing the optimal set of control variables. Unfortunately, few researchers have a solid grasp of what is meant by the concept of holding other factors constant, and they poorly understand when it is optimal not to attempt to hold a factor constant. (Students I had in an "applied-regression" course after they had two-quarters of econometrics with the conventional approach could not describe what this concept means. Thus, I offer this new approach in this chapter.)

In this chapter, you will learn:

- What "holding other factors constant" theoretically means
- How it works when it is cleanly done
- When you do not cleanly hold other factors constant
- When you want to hold a factor constant and when you don't want to.

I will give away a few dirty little secrets before we get started. First, regarding the third bullet, other than with dummy variables, we cannot fully hold other factors constant. Rather, the best we can do in most cases is "adjust (non-completely) for the factors." Second, economists rarely disclose this point and portray unwarranted certainty in their ability to rule out confounding factors that they include in a model but are imperfectly held constant.

DOI: 10.4324/9781003285007-4

Regressions are "models" because we are trying to, well, *model* or simulate how an outcome is determined. When we say we want to **hold some factors constant**, we want to design the model so that one explanatory variable moves without the other factor moving with it. For example, when estimating the effects of schooling on income, we want to design a model in which we compare people with different levels of education without those differences being accompanied by differences in inherent intelligence and other things that typically come with higher levels of schooling (but are not a product of schooling). We want to hold constant those other factors as educational levels vary. This should help us get closer to the true causal effect of a year of schooling on income.

As you will see, there are going to be times in which it is optimal not to hold a factor constant. That is, after a treatment, you might want to allow factors to move with the treatment in the model rather than making them "constant."

In this chapter, I use a few approaches to describe what "holding other factors constant" means. (This is also known as *ceteris paribus*, which may have come from Latin, meaning "all other things equal" or from French, meaning "Don't put all of those darn things in my coffee at once so that I know what particular ingredients make it perfect.")

4.1 Why do we want to "hold other factors constant"?

Let us start with an example inspired by a chocolate-cinnamon ice cream cone I once had. Say you want to test whether adding cinnamon to your chocolate-chip cookies makes them tastier. You would want to make a control and treatment batch. These two batches should be as similar as possible, with as close to the same amounts of butter, sugar, and chocolate. When comparing the treatment to the control batch, we would want nothing else to be different between the two batches other than the inclusion of cinnamon. That is, we want to **hold constant** all other factors that could vary with whether cinnamon is added. When we go from the non-cinnamon batch (the control group) to the cinnamon batch (the treatment group), hopefully, the amount of butter, sugar, chocolate, and other things that affect the taste of the cookies would be the same or would be "constant" between the two batches. This is how we would be sure that any taste differences between the two batches would be due to just the cinnamon.

This is how we would wish to test for any causal effect. We would want it so that, in the model we design, the key-explanatory variable changes by itself and not with other "confounding" factors that could affect the outcome. For example, when estimating how TV watching affects Body Mass Index for children, we would want TV-watching to change on its own and not be accompanied by the factors that might come with TV-watching and possibly affect BMI (e.g., perhaps busyness of parents, the weather, parks nearby, etc.). Doing so would involve including these factors in the model as control variables. Not surprisingly, it is often quite a difficult task to fully hold all other factors constant.

4.2 Operative-vs-"held constant" and good-vs-bad variation in a key-explanatory variable

Part of gauging whether a model is validly (accurately) estimating a causal effect, one needs to understand what causes variation in the key-explanatory variable. Let me define **sources of variation** (in the key-X or treatment variable) as the reasons why the key-X variable has high values for some

	Good variation	Bad variation
Held-constant variation	V1	V2
Operative variation	V3	V4

Figure 4.1 Types of variation in the key-explanatory variable

observations and low values for other observations, or why some receive the treatment and others do not. For example, if the key-X variable were the state unemployment rate in a given month, then the major sources of variation would be state (some states tend to have higher or lower unemployment than others), time (year-month) effects due to changes in the strength of the national economy affecting what happens in most states, and industry shifts affecting employment in particular states.

Figure 4.1 separates the variation in the key-explanatory variable into four categories. I first distinguish the variation as either *good* vs. *bad variation*, which I will give a little information on here but go into greater detail in Section 6.2:

- **Good variation**: variation in the key-X variable due to factors that are not correlated with the dependent variable, other than by affecting the key-X variable.
- **Bad variation**: variation in the key-X variable due to factors that could be correlated with the dependent variable beyond through the key-X variable.

Note that determining whether the variation in a key-X variable is good-vs-bad depends on what the dependent variable is. In addition, *bad variation* is only applicable to the regression objectives of estimating causal effects and adjusting outcomes; it is not applicable if the objective is forecasting or determining predictors. Regardless of whether the variation is good or bad, the variation can also be distinguished between *held-constant* and *operative variation*:

- **Held–constant variation**: variation in the key-X variable that is "held constant" and does not go into determining how the variable is related to the dependent variable.
- **Operative variation**: variation in the key-X variable that is used to determine how the key-X variable is related to the dependent variable.

In a regression model, the *operative variation* would be the variation that is not held constant with control variables. As you will see below, this could include variation from factors that have variables included in a model but that imperfectly hold the factor constant. Moving variation from *operative* to *held-constant* does not change whether it is *good* or *bad variation*. Good is good and bad is bad, regardless of whether they are held constant.

As an example, consider the sources of variation for years-of-schooling, as one estimates how years-of-schooling affects income (say, at age 45). Note that most variation would be considered *bad variation* because they come from sources that could also affect income beyond through any effect on years-of-schooling attained. For example, having more-educated parents could impact income not just through year-of-schooling but also by building other skills that would come in handy in the labor market. The only *good variation* that came to mind is from luck in SAT (or other entrance exam)

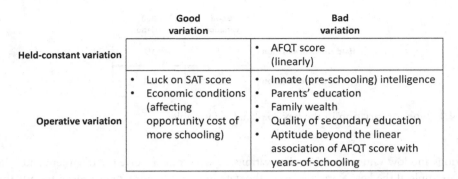

	Good variation	Bad variation
Held-constant variation		• AFQT score (linearly)
Operative variation	• Luck on SAT score • Economic conditions (affecting opportunity cost of more schooling)	• Innate (pre-schooling) intelligence • Parents' education • Family wealth • Quality of secondary education • Aptitude beyond the linear association of AFQT score with years-of-schooling

Figure 4.2 Types of variation for years–of–schooling (for how it affects income)

scores and the current economic conditions, which would likely not have much effect on income about 25 years later (Figure 4.2).

In this example, I have controlled for the AFQT score, which (as mentioned in Chapter 2) is meant to capture aptitude. This adjusts for any linear relationship between the AFQT score and income (or between the AFQT score and years-of-schooling, as discussed below). However, there would undoubtedly be other aspects of aptitude not measured by the AFQT score (and beyond any linear relationship) that could affect income. Thus, even though the AFQT score falls under the *held-constant variation*, a part of aptitude falls under the *operative variation*, which is a bad thing because it is a *bad variation* due to potentially having its own effect on income other than by affecting years-of-schooling.

As a preview of Chapter 6, one of the goals of any analysis aiming to estimate causal effects is to make it so the *bad-operative variation* (V4 in Figure 4.1) equals zero. That is, the factors being controlled for would hopefully make it so V4 = 0. I should note that how much variation there is in each cell cannot be determined or tested for. Rather, assessing whether any *bad-operative variation* remains would be based on understanding how various factors are related to each other and the outcome. As you will learn in Chapter 6, making it so there is no *bad variation* among the *operative variation* does not guarantee that a model is valid. There could be other PITFALLS that apply. But *bad-operative variation* is a large source of invalidity.

For now, the important distinction is between *held-constant* and *operative variation*. In the Simple Regression Model, there is no *held-constant variation*, as all variation in the key-explanatory variable is used in determining the slope of the regression line. This would likely include both *good* and *bad variation*. Adding variables, to some extent, holds constant those factors being controlled for, which reduces the *operative variation*, moving it to *held-constant variation*.

To demonstrate how controlling for a factor affects the *operative variation*, let's consider the data we have used on how years-of-schooling is related to income. I took a random sample of 100 from the sample of 2772 observations we used in Chapter 2. I then, for the sake of tractability for the example, deleted 7 of the observations who had a top-coded income of about $265,000. Thus, I have 93 observations. I plot out their years-of-schooling and income in the top panel of Figure 4.3.

In the bottom panel of Figure 4.3, I show a plot of "adjusted years-of-schooling" and income. The adjusted years-of-schooling is effectively the same as equation (2.21) in Section 2.9, as it takes out the

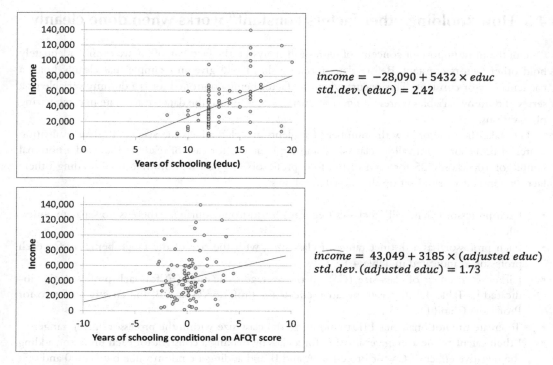

$$income = -28{,}090 + 5432 \times educ$$
$$std.dev.(educ) = 2.42$$

$$income = 43{,}049 + 3185 \times (adjusted\ educ)$$
$$std.dev.(adjusted\ educ) = 1.73$$

Figure 4.3 Demonstrating how adjusting for factors reduces operative variation

linear contribution of the AFQT score to years-of-schooling. The most important point is that there is now less *operative variation*, as the standard deviation of years-of-schooling is 2.42, and the standard deviation of adjusted-years-of-schooling (adjusted for AFQT) is 1.73.

The regression equations for Figure 4.3 are:

$$\widehat{income} = -28{,}090 + 5432 \times educ \tag{4.1a}$$

$$\widehat{income} = -8701 + \mathbf{3185} \times educ + 248 \times afqt \tag{4.1b}$$

$$\widehat{educ} = 10.907 + 0.054 \times afqt \tag{4.1c}$$

$$(adjusted\ educ) = educ - \widehat{educ} = educ - (10.907 + 0.054 \times afqt) \tag{4.1d}$$

$$\widehat{income} = 43{,}049 + \mathbf{3185} \times (adjusted\ educ) \tag{4.1e}$$

Note that the model that has *afqt* as a control variable (4.1b) gives the same coefficient estimate on years-of-schooling (*educ*) as the model that uses *adjusted-educ* (4.1e), which factors out *afqt* from the years-of-schooling variable (4.1c and 4.1d). Thus, we can think of the coefficient estimate on *educ* in (4.1b) and (4.1e) as how *educ* is related to *income*, after adjusting for the linear relationship between *afqt* and *educ*.

4.3 How "holding other factors constant" works when done cleanly

One of the most important concepts of regression analysis is the fact that, often, we cannot adequately hold other factors constant. Before demonstrating this, I will give an example that cleanly holds a particular factor constant. This occurs when the factor being controlled for is a dummy variable or a series of dummy variables representing a categorization, as long as the data are accurate in categorizing observations.

Let's take the issue of how the number of students in a class affects the average student-evaluation scores of professors – I'll call it "class-size" and hyphenate it for ease of reading. I created a notional sample of 100 classes, 25 for each of the four professors. To best demonstrate how holding-other-factors-constant works, I set up the model as follows:

- Each professor teaches all 25 classes (sections) for just one course (so there is no separate course effect).
- Each professor has a distinct range of class sizes, with the size of the range being 40 for each professor, as indicated in Table 4.1.
- I impose an effect of class-size (CS) on the average evaluation (E) for each professor, also indicated in Table 4.1. (I create negative effects for Professors A and B, and an effect of zero for Professors C and D.)
- To create the notional data, I first randomize the class-size within the professor's given range.
- I then calculate the average evaluation for a class by making a constant for each professor, adding the negative effect of CS for Professors A and B, and adding a random value between 0 and 0.5.

If I were not to add that last random value, then the data would all be on a straight line for each professor, with the slope being the exact effect I impose and the R^2 being 1.0. What this randomness means is that separate regressions of the evaluation on class-size for each professor would not give coefficient estimates that exactly match the effects I impose. However, if I were to repeat this randomization and exercise an infinite number of times, then the average coefficient estimate on the class-size for each professor would be exactly the effects I imposed.

My thinking behind the effects that I impose is that, perhaps for larger classes, an extra few students would not make a difference in a student's experience. For the smaller classes, the class-size would make a larger difference in how much interaction a student would have with the professor and how much a student could participate.

Researchers are often interested in the Average Treatment Effect (ATE), which is how much an outcome would move, on average, if all subjects were given (or were exposed to) one more unit of the key-explanatory variable. For this topic, the ATE would be the average effect on the average evaluation of the class from adding one more student to the class. In our case, the ATE would be the average

Table 4.1 Model set-up for class-size and professor evaluations

Professor	Range of class size	Class-size effect on the average evaluation that I imposed
A	20–60	−0.03
B	100–140	−0.01
C	180–220	0
D	260–300	0

of the effects for each professor because they have the same number of observations in the sample. The true ATE is, thus, the average of −0.03, −0.01, 0, and 0, which comes to −0.01. Whereas you and I know what the true ATE is overall and for each professor, the researcher collecting and analyzing these data does not know these effects.

In Figure 4.4, I show the same data for two scenarios. In the top chart, I draw the line from a Simple Regression Model (no control variables). The regression equation is:

$$\hat{E}_i = 3.30 + 0.0040 \times CS_i \tag{4.2}$$

Note that the subscript i refers to one of the 100 individual classes. In the top chart, all classes are compared to all other classes, which means that classes for one professor are compared to classes of other professors. This means that, as class-size changes, eventually the professor changes as well. Thus, the *operative variation* in the key-X variable, the class-size, is not just from the randomization of class-sizes but also who the professor is. There is no *held-constant variation*.

In that simple model, the coefficient estimate is positive (0.0040), suggesting that higher class-sizes increase evaluations. We know this is wrong from the negative or zero effects that I imposed for the

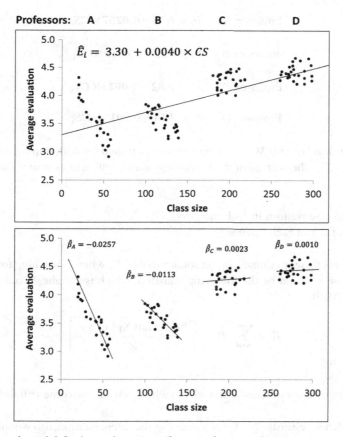

Figure 4.4 Notional model for how class-size affects professor evaluations

professors. The problem is that the *operative variation* in class-size from the professor is *bad variation* because the effectiveness of the professor affects the dependent variable (E). Thus, we need to move the variation in class-size due to the professor from *operative* to *held-constant variation*. This is simply done by adding three dummy variables for the professor, leaving one out as the reference group. (Because these are control variables, it would not matter which professor is left as the reference category.) In contrast with the variation in class-size from the professor, the randomness determining class-size within a professor's classes would be *good variation*, as that would only be connected to the outcome by affecting the class-size.

When the professor is controlled for, the regression equation becomes:

$$\hat{E}_i = 3.92 - \mathbf{0.0098} \times \mathbf{CS_i} + 0.081 \times (Prof\ B)_i + 2.29 \times (Prof\ C)_i + 3.23 \times (Prof\ D)_i \quad (4.3)$$

Now, the coefficient estimate on CS has turned negative (-0.0098), and it is close to the ATE of -0.0100.

To demonstrate how we know that the professor is held constant and what that does, in the bottom chart, I estimate separate models for each professor. I show these coefficient estimates and the slopes for each professor in the bottom chart of Figure 4.4. The regression equations are:

$$\text{Professor A}: \quad \hat{E}_i = 4.57 - \mathbf{0.0257} \times \mathbf{CS_i} \quad (4.4a)$$

$$\text{Professor B}: \quad \hat{E}_i = 4.92 - \mathbf{0.0113} \times \mathbf{CS_i} \quad (4.4b)$$

$$\text{Professor C}: \quad \hat{E}_i = 3.82 + \mathbf{0.0023} \times \mathbf{CS_i} \quad (4.4c)$$

$$\text{Professor D}: \quad \hat{E}_i = 4.14 + \mathbf{0.0010} \times \mathbf{CS_i} \quad (4.4d)$$

This is where it gets kind of neat. When categories are controlled for with dummy variables, the coefficient estimate on CS is the average of the within-category coefficient estimates on CS, weighted by the product of:

- The number of observations in each category
- The variance of CS in each category.

More formally, the coefficient estimate, $\hat{\beta}_1$, on some variable X_1, when controlling for a categorization of groups marked by g, would be the following equation, which is a slight variant of one presented by Gibbons et al. (2019):

$$\hat{\beta}_1 = \sum_g \hat{\beta}_{1g} \times \left[\frac{N_g \times \text{var}(X_1 \mid g, X_2)}{Z} \right] \quad (4.5)$$

where:

- $\hat{\beta}_1$ would be the overall estimated effect of variable X_1 on the outcome ($-\mathbf{0.0098}$ from equation (4.3)).
- $\hat{\beta}_{1g}$ is the coefficient estimate on X_1 for group g in the categorization; this would be the four bold coefficient estimates in equations (4.4a–d).

- N_g is the number of observations in group g. (This assumes there are no sample weights. If there were sample weights, N_g should be replaced by $(N_g \times w_g)$, where w_g is the average sample weight for observations in group g.)
- $\text{var}(X_1 \mid g, X_2)$ is the variance of X_1 in group g, conditional on all other variables, as represented in X_2. (In our case, there are no other variables.)
- Z is the sum of $[N_g \times \text{var}(X_1 \mid g, X_2)]$ across groups. (Including this in the denominator scales the bracketed part, the "weight," so that the sum of the weights equals one.)

Just so you believe me, I'll show the calculations in Table 4.2:

- Column (2) indicates the number of observations in each group.
- Column (3) has the proportion of the observations for each professor (group). This is the probability that an observation is in group $g = \text{Pr}(g)$, which is just 0.25 for each professor. I include this to allow for initial sample weights if there were any.
- Column (4) has the coefficient estimate on CS for each professor, from equations (4.4a–d).
- Column (5) has the variance of CS within each professor's set of observations.
- Column (6) is the numerator of the weight in brackets in equation (4.5).
- Column (7) divides the weights in column (6) by the sum of the weights (146.6332) so that they sum to 1.0.
- Column (8) multiplies the coefficient estimates in column (4) by the final weights in column (7). The sum of these is the weighted average of the coefficient estimates within each quartile.

Note that the weighted average of the coefficient estimates, -0.0098, is the same as that from equation (4.3), when all professors are included in the model and there are dummy variables to control for the professor. This demonstrates the point made above, that including a set of dummy variables in a model to control for groups effectively makes it so the coefficient estimate on the key-X variable is the average of the within-group coefficient estimates on that X variable, with the average weighted by the share of observations and the variance of that key-X variable within each group. When the professor is controlled for (i.e., held constant), no longer does the coefficient estimate on CS capture comparisons of classes across professors. Rather, the coefficient estimate on CS is the weighted average of coefficient estimates from four models in which the professor does not change.

Table 4.2 Demonstrating "holding other factors constant" in the presence of dummy variables

(1)	(2)	(3)	(4)	(5)	(6)	(7)	(8)
Professor	Number of Observations (N_g)	$Pr(g)$	$\hat{\beta}_{1g}$	Variance of class-size	Weight numerator $(3) \times (5)$	Final weight	$\hat{\beta}_{1g} \times final$ weight $(4) \times (7)$
A	25	0.2500	−0.0257	172.1344	43.0336	0.2935	−0.0075
B	25	0.2500	−0.0113	155.0025	38.7506	0.2643	−0.0030
C	25	0.2500	0.0023	129.5499	32.3875	0.2209	0.0005
D	25	0.2500	0.0010	129.8460	32.4615	0.2214	0.0002
	100				146.6332	1.0000	**−0.0098**

Here's the important point: **Once we control for the professor, then as the class–size varies in the sample, the professor does not change.** Starting from the left–most observation in the bottom chart of Figure 4.4, as we move right for those first 25 observations, it stays as Professor-A observations. After that 25th observation, in the model, we stop and no longer compare further observations to Professor A. Then a new regression line is estimated for Professor-B's observations, and when they get to the end for Professor B, again they stop. The overall estimate of -0.0098 is the weighted average of four within-professor coefficient estimates. Thus, the *operative variation* in class-size – the variation that goes into calculating the overall coefficient estimate on class-size – is within-professor variation. Because that within-professor variation in class-size is just from my randomization, it should be *good variation*. The professor is held constant and does not change when class-size changes. Bingo!

Assuming the data were correct, we have fully held the professor constant. Fully holding some factor constant only occurs for dummy variables that correctly classify observations into different groups. We will see an example in the next section of (imperfectly) adjusting for a quantitative (non-dummy) variable.

Another great aspect of this feature of controlling for a categorization is that it hardly matters if the coefficient estimate on the professor is mis-estimated due to imprecision. The important comparisons are done within each professor's observations. However, it is possible that mis-estimated professor effects could impact other coefficient estimates (if there were any), which could likely-only-slightly impact the estimated effect of the class-size.

Returning to the types of variation breakdown, Figure 4.5 shows the basic change when we control for the professor. In the top panel, based on the simple model without any controls for the professor, the *bad-operative variation* is from the professors. In contrast, in the bottom panel in which there are controls for the professor, the variation from the professor switches over to *held-constant variation*. Thus, in this example, the *bad-operative variation* (V4) now equals zero.

As a preview of one of the PITFALLS you will see in Chapter 6, we actually got a little lucky with our estimate of -0.0098 being so close to the true ATE of -0.0100. If you take the four individual professor's coefficient estimates (-0.0257, -0.0113, 0.0023, 0.0010), the average comes to -0.0084. The overall coefficient estimate of -0.0098 was more negative than the average because

	Good variation	Bad variation	
Held-constant variation	V1 = 0	V2 = 0	$E = \beta_0 + \beta_1 \times CS + \varepsilon$
Operative Variation	V3 = Random-ness	V4 = Professor	

	Good variation	Bad variation	
Held-constant variation	V1 = 0	V2 = Professor	$E = \beta_0 + \beta_1 \times CS + \beta_2 \times (\text{Prof B})$ $+ \beta_3 \times (\text{Prof C}) + \beta_4 \times (\text{Prof D}) + \varepsilon$
Operative Variation	V3 = Random-ness	V4 = 0	

Figure 4.5 Demonstrating how types of variation change when adding control variables

the larger negative coefficient estimate for Professor A had a higher weight in determining the weighted average of the individual coefficient estimates than that for Professor's C and D (column 7 of Table 4.2) due to the higher variance of class-size (column 5). This occurred even though Professor A's estimated effect was less negative at −0.0257 than his/her true effect (−0.0300), just due to randomness. Recall that the researcher studying this does not know that the true overall effect is −0.0100, and so they would hope to obtain an average of the coefficient estimates across professors, with each professor weighted the same due to having the same number of observations in the sample. Thus, as strange as this sounds, it actually would have been better for the researcher to obtain an estimate of −0.0084 instead of **−0.0098**. Even though the estimate obtained was closer to the true effect than the average, there is still bias here from some professors being over-weighted in the sample due to the higher variance. This bias will be PITFALL #7 in Chapter 6.

This highlights the point made above on how there still could be bias from other sources even if you rid the model of *bad-operative variation*. Furthermore, imprecision could cause the estimate to be off from the true effect, as it was the imprecision that gave us the average across professors of −0.0084 instead of the true average of −0.0100.

(You might wonder why a researcher doesn't just take an average of the coefficient estimates across groups rather than estimate the full model. The reason is that a regression with all groups included is a much more efficient method of doing the proper calculations. There might be a very large number of groups, making it cumbersome to estimate and collect all the coefficient estimates. The regression compiles them in milli-seconds, and appropriately minimizes some groups in weight/importance due to sample size. Furthermore, the regression can easily calculate the standard error, covered in the next chapter, which is important for hypothesis tests or some assessment of the strength of the evidence.)

Let us consider an example with two dummy variables as the explanatory variables to explain income (Y) – whether a person has a college degree (*CollDeg*) and whether a person is Hispanic. The use of two dummy variables like this allows us to see in a table who is compared to whom, or what observations are compared to what observations. The regression model is:

$$Y_i = \beta_0 + \beta_1 \times (CollDeg)_i + \beta_2 \times (Hispanic)_i + \varepsilon_i \qquad (4.6)$$

This model would probably not produce the true causal effect of having a college degree or of being Hispanic, as it remains unlikely that the college degree is randomly assigned. Nevertheless, the model produces our "estimates" of these effects. And so we are estimating the effect of having a college degree, holding Hispanic constant; and we are estimating the effect of Hispanic, holding college degree constant.

Let's consider who is being compared to whom in the model to determine the coefficient estimates, based on the average incomes for each group, as defined in Table 4.3. For β_1, since *Hispanic* is being held constant, we are comparing the average incomes for those with and without a college degree for Hispanics and for non-Hispanics. Thus, we have two comparisons: ($\bar{Y}_C$ to $\bar{Y}_A$) and ($\bar{Y}_D$ to $\bar{Y}_B$). The estimate for β_1 would then be a weighted average of the differences in average incomes, with the weights being based on the percentage (or number) of observations in the non-Hispanic and Hispanic groups and the variance of *CollDeg* in each group – see equation (4.5) above. Note that, given the groups that are being compared to each other, the value of the *Hispanic* variable does not change as we go from a value of 0 to 1 for *CollDeg*. That is, in the comparisons determining the estimated effect of *CollDeg*, we are not comparing across Hispanic and non-Hispanic groups. Thus, *Hispanic* is "held constant."

Table 4.3 Average income for each group

	Hispanic = 0	Hispanic = 1
CollDeg = 0	$\overline{Y}_A$	$\overline{Y}_B$
CollDeg = 1	$\overline{Y}_C$	$\overline{Y}_D$

Likewise, since *CollDeg* is held constant, the estimate for β_2 is based on the weighted average of the difference in average incomes between: ($\overline{Y}_B$ and $\overline{Y}_A$) and ($\overline{Y}_D$ and $\overline{Y}_C$). In our model, as we vary whether a person is Hispanic, we are holding constant whether they have a college degree.

Note that when we say we are holding the variable *Hispanic* constant, it does not mean that we are only including Hispanics or only including non-Hispanics. Rather, the value of *Hispanic* does not change as we, effectively, change *CollDeg* in the model and see how average income changes.

There is a situation in which having dummy variables for a categorization does not hold a factor constant as purely as I describe here. If there were two separate categorizations among the control variables, then only one of those categorizations would be held constant (with the effects of the treatment being estimated within each category), and the variables for the other categorization would be merely adjusted for and not fully held constant. This would occur, in the example above, if the professors taught different courses. In this case, as we aim to estimate the effect of the class-size (the treatment), there are two types of categorizations among the control variables: the professor and the course. By controling for both categorizations, the model estimates: (1) the relationship between class-size and average evaluation in the class within each professor's set of classes, factoring out the estimated course effects; and (2) the relationship between class-size and average evaluation in the class within each course's set of classes, factoring out the estimated professor effects. It turns out that both arrive at the same overall estimated class-size effect, but only one categorization is purely held constant. Despite it being imperfect, it is still better to control for both sets of categorizations than just one to help reduce potential omitted-factors bias. This will be discussed in some more detail in Section 8.1.3. The example above with estimating the effect of a college degree while controlling for Hispanic would not apply because there is only one control variable (*Hispanic*).

4.4 Why is it difficult to "hold a factor constant"?

In the example in the prior section examining how class-size affects average evaluations, we cleanly held constant the professor because controlling for the professor meant that we were estimating the model separately for each professor (category), and the four coefficient estimates from those separate models were what determined the overall coefficient estimate. When one needs to hold constant a factor that is quantitative and not categorical, then it is not as clean.

Let's consider an example from our list of regression topics from Section 1.1: "how does oatmeal consumption affect cholesterol levels?" This was an issue back in the late 1980s when cholesterol was considered one of the leading causes of heart disease. Researchers noticed that oatmeal consumption was associated with lower cholesterol levels. They probably created some graph that looked something similar to the notional one I create below in Figure 4.6, in which each observation represents one person's cholesterol level and reported oatmeal consumption. And they likely found the best-fitting line for the data to be downward-sloping, as this one is. They probably argued from this that oatmeal *reduces* cholesterol.

What is wrong with this conclusion? The problem is that we probably cannot rule out other reasons why those who consume more oatmeal have lower cholesterol. I can think of two such general reasons:

1. Eating oatmeal may replace other high-cholesterol breakfast foods. My guess is that people who eat oatmeal probably are not eating eggs, bacon, or sausage for breakfast. This would mean that any cholesterol-neutral food would be associated with lower cholesterol if it replaced high-cholesterol food.
2. It probably is not random who eats oatmeal. People who eat oatmeal tend to be health-conscious, so they likely tend to exercise regularly and avoid eating Big Macs or Loco-Mocos (a Hawaiian double cheeseburger with bacon, two fried eggs, and gravy on top). Thus, it is possible that the negative association we see between oatmeal and cholesterol – meaning that when one is higher, the other is generally lower – is due to oatmeal being a marker for other healthy behaviors.

Before we conclude that oatmeal *causes* lower cholesterol, we need to rule out these other possible explanations. This means that we need to make sure that variation across people in the amount of oatmeal consumption occurs in isolation and not with variation in other dietary or health-conscious behaviors. To address these issues from a simple model of equation (4.7) below (representing Figure 4.6), we could attempt to adjust for these factors by adding variables representing breakfast food, other dietary characteristics, and exercise to the model, in equation (4.8):

$$Y_i = \beta_0 + \beta_1 X_{1i} + \varepsilon_i \tag{4.7}$$

$$Y_i = \beta_0 + \beta_1 X_{1i} + \beta_2 X_{2i} + \beta_3 X_{3i} + \beta_4 X_{4i} + \varepsilon_i \tag{4.8}$$

where:
* Y = cholesterol
* X_1 = oatmeal consumption per week
* X_2 = sausage and bacon servings per week
* X_3 = Big Macs and Loco-Mocos per week
* X_4 = days exercising per week.

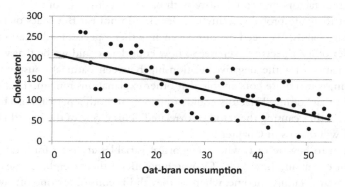

Figure 4.6 Notional scatterplot of oat-bran consumption and cholesterol

When we control for a categorical variable, we only estimate the treatment-outcome relationship within each category. In contrast, when we control for a quantitative variable (i.e., not categorized), we are merely removing the estimated linear relationship between that variable and the key-X variable (and other variables). Any non-linear relationship between the control variable and the key-X variable would mean that, as the key-X variable (the treatment) varies in the sample, so does the control variable. Even if a polynomial version of the control variable were included in a model, such as a quadratic form with both the value and the squared value of the control variable, any part of the relationship between that control variable and the key-X variable that is not explained by the quadratic would mean that the factor is still changing as the treatment changes. Thus, there would still be *bad-operative variation* in the amount of oatmeal the subjects eat from these factors that have variables included in the model.

Furthermore, just like there will be error in the estimated causal effect of some treatment on an outcome, there will be error in the estimated relationship between a control variable and the key-X variable and between the control variable and the outcome. This could be due to:

- Imprecision or uncertainty from natural randomness in sampling or in how an outcome is determined.
- Almost certain non-linear relationships.
- A bias in the coefficient estimate from the PITFALLS that will be discussed in Chapter 6.

The estimated effect of oatmeal on cholesterol, $\hat{\beta}_1$, would probably be smaller (less negative) in equation (4.8). In (4.7), when oatmeal is higher, there is probably less sausage/bacon/Big-Mac/Loco-Moco consumption and probably more exercise. But, in (4.8), when oatmeal is higher, the amount of sausage/bacon/Big-Mac/Loco-Moco consumption and exercise would change less with higher oatmeal than it would in equation (4.7) because they were controlled for. Technically, controlling for these factors might not take the factor of Big Macs and Loco-Mocos out of the oatmeal-cholesterol relationship for the three bulleted reasons stated above. Using more detail to represent these factors could do a better job of adjusting for them.

Besides these issues for the variables we do control for, we need to ask ourselves whether there are any unobservable factors we are missing. Also, are we accurately identifying "breakfast food" with our variable for sausage and bacon servings or "health consciousness" with our variables for Big-Mac and Loco-Moco consumption and the number of days per week a person exercises? Are we adequately adjusting for the other factors that could move with oat-bran consumption?

My guess is that there are probably many people who do not eat Big Macs or Loco-Mocos who still have poor dietary habits. We need to consider many other aspects of a diet, and we would probably need to consider other aspects of exercise. So how confident could we be that we have controlled for all other explanations for the negative relationship between oatmeal consumption and cholesterol? It is uncertain, as it is quite conceivable that other explanations remain. That is, there could be *omitted-factors bias* in that "omitted" factors could contribute to both a person's oat-bran consumption and cholesterol levels, thus causing them to be correlated. This is one of the key PITFALLS of regression analysis that I will discuss in Chapter 6.

Another situation to beware of is when categorical variables are used for a quantitative variable. For example, when estimating how kids' TV-watching affects their weight, a researcher might state that they "held constant" family income, when all they did is control for one of, say, three categories of income. The three income groups are indeed held constant, assuming that the data are accurate. However, within each of the three income groups, incomes will vary greatly and would be a potential source of omitted-factors bias. There would still be plenty of *bad-operative variation* from income, despite controlling for income groups.

These stories are emblematic of an often-ignored truth in regression analysis:

> In a study in which the treatment variable is a choice for an individual (such as how much oatmeal to eat) or for a city or state (such as the income tax rate or minimum wage), controlling for observable characteristics only takes you so far in addressing alternative explanations. The unobserved reasons why a subject receives a treatment or how much exposure the subject gets to the treatment may greatly impact the estimated association between the treatment variable and the dependent variable. Including control variables is much more effective to fully address potential problems (from omitted-factors bias) when it is aiming to adjust for cases of incidental correlation when the treatment (key-X variable) is inherently random to the subject.

In the cases presented in this section, the model is unable to fully hold constant the relevant factors. Special methods might be able to address these problems. Chapter 8 will introduce some of those methods.

4.5 When you do *not* want to hold a factor constant

A few years ago, my wife and I were walking through the Vancouver, BC airport, with a little time to spare. We came across one of those ball-machine sculptures, in which a metal ball is dropped from above and goes through various paths to get to the bottom. It had three levers that swung with a pendulum and determined the path a given ball would follow, resulting in a variety of dings, bings, bips, bops, and whirls that mesmerized us – it should be the first video that comes up if you search "limited edition creative machines" on YouTube.

My inner geek wanted to calculate the probability that a ball went on each path. And then I thought about the concept of holding a factor constant, and I pondered a situation in which I were to hold constant one of the levers so that it did not swing. The proportion of balls traveling down a certain path would no longer represent the true probabilities. This might seem like an obvious point, but many researchers make an analogous mistake in their regressions.

The general tendency of researchers is to include as control variables anything that could affect the outcome. But doing so can be detrimental to a model, especially if the control variable is determined after the treatment. The examples I have used so far in this chapter involve situations in which we would need to control for a factor to reduce the influence of a confounding factor when attempting to estimate how a treatment affects an outcome. Controlling for the factor, in most cases, should result in a coefficient estimate on the treatment variable that is closer to the true causal effect. There are some situations, however, in which including certain control variables would push an estimate away from the true causal effect. The most common situation in which this would occur is when the variable one was controlling for was a mediating factor, as introduced in Section 2.14, representing one of the reasons why the treatment affects the outcome. We will review two examples to demonstrate this.

4.5.1 Case 1: How much should lemon trees be watered?

Let's say that we are interested in determining how the amount of water affects the production of lemon trees. Consider these details:

- On Day 1, you plant 50 baby lemon trees that appear to be the same.
- Half are planted in the good-soil part of the yard.
- Half are planted in the bad-soil part of the yard.
- Upon planting the trees, you randomly assign each tree one of ten different amounts of water that the tree is then given weekly for five years – each of the ten water amounts will be given to five trees.
- Assume that trees are covered when it rains so that the only water they receive is what you give them.

The setup for the model would be:

- Dependent variable: Number of lemons the tree produces in the 5th year (L)
- Key-explanatory variable: Amount of weekly water (W)
- Possible control variables:
  - Indicator variable for being in the "good soil" part of the yard (G)
  - The height of the tree at the start of the 5th year (H) – this could be measured in feet or meters or any other unit.

The important issue is what control variable(s) should be used. That is, what factor(s) should we attempt to adjust for and what factor(s), if any, should we allow to change as the amount of water changes?

I think most of us would agree that we would want to control for the indicator of being in the "good soil" part of the yard (G). Even though the amount of water is randomized, for this small sample of 50 trees, it is quite likely that the randomness would not make it even for how many trees watered a given amount are in the good vs. bad soil. Thus, we want to hold constant the "good soil" factor so that this would not vary when we allow the amount of water to vary, just as we do not want the amount of other ingredients to vary as we add cinnamon to our cookies. From what we learned in Section 4.3, this would make it so the effect of water on the number of lemons produced would be estimated separately for those trees in the good soil and those trees in the bad soil.

Do we also want to control for the height of the tree at the beginning of the 5th year (H)? This comes down to whether, in our model, we want the height to be allowed to change or to be partly held constant when the amount of water changes.

We are injecting a treatment of the amount of water into this model of lemon-tree production. In the model, we want to see how lemon production changes as the amount of water varies. I would argue that part of the reason why the amount of water could affect the number of lemons produced by the tree is that it affects how large the tree grows. If we were to control for the height (i.e., not allow it to fully change as the amount of watering changes), then we are factoring out part of the watering effect. We would not capture the full effect of the watering on the number of lemons. Yet, this would be the tendency of many researchers, as the height would be correlated with the amount of water and could affect the outcome. This would be similar to holding a lever constant on the ball machine sculpture.

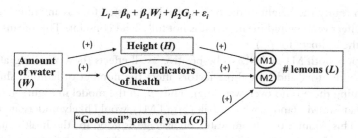

Figure 4.7a Flow chart showing mechanisms for lemon-tree example when excluding "height"

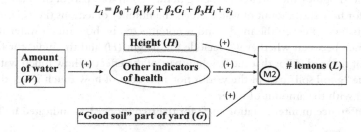

Figure 4.7b Flow chart showing mechanisms for lemon-tree example when including "height"

To demonstrate this, let's consider the flowcharts in Figures 4.7a (*not* controlling for the height) and 4.7b (controlling for the height), along with the accompanying Table 4.4 describing the differences. I include in Figure 4.7a the mechanisms for how the amount of water (W) affects the number of lemons (L):

- Mechanism M1 is that the water affects the height (H), which in turn affects the number of lemons.
- Mechanism M2 is that the water affects the overall health of the tree in other ways besides the height, or "other indicators of health" for the tree, which again affects the number of lemons.

(I use an oval for the "other indicators of health" because it is non-quantifiable, unlike the other variables.)

The height and the "other indicators of health" are considered mediating factors, which again are factors through which the key-X variable affects the dependent variable. Mediating factors are products of the key-X variable that, in turn, affect the dependent variable.

In Figure 4.7a, the estimate for β_1 in the equation at the top of the figure will capture both mechanisms M1 and M2 because both the height and "other indicators of health" are allowed to change when the amount of water changes. That is, neither the height nor any other indicator of the tree's health is controlled for.

In contrast, in Figure 4.7b, $\beta_3 H_i$ is added to the model. This means that the model is effectively making it so that when the amount of water (W) is higher, the height (H) theoretically does not change (or, is sort of held constant), as seen by the lack of an arrow from "water" to "height." Thus, β_1 would no longer capture mechanism M1 since there is no longer an effect of the amount of water on the height. (In reality, the height of the tree is merely "adjusted for," as any non–linear relationship or mismeasured effect of H would mean that it is not fully held constant. This means that part of M1 might still be in the estimate for β_1.)

We would expect both M1 and M2 to be positive, as all effects (how watering affects the height and other health indicators, and how those factors affect the number of lemons) should be positive in this case (assuming there is no over-watering). Thus, β_1 in the model in Figure 4.7b, which should just capture mechanism M2 (and maybe a small part of M1), would likely understate the full effect of watering a tree. (This assumes that more water, on average, is good for the health and production of the tree. We may be able to improve the estimate of the optimal amount of water by using a quadratic model, with W and W^2, but I use the linear model for simplicity.)

Note that, in both figures, the variable for being in the "good soil" part of the yard (G) is not part of the mechanisms for how the amount of water affects the number of lemons (i.e., G is not a mediating factor), as it has its own effect in the model and is not affected by how much water the tree is given (W). The difference between whether we include the height (H) and the indicator for being in the "good soil" part of the yard (G) is that the height is part of the effect of how much water the tree gets, while being in the "good soil" part of the yard is not a product of how much water the tree gets, but *may* be correlated with the amount of water.

What is the difference in interpretation of β_1 for the two models? As indicated in Table 4.4:

- β_1 in the model in Figure 4.7a tells us how the amount of lemons produced varies with the amount of water, holding constant whether the tree is in the "good soil" part of the yard.
- β_1 in the model in Figure 4.7b tells us how the amount of lemons produced varies with the amount of water, holding constant being in the "good soil" part of the yard and adjusting for the height of the tree. Alternatively, we can think of it as how the amount of water affects the number of lemons by affecting aspects of the tree's health other than the tree's height. This is no longer informative on how water affects the number of lemons produced, as it is only part of the effect we want.

Table 4.4 A summary of the two cases for the lemon–tree example

	$L_i = \beta_0 + \beta_1 W_i + \beta_2 G_i + \varepsilon_i$ (Figure 4.7a)	$L_i = \beta_0 + \beta_1 W_i + \beta_2 G_i + \boldsymbol{\beta_3} H_i + \varepsilon_i$ (Figure 4.7b)
Is the variable H (height) included in the model? That is, is it controlled for?	No	Yes
In the model, does H vary with the amount of water (W)?	Yes	Theoretically no (it's controlled for)
What mechanisms are captured by β_1 (the coefficient on W)?	M1 and M2	Just M2
What is the interpretation of β_1?	How the # lemons is affected by the amount of water	How the # lemons is affected by the amount of water beyond the mechanism of increasing the height of the tree
Does this estimate the full causal effect of the amount of water?	Yes	No

As you are probably thinking, the model in Figure 4.7a gives the full effect of the water given, and the model in Figure 4.7b gives only part of the effect, as the effect from how water affects the height is mostly factored out of the estimated effect of the amount of water.

The main lessons are:

- We control for the factors we want to not change as the key-explanatory variable changes.
- We do not control for the factors we want to allow to change when the key-explanatory variable changes. (These are typically mediating factors, or variables that are products of the key-explanatory variable and affect the dependent variable.)
- We want to basically design the model so that water changes and then we let it play out to see what happens. Controlling for a mediating factor is not letting it play out, which would prevent the model from accurately estimating the full effects of water on the number of lemons.

Referring back to the ball-machine sculpture, holding constant a lever would be equivalent to controlling for a mediating factor, as the lever comes after the initial treatment of the ball dropping from above. Rather than hold constant the lever, once the treatment is set, we should let it play out and see what happens.

4.5.2 Case 2: An example with domino chains

This would not be a typical regression one would do, as it certainly does not inform us on a health, economic, or public-policy issue (to the best of my knowledge). But it is a fun and efficient example for demonstrating what a model is and what happens when you hold a factor constant. Imagine that you have 10 distracted participants each set up a simple domino chain, with a length of five dominos each. (I'll let you imagine the reasons why they are distracted.)

The situation is as follows:

- We want to know what the causal effect of tipping the first domino (D_1) is on the probability of the last domino falling (D_5). Theoretically, it should be a 1-to-1 relationship, so the causal effect of D_1 on D_5 should be 1.0. But, because the participants were distracted, there are a few chains with problems.
- The constructed domino chains are depicted in the left image in Figure 4.8.
- When asked to tip the first domino, the last five domino chains are not tipped due to the participants being distracted. (This is beneficial for us to create variation in the key-X variable, D_1.)
- The data generated by this exercise are in Table 4.5, with $D_i = 1$ if the ith domino in the chain gets tipped over and $D_i = 0$ otherwise.
- Observations 1–3 go as planned, with the first domino being tipped ($D_1 = 1$) and the last domino eventually falling ($D_5 = 1$), as seen in the middle image of Figure 4.8.
- Observations 4 and 5 had a miscue, with the first domino being tipped, but the error occurring before the third domino for observation 4 and after the third domino for observation 5.
- Observations 6–10 had the first domino never being tipped ($D_1 = 0$), and so the last domino did not fall ($D_5 = 0$).

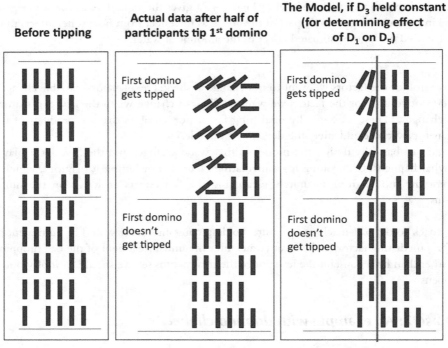

Effectively, no 5th dominoes get tipped as a result of D_1 being tipped, in the model.

Figure 4.8 Initial chains before and after tipping the first domino, and the model with D3 held constant

Table 4.5 Notional data on dominos chains to understand "holding other factors constant"

Observation number	First domino got tipped (D_1)	2nd domino fell (D_2)	3rd domino fell (D_3)	4th domino fell (D_4)	Last (5th) domino fell (D_5)
1	1	1	1	1	1
2	1	1	1	1	1
3	1	1	1	1	1
4	1	1	1	0	0
5	1	1	0	0	0
6	0	0	0	0	0
7	0	0	0	0	0
8	0	0	0	0	0
9	0	0	0	0	0
10	0	0	0	0	0

The true causal effect of D_1 on D_5 equals 0.6 in this exercise. This is just the difference in means of D_5 between when $D_1 = 1$ (0.6) and when $D_1 = 0$ (0.0).

Now, let's consider two regressions to attempt to come up with this true causal effect of 0.6.

$$D_5 = \beta_0 + \beta_1 D_1 + \varepsilon \tag{4.9}$$

$$D_5 = \beta_0 + \beta_1 D_1 + \beta_2 D_3 + \varepsilon \tag{4.10}$$

These two models are depicted in the two panels of Figure 4.9. As described in Section 2.14, each arrow represents the causal effect of a one-unit change in the source variable on the variable being pointed at. The top model represents equation (4.9):

- Tipping the first domino always results in the second domino falling (whereas the second domino never falls when the first domino does not), so the causal effect of D_1 on D_2 is 1.0.
- The third domino falls 80% of the time (4 of 5 times) that the second domino falls, so the causal effect of D_2 on D_3 is 0.8.
- The fourth domino falls 75% of the time (3 of 4 times) that the third domino falls, so the causal effect of D_3 on D_4 is 0.75.
- The fifth domino falls each time (3 of 3 times) that the fourth domino falls, so the causal effect of D_4 on D_5 is 1.0.

Whereas the effect of water on lemon-tree production had multiple mechanisms, there is only one mechanism for how tipping the first domino affects whether the last domino falls. That mechanism simply has the first domino tipping the second, which tips the third, which tips the fourth, which then tips the fifth. So D_2, D_3, and D_4 are mediating factors for the effect of D_1 on D_5.

Note that the coefficient on tipping the first domino, in the top panel, is 0.6, which is the product of the four values of the arrows in the one mechanism: $1.0 \times 0.8 \times 0.75 \times 1.0 = 0.6$. This value of 0.6 is the correct causal effect of D_1 on D_5 for this sample of 10 domino chains, as indicated above.

Now, what would happen if we controlled for one of the mediating factors? In the bottom panel, we control for D_3 (whether the third domino fell) by including it as a control variable.

This would make it so, as D_1 varied in the sample (or, changed in the model), D_3 would not be allowed to vary because it would be held constant. In the model, that breaks the chain, and so D_2 changing does not affect D_3. This is depicted in the right-most image in Figure 4.8, with the model

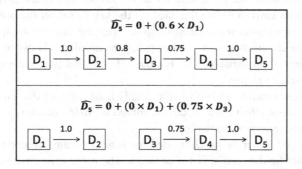

Figure 4.9 Mechanisms for how tipping the first domino affects whether the last domino falls

effectively imposing a wall (or blocker) before the third domino for each chain. That means that the final domino would not fall as a result of the initial tip of the first domino.

The regression model would now be:

$$\hat{D}_5 = 0 + 0 \times D_1 + 0.75 \times D_3. \tag{4.11}$$

The coefficient estimate of 0 on D_1 understates the true causal effect of D_1 on D_5, which should be 0.6.

Also, note that the coefficient on D_3 is the product of the causal effects in the mechanism for how D_3 affects D_5: $0.75 \times 1.0 = 0.75$.

We have controlled for part of the reason why D_1 affects D_5. This is similar to controlling for the height of the lemon tree. And it is similar to fixing a lever in the ball-machine sculpture. We no longer are estimating the true causal effect. We need to be careful what we actually want to hold constant. Basically, we want to implement a treatment and then, as they say, let it go and let it play out rather than controlling for what happens after the treatment.

4.6 Proper terminology for controlling for a variable

From the lessons in this chapter, we can only say we are "holding a factor constant" if that factor is categorical and not based on a quantitative variable. Fully holding a factor constant also requires that we are fairly certain that the data have observations properly assigned to categories. For example, if a data set had errors in race/ethnicity, then if we included racial/ethnic categories as control variables, we would not fully hold constant race and ethnicity.

For quantitative (non-categorical) variables, the best we can do is say that we "adjust for" or we "control for" the factor. Some argue that we should only say we "attempt to adjust for" the factor, or even that we "imperfectly adjust for the factor." I will not decide which is more appropriate, but what is important is that one should be cautious to make sure not to over-sell the model's ability to hold the factors constant. There is a huge difference in how a reader of a study would assess a study if the authors report that they "held constant" vs. "adjusted for" a certain factor.

4.7 Chapter summary

- "Holding a factor constant" means that, in the model, as one key factor changes, the other factor does not change. This aims to isolate the effect of the key factor on the outcome.
- Controlling for groups within some categorization (with dummy variables) means that the over-all coefficient estimates are based on within-group relationships between the key-explanatory variable and the dependent variable. This is what tells you that the group is held constant as the key-explanatory variable changes.
- Controlling for a quantitative factor does not cleanly hold constant that factor.
- When estimating causal effects, not all factors should be held constant, particularly factors that occur after the key-explanatory variable.
- Technically, unless the factor being controlled for is an accurate categorization (set of dummy variables), we cannot hold a certain factor constant. The more appropriate description is that we "adjust for" or "control for" certain factors.

Exercises

1. Consider the regression model from Chapter 2, Question #2,

$$\widehat{price} = 100,000 + 45,000 \times bedrooms + 10 \times sqft$$

   If you observed home prices listed for 1000-square-foot homes and for 3000-square-foot homes (without any other information), why would the difference in average home price between the two sets of homes likely be more than $20,000 (which is $10×2000, with 2000 being the difference between 3000 and 1000)? Why would this be different from what the regression indicates?

2. Use the logic from the cookie example in Section 4.1 to describe why it would be difficult to estimate how a parental divorce affects outcomes for children.

3. Use the logic from the cookie example in Section 4.1 to describe why it would be difficult to estimate how the marginal income tax rate affects GDP growth.

4. Consider the model that aims to estimate how hours-studied affects a test score for people in a single large class:

   (test score) $= \beta_0 + \beta_1 \times$ (# hours studied for test) $+ \beta_2 \times$ (major) $+ \varepsilon$

   where major is a dummy variable for whether the course is part of the student's major. Come up with a table for the source of variation in the key-X variable of "hours studied" (as in Figures 4.1 and 4.2 in Section 4.2), with a factor in V3, V4, and either V1 or V2.

5. With the data on the book's website, **income_coll_hisp_data**, regress income on coll and hisp (for the purpose of estimating the effect of a college degree on income, holding constant whether the person is Hispanic).

   a. Create a table similar to Table 4.2 to demonstrate how the coefficient estimate on coll is based on the weighted average of the coefficient estimates on coll for the two groups identified by the variable, hisp.

   b. How do you know that Hispanic is held constant?

6. Set up a notional model of a research issue you choose and draw a chart similar to Figure 4.7a, that has: (a) at least one mediating factor that should not be controlled for (similar to the height of the lemon tree); and (b) one variable that is not a mediating factor and should be controlled for (similar to the variable for the "good soil part of the yard").

Reference

Gibbons, C. E., Serrato, J. C. S., & Urbancic, M. B. (2019). Broken or fixed effects? *Journal of Econometric Methods*, 8(1).

5 Standard errors, hypothesis tests, p-values, and aliens

DOI: 10.4324/9781003285007-5

Sometimes I think the surest sign that intelligent life exists elsewhere in the universe is that none of it has tried to contact us.

– Calvin (of Calvin and Hobbes)
CALVIN AND HOBBES © Watterson. Reprinted with permission
of ANDREWS MCMEEL SYNDICATION. All rights reserved.

Recall from Section 2.13 that there are two main reasons why a coefficient estimate from a regression can be wrong: imprecision and inaccuracy/bias. Whereas the next chapter will focus on identifying sources of inaccuracy or bias, this chapter presents the measure of imprecision in coefficient estimates (the standard error) and how that is used for hypothesis testing and determining a range of likely estimates (confidence intervals).

In this chapter, you will learn:

- What is the standard error (the measure of imprecision of a coefficient estimate) and what determines how large the standard error is
- How the standard error determines the likelihood of various ranges of values for a coefficient estimate
- The basics of hypothesis tests and how to properly interpret hypothesis tests, including an insignificant estimate
- How to calculate a confidence interval
- What could bias a standard error (multicollinearity, heteroskedasticity, and clustering) and how to fix those problems
- Why the p-value is not what you think it is and why many researchers incorrectly interpret the p-value
- How statistical significance is not your goal
- Perhaps a better approach than using hypothesis tests to form the basis of conclusions from a regression.

In the end, I will tell you why I personally believe that hypothesis tests should not be used and instead that regression results be characterized by the strength of evidence. To make this argument, I first need to describe hypothesis tests – as your professor might not agree with me that hypothesis tests should not be used.

5.1 Standard errors

Let's return again to the National Longitudinal Survey of Youth (NLSY) sample from Chapter 2 that we used to estimate the relationship between years-of-schooling and income. Let's now estimate a model with more control variables. From the original data set **income_data**, the variables for determining income in 2003, are:

- *income* (the dependent variable) = the person's income in 2003
- *educ* = years-of-schooling completed

- *afqt* = AFQT percentile
- *age* = age in 2003
- *black* = 1 if the respondent is Black; = 0 otherwise
- *hisp* = 1 if the respondent is Hispanic; = 0 otherwise
- *mom_hs* = 1 if the respondent's mother completed at least 12 years-of-schooling; = 0 otherwise
- *mom_coll* = 1 if the respondent's mother completed at least 16 years-of-schooling; = 0 otherwise
- *dad_hs* = 1 if the respondent's father completed at least 12 years-of-schooling; = 0 otherwise
- *dad_coll* = 1 if the respondent's father completed at least 16 years-of-schooling; = 0 otherwise.

Table 5.1 shows the output from Stata, while Table 5.2 shows the R output. Note that there are differences in the output that is produced.

From Table 5.1, the top panel has overall regression statistics – the top-left three numbers (under SS) are *ExSS*, *RSS*, and *TSS*. The R^2, in the top-right panel, is 0.210 (which is roughly 1.47 ÷ 7.01) In the bottom panel of the table, the variables used in the model are listed.

Note that the variables for the highest-grade-completed of the mother were missing for 808 respondents (6.4% of the initial 12,686 respondents), and the variables for the highest-grade-completed of the father was missing for 1806 respondents (14.2%). For the sake of keeping the observations for this exercise, I did the technically-incorrect thing of assigning a value of zero for the mother and father's educational variables if they were missing. In Section 12.2.7, I discuss a better option for dealing with missing data.

The first number in each row represents the coefficient estimate on the given variable. The second number is the **standard error** of the given coefficient estimate. The standard error is a measure of how precise the coefficient estimate is. Often standard errors are reported in studies in parentheses next to or under a coefficient estimate.

Table 5.1 Stata output for regression of 2003 income on various factors

Source	SS	df	MS	Number of obs = 2772
				F(9, 2762) = 81.43
Model	1.47E+12	9	1.63440E+12	Prob > F = 0.0000
Residual	5.54E+12	2762	2.00710E+10	R-squared = 0.2097
Total	7.01E+12	2771	2.531.40E+10	Adj R-squared = 0.2071
				Root MSE = 44,800

income	Coef. estimate	Standard error	t value	[p-value]	[95% Conf. Interval]	
educ	5119	461	11.10	0.000	4215	6023
afqt	250	43	5.76	0.000	165	335
age	753	386	1.95	0.051	−4	1510
black	−6868	2331	−2.95	0.003	−11,439	−2298
hisp	−76	2517	−0.03	0.976	−5012	4859
mom_hs	2025	2158	0.94	0.348	−2206	6256
mom_coll	2135	3638	0.59	0.557	−4999	9269
dad_hs	996	2126	0.47	0.639	−3173	5165
dad_coll	14,840	3011	4.93	0.000	8936	20,744
_cons	−59,671	17,699	−3.37	0.001	−94,377	−24,966

Source: Bureau of Labor Statistics, 2014.

Table 5.2 R output for regression of 2003 income on various factors

From summary() command

Residuals:

Min	1Q	Median	3Q	Max
−106,269	−22,127	−6816	9387	242,031

	Estimate	Std. Error	t value	[p-value]
(Intercept)	−59,671	17,699	−3.37	0.001
Educ	5119	461	11.11	< 2.00E−16
Afqt	250	43	5.76	0.000
Age	753	386	1.95	0.051
Black	−6868	2331	−2.95	0.003
Hisp	−76	2517	−0.03	0.976
mom_hs	2025	2158	0.94	0.348
mom_coll	2135	3638	0.59	0.557
dad_hs	996	2126	0.47	0.639
dad_coll	14,840	3011	4.93	0.000

Residual standard error: 44,800 on 2762 degrees of freedom
Multiple R-squared: 0.2097, Adjusted R-squared: 0.2071
F-statistic: 81.43 on 9 and 2762 DF, p-value: < 2.2E − 16

From confint() command
(lower and upper bounds of 95% confidence intervals)

	2.5%	97.5%
(Intercept)	−94,377	−24,966
Educ	4215	6023
Afqt	165	335
Age	−4	1510
Black	−11,439	−2298
Hisp	−5012	4859
mom_hs	−2206	6256
mom_coll	−4999	9269
dad_hs	−3173	5165
dad_coll	8936	20,744

Source: Bureau of Labor Statistics, 2014.

From the Appendix of Background Statistics Tools, an "estimator" is the best guess we have for what the true population estimate is. The coefficient estimate in a regression is an estimator as well. There is inevitably randomness in the estimate due to two major sources: (1) often having just a sample of the population; and (2) the outcome itself being subject to randomness. A **standard error** is the standard deviation of the sampling distribution for the coefficient estimate.

In some sense, the coefficient is a random variable in the population. For example, being Hispanic wouldn't affect income the same for all Hispanics. What would be estimated, if proper controls were included, would be an average association of being Hispanic with income for the selected sample (Section 2.11). If we were to select a different sample, we would likely obtain a different coefficient estimate.

The second major source of randomness comes from unexpected and random things affecting outcomes. A student may be sick and perform worse on an exam than would be expected. An incorrect referee call can determine who wins a basketball game. A judge wavering between giving a score of 5.3 or 5.4 can determine who wins a gymnastics competition. As the outcome changes with these random events, the coefficient estimates linking explanatory variables to these outcomes will change. The more random the outcome is (marked by not being explained well by the set of explanatory variables), the greater would be the standard errors.

The formula for the standard error (SE) on a coefficient estimate on a variable, X_j, is the following:

$$SE\left(\hat{\beta}_j\right) = \frac{\hat{\sigma}}{\sum\left(X_j - \bar{X}_j\right)^2 \times \left(1 - R_j^2\right)} \tag{5.1}$$

where:
- $\hat{\sigma}$ is the Standard Error of the Regression or Root Mean Square Error (Section 2.5 and equation (2.16)), which has in the numerator the sum of the squared residuals
- R_j^2 is the R^2 from a regression of the variable X_j on the other X variables and a constant.

Note that, if there were no other X variables in the model other than X_j, then the second quantity in the numerator of (5.1) would be equal to one.

From the formula for the standard error of the coefficient estimate, we can determine that the following main factors would be associated with a *lower* standard error (which is always better) for some variables, X_j:

- A larger sample size (n is in the denominator in the formula for $\hat{\sigma}$ in equation (2.16))
- A smaller amount of unexplained variation in Y (i.e., based on the standard-error-of-the-regression
- A larger standard deviation in X_j (which gives more variation to explain Y)
- Less variation in X_j explained by the other X variables (which leads to a greater *operative variation* in X_j and allows the relationship between X_j and Y to be more easily separated from the relationships between other X variables and Y).

This means that adding a control variable would contribute to a lower standard error for variable, X_j, by reducing the standard-error-of-the-regression, but it would contribute to a higher standard error by leaving less variation in X_j not covered by other variables. Thus, adding a variable that is more-highly correlated with X_j is more likely to increase the standard error than would a variable that is not highly correlated with X_j.

To demonstrate the importance of sample size and variation in the explanatory variable, consider Figure 5.1. As a preview of the discussion of confidence intervals in Section 5.3.5 below, I provide not just the estimated slopes, but also the slopes characterizing the 95% confidence intervals for the coefficient estimates, which indicate that we can be 95% certain that the true population coefficient (but not necessarily the true causal effect) lies in this range. This is notional data that I created. It could be any topic, but I made this an analysis of the relationship between average daily TV hours and Body

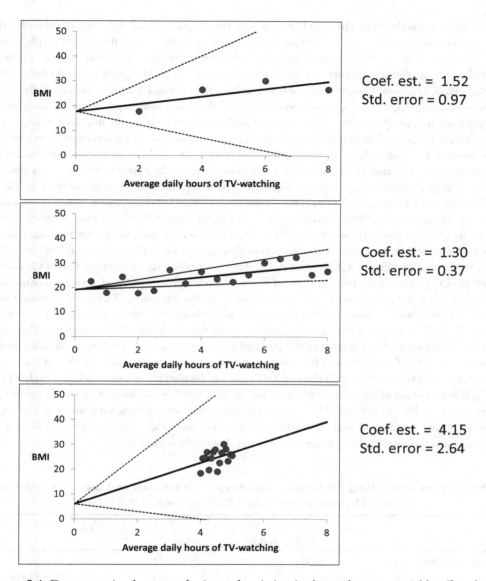

Figure 5.1 Demonstrating how sample size and variation in the explanatory variable affect the standard error

Mass Index (BMI). The outcome for each observation, in all three charts in Figure 5.1, is determined by the same formula:

$$BMI = 20 + 1.0 \times (Average\ TV\ hours) + 12 \times [\text{a random number between 0 and 1}] \qquad (5.2)$$

(The random component, meant to mimic how other factors besides TV watching affect BMI, is needed to make sure there is some imprecision and a positive standard error for all three models.)

What differ across the three charts in Figure 5.1 are the sample size and the range of values for the key-X variable (average TV hours). The first comparison is from the first to the second graph, which shows the power of more observations. It shows that the coefficient estimate would be more precisely estimated (with a smaller standard error) with 16 observations in the middle graph vs. just 4 observations in the top graph. The confidence interval for the regression slope is much narrower in the middle graph, with more observations, which I adjusted vertically to have the same y-intercept, for ease of comparison.

To demonstrate the effect of the variation in the explanatory variable on the imprecision, let's compare the middle to the bottom graph. For the bottom graph, I made it so all 16 observations were in the narrow range of 4–5 (rather than 0.5–8 in the middle graph). This would mean that the left quantity in the denominator of equation (5.1) would be smaller, causing the standard error to be higher. As you can observe, the slope characterizing the data is much less certain with the smaller range/variance for the X variable, which can be seen with the much higher standard error and resulting wider confidence interval.

The true coefficient in all three models is 1.0, as seen in equation (5.2). Yet, all three coefficient estimates are far from 1.0 due to the imprecision. The larger the standard error, the greater potential there is to have a coefficient estimate farther from the true coefficient, as we see in the bottom graph of Figure 5.1.

Let's tie this back to Figure 4.3 in Section 4.2. After controlling for the Armed Forces Qualification Test (AFQT) score (in the bottom panel of Figure 4.3), the *operative variation* in years-of-schooling was less than when the AFQT score was not controlled for (the top panel). This would translate into a higher standard error (less precision) for the coefficient estimate on years-of-schooling. This is what occurs in Table 5.3, in which I show the results of those models (with all observations rather than the small random sample) and now with the standard errors. As expected, when years-of-schooling is adjusted for the AFQT score, there is less *operative variation*, as seen in the lower variance of the years-of-schooling variable, as well as with the standard error on the coefficient estimate being higher (475 vs. 347). When, instead of adjusting the years-of-schooling variable for the AFQT score, the AFQT score was simply added to the model (in column (3)), the coefficient estimate on years-of-schooling is the same as using the adjusted-year-of-schooling (5395), but the standard error is lower (436 vs. 475) because the standard-error-of-the-regression is lower due to the higher R^2.

Table 5.3 How controlling for factors reduces *operative variation* and increases standard errors (Dependent variable = 2003 income, n = 2772)·

	Variance of years-of-schooling variable	(1)	(2)	(3)
Years-of-schooling	**6.35**	8121		5395
		(347)		(436)
Years-of-schooling adjusted for the AFQT score	**3.87**		5395	
			(475)	
AFQT score				368
				(37)
Constant		−54,299	54,019	−34,027
		(4703)	(934)	(5045)
R-squared		0.165	0.045	0.195

Standard errors are in parentheses.

Data source: NLSY 1979.

Box 5.1   Why macroeconomists are so bad at predicting recessions

Economists in the November 2007 Philadelphia Federal Reserve's Survey of Professional Fore-casters predicted 2008 GDP growth of 2.5% and estimated just a 3% chance of a recession (Research Department, Federal Reserve Bank of Philadelphia, 2007). What makes this laughable is that this occurred just *one month before the Great Recession/Financial Crisis officially began.*

On a related note, in the Summer of 2015, I had a foul-shooting contest with LeBron James. The final score was:

   LeBron: 60 of 68
   Me: 56 of 68

Why did we shoot 68 free throws? (LeBron wondered the same thing.) You will see in a moment.

Can one conclude from this contest that LeBron is a better free-throw shooter? Some may say yes, but a statistician would say that there are not enough observations to make such a conclusion, particularly given the small difference in our shooting percentages.

Now, imagine trying to predict a recession. Decent macro-economic data has been collected since 1947. Thus, there were only **68** years of good data on the economy (at the time of my ~~imaginary~~ contest with LeBron). In that time, there had only been 11 recessions. With so few observations, there would be very large standard errors on the coefficient estimates for the variables used to predict recessions because of the larger role that randomness has in smaller samples. Thus, it would be difficult to identify things that lead to a recession.

Referring back to an earlier point (Section 2.12), the economy has changed: a shift from manufacturing to technology, more energy-efficient technologies and vehicles, more financial instruments to spread risk which could stabilize (or destabilize) the economy, etc. Thus, what caused recessions in the past might be very different from what would cause a recession today. In the same vein, what helped stave off recessions in the past may be different from what helps stave off recessions today. In other words, causal effects can change over time. And, next time, I might beat LeBron.

Sometimes, the standard error needs to be adjusted given the nature of the data or the model being used. I will discuss these issues and corrections in Section 5.4.

5.2 How the standard error determines the likelihood of various values of the true coefficient

The standard error is important for hypothesis testing but also for informing us on the range of likely values and even the likelihood of certain values for the true coefficient. First, let me put on my broken-record hat again and note that the true coefficient is for a given model, which is not necessarily the true causal effect. For the true coefficient to be the true causal effect, there would need to be no biases in the model. A researcher would estimate the true causal effect only if there were no bias and no imprecision – in other words, never, unless the error from the bias exactly matched the error from the imprecision.

In most cases, we can assume that the coefficient estimate is a random variable that follows a normal distribution. For small samples, this might not necessarily be the case. However, in almost all cases, the normal curve would still offer a reasonable approximation of the true distribution of possible values.

For a useful example, I will use one that I created in my book, *Confessions of a Recovering Economist* (Arkes, 2022). The example is based on a study on how greater gender and racial/ethnic diversity in the first ship assignment for U.S. Navy enlisted sailors affect their reenlistment decisions (Arkes et al. 2022). The regression equation regarding gender diversity, for a sample of about 81,000 males, is roughly:

$$\widehat{(reenlist)} = \underset{(0.030)}{0.065} \times (\text{proportion of officers who are female}) + \ldots \tag{5.3}$$

(The actual coefficient estimate and standard error were 0.064 and 0.031, but I will use **0.065** and **0.030** to simplify some calculations below. The "…" just indicates that there were other diversity measures and demographic characteristics in the model.)

The estimate of **0.065**, if correct, would say that going from 0% to 100% female officers (who are superiors to the enlisted sailors) would increase the reenlistment rate for male enlistees by 6.5 percentage points. More realistically, going from 10% to 20% of officers who were female (the value of the key-X variable would go from 0.10 to 0.20) would increase the reenlistment rate for enlisted males by 0.65 percentage points.

We believe we had a valid model in that there were not likely any meaningful systematic biases, but the value of 0.065 was still likely wrong. Figure 5.2 shows the likelihood of various ranges of values for the true coefficient for this model. I mark several of the possible values of the true coefficient:

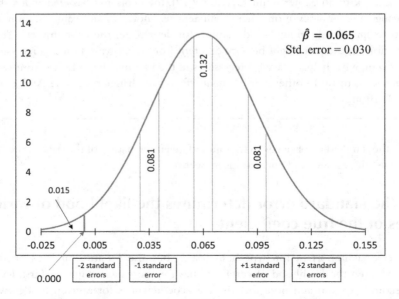

Figure 5.2 Various probabilities of the true coefficient, given the estimate and standard error

- The coefficient estimate of 0.065
- Both one standard error below and above the coefficient estimate (0.035 and 0.095)
- Both two standard errors below and above the coefficient estimate (0.005 and 0.125)
- Zero.

In addition, I create 0.1-wide bands around the coefficient estimate and the values one standard error below and above the coefficient estimate. The number in each band indicates the likelihood that the true coefficient lies in that range. The figure tells us that:

- There is only a 13.2% chance that the true coefficient is between 0.060 and 0.070, which is centered around the coefficient estimate of 0.65.
- The likelihood that the true coefficient is about one standard error lower than the coefficient estimate (in the 0.030 to 0.040 range) is 0.081, which is about 61% as likely as being in the 0.060–0.070 range. The same applies to the true coefficient being about one standard error higher (in the 0.090–0.100 range).
- There is a greater likelihood that the true coefficient is in one of the two ranges that is one standard error away than in the band centered on the coefficient estimate (0.081 + 0.081 = 0.162 vs. 0.132). Note that all of these numbers would be a bit different for different-sized bands.
- There is a 1.5% chance that the true coefficient is below zero.

A common characterization of the range of likely values is a confidence interval, particularly the 95% confidence interval. This is based on the same concept here. I introduced confidence intervals in the prior section, but I will give more detail on the calculations below in Section 5.3.5.

I stated, back in the opening of Chapter 2, how it is comical that regressions often produce numbers (coefficients and standard errors) with such a large number of decimal places. The concept in this section explains why I find it comical, as the numerous decimal places portray great precision, whereas there is often a wide range of possible values for the true coefficient. What good is the eighth decimal place when there is such uncertainty on the second decimal place, and even the first decimal place?

5.3 Hypothesis testing in regression analysis

5.3.1 Setting up the problem for hypothesis tests

Let's say that you want to explore the theory that the anti-bullying campaigns that today's teenagers are exposed to affect their empathy. In particular, you want to test whether current teenagers have a different level of empathy from the historical population of teenagers. Suppose you have a random sample of 25 teenagers. And let's say that there is a questionnaire with a multitude of questions that are combined to give a standardized score on empathy that has, in the historic population of teenagers, a normal distribution with a mean of 100 and a standard deviation of 15. From your sample of current teenagers, let's say that you find that their average empathy score is 104, a little higher than the historical average of 100. So you want to conduct a hypothesis test to see whether there is evidence confirming the contention that current teenagers do indeed have a different level of empathy from the historical teenage average. (Note that I am initially testing for a *different level* and not a *higher level* of empathy. We will consider directional hypothesis testing later on.)

The test is really about how certain we can be to rule out randomness giving you the sample mean that is different from 100, the historical mean. Randomness pervades our life. Randomness in getting the right coach could dictate the difference between making it or not in professional sports. For a student growing up in poverty, randomness in the teacher she gets could determine academic and financial success in life. Randomness on questions you are guessing on when taking college entrance exams could determine whether you get into your desired college, which could change the course of your life. And randomness would likely determine who you marry, unless destiny has a greater role than what I give it credit for.

In statistics, randomness in outcomes brings on uncertainty in a statistic. It dictates the sample that you get when you draw from a larger population. Having more observations, to some extent, counteracts the uncertainty that randomness brings, and we can better gauge whether any relationships observed are real (whether large, small, or zero).

Assuming this was a random sample of the population of teenagers, the higher mean level of empathy in the sample of current teenagers means that either:

- They do have the same mean empathy level as the historical population of teenagers, and it was random variation that caused this sample of 25 teenagers to have a mean level of empathy that is 4 points off from the population mean of 100 or
- Current teenagers indeed have a different mean empathy level from the historical population of teenagers.

We want to determine whether 104 is far enough from 100 that we can rule out, with an adequate level of certainty, that the mean of current teenagers is still 100 and randomness is giving us the sample mean of 104. This would allow us to conclude, with a given degree of certainty, whether current teenagers do indeed have a significantly different empathy level from the historical teenage population.

The test procedures are:

1. Define the hypotheses:
   Null hypothesis: H_0: mean empathy of current teenagers $= \mu = 100$
   Alternative hypothesis: H_1: mean empathy of current teenagers $= \mu \neq 100$
2. Determine the standard error of the estimate. To keep the calculations simpler for the sake of the exercise, let's assume that the sample of current teenagers has the same standard deviation of empathy (σ) of 15 as in the historical population – this allows us to use the normal distribution rather than the Student's t-distribution, which we would use if we didn't know the true standard deviation and had to use the sample standard deviation (s) instead. The standard error of the mean is equal to: $\dfrac{\sigma}{\sqrt{n}} = \dfrac{15}{\sqrt{25}} = 3$. (See Appendix Section A.3.)
3. Determine how certain you want to be for the test by establishing a statistical significance level. Most people use 95% certainty, which translates into a 5% (statistical) significance level. This would say that, if the null hypothesis were true, you allow a 5% chance that the random sample you have would show that the alternative hypothesis was true. That is, if the null hypothesis were true, you would make the wrong conclusion 5% of the time. (This does not say that there is a 5% chance that the conclusion is wrong, as it just speaks to what happens if the null hypothesis were true. More on this later.)

4. Starting with the assumption that the null hypothesis were true (the mean empathy for current teenagers is 100), determine whether 104 is different enough from the hypothesized value of 100 that we can rule out (with a high degree of certainty) that randomness gave us the sample mean (104) this far from the hypothesized value of 100. If so, we can *reject* the null hypothesis and *accept* the alternative hypothesis.

We can see this graphically in Figure 5.3. In this figure, we make the safe assumption that there is a normal distribution for the current teenagers given that the underlying population has a normal distribution. I shade in the **rejection regions**, which mark the parts of the distribution of mean scores that would make us "reject" the null hypothesis that current teenagers have the same empathy as the rest of the population. They represent the "unlikely-to-occur" ranges. In this case, I make the rejection region represent 5% of the area under the curve, split between the left and right tails of the distribution. Again, we would accept a 5% chance of being wrong if the null hypothesis were true. The critical values defining the rejection regions are:

$$100 \pm 1.96 \times 3 = 94.12, \ 105.88$$

(The value 1.96 is the z value that leaves 0.025 in each tail, or 0.05 total area or probability in the rejection regions. This comes from the standard normal distribution, as described in Appendix Section A.2. The value 3 is the standard error for the mean as calculated above.)

The teenagers' sample mean (104) is not in one of those rejection regions, so the sample mean is not far enough away from 100 that we can rule out randomness producing a different mean empathy level from that of the historical population. Thus, we cannot conclude that current teenagers have a different mean level of empathy. Note that we do not conclude that current teenagers have the same mean level of empathy, as we cannot prove a null hypothesis.

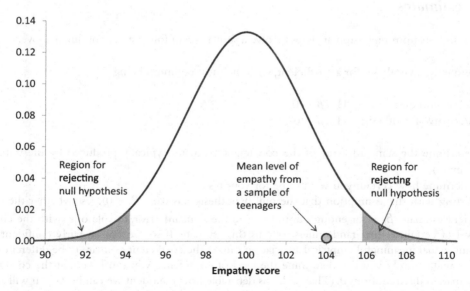

Figure 5.3 Hypothesis test example for a sample mean

This was a two-sided test, formally testing whether current teenagers have a *different* mean level of empathy from the historical population. Alternatively, you could do a one-sided test, testing whether current teenagers have *higher* empathy than the population. In this case, the hypotheses would be:

$H_0 : \mu \leq 100$
$H_1 : \mu > 100$

The critical value would be: $100 + 1.645 \times 3 = 104.935$. (The z value of $+1.645$ is the z value that leaves all 0.05 in the right tail in the standard normal distribution.) Again, with the sample mean of 104, we could not conclude that current teenagers have a higher empathy level than the historical population of teenagers.

There is always the possibility that the conclusion of the test could be wrong. The two types of errors will be discussed in more detail in Section 5.3.7. Briefly, they are:

- Type I error (False Positive) – current teens have the same level of empathy as historical teens, but random sampling happens to produce a level of empathy that is significantly different from the historical value of 100.
- Type II error (False Negative) – current teens do have a different level of empathy, but we are not able to detect a statistically-significant difference.

The reason for going through this exercise is that the same concepts are used to determine if randomness can reasonably be ruled out for a coefficient estimate to be different from zero or different from a particular number.

5.3.2 The four steps for hypothesis testing for regression coefficient estimates

Hypothesis tests from regression analyses involve a similar set of four steps, as outlined above:

1. Define the hypotheses for a coefficient, with the most common being:

   Null hypothesis: $H_0 : \beta_i = 0$
   Alternative hypothesis: $H_1 : \beta_i \neq 0$

2. Determine the standard error of the coefficient estimate (typically produced by the statistical program).
3. Determine how certain you want to be for your test.
4. Starting with the assumption that the null hypothesis was true ($\beta_i = 0$), test whether the coefficient estimate, $\hat{\beta}_i$, is far enough from 0, given the standard error, to rule out (with the chosen level of certainty) that randomness gave us this estimate. If so, we can be fairly confident that some actual meaningful empirical association caused the coefficient estimate to be different from 0. Simultaneously, you can determine the level of confidence you can have that the coefficient estimate is different from 0. (That said, it is debatable how confident we can be, as you will see in Section 5.5 below.)

5.3.3 *t-statistics*

With regression analysis, the Student's *t*-distribution is used. The Student's *t*-distribution (or, just *t*-distribution) is very much like the *standard normal* distribution, but it is a little wider. With samples of around 100 or more, the Student's *t*-distribution gets pretty close to the standard normal distribution. While one should have some understanding of reading a Student's *t*-distribution, statistical programs typically indicate the significance and certainty levels.

The observed ***t*-statistic** or ***t*-stat** ($t_{observed}$ or t_o) for a coefficient estimate is simply:

$$t_o = \frac{coefficient\ estimate\left(\hat{\beta}\right)}{standard\ error\left(SE\left(\hat{\beta}\right)\right)} \tag{5.4}$$

In rare cases, the hypothesized value for the null hypothesis will be some number other than zero. In those cases, the numerator for the *t*-stat would be the coefficient estimate minus the hypothesized value.

The *t*-stat is the statistic that is used to test whether the coefficient estimate is statistically significant. This is the third number in each row in Table 5.1 (for Stata) back in Section 5.1. As an example, the *t*-stat for the years-of-schooling variable (*educ*) is, rounding off, $5119.4/461.0 = 11.10$.

Note that, similar to the transformation to Z for the standard normal distribution (in Appendix Section A.2), the *t*-stat transformation involves subtracting out the hypothesized value (which is normally zero) and dividing by the standard error. And so the *t*-stat is similar to the Z value in that it represents the number of standard errors away from zero that the coefficient estimate is. The more standard errors away from zero it is, the more certainty we can have that the true coefficient is not zero.

An important ingredient for the *t*-stat (for hypothesis tests) is the degrees of freedom. The number of **degrees of freedom** indicates the number of values that are free to estimate the parameters, which equals the number of observations minus the constraints (parameters to be estimated). The definition is:

$$\text{Degrees of freedom} = n - K - 1 = n - k$$

where
- n = sample size
- K = # explanatory variables
- $k = K + 1$ = # parameters to be estimated (the explanatory variables and the constant).

While computer programs typically indicate the degrees of freedom, you may need to calculate it in order to conduct manual tests or to construct confidence intervals, as demonstrated below.

In the next few sub-sections, we apply the standard errors and the *t*-distribution in order to conduct the hypothesis tests and calculate p-values and confidence intervals. This would be appropriate as long as the error terms were normally distributed or at least approximately normally distributed (Assumption A.3 from Section 2.10). In cases in which the error terms were not normally distributed, these calculations would be incorrect. A simple solution to address the possibility of miscalculations due to non-normal error terms would be to require higher levels of significance to make certain conclusions. This will be discussed in more detail in Sections 5.5 and 5.6.

5.3.4 Statistical significance and p-values

In a criminal trial, the hypotheses a jury weighs are:

- Null H_0 : The defendant is innocent.
- Alternative H_1 : The defendant is guilty.

The jury needs to determine if there is enough evidence to reject the null hypothesis with a high level of certainty (i.e., beyond a reasonable doubt) and accept the alternative hypothesis that the defendant is guilty. The jury does not need to establish that the null hypothesis is true, that the defendant is innocent.

5.3.4.1 Two-sided hypothesis tests

To test for the significance of a coefficient estimate, as stated above, you would start with the hypotheses:

- Null $H_0 : \beta_i = 0$.
- Alternative $H_1 : \beta_i \neq 0$.

Just as in a criminal trial, we aim to test whether the null hypothesis can be disproven beyond a reasonable doubt. That is, we aim to test whether the coefficient estimate is far enough away from zero to conclude that it is "**statistically significant**" or "**significantly different from zero,**" indicating that the true coefficient is likely not zero. We do not aim to prove that the null is true (i.e., that $\beta_i = 0$).

    With the t-stat, the statistical significance of a coefficient estimate can be determined. Note the language: *It is not a variable but rather it is the coefficient estimate that is statistically significant or insignificant.*

    The test for significance for a coefficient estimate involves comparing the t-stat to critical values on the Student's t-distribution. As with the example with the mean level of empathy from a sample of current teenagers above, if the t-stat is beyond one of the critical values, in one of the tails of the distribution, then we can conclude that it is unlikely that randomness caused the estimate to be that far away from zero. We would then conclude whether the coefficient estimate is statistically significant.

    Figure 5.4 shows the rejection regions for the hypothesis tests for the model used in Tables 5.1 and 5.2, based on having a 5% significance level. That is, the rejection regions are defined so as to have the probability of rejecting a true null hypothesis of 5%. To determine the critical t value ($t_{critical}$ or t_c) that defines the rejection regions, you can easily find online calculators to do this, or, in Excel:

- Use the command T.INV.2T (two–tail test).
- Plug in 0.05 for a 5% level of significance (or 0.01 for a hypothesis test based on a 1% level of significance).

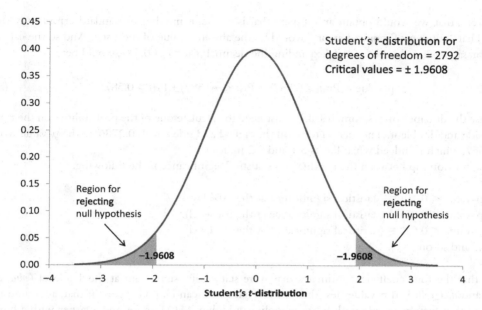

Figure 5.4 Rejection region for Student's *t*-distribution (d.f. = 2762)

- Plug in "degrees of freedom" = $n - K - 1 = 2772 - 9 - 1 = 2762$.
  (This is for the coefficient estimate in Tables 5.1 and 5.2, with nine explanatory variables.)
- It should give you a critical value of $t_c = 1.9608$, which is pretty close to the equivalent critical value of 1.9600 for the standard normal distribution.

One would reject the null hypothesis (that the coefficient estimate equals 0) if the *t*-stat were in the rejection region of greater than 1.9608 or less than −1.9608.

Based on the rejection regions, we can conclude from Tables 5.1 and 5.2 that *educ, afqt, black, dad_coll*, and the constant term have coefficient estimates different from zero (using the 5% significance level). That is, we can reject the null hypothesis at the 5% level for these four variables and the constant term. Note that the *t*-stat for *age* is 1.95, which is close to the critical value, but not quite there. The other variables (*hisp, mom_hs, mom_coll*, and *dad_hs*) all have *t*-stats with an absolute value below 1.9608. Thus, their coefficient estimates are statistically insignificant. The critical values for significance at the 1% level would be ±2.578. These four variables (*educ, afqt, black*, and *dad_coll*) have *t*-stats exceeding these critical values, as well. Thus, they are also significant at the 1% level. Normally, we do not have to look up these critical values, as most statistical programs will indicate the statistical significance for us, as Stata does above, with the p-value.

The **p-value** indicates the likelihood that, if the true coefficient were actually zero, random processes (i.e., randomness from sampling or from determining the outcomes) would generate a coefficient estimate as far from zero as it is. From Tables 5.1 and 5.2, note how the larger the *t*-stat is, the lower the p-value is.

These calculations are similar to equation (A.18) in the Appendix, in which we estimate the probability of obtaining a sample mean for IQ at least 2 standard deviations from the mean. Here we are calculating how likely it would be, if the null hypothesis were true that the population coefficient were zero, that we would obtain an estimate that is a certain number of standard errors away from zero. That "number of standard errors" would be the absolute value of the *t*-stat. And so the calculation for, say, *mom_coll*, with a *t*-stat (expanding the decimal places) of 0.587, would be:

$$\text{p-value} = \Pr(|t| > 0.587) = \Pr(t < -0.587) + \Pr(t > 0.587) \tag{5.5}$$

Because the distribution is symmetrical, we just need to calculate one of the probabilities on the right-hand side and double it. The second term on the right-hand side equals 0.2786, so the p-value would be 0.557, which is indeed what Tables 5.1 and 5.2 indicate.

The relationship between the p-value and statistical significance is the following:

- (p-value < 0.10) = (statistical significance at the 10% level).
- (p-value < 0.05) = (statistical significance at the 5% level).
- (p-value < 0.01) = (statistical significance at the 1% level).
- … and so on.

Note that the four coefficient estimates that were statistically significant at the 1% level (*educ*, *afqt*, *black*, and *dad_coll*) had p-values less than 0.01. That is, we can be pretty certain that, after adjusting for the other factors, people with more schooling, a higher AFQT score, and a father with a higher level of education have higher income on average, while those who are Black have lower income on average. The coefficient estimate on "age" has a p-value of 0.051. This means that it is not significant at the 5% level. However, it is significant at the 10% level. Note that, even though this is a two-sided test, it is safe to give directional conclusions. You will see why in the next sub-section.

Remember, we have *not* made the case that these are causal effects. We need some theory and stories to sort through the alternative explanations before concluding whether any of these are causal effects or possibly related to each other for other reasons.

The coefficient estimates on Hispanic, the two variables for mother's education, and the variable on father's college degree are statistically insignificant, as the p-values are above 0.10, which is considered the maximum p-value for even weak statistical significance.

All this said, the p-value does not indicate how certain one can be that a given estimate signifies a real empirical relationship between an explanatory variable and the outcome. As I will discuss in Section 5.5, there are many problems with using the p-value, despite it being the standard statistic used to gauge how confident we can be that an empirical relationship is real.

Furthermore, people tend to put too much weight on the primary thresholds of statistical significance, 5% and 10%. Researchers tend to label an estimate with a p-value of 0.049 to be a "significant predictor," but an estimate with a p-value of 0.051 to be a "weakly significant predictor," or "insignificant predictor." As you can see, there is little difference between how significant they are, so randomness or bias could cause the difference in significance.

Finally, let me note that, if two or more explanatory variables are highly correlated, they may be sharing any "effect" or empirical relationship with the dependent variable. This may cause the variables to, individually, have statistically-insignificant coefficient estimates even though the variables are collectively significantly related to the dependent variable. One option in such a situation is to exclude one or more of the correlated explanatory variables to see if the one remaining in the model has a significant coefficient estimate. A second option is to test the joint significance of the coefficient estimates. I will demonstrate this "joint significance test" test in Section 5.3.6.

5.3.4.2 One-sided hypothesis tests

While most tests on statistical significance are based on two-sided tests, the more appropriate test may be one-sided. This should be used when it is clear, theoretically, that an X variable could affect the outcome only in one direction. For example, we can be pretty certain that, on average and adjusting for other factors, Blacks will get paid less than Whites and older people would be paid more than younger people at least for the age range of our data (38 to 46). Thus, we can form a hypothesis test on whether the coefficient on the variable, *black*, is negative and that on the variable, *age*, is positive. Making the test one-sided makes it easier to reject the null hypothesis (which may not be a good thing).

For *age*, the hypotheses would be:

- $H_0 : \beta_i \leq 0$.
- $H_1 : \beta_i > 0$.

In contrast with the procedures for the two-sided test in Figure 5.4, the rejection region for this one-sided test will be entirely in the right tail of the *t*-distribution. To find the critical value that defines the rejection region for a hypothesis test, based on having a 5% significance level, in Excel:

- Use the command T.INV (one-tail test) – this is a left-tail test, so you may have to reverse the sign.
- Plug in 0.05 for a 5% level of significance (or 0.01 for a hypothesis test based on a 1% level of significance).
- Plug in "degrees of freedom" = 2762.
- It should give you $t_c = -1.6454$.
- Reverse the sign to $t_c = 1.6454$, since it is a right-tailed test and the *t*-distribution is symmetric.

You would then compare the *t*-stat on the coefficient estimate on the variable, *age*, with that critical value of 1.6454. The graphical representation of this test is Figure 5.5. The *t*-stat on *age* is 1.95

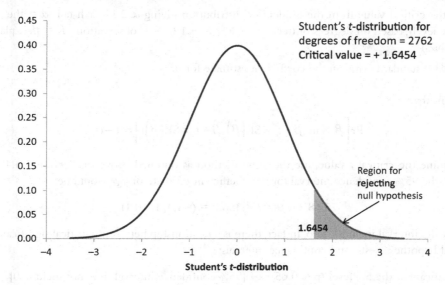

Figure 5.5 Rejection region for a one-sided hypothesis test, Student's *t*-distribution (d.f. = 2762)

(from Tables 5.1 and 5.2), so it now lies in the rejection region, and we can reject the null hypothesis that the true coefficient on *age* is less than or equal to zero and accept the alternative hypothesis that age is positively related to income, adjusting for the other factors.

Pretty much all researchers (me included) make the wrong official interpretation of two-sided tests. We would take, say the coefficient estimate and *t*-stat (-3.13) on *black* from Tables 5.1 and 5.2 and conclude: "being Black is associated with significantly lower income than non-Hispanic Whites (the reference group)." But the proper interpretation is "being Black is associated with significantly different income from non-Hispanic Whites."

The reason why it is okay is that people make this incorrect interpretation is that, if it passes a two-sided test, then it would pass the one-sided test in its direction as well. This is because the rejection region for a one-sided test would be larger in the relevant direction than for a two-sided test. Thus, the two-sided test is a stricter test.

5.3.5 Confidence intervals

Confidence intervals indicate the interval in which you can be fairly "confident" that the value of the true coefficient lies. Assuming that the sample is randomly drawn from the population of interest, a 95% confidence interval (the standard percentage) is the one in which you can be 95% confident that the true coefficient lies in that interval. This does not mean that we can be 95% confident that the true *causal effect* lies in that interval, as this requires that the coefficient estimate is unbiased as an estimate of the causal effect.

The formula for a confidence interval for the true population value of a coefficient, β, in a given model is:

$$\hat{\beta} \pm t_c \times SE\left(\hat{\beta}\right) \text{ or } \left[\hat{\beta} - t_c \times SE\left(\hat{\beta}\right), \hat{\beta} + t_c \times SE\left(\hat{\beta}\right)\right] \tag{5.6}$$

where
- t_c = the critical value from the Student's *t*-distribution giving $\alpha/2$ in each tail (α = the significance level), based on degrees of freedom = $n - K - 1$ (n = # observations; K = # explanatory variables)
- $SE\left(\hat{\beta}\right)$ = standard error on the coefficient estimate for β.

This means that:

$$\Pr\left[\beta \text{ is in } (\hat{\beta} - t_c \times SE\left(\hat{\beta}\right), \hat{\beta} + t_c \times SE\left(\hat{\beta}\right))\right] = 1 - \alpha \tag{5.7}$$

To determine the critical t value, use the same method as outlined above (in Section 5.3.4). From Table 5.1, the 95% confidence interval for the coefficient estimate on *age* would be:

$$752.8 \pm 1.9608 \times 386.2 = (-4.4, 1510.1)$$

Note that the interval includes zero. In fact, there is a relationship between statistical significance (for two-sided hypothesis tests) and confidence intervals:

- [Significant at the 5% level (p < 0.05)] ↔ [95% confidence interval does not include 0]
- [Insignificant at the 5% level (p > 0.05)] ↔ [95% confidence interval includes 0]

In Tables 5.1 and 5.2, the 95% confidence intervals for *educ*, *afqt*, and the other variables with estimates with p < 0.05 do not include zero.

Confidence intervals do not receive the credit and use that they should. As shown in Figure 5.2 in Section 5.2, the coefficient estimate is typically just the central and best guess on the true estimated effect or association. The confidence interval has much more information, as it indicates the range of likely values. This is especially important for estimates that are only borderline statistically significant, as an estimated large effect could have a small and inconsequential effect within the realm of possibilities. For example, the best guess for the association between *age* and *income* is an extra $780 per year. But an estimate as low as $0 is in the "plausible" range, as it is within the 95% confidence interval.

5.3.6 F-tests for joint hypothesis tests and overall significance

The hypothesis tests so far have dealt with one coefficient estimate. In some cases, one may be interested in whether a set of variables is collectively statistically significant. Likewise, one may want to understand whether all the explanatory variables together in a model have statistical significance – something that the R^2 statistic, by itself, does not indicate. In addition, sometimes researchers test for the value of linear combinations of coefficient estimates. All of these tests use the F-distribution.

5.3.6.1 Joint hypothesis tests

The formal hypothesis test, for four variables, X_1–X_4, would be:

- $H_0 : \beta_1 = \beta_2 = \beta_3 = \beta_4 = 0$ (for corresponding explanatory variables X_1, X_2, X_3, X_4).
- H_1 : one of the β's does not equal 0.

This joint hypothesis test (sometimes called the Chow/Wald test) involves calculation of the F-statistic, which is:[1]

$$F_{n-k}^{k-1} = \frac{\left(\sum \hat{\varepsilon}_{RR}^2 - \sum \hat{\varepsilon}_{UR}^2\right)/m}{\left(\sum \hat{\varepsilon}_{UR}^2\right)/(n-k)_{UR}} \tag{5.8}$$

where:
- $\sum \hat{\varepsilon}_{UR}^2$ is the Sum of Squared Residuals in the unrestricted regression (UR), in which all variables are included
- $\sum \hat{\varepsilon}_{RR}^2$ is the Sum of Squared Residuals in the restricted regression (RR), in which variables X_1, X_2, X_3, and X_4 are excluded from the model (assuming there is at least one other explanatory variable that remains)
- m is the number of variables being excluded (4, in this case)
- $(n-k)_{UR}$ is the degrees of freedom in the original unrestricted regression, with n being the sample size and k being the number of explanatory variables (K) plus one.

As an example of the joint hypothesis test, let's consider the four variables on parents' education in Table 5.1 in Section 5.1. Estimating the original model, with all four parents' education variables, produces an *RSS* of (5.5436e + 12) or (5.5436 × 10¹²). The model without those four variables produces an *RSS* of (5.6190 × 10¹²). Thus, the *F*-statistic is:

$$F_o = \frac{\left(5.6190 \times 10^{12} - 5.5436 \times 10^{12}\right)/4}{\left(5.5436 \times 10^{12}\right)/(2772 - 9 - 1)} = \frac{0.018885 \times 10^{12}}{0.0020007 \times 10^{12}} = 9.40 \tag{5.9}$$

The critical *F* value at the 5% significance level, with degrees of freedom of 4 (*m*) in the numerator and 2762 (*n* − *K* − 1) in the denominator, is 2.375. This can be determined in Excel with the function, F.INV.RT (using 0.05 probability and 4 and 2762 as the degrees of freedom). Given that the *F*-statistic of 9.40 exceeds the critical value of 2.375, we can reject the null hypothesis and conclude, at the 5% significance level, that the variables are jointly significant. If we wanted to calculate a p-value, we use the Excel command F.DIST.RT, and plug in the test statistic of 9.40 and the degrees of freedom, which should give you 0.00000015. If we were to just test the two mother's education variables, we get an *F*-statistic of 0.67, which is statistically insignificant.

Thus, we would say that all the coefficient estimates on the four parents' education variables are jointly significant, but the coefficient estimates on the two mother's education variables are not jointly significant.

5.3.6.2 Overall-significance test

For overall significance, the hypothesis test would be:

$H_0 : \beta_1 = \beta_2 = \ldots \beta_K = 0$ (for a model with *K* explanatory variables $X_1, X_2, \ldots X_K$).
$H_1 :$ one of the *β*'s does not equal 0.

With *k* = *K* + 1 (the number of parameters to be estimated equals the number of explanatory variables plus one), the test statistic is:

$$F_{n-k}^{k-1} = \frac{(ExSS)/(k-1)}{(RSS)/(n-k)} = \frac{R^2}{\left(1-R^2\right)} \times \frac{(n-k)}{(k-1)} \tag{5.10}$$

This would actually be the same as equation (5.8) above if all of the variables were being tested. In the original model from Table 5.1, the regression output automatically gives the test statistic, with *K* = 9 (nine variables) of *F*(9, 2792) = 81.43, which is easily statistically significant, with a p-value of zero.

The overall-significance test is not that common a test. Most regressions that see the light of day would have some significant coefficient estimates, which is a good sign that the overall regression has significance. Furthermore, the test itself has minimal bearing on any of the four main objectives of regression analysis. I rarely see the overall-significance test in published research studies.

The joint hypothesis test is also rare, but it has more value. This is particularly the case when there are two variables that are highly correlated. They may both be individually statistically insignificant (due to splitting explanatory power for the dependent variable), but they may be collectively or jointly significant.

5.3.6.3 Tests for linear combinations of variables

In some cases, one may want to test whether two coefficients are equal. From a regression equation

$$Y = \beta_1 X_1 + \beta_2 X_2 + \beta_3 X_3 + \varepsilon_i$$

one could test whether $\beta_2 = \beta_3$. This would be equivalent to the test for whether $\beta_2 - \beta_3 = 0$. Under the null hypothesis (that $\beta_2 - \beta_3 = 0$):

$$\left(\hat{\beta}_2 - \hat{\beta}_3\right) \sim Normal\left(0, Var\left(\hat{\beta}_2 - \hat{\beta}_3\right)\right)$$

$$\text{with } Var\left(\hat{\beta}_2 - \hat{\beta}_3\right) = Var\left(\hat{\beta}_2\right) + Var\left(\hat{\beta}_3\right) - 2 \times Cov\left(\hat{\beta}_2, \hat{\beta}_3\right). \tag{5.11}$$

The test for this would then use the Student's t-distribution:

$$t_o = \frac{\left(\hat{\beta}_2 - \hat{\beta}_3\right)}{SE\left(\hat{\beta}_2 - \hat{\beta}_3\right)} \tag{5.12}$$

with the same degrees of freedom as with the test for a single parameter ($n - K - 1$).

Note that if one were testing whether $\beta_2 + \beta_3$ equalled some value, the variance of the distribution would be $Var\left(\hat{\beta}_2 + \hat{\beta}_3\right) = Var\left(\hat{\beta}_2\right) + Var\left(\hat{\beta}_3\right) + 2 \times Cov\left(\hat{\beta}_2, \hat{\beta}_3\right)$.

5.3.7 False positives and false negatives

As Jay Leno alluded to (in Chapter 1), a good portion of research will be wrong. Many of the reasons that will be given in Chapter 6 have to do with modeling and data problems, or the PITFALLS of regression analysis. But, even with a valid regression (i.e., without any PITFALLS or biases), the wrong conclusion may result from any hypothesis test. We can classify incorrect conclusions from hypothesis tests into two categories:

- **Type I error** (false positive), in which the null hypothesis is true, but it is rejected. In practice, this means that the variable has no significant relationship with the outcome, but the regression mistakenly finds statistically-significant evidence for a relationship. In a criminal trial, this would be convicting an innocent defendant. (The "positive" term in "false positive" refers to a non-zero relationship – not necessarily a positively-correlated relationship.)
- **Type II error** (false negative), in which the null hypothesis is false (the factor is related to the outcome), but the regression does not find evidence for a statistically-significant estimate. In a criminal trial, this would be acquitting a guilty defendant. (The "negative" term refers to no empirical relationship – not a negatively-correlated relationship.)

Conventionally, the probability of a Type I error (a false positive), typically labeled as α, would be the significance level at which one is using to test the coefficient estimate. Typically, 5% is used, so 5% would be the probability of a Type I error. However, as you will see in Section 5.5, the conventionally used probability of a Type I error (the significance level) can severely understate the true probability of a Type I error. That is, there are many more false positives in the research world than has been conventionally thought.

Calculating the probability of a Type II error, typically labeled β (not to be confused with a coefficient estimate), is complicated. It requires an alternative hypothesis for the coefficient estimate. I will spare you the calculation – it's ugly – but this probability will be lower if:

- The alternative hypothesis for the population coefficient is further from zero
- The probability of a Type I error (α) is higher.

Many proposals to obtain research grant funding require a calculation of **statistical power** (or, just "power") for reasonable coefficient estimates. The power of a model is the probability that a model rejects the null hypothesis if the null hypothesis were false – that is, what is the probability that, if there were a real empirical relationship of a particular size, the model would capture that relationship with statistical significance? The power of a model is the opposite of a Type II error: power = $1 - \beta$. Such calculations are somewhat arbitrary and involve many assumptions, such as the size of a given effect, but a power of 0.80 is typically considered adequate.

5.3.8 Choosing the optimal significance level for the hypothesis test

From the prior sub-section, there is an inverse relationship between the significance level (the probability of a Type I error, α) and the probability of a Type II error (β). Thus, trying to reduce the probability of one of these errors increases the likelihood of the other type of error. I will argue below in Section 5.10 why I do not believe hypothesis tests should be used. However, if they are used, then a significance level needs to be selected in order to make the final conclusion of whether the null hypothesis can be rejected.

Whereas the most common significance level used is 0.05, there are a few important considerations for selecting a significance level. First, a very large sample would mean that all coefficient estimates would have a good chance of being statistically significant, so the significance level should be lowered. Second, as Kim and Ji (2015) and Kim (2020) argue, the cost of being wrong one way or the other should be a factor. If there is a high cost from a false positive, then the significance level should be lowered. A third reason will come from Section 5.5 regarding the likelihood that there would be an empirical relationship in the first place.

5.3.9 Statistical vs. practical significance

With enough observations, standard errors decrease and the likelihood of a coefficient estimate being statistically-significant increases. But just because it is statistically significant does not mean that the estimated effect is meaningful. That is, it may not be practically significant.

A good example comes from Box 8.1 in Section 8.1. I describe Pope and Schweitzer's (2011) study on whether professional golfers' strategy is subject to "loss aversion," a cognitive bias that people go to costly efforts to avoid a loss. The "loss" in this situation would be a score worse than par – a bogey or worse. So loss aversion would mean that the golfers try harder for a par putt than for a birdie or eagle putt because missing a par putt would put them in "the domain of losses." Of the eight models in Table 3 of their article, I personally prefer column (4), and I'll describe why in Box 8.1. One practically and economically significant result is that players are less likely to make a birdie or eagle putt than a par putt by about 3–4 percentage points, holding constant the distance and many other factors. This does suggest that they play it too safe on the birdie putts particularly to avoid making a difficult putt for par and getting bogey (a relative loss). But another result is that players have a higher probability of making a putt for bogey by 0.3 percentage points. This estimate is statistically significant ($p < 0.01$), but I would call it practically insignificant. It means that any difference in effort or risk for bogey putts causes one extra made putt every 300 or so bogey putt attempts. Given that the median player has less than 3 bogeys per round, this result appears not to be practically important, despite its statistical significance.

The opposite is that, when there are too few observations, standard errors are higher, making it difficult to detect statistical significance. Thus, there could be a meaningful estimated effect that is unbiased but is deemed insignificant because the standard errors are too high. This would be a "false negative," or Type II error.

Box 5.2   Do we really know who the best hitters in baseball are each year?

Can there be a case in which something is not statistically significant but is perceived to be practically significant? Think of baseball batting crowns, which go to the player with the highest batting average in each (American and National) league. The player who has the highest batting average in a league is considered to have a *practically significant* advantage because they are crowned the best hitter in the league. But it is very rare that the difference between the batting champion and the runner-up is *statistically significant.*

For a 0.350-hitting batting champion (35 hits for every 100 at-bats), assuming 600 at-bats, the runner-up would need a batting average of less than 0.323 (at least 0.027 lower) for us to be able to conclude that the batting champion was indeed the better hitter. (This, of course, assumes that other factors are the same between the top hitters, including opponent-pitcher quality.) In the past 25 years from the writing of this (1994–2018), only 4 of the 50 batting champions (two in each league) have beaten the runner-up by a statistically-significant margin (at the 5% level). This would just be 1.5 more times than the expected 2.5 times that it would occur (in 50 instances) just by chance or a Type I error, if the top two hitters had exactly the same batting skills every year. So batting champions are crowned even though we are rarely certain that they are indeed the best hitters in a given year.

5.4 Problems with standard errors (multicollinearity, heteroskedasticity, and clustering) and how to fix them

In Chapter 6, I will discuss seven major PITFALLS in a model that could cause inaccuracy, moving the *coefficient estimate* away from the true causal effect of a variable. Having a biased coefficient estimate would, of course, affect any hypothesis tests and confidence interval for how one variable affects another. The validity of hypothesis tests and the accuracy of confidence intervals could also be affected by whether the *standard errors* are properly estimated or minimized as much as possible. Some aspects of a model or the data could lead to a bias (an overstatement or understatement) of the true standard errors; and some strategies may be able to reduce the bias in the standard errors.

This section discusses the three main sources of bias on standard errors: multicollinearity, heteroskedasticity, and clustering. I give significantly less attention to these biases and corrections for the standard errors than to the biases for coefficient estimates in Chapter 6 for three reasons: (1) they are much less likely to lead to incorrect conclusions because the bias tends to be smaller, although that is not universally the case; (2) they are much easier to assess whether they could be problematic; and (3) the corrections are mostly much simpler. Nevertheless, these biases in the standard errors are important to correct for. But we need to keep in mind that getting the standard errors correct doesn't help much if you are off-target with a biased coefficient estimate.

5.4.1 Multicollinearity

Multicollinearity is a situation in which having explanatory variables that are highly correlated with each other causes the coefficient estimates to have inflated standard errors. **Perfect multicollinearity** occurs when one X variable is an exact linear transformation of another X variable or set of X variables—the R^2 would equal 1.000 if that X variable were regressed on the other X variable(s). When this occurs, the model is unable to distinguish between the effects of the two-or-more variables. Either the model will not run, or it will run and just not be able to estimate the coefficient for at least one of the collinear variables.

The logic behind how multicollinearity leads to inflated standard errors comes from two earlier charts. In Figure 4.3 from Section 4.2, we saw that when estimating the relationship between years-of-schooling and income, controlling for the AFQT score reduced the *operative variation* in the years-of-schooling variable that goes into explaining income. And, from the middle and bottom charts in Figure 5.1 in Section 5.1, we learned that a narrower range (less variation and lower standard deviation) in an explanatory variable causes higher standard errors in the coefficient estimate on that explanatory variable. Thus, controlling for a variable that is highly correlated with the key-X variable would significantly reduce the *operative variation* in the key-X variable, which would cause higher standard errors.

The inflated standard error from multicollinearity for the key-X variable does not necessarily mean that a potential control variable that is correlated with the key-X variable should be excluded, as doing so could cause omitted-factors bias, which you will see in Chapter 6. A researcher should assess the benefits of including a control variable (reducing omitted-factors bias) and the costs (inflated standard errors). Typically, reducing the bias in the coefficient estimate is more important, so variables should be included if they would reduce omitted-factors bias.

In the case of estimating how years-of-schooling affects income, the benefit of including the AFQT score (reducing the bias on the estimated effect of years-of-schooling) likely outweighs the cost (higher standard error on the years-of-schooling estimate). And so, in Table 5.3 above, the higher standard error for the years-of-schooling coefficient estimate when that variable is adjusted for the AFQT score (column (2)) or when the AFQT score is simply included in the model (column (3)) is a reasonable price to pay for reducing bias from not adjusting for the AFQT score.

There is no scientific standard to use when assessing whether to include a control variable that is highly correlated with the key-X variable. The criterion I like to use is, if the control variable were included, whether there would be any independent variation in the key-X variable. That is, can the key-X variable move on its own much without the correlated control variable also moving? If so, then I consider it okay to include the control variable. In the example above, years-of-schooling can certainly vary in the population independently of the AFQT score.

Let's consider a different situation in which the key-explanatory variable might be so highly correlated with another variable that its effects get confounded with and (possibly) partly captured by the other variable. Ruhm and Black (2002) examine how "the strength of the economy" affects alcohol use. A weak economy could increase alcohol use as people have more time to drink and may be depressed from being unemployed; but a weak economy could reduce income and stress from working too much, which could reduce drinking. Thus, the causal effect could go in either direction. Table 5.4 shows results from two models that Ruhm and Black estimated on the log of the number of drinks, with only the coefficient estimates on the key-X variables being presented.

In Model (1), the authors just include the unemployment rate as the measure of the strength of the economy. In Model (2), they add state personal income per capita (PI/C). As you can see, the coefficient estimates all point to the result that the number of drinks is lower in a weaker economy and higher in a stronger economy, with the coefficient estimates being statistically significant.

Multicollinearity could occur here because, in Model (2), both the unemployment rate and PI/C are included at the same time, and they are likely highly negatively correlated with each other. As a result of the inclusion of PI/C, the standard error on the unemployment-rate estimate increases a little. More importantly, in this case, the coefficient estimate on the unemployment rate is reduced in magnitude from −0.313 to −0.231.

So which estimate is better, −0.313 or −0.231? It depends on the question you are asking. For Ruhm and Black, who were interested in whether drinking increases or decreases in bad economic times, either model is correct, with Model (2) giving even stronger support for the evidence than Model (1).

However, let's say that the question you are asking is: "How does the amount of drinking change if the state unemployment rate were to increase by one percentage point?" In this case, the best strategy (in my view) would be to exclude PI/C. The unemployment rate typically does not move on its own. Rather, it usually moves with other economic variables. Controlling for PI/C would give an estimate that represents: "How a one-percentage-point increase in the unemployment rate affects the number of drinks a person has beyond any effect that PI/C has." The state unemployment rate and PI/C would likely be coinciding variables rather than variables coming in a specific sequential order. And I imagine that there likely would not be much independent variation in the unemployment rate, as changes in the unemployment rate likely come with changes in personal income per capita.

Table 5.4 Results on how the economy affects alcohol use – from Ruhm and Black (2002)

	Dependent variable = ln(# drinks in prior month)	
	Model (1)	Model (2)
State unemployment rate	−0.0313	−0.0231
	(0.0048)	(0.0052)
State personal income per capita (PI/C)		0.0537
		(0.0080)

Standard errors are in parentheses. Also included in the models are controls for personal characteristics, state, state-specific time trends, beer taxes, and month.

So, if you wanted to estimate the effect of the unemployment rate, I would maintain, based on these arguments, that they would not want to hold PI/C constant because the model would effectively hold constant part of the unemployment-rate effect.

One situation in which you do not have to be concerned with multicollinearity is if it occurs for two or more control variables (and not the key-explanatory variable). Typically, the more relevant information from control variables that are included in the model, the better a model would be in terms of minimizing any bias.

5.4.2 Heteroskedasticity

One of the assumptions for the Multiple Regression model in Section 2.10 was **A4**: the model has **homoskedasticity** in that the error terms have the same variance, regardless of the values of X or the predicted value of Y. That is, $var(\varepsilon \,|\, X) = var(\varepsilon)$, for all explanatory variables. A violation of this assumption would be called **heteroskedasticity**, which occurs when the variance of the error term is not the same at all values of a given X variable or set of X variables. Some say the word "heteroskedasticity" comes from the Greek terms "hetero" (meaning different) and "skedasis" (meaning dispersion); another theory says it comes from French, meaning "On Thursdays, I like to let the barista choose how to prepare my coffee, and I'm okay with the wider variance in quality."

Figure 5.6 shows a notional example of what homoskedasticity would look like between the AFQT percentile and income. Note that there is a relatively consistent distribution of values of income across the whole range of the AFQT percentile scores. If there were a line going through the middle of these data, the spread of the residuals would probably be generally similar at different values of the AFQT score.

Now, I show, in Figure 5.7, the true data from the NLSY, with just a small partly-random sample to make the graph tractable. In this case, the distribution of income is much narrower for low percentiles for the AFQT score than for higher percentiles. This is heteroskedasticity. The pattern makes sense, as those with lower aptitude would tend to have a narrower range of economic opportunities.

Heteroskedasticity causes biased standard errors in regression models. This occurs because, at the values of the X variable where there is greater variation in the Y variable, we have less certainty on where the central tendency is, but we assume that we have the same certainty that we do for the

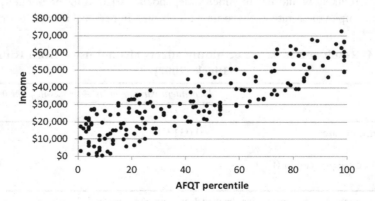

Figure 5.6 A notional example of homoscedasticity

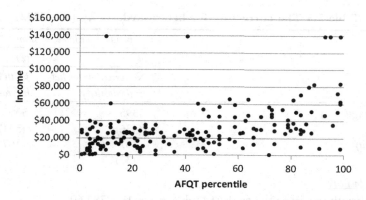

Figure 5.7 A sample of real data on AFQT and income, demonstrating heteroskedasticity

Data source: NLSY 1979.

other values for the X variable. With the variation in the Y variable greater at some values of the X variable, the weight should be less for those observations to calculate the standard errors due to the greater uncertainty in the value of Y. Thus, the estimated standard errors would be biased estimators of the true population standard deviation of the coefficient. Given that the estimated *standard errors* are biased, any hypothesis tests would be affected. (Heteroskedasticity does not bias the *coefficient estimates*.)

The correction is simply to use **robust standard errors**, also known as Huber–White estimators. This allows the standard errors to vary by the values of the X variables. The equation for the robust standard errors is highly mathematical, so in the spirit of the book, I will leave it out. In research, it is typically adequate to just mention that you are using robust standard errors; showing the equations is typically not necessary in a research report or article.

Table 5.5 shows, from our basic model of regressing *income* on *educ* and *afqt*, the **Breusch–Pagan tests** for heteroskedasticity with respect to the predicted value of income, years-of-schooling, and AFQT score. All are statistically significant (with $p = 0.000$), providing strong evidence for heteroskedasticity for each case. In Model (2), I show the heteroskedasticity-corrected model. Note that the coefficient estimates do not change with the correction. It is just the standard errors that change. For *educ*, there is a large increase in the standard error, but that for *afqt* has a small decrease.

In most cases, the direction of the bias on the standard errors is downwards, so robust standard errors (those corrected for heteroskedasticity) are usually larger. Corrected standard errors will be smaller in the atypical cases in which there is wider variation in the error terms for the central values of an explanatory variable than for the extreme values. This could occur if, say, most low-education people have a small variance in their income (due to being mostly blue-collar workers), most high-education people have a small variance (perhaps being mostly white-collar workers), and those with a middle amount of education have higher variance because they could get on either a blue-collar or white-collar career track.

The test for heteroskedasticity might not be that useful. Just as an insignificant coefficient estimate on a variable does not indicate that the variable is not related to the dependent variable (more on this in Section 5.8), an insignificant test for heteroskedasticity does not prove that there is no heteroskedasticity. The best approach may be to do a visual inspection of the data. **Yet, given the simplicity of the correction for heteroskedasticity in most statistical programs, it is worth making the correction when there is even a small possibility of heteroskedasticity.**

Table 5.5 The correction for heteroskedasticity (n = 2772)

	Dependent variable = income	
	(1)	(2)
	No correction for heteroskedasticity	With a correction for heteroskedasticity
Years-of-schooling (*educ*)	5395	5395
	(436)	(531)
AFQT score (*afqt*)	367	367
	(37)	(36)
Tests for heteroskedasticity:		
heteroskedasticity with respect to the predicted value of income	$\chi^2(1) = 782.60$, $p = 0.000$	
heteroskedasticity with respect to *educ*	$\chi^2(1) = 718.04$, $p = 0.000$	
heteroskedasticity with respect to *afqt*	$\chi^2(1) = 544.23$, $p = 0.000$	

The standard errors are in the parentheses.

Data source: NLSY 1979.

If you find yourself assessing another study and do not have the data, then consider the issue theoretically. You do not have to think about whether the error terms would have a different variance for different values of each explanatory variable. Rather, just focus on the key-explanatory variable(s).

Note that correcting for heteroskedasticity is important, but the egregiousness from not correcting for heteroskedasticity is fairly small compared to the egregiousness from having a poorly-specified model or having a meaningful unaddressed PITFALL, among those that will be described in Chapter 6.

Also, note that different statistical programs might produce different standard errors from the correction for heteroskedasticity, due to slightly different methods. In particular, the two programs I used, Stata and R, generate different standard errors with the corrections. (There are discussions of these discrepancies on the internet.) The differences are typically small enough that it would not matter which one is correct, but that is not the case all of the time. This is another situation, adding to Bayes' critique of p-values that I will discuss in Section 5.5, in which extra care needs to be used when interpreting p-values.

5.4.3 Correlated observations or clustering

Imagine that, in a school of 10 classes of 30 students each, 5 of the classes are randomly selected to have a new-math program that is given to all students in those 5 classes. You then estimate a model as follows:

$$Y_{ic} = X_{ic}\beta_1 + \beta_2 T_c + \varepsilon_{ic} \tag{5.13}$$

where
- subscript i refers to student i
- subscript c refers to class c

- Y is the math score growth in the given year
- X is the student's other characteristics
- T_c is the treatment of having the new math program for class c.

So 150 students get the new math program, and 150 students receive the old program. Are the 150 students randomized? Not exactly. Really, only 5 of 10 entities were randomized – the classes. Randomizing 5 of 10 classes is not as powerful as randomizing 150 of 300 students would be, in part because there is a greater likelihood that there are non-trivial differences between the classes in terms of teacher quality or overall student aptitude when 5 of 10 are chosen randomly. If we chose 150 students of 300 randomly (and held constant the teacher), then there would likely be fewer differences between the randomly-selected treatment and control groups in factors that could affect the outcome.

Because it is likely that at least one of the 10 teachers is really good or really bad, teacher quality would have effects that incidentally vary with the treatment and are not held constant. Thus, if we observe one child in a class with a positive residual, then we would expect others in that class to be more likely to have a positive residual than a negative residual—the students in that class would tend to benefit from the good teacher, beyond the effect of the treatment. If this were the case, the error terms for observations would tend to be positively correlated for people from a particular class. This means that the "effective sample size" would be much less than 300.

In this situation, we would say that there is "**clustering**" at the class level. Another way to look at this is that we have violated one of the original assumptions of the regression model—that the error terms are independently and identically distributed across observations (Assumption **A2**). Because of this violation, the standard errors would need to be corrected. The reason for this is that the "effective sample size" is lower because, with a sample size of N, there are not N independent observations. The bias in the standard errors is typically that they are lower than they should be, so the correction results in larger standard errors.

Sometimes, there may be some vagueness over how to specify the clusters (i.e., the potentially correlated sets of observations). Moulton (1990) argues that one should cluster at the level of the aggregated explanatory variable. For example, with a key-explanatory variable being the annual state unemployment rate, the cluster would be specified at the state-year level. This would mean that everyone observed from a state in a given year would be allowed to have correlated error terms. Pepper (2002), on the other hand, argues that the clusters should be specified at the highest level possible. Thus, people would be clustered at the state (or, perhaps year) level, or two sets of clusters at the state and year level.

The correction is typically pretty simple in most statistical packages. It basically involves an indication that observations should be allowed to be correlated based on the value(s) of a particular variable or set of variables that you stipulate.

5.5 The Bayesian critique of p-values (and statistical significance)

A thousand phenomena present themselves daily which we cannot explain, but where facts are suggested, bearing no analogy with the laws of nature as yet known to us, their verity needs proofs proportioned to their difficulty.

–Thomas Jefferson

5.5.1 The problem

The main statistic to determine how certain one can be that an observed empirical relationship is real has been the p-value. In the last several years, however, there has been increased criticism of using p-values. *The p-value, as it turns out, is not an accurate indicator of whether the estimate you find is different from the hypothesized value (typically zero).*

As described above, the p-value indicates the likelihood that, if the coefficient were actually zero, random processes would generate a coefficient estimate as far from zero as it is. But, whereas most perceive this to mean that the probability that the statistical relationship is real is one minus the p-value (as I mistakenly did for the first 17 years of my career), the actual probability the statistical relationship is legitimate requires extra information. John Ioannidis (2005) argued that the probability that a research finding is true depends on three important pieces of information:

• The *prior* probability that there is an effect or relationship (pretty nebulous, eh?)
• The **statistical power** of the study (which depends on the probability of a false negative and requires an alternative hypothesized value)
• The t-statistic for the coefficient estimate (along with the degrees of freedom).

The p-value is based just on the last one.

Regina Nuzzo (2014) demonstrated how these *prior* probabilities matter. She calculated the probability that an estimated relationship is real for a given p-value, given various levels of the prior probability. Table 5.6 shows her calculations.[2]

• A p-value of 0.05 is usually the standard for determining statistical significance and is typically interpreted as there being a 95% certainty that the empirical relationship is real. But the calculations show that, if the prior probability were a toss-up (i.e., a 50% chance that there is a non-zero relationship between two variables), then a p-value of 0.05 would mean that there is only a 71% chance that there is a real empirical relationship.
• A p-value of 0.01, which is usually considered very strong evidence, is only correct 89% of the time for a toss-up. (This blew my mind when I read about this! This conventionally-used indicator of "strong evidence," a p-value less than 0.01, actually does not meet the criteria for "weak evidence," which is typically 90% certainty.) And, for a long shot (such as whether a newly developed drug could affect certain medical conditions), an estimate that is significant at even the 1% level has less than a 1-in-3 chance of being correct. Wow!!

Table 5.6 The probability that an estimated relationship is real for various p-values and prior probabilities

	Prior probability of an effect	p-value for estimate	Probability that the effect is real
"Long-shot"	5%	0.05	11%
	5%	0.01	30%
"Toss-up"	50%	0.05	71%
	50%	0.01	89%
"Good-bet"	90%	0.05	96%
	90%	0.01	99%

Source: Nuzzo (2014).

Let me demonstrate the problem with some real data. It has been shown that, from 1999 to 2009, the number of films Nicolas Cage appeared in for a given year was highly correlated with the number of people who drowned in a swimming pool in the United States, with a correlation coefficient of 0.67.[3] A regression using the 11 observations gives:

$$\left(\# \ pool \ \widehat{drownings}\right) = 87.1 + 5.8 \times \left(\# \ Nicolas \ Cage \ movies\right) \tag{5.14}$$

The coefficient estimate of 5.8 has a p-value of 0.025.[4] The conventional interpretation would say that we can conclude at the 5% level of significance (i.e., with greater than 95% certainty, or more precisely, 97.5% certainty) that the number of Nicolas Cage movies is empirically related to the number of pool drownings. But it would be misguided to think that there was a causal effect or a systematic empirical relationship occurring. His movies are not *that* bad! (I'm sure Thomas Jefferson liked a few of his movies.)

The problem is that we could do the same for the top 1000 actors/actresses, and we would get some statistically-significant relationship (at the 5% level of significance) for about 5% of them – this is a Type I error, as described in Section 5.3.7. I'd bet my Nicolas Cage movie collection (even *Moonstruck*) that his movies do not cause drownings nor are systematically related to the number of drownings. Rather, Nicolas Cage just happens to be one of those 50 or so out of 1000 for the 1999–2009 period.

To account for the likelihood that 5% of actors/actresses would have a significant coefficient estimate by chance, the prior probability that there is a relationship needs to be accounted for. This is **Bayes' critique of p-values**. If we were to consider the before-the-fact (called "*a priori*") probability that there would be a relationship, then we would probably come to the correct conclusion, which I am guessing is that the number of films for any actor/actress in a year is not empirically related, in any meaningful way, to the number of drownings.

A related problem that also casts doubt on the p-value is that those null hypotheses are almost always false – almost everything is related statistically by a non-zero amount. Many of these relationships are so small that they are meaningless, but with a large enough sample, p-values would indicate significance and null hypotheses would be rejected. (This is where the statistical significance vs. practical significance issue comes into play.) What this suggests is that, with larger samples, the p-value thresholds for determining significance should be lower.

Does all of this mean that the typical approach of using p-values, called the "frequentist approach," is no longer any good? Probably not. I doubt it's going away anytime soon. The resistance to changing approaches is that once you introduce the prior probability, as is needed in the new approach, the statistical testing becomes subjective. There would no longer be the nice objectiveness of the current standard of using p-values.

Now you know an integral interpretation of regression analysis that I did not know until 18 years into my career and that few researchers are aware of, from what I have seen.

5.5.2 What is the best approach given these issues?

This lesson indicates that we should heed the (Carl) Sagan Standard, that "extraordinary claims require extraordinary evidence." This is in line with the Thomas Jefferson quote to open this section. Unfortunately, there is no straightforward solution to this problem. One approach is to calculate the likelihood that the null and alternative hypotheses are correct – see Kass and Raftery (1995) and Startz (2014). However, such calculations of the true probability that an empirical relationship is real require some assumptions on the prior probabilities of various magnitudes of the relationship or an *a priori* likelihood that there would be a relationship. This involves a great amount of subjectivity. Theoretically, it shouldn't just be an *a priori* likelihood on whether there is a relationship but also on the magnitude of the relationship. But I recognize this introduces a major complexity that no one has tackled, to the best of my knowledge.

Instead of going down this path, what some researchers do these days is an "informal Bayesian approach," which involves:

- Using p-values of 0.01 as the benchmark, and being skeptical of results with p-values above 0.01 unless they are backed by strong prior probabilities of there being a relationship.
- Lowering those p-value thresholds even more when sample sizes are very large. Unfortunately, no one has come up with a theoretically-based rule of thumb on what thresholds to use.
- Focusing on practical significance as well as economic significance.
- Being cautious with interpretations. When significance is not strong (e.g., a p-value greater than 0.01), then perhaps the most that can be said is that the data "support the theory." A typical interpretation of "strong evidence" may be misleading.

5.6 What model diagnostics should you do?

None! Well, most of the time, none. This is my view, and I might be wrong. Others (including your professor) may have valid reasons to disagree. But here is the argument why, in most cases, there is no need to perform any model diagnostics.

The two most common model diagnostics that are conducted are:

- checking for heteroskedasticity
- checking for non-normal error terms (Assumption **A3** in Section 2.10).

One problem is that the tests are not great. The tests will indicate whether there is statistically-significant evidence for heteroskedasticity or non-normal error terms, but they certainly cannot prove that there is not any heteroskedasticity or non-normal error terms.

Regarding heteroskedasticity, your regression probably has heteroskedasticity. And, given that it is costless and painless to fix, you should probably include the heteroskedasticity correction.

Regarding non-normal error terms, recall that, due to the Central Limit Theorem, error terms will be approximately normal if the sample size is large enough (i.e., at least 200 observations at worst, and perhaps only 15 observations would suffice). However, this is not necessarily the case if: (1) the dependent variable is a dummy variable; and (2) there is not a large-enough set of explanatory variables. That said, a problem is that the test for non-normality (which tests for skewness and kurtosis) is highly unstable for small samples.

Having non-normal error terms means that the t-distribution would not apply to the standard errors, so the *t*-stats, standard levels of significance, confidence intervals, and p-values would be a little off-target. The simple solution for cases in which there is the potential for non-normal errors is to require a lower p-value than you otherwise would to conclude that there is a relationship between the explanatory and dependent variables.

I am not overly concerned by problems with non-normal errors because they are small potatoes when weighed against the Bayes critique of p-values and the potential biases from PITFALLS (Chapter 6). If you have a valid study that is pretty convincing in terms of the PITFALLS being unlikely and having low-enough p-values in light of the Bayes critique, then having non-normal error terms would most likely not matter.

One potentially-useful diagnostic would be to check for outliers having large effects on the coefficient estimates. This would likely not be a concern with dependent variables that have a compact range of possible values, such as academic achievement test scores. But it could be the case with dependent variables on individual/family income or corporate profits/revenue, among other such outcomes with potentially large-outlying values of the dependent variable. Extreme values of explanatory variables could also be problematic. In these situations, it could be worth a diagnostic check of outliers for the dependent variable or the residuals. One could estimate the model without the big outliers to see how the results are affected. Of course, the outliers are supposedly legitimate observations, so any results without the outliers are not necessarily more correct. The ideal situation would be that the direction and magnitude of the estimates are consistent between the models with and without the outliers.

Outliers, if based on residuals, could be detected by residual plots. Alternatively, one potential rule that could be used for deleting outliers is based on calculating the **standardized residual**, which is the actual residual divided by the standard deviation of the residual—there is no need to subtract the mean of the residual since it is zero. The standardized residual indicates how many standard deviations away from zero a residual is. One could use an outlier rule, such as deleting observations with the absolute value of the standardized residual greater than some value, say, 5. With the adjusted sample, one would re-estimate a model to determine how stable the main results are.

5.7 What the research on the hot hand in basketball tells us about the existence of other life in the universe

A friend of mine, drawn to the larger questions on life, called me recently and said that we are all alone – that humans are the only intelligent life in the universe. Rather than questioning him on the issue I have struggled with (whether humans, such as myself, should be categorized as "intelligent" life), I decided to focus on the main issue he raised and asked how he came to such a conclusion. Apparently, he had installed one of those contraptions in his backyard that searches for aliens. Honestly, he has so much junk in his backyard that I hadn't even noticed. He said that he hadn't received any signals in two years, so we must be alone.

While I have no idea whether we are alone in the universe, I know that my curious friend is not alone in his logic. A recent *Wall Street Journal* article made a similar logical conclusion in an article with some plausible arguments on why humans may indeed be alone in the universe. One of those arguments was based on the "deafening silence" from the 40-plus-year Search for Extraterrestrial Intelligence (SETI) project, with the conclusion that this is strong evidence that there is no other intelligent life (Metaxas, 2014). Never mind that SETI only searches our galaxy (of the estimated 170-plus billion galaxies in the universe) and that for us to find life on some planet, we have to be aiming our SETI at that planet (instead of the other 100 billion or so planets in our galaxy) at the same time (within the 13.6 billion years our galaxy has been in existence) that the alien geeks on that planet are emitting strong-enough radio signals in our direction (with a 600-plus-year lag for the radio signals to reach us). It may be that some form of aliens sent radio signals our way 2.8

billion years ago (~~before they went extinct after eliminating their Environmental Protection Agency~~), and our amoeba-like ancestors had not yet developed the SETI technology to detect the signals.

The flawed logic here, as you have probably determined, is that lack of evidence is not proof of non-existence. This is particularly the case when you have a weak test for what you are looking for.

This logic flaw happens to be very common among academics. One line of research that has been subject to such faulty logic is that on the hot hand in basketball. The "hot hand" is a situation in which a player has a period (often within a single game) with a systematically higher probability of making shots (adjusting for the difficulty of the shot) than the player normally would have. The hot hand can occur in just about any other sport or activity, such as baseball, bowling, dance, test-taking, etc. In basketball, virtually all players and fans believe in the hot hand, based on witnessing players such as Stephen Curry go through stretches in which they make a series of high-difficulty shots. Yet, from 1985 to 2009, plenty of researchers tested for the hot hand in basketball by using various tests to essentially determine whether a player was more likely to make a shot after a made shot (or consecutive made shots) than after a missed shot. They found no evidence of the hot hand. Their conclusion was "the hot hand is a myth."

But then a few articles, starting in 2010, found evidence for the hot hand. And, as Stone (2012), Arkes (2013), and Miller and Sanjurjo (2018) show, the tests for the studies in the first 25 years were pretty weak tests for the hot hand because of some modeling problems, one of which I will describe in Box 6.4 in the next chapter.

The conclusions from those pre-2010 studies should not have been "the hot hand is a myth," but rather "there is no evidence for the hot hand in basketball." The lack of evidence was not proof of the non-existence of the hot hand. Using the same logic, in the search for aliens, the lack of evidence is not proof of non-existence, especially given that the tests have been weak.[5] I'd bet my friend's SETI machine that the other life forms out there, if they exist, would make proper conclusions on the basketball hot hand (and that they won't contact us until we collectively get it right on the hot hand).

5.8 What does an insignificant estimate tell you?

The basic reason why the lack of evidence is not proof of non-existence is that there are alternative reasons for the lack of evidence. As mentioned earlier, when a jury in a criminal trial deliberates on whether a defendant is guilty, the jury members are not directed to conclude that the defendant has been proven innocent. Rather, they are supposed to determine whether there is significant evidence (beyond a reasonable doubt) that indicates the defendant was guilty. Thus, one reason why a defendant may be found "not guilty" is that there was not enough evidence.

The same concept is *supposed to* be used for statistical analysis. We are often testing whether a coefficient estimate is different from zero. Let's say we are examining how class-size affects elementary-school students' test scores, and let's say that we find an insignificant estimate on the variable for class-size. In a study of mine (Arkes 2016), I list four general possible explanations for an insignificant estimate:

1. There is actually no effect of the explanatory variable on the outcome in the population.
2. There is an effect in one direction, but the model is unable to detect the effect due to a modeling problem (e.g., omitted-factors bias or measurement error – see Chapter 6) biasing the coefficient estimate in a direction opposite to the actual effect.

3. There is a small effect that cannot be detected with the available data due to inadequate power – i.e., not a large enough sample given the size of the effect.
4. There are varying effects in the population (or sample); some people's outcomes may be affected positively by the treatment, others' outcomes may be affected negatively, and others' outcomes may not be affected; and the estimated effect (which is the average effect) is insignificantly different from zero due to the positive and negative effects canceling each other out or being drowned out by those with zero effects.

So what can you conclude from the insignificant estimate on the class-size variable? You cannot conclude that class size does not affect test scores. Rather, as with the hot hand and the search for aliens, the interpretation should be: "There is no evidence that class-size affects test scores."

Unfortunately, a very common mistake made in the research world is that the conclusion would be that there is no effect. This is important for issues such as whether there are side effects from pharmaceutical drugs or vaccines. The lack of evidence for a side effect does not mean that there is no effect, particularly if confidence intervals for the estimates include values that would represent meaningful side effects of the drug or vaccine.

All that said, there are sometimes cases in which an insignificant estimate has a 95% or 99% confidence interval with a fairly narrow range and outer boundary that, if the boundary were the true population parameter, it would be "practically insignificant" (see Section 5.3.9). If this were the case and the coefficient estimate were not subject to any meaningful bias, then it would be safe to conclude that "there is no meaningful effect."

Sometimes, there could be hidden information behind an insignificant estimate. Consider the fourth reason for the lack of a significant estimate: that different segments of the population could experience different effects of a treatment. An important issue in the world of military manpower is how servicemen and servicewomen are affected by hostile deployments, which are basically deployments that involve being put in danger by an enemy combatant. Of great concern to the military is how hostile deployments affect the probability that someone reenlists. For some who do not like danger, a hostile deployment could reduce the probability of reenlisting. However, for others, a hostile deployment might be exciting or give them more of a sense of protecting the country. For these latter types, a hostile deployment could increase the probability of reenlistment. It is possible that, when estimating the effects of a hostile deployment, these negative and positive effects cancel each other out. Thus, the hidden information could be that there are real effects (in one or both directions), but the model is unable to capture those effects.

In some cases, the counteracting positive and negative effects are not important, as a researcher may be interested only in the average effect. For example, the military might be more concerned with how reenlistment rates would be affected. But it would be incorrect to conclude from an insignificant estimate that a hostile deployment has no effect on servicepersons' reenlistment decisions.

Let me also note that a statistically-significant estimate may also be subject to some of these issues/interpretations from the list above. Any estimate (insignificant or significant) is potentially subject to modeling problems (reason #2). Inadequate power could mean that a significant estimate still has wide confidence intervals that include numbers that would indicate a practically insignificant relationship between variables (reason #3). And a significant estimate in one direction could be mitigated, to some extent, by a counteracting effect in the other direction for some segment of the population (reason #4).

In sum, in Section 2.8, I discussed how there could be a correlation without causation. What I have discussed in this section is an example of there being causation without a correlation, or at least without an observed or statistically-significant correlation. One variable may have a causal effect on another variable, but inadequate data or modeling problems may preclude the detection of any correlation, or opposing effects may cancel each other out.

5.9 Statistical significance is not the goal

As we conduct research, our ultimate goal should be to advance knowledge. Our goal should not be to find a statistically-significant estimate. Advancing knowledge occurs by conducting objective and honest research.

A statistically *insignificant* coefficient estimate on a key-explanatory variable is just as valid as a *significant* coefficient estimate. The problem, many believe, is that an insignificant estimate may not provide as much information as a significant estimate. As described in the previous section, an insignificant estimate does not necessarily mean that there is no meaningful relationship, and so it could have multiple possible interpretations. If the appropriate confidence intervals for the coefficient were narrow (which would indicate adequate power), the methods were convincing for ruling out modeling problems, and the effects would likely go in just one direction, then it would be more reasonable to conclude that an insignificant estimate indicates there is no meaningful effect of the treatment. But meeting all those conditions is rare, and so there are multiple possible conclusions that cannot be distinguished.

As mentioned in the previous section, a statistically-significant estimate could also be subject to the various interpretations of insignificant estimates. But these are often ignored and not deemed as important, to most people, as long as there is statistical significance.

Statistical significance is valued more, perhaps, because it is evidence confirming, to some extent, the researcher's theory and/or hypothesis. I conducted a quick, informal review of recent issues of leading economic, financial, and education journals. As it has been historically, almost all empirical studies had statistically-significant coefficient estimates on the key-explanatory variable. Indeed, I had a difficult time finding an insignificant estimate. This suggests that the pattern continues that journals are more likely to publish studies with significant estimates on the key-explanatory variables.

The result of statistical significance being valued more is that it incentivizes researchers to make statistical significance the goal of research. This can lead to **p-hacking**, which involves changing the set of control variables, the method (e.g. Ordinary Least Squares (OLS) vs. an alternative method, such as in Chapters 8 and 9), the sample requirements, or how the variables (including the outcome) are defined until one achieves a p-value below a major threshold. (I describe p-hacking in more detail in Section 13.3.)

It is unfortunate that insignificant estimates are not accepted more. But, hopefully, this book will be another stepping stone for the movement to be more accepting of insignificant estimates. I personally trust insignificant estimates more than significant estimates (except for the hot hand in basketball).

The bottom line is that, as we conduct research, we should be guided by proper modeling strategies and not by what the results are saying.

5.10 Why I believe we should scrap hypothesis tests

I have so many problems with hypothesis tests that I think they ought not to be used in statistical studies, or at the very least, not tried at home without supervision by a trained professional. My main problems are the following:

- They are often wrong, with Type I and Type II errors, which occur more frequently than people believe.
- They do not take into account the Bayesian critique, or how likely the empirical relationship was before-the-fact.
- They are often misinterpreted, although this problem could be fixed.
- They do not consider how likely or unlikely potential PITFALLS might be biasing the estimated effect (as described in the next chapter).
- They do not consider the magnitude and the practical significance of the estimate (not to mention the practical significance of the lower bound of a reasonable confidence interval).
- The focus on meeting certain thresholds likely increases the prevalence of using statistical significance as the goal of research (and p-hacking).
- Given all the above, the term "reject null hypothesis," or even just "statistically significance," conveys much greater certitude for a hypothesis test than it deserves. It can give readers a subconscious belief that the result is legitimate.

A good example of why the seeming finality of a hypothesis test is not optimal comes from Paolella (2018). He gives a scenario in which a new potential cancer drug is tested for improving outcomes and has a p-value of 0.06. Thus, it would fail to reject the null hypothesis when using the conventional 0.05 significance level, and one might conclude "there is no evidence that this drug is effective." A better interpretation would be that there is very weak evidence for this drug being effective, and it might merit another trial to test again for its effectiveness.

This example demonstrates a good alternative to using hypothesis tests. I believe a regression result should be objectively characterized by the strength of the evidence for a relationship. This should be based on information on the p-value, the before-the-fact (*a priori*) likelihood that the empirical relationship you are testing exists, the range of likely estimates, the practical significance of values in a conventional confidence interval, and the likelihood that the model was able to adequately address any potential biases. Thus, I do not espouse eliminating the use of p-values, but using them in context with all the other important bits of information to allow a reader to make a final judgment on the legitimacy of a research result. A p-value of 0.05, which is typically considered "strong" evidence, should no longer be considered as such. And a p-value around 0.01 could be considered "strong" evidence only if the *a priori* likelihood of the empirical relationship was relatively high, the lower end of a reasonable confidence interval has a value that would be meaningful, and the study reasonably rules out or addresses potential biases.

The typical characterization would be describing the overall evidence as non-existent, weak, moderate, strong, overwhelming, or one of many other such characterizations speaking to the strength of the evidence. I personally also like more descriptive terms (particularly when it is difficult to judge), such as mushy, squishy, questionable, dubious, granitic, rebellious, and more – but I should note that your professor or a journal might not appreciate such characterizations as much as I would.

5.11 Chapter summary

Figure 5.8 summarizes the main points of this chapter. Standard errors are important for indicating how precise your coefficient estimates are. The standard errors from your regression will help to produce a range of likely values (confidence intervals) as well as hypothesis tests and significance indicators (p-values) for the coefficient estimates.

However, the standard approach to using p-values has been called into question. The true probability that a given estimated relationship is real depends on, among other things, its size relative to the standard error and the prior probability that such an empirical relationship could exist. That said, it is impossible to objectively calculate these probabilities.

The best approach is to reduce the p-value threshold for what constitutes "strong evidence" for an empirical relationship (particularly when the sample size gets larger), focus on practical significance as well as statistical significance, and be cautious about interpretations of significance.

Another common misinterpretation is for an insignificant effect. Often, an insignificant effect is interpreted as "there is no effect," whereas the more appropriate interpretation would be that "there is no evidence for an effect." Furthermore, there could be hidden information behind an insignificant

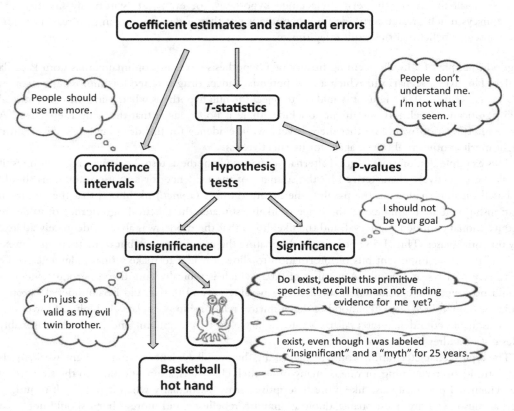

Figure 5.8 Summary of Chapter 5

Credit: Abigail Soong.

estimate. Given that a coefficient estimate represents an average effect or association, it is possible that a given treatment positively affects (or is positively associated with) the outcome for some people and negatively affects others. Distinguishing between these positive and negative effects could be quite fruitful for a better understanding of the research issue.

Regarding hypothesis tests, do not try these on your own. Only conduct a hypothesis test with a trained and ethical professional.

Exercises

1. From the data, **temperature_gdp**, restrict the sample to observations with *condition1*=1 (having non-missing data on GDP growth and temperature) and to three countries: Iceland, Kenya, and Saudi Arabia.
   a. Calculate the means and standard deviations of *gdpgrowth* and *temp* for each country.
   b. Regress GDP growth (*gdpgrowth*) on average temperature (*temp*) for the three countries, separately, and report the coefficient estimates and standard errors.
   c. What is a likely reason why Kenya has the highest standard error on the coefficient estimates on *temp* (at 2.316)?
   d. Why does Iceland have a lower standard error on the coefficient estimate on temp than that for Saudia Arabia, despite having a lower standard error on temp?

2. Borrowing from Table 8.4 in Section 8.4, consider the regression model:

$$\widehat{MJ} = \hat{\beta}_0 + \hat{\beta}_1 * (UR)$$

where *MJ* is the past-month-marijuana-use rate for 12–17-year-olds in a state in 2009–10, *UR* is the average state unemployment rate for 2009–10, and there are 51 observations (50 states plus DC). The results are the following, with the standard errors in parentheses below the coefficient estimate:

$$\widehat{MJ} = 8.971 + 0.244 * (UR)$$
$$(1.406) \quad (0.148)$$

   a. Give the formal null and alternative hypotheses for whether the variable *UR* has a coefficient that is different from zero.
   b. Give the formal null and alternative hypotheses for whether the variable *UR* has a positive coefficient.
   c. Calculate the *t*-stat for the coefficient estimate on *UR*.
   d. Determine the critical values for the two-sided test on that coefficient for tests at the 1%, 5%, and 10% levels. Is the coefficient estimate statistically significant at those levels?
   e. Determine the critical value for the one-sided hypothesis test (at the 5% significance level) on that estimate to test if it is positive. What is the conclusion of the hypothesis test?
   f. Calculate the 95% confidence interval for the coefficient estimate on *UR*.

3. Use **democracy2**, re-estimate the regression in Question #1a in Chapter 3, regressing life_exp on *democracy, avgeduc, educgini, urbanpct, africa, asia, oceania,* and *america* (for 1985 observations and *condition1* = 1).

    a.   Which coefficient estimates are statistically significant at the 1, 5, and 10% levels?

    b.   Test for the joint significance of the coefficient estimates on *africa*, *asia*, *oceania*, and *america*.

4.   Suppose that some researcher, with nothing else better to do, were to estimate a model for each of the 500 baseball players with the most plate appearances in 2017. The model is: (*# lightning strikes in the U.S. that night*) $= \beta_0 + \beta_1 \times$ (*# hits player had in game that day*) $+ \varepsilon$.
The researcher is surprised to find that seven of the 500 players had a statistically-significant estimate of β_1, with a p-value below 0.01 – four were positive and significant, and three were negative and significant. Thus, this researcher concluded that four players generate so much excitement with their hits that it must change the weather and produce lightning.

    a.   What is wrong with this conclusion?

    b.   What other information needs to be considered before concluding that there is a real empirical relationship between the number of hits for these players and the number of lightning strikes?

5.   Suppose that some researchers regressed, for graduating high-school seniors, "high-school-GPA" on "tablet-use-in-high-school" and found an insignificant estimate on "tablet-use." What are three reasons why "tablet-use" may indeed affect GPA, despite the finding of this research?

6.   Consider the following model to estimate the effect of college quality on the natural logarithm of income (among a sample of 40-year-old college graduates):

$$\ln(income)_i = \beta_1 \times (CQ)_i + \beta_2 \times (score)_i + \beta_3 \times (C\_score\_AVG)_i + X_i\beta_4 + \varepsilon_i$$

where
CQ = person i's college quality (key-X variable)
score = person's college-entrance-test score
C_score_AVG = college's average entrance-test score of attending students
X = demographic characteristic

    a.   Describe why there could be multicollinearity in this model, with regard to CQ.

    b.   Describe why there could be heteroskedasticity in this model, with regard to CQ.

    c.   Describe how there could be correlated error terms in this model.

7.   Based on the available evidence, is there intelligent life elsewhere in the universe?

Notes

1 With large samples, this F-test is equivalent to a χ^2 test in which the observed F-stat (F_o) multiplied by the number of restrictions (*m*) is distributed χ^2 with *m* degrees of freedom:

$$F_o \times m = \frac{\left(\sum \hat{\varepsilon}^2_{RR} - \sum \hat{\varepsilon}^2_{UR} \right)}{\dfrac{\left(\sum \hat{\varepsilon}^2_{UR} \right)}{(n-k)_{UR}}} \sim \chi^2(m)$$

2 These are complicated calculations that require a few assumptions. In a one-to-one conversation with the author, I was told that conservative assumptions were made.

3 www.tylervigen.com/, accessed July 10, 2018.

4 This regression was based on a simple cross-sectional regression. A more complicated time-series model (borrowing methods from Chapter 10) produces a coefficient estimate on the number of Nic Cage movies of 6.0, with a p-value of 0.012 – i.e., it's ever more strongly significant.
5 Now, scientists are arguing for the possibility that there are multi-verses – other universes. Maybe, in a Bizarro World in a different universe, Bizarro Me is an NBA star and Bizarro LeBron James is a geeky sports fan writing a book about regressions.

References

Arkes, J. (2013). Misses in "hot hand" research. *Journal of Sports Economics*, *14*(4), 401–410.

Arkes, J. (2016). On the misinterpretation of insignificant coefficient estimates. SSRN Working Paper. (Available at http://papers.ssrn.com/sol3/papers.cfm?abstract_id=2821164, accessed July 10, 2018).

Arkes, J. (2022). *Confessions of a Recovering Economist: How Economists Get Almost Everything Wrong*. (Self-published), https://www.amazon.com/dp/B0BLG2PFHF/.

Arkes, J., Tick, S., & Mehay, S. (2022). The Effect of the Diversity on First-Ship Assignment on First-Term Retention Decisions. Working Paper.

Bureau of Labor Statistics, U.S. Department of Labor. (2014). *National Longitudinal Survey of Youth 1979 cohort, 1979–2012 (rounds 1–25)*. Columbus, OH: Center for Human Resource Research, The Ohio State University.

Ioannidis, J. P. (2005). Why most published research findings are false. *PLoS Medicine*, *2*(*8*), e124. doi:10.1371/journal.pmed.0020124.

Kass, R. E., & Raftery, A. E. (1995). Bayes factors. *Journal of the American Statistical Association*, *90*, 773–95.

Kim, J. H. (2020). Decision-theoretic hypothesis testing: A primer with R package OptSig. *The American Statistician*, *74*, 370–379.

Kim, J. H., & Ji, P. I. (2015). Significance testing in empirical finance: A critical review and assessment. *Journal of Empirical Finance*, *3*, 1–14.

Metaxas, E. (2014). Science increasingly makes the case for god. *Wall Street Journal*, December 25, 2014. (Available at www.wsj.com/articles/eric-metaxas-science-increasingly-makes-the-case-for-god-1419544568, accessed July 10, 2018).

Miller, J. B., & Sanjurjo, A. (2018). Surprised by the hot hand fallacy? A truth in the law of small numbers. *Econometrica*, *86*(6), 2019–2047.

Moulton, B. R. (1990). An illustration of a pitfall in estimating the effects of aggregate variables on micro units. *The Review of Economics and Statistics*, *72*(2), 334–338.

Nuzzo, R. (2014). Statistical errors. *Nature*, *506*(7487), 150–152.

Paolella, M. S. (2018). *Fundamental statistical inference: A computational approach* (Vol. 216). Hoboken, NJ: John Wiley & Sons.

Pepper, J. V. (2002). Robust inferences from random clustered samples: an application using data from the panel study of income dynamics. *Economics Letters*, *75*(3), 341–345.

Pope, D. G., & Schweitzer, M. E. (2011). Is Tiger Woods loss averse? Persistent bias in the face of experience, competition, and high stakes. *The American Economic Review*, *101*(1), 129–157. (Available at http://faculty.chicagobooth.edu/devin.pope/research/pdf/Website_Golf.pdf, accessed July 10, 2018).

Research Department, Federal Reserve Bank of Philadelphia (2007). Survey of Professional Forecasters, November 13, 2007. https://www.philadelphiafed.org/-/media/research-and-data/real-time-center/survey-of-professional-forecasters/2007/spfq407.pdf, accessed October 23, 2018.

Ruhm, C. J., & Black, W. E. (2002). Does drinking really decrease in bad times? *Journal of Health Economics*, *21*(4), 659–678.

Startz, R. (2014). Choosing the more likely hypothesis. *Foundations and Trends in Econometrics*, *7*, 119.

Stone, D. F. (2012). Measurement error and the hot hand. *The American Statistician*, *66*(1), 61–66.

6 What could go wrong when estimating causal effects?

DOI: 10.4324/9781003285007-6

Box 6.1   A regression is like a glass of beer

On the rare occasions in graduate school when we weren't neck-deep in proofs, my friends and I would share a pitcher or two (or more) of beer on the terrace at the Student Union on the shore of Lake Mendota in Madison, Wisconsin. One day, I had a half-filled cup of beer. I held up my cup, and told my friends, "This … is a good regression." I then poured the contents of the pitcher into my beer, causing beer to spill onto the table and giving me a mostly-foam glass of beer. In response to their query on what the heck I was doing wasting all that beer, I said, "This is what happens when you put too many variables into your regression." If my friends were not so upset over the spilt beer, I would have explained that important information becomes lost as you add more variables, and the meaning of the estimates on the existing variables becomes "foamier." Deciding on the best set of variables in a regression model is an art, as is pouring a glass of beer.

Doesn't it seem magical that a computer can take the data you input and produce all of these regression results, indicating how the dependent variable moves with each explanatory variable, adjusting for the other explanatory variables? Well, it's not that magical after all. You see, the secret is that there are little green elves inside the computer doing these calculations. These remarkably error-free and fast-computing creatures are concerned about one thing: *how* the variables move with each other, after adjusting for other variables included in the model. We don't pay the green elves enough for them to give a hoot about *why* the variables move (or don't move) together, whether it is due to a causal effect of X on Y (as you may hypothesize), a causal effect in the other direction of Y on X, common factors creating a correlation, incidental correlation (think Nic Cage from Chapter 5), or some other explanation.

The green elves don't really get out much … they're happy spending most of their time waiting in our computers for the next regression command to be sent. Not getting out much, they don't know our world very well – can't say I understand it well either – and so even if we paid them to tell us why the variables moved together, they probably would not do as good a job as they do in their calculations. This is where we collectively come in, to determine why the variables move together or not. We need to determine how certain we can be that the coefficient estimate is representative of the causal effect of an X variable on the Y variable (or lack thereof), if that is our objective. There are two general ways you can look at this:

- Is there a bias that is systematically (or incidentally) moving the coefficient estimate away from the true causal effect?
- Is there a plausible alternative explanation for the coefficient estimate being the value you found, other than the hypothesized reason why they are related as such (e.g., X causes Y)?

The main focus of this chapter is on seven of the most likely **sources of bias** or **alternative explanations** to regression results. They are presented based on seven relatively straightforward PITFALLS on characteristics of variables or relationships between variables that could bias the coefficient estimate, which in turn could bias a hypothesis test or an equivalent assessment of the strength of evidence for a regression result. These PITFALLS are what need to be considered when assessing your own research or when scrutinizing others' research. This may not be a complete list of the things that can go wrong, as one of the biases was just discovered a few years ago. But these PITFALLS likely explain most of the things that could bias coefficient estimates when estimating causal effects. These PITFALLS are described with simple and direct terms, basic flow charts, examples of situations in which the bias could arise, and stories relating the concepts through the lens of everyday events – rather than the complex mathematical equations that you would see in other textbooks.

To put this in proper perspective, recall from Section 2.13 that the two reasons why a given regression result would be incorrect are imprecision and inaccuracy. Whereas measures of and interpretations based on imprecision were covered in the prior chapter, this chapter discusses the sources of inaccuracy, which are biases that systematically move a coefficient estimate away from the true causal effect. With a bias, you would not get the correct answer even if you had an infinite number of observations.

So, in this chapter, you will learn:

- More detail on what constitutes *good* vs. *bad variation* in the key-X variable
- The seven most prevalent sources of bias in regression analysis
- How to detect those biases or assess the likelihood of them
- How to determine the direction of those biases
- How to determine the optimal set of control variables to address and avoid potential biases (and not create new biases).

The PITFALLS (sources of bias) discussed in this chapter all apply to the regression objective of estimating causal effects. In Chapter 7, I will discuss which of these PITFALLS apply to the other main regression objectives of forecasting, determining predictors, and adjusting outcomes to gauge relative performance or anomaly detection. Before getting into the PITFALLS, I will define and set up the problem.

Recall the discussion I gave to open Chapter 2 on how the great power one has by estimating a regression brings on a great responsibility to make proper interpretations and conclusions. Making responsible conclusions includes properly interpreting the imprecision of an analysis, as we discussed in Chapter 5. Making responsible conclusions also includes giving an objective and thorough assessment of any biases that could not be addressed and might be affecting the coefficient estimates. This chapter will help you identify those biases.

6.1 Setting up the problem for estimating a causal effect

The classic model in quantitative research is to examine the effect of some treatment on an outcome. The treatment could be the conventional meaning of treatment for, say, some medical condition. Or the treatment could refer to any other intervention or even a choice by a person. Whereas the treatment is often considered a dummy variable (for whether the subject had exposure to the treatment), it could also be a quantitative variable representing different levels of exposure to the treatment (such as years-of-schooling). For the sake of this current discussion, it is easier to think of the treatment as a yes/no situation.

What researchers would typically be interested in is the **Average Treatment Effect** (ATE) on an outcome, or the average effect of the treatment on a given outcome in the relevant population. That is, if the treatment were assigned to everyone in the relevant population, how would a given outcome change, on average? This is equivalent to: if a random person were to be assigned the treatment, what is our best guess for how his/her outcome would change? For a quantitative variable, the ATE would be the average change in the outcome if everyone received one extra unit of the treatment (e.g., one extra year of schooling).

To understand the difficulty in estimating the ATE, let's define the following:

- $T = 1$ if the person received the treatment; $T = 0$ otherwise
- $Y_i(1)$ = the outcome for person i if he/she *received the treatment*
- $Y_i(0)$ = the outcome for person i if he/she *did not receive the treatment*

The treatment effect for individual i would be: $Y_i(1) - Y_i(0)$. Thus, the ATE would be the average of everyone's treatment effect:

$$\text{ATE} = \sum_{i=1}^{N} \frac{[Y_i(1) - Y_i(0)]}{N}$$

$$= E(Y_i | \text{Treatment}) - E(Y_i | \text{No treatment}) \tag{6.1}$$

where N is the number of people in the population.

Unfortunately, we only observe people in either the treatment or the non-treatment state; we cannot observe the counterfactual for any given person. Incidentally, this is the reason why we rarely can know whether some government policy/investment (a tax increase, the Iraq War, the Bridge to Nowhere) was beneficial in the long run. We will never know what the counterfactual outcomes would have been.

Given that we do not know the counterfactual for each person, what a model would typically estimate for the treatment effect would be:

$$\hat{\beta} = \left\{ E\left[Y_i(1 | T = 1) \right] - E\left[Y_i(0 | T = 0) \right] \right\}$$

$$= \begin{array}{cc} \text{Average outcome} & \text{Average outcome} \\ \text{for those who} & \text{for those who} \\ \text{receive the} & \text{do not receive the} \\ \text{treatment} & \text{treatment} \end{array} \tag{6.2}$$

$$\left(\text{Treatment group} \right) \left(\text{Control group} \right)$$

This would provide a decent estimate of the ATE only if the two sets of people (the treatment group and the control group) were similar in all relevant characteristics other than whether they received the treatment. This is the same concept as with the example we had back in Section 4.1 on how to test whether adding cinnamon improves your chocolate chip cookies. We wanted to make sure that, when cinnamon varies among the cookies (in that some cookies have cinnamon and some don't), nothing else was different between the two batches that could affect the taste. That is, the amount of chocolate, butter, sugar, etc. should be the same in the cinnamon and non-cinnamon sets of cookies so that we know that any differences in taste are attributable to the presence of cinnamon.

In our situation, we want to make sure that there are no differences in the treatment and control groups that could affect the outcome. That would be necessary for us to attribute any differences between the two groups to the treatment itself. Obviously, there will be many individual differences between those in the two groups. But that would be okay if the two groups, on average, were similar in the other factors that could affect the outcome. Random assignment to the treatment and an adequate sample size would present such a scenario.

The problem is that most treatments are not randomly assigned, but rather are determined by some factor that could also affect the outcome. For example, families that end up divorcing are, on average, different in meaningful ways from families that remain intact in ways that could impact children's outcomes. In this case, the treatment (divorce) is probably not the only relevant factor that is different between the treatment and control group. These things that are different could include observable characteristics (e.g., parents' education), but it would also, almost certainly, include unobserved or non-quantifiable characteristics. And so other (unobservable) factors are not held constant, as we estimate the effects of these treatments (divorce) on various outcomes. These could present alternative stories as to why the estimated treatment effect is what it is, other than it being the causal effect.

The same idea would apply if the key-X variable were a non-dummy variable, such as years-of-schooling or the unemployment rate. Those with different values of the key-X variable must be similar to each other, on average, after adjusting for other factors. Otherwise, we cannot attribute the change in outcome related to a change in the key-X variable to being a product of the key-X variable itself.

Whether it is problematic to only observe a subject in one scenario (being in either the treatment or control group) and not the counterfactual ultimately depends on the reasons why subjects receive the treatment. Or, for a quantitative variable on the treatment, we need to know why some receive greater exposure to the treatment. This is the focus of the next section.

6.2 Good variation vs. bad variation in the key-explanatory variable

Recall the discussion from Section 4.2 on the sources and types of variation in the key-explanatory (treatment) variable. I will copy that figure here for easy reference. Recall that the **sources of variation** are the reasons why (or factors determining why) the key-X variable has high values for some observations and low values for other observations, or why some receive the treatment and others do not.

Whereas I focused on the distinction between *held-constant* and *operative variation* in Chapter 4, here I will dive further into distinguishing between *good* and *bad variation*, as *bad-operative variation* is a common source of bias in regression models. In Chapter 4, I defined *good* and *bad variation* as:

- **Good variation**: variation in the key-explanatory variable due to factors that are not correlated with the dependent variable, other than by affecting the key-explanatory variable.
- **Bad variation**: variation in the key-explanatory variable due to factors that could be correlated with the dependent variable, beyond through the key-explanatory variable.

The last phrase of both of these definitions is important. If a key-X variable affected the dependent variable, then any factor that caused variation in the key-X variable would be correlated with the dependent variable through the key-X variable. If that was the only reason why the factor creating the variation in the key-X variable was correlated with the dependent variable, then it would be *good variation*. If there were other reasons for that factor to be related to the dependent variable, then those other reasons would constitute *bad variation*.

	Good variation	Bad variation
Held-constant variation	V1	V2
Operative variation	V3	V4

Figure 6.1 Sources of variation: good vs. bad and held-constant vs. operative variation

The ideal situation, from the last section, was that assignment to the treatment is random, such as in a randomized control trial (RCT). In such a situation, the variation in the key-X variable would be purely from the randomness (e.g., a random-number generator) determining whether or not someone received the treatment. This would be classified as *good variation* because it would only affect the dependent variable by affecting whether the subject received the treatment. In fact, in an RCT, all variation would be *good variation*, and it would almost all be *operative*, unless a model controlled for certain demographic factors that, by chance, were correlated with the random determination of who received the treatment.

This, however, would not guarantee that a study is valid. The sources of variation speak to the systematic reasons why some get the treatment (or higher level of treatment exposure) and others do not. There could be an incidental correlation causing problems. For example, in an RCT, it is possible that either the treatment or control group, just due to random chance, has a disproportionate share of people who tend to have characteristics contributing to higher values of the outcome (such as being in the "good soil" part of the yard in the lemon-tree example). Having a large sample would reduce the possibility of this problem.

Unfortunately, most studies having pure randomness determining the treatment have generous financial support to conduct an RCT or are from academics who can choose their topic to research. The latter often search for randomness in a treatment and build an analysis around that randomness.

The more realistic situation, however, is that the key-X variable will have some sources of variation that are not random with respect to the dependent variable. This is where there is likely *bad variation* that can be the source of some of the PITFALLS covered in this chapter.

Let me tie the different types of variation to common terms used in regression analysis to describe a variable or its variation: **endogenous** and **exogenous**. In Table 6.1, I give the formal definitions of endogenous and exogenous variables in the first row below the heading. The difference is that the values of an endogenous variable are determined by variables *within* the model, whereas an exogenous variable has its values determined by factors *outside* the model.

There are two reasons why I now do not like these terms, even though I have used them in the past. First, the formal definition can create confusion. In my view, they should be opposite to what they are. Exogenous is supposed to connote random variation in the key-X variable that should not create bias, but a factor of the key-X variable outside the variables in the model would create *bad-operative*

Table 6.1 Exogenous vs. endogenous variables

	Endogenous variable	*Exogenous variable*
The not-so-great definition (para-phrased to put in proper context with our terminology)	The values of the variable are determined by factors *within* the model	The values of the variable are determined by factors *outside* the model
What it means to say	*Bad-operative variation* $\neq 0$, so it could cause bias if not corrected for	*Bad-operative variation* $= 0$, so there should not be any bias from *bad variation*
What it means to say, in terms of "randomness"	The variable is *non-random* with respect to the out-come	The variable is *random* with respect to the outcome
Relationship with the error term (ε)	Correlated	Uncorrelated

variation if that factor were related to the dependent variable. And the definition of endogenous (being determined by variables within the model) can be a good thing, as such variation would be controlled for if the key-X variable were determined just by variables within the model rather than by factors not controlled for in a model.

As an example, consider the issue of how years-of-schooling affects income and these two sources of variation for years-of-schooling: race/ethnicity and motivation, both of which could have their own effects on income, other than through years-of-schooling. Typically, a model could control for race/ethnicity but could not control for motivation. According to the definitions, this would imply that variation in years-of-schooling from race/ethnicity would be endogenous because it is determined by variables in the model, while that for motivation would be exogenous. However, the problematic source of variation would be from motivation – because it could not be controlled for.

My second reason for not liking the definitions is that it is rare that a variable is purely exogenous or endogenous. A key-X variable from something other than an RCT would likely have both exogenous and endogenous variation, which we can think of as *good* and *bad variation* (even though that is not the definition). Thus, technically, almost all key-X variables are endogenous variables because they have some endogenous variation. Whether the endogenous variation creates bias depends on whether that variation is held constant or whether, somehow, the *good-variation* part of the key-X variable can be isolated. But the connotation is that endogenous variables create bias.

The second row of Table 6.1 on the previous page shows what is meant by an endogenous vs. exogenous variable in terms of the classification we have used. It would be exogenous if the *bad-operative variation* were zero and endogenous otherwise.

The third row indicates what endogenous vs. exogenous means, in terms of the randomness of the variable. An exogenous variable is equivalent to a variable being random with respect to the outcome. This does not mean that the variable was randomly assigned, but rather it means that the variable would not be subject to any *bad-operative variation*, nor any omitted-factors bias from incidental correlation (as you will see with PITFALL #2 below).

The last row then ties what is meant by endogenous vs. exogenous variables to Assumption **A5** back in Section 2.10. That assumption was that the key-X variable, conditional on the other variables in the model, was uncorrelated with the error term. If there were *bad-operative variation*, it would violate Assumption **A5**, and the coefficient estimate would pick up part of the error term, causing a bias.

In my view, the characterization of *"good vs. bad variation,"* however basic the terms are, is more logical and descriptive. In the presence of *bad variation*, the model needs to be designed to convert the *bad variation* from *operative* to *held-constant variation*, which would leave only *good variation* among the *operative variation*.

Let's take an example of how the state unemployment rate affects crime rates. Variation in the state unemployment rate coming from the state and year would be *bad variation* because certain states would have characteristics (from weather, wealth, and other factors) that could cause a state to have higher (or lower) crime rates than other states, and crime rates sometimes vary based on the national trends (i.e., the year), such as drug-use pandemics. Because state and year create *bad variation* in the unemployment rate, they should be controlled for with sets of dummy variables (or equivalently with fixed effects, as will be shown in Chapter 8). That would shift the *bad variation* in the state unemployment rate from the state and year from *operative variation* to *held-constant variation*.

Hopefully, controlling for the state and year would make it so variation in the unemployment rate would then come from sources that affect crime only by affecting the unemployment rate, such as a decline in an industry that is concentrated in a particular state. In this case, V4 would hopefully equal zero in Figure 6.1.

The reality is that there could be part of variation from the state and year that is *good variation* in that it has no connection with the outcome. It is unfortunate to lose *good-operative variation* by controlling for the sources (the state and year), but that is better than keeping *bad-operative variation*.

In sum, one of the goals of any study aiming to estimate causal effects is to design the regression model so that there is no *bad-operative variation* (V4 = 0). Ideally, the coefficient estimate on the key-X variable would be identified by the *good-operative variation* (V3). Still, there are other potential biases that could occur even if there was no *bad-operative variation*.

6.3 An introduction to the PITFALLS

The PITFALLS in the following sections, along with a general classification for them, include:

Non-random key-X variables (with *bad-operative variation*)

- o PITFALL #1: Reverse causality
- o PITFALL #2: Omitted-factors bias
- o PITFALL #3: Self-selection bias

Bad data

- o PITFALL #4: Measurement error

Common modeling mistakes

- o PITFALL #5: Using mediating factors or outcomes as control variables
- o PITFALL #6: Using an improper reference group
- o PITFALL #7: Over-weighting groups (when using fixed effects or dummy variables)

These PITFALLS create biases in the coefficient estimate for the key-X variable. Recall that a bias, when estimating causal effects, is something other than imprecision that moves a coefficient estimate away from the true causal effect.

The first three PITFALLS can best be classified (though not perfectly) as being due to non-random key-explanatory variables. Basically, the sources of variation of the key-X variable could be related to the dependent variable, meaning it has *bad variation*. This could be from the following sources of variation in the key-X variable: the outcome itself (reverse causality), other factors that could affect the outcome (omitted-factors bias), and how the subject expects the key-X variable to affect the outcome (self-selection bias). That said, as you will learn in Section 6.5, some parts of omitted-factors bias are not due to *bad variation* and could even result if there were an RCT.

The other PITFALLS fall into the categories of "bad data" (PITFALL #4 on measurement error) and "common modeling mistakes" (PITFALLS #5–7). The following notes whether the PITFALLS are fixable:

- **Non-random key-X variables**: Sometimes fixable, but difficult
- **Bad data**: Pretty much never fixable
- **Common modeling mistakes**: Most of the time fixable.

I should note that biases, other than from the common modeling mistakes, can rarely be proven to apply. Sometimes, applying the methods that I will discuss in Chapter 8 to address the biases can demonstrate the extent of a bias, but there are often alternative explanations for why the new estimates are different from the estimates from before the fix. Thus, as you assess a study, it's not about proving that there is a bias but rather assessing whether there are potential biases or alternative explanations for the results.

Ultimately, a study should be judged based on how well the model can avoid PITFALLS and how forthright the study is on any remaining potential biases the study might have.

6.4 PITFALL #1: Reverse causality

6.4.1 The basics of reverse causality" before chapter text begins

Reverse causality deals with the simple question of "which came first?" or "what caused what?" Sugar or the sweet tooth? The rude teenager or the overbearing parent? The E! Network or the Kardashians? The Chicken McNugget or the Egg McMuffin?

Reverse causality is a situation in which the dependent variable (Y) affects the key-explanatory variable (X), or something closely-tied with the dependent variable affects an explanatory variable. This would mean that any empirical relationship between two variables, even after adjusting for other factors, could be partly-to-fully attributable to Y affecting the key-X variable rather than what we aim to estimate of how the key-X variable affects Y. This means that the coefficient estimate on the key-X variable would be biased. The direction of the bias is simply the direction of the reverse causality: if Y positively (negatively) affected the key-X variable, then it would contribute positively (negatively) to the relationship between the two variables and the bias would be positive (negative).

Let's say that you are examining whether marijuana use affects the probability that a person experiences depression. Perhaps marijuana affects the brain in some physical fashion, making a person more susceptible to depression. Or perhaps marijuana use effectively relieves anxiety, which can help a person be more social, which in turn could help to relieve depression symptoms. The model would be the following:

$$Y_i = X_i \beta_1 + \beta_2 \times MJ_i + \varepsilon_i \tag{6.3}$$

where:
- Y = a measure of depression
- X = a set of control variables
- MJ = some measure of marijuana use.

Assuming that you had a random sample, would you consider the estimate on β_2 to be a good indicator of how much using marijuana *affects* the extent of depression? Figure 6.2 demonstrates the problem. You aim to estimate the value of **A**, which is the effect of a one unit increase in marijuana use on the extent of depression, however, depression is measured. But, as shown with the line labeled

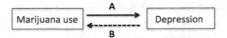

Figure 6.2 A demonstration of reverse causality between marijuana use and depression

B, there could be reverse causality. That is, a person's depression (the outcome) could affect whether he/she uses marijuana (the key-X variable), even after controlling for other determinants of marijuana use and depression. Perhaps some depressed people use marijuana to self-medicate (Harder et al., 2006). If that effect, **B**, were positive, then the reverse causality would contribute positively toward the coefficient estimate. That is, the coefficient estimate, $\hat{\beta}_2$, would capture both **A** and **B** – *remember that the coefficient estimate indicates how the variables move together, regardless of the direction of causality.* Thus, it is possible that the true effect, **A**, might be zero (that marijuana use does not affect the extent of depression), but a positive reverse causality may lead to a positive coefficient estimate on *MJ*, giving the impression that there is a positive effect of marijuana use on depression. Regardless of the true effect of **A**, the estimate would probably not be trustworthy, as it would be upwardly biased in this situation, provided that **B** was positive.

If there were reverse causality, we would say that marijuana had *bad-operative variation* and that *marijuana use is not random with respect to depression.* That is, a source of variation in marijuana use is the outcome itself. This, in turn, means that, unlike our cinnamon-cookie case back in Section 4.1 (in which we had cinnamon be the only relevant thing different between two batches of cookies), marijuana use is not the only relevant thing that is different across people with different levels of marijuana use, as some underlying depression may already exist. In terms of the assumptions of the Multiple Regression Model, **A5** would be violated because the error term (representing the unexplained propensity to suffer from depression) would be higher for those who use marijuana.

Reverse causality can rarely be proven. In this marijuana-depression example, it is virtually impossible to determine which is causing which because the effects in both directions (**A** and **B** in Figure 6.2) could be the same sign. But there are situations in which your model may provide evidence suggesting reverse causality. Consider a problem a student of mine had explored: whether omega-3 consumption affects depression. In that situation, the effect of omega-3's on the probability of depression should be zero or negative, as it is unlikely that omega-3's would increase the likelihood of depression. The reverse causality should be positive, if anything, as having depression could lead to higher omega-3 consumption to help medicate the depression, based on speculation of such an effect. In this case, the expected causal effect and the reverse causality worked opposite to each other. Thus, when the student estimated a positive coefficient estimate on omega-3 consumption, the most likely explanation was that reverse causality was dominating any potential negative causal effect of omega-3s on depression. When the likely causal effect is opposite in sign to the expected reverse causality and the coefficient estimate is of the sign consistent with reverse causality, then this suggests that your estimate is affected by reverse causality.

6.4.2 Demonstrating reverse causality

I created two worlds today. I created a Random (good) World that is free from reverse causality or any other issue with non-random key-explanatory variables, and I created a Non-random (bad) World, which does have reverse causality.

The research issue for these worlds is how much a college student's friends' grade point average (GPA) affects his/her own GPA. Perhaps having friends with better study habits affects one's own study habits. Similarly, having friends who are not so interested in grades and easily get distracted to party, or play video games could distract a student, so poor grades of one's friends (representing the importance they place on studying) could lead to worse grades for the given student. The almost certain potential reverse causality is that, just as a given student's friends can affect his/her GPA, the student him/herself can affect friends' GPA.

In these two worlds, I created 1,000 observations (500 Type A students and 500 Type B students—with no connection with the standard labels for personality types). And I created two variables: the student's own GPA and the average GPA of his/her closest three friends. For the sake of simplicity in creating this example, I use a standardized GPA so that it has a mean of zero and a standard deviation of one. I first randomized both friends' average GPA and the subject's own GPA based on a standard normal distribution.

For both worlds, I then added in the causal effects and reverse causality, as seen in Figure 6.3. Recall that the value of the arrow represents how much a one-unit increase in the source variable affects the value of the variable that is being pointed at. The traits are:

- For Type A:
  o Each one-point higher value of friends' GPA (i.e., one standard deviation) causes an increase in the subject's standardized GPA of 0.5 points.
  o There is no reverse causality, as they do not affect their friends' GPA.
- For Type B:
  o Friends' GPA has no effect on the subjects' own GPA.
  o In the Non-random World (but not the Random World), there is reverse causality, as each point of own standardized GPA affects their friends' average standardized GPA by 0.8 points (0.8 standard deviations).

So there is reverse causality in the Non-random (bad) World, but not in the Random (good) World.

When some researchers (who don't know these relationships I've created) come in and attempt to estimate the causal effect of friends' GPA on the subject's own GPA, they hopefully will estimate the average causal effect in the population. In both worlds, that average effect would be the average of the effect for Type A's (0.5) and for Type B's (0.0), which comes to 0.250.

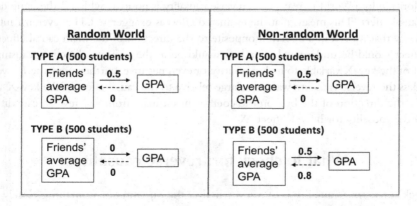

Figure 6.3 Demonstrating reverse causality in Random and Non-random worlds

Table 6.2 Demonstration of the biases from reverse causality (n = 1000)

| | Random (good) World | Non-random (bad) World |
	Standardized GPA	Standardized GPA
Friends' average standardized GPA	0.272	0.492
	(0.034)	(0.025)
Constant	−0.044	−0.039
	(0.033)	(0.029)
R-squared	0.060	0.279

Note: Standard errors are in paretheses.

In the Random World, it is likely that the researchers will find a coefficient estimate on friends' GPA relatively close to 0.250, as there is no reverse causality (nor other problem) affecting their estimates. Note that this does not mean that the coefficient estimate would be exactly 0.250 because of the random component to the test score I initially created before adding in the peer effects. If I were to re-randomize the data and estimate the model an infinite number of times, the average coefficient estimate would be 0.250.

In contrast, in the Non-random World, there should be a positive bias from the reverse causality, so we would expect the researchers to find a coefficient estimate on *friends' GPA* to be considerably higher than 0.250.

Table 6.2 shows the results of the model. (Note that if I were to allow Excel to re-randomize the variables, I would get a little different numbers, but they should follow the same general patterns.) In the Random World, the estimated effect of *friends' GPA* (0.272) is indeed close to 0.250 – less than one standard error away. However, in the Non-random World, as would be predicted, the estimate (0.492) is upwardly-biased from the true causal effect, well beyond how much imprecision could conceivably move the coefficient estimate away from the true effect. As the creator of this world, I know this to be the case, but the researcher/reader wouldn't know how much of that 0.492 was a causal effect of the friends' GPA on the subject or the subject's GPA on his/her friends' GPA (the consequences of reverse-causality).

This is also a good example of a case in which the R^2 is not relevant. One may look at these two worlds and conclude that the model is better in the Non-random World because it has an R^2 that is over four times higher than that in the Random World. But the higher R^2 is attributable to a reverse causality that hinders the model from estimating the true causal effect.

In the Non-random World I created, the reverse causality is positive, which is the same direction as the actual causal effect. This means that the estimated effect is exaggerated. However, if I introduced a reverse causality that moved in a direction opposite to the direction of the main causal effect, then the estimated effect would be understated. The bias would be in the negative direction, causing the estimated effect of the key-X variable to be less positive or even negative. Furthermore, the R^2 would likely decrease unless the reverse causality was quite large relative to the causal effect of the key-X variable.

Generally, the direction of the bias on the coefficient estimate from any reverse causality is in the direction of the causality for how Y affects X.

What to check for: reverse causality

The check for reverse causality is to assess whether the outcome or something closely tied to the outcome could affect an explanatory variable, particularly the key-explanatory variable.

Box 6.2   Testing for what's more important in the NFL: running or passing

A big topic in football is whether the running (rushing) game or passing game is more important, although the debate has historically been one-sided. The great coach and famous commentator, John Madden, would often argue that it is the running game, usually citing some statistic, for example, that a given team has a 7-2 win-loss record when their main running back rushes for 100 yards.

For years, I wanted to yell at the television: "RUSHING YARDS IS ENDOGENOUS." (This was from before I realized how misleading the term "endogenous" is.) That is, teams run the ball more (and pass less) when they are winning. It helps reduce the likelihood of a turnover and run the clock down. Thus, having a 100-yard rusher could be more of a *marker for winning* than a cause of winning. So, if you are estimating how having a rushing and passing advantage increases the probability of winning, you would set up a model, perhaps in terms of the home team, as follows:

$$Y = \beta_1 (Rush) + \beta_2 (Pass) + X\beta_3 + \varepsilon$$

where
- Y = whether the home team won a given game
- $Rush$ = a measure of the rushing advantage of the home team over the visiting team
- $Pass$ = a measure of the passing advantage of the home team over the visiting team
- X = Other factors, including controls for the teams playing

Figure 6.4 demonstrates the problem. You want to estimate the causal effects represented by the solid lines, **A** and **C**. But potential reverse causality, represented by the dashed lines (**B** and **D**), could affect the estimates. In particular, the coefficient estimate on rushing advantage ($\hat{\beta}_1$) would capture both **A** (the true causal effect) and **B** (the reverse causality part of the relationship between rushing advantage and the probability of winning). It is likely that **B** > 0 – that is, as the probability of winning increases, teams will generally rush the ball more. Thus, $\hat{\beta}_1$ would be biased upwards.

The estimate for **C** ($\hat{\beta}_2$) would capture both **C** and **D**, regardless of the direction of the causality. **D** would likely be negative – teams pass less as their chance of winning increases – so the estimate of **C** would be biased downwards.

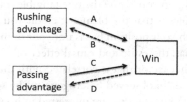

Figure 6.4 Reverse causality in football

The key to eliminating such biases, as I have discussed and will discuss more in Section 6.11 and Chapter 8, is to eliminate the *bad variation* from the key-explanatory variables. That is, I want all *operative variation* to be *good variation* that is not subject to reverse causality (or any other bias). My solution, in this case, is to use first-half statistics (on rushing yards, passing yards, and other factors) to predict the eventual winner rather than full-game statistics, as teams typically would not change run-vs-pass strategies in the first half based on a lead or deficit (Arkes, 2011). That is, hopefully, first-half statistics are mostly random, containing only *good variation*. The first-half statistics, after adjusting for the home and away team, would be the *operative variation*.

Using full-game statistics produced results consistent with the conventional argument: controlling the rushing game was associated with a higher probability of winning, but no evidence for having a passing advantage mattered. However, these results were subject to the biases mentioned above. Using first-half statistics reversed the results, so there was evidence that controlling the passing game increased the probability of winning, but no evidence that controlling the rushing game mattered, on average. These results were more credible because they were less subject to reverse causality. Maybe if this whole regression-book thing doesn't work out, I can be a football commentator. (And, perhaps if I had yelled at the TV, "THERE IS REVERSE CAUSALITY," instead of using the vague term "ENDOGENOUS," someone would have listened to me.)

6.5 PITFALL #2: Omitted-factors bias

6.5.1 *The basics of omitted-factors bias*

Yogi Berra once said, "I never blame myself when I'm not hitting. I just blame the bat and if it keeps up, I change bats."

Omitted-factors bias, known to most mortals as *omitted-variables bias*, is like getting blamed for (or credited with) something that you didn't do because it happened in your vicinity or on your watch. Perhaps you were the Admiral in charge of Navy recruiting during the dot-com boom, and you get fired because the Navy does not meet its recruiting goal, even though no one would have met the goal given how strong the economy was. Or you are the coach of the U.S. Olympic basketball team before the rest of the world started catching up with the United States in talent, and you lead them to the gold medal. You get honored as a great coach, even though there was so much talent on the team that they could have won with Elmer Fudd as the coach. Or you are a baseball superstar, and you are in the middle of a slump. You can't pinpoint any intangible factor causing the slump (such as your concentration or randomness), so you blame the one tangible thing that is in plain sight: your bat.

The idea in all of these examples is that the blame or credit you (or the bat) receive is partly for something that is "correlated" with your position but is not your doing (or the bat's doing). This is the concept behind omitted-*factors* bias: the estimated causal effect of some treatment on an outcome is picking up the effects of some other factor that is correlated with the treatment but is not accounted for in the model. This is also called "unobserved heterogeneity" by some researchers.

To understand this formally, let's say that you are interested in how some key-explanatory variable, X_1, affects some outcome, Y, and you start with a "simple regression model":

Box 6.3   The conventional not-so-great definition

I'm pretty sure that I am not immortal, but I do believe that the immortals among us do not use the conventional term and definition for this PITFALL (used in other textbooks and on the internet), as described here:

Omitted-variables bias for the coefficient estimate on a variable, X_1, occurs when some other variable, X_2:

- is not included in the model
- affects the outcome Y, and
- is correlated with the key-explanatory variable, X_1.

$$Y_i = \beta_0 + \beta_1 X_{1i} + \varepsilon_i \tag{6.4}$$

The name I prefer using is **omitted-factors bias**. The conditions, with the new parts underlined, are that there is some other factor (F) that:

- is not included in the model (or is not fully held constant in the model),
- affects the outcome Y, and
- is correlated with X_1 (not solely due to X_1 affecting F).

The reasons for the changes from the conventional name and definition are as follows:

- I call it omitted "factors" rather than "variables" because there could be an important "factor" that is not fully quantifiable or observable (such as health consciousness) and thus has no "variable."
- I add the term "is not fully held constant in the model" because there could be a variable for a factor that does not fully represent that factor. For the factor of aptitude, there is the AFQT score that we have used, but there is much more to aptitude than what the AFQT score measures. (In the first edition of this textbook, I called such situations "quasi-omitted-variables bias.")
- The addition to the third bullet has to do with mediating factors, which was discussed in Section 4.5 with the lemon-tree and domino-chain examples and will be formalized in PITFALL #5 below. The conventional definition implies you would want to control for a mediating factor because it satisfies all three conditions for "omitted-variables bias" (in Box 6.3). Thus, in the lemon-tree and domino-chain examples, the conventional definition of "omitted-variables bias" would tell us to control for the height of the lemon tree and whether the third domino fell. However, doing so would create a bias because we would only estimate part of the causal effect (or none of the causal effect in the domino-chain example).

If the above conditions apply for omitted-factors bias, then the estimate for β_1 in equation (6.4) would not just capture the effects of X_1, but also reflect to some extent the effects of F. Thus, it would be a biased estimator of the causal effect of X_1 on Y. In other words, X_1 would be blamed for (or credited with) the variation in F that affects Y and happens to come along with a one-unit higher value of X_1. This presents an alternative story (to the "causal effects" story) for why the coefficient estimate, $\hat{\beta}_1$, is what it is. The factor, F, would be part of the "sources of variation" for the key-X variable, and it would create *bad-operative variation* because it is not held constant and affects the outcome.

Consider again the example we have used of estimating how an extra year of schooling affects income. From the simple model of

$$income = \beta_0 + \beta_1 \times educ + \varepsilon,$$

the issue was what tends to come with an extra year of schooling in the data. Not only would it tend to come with the skills and perhaps network connections that result from an extra year of schooling, but it also comes with the factors that determine who gets an extra year of schooling. Two such factors could be innate intelligence and motivation, and these certainly could affect income.

In the simple model above, there would be omitted-factors bias because innate intelligence and motivation:

- are not fully held constant in the model,
- affect income, and
- are correlated with years-of-schooling (not because years-of-schooling affects them).

The years-of-schooling variable would be incorrectly credited with the effects of innate motivation and intelligence on income, and that undue credit would show up in the coefficient estimate on years-of-schooling, making the estimated effect of one extra year-of-schooling appear higher than it actually is. We would say that years-of-schooling is not random in the population, as certain relevant factors cause some people to obtain more years-of-schooling. The assumption on the Multiple Regression Model that is being violated, again, is **A5** because the error term would be correlated with the amount of schooling the person obtains.

In contrast, *not* controlling for workplace skills and network connections would *not* lead to omitted-factors bias, despite these factors being correlated with years-of-schooling, because the number of years-of-schooling affects them and not *vice versa*. (These two factors would be similar to *height* in the lemon-tree example and whether the third domino falls, D_3, in the domino-chain example from Section 4.5 because they come after the treatment.) Note that the conventional definition of omitted-variables bias would <u>incorrectly</u> imply that workplace skills and network connections (and even a person's occupation) resulting from greater years-of-schooling should be included as control variables if data were available.

6.5.2 How to determine the direction of omitted-factors bias

Let's return to the oatmeal-cholesterol example from Section 4.4. In that example, we aimed to estimate how oatmeal consumption affected cholesterol levels. And we were concerned about controlling for "health consciousness." For the sake of the argument, let's say that "health consciousness" has a positive effect on oatmeal consumption (represented by **C** in Figure 6.5) and a negative effect on cholesterol (represented by **D**). The product of effects **C** (positive) and **D** (negative) would be negative. This means that the omitted factor of "health consciousness" contributes negatively to the estimated causal effect of oatmeal consumption on cholesterol, leading to a negative bias for estimating the value of **A**. This could create a correlation without there being causation. That is, it is possible

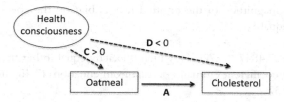

Figure 6.5 Omitted-factors bias for the relationship between oatmeal and cholesterol

that oatmeal has no effect on cholesterol ($\mathbf{A} = 0$), but the omitted-factors bias produces a negative relationship observed between oatmeal consumption and cholesterol. Again, this is an alternative story (to the "causal effects" explanation) for why there would be a negative relationship between oatmeal consumption and cholesterol.

6.5.3 The formula for omitted-factors bias

Let's go back to the generic case, starting with this equation,

$$Y_i = \beta_0 + \beta_1 X_{1i} + \varepsilon_i \tag{6.5}$$

and adding in a known variable, X_2 (and using δ's instead of β's)

$$Y_i = \delta_0 + \delta_1 X_{1i} + \delta_2 X_{2i} + u_i \tag{6.6}$$

This is a model in which we have a known variable (X_2) for the missing factor. Let's create one more model of regressing X_2 on X_1:

$$X_{2i} = \lambda_0 + \lambda_1 X_{1i} + v_i \tag{6.7}$$

The omitted-factors bias for β_1 in equation (6.5) is $\delta_2 \times \lambda_1$. Basically, the bias on β_1 will be the product of: (1) how much X_2 moves with a one-unit change in X_1 in equation (6.7); and (2) how much Y moves with a one-unit change in X_2, after adjusting for X_1 in the model of equation (6.6). This is equivalent in theory to $\mathbf{C} \times \mathbf{D}$ in the oatmeal-cholesterol example in Figure 6.5.

As an example, let's take equations (2.4b) and (2.21), expanding to 3 or 4 decimal places for the relevant coefficient estimates,

$$\left(\widehat{income}\right)_i = -54,299 + 8120.978 \times (educ)_i \tag{2.4b}$$

$$\left(\widehat{income}\right)_i = -34,026 + 5394.537 \times (educ)_i + 367.4847 \times (afqt)_i \tag{2.21}$$

and add the equivalent of equation (6.7),

$$\left(\widehat{AFQT}\right)_i = -55.165 + 7.419 \times (educ)_i \tag{6.8}$$

In equation (2.4b), the magnitude of the omitted-factors bias on the coefficient estimate on *educ*, when *afqt* is excluded, equals:

$\delta_2 \times \lambda_1 = 7.419 \times 367.4847 = 2726.44$, which is exactly equal (other than rounding) to the difference in coefficient estimates on *educ* from equations (2.4b) and (2.21): $8120.978 - 5394.537$.

Again, the amount of omitted-factors bias would be how much *afqt* changes (on average) with a one-unit increase in *educ* (7.419) times how much income is higher (on average) with a one-unit higher value of *afqt* (367.4847).

6.5.4 The three main sources of omitted-factors bias

Understanding the sources of omitted-factors bias is important to help assess whether a study is subject to the bias. The main sources are:

1. **Spurious correlation** between the *key-explanatory variable* and the *dependent variable*. The two variables would be naturally correlated with each other due to having a common factor. This is the most common source of omitted-factors bias, involving an unobserved factor (F) affecting both the key-X variable (X_1) and the outcome (Y). That is, F creates *bad-operative variation* in X_1.
2. **Incidental correlation** between the *key-X variable* and an *omitted factor*. The correlation would just be by coincidence and not by any deterministic or systematic relationship. (This type of omitted-factors bias would not be due to *bad-operative variation* because the omitted factor is not creating variation in the key-X variable, but rather, is merely correlated with it incidentally, or by accident.)
3. **Replacement action** from not receiving a treatment or not engaging in a behavior representing the key-explanatory variable. This means that, instead of receiving a treatment (for a yes/no treatment) or instead of having greater exposure to the treatment (for a quantitative variable), the subject engages in another behavior that would affect the outcome and which could not be fully held constant. An example that I will use below is that, for estimating the effect of oatmeal on cholesterol, those who do not eat oatmeal might eat bacon-and-eggs or other high-cholesterol foods as a replacement. If the replacement action were not fully held constant, the oatmeal would get credited with the benefits of not eating high-cholesterol foods. (This is tied to one of the issues involved in PITFALL #6 on having improper reference groups. It too is not the result of *bad-operative variation*.)

The most difficult to conceptualize is probably omitted-factors bias from incidental correlation. Examples of all of these will be given below, after discussing the strategies for identifying them. Note that *bad variation* in the key-X variable would only be at play for the first case of spurious correlation. The others sources of omitted-factors bias are not attributable to factors that determine the value of the key-X variable.

6.5.5 Strategies to identify each of the three main sources of omitted-factors bias

The ability to gauge whether there is any omitted-factors bias is important for both scrutinizing a model and also determining what variables to control for in a model, provided the variables are available (Section 6.11). Omitted-factors bias, in most cases, cannot be proven to exist. Rather, researchers must think about whether omitted-factors bias may be affecting their estimates. There are two basic steps for each of the three sources of omitted-factors bias, all of which need to be considered. They are:

1. Spurious correlation (*bad variation*):
   o **Step 1**: Determine the factors of the key-X variable. Think about what causes the key-X variable to be high for some observations and low for others. Or, for a dummy variable, what causes some observations to get the treatment (have a value of 1) vs. not get the treatment (0)?
   o **Step 2**: Determine if any of those factors could affect the outcome independently (i.e., beyond through its effects on the key-X variable) and are not fully held constant in the model.
2. Incidental correlation:
   o **Step 1**: Determine major factors that could affect the *dependent* variable, Y.
   o **Step 2**: Assess whether any of those factors that are not fully held constant in the model could be incidentally correlated with the key-X variable. (This is the difficult one.)
3. Replacement action:
   o **Step 1**: Assess whether there would be a tendency to respond to having low values of the key-X variable or not receiving the treatment.
   o **Step 2**: Assess whether any response could be something that could affect the dependent variable and is not fully held constant.

Note that the strategies for the first and second sources of omitted-factors bias are sort of reversed, as shown in Table 6.3. For spurious correlation, the idea is to assess what factors could affect the key-explanatory variable and then assess if those factors could affect the outcome. For incidental correlation, because there would be no systematic correlation, it is reversed.

Table 6.3 Detecting spurious vs. incidental correlation as a source of omitted-factors bias

	Step 1: Assess major factors of the _____	*Step 2: Assess whether those factors could independently* _____
Spurious correlation	key-explanatory variable	affect the dependent variable
Incidental correlation	dependent variable	be correlated with the key-explanatory variable

I will now give examples of the three types of omitted-factors bias, using these strategies to identify them. As stated above, this discussion will also speak to the issue of what control variables should be included in a model (Section 6.11). Quite simply, anything that could be a source of omitted-factors bias should be controlled for.

6.5.6 Examples of omitted-factors bias from spurious correlation

Let's say that you were estimating how the state unemployment rate affects teenage marijuana use (with observations over a 10-year period). It could be aggregated state-level data, or it could be individual-level data on marijuana use but using state unemployment rates.

- **Step 1**: The main factors that determine the state unemployment rate are state and year effects, as well as sector-specific growth or decline affecting states differently based on the composition of different sectors (industries) in their economy.
- **Step 2**: States and years certainly could have effects on the teen-marijuana-use rate (beyond through their effects on the unemployment rate): we know that certain states (e.g., California) tend to have higher rates of teen marijuana use, and teen marijuana use certainly has patterns over time. It's less likely that sector-specific growth or decline would have impacts on teen marijuana use beyond its effect on the unemployment rate. Thus, state and year would need to be controlled for to avoid omitted-factors bias from spurious correlation.

This example of how state unemployment rates affect teenage marijuana use was an interesting case that I had to ponder for a while as to whether not controlling for state or year was omitted-factors bias due to spurious correlation or incidental correlation. Taking the general factor, *state*, I do not believe there is any systematic reason why states with higher unemployment rates would tend to have higher-vs.-lower teenage drug use for reasons other than the causal effect of the unemployment rate on teenage marijuana use. However, if you take a certain state, as I did above with California, the characteristics of California (culture, industrial composition, demographics, marijuana laws, etc.) have contributed to a higher unemployment rate and higher teenage drug use, compared to other states. Thus, the individual state of California would systematically contribute to a positive omitted-factors bias due to spurious correlation. Each of the 50 states plus D.C. would have its own potential omitted-factors bias, which could be negative or positive and large or minimal. Likewise, each individual year could be a source of its own omitted-factors bias. Controlling for state and year addresses these sources of bias.

In another example, suppose that you were estimating how individual wine consumption affects health.

- **Step 1**: The main factors that determine wine consumption include demographic characteristics, income, wealth, state, type of community (blue- vs. white-collar) the person lives in, and more.
- **Step 2**: All of these factors could potentially affect health. Thus, without adequate controls for these factors, there could be omitted-factors bias.

One other wonderful example comes from a 2012 study, in the highly-respected *New England Journal of Medicine*, that found a very strong positive correlation (0.791) between a country's per-capita chocolate consumption and the number of Nobel laureates per capita (Messerli, 2012). The correlation was highly significant, with $p < 0.0001$. The author notes that this is consistent with the idea that the flavonoids in chocolate improve cognitive functioning so much that it creates more Nobel Laureates.

While the author recognized that correlation does not mean causation, he argues there is no common factor between chocolate and Nobel laureates. Let's think about this with our steps.

*   **Step 1:** What main factors determine chocolate consumption in a country? I imagine the primary factor is a country's wealth, as chocolate is a luxury good.
*   **Step 2:** Could wealth affect the number of Nobel laureates from the country? Most definitely. Richer countries tend to have better educational systems, which is probably the main contributor to producing Nobel laureates.

Thus, there is an alternative explanation to this correlation, as the chocolate is getting credited with the contribution of a country's wealth and educational system for producing Nobel laureates.

6.5.7 Examples of omitted-factors bias from incidental correlation

Let's return to the lemon-tree example from Section 4.5. Recall that one-half of the trees were planted in the "good-soil" part of the yard and the other half were planted in the "bad-soil." We then randomized the amount of water to each tree. And so our steps for detecting omitted-factors bias from incidental correlation are as follows:

*   **Step 1:** The known factors that could affect the dependent variable, lemon production, (besides the amount of water) are being in the good soil part of the yard and being innately healthy.
*   **Step 2:** These could certainly be correlated with the amount of water, by chance. From the binomial probability distribution, the probability that the good-soil or bad-soil part of the yard had at least a 10-tree advantage (at least 30 of the 50 trees) in having trees assigned in the upper half of the randomly-assigned water amount is slightly higher than 20%. In fact, there is only an 11% chance that the high-water trees would be evenly split 25–25 between the good- and bad-soil parts of the yard. Similarly, the innate health of the tree, at the time of planting, could be different based on the amount watered.

Thus, if being in the "good soil" part of the yard were not controlled for, there could be omitted-factors bias. And, because we cannot control for the innate health of the tree (as it is non-quantifiable), there could be omitted-factors bias from that factor. This demonstrates that there could be omitted-factors bias from randomized control trials if the samples were not large enough. It would be incidental, as there would not be a systematic reason for there to be a bias one way or the other. If there were a much larger sample size, it would be less likely that any incidental correlation would lead to meaningful omitted-factors bias. Technically, there would not be any *bad variation* because these factors (good soil and innate health of the tree) did not determine the exposure to the treatment, but rather it was just the randomization. Still, it would be considered omitted-factors bias.

Let's consider another example, on the effects of tax rates. U.S. President Bush (the first one), along with Congress, raised the top marginal income tax rate from 28% to 31% in 1991. President Clinton and Congress then raised the top tax rate to 39.6% in 1993. We normally think that tax-rate increases lead to lower GDP growth and higher unemployment rates, but the economy started a long expansion after Bush's first tax hike, and continued strongly after Clinton's tax increase, up until the 2001 recession, which set a record for the longest period in U.S. history without a recession.

If we expand the data to the 1991–2017 period and test this a bit more formally, the general pattern from the 1990s is confirmed. Time-series regressions, which include lags of the dependent

Table 6.4 Likely-biased (from omitted-factors bias) estimates of top marginal tax rates on the unemployment rate and real GDP growth rate, 1991–2017 (n = 27)

	(1) Dependent variable = unemployment rate	(2) Dependent variable = real GDP growth rate
Top marginal tax rate	−0.177***	0.120
	(0.058)	(0.122)
	[−0.297, −0.057]	[−0.131, 0.372]
1-year lagged unemployment rate	0.763***	
	(0.106)	
1-year lagged real GDP growth rate		0.334
		(0.206)
Constant	7.982***	−2.847
	(2.377)	(4.323)
R-squared	0.752	0.220

Standard errors in parentheses. The 95% confidence intervals for key-explanatory variables are in brackets.

*** $p < 0.01$, ** $p < 0.05$, * $p < 0.1$.

variables, are presented in Table 6.4. (I am getting ahead of myself, as I will cover time-series models in Chapter 10.) The model consists of:

- Dependent variable = annual national unemployment rate or real GDP growth rate
- Key-explanatory variable = top marginal income tax rate
- Control variables = 1-year-lagged unemployment rate or real GDP growth rate

The results show that the top tax rate has a significant estimated negative association with the unemployment rate ($p < 0.01$, as indicated by the stars on the coefficient estimate), but an insignificant positive association with the real GDP growth rate. Each percentage point of the tax rate is associated with an estimated *lower* unemployment rate, on average, by 0.06–0.30 percentage points (the 95% confidence interval). The coefficient estimate on the tax rate in the unemployment-rate model (and the insignificant estimate in the GDP-growth model) are opposite to what most would have predicted – that higher tax rates hinder economic growth.

It is always possible that the higher tax rates helped towards balancing the budget and that contributed to a stronger economy. But the more likely explanation for these estimates is that events unrelated to but *incidentally correlated* (or occurring) with the tax rates were strong determinants of the strength of the economy.

For assessing whether there could be an incidental correlation, let's do the two steps:

- **Step 1**: Many factors could determine the strength of the national economy. The big events during the 1991–2017 period were the first Iraq War (and resulting high gas prices, 1991), the dot-com boom (the late 1990s), the September-11 attacks (2001), the housing boom (roughly 2004–2006), and the Financial Crisis (roughly 2008–2010).
- **Step 2**: These certainly could be incidentally correlated with the tax rate. Two of the three harmful events (the first Iraq War and the Financial Crisis) just happened to occur when the tax rate was low, and one of the positive events mentioned (the dot-com boom) occurred in a high-tax period.

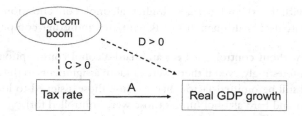

Figure 6.6 Omitted-factors bias from incidental correlation (for how the tax rate affects GDP growth)

This can be depicted graphically. In Figure 6.6, we are interested in estimating how the tax rate affects GDP growth. (We can think of it as the average tax rate or top-marginal tax rate.) There are many possible omitted factors to consider, and I use the example of the dot-com boom, for which I use an oval because we can't really quantify the dot-com boom. This certainly had a positive effect on GDP growth. The question then is whether it is incidentally correlated with the key-X variable. And it is. The dot-com boom just happened to occur in a high-tax period, so there is a positive correlation. I call it "incidental" because, in my view, the dot-com boom was destined to happen regardless of the tax rate. Even though this is just a correlation between the dot-com boom and the tax rate instead of an "effect" (thus line **C** is not an arrow), there would still be omitted-factors bias. Because both **C** and **D** are positive, the bias would be positive, making it seem that higher tax rates have a more positive (or less negative) effect than it actually does.

We can think of this as the low tax rates getting unfairly blamed for the effects that September 11 and the financial crisis had on the economy, and the high tax rates are getting inappropriately credited with the effects of the dot-com boom. This is reason #854 why macroeconomic outcomes are so difficult to correctly model and predict, as there are too many moving parts, many of which are unobservable or difficult to quantify.

Note that there is a difference here from the example above on how the state unemployment rate affects teenage marijuana use. We could control for the year in that example because there were multiple subjects in each year. However, with just the single subject of the U.S., controlling for the year with dummy variables would fully control for the tax rate so that the model would be unable to estimate a coefficient on the tax rate. One potential solution is to estimate how state tax rates affect state economic growth or unemployment rates, which I will show in Section 6.8. However, even this model will be problematic, as you will see.

Omitted-factors bias from incidental correlation is less likely and of lower magnitude with a larger sample and with greater variation in the key-X variable. For example, in a randomized control trial, any differences by chance between the treatment and control groups in the factors determining the outcome would be smaller on average.

6.5.8 Examples of omitted-factors bias from replacement actions

Let's return to the example from above on how wine consumption affects health. The steps for assessing whether there is omitted-factors bias from replacement actions are:

- **Step 1:** Would those not drinking wine be doing something else instead? I would imagine they would be more likely to drink beer and hard alcohol.
- **Step 2:** Would those replacement actions affect health? I imagine they would, in some ways similar to how wine would, but there could be extra harmful effects on health from potentially

more calories (with beer) and perhaps higher alcohol concentrations (for hard alcohol), all without the potential health benefits of Resveratrol and other compounds found in wine.

Thus, any such study without controls for beer and hard-alcohol consumption might be subject to omitted-factors bias. Interestingly, even if there were random assignments to the amount of wine consumption, there could still be omitted-factors bias because those assigned to low wine consumption might drink more beer and hard alcohol (unless those were controlled for).

For another example, we'll return to the case of estimating how oatmeal consumption affects cholesterol.

*   **Step 1**: Would those eating less oatmeal be doing something else instead? Yes, as they would likely be eating something else for breakfast, and one common breakfast is bacon-and-eggs.
*   **Step 2**: Would those replacement actions affect cholesterol? Yes, bacon-and-eggs certainly would increase cholesterol levels if eaten regularly.

Thus, there would be omitted-factors bias in that oatmeal is being credited with *not* eating the cholesterol-filled bacon-and-eggs. This raises an important consideration. What I imagine most people would be interested in is the mechanism of whether oatmeal physiologically reduces cholesterol. Others, however, might be interested in the mechanism that eating oatmeal replaces bad foods that people would otherwise be eating. In the latter situation, there would not be omitted-factors bias from the replacement action. But I believe most would be interested in physiological effects rather than replacement effects.

6.5.9 What are false flags for omitted-factors bias?

A common mistake is to believe that there is omitted-factors bias if there is something else that could affect the outcome. There are always other factors that could affect an outcome, as long as R^2 does not equal 1.000. The omitted factors would need to be non-trivially correlated with the key-explanatory variable to cause the bias.

Another common mistake is to consider mediating factors as sources of omitted-factors bias. But Chapter 4 demonstrated that controlling for mediating factors is what causes a bias by preventing a model from capturing the full effect. There will be more on this for PITFALL #5.

6.5.10 How omitted-factors bias can describe reverse causality

Reverse causality can often be described using omitted-factors bias. For the issue of how marijuana affects depression, one could apply omitted-factors bias in that the factors leading to depression could cause both marijuana use and depression. Even though almost all cases could fall under omitted-factors bias, the concept of reverse causality is still important because it may sometimes describe a problem more efficiently or with more clarity.

6.5.11 The truth on when control variables can address omitted-factors bias

Here is a dirty little secret of regression analysis: if the key-X (treatment) variable is based on subjects' conscious decisions, then it would almost be impossible to fully address omitted-factors bias. This would include decisions for individuals (such as how much wine to drink) and decisions for states or localities (such as the tax rate or the minimum wage). It would be virtually impossible to hold constant all the factors that went into the decision on whether or how much of the treatment to have. There might be some fancy method (as you will see in Chapter 8) that can be used to address the omitted-factors bias, but those need to be done with care to ensure that new problems are not created and the results would apply to the relevant population rather than a limited segment of the population.

Omitted-factors bias is much more likely to be able to be adequately addressed by including control variables when the key-X variable is not a conscious choice (such as the state unemployment rate) and in a situation in which the treatment is randomly-determined but there could be incidental omitted-factors bias. This was the case in the lemon-tree model and there being a potential correlation between the good-soil part of the yard and the amount of water being randomly-assigned. Including the good-soil indicator variable fully addresses that omitted-factors bias, although not the omitted-factors bias from the health of the tree.

What to check for: omitted-factor bias

All three sources need to be considered: spurious correlation, incidental correlation, and replacement actions. The three checks are:

a.   Could any factor that is not fully held constant systematically affect both the key-X variable and the outcome?
b.   Could any factor of the outcome be incidentally correlated with the key-X variable?
c.   Would subjects receiving no treatment or low exposure to the treatment tend to do some other action that could affect the outcome?

6.6 PITFALL #3: Self-selection bias

6.6.1 The basics of self-selection bias

Recall from Section 2.11 that everyone has (or all subjects have) their own effect(s) rather than there being a single effect of a treatment on an outcome that everyone would experience if given the treatment. One of the examples I gave was that a parental divorce could affect children differently, depending on the situation and the child.

Self-selection bias involves the individual effect being a factor in determining whether the subject receives the treatment or how much of the treatment they get. It reminds me of a Yogi Berra quote (slightly modified): "When you come to a fork in the road, take it … rather than choosing your path randomly, as this will vex academic researchers who aim to estimate the causal effects of your choices."

There are various forms of what is called "selection bias." I will address "sample-selection bias" in Section 6.12. Self-selection bias, sometimes called just "selection bias,"[1] occurs when the following two conditions occur:

•   the subject (a person or entity such as a city or state) can, to some extent, select him/her/itself into a category (i.e., choose a value) for the key-explanatory variable; and

- the reason(s) for that choice or determination of the key-explanatory variable are related to the individual benefits or costs of that factor on the dependent variable.

For the case of estimating how parental divorce affects children's outcomes:

- It's not exactly the subject (the child) who chooses but the parents do
- Parents might make that choice based on how much the divorce would benefit or harm their children's well-being (and outcomes).

Of course, subjects would not always know what their impact would be from the treatment, but as long as there is some connection between their perceived impact and the true impact, along with that being an input in the decision for receiving the treatment, there could be self-selection bias. What results from self-selection bias is that those with more-beneficial or less-harmful impacts would be more likely to receive the treatment (or have greater exposure to the treatment). Thus, the bias would be in the direction of overstating beneficial effects and understating harmful effects of a treatment. Because the expected benefits/costs of the treatment are not known to the researcher, there would be *bad-operative variation* in the treatment and result in a biased estimated treatment effect.

6.6.1 A basic two-person example of the effects of a college degree on income

Consider the following example, in Table 6.5, based on a sample of two people: Charlie (who wants to work in Silicon Valley for a big tech company) and David (who wants to do a construction job or some other manual labor). The big tech firms in Silicon Valley typically do not consider people for programming jobs if they do not have a college degree, so Charlie needs to go to college to land such a job and would be handsomely rewarded if he does so. David, on the other hand, would receive much less of a benefit for going to college; maybe a college degree would boost his earnings a little by improving his business sense and networking skills.

The Average Treatment Effect we would hope to estimate would be $50,000, which is the average of the effects of $80,000 for Charlie and $20,000 for David. However, the likely scenario would be that Charlie gets his college degree and David does not because the expected effect of college on his income may not be worth the costs of college for David. And so we would likely observe $110,000 for the person who went to college and $40,000 for the person who did not go to college, translating to an estimated $70,000 effect of college. Thus, we would be overstating the true average effect of college on income (which was $50,000) for this sample because the person who chose college did so because he (correctly) expected to receive the larger effect. (There could also be omitted-factors bias here, as earning potential without a college degree could determine who goes to college and affect income.)

Table 6.5 An example of self-selection bias

	Charlie (likes to work with computers)	David (likes to get his hands dirty)
Income without a college degree	$30,000	$40,000
Income with a college degree	$110,000	$60,000
Effect of a college degree	$80,000	$20,000

In this case, assignment to different levels of education is not random, but rather tied to something related to the benefits of the education in terms of future earnings potential. Of course, people do not always know what the effect of college would be for them, but many people have a sense of how their income potential would be affected based on what type of career they plan on pursuing. There would be *bad variation* from "expected benefit of college" determining whether people get their college degree. This, of course, is not an observable trait in any data, and so it would be *bad-operative variation*.

More generally on this issue of the effects of years-of-schooling on income, there is a distribution of individual effects, and people choose the level of schooling for which their individual expected net benefit is maximized (considering the individual costs of schooling as well). Thus, the benefit of schooling (or average effect) for those who actually acquire more schooling is likely higher than the average effect for those who have less schooling. This contributes to a positive bias on the estimated effect of schooling on income.

6.6.2 An example with a wider range of effects

Consider another example of the optimal assignment of military recruiters. Military personnel assigned as recruiters can typically request their duty locations, and many often request locations near their family or where they grew up. A service, say the Army, may be interested in estimating how assigning recruiters to their home county, on average, affects their productivity as a recruiter, or the number of contracts they get. The Army may estimate the following model:

$$C_i = X_i\beta_1 + \beta_2 H_i + \varepsilon_i \tag{6.9}$$

where
- C = # contracts (or recruits) for a given recruiter in a given time period
- X = a set of characteristics of the recruiter and the location
- H = an indicator for being assigned to one's home county.

The effect of recruiting in one's home county would not be the same for all recruiters. Being back at home may positively affect productivity if the recruiter has old contacts or if the recruiter would be more trustworthy to potential recruits, being from the neighborhood, than other recruiters would be. On the other hand, for some people, being back home could negatively affect productivity because the recruiter spends more time with family and his/her homies.

Self-selection bias would apply if those who would be more successful at recruiting back home (relative to other areas) were more likely to be assigned to their home county (likely by requesting to do so). In contrast, the ideal situation for the researcher would be that recruiters are assigned to their home county regardless of their individual causal effect.

As a visual depiction, consider the sample of seven recruiters in Figure 6.7, which shows in the top chart the frequency distribution of the true effect for a sample of seven recruiters. So the effect of home-county (H) on the number of monthly contracts varies from -0.3 to 0.3 in 0.1 increments, with each recruiter having their own effect. The Average Treatment Effect is 0.0, which is the average of the seven individual effects. This would be the average impact on recruiting if all seven were assigned to their home county.

In the bottom chart, I show a likely situation in which only some of the recruiters are assigned to their home county, marked by the bars being filled in for the four recruiters assigned to their home

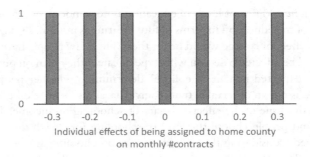

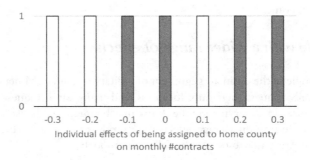

Figure 6.7 Demonstrating self-selection bias

county ($H = 1$) and the bars being unfilled for the other three ($H = 0$). I purposefully made it so it is not just those with the higher effects who are assigned to their home state, as recruiters might not correctly predict how successful they would be back home, and other factors, such as the Army's needs, could determine where a recruiter would be assigned.

What the researcher observes is the impact just for those who receive the treatment. For completeness of the example, let me assume that the recruiters would be equally successful if all were *not* assigned to their home county. The average effect we would observe would be $(-0.1 + 0 + 0.2 + 0.3) \div 4 = 0.1$. This overstates the true average effect of 0.0. Thus, there is a positive bias from the tendency of recruiters to request their home county if they think they'd be successful there.

6.6.3 An example of the effects of minimum-wage increases

At the time I write this, there has not been a U.S. federal minimum-wage increase in 13 years, as it currently stands at $7.20. There have been discussions to raise it to $15, but there is great opposition to that proposal. At the same time, some high-cost cities have already raised the minimum wage to around that figure (e.g., $14.49 in Seattle and $16.32 in San Francisco).

There have been hundreds of studies examining how minimum-wage increases affect employment levels. The results have been all over the map, with some studies finding negative impacts and other studies finding positive impacts, but they tend towards minimum-wage increases leading to reduced employment.

This is a classic case of there not being a single effect for all subjects (in this case, the subject is a city or state). For example, if the federal minimum wage were increased to $15, there would be minimal-to-no impact in Seattle, San Francisco, and many other high-cost cities and states in which wages are already fairly high. In contrast, in low-cost areas (e.g., Mississippi), there is the potential for greater negative effects on employment.

Most minimum-wage studies rely on data on state-level (or city-level) minimum-wage changes. However, because of these varying effects, there is great potential for self-selection bias in such studies. It is not random as to which cities or states enact minimum-wage increases, as they would tend to be the ones that would be able to more easily absorb the minimum-wage increase. Perhaps average wages for low-skill workers are already high, or maybe a city has such strong economic growth that people would pay higher prices for their coffee or other products that would have greater costs with the minimum-wage increase.

This would mean that we would have self-selection bias in that we would be more likely to observe minimum-wage increases with less-harmful or less-negative effects than would be the average effect across the country. Again, this would bias the estimated effect in the more-beneficial direction, which would be less employment loss in this case.

6.6.4 The simple rule for the direction of the bias

Self-selection bias could be either in the positive or negative direction. It simply comes down to whether the outcome is good or bad – that is, whether high values of the outcome are good or bad. Let's return to the first example in this section, in which one was estimating how a parental divorce would affect children's outcomes, and let's consider both a good and bad outcome as follows:

$$S_i = X_i\beta_1 + \beta_2 D_i + \varepsilon_i \tag{6.10a}$$

$$B_i = X_i\delta_1 + \delta_2 D_i + \upsilon_i \tag{6.10b}$$

where
- S = achievement test score
- B = behavioral problems index score (a higher score indicates more problem behavior)
- D = a dummy variable for whether the child has experienced a parental divorce
- X = a set of demographic variables.

Parents might have a good sense of how a divorce would affect their children. (In fact, they probably would have a better sense of how their children would be affected than what a regression analysis estimating an average effect would say.) Whereas some parents make the decision regardless of how the children would be affected, some parents might hinge their decision on how beneficial or harmful the divorce would be for their children. This, in turn, would depend on many factors, including the existing conflict in the household and what the living arrangements would be after the divorce.

And so the children who end up experiencing a parental divorce could tend to be those who would benefit more or be harmed less by the divorce in terms of their test scores (and so would have higher values of β_2 than would a sample of all children). Likewise, they would tend to be the ones who have the lower (less positive and perhaps more negative) effects of divorce on behavioral problems, so they would tend to have lower values of δ_2.

Thus, in equation (6.10a), we would have a *positive* bias on the estimated effect of divorce on the *good* outcome of test scores. And, in equation (6.10b), we would have a *negative* bias on the estimated effect of divorce on the *bad* outcome of behavioral problems. It is that straightforward.

6.6.5 Summary

In a basic model (without fancy methods to address the PITFALLS), self-selection bias is unlikely to be acting on its own. It occurs when it isn't random whether a subject receives a treatment or how much treatment the subject is exposed to. And omitted-factors bias typically comes with non-random assignment in a basic model. Where self-selection bias could act on its own is with the quasi-experimental methods for addressing the PITFALLS, which will be discussed in Chapter 8. Such methods can sometimes address omitted-factors bias but not self-selection bias.

Regarding Yogi's para-phrased quote to open this section, I wish he had said, "When you come to a fork in the road, flip a coin."

What to check for: self-selection bias

The key question here is whether the subject, to some extent, can "choose" the value of the key-explanatory variable (the treatment) and whether that choice depends in part on the benefits/costs of the treatment.

6.7 PITFALL #4: Measurement error

Bias from **Measurement error** occurs when an explanatory variable is measured with error. It causes the estimated effect of the explanatory variable on the outcome to be biased, with the bias usually being in the direction of zero.

6.7.1 Causes of measurement error

Just like humans have flaws, most data have errors (but not always due to human errors). Here are several examples where one might experience a non-trivial amount of measurement error.

- **Lying**: In surveys, respondents may lie about sensitive topics such as health, unlawful behaviors, or the bad things that they eat.
- **Poor recollection**: Respondents in surveys may not remember their experiences correctly – e.g., people may not remember how much marijuana they smoked in the past year.
- **Mis-coding**: Coders who are inputting data may type in a wrong number.
- **Poor representation of the intended concept**: The data may not accurately represent the concept of interest. For example, diagnosing depression or Post-Traumatic-Stress-Disorder (PTSD) is often based on just a few questions, and so the algorithm likely incorrectly diagnoses some cases and fails to diagnose others.

Note that, in the last bullet on measuring depression or PTSD, the data may indeed be coded perfectly and the respondents may have told the truth on the questions that are used for a diagnosis. The measurement error would come from the questions not accurately identifying whether a person has PTSD.

6.7.2 Consequences of measurement error

Suppose that the average income for those without and with a college degree is as depicted in Figure 6.8. On average, those with a college degree earn $40,000 more than those without a college degree.

Now suppose that a random sample of people with a college degree were misassigned to the no-college-degree group. Assuming that this sample of the misassigned were fairly representative of the college-degree group, this would raise the average income for the no-college-degree group. This would then reduce the difference in average income between the two groups. Conversely, let's say that part of the no-college-degree group is misassigned to the college-degree group. This would likely lower the average income of the college-degree group, again reducing the difference. The measurement error would cause the observed difference in incomes between the two groups to be lower than the actual differences.

This demonstrates the effects of an explanatory variable being measured with error. It typically causes the coefficient estimate to be biased towards zero, which is called **attenuation bias**. If the explanatory variable were a variable with many possible values (such as years-of-schooling) rather than just a dummy variable, the same concept applies: the misclassification from measurement error would typically cause a bias towards zero in the coefficient estimate on the variable.

Let's use some actual data to test for the effects of measurement error. In Table 6.6, I show the results of two models:

- Column (1) is the same as the Multiple Regression model from Table 5.1 in Section 5.1, except that a dummy variable for having a "college degree" is used instead of "years-of-schooling" and the standard errors are now corrected for heteroskedasticity
- Column (2) is the same except that I switched the "college degree" assignment for a randomly-selected part of the sample. That is, for about 10% of the sample (those who had a randomly-generated variable in the [0,1] range be <0.1), I set the college-degree variable equal to 1 if it was originally 0 and *vice versa.*

What we see is that the coefficient estimate on "college degree" is reduced significantly: from $28,739 to $15,189. Thus, the measurement error in the college-degree variable is causing a bias in the coefficient estimate towards zero. (Note that if you try to replicate this with the code on the book's website, you will obtain different numbers due to the randomization, but the general story should be the same.)

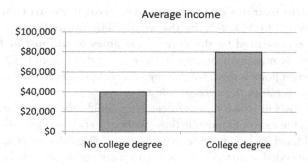

Figure 6.8 Notional example to demonstrate measurement error

Table 6.6 Regression models demonstrating the effects of measurement error (n = 2772)

	Dependent variable = income in 2003	
	(Model 1)	(Model 2)
College degree	28,739***	15,189***
	(2,953)	(2,340)
AFQT score	321***	438***
	(39)	(41)
Age	671*	398
	(404)	(407)
Black	−3898*	−2177
	(2,073)	(2,137)
Hispanic	907	1703
	(2,176)	(2,222)
Mother has an HS diploma	3469*	3574*
	(1,928)	(1,970)
Mother has a college degree	1407	4465
	(4,831)	(4,863)
Father has an HS diploma	1038	1040
	(2,011)	(2,052)
Father has a college degree	14,197***	17,363***
	(3,836)	(3,945)
Constant	9296	8345
	(17,198)	(17,363)
R-squared	0.212	0.190

Source: 1979 National Longitudinal Survey of Youth.

Standard errors are in parentheses and corrected for heteroskedasticity.

***$p < 0.01$, **$p < 0.05$, *$p < 0.1$.

It is not just the coefficient estimate on the mismeasured variable that is affected. Note that the other coefficient estimates change as well. In particular, the one variable that has a very strong positive association with schooling, *afqt*, has a much higher coefficient estimate when the measurement error is added into the college-degree variable. This is likely because the *afqt* variable is now picking up the variation in income that the college-degree variable is failing to do because of the measurement error. The same is true for the other factors that are likely positively correlated with having a college degree. **This demonstrates that measurement error in control variables could cause omitted-factors bias (PITFALL #2) in the coefficient estimate on the key-X variable because the factors represented by the control variables would not be fully adjusted for.**

There was undoubtedly measurement error in the existing data before I added my own measurement error. The important point is this: *Added to any other biases, measurement error will typically contribute to a downward-in-magnitude bias on the coefficient estimate.*

That said, there are cases in which measurement error could cause an upward-in-magnitude bias. This would occur if, in the case of Figure 6.8, those without a college degree but miscoded as having a college degree had higher average income than the true college-degree people. Alternatively, this could result from those coded incorrectly as not having a college degree and having a lower average income than the true non-degree people.

The general rule is:

* If the error in an explanatory variable is likely to be uncorrelated with the outcome or any explanatory variable (*non-differential measurement error*), then the near-certain direction of the bias is towards zero. This would be the case with any coding errors, as well as any sort of economic statistic used as an explanatory variable, as all economic statistics have measurement error that is more likely to be due to sampling variation than anything intentional.
* If there is a reason to believe that there could be a non-trivial correlation between the error in the explanatory variable and the outcome or any explanatory variables (*differential measurement error*), then the direction of the bias from measurement error is in an uncertain direction that needs significant efforts to calculate. This is more likely to occur with survey data, which could be subject to lying or poor recollection.

A researcher should assess whether any error in a given explanatory variable would naturally be greater at certain values of that variable. For something like marijuana use in the past year, there probably would be greater measurement error at higher values.

6.7.3 Can bias from measurement error be corrected?

There have been various methods suggested for correcting measurement errors. The most common methods have been summarized well in Guolo (2008) and Carroll et al. (2006). Unfortunately, all methods rely on many assumptions about the relationship of the error with the other explanatory variables. They also result in higher standard errors. Furthermore, these methods are computationally intensive, which makes it questionable whether it's worth the unknown benefit of improved estimates.

Theoretically, the instrumental-variables (two-stage-least-squares) method that will be introduced in Chapter 8 could address the problem of measurement error. That, however, is a rare option, as it requires a variable that affects the key-explanatory variable and has no other effect on the outcome. Furthermore, the instrumental-variables method produces results that typically apply to a narrow slice of the population, and so such results are of questionable value.

6.7.4 How controlling for more variables can increase bias from measurement error

The extent of bias from measurement error depends on the proportion of the *operative variation* that is due to measurement error. Controlling for other factors would almost certainly reduce the amount of *operative variation* by a larger amount than the measurement error is reduced. In fact, controlling for dummy variables can reduce *operative variation* without reducing measurement error at all. This means that any existing bias from measurement error would likely increase with the inclusion of more control variables, particularly dummy variables for a categorization. This does not mean that important factors should not be controlled for, as excluding variables as control variables has the potential to introduce greater bias from omitted-factors bias than that from measurement error.

Table 6.7 demonstrates this with the instructor-evaluation models from Chapter 4 – equations (4.2) and (4.3) from Section 4.3. For a randomly chosen set of about 10% of the sample, I subtracted

Table 6.7 Demonstrating how adding control variables can exacerbate bias from measurement error (n = 100)

Variables	(1)	(2)	(3)	(4)
	Dependent variable = Average evaluation in class			
Class-size	0.0040***		−0.0098***	
	(0.0003)		(0.0017)	
Class-size with error for ~20%		0.0040***		−0.0077***
		(0.0003)		(0.0015)
Prof. B			0.811***	0.634***
			(0.144)	(0.130)
Prof. C			2.294***	1.957***
			(0.268)	(0.241)
Prof. D			3.230***	2.724***
			(0.401)	(0.359)
Constant	3.299***	3.298***	3.917***	3.846***
	(0.060)	(0.061)	(0.078)	(0.075)
R-squared	0.603	0.599	0.828	0.816

Standard errors in parentheses.

***$p < 0.01$, **$p < 0.05$, *$p < 0.1$.

15 from the class-size, and for another randomly chosen 10% of the sample, I added 15 students to the class-size – all without changing the dependent variable. The odd-numbered columns show the original results from equations (4.2) and (4.3), while the even columns show the results from the models with the error in the class-size variable. From the Simple Regression Model in column (1), adding the error to the class-size variable in column (2) had hardly any impact on the coefficient estimate on the class-size. However, when the professor is held-constant, in columns (3) and (4), the error added to the class-size variable caused over a 20% reduction (that is, a bias) in the coefficient estimates. I will discuss this further in Chapter 8 when describing fixed effects.

6.7.5 Measurement error in the dependent variable

Measurement error in the dependent variable is much less problematic. In fact, it results in no bias in the estimated effect of the explanatory variables as long as the reason for the measurement error is unrelated to the key-explanatory variable. To see why this is the case, consider again Figure 6.8. Let's suppose that 10% of the people lie and add an average of $5,000 to their income. As long as there is not too large of a discrepancy between the two groups in the propensity to lie, then the averages for both groups would increase by about $500, and the difference in their average income should stay about the same.

The one effect that measurement error in the dependent variable may have is that the standard errors on the coefficient estimates become larger. The greater is such an error in the dependent variable, the larger will be the standard errors, and the more likely it is that a coefficient estimate would be far off from the true coefficient due to imprecision.

What to check for: measurement error

Check if there could be a non-trivial error in the survey response or the coding of the explanatory variable. Or consider whether the explanatory variable is imperfect in representing the intended concept.

Box 6.4   The Hot Hand in Basketball: 25 years of measurement error

As discussed in the Preface, the inspiration for this book came from incorrect interpretations of results from research on the "hot hand" in basketball—I fully recognize that this sounds like a strange motivation. I described back in Section 5.7 that the "hot hand" is a period of elevated performance in which a person has a higher-than-normal probability of making a shot. It is often called "being in the zone" or "*en fuego*." The hot hand can show up in any sport, but it is most known in basketball, where a player gets in a groove and plays well above their normal playing level. I played a ton of basketball in my youth. I had regular experiences with the "hot hand."

So I knew something was wrong when I discovered that all published research on this topic claimed that the hot hand in basketball was a "myth." That is, whenever we see someone hit several shots in a row, these authors argue, it is just part of random variation, just as we would get several instances of six or so heads or tails in a row if we flip a coin enough times. As my friend, Dan Stone, pointed out, this conclusion implies that there can be no improved performance from temporary increases in confidence. So, according to these researchers, 100% of basketball players and coaches and almost all basketball fans who believe in the hot hand are wrong and are committing the common human fallacy of seeing patterns in data that are actually random. This was such a great story that it has shown up in many pop-economics books (even a few by Nobel-prize-winning-economists). Even an almost Fed-Chairman-nominee lectured the Harvard basketball team that the hot hand didn't exist (Brooks, 2013).

Given that I knew they were wrong (from my own experiences), I had to figure out what was wrong with their research. First, I combined all players into one model to generate greater power (rather than the prior studies examining one player at a time). I found a small hot-hand effect with free throw data (Arkes, 2010)—that players were 3–5 percentage points more likely to make a second of two free throws if they hit their first free throw.

The real breakthroughs, however, came from Daniel Stone (2012) and Josh Miller and Adam Sanjurjo (2018), who found biases in prior studies, including my own. Stone demonstrated that *measurement error* caused by the mis-assignment of players into the hot or normal state causes the estimated hot-hand effects to be severely underestimated. That is, the "hot" state may have been indicated in the research by hitting one's last shot or last few shots. But a person with a hot hand will not necessarily hit every shot. So sometimes a person is "hot" but classified as "not hot" and *vice versa*. (The data may be coded correctly but not reflect the intended concept, "hot hand," accurately.) In Arkes (2013), building off of Stone's work, I simulated a world with a hot hand occurring regularly and demonstrated how the prior research, given their methods and sample sizes, severely understated the hot-hand effect and would have had a very low probability of detecting a significant effect for the hot hand. Importantly, what this also implied was that the small hot-hand effect I found with free throw data in 2010 (which was also subject to the same measurement error) is likely representative of a much larger hot-hand effect. The breakthrough Miller and Sanjurjo (2018) had was recognizing a bias related to the Gambler's Fallacy. They demonstrate that, if you take all "heads" in a finite sequence of coin flips, the probability that the following flip is a "heads" is <50%. They actually reverse the result from the seminal hot-hand study by Gilovich et al. (1985), using that study's data to demonstrate that correcting for the gambler's-fallacy bias leads to significant hot-hand effects.

So, as mentioned in Section 5.7, the proper interpretation of the prior research should not have been, "the hot hand is a myth." Rather, it should have been, "We found no evidence for the hot hand."

What a delicious irony here! *The original researchers (and Nobel Prize winners) who claimed that basketball players and fans were mistakenly seeing patterns in data that are actually random were actually the ones making the error, concluding randomness in data that are almost certainly patterned.* (And good thing that the near-Fed-Chairman-nominee didn't become the Fed Chairman.)

Let me add that in my even-funner-book-than-this-one, *Confessions of a Recovering Economist*, I explain how the hot-hand research is a microcosm of several major problems with economic research, including how even those deemed the best among us (Nobel laureates) fail to recognize biases.

6.8 PITFALL #5: Using mediating factors or outcomes as control variables

This PITFALL combines two PITFALLS (called BIG QUESTIONS) from the first edition of this book. Both remind me of a Yogi quote and make me think of something else he might say. Regarding using outcomes as control variables, Yogi once said: "Congratulations. I knew the record would stand until it was broken." On the use of mediating factors as control variables, I'm sure, even though it is not documented anywhere to my knowledge, that he said "I wouldn't have hit so many homers if I hadn't hit the ball so hard." The difference is that, whereas a "record" is an outcome in itself, hitting the ball hard is not an outcome but is a good indicator of several batting outcomes that should not be controlled.

6.8.1 Why mediating factors and outcomes should not be included as control variables

This PITFALL formalizes the concept from Chapter 4 of not controlling for factors that are products of the key-explanatory variable. This is the underappreciated star of regression PITFALLS, as it is often overlooked. This is a mistake few researchers are conscious of and something you won't see in other textbooks, at least as of this writing.

Recall from earlier discussions:

- From Section 6.5, omitted-factors bias is not a problem if the omitted factor is a product of the key-explanatory variable.
- In the lemon-tree example from Section 4.5 and Figure 4.7a and b, we did not want to control for the height of the tree, as that was part of the reason why the amount of water affected how many lemons the tree produced.
- In the domino-chain example from Section 4.5 and Figure 4.9, as we aimed to estimate how tipping the first domino affected whether the last domino fell, we did not want to hold constant whether the third domino fell. That too was part of the mechanism we wanted to capture.

The products of the explanatory variable could be mediating factors, as in the lemon-tree and domino-chain examples. In addition, they could be outcomes themselves, which is similar in that controlling for an outcome would be removing part of the effect a researcher is attempting to capture. Either way, including mediating factors or outcomes as control variables, would cause a bias in the estimated causal effect.

6.8.2 An example of including mediating factors as control variables

Let's consider a case that comes from one of my publications (Arkes, 2007). In that study, I examined what happens to teenage drug use when the state unemployment rate increases, similar to the basic regression from Section 3.3. From the more-recent NLSY (starting in 1997), I had individual-level data of teenagers from all states and over several years. I specified the model as follows:

$$Y_{ist} = X_{ist}\beta_1 + \beta_2 UR_{st} + \varepsilon_{ist} \qquad (6.11)$$

where Y is the measure of teenage drug use, UR is the state unemployment rate for state s in year t. The vector X would include a set of demographic variables, year dummy variables, and state dummy variables. This is nearly equivalent to using state and year fixed effects, which will be covered in Section 8.1. The i subscript indicates that individual-level data is used.

When writing this article, I conceived of several mechanisms for how a higher unemployment rate could lead to a change in teenage drug use. They are represented in the top chart in Figure 6.9, which is similar in nature to Figures 4.7a and 4.7b. The first set of arrows on the left represents how an increase in the unemployment rate (by one percentage point) would affect three mediating factors.

Recall from Chapter 4 that mediating factors (also called "intervening factors" or "mechanism variables") are factors through which the key-explanatory variable affects the dependent variable. For example, in the lemon-tree example, the tree's height was a mediating factor for how watering affected the number of lemons the tree produced.

The second set of arrows represents how one-unit *increases* in those mediating factors would affect teenage drug use. *Decreases* in the mediating factors would cause the opposite effect. A **mechanism** would be a full reason why a change in the unemployment rate caused a change in teenage drug use, represented in Figure 6.9 as a full pathway, or one set of the left and right arrows. There are three mechanisms, labeled with circled M1, M2, and M3. Properly estimating the values of these mechanisms would be impossible because two of the mediating factors are unobservable and non-quantifiable, and there would be numerous biases in estimating how teenage income affected teen drug use. Furthermore, there could be a correlation between the various mechanisms, so the sum of the three mechanisms, if this were the complete set of mechanisms, would not necessarily be the true causal effect. Nevertheless, all of the mechanisms contribute to the overall effect of the unemployment rate on teen drug use, along with other mechanisms I might have missed.

The mechanisms and the likely sign of the effect are that a higher state unemployment rate would:

- **M1**: reduce teenage income, making drugs less affordable → reducing drug use (NEGATIVE EFFECT)
- **M2**: lead to greater free time and boredom, creating more opportunities to use drugs or greater motivation to use drugs to add excitement to their life → increasing drug use (POSITIVE EFFECT)
- **M3**: increase the number of drug sellers, which makes drugs more available and perhaps easier to obtain → increasing use (POSITIVE EFFECT).

Because there are both negative and positive mechanisms, the overall effect could be negative or positive.

Also in Figure 6.9 are the variables in the vector, X – state, year, and demographic variables (e.g., gender and race/ethnicity). These are *not* part of a mechanism for how the unemployment rate would affect teenage drug use, as they probably would not be affected by the unemployment rate.

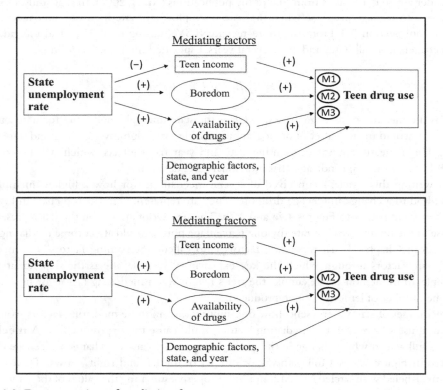

Figure 6.9 Demonstration of mediating factors

The classic definition for the conventionally-named omitted-variables bias from all textbooks I have seen implies one should control for these mediating factors (particularly teenage income) because they are correlated with the unemployment rate and likely affect the outcome. Changes in teenage income, however, represent part of the reason why the unemployment rate affects teenage drug use.

If we were to estimate equation (6.11), which does not include the teenager's income (or any proxy for boredom or availability), then the estimate for β_2 would capture the effects of the unemployment rate on teenage drug use from all three mechanisms (M1, M2, and M3) plus any other mechanisms that I may not have conceived of.

In this case, assuming the model has no other biases, the estimate for β_2 would be an unbiased estimate of the "full effect" – or, how teenage drug use should move if the unemployment rate were to increase by one percentage point, after adjusting for the factors in X.

As for identifying each of the six effects (the six arrows) that are part of the mechanisms, as mentioned above, that would be very difficult to accurately identify for many reasons. But we do not have to be concerned about those if you are interested in the *full effect* for β_2.

At the beginning of this section, I said many researchers were not aware of this issue. Here is an example for why I say this. When I submitted this article for publication, a referee at the well-respected journal where it is now published said that I needed to include the teenager's income in the model. I responded that I cannot do that. Let's look at what would have happened to the model if I had controlled for teenage income.

The model would be the following:

$$Y_{it} = X_{it}\beta_1 + \beta_{2a}UR_{it} + \beta_3 \left(\text{teenager's income}\right)_{it} + \varepsilon_{it} \tag{6.12}$$

This model is represented in the bottom chart of Figure 6.9. Teenage income now has its own separate effect outside of the unemployment-rate effect. **Thus, in the model, when the unemployment rate changes, boredom and availability would increase (not that we observe it), but income would theoretically not change because it is being controlled for.** Effectively, any variation in teenage income not part of the linear relationship with the unemployment rate could still be captured by part of the unemployment-rate effect on drug use. This means that drug use would change from the full increases in boredom and availability, but only change from a small part of the changes in income. So the unemployment-rate effect would mostly reflect the other two mechanisms, M2 and M3, and just capture a small part of M1. The interpretation of the estimate for β_{2a} in equation (6.12) would now, roughly, be: how a one-percentage-point increase in the unemployment rate affects teenage drug use beyond any effect through teenage income (and adjusted for the other factors represented in X). It would no longer represent the "full effect" of the unemployment rate or how teenage drug use moves with the unemployment rate.

Is the new coefficient estimate on the unemployment rate ($\hat{\beta}_{2a}$) interesting? Maybe … if you want to gauge the size of those other effects. But, from a practical standpoint, it is not as interesting or relevant as the "full effect" of the unemployment rate on teenage drug use.

In what direction would the estimated unemployment-rate effect be biased? Because the teen-income mechanism (M1) contributed negatively to the effect of the unemployment rate on drug use, eliminating (or reducing) this mechanism from the unemployment-rate effect would cause a positive bias on the estimate—i.e., we would be reducing a negative mechanism, causing the estimate to increase. Thus, if I had followed the referee's suggestion, I would have only estimated a *partial effect* of the unemployment rate on teen drug use rather than the *full effect*.

(The term "partial effect" – used here to contrast with the "full effect" – is also used when describing coefficient estimates in a Multiple Regression Model. A "partial effect," like a partial derivative, is the effect of some variable on the outcome while controlling for other factors. I personally believe that using those terms here – in the context of capturing a "full causal effect" as opposed to only "part of a causal effect" – is a better use of the term "partial effect" in regression analysis.)

Note that even if the coefficient estimate were higher in equation (6.12), as we may expect, it would still be a partial effect because it does not include every mechanism. Yes, a partial effect can be larger in magnitude than a full effect if the excluded mechanisms are in the opposite direction of the net effect of the other mechanisms.

As stated in Chapter 4, the ideal modeling strategy is to design the model so that the treatment occurs and the model allows the effects to play out rather than control for the mechanisms that occur along the way.

6.8.3 An empirical example: how TV watching affects body-mass index

This source of bias has not been accepted by all practitioners. Thus, I thought I would provide proof of how controlling for mediating factors causes bias beyond what I showed with the domino-chain example in Section 4.5.2. I created the notional model, depicted in Figure 6.10, on how TV-watching affects BMI. The top flowchart in Figure 6.10 shows that the true Average Treatment Effect of an extra hour of TV on BMI is 1.2. In the bottom flowchart, I show two mechanisms:

- **M1**: An extra hour of TV watching increases junk-food consumption by 0.8 units, and each unit of junk-food increases BMI by 1.0.
- **M2**: This is a generic mechanism covering all other avenues through which TV-watching affects BMI.

Because the overall causal effect of TV-watching on BMI is 1.2 and M1 = 0.8 (0.8 × 1.0), M2 would equal 0.4 if M1 and M2 were independent of each other.

In a notional sample of 1,000 observations, I imposed these effects and added some randomness so that the estimated effects would not be exactly the true effects. The results are in Table 6.8. First, note that the coefficient estimate on junk food in Model (1) of 0.963 is fairly close to the effect of 1.0 that I imposed on the right half of mechanism M1.

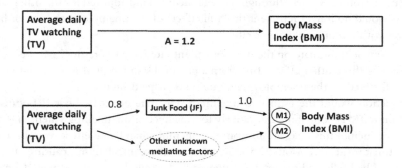

Figure 6.10 Notional model of TV-watching and BMI

Table 6.8 Regression results from notional models of TV-watching and BMI (n = 1000)

	(1)	(2)
	Dependent variable = Body-Mass Index	
	Model with the mediating factor of "junk-food"	*Model without the mediating factor of "junk-food"*
TV hours	0.442***	1.215***
	(0.040)	(0.023)
Junk food	0.963***	
	(0.044)	
Constant	17.47***	17.48***
	(0.09)	(0.11)
R-squared	0.817	0.730

Standard errors are in parentheses.

***$p < 0.01$, **$p < 0.05$, *$p < 0.1$.

The important comparison is for the coefficient estimates on TV hours in the two models. Only in Model (2), in which the mediating factor of junk food is excluded, is the coefficient estimate on TV hours close to the true causal effect of one extra hour of TV-watching on BMI of 1.2. The corresponding coefficient estimate in Model (1) of 0.442 severely underestimates the effect. Note that it is close to the value of M2 of 0.4. The direction of bias is negative in this case because I was eliminating a positive mechanism.

6.8.4 Mediating factors vs. omitted-factors bias

Someone may argue that not controlling for teenage income would cause omitted-factors bias. However, recall that I said back in Section 6.5 that omitted-factors bias is not a problem if the key-explanatory variable is affecting the omitted factor and not *vice versa*. That is the case here with the key-explanatory variable (the state unemployment rate) and the omitted factor (the teenager's income). Thus, omitting teenage income should not be a concern because the only reason that the teenager's income would be correlated with the unemployment rate is that the unemployment rate affects teenage income.

However, there are other situations in which it would not be as clear as to whether to control for some variables. Take the case in Figure 6.11, a political-science issue, in which you want to estimate the effects of campaign donations from the National Rifle Association (NRA) on the probability that a Congressman votes for a certain pro-gun legislative bill.

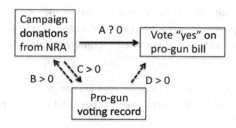

Figure 6.11 The effect of campaign donations on voting behavior

The issue is whether a Congressman's "Pro-gun voting record" should be included as a control variable. Excluding the variable would present a potential omitted-factors bias problem because the Congressman's voting record, which proxies for views on guns, could lead to NRA campaign donations and the eventual vote on the current bill. However, including "pro-gun voting record" would mean that you may only be estimating a "partial effect" rather than the "full effect" of NRA campaign donations on the probability of the "yes" vote because the campaign donations could increase their pro-gun leanings (which the pro-gun voting record represents).

So what do you do? The best thing to do is:

1. Acknowledge the dilemma in your article.
2. Estimate the model both with and without "voting record."
3. If the estimated effect of "NRA campaign donations" is similar with and without "voting record" included, then you probably are okay.
4. If the estimated effect of "NRA campaign donations" is different with "voting record" included vs. not included, then you should report both, or perhaps explore further what precedes what in terms of donations and voting record, if data were available.

The example in Figure 6.11 provides a nice opportunity to practice determining the direction of bias for omitted-factors bias and the bias from including mediating factors as control variables.

- Not controlling for "pro-gun-voting-record" would contribute to a positive omitted-factors bias on the estimated effect of campaign donations on the likelihood of voting yes (**A**). This is because the product of **B** and **D** is positive.
- Controlling for "pro-gun-voting-record" would contribute to a negative bias on the estimated effect, as the positive mechanism of **C** × **D** would be eliminated or reduced.

6.8.5 Example of using an outcome as a control variable

If you were to investigate the research articles on how state tax rates affect state economic growth, you would find that nearly all articles on this topic included outcome variables as control variables. This was to make the regression model consistent with a theoretical model, but it results in biased estimates, typically leading to an understatement of the true effect.

Rather than singling any study out, I use mostly my own data that I compiled. Table 6.9 shows the estimated effects of state income tax rates on the growth rate in Gross State Product (the state version of Gross Domestic Product) for three models:

- Model (1) has just state and region-year-interacted dummy variables as control variables, as well as a few other tax rates (indicated in the Notes section of the table)
- Model (2) adds state employment growth as an explanatory variable
- Model (3) further adds growth in real personal income per capita for the state as an explanatory variable.

These two variables that are added in Models (2) and (3) are outcomes of the key-X variable (the tax rate). That is, growth in state employment and real personal income per capita are likely, to some extent, products of the tax rate.

The important result in Table 6.9 is that the coefficient estimates on the key-X variable, "maximum marginal income tax rate," are reduced in magnitude as the outcome variables are added as

Table 6.9 The effects of state tax rates on Gross State Product growth (n = 1440), 1980–2009

Examining the effects of maximum marginal income tax rate

	Dependent variable = Growth rate in Gross State Product		
	Model (1)	Model (2)	Model (3)
Maximum marginal income tax rate	−0.366***	−0.295**	−0.142
	(0.140)	(0.133)	(0.117)
	[−0.640, −0.092]	[−0.556, −0.034]	[−0.371, 0.087]
Employment growth		0.762***	0.536***
		(0.069)	(0.062)
Real personal income per capita growth			0.770***
			(0.042)

The sample includes the lower 48 states for 30 years (1980–2009). Standard errors are in parentheses. The 95% confidence intervals are in brackets. Models also include state and region-year-interacted dummy variables. In addition, they include maximum corporate income tax, sales tax, and long-term capital gains tax rates. ***$p < 0.01$, **$p < 0.05$, *$p < 0.1$.

control variables, in Models (2) and (3). The reason is that the outcomes included as control variables are soaking up a good part of the effect of the tax rate on the general strength of the economy, leaving less of that effect that the tax rates can have.

The logic of the interpretation here is similar to that of mediating factors. In Model (3), we are now estimating the effect of the state tax rate on growth in Gross State Product beyond any effects that state tax rates have on employment and income growth – not exactly an interesting nor useful concept. The more useful regression would be Model (1), which tells us how Gross State Product changes with a one-percentage-point increase in the tax rate, controlling for the state and region-year.

An important point to note is that many variables could be considered as outcomes. For example, we have used years-of-schooling as a key-X variable, but it could be an outcome. That is okay and does not cause a bias, as long as the variable is not a product of the key-X variable in a given model.

6.8.6 The correction

This PITFALL is a modeling problem rather than an inherent problem with the data or with how factors are related to each other. Thus, as long as there are no biases created by doing so, the simple fix is to eliminate from your model variables that could be the product of the key-explanatory variable. As described in Chapter 4, you want to allow the key-X variable to vary in the sample and then, rather than controlling for what happens next, let it go, let it play out, and see what happens to the outcome.

What to check for: using mediating factors and outcomes variables as control variables

The check is to assess whether any control variable could be a product of the key-explanatory variable(s). If so, the best practice is to drop the variable from the model.

6.9 PITFALL #6: Improper reference groups

This PITFALL is about ensuring that optimal comparisons are being made. Imagine if Yogi Berra had said, "Compared to my worst game ever, I did pretty good out there today." This would not have been very informative, as his worst game is not the ideal reference point to gauge how well he played today.

This is an important PITFALL because researchers can manipulate research results based on which reference group is used. If corporations were conducting research on whether there are harmful effects of their products, they could change who is part of the reference group in order to show that the harmful effects of the product are minimal or non-existent, when the reality might be that there are significant harmful effects.

The standard meaning of a reference group is that, in a categorization of two or more mutually-exclusive groups, it is the group/category that is not included in the model as an explanatory variable. The coefficient estimates on the variables for the other groups would then be based on the comparison of the outcome for a given group to that for the reference group.

For the sake of estimating causal effects, the reference group for the key-X variable could refer to:

- Those not receiving the treatment (if the key-X variable is based on yes/no for receiving a treatment)
- The group that does not have a variable representing it in the model (for key-X variables for a multi-group categorization)
- In a practical sense, those with low values of the key-X variable when the key-X variable is quantitative or non-categorical. (I took the latitude here to expand the definition of a reference group to something not quite fitting the normal definition but that is essentially the same thing.)

The issue of whether a study has the optimal reference group or an improper reference group for the key-X variable comes down to three sub-questions, of which one or more might apply:

A. Does the reference group represent an incorrect counterfactual?
B. Would those in the reference group be more likely to be doing something instead of the treatment that could affect the dependent variable?
C. Do those in the reference group experience a lower-intensity effect of the treatment?

Which of these sub-questions should be used depends on the situation. And the direction of the bias is determined differently for each sub-question. I will give some examples, and then I will give inexact guidance on which of these sub-questions to use in different situations. But first, let me note that, for control variables, it does not matter what reference group is used, as it would not affect the result of interest (the coefficient estimate on the key-X variable).

6.9.1 Does the reference group represent an incorrect counterfactual?

This sub-question is important for issues for which it is not just a yes/no treatment, but rather at least three categories for the treatment. A good example comes from a RAND Corporation analysis of how "hostile deployments" affect the probability of first-term enlisted personnel reenlisting for a second term (Hosek and Martorell, 2009). A hostile deployment, in the military, is the case of a serviceperson being deployed to a location that is deemed to present a danger to the serviceperson. In administrative military data, having a hostile deployment is indicated by whether the serviceperson received extra hostile-duty pay in a given month. It is normally given to everyone who is part of a unit (e.g., an Army company) that had members in an area exposed to danger in a given month.

Hosek and Martorell (2009) essentially put everyone into one of three groups:

- no deployment
- a non-hostile deployment
- a hostile deployment.

(Technically, a person could be in both of the latter two groups, with two separate deployments, but the lesson here still holds.)

They included variables for the second and third groups in the model, which made the "no deployment" category as the reference group. Is this the correct reference group?

The implied objective of the analysis was to determine how the increased danger servicepersons were facing, as a result of the Global War on Terrorism (GWOT), was affecting reenlistment rates. And so we need to think about what category would those having a hostile deployment due to the GWOT have been in had there not been the GWOT. Would they have been on no deployment? Would they have been on a non-hostile deployment? Or would servicepersons have been in a mix of those two categories had there not been the GWOT?

By making the reference group "no deployment," it implicitly assumes that all the "hostile deployments" would have had the counterfactual of "no deployment." Based on this, as seen in Table 6.10, they estimate the hostile-deployment effect on the probability of reenlistment to be −0.5 percentage points for Army soldiers (not significant at the 5% level) and +1.7 percentage points for Marines (which was highly significant).

But what if the correct counterfactual were a non-hostile-deployment? That is, what if those on hostile deployments would have had a non-hostile deployment had it not been for GWOT? If that category were used instead as the reference group, the estimated effect of a hostile deployment would have been −8.7 percentage points for Army soldiers (−0.005 minus 0.082) and −4.8 percentage points for Marines (0.017 minus 0.065), both of which would be statistically significant. This can be seen in Figure 6.12, in which I depict the Army results. I start with a baseline reenlistment rate of 30% for non-deployers, and the rates for the other two groups add the coefficient estimates from Table 6.10 above. We can see that the hostile deployers have lower reenlistment rates than the non-hostile deployers

Table 6.10 Summarizing the main model from Hosek and Martorell (2009, Table 7.1, p. 40)

	Army	Marine Corps
Non-hostile deployment	0.082***	0.065***
	(0.006)	(0.004)
Hostile deployment	−0.005	0.017***
	(0.003)	(0.002)

The dependent variable is a dummy variable for whether the enlisted person reenlists. The reference group is those with no deployment. These results come from the bottom model of Table 7.1 in the report, which uses interacted fixed effects for occupation (MOS) and a quarter of the reenlistment decision.

***$p < 0.01$, **$p < 0.05$, *$p < 0.1$.

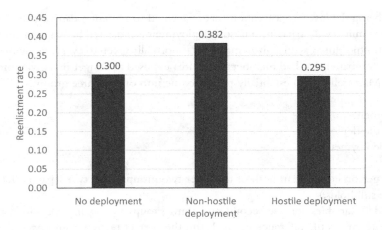

Figure 6.12 Depicting the Army results from Table 6.10 to demonstrate improper reference groups

by 8.7 percentage points (29.5% minus 38.2%). This is a completely different story from what comes out in the table in the report, as using non-hostile deployments as the reference group would result in a large negative estimated effect of a hostile deployment. (My military student leaned heavily towards believing the "non-hostile deployment" was the best counterfactual and reference group.)

If the actual counterfactual were some mix of "no deployments" and "non-hostile deployments," then one option would be to add "non-hostile deployments" to the reference group. What would the estimated effect of "hostile deployments" be then? From Figure 6.12, the reenlistment rate for the reference group would be somewhere between 0.300 and 0.382. The estimated effect of a hostile deployment would then be somewhere between the −0.005 that the authors estimate and −0.087.

I hate to complicate things, but the solution for the proper reference group is not simply to combine the first two groups, but rather to weight the first two groups based on the percentages of each that the hostile deployers would have as the counterfactual (had they not had a hostile deployment). And who knows what that mix would be? Perhaps it should be based on what the mix was before GWOT started.

Whatever the reference group would be, it would probably come out that a hostile deployment does have a sizable negative impact on the probability of reenlisting. Hosek and Martorell (2009) likely had a large positive bias on their estimates, which ended up understating the negative effect of hostile deployments, even incorrectly turning the estimate positive for the Marine Corps.

The important point is that, when there are three or more categories for the key-X variable (the treatment), choosing the correct counterfactual might be difficult. It has to be done carefully.

Let me describe a mistake made in one of my own articles with a colleague and student as another example (Shen, Arkes, and Pilgrim, 2009). Also dealing with military deployments, we aimed to estimate how the length of the deployment affected the detection of Post-Traumatic Stress Disorder (PTSD) for Navy enlisted personnel. We classified people into three groups based on the length of the most recent deployment, which I depict in Figure 6.13. The figure shows an initial rate for those in the reference (left-most) group of short deployments of 1–60 days. (I do not still have the data, so I guessed at the initial rate of 3.0%.) What is important is that the coefficient estimates on the other two groups were 0.011 (1.1 percentage points) and 0.022 (2.2 percentage points), so the other groups would have then had rates of 4.1% and 5.2%.

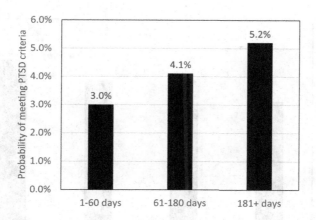

Figure 6.13 How the length of a Navy deployment affects the likelihood of PTSD

What I believe we got wrong was that we had the incorrect counterfactual. In particular, if those in the long deployments of more than 180 days did not have such a long deployment, the most likely case would be that they would have had a deployment of 61–180 days, not a rare deployment of 1–60 days. This is the tendency of researchers to make the lowest group the reference group, but it could lead to overstating the effects. Indeed, in this case, I would say that the effect of a long deployment on the probability of meeting the criteria for PTSD would be closer to 1.1 percentage points (5.2% minus 4.1%) rather than the 2.2 percentage points we reported.

The direction of the bias, for this sub-question on whether the incorrect counter-factual is used, is based on whether the true counterfactual groups (whether some are added or taken out) have a higher or lower average of the dependent variable than the existing/initial reference group, after adjusting for other factors. The rule is the following:

- If the optimal reference group has a mean of the dependent variable (after adjusting for other factors) that is *more positive* than the current reference group (as in the case of the Army and Marine Corps above), then the estimated effect of the key-X variable should be *more negative* than it is, meaning that it was *positively biased* beforehand.
- If the optimal reference group has a mean of the dependent variable (after adjusting for other factors) that is *more negative* than the current reference group, then the estimated effect of the key-X variable should be *more positive*, meaning that it was *negatively biased* beforehand.

This use of incorrect counterfactuals appears to be most applicable when there is a policy intervention and there are more than two treatment categories. Perhaps the best approach to determine the direction of the bias is to draw it out, as in Figures 6.12 and 6.13.

6.9.2 Would those in the reference group be more likely to be doing something instead of the treatment that could affect the dependent variable?

This sub-question is directly tied to the third source of omitted-factors bias in Section 6.5, *replacement actions*. Consider the oatmeal-cholesterol from that discussion. This would be a case in which

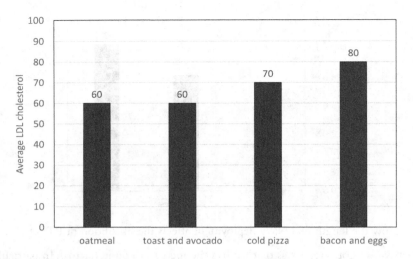

Figure 6.14 Notional bad cholesterol levels based on the typical breakfast

the treatment is a numeric variable, and so the effective reference group would be those with low amounts of oatmeal consumption. The question becomes whether those who have low oatmeal consumption are doing something else instead (of eating oatmeal) that could affect cholesterol. What you are probably thinking is that oatmeal tends to be a breakfast food, and of those not eating oatmeal, many might be eating bacon-and-eggs or cold pizza, both of which probably increase cholesterol levels.

Let's simplify this a bit and separate people into four groups, distinguished by their typical breakfast, as depicted in Figure 6.14. The figure shows notional numbers I created on the average cholesterol levels for each group. Separating people into four groups demonstrates that if people aren't eating oatmeal, they are eating something else. This means that, as oatmeal consumption changes in the sample, bacon-and-eggs and cold-pizza consumption is probably also changing. And so it could be that oatmeal has no effect on cholesterol, but it might look like it does because the reference group has high cholesterol due to eating more bacon and eggs.

In the following regression

$$\text{Cholesterol} = X\beta_1 + \beta_2 \times (\text{oatmeal}) + \varepsilon, \tag{6.13}$$

if X did not include other things for breakfast people eat, the bacon-and-eggs and the cold-pizza people would be part of the reference group in the model. So it would be possible that oatmeal does not affect cholesterol, but looks like it did because oatmeal people are being compared to people consuming high-cholesterol foods. Putting this in the perspective of omitted-factors bias, bacon-and-eggs and cold-pizza would be negatively correlated with oatmeal and would positively affect cholesterol, and so the estimate for β_2 would be biased negatively if they were not controlled for.

The ideal reference group would be one that was most neutral to the outcome. Out of the categories, what I would think would be the most cholesterol-neutral category would be the second one, "toast and avocado." If that were the reference group, then the model would show no evidence for any effect of oatmeal on cholesterol (based on my notional data). Making "toast and avocado" the reference group would simply entail adding the other groups as control variables as follows:

$$\text{Cholesterol} = X\beta_1 + \beta_2 \times (\text{oatmeal}) + \beta_3 \times (\text{bacon-eggs}) + \beta_4 \times (\text{cold-pizza}) + \varepsilon \qquad (6.14)$$

Whereas I turned this into a discrete problem of categories, it would also apply if the oatmeal, bacon-and-eggs, and cold-pizza variables represented the amounts of the breakfast eaten.

This problem of replacement actions could also apply to studies estimating the effects of wine consumption on health. The reference group of no wine could include alcohol-abstainers, as well as those consuming large amounts of beer and hard alcohol. If the variables representing beer and hard-alcohol consumption were not included as control variables, the estimated effects of wine consumption could pick up the effects of not being big beer and hard-alcohol drinkers.

Even with a randomized control trial assigning different amounts of wine for people to drink (and somehow properly enforcing it), there still could be bias in the estimated health effects of wine because those assigned to have zero wine could turn to beer and hard alcohol.

For this sub-question of the PITFALL for improper reference groups, the direction of bias would be the opposite direction of the effects of the replacement actions on the outcome. For example, in equation (6.13), because bacon-and-eggs and cold-pizza have positive effects on cholesterol, having them as part of the reference group would produce a negative bias on the estimated effect of oatmeal consumption. This could also be determined from a flowchart and the corresponding omitted-factors bias.

This source of bias from improper reference groups appears to be common among studies on the effects of health behaviors on health outcomes. Not doing one activity (e.g., eating oatmeal, drinking wine, watching TV) means the subjects are doing something else, and that something else could have its own effect on their health.

6.9.3 Do those in the reference group experience a lower-intensity effect of the treatment?

Suppose you wanted to estimate the following:

$$\text{Postural problems} = \beta_0 + \beta_1 \times (\text{whether had } 5+ \text{ hours on cell phone}) + \varepsilon \qquad (6.15)$$

The key-X variable is a dummy variable for whether the person spends 5-or-more hours per day on their cell phone. The reference group would be those who spend <5 hours on their cell phone.

In this situation, those in the reference group would have some lower-intensity effects of the treatment. They could have 4.99 hours on their cell phone, on average, and yet be considered part of the reference group in this model. Any harmful effects of too much use of cell phones on posture might be already ingrained in a body from 3 hours per day. At the same time, perhaps those having 0 hours of cell phone use might not be a good reference group, as that would not be the counterfactual for someone if they did not spend 5+ hours on their phone.

Thus, estimating equation (6.15) could understate the impact. This strategy could be used by someone researching a pharmaceutical drug (or cell phone use) if they wanted to show that the side effects of the drug (the pharmaceutical one or the phone) are minimal.

The direction of the bias for this sub-question is more straightforward than the others, as it would be a muted estimated effect (downward in magnitude). This use of improper reference groups could be common in health-related studies.

Perhaps step-wise effects should be estimated. For instance, the variables could be:

* 0–1 hours per day (the excluded category)
* At least 1 hour per day
* At least 3 hours per day
* At least 5 hours per day.

Based on the discussion from Section 3.1 on the highest degree and income, the coefficient on "At least 5 hours" would now be a comparison to the "At least 3 hours" group. All that said, it would be difficult to know what the likely counterfactual (range of hours using the cell phone) would be for someone who chooses not to use the cell phone for at least 5 hours per day, and generally what the groups (variables) should be. It could be useful to examine the data to determine if there were any natural breaks in the data in the distribution of average daily cell phone use. Perhaps the better approach is to just use actual hours per day as the key-X variable.

What to check for: improper reference groups

Assess whether the reference group to the treatment (the key-X variable) represents the correct counterfactual (what a subject would have experienced had they not had the treatment), whether there is a replacement action for not receiving the treatment that could affect the outcome, and whether those in the reference group are receiving a lower-intensity effect of the treatment.

6.10 PITFALL #7: Over-weighting groups (when using fixed effects or dummy variables)

6.10.1 The conditions for and an example of this bias

This bias occurs when the following three conditions hold:

* a control variable (or set of variables) is based on a categorization of the sample into groups; this includes basic dummy variables
* the effect of the key-X variable on the outcome is meaningfully different across those groups
* the variance (and standard deviation) of the key-X variable is different across those groups.

Back in Section 4.3, we saw how a coefficient estimate is calculated, with the presence of control variables using a categorization. The case was estimating how class-size (CS) affects the average evaluation of the professor for a class (E), with the effects imposed on each professor, along with what was estimated for each professor, being:

- **Professor A**: −0.0300 (estimated as −0.0257)
- **Professor B**: −0.0100 (estimated as −0.0113)
- **Professor C**: 0.0000 (estimated as 0.0023)
- **Professor D**: 0.0000 (estimated as 0.0010)

The overall equation when the professor was controlled for was:

$$\hat{E}_i = 3.92 - 0.0098 \times CS_i + 0.081 \times \left(\text{Prof B}\right)_i + 2.29 \times \left(\text{Prof C}\right)_i + 3.23 \times \left(\text{Prof D}\right)_i \qquad (4.3)$$

The equation for how a coefficient is estimated in the presence of a set of dummy variables, as in for professors, is:

$$\hat{\beta}_1 = \sum_g \hat{\beta}_{1g} \times \left[\frac{N_g \times \text{var}\left(X_1 \mid g, X_2\right)}{Z} \right] \qquad (4.5)$$

Note that the weight for a group (the numerator of the fraction) depends on:

- (Not surprisingly) the sample size of group g (N_g)
- (Not as obvious) the variance of X_1 in group g, adjusted for the other variables in the model (X_2).

Think of it this way. If one professor always had classes of 30 people, then there is no within-professor variation in class-size, and there would be no way to estimate a β_{1g} for that professor, so that professor's weight in the model would be zero. The estimation of β_1 would have to come from other professors. As the variation (or variance) in class-size increases for a professor, the coefficient would be estimated more precisely for that professor, with lower standard errors – see Figure 5.1 in Section 5.1. The model then naturally gives more weight to the professors with the more-precisely-estimated coefficients to compute the overall estimate.

This weighting scheme would make sense if there were indeed a constant effect (β_1) across all groups in the population, as the groups with the greater variance in the key-X variable would be more precisely estimated. But it is an unlikely scenario that the effect would be the same across all groups.

In that earlier example, I had used the same-sized range of values of 40 (but at different levels) for the key-X variable (CS) for the professors, so the var(CS) was relatively close for each group and the professors had somewhat similar weights. Still, Professor A and B's coefficient estimates had greater weight because of a little higher var(CS), just due to chance, and the stronger negative coefficient estimate for Professor A, along with the higher weight, caused the overall coefficient estimate to be different from the average of the coefficient estimates. Being close to the average coefficient estimate across professors would have been more ideal, with there being the same number of observations (25) for each professor. Still, the coefficient estimate was very close to the true effect, partly due to luck.

Despite not being planned this way (as I made the same-sized range of class-sizes across professors), there was bias because:

- a set of control variables grouped the sample by the professor
- there was a different class-size effect on evaluations for the various professors
- the variance (and standard deviation) of the key-X variable (class-size) was different across professors, due to randomness.

(This was a somewhat-rare case in which the bias moved the coefficient towards the true effect. Whereas I had the impulse to re-randomize and create a new set of data, in the spirit of the main lesson of the book of not changing the model or sample to seek a certain result, which would be the equivalent of p-hacking, I decided to keep this example.)

Still, this bias was fairly minor in our Chapter 4 example. If, on the other hand, the professors had significantly-different variances in the class-size variable, then some professors would be even more over-weighted in the sample (and other professors would be under-weighted), and it could cause a much greater bias.

Let's return to that example and add the realistic twist of large differences in variance in class-size across professors. The setup, largely following the earlier example, is the following:

- A university has four professors (A, B, C, and D), and we will assume they each teach a different course. (Thus, there are effectively four professor-course-interacted groups, but we can ignore the course.)
- There are 25 observations (classes) per professor … obviously this would be over several years, but we will not worry about the time factor.
- There is a range of class sizes for each professor that is indicated in Table 6.11. Whereas the range in class size was 40 for each professor in the Chapter 4 example, the range will be different for each professor in this case.
- The true effect of class-size on the average evaluation, for each professor, is also indicated in Table 6.11, with the same effects as the earlier example and there being no effect for Professors C and D. The true Average Treatment Effect that we hope to estimate is -0.01, which is the average of the four effects for the four professors, of -0.03, -0.01, 0, and 0 (since each professor has the same number of classes).
- I added randomness to the evaluation, so the coefficient estimates on class-size will not equal the effects I imposed, but should be in the general ballpark of the true effects.
- But the researcher does not know these individual effects, nor the overall Average Treatment Effect.

Figure 6.15 shows the new data, with the top chart showing the model without controlling for the professor, and the bottom chart having separate models for each professor. Table 6.12 then summarizes the results from the regression models. In the model without controls for the professor, the given line is the estimated regression model, which has an unexpected positive and significant coefficient estimate on class-size of 0.0007. We know this isn't correct from how I constructed the data to have a negative effect for two of the professors and a zero effect for the other two professors. And so it is likely due to omitted-factors bias because, as class size changes (moving from left to right in Figure 6.15), so does the professor. This shows why it is necessary to control for the professor. Some professors just tend to get higher ratings, and some tend to get lower ratings.

Table 6.11 Model set-up for class-size and professor evaluations

Professor	Range of class size	Class-size effect on the average evaluation that I imposed
A	10–40	-0.03
B	100–150	-0.01
C	175–250	0
D	300–400	0

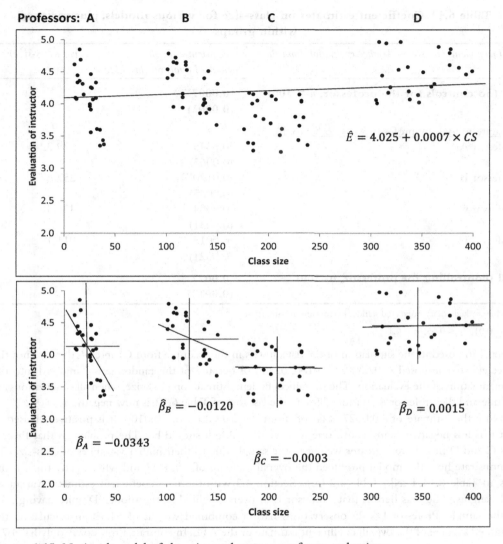

Figure 6.15 Notional model of class–size and average professor evaluations

Recall that including the set of professor dummy variables makes it so that classes are just being compared to other classes for the same professor and not to classes from other professors. In the bottom chart in Figure 6.15, the *operative variation* in class-size is from within the classes for a given professor – as class-size changes, the professor does not change. That is, again moving left to right, once you get to the right-most observation for each professor, it moves to a separate sub-model for the next professor and is not compared to the prior professor.

Table 6.12 also shows the coefficient estimates from the individual within-professor models, which are also embedded in the bottom chart of Figure 6.15. These models for individual professors are the same sub-models that the green elves are calculating behind the curtains and that will go into calculating the overall estimated effect. The coefficient estimates on class-size are consistent with the class-size

Table 6.12 Coefficient estimates on class-size for various models, plus variance within groups

Dependent variable = Average evaluation from the class	Coefficient estimate (standard error) on class-size	var (class-size)
All (no controls for the professor, n = 100)	**0.0007**** (0.0003)	
Separate models by professor (n = 25 for each)		
Professor A	−0.0343*** (0.0063)	79.32
Professor B	−0.0120*** (0.0035)	257.67
Professor C	−0.0004 (0.0031)	426.46
Professor D	0.0015 (0.0021)	911.19
All (controlling for professor, n=100)	**−0.0027** (0.0037)	

The heteroskedasticity-corrected standard errors are in parentheses.

***$p < 0.01$, **$p < 0.05$, *$p < 0.1$.

effects I imposed in the simulation of the data. Just as in the example from Chapter 4, they are not the exact effects I imposed (−0.0300, −0.0100, 0, and 0) because of the randomness I injected into the determination of the evaluation. The overall coefficient estimate on class-size, when all observations are include and the professor is controlled for, in the last row of Table 6.12, is now negative (−0.0027).

Now, the estimate of −0.0027 is far off from the true ATE of −0.0100. It is positively biased in that it is less negative, being about one-quarter the value it should be. The problem is that Professors C and D now have a greater weight in the sample due to their higher variances of class-size. To demonstrate how the model produced the overall estimate of −0.0027 and why exactly there is the bias, in Table 6.13, I redo Table 4.2 from Section 4.3 with the new coefficient estimates, variances, and weights. The bias here is that Professor D is over-weighted in the model. Despite having 25% of the sample, Professor D's 25 observations have a combined weight of 54.4% in calculating the weighted average of the overall coefficient estimate or the ATE. In contrast, Professor A only has 4.7%

Table 6.13 Demonstrating bias in how the overall coefficient estimate is estimated when controlling for categories

(1) Prof.	(2) N_g	(3) Pr(g)	(4) $\hat{\beta}_{1g}$	(5) var(CS)	(6) Weight numerator (3) × (5)	(7) Final weight	(8) $\hat{\beta}_{1g} \times$ weight (4) × (7)
A	25	0.2500	−0.0343	79.3100	19.8275	0.0474	−0.0016
B	25	0.2500	−0.0120	257.6767	64.4192	0.1539	−0.0018
C	25	0.2500	−0.0004	426.4601	106.6150	0.2547	−0.0001
D	25	0.2500	0.0015	911.1898	227.7974	0.5441	0.0008
	100				418.6591	1.0000	−0.0027

of the weight in the model. Note that this weighting naturally occurs with models that control for a classification.

As mentioned above, the rationale for why this weighting makes some (but not complete) sense is that the β_1's for Professors C and D will be more precisely estimated, as can be seen in Table 6.12 with the lower standard errors for Professors C and D and the highest standard error for Professor A, who had by far the lowest variance in CS. However, as described above, this weighting scheme has the underlying assumption that there is one universal effect that applies to everyone, which we know is not the case. And this is why our estimate of -0.0027 is so far off from the true ATE of -0.0100. (Note that the pure average of the four coefficient estimates for each professor is -0.0113, which is not too far off from the true ATE of -0.0100.)

I classify this bias as a "modeling mistake" because it is correctable by changing the model. It requires using sample weights for the observations that are the inverse of the variance, a correction developed by Gibbons et al. (2019). I will describe the correction in Section 8.2, after introducing the fixed-effects method.

Let me also draw a connection to an earlier lesson on what an insignificant estimate on the key-explanatory variable could mean (Section 5.8). The fourth reason given was that an insignificant estimate could be due to there being varying effects in the population (or sample), and the estimated effect is insignificant due to positive and negative effects canceling each other out or being drowned out by those observations with zero effects. That is part of what has occurred here, besides the bias from over-weighted groups. There actually were real effects for Professors A and B, but they were drowned out by the near-zero estimates for Professors C and D, and no meaningful nor significant overall effect was detected.

6.10.2 Direction of the bias

The direction of this bias is based on whether the over-weighted groups have effects that are below or above the Average Treatment Effect. This could be determined by estimating the model separately for each group after the other variables have been adjusted for. In the model above, the bias was positive (less negative) because the professors with the wider variance (Professors C and D) had more positive estimated effects than the other professors: i.e., near-zero estimated effects for Professors C and D, versus larger negative estimated effects for Professors A and B. (There were no other factors to adjust for in this model.)

6.10.3 Common cases in which groups could get over-weighted

Basically, this bias could occur in any situation in which the variance of the key-X variable could be different across groups. Just due to natural variation, there will always be some difference in variance across groups, causing some over-weighting of certain groups. The question is whether the differences across groups in the variance of the key-X variable and the differences in the causal effects are large enough to meaningfully bias the estimated effects of the key-X variable.

There is a multitude of cases in which this could occur. A generic case that I believe has a great risk for such bias would be policy analysis at the state or local level. Many studies estimating policy effects will use city- or state-level data. For example, from PITFALL #5, there are studies that attempt to estimate the effects of state income tax rates on state economic growth. Other studies examine the effects of state minimum-wage laws, medical-marijuana laws, drunk-driving laws, welfare laws, and more. These studies typically would use panel data with either pooled cross-sections or aggregate state-level data across numerous years. And the studies would typically control for the state with a set of dummy variables or fixed effects.

Let me note that such studies would also typically weight states or cities, to some extent, by population size. This would either be by having more individual-level observations for the larger states or using sample weights related to state populations for aggregate-level analyses. The over-weighting discussed here would be over- and under-weighting beyond differences in group weights based on the population size.

Controlling for the state (or city) would be essential to avoid omitted-factors bias. However, there would certainly be large differences in the variance of the key-X (policy) variable across states. For example, some states have no income-tax rate or have a rate that had not changed during a period of analysis. Those states would be under-weighted in the model; in fact, they would not contribute at all to the overall estimated tax-rate effect because a coefficient estimate on the tax rate could not be estimated for those states. The states that had the larger changes in the tax rate would be over-weighted.

The same would apply to evaluating state minimum-wage laws. The states with the larger changes would have greater variances in the minimum wage and consequently be over-weighted. And, if states that choose the larger minimum-wage increases are those that could handle the larger changes without too much employment loss, then there would be a bias in the estimated effects of minimum-wage increases towards zero.

This could also occur for cases in which a policy is implemented, represented as a dummy variable. For example, about half of all states have implemented medical-marijuana laws, allowing people to legally use marijuana to address a medical condition. If there were a study on how such laws affect some outcomes (say, overall marijuana use) over the 2000–2020 time period, then the states with the law implemented closer to the middle of the period (2010) would have a larger variance in the policy variable and would consequently be over-weighted. To demonstrate this, in a sequence of six numbers:

- The sequence of $(0, 0, 0, 1, 1, 1)$ – equivalent to implementing the policy halfway through a six-year period – has a variance of 0.30.
- The sequence of $(0, 1, 1, 1, 1, 1)$ or $(0, 0, 0, 0, 0, 1)$ – equivalent to implementing the policy before the second year or the last year – has a variance of 0.17, and would have just over one-half the weight of the state implementing the law half-way through the period.

And so, in the 2000-2020 period, Arizona (implementing the law in 2010), New Jersey (2010), and Massachusetts (2012) would be over-weighted, whereas Hawaii (2000) and Missouri (2018) would be under-weighted.

I would be amiss if I were not to also mention how this bias would apply to several of my research articles that examined how state unemployment rates affected various outcomes, such as teenage drug use (Arkes, 2007, 2011), teenage weight problems (Arkes, 2009), cigarette use (Arkes, 2012), and divorces (Arkes and Shen, 2014). Many others have had similar studies. As I will show in the next section, some states have a greater variation in the unemployment rates (e.g., California and Ohio) than others (Nebraska). This is a sustained pattern – that agricultural states have lower variances than other states in the unemployment rate. Thus, in any analysis on the effects of state unemployment rates, agricultural-dominant states would tend to be under-weighted beyond having low weights due to smaller populations.

Another situation in which there could be over-weighting is across demographic groups. As a basic example, Black adults tend to have a lower variance in years-of-schooling than non-Black adults, likely due to fewer Blacks graduating from college and attending graduate school. Thus, if estimating the effects of years-of-schooling on income, non-Blacks might be over-weighted relative to Blacks.

6.10.4 Evidence for the bias

Gibbons et al. (2019) examine whether there is evidence for such bias from eight "influential" articles using fixed effects (which effectively controls for a categorization) from one of the top economics journals, *The American Economic Review*. They first find evidence for what they call "heterogeneous treatment effects" in six of the eight studies. This is basically that different groups have different effects, a result that is not surprising to me at all but is worth mentioning to highlight how preposterous is the implicit assumption that there is a single universal effect. The authors then find that correcting for the bias (with the procedure I will describe in Section 8.2) produced estimates that were different from the reported estimates in these articles by economically- or statistically-significant amounts for six of the eight studies. This is a source of bias that still has received little attention. It's time to change that.

6.10.5 Could the same bias occur when adjusting for quantitative variables?

Yes, this is possible. However, I am not aware of any formula that could calculate this bias. And, for what it is worth, my intuition tells me this would be less pronounced than it is for controlling for a categorization.

As a brief informal example, from the model in Section 2.9,

$$\left(\widehat{income}\right)_i = -34{,}027 + 5395 \times (educ)_i + 367 \times (afqt)_i \tag{2.21}$$

I found that adjusting for the AFQT score decreased the *operative variation* in the years-of-schooling variable (measured as the variance) more for those in the top third of AFQT scores relative to the others.

Furthermore, in these models:

$$income = \beta_0 + \beta_1 \times (educ) + \beta_2 \times (black) + \varepsilon \tag{6.16}$$

$$income = \beta_0 + \beta_1 \times (educ) + \beta_2 \times (black) + \beta_3 \times (afqt) + \varepsilon \tag{6.17}$$

when I include the AFQT score (again, a quantitative variable), the variance of years-of-schooling-adjusted-for-AFQT decreases more for Blacks than non-Blacks, causing the effective weight for Blacks to decrease by about 2.1 percentage points. Whereas this is not a large amount, it shows that adding a quantitative variable could impact the effective weights across groups in the model. This is something that I think should be investigated by people smarter than I am.

What to check for: over-weighted groups

Assess whether the variance of the key-X variable and the effect of the key-X variable on the outcome vary, by a meaningful amount, across groups that are controlled for.

6.11 How to choose the best set of control variables (model selection)

In this section, I discuss another highly-misunderstood topic: choosing the optimal set of control variables. This is often called **model selection**. Recall that control variables are those that are included in a model to help identify the true causal effects of the key-explanatory variables (or the key empirical relationships for other regression objectives). Opinions vary widely on the criteria for choosing the right set of control variables. Poor choices in choosing control variables contribute to the plethora of incorrect research results.

The purpose of using control variables is to address any potential PITFALLS, particularly omitted-factors bias and improper reference groups. That is, for the objective of estimating causal effects, control variables help toward ruling out alternative explanations for why the empirical relationship is what it is. At the same time, including the wrong control variables might introduce PITFALLS (using mediating factors or outcomes as controls, and improper reference groups), causing bias in the coefficient estimate.

The generally easy part of choosing which control variables to use is avoiding mediating factors and outcomes of the key-X variable. The more difficult part is determining what control variables to include to address the three types of omitted-factors bias. The third type, whether there is a replacement action for receiving low values of the treatment, is also part of PITFALL #6 of improper reference groups. The other issues with improper reference groups (having the correct counterfactual and whether the control group has a lower-intensity amount of the treatment) are more about characterizing the treatment correctly than choosing the correct set of control variables.

6.11.1 Choosing control variables to minimize omitted-factors bias from spurious correlation

Recall the steps for assessing whether there is omitted-factors bias from spurious correlation:

*   **Step 1**: Determine the factors of the key-X variable. Think about what causes the key-X variable to be high for some observations and low for others. Or, for a dummy variable, what causes some observations to get the treatment (have a value of 1) vs. not get the treatment (0)?
*   **Step 2**: Determine if any of those factors could affect the outcome independently (i.e., beyond through its effects on the key-X variable) and are not fully held constant in the model.

So we want to control for any factor that could affect the key-X variable and the outcome. That is, we want to convert such *bad variation* from *operative* to *held-constant variation*. Thus, we need to determine the main sources of variation in the key-X variable.

Let's take the example from Section 6.8 on how the state unemployment rate (UR) affects teenage drug use (Y). Recall that this involves a sample of individual teenagers across the country from a range of years. Figure 6.16 shows the breakdown of the sources of variation for two models: a model with just the unemployment rate and a model that adds state and year dummy variables. The subscripts are important here:

*   subscript i is the individual teenager
*   subscript s is the individual teenager's state
*   subscript t is the year (time) the individual teenager is observed.

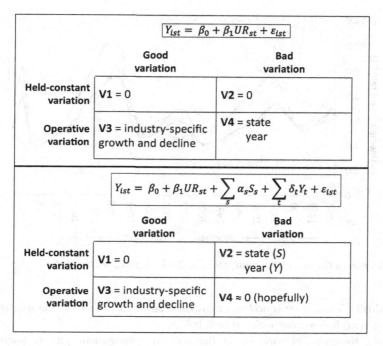

Figure 6.16 Sources of variation for state unemployment rates (with the outcome of teenage drug use)

In the top panel, because there are no control variables, there is no *held-constant variation*. All variation in the state unemployment rate is *operative* in that it is used to determine how the state unemployment rate is related to teenage drug use. Because states have different levels of the unemployment rate and teenage drug use, there are 51 potential sources of omitted-factors bias from 50 states plus Washington, DC. For example, over the 1986–2021 period, California had a higher average unemployment rate (7.1%) than the U.S. (5.9%) and likely had a higher teen drug use rate due to medical-marijuana laws. Thus, California would create a positive omitted-factors bias if not controlled for. Likewise, because the national unemployment rate and nationwide teenage drug use naturally ebbs and flows, the year could create omitted-factors bias. Thus, the state and year are considered sources of *bad variation* in the state unemployment rate.

The variation in the state unemployment rate from industry-specific growth and decline, on the other hand, should be *good variation* in that there would not be any systematic reason why a certain industry growth or decline would be correlated with other factors determining the extent of teen drug use in a state (with the notable exception of the marijuana industry). That said, omitted-factors bias from the incidental correlation between industry-specific growth for a state's industries and other factors contributing to teen drug use could not be ruled out.

In the bottom panel of Figure 6.16, in which I include control (dummy) variables for each state and year (excluding one for a reference group), the state and year are converted from sources of *operative* to *held-constant variation*. (Given that these are control variables, it does not matter which state or year is left out as the reference group.) Now, in the model, the *operative variation* in the state unemployment rate for the estimation of its effect on teen drug use no longer comes from state or time

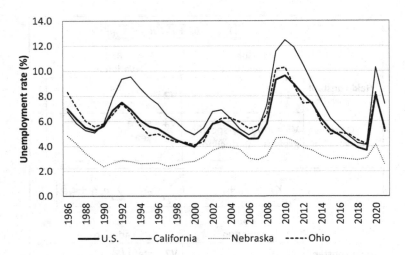

Figure 6.17 Trends in the unemployment rate for the U.S. and selected states

periods, individually. Thus, there is no longer any omitted-factors bias from the state or time period. Hopefully, there is no *bad-operative variation* (V4) left.

So, hopefully, the *operative variation* in the state unemployment rate is coming from the industry-specific growth and decline, which causes "within-state changes relative to other states." I believe this would be *good variation* (V3) because there is no systematic reason I envision for how that could affect teenage drug use. What exactly would the "within-state change relative to other states" look like? Consider Figure 6.17, which shows (1986–2021) annual unemployment rates (UR) for the United states and for three states: California, Nebraska, and Ohio. Here are a few points:

- Compared to the United States, California almost always has higher URs, Nebraska has lower URs, and Ohio has about the same URs. These average differences would be part of the variation in the UR variable due to states.
- Any change in the UR for the United States would represent variation in UR due to year effects.
- The within-state changes relative to other states can be seen in how states have different changes relative to other states (or relative to the country as a whole). Note that, from the Financial Crisis (2008 to 2010), whereas the national UR increased by about 5 percentage points (roughly 4.5% to 9.5%), California's UR increased by over 7 percentage points, and Nebraska's UR increased by less than 2 percentage points.

The estimate for β_1 in the bottom chart in Figure 6.16 would be based on this within-state variation, which hopefully is *good variation*. It would estimate how much higher or lower teenage drug use tends to be with a one-unit higher unemployment rate in a given state relative to other states. Note that this is similar to the example of how class-size affects instructor evaluations from Section 4.3. Just as the estimated class-size effect was based on within-instructor variation, the estimate for β_1 here would be based on within-state variation, after factoring out the year effects. I get into more details on this in Section 8.1, on the discussion of fixed-effects models.

6.11.2 Choosing control variables to minimize omitted-factors bias from incidental correlation

From Section 6.5, the steps for identifying omitted-factors bias from incidental correlation were:

- **Step 1**: Determine major factors that could affect the dependent variable.
- **Step 2**: Assess whether any of those factors that are not fully held constant in the model could be incidentally correlated with the key-X variable.

Let's consider here a randomized control trial. Let's say that a university wished to study the merits of reducing by one-half the number of core-curriculum courses a student must take, in order to give students more choice on the courses they take. We'll say that the university randomizes students in a single cohort based on whether they had an even or odd birthdate so that odd birthdays have reduced core-curriculum courses. (We'll ignore the fairness issue.) The outcomes they could examine could include whether the student: dropped out, graduated in four years, and attended graduate school within two years of graduation.

The randomization process should help to reduce any omitted-factors bias from a spurious (systematic) correlation. However, it is always possible that students with a greater propensity to drop out or not graduate in time would, *incidentally*, be disproportionately more or less likely to be assigned to the treatment group receiving the new core curriculum standards. This would especially be a concern for a sample that was not too large. Thus, controlling for certain characteristics (e.g., high school GPA, entrance-test scores, etc.) could help reduce potential omitted-factors bias that could result, even with a randomized treatment.

6.11.3 Choosing control variables to minimize omitted-factors bias from replacement actions or to set the proper reference group

The steps for assessing whether a replacement action could create omitted-factors bias (or bias from improper reference groups), the steps were:

- **Step 1**: Assess whether there would be a tendency to respond to having low values of the key-X variable or not receiving the treatment.
- **Step 2**: Assess whether any response could be something that could affect the dependent variable.

The example I had used earlier on this topic was that, when examining how wine consumption affects health, those not drinking wine might be drinking beer or hard liquor instead. Thus, to minimize this type of omitted-factors bias, one should include in the model control variables for beer and hard-liquor consumption, or whatever the replacement action could be. As mentioned above, this addresses the first type of bias in PITFALL #6 on improper reference groups.

6.11.4 When it is not necessary to control for a variable

If a potential control variable does not meet the criteria for being included, based on the three scenarios I just discussed, then it would actually be okay to exclude it from a model.

Let me commit econometric heresy and make the argument that there are some cases in which it is not necessary to control for demographic characteristics. Let's return to the issue of how the state unemployment rate affects teenage drug use, and let's suppose that we have individual-level data on teenagers from each state over ten years and assess whether it meets any of the criteria above.

Demographic characteristics could affect the outcome – for example, teen males are more likely to use drugs than teen females. But such characteristics should not affect nor be correlated in any meaningful way with the state unemployment rate, which is based on hundreds of thousands or even millions of people over age 16 in the state. Furthermore, the demographic characteristics are in no way representative of a replacement action. And, with a large-enough sample, there should not be any meaningful incidental correlation between the demographics of the subject and the state unemployment rate. Thus, there should not be any omitted-factors bias by excluding demographic characteristics as control variables.

That said, controlling for demographic characteristics would not harm the model, as they are not mediating factors. Basically, you could control for these characteristics or not, and it shouldn't make that much difference.

6.11.5 Criteria to use and not use for deciding whether to include a control variable in a model

I will now lay out criteria here for whether to include a control variable in a model that has the objective of estimating causal effects. These criteria mostly follow from the discussion so far, particularly from the PITFALLS and the example just discussed. The criteria are:

1. Theory suggests that one of the following could be the case:
   a. the *control variable* could affect the outcome *and* the key-explanatory variable(s)
   b. the *control variable* could affect the outcome and be incidentally correlated with the key-explanatory variable
   c. the *control variable* represents a replacement action from not receiving the treatment, or having low exposure to the treatment
   d. the *control variable* helps towards establishing the optimal reference group for the key-explanatory variable.
2. The *control variable* is not a product of the key-explanatory variable and is not an outcome itself.
3. For quantitative variables, the coefficient estimate on the *control variable* is not in an inconceivable direction or of an inconceivable magnitude. (This is less of an issue with dummy variables, as they merely involve estimating within-group coefficient estimates.)
4. The *control variable* is not too highly correlated with the key-explanatory variable.
5. The *control variable* does not violate these PITFALLS:
   o It is not affected by the outcome (reverse causality)
   o People do not select different values of the *control variable* based on expectations of the effects of that variable on the outcome (self-selection bias)

The first criterion is the basis for including any control variable, with (a) – (c) addressing omitted-factors bias and (d) addressing improper reference groups. If the variable should not affect the outcome or is not possibly correlated with the key-explanatory variable, then there is no need to control for the variable. The second criterion just speaks to whether the control variable would be a mediating factor or outcome for the key-explanatory variable (PITFALL #5).

The third criterion is a bit controversial. The idea here is that, for a quantitative variable that could only have a positive effect (if any), according to theory, a few non-representative outlying observations could cause its coefficient estimate to be negative. The incorrect estimate may exacerbate any omitted-factors bias. The important part of this criterion is being certain that the coefficient estimate cannot conceivably be in the direction it is. Also, if a variable has an inconceivably large estimated effect, then give some thought as to whether this apparently-overstated estimate would affect other estimates and whether it is best to exclude the variable from the model. This is part of the "art" in regression modeling.

For the fourth criterion, if a control variable were too highly correlated with the key-explanatory variable or would not allow much independent variation in the key-explanatory variable, then it would be difficult to generate precise effects of the key-explanatory variable. The effects of the key-explanatory variable would be split between the key-explanatory variable and other factors that almost always move with the variable. This was discussed in Section 5.4.1 on *multicollinearity*.

For the fifth criterion, if a control variable were subject to reverse causality or self-selection bias, then the coefficient on it may absorb too much of the variation in the dependent variable, leaving less to be explained by the key-explanatory variable. This is like PITFALL #5 regarding using outcomes as control variables, as part of the effect is being factored out.

The other PITFALLS are not important for a control variable. If a control variable were subject to omitted-factors bias or measurement error, it does not mean that the variable should not be included, as it would still likely reduce any bias. Omitted-factors bias on the control variable can actually be a good thing, as it could capture the effects of other important variables that could be correlated with the key-explanatory variable. This means that it is okay if a control variable is not fully random with respect to the outcome, as long as it is not subject to reverse causality or self-selection bias.

In addition, a variable that has measurement error still could provide value to the model in helping to control for an important factor. Any bias from measurement error should just change the magnitude of the coefficient estimate without changing its sign. With a biased estimate on the control variable, there would likely still be omitted-factors bias for the key-explanatory variable, but less bias than one would get from not including that control variable. Finally, it is also okay if a control variable has its own mediating factor as another control variable, as it would just provide more information.

There may be some potential control variables that satisfy some of the criteria but not all. This is where judgment needs to be used to determine which PITFALL causes the least bias.

One criterion that some believe should be used is that the variable has to be statistically significant. I do not use this criterion because of what we learned in Section 5.8 about how an insignificant estimate does not mean that the variable has no effect/association. Regardless of the significance, the coefficient estimate is usually the best guess on the contribution of the variable in explaining the outcome. Furthermore, an insignificant coefficient estimate still imparts information, provided it satisfies the third criterion above on the estimate being conceivable.

Also, many use as a guide some goodness-of-fit measures. We saw R^2 and Adjusted R^2 back in Section 2.5, with higher values being indicative of a better fit of the model. There is also the Akaike Information Criterion (AIC), the corrected-AIC (AICc), and the Bayesian Information Criterion

Table 6.14 Reasons for including and excluding a potential control variable and what criteria *not to use*, when estimating causal effects

Reasons to include	*Reasons to exclude*	*Criteria not to use*
• It could affect both the key-X variable and the outcome • It could be incidentally correlated with the key-X variable and affect the outcome • It could be a response action to getting minimal-to-no treatment • It helps set the proper reference group for the key-explanatory variable	• It is a mediating factor for the key-X variable • It is an outcome of the key-X variable • It is too highly correlated with the key-X variable so that the key-X variable has an inadequate amount of independent variation • It could be affected by the outcome • It is subject to self-selection bias • Its coefficient estimate, when included in the model, has an inconceivable sign or magnitude	• Whether the control variable itself is subject to omitted-factors bias • Whether it has measurement error • Whether it is a mediating factor for another control variable (not for the key-X variable) • Whether it is significant • Whether it affects the goodness-of-fit (R^2, Adjusted-R^2, AIC, BIC) … except for choosing how to characterize variables

(BIC). I will leave details on these measures to Chapter 10 on time series models, but the lower values are the better fits. These are the criteria that are usually considered when one discusses "Model Selection." However, I would argue against using these to decide whether a control variable should be included in a model, as the set of criteria described above is more useful and appropriate. But these goodness-of-fit measures could help in deciding how to best characterize a key-explanatory variable or a control variable. For example, these criteria may speak to whether, in order to provide a better fit of the data, a certain control variable should be represented in a quadratic form, as a spline, or as a set of dummy variables for various values of the variable.

Table 6.14 summarizes the rules on whether to include or exclude a potential control variable, along with giving the criteria that should *not* be used to determine whether a control variable should be included. When it says "not to use" the criteria, it means that this should not be a consideration. Again, this is for the regression objective of estimating causal effects.

6.12 What could affect the validity of the sample?

In some cases, the sample for a regression includes the whole population that is being evaluated. But, in most cases, a sample is just that—a sample of the intended population that you are attempting to describe. For example, a clinical trial for a cancer procedure would be intended for the population of patients for a particular cancer. When you only have part of a population, the important question is whether the sample is representative of the intended population. If the sample were non-representative, then making inferences on the population would be questionable.

There are three main causes of samples being non-representative of the intended population. The first is **sample-selection bias**, which occurs when the sample is non-random due to subjects (observations) being selected for the sample based on some factor related to the outcome. Note that *self-selection bias* (Section 6.6) is that people are selecting themselves into a certain value of the key-X variable, whereas *sample-selection bias* is selecting oneself or being selected into a sample for a reason connected to the outcome.

Consider researchers who want to examine the impact of a pharmaceutical drug to treat a certain medical condition. They need the approval of subjects to participate in the study. Who is going to participate? It would probably tend to be those who suffer more or were more concerned about the toll of the health condition, which may not be a random sample of people with the medical condition. Even if the researchers design a valid randomized experiment among the study volunteer subjects, there may still be sample-selection bias based on who volunteers. This would cause bias in the estimated effect if the drug had different effects on mild versus severe forms of the medical condition.

A second cause for non-representative samples is attrition bias in longitudinal surveys, which are surveys that track people over time. **Attrition bias** occurs when those who stay in the sample are different from those who leave or stop responding (or "attrite"). The reasons for attriting from a longitudinal survey could be positive or negative: they might attrite due to becoming homeless and not reachable for surveyors, being too busy in an important job, moving overseas due to a good job offer, or escaping authorities for tax evasion. So, if you were estimating the effects of schooling on income with longitudinal data, the estimate may not be representative of the population parameter if the effect is higher or lower for attriters than for those still in the sample at the time the data are used.

A third cause of non-representative samples is strategic sampling for a survey, where certain parts of the population (e.g., low-income groups) may be oversampled. Strategic sampling may be for the purpose of ensuring that there are enough observations for separate analyses of particular subpopulation groups, which occurs often in social science surveys. Fortunately, the surveys often provide sampling weights, which can typically be applied to regression models to make it nationally representative – see Section 3.3.

While the latter cause of non-representative samples can be addressed with sample weights (when available), the other two causes of non-representative samples are not easily addressed. One method that has been used is the Inverse Mills Ratio – also known as the Heckman correction (Heckman, 1979). However, this method requires an identifying variable that affects sample inclusion, but not the outcome, as well as data on non-participants in the sample. Because such an identifying variable is very difficult to find, it is rare that adequate corrections can be made in the case of sample selection or attrition bias.[2]

One other (less prevalent) cause of non-representative samples is that the period of analysis may not be relevant for making inferences about what would happen today. For example, in examining the effects of parental divorce on children's outcomes, an analysis of data from 30 years ago (when divorce was less frequent) may not be relevant for today, as there would likely be less stigma and feelings of being an exception with being from a divorced home due to the greater prevalence today.

What to check for: non-representative samples

Is some factor causing the sample to be different in nature from the population for which you are trying to make inferences? Typical causes include sample-selection bias, attrition bias, and strategic sampling for a survey.

6.13 Applying the PITFALLS to studies on estimating divorce effects on children

It has been estimated that 40% of all children born to married parents experience their parents divorcing by age 18 (Amato, 2005; Kennedy and Ruggles, 2014). Divorces (and separations) can be quite harmful to children. Immediate effects could be that their academic achievement is affected, which could then have lasting effects on their future academic and economic success. Any subsequent co-parenting conflict or instability from later parental relationships and marital transitions could cause further problems for children. All that said, divorces could be helpful for some children whose families have so much conflict that the parents divorcing may help foster a more peaceful upbringing.

Many researchers have attempted to estimate the effects of divorce on children's outcomes, including myself. This is not easy, as it is not random which parents end up divorcing. These researchers (including yours truly again) have argued that such studies are important because they could help inform parents on how their children would be affected if they were deciding how much effort to exert to avoid a divorce. I now disagree with that. I believe that this is a situation in which parents, if they were being objective, would be able to better gauge how a divorce would affect their children than what they could learn from a research study. This is because all situations (e.g., the conflict and the functionality of the household) are different, and children vary in how much they would be affected by parental divorce. In addition, such studies suffer from several biases, so a given study probably could not be trusted to give an unbiased estimated effect, including my own studies. These biases, however, make for a great case study to apply numerous PITFALLS.

The basic model would be some form of:

$$Y_i = X_i\beta_1 + \beta_2 D_i + \varepsilon_i \tag{6.18}$$

where:
- Y is some outcome for a child (academic achievement, behavior problems, substance use)
- D is an indicator (dummy) variable for the parents being divorced
- X is a set of other factors that could help towards estimating the true causal effect of the divorce.

The variables in X would represent factors that could affect both whether a child's parents may divorce and the child's academic achievement. This could include demographic or socio-economic factors, such as parents' income and education. What I describe next are all of the potential PITFALLS that would need to be addressed to properly estimate the causal effects of divorce on children.

Reverse causality: This is probably minor enough so that it would have minimal effects on the estimated effect of a divorce, but it is possible that the child's academic or behavioral problems could lead to greater tension for the parents, which increases the likelihood of a divorce.

Omitted-factors bias: This is likely the most applicable and important PITFALL for this issue. There are many potential factors that could affect both the probability that the parents divorce and the child's outcomes. Such factors could include family income, the level of dysfunction in the family, the intensity of parental arguments, and parental substance abuse. To the extent that these factors were not controlled for, they would likely contribute to a bias in the estimated effect of the divorce in the direction of divorce being more harmful (e.g., a negatively-biased effect of divorce on academic achievement).

Self-selection bias: The idea behind self-selection bias is that the parents may choose whether to divorce partly based on how they believe it would affect the child. If the parents believe that their child(ren) would suffer from a divorce, the parents may make an extra effort to avoid a divorce. On the other hand, if the conflict is so great that the divorce would likely make for a better environment for the child(ren), or if the parents believe they could have a seamless divorce without too much co-parenting conflict, then they could be more likely to divorce. Basically, the divorce is not random, and it may be partly dictated by what the expected effect would be on the child. Of course, parents may not know exactly how their child would be affected, and some parents may make this choice regardless of how their children are affected. But assuming that there is some connection between parents' beliefs and the reality of how children would be affected, there could be self-selection bias, contributing, in this case, towards "beneficial effects" (i.e., divorce improving the child's outcomes). Thus, the harmful effects of a divorce could be understated.

Measurement error: What may be the consequential event for children is the separation, and this may occur long before an actual divorce. Sometimes, surveys ask parents about separation dates, but most surveys I have seen only ask parents about the divorce. It is possible that some parents may answer survey questions based on the separation date rather than the divorce date, but it would be impossible to know which parents do this. If there were any appreciable measurement error, it would likely contribute to a bias towards zero.

Improper reference group: One concern would be making sure the reference group ("no parental divorce") is what you want. This group could theoretically include those children who always lived in a single-parent household. They technically do not experience parental divorce, and so their experiences may not be the ones to compare to those experiencing a divorce, as this would not speak to the policy issues described above. In addition, children whose parents separated but have not divorced would technically be in the reference group, which is tied to the measurement-error issue mentioned above. One way to address this could be to classify these children whose parents were never married or are now separated to be in separate categories, so there could be four categories of children (the reference group of parents being married, parents never married, parents are separated, and parents are divorced). Alternatively, one could start with a sample of children whose parents were married in an initial period and compare the outcomes in a period several years later for those whose parents divorced (and maybe separated) to those children whose parents' marriage remained intact. There is also the possibility of remarriage of a parent. Perhaps, this could be ignored, and the focus would be on the divorce of the child's biological parents, with the remarriages (after a divorce) being part of the overall effect of the initial divorce.

Over-weighted groups: The typical control variables for racial/ethnic groups and parents' education could cause some groups to be over-weighted. For example, if there were a variable to separate families based on low-vs.-high parents' education, then it is possible that the effect of parental divorce on children's outcomes was different for these two groups. In addition, I believe divorce rates are higher for parents with low education, which would mean that their divorce rate is closer to 50%, which would maximize the variance in the key-X variable of whether the parents are divorced. Thus, children with less-educated parents would have greater weight, which, combined with any different causal effects, would bias the overall estimated effect.

6.14 Applying the PITFALLS to nutritional studies

It is difficult to go onto your favorite news website without seeing the results of a new study on what foods or vitamins contribute to or help prevent certain illnesses. There may be studies that say that certain foods are not as harmful as we had thought. What does John Ioannidis, the Greek doctor/ medical researcher mentioned in Chapter 1, say about these studies? According to Freedman (2010), Ioannidis says, "Ignore them all."

Well, maybe that's going too far. Or maybe it isn't. I won't single out any particular study, but just discuss them in general. Let's think about all of the potential problems with such studies and the questions to ask.

First, the benefits or harms from foods could take years to surface. Most nutritional studies have not tracked people very long. Thus, there may not be enough variation in the outcomes to identify the effects.

Second, people routinely misreport their food/nutrition intake. For long-term retrospective studies, it is doubtful that people can remember what they would typically eat. This means that there would be significant measurement error, which would likely bias the estimates toward zero (PITFALL #4).

Third, eating certain foods is not random, and the estimated effects of certain foods may be subject to omitted-factors bias (PITFALL # 2). The factors that determine how much of certain kinds of foods people eat are likely correlated with other factors that affect people's health. For example, people who tend to eat oatmeal may be more health-conscious and less likely to eat Big Macs or Loco-Mocos. Likewise, those who do not eat fresh fruits and vegetables probably are not very health-conscious. Thus, diet is not assigned randomly.

Fourth, researchers can design the reference group (or equivalently, what other factors to control for) so as to maximize an effect (PITFALL #6). For example, for the oatmeal/cholesterol issue, eaters of bacon and sausage (high-cholesterol foods) may eat less oatmeal because they are having their bacon/sausage instead. Thus, it would be easier to find a significant difference in cholesterol levels across different levels of oatmeal consumption if bacon and sausage were not controlled for (making them part of the reference group). Factoring out the bacon/sausage eaters from the reference group (which could be at least partly accomplished by controlling for bacon/sausage consumption) would provide a more appropriate comparison group.

Fifth, there is the possibility of reverse causality (PITFALL #1). If someone develops high cholesterol, they might increase how much oatmeal they eat.

Sixth, if you examine enough types of food/nutrition and enough types of illnesses, there will undoubtedly be some significant relationships. In fact, if the food had no effect on any illness, then 5% of different types of food would, by randomness, be significantly related (positively or negatively) to a given illness at the 5% significance level. These factors need to be considered when evaluating statistical significance – see Section 5.5.

Seventh, consider who funded the research. If the dairy industry funded a study on the effects of dairy consumption, I can guess what it would say. I doubt the funder would allow a bad result to be published. (Coincidentally, I find myself eating cheese as I write this.)

Ioannidis (2013) noted the extremely poor results from replicating nutritional research claims with randomized trials. He notes how difficult it is to accurately measure nutritional intake and that, while the new randomized trials have been promising, we need to significantly increase the size of these studies to tens of thousands in order to obtain any meaningful results.

A new study examined the extent of agreement and potential reasons for differences between observational and randomized studies (Schwingshackl et al., 2021). They generally found no systematic bias for the observational studies consistently overstating or understating nutritional effects, relative to the results of randomized studies. That said, any individual observational study could be highly-biased, as could a randomized study. The main reasons for this are differences in samples (and their characteristics such as age), the amount or type of exposure to the nutritional component, and the comparison (control) group. The sample is important because certain interventions (such as fish oil) would be more beneficial for older people who are more likely to have cardiovascular issues. An example of differences in exposure could be an observational study examining the effects of beef consumption vs. a randomized study examining the effects of grass-fed beef consumption. And the comparison group is important, as the standard American diet (now growing to other countries, unfortunately) that would often be the control group in an observational study would be different from a well-designed randomized study that made the comparison group some other type of diet.

So, if you can't trust these studies, what can you do? The best thing to do may just be to use common sense. What types of foods do obese people tend to eat more of than other people? Does a certain type of food taste unnatural (think of some sweeteners in diet soft drinks)? If pesticides kill insects, is it reasonable to conclude that they would be harmless to humans? Would variety be better than eating the same types of food (for different nutrients and to avoid too much of something that may be bad for you)?

6.15 Chapter summary

If there were only two takeaways you receive from this entire book, I would hope they would be:

1. The hot hand in basketball is real and not a myth, as many famous economists, statisticians, psychologists, authors, and Nobel Prize winners continue to argue.
2. Whenever you hear a research finding from a friend or on the news, before believing it, you would ask yourself "Is there an alternative reason for this finding?"

This chapter focuses on those alternative reasons for results for the main objective of regression analysis: estimating the causal effect of a treatment on an outcome. The general story of this chapter is:

- Regressions indicate how two variables move together, after adjusting for other factors.
- There are many reasons why two variables could move together (or not move together), other than due to the causal effect of the treatment on the outcome (or lack of any effect).
- The PITFALLS present some of these common reasons, and they result in a biased estimate of the causal effect.
- These PITFALLS need to be considered as you select the optimal set of control variables to use in a model.
- These PITFALLS need to be considered when assessing the soundness of other studies and when properly assessing how likely it is that your estimates represent the true causal effect.
- To the extent that the biases cannot be addressed, it is important to acknowledge this so that readers can properly judge a study.

Table 6.15 summarizes the PITFALLS in terms of what to check for to assess whether the PITFALL applies to a study and the direction of the bias.

Table 6.15 A summary of the 7 PITFALLS

PITFALL	What to check for	Direction of bias
Non-random explanatory variables		
1. Reverse causality	Does the outcome affect an X variable?	The direction of how the outcome affects the treatment variable
2. Omitted-factors bias	Does some omitted factor affect both the key-X variable and the outcome? Might there be an incidental correlation between factors of the key-X variable and the outcome? Could those receiving little-or-no treatment engage in a replacement action that affects the outcome?	The sign of the product of the correlations between the omitted-factor to the treatment variable and to the outcome
3. Self-selection bias	Did the subject choose or get assigned to the key-X variable by some means that is related to the personal benefits or costs of the X variable?	Positive if higher values of the outcome are good; negative if higher values are bad
Data issues		
4. Measurement error	Is there non-trivial error in the coding of the explanatory variable? Is the X variable imperfect in representing the intended concept?	Towards zero if the measurement error is random; uncertain otherwise
Common modeling mistakes		
5. Using mediating factors or outcomes as control variables	Is there a control variable included in the model that is a product of the key-X variable (or determined after the key-X variable)?	The opposite of the sign of the mechanism of how the treatment affects the outcome
6. Improper reference groups	Does the reference group represent the correct counterfactual? Is there a replacement action that impacts the outcome? Does the reference group have a lower-intensity effect of the treatment?	Positive if the reference group in the analysis has lower values of the outcome than what the proper reference group has
7. Over-weighted groups	Could the variance of the key-X variable and the effect of the key-X variable on the outcome vary across groups that are controlled for?	Positive if the groups being over-weighted have more-positive treatment effects than the other groups; negative otherwise

It is rare that an analysis will come out of an overall assessment 100% clean. In survey data, there is often some degree of measurement error, perhaps due to people misreporting parts of their life such as substance use or income. There may be omitted factors that you cannot do anything about. Also, in some cases, fixing some problems may create other problems.

In Chapter 8, I will introduce several methods of addressing the issues related to non-random explanatory variables. Sometimes, the fix is near perfect … other times, it just improves the model but still may leave doubt.

Not being able to perfectly address some of the PITFALLS does not mean that you should automatically throw away or discount the research. Rather, you would want to take into account how much it violates the issue and how egregious a problem that specific PITFALL turns out to be. It is important to understand that in such cases in which the inherent problems are potentially large, the problem would need to be addressed for the research to have any credibility.

Alternatively, you could call the relationship you are analyzing a *correlation* or an *association* that suggests the possibility of a causal effect. Hopefully, your analysis would be considered a stepping stone for further efforts to better capture the causal effect rather than anything that would guide policy. It would be important to acknowledge the limitations of such a study.

When conducting research, it is best to do the responsible thing and acknowledge all potential biases and PITFALLS of the research. Be careful with your interpretations. If any PITFALLS remain, use more modified language such as "the evidence in this analysis *supports* the theory that …" rather than "the evidence *proves*" or "the results *provide strong evidence for* the theory." And add the necessary caveats.

Exercises

1. Explain how the Yogi quote in the second paragraph of Section 6.6 relates to PITFALL #3 on self-selection bias.
2. Explain how the Yogi quote in the first paragraph of Section 6.8 relates to PITFALL #5 on including outcomes as control variables.
3. Explain how the Yogi quote in the first paragraph of Section 6.9 relates to PITFALL #6 on using improper reference groups.
4. For an analysis of how meditation affects the number of hours a person sleeps, give an example of at least one source of *good variation* and at least one source of *bad variation*.
5. Use the data set, **tv–bmi–ecls**. A version of this data was used for a 2015 study examining the relationship between TV watching and BMI (Peck et al., 2015). The data come from the Early Childhood Longitudinal Survey (ECLS).
   a. Estimate the following model:
      - Dependent variable = *zbmi2* (this is the percentile for BMI, measured in the Spring of first grade, based on the standard-normal z-score, adjusted for gender and age-in-months)
      - Key-X variable = *tv2* (this is the average daily hours of TV reported by the child's parents)
      - Weight the model by the sample weight, *wt2*
      - Correct for heteroskedasticity.
   b. Estimate the model again, adding in the following control variables:
      - race/ethnicity (*black hisp other unknown*) with "white" the excluded group
      - demographics (*female age2*)
      Comparing the coefficient estimate on *tv2* with that from (a), what can you learn?
   c. Explain how "family income" could potentially lead to omitted-factors bias in estimating how TV hours affect BMI.

d. Estimate the model in (b) again, but add in the following two income variables to mimic what Peck et al. (2015) used:
- *faminc2_40_100k* (family income between $40,000 and $100,000)
- *faminc2_100k_plus* (family income >$100,000)
- the excluded group is <$40,000)

e. Could there still be omitted-factors bias from "family income" in the model in (d)?

f. Instead of the family-income variables used in (d), use the following as control variables:
- *income2* (this is the median of $5,000-wide categories of family income that parents indicated on the survey)
- *incsq2* (the square of *income2*)
- *income2_75, income2_100, income2_200* (which are three categories at the high end that have ranges larger than $5,000)

What does the change in the coefficient estimate on *tv2* tell you?

6. Which of these is more likely to suffer from self-selection bias? Explain and give the likely direction of the bias.

Case 1: Estimating how participating in a voluntary meditation program affects an 11th grader's GPA?

Case 2: Estimating how having an unemployed father affects an 11th grader's GPA?

7. Which of the following would be more likely to suffer from reverse causality? Explain.

Case 1: With observational (non-experimental) data, estimating how blood-pressure medicine affects the likelihood of getting the flu.

Case 2: With observational (non-experimental) data, estimating how meditation affects blood pressure.

8. Which of the following is more likely to suffer from bias due to measurement error? Explain and give the likely direction of the bias.

Case 1: Estimating how a person's reported cocaine use affects their income.

Case 2: Estimating how the number of murders per capita in a county affects the county's unemployment rate.

9. Which of the following control variables would be more likely to cause bias due to being a mediating factor for estimating the effect of class size on 6th-grade student math achievement? What would be the likely direction of the bias from including the control variable? Explain.

Control variable 1: The amount of parental help on homework.

Control variable 2: The amount of individual time with the teacher.

10. Consider the following model estimating peer effects on marijuana use among teenagers:

$$MJ_i = \beta_1 \times (MJ\text{-}P)_i + X_i\beta_2 + \varepsilon_i,$$

where *MJ* is a measure of the person's marijuana use, *MJ-P* is a measure of the marijuana use of the person's peers, and *X* is a set of demographic factors.

a. Describe why and how (i.e., in what direction) reverse causality could bias the estimate for β_1.

    b. Describe why and how omitted-factors bias could affect the estimate for β_1.

    c. Describe why and how self-selection bias could affect the estimate for β_1.

    d. Describe why and how measurement error could bias the estimate for β_1.

11. A research finding was recently given on one of those "health-advice" radio shows: "Those who are more optimistic at the start of a week have a better week." The host then said that you can make your week better if you are optimistic at the start of the week. Critique this conclusion. Is there an alternative story to the causal-effects interpretation, involving a systematic reason why optimism and the quality of a person's week would be positively related?

12. Suppose that a study used self-reported consumption of potato chips and overall health index score from self-reported health measures to estimate how potato-chip consumption affected health.

    a. Why could there be reverse causality?

    b. Why could there be omitted-factors bias from spurious correlation?

    c. Why could there be bias from measurement error?

13. Consider the following model to estimate the effects of certain foods on health for a sample of 60-year-olds:

$$health60_i = \beta_0 + \beta_1 * (bb)_i + \beta_2 * (bigmacs)_i + X_i\beta_3 + \varepsilon_i,$$

where:

health60 = a measure of health at age 60

bb = average annual pounds of blueberries eaten over the past 30 years

bigmacs = average annual number of Big Macs eaten over the past 30 years

Based on the rules for deciding what control factors to include in a model (Section 6.11), indicate whether and explain why the following potential control variables: "should be excluded"; "should be included"; or "could be included or excluded."

    a. A measure of health at age 50

    b. Average days of exercise over the past 30 years

    c. Racial/ethnic indicator variables

    d. Of one's 5 best childhood friends, the number who regularly ate Big Macs.

14. Use the data set, **temperature_gdp**, and restrict the sample to these five countries: Australia, Iceland, Italy, Japan, and Peru. The data set has information on average temperature and GDP growth for each year. Consider a model that estimates the effect of temperature (*temp*) on GDP growth (*gdpgrowth*), as follows

$$gdpgrowth = \beta_0 + \beta_1 \times temp + \beta_2 \times \text{Iceland} + \beta_3 \times \text{Italy} + \beta_4 \times \text{Japan} + \beta_5 \times \text{Peru} + \varepsilon$$

    a. Estimate the model.

    b. Estimate a separate model of

$$gdpgrowth = \beta_0 + \beta_1 \times temp + \varepsilon$$

    for each of the five countries.

    c. Using the criteria established in Section 6.10, assess whether there could be bias from over-weighted groups, with the controls for the country.

    d. Calculate the average of the coefficient estimates on *temp* from the five models in (b). (Normally, this would be weighted by the number of observations, but there are the same number, 43, observations for each country.)

    e. Construct a table similar to Table 6.13 in Section 6.10. What is the weighted average of the coefficient estimates based on the sample size and variance of temp within each country? How does this compare to the coefficient estimate in (a)?

    f. Why is the coefficient estimate on *temp* in (a) different from the answer in (d)?

15. Is the hot hand in basketball a real phenomenon?

16. In the movie, *Saving Private Ryan*, one of the soldiers said to another, something like, "The best way to fall asleep is trying to stay awake, as that's when I most-easily fall asleep." Use one of the PITFALLS to critique this statement.

Notes

1 Let me note here that some people (particularly those writing on Wikipedia) have tried to take the term, "self-selection bias," and make it mean the same thing as "sample-selection bias." I am taking the meaning back to its original form, as the term "self-selection bias" better describes the source of bias described in this sub-section.

2 The Heckman correction requires having data on subjects that do not make the final sample—e.g., for attrition bias, those who were in the earlier surveys but not the primary-analysis sample. Let's say that the primary-analysis sample is for 2008. The procedure involves first modeling the probability that the person is in the 2008 sample. It then calculates a propensity to be in the 2008 sample based on the explanatory variables. Next, it includes that propensity variable in the final regression for the 2008 sample. Unfortunately, this model is highly volatile with respect to variables included. Furthermore, to achieve any reasonably-valid results, the model requires having an "identifying" variable that: (1) explains whether the person is in the 2008 sample; and (2) has no independent effect on the outcome. It is quite rare to find such an "identifying" variable.

References

Amato, P. R. (2005). The impact of family formation change on the cognitive, social, and emotional well-being of the next generation. *The Future of Children, 15,* 75–96.

Arkes, J. (2007). Does the economy affect teenage substance use? *Health Economics, 16*(1), 19–36.

Arkes, J. (2009). How the economy affects teenage weight. *Social Science & Medicine, 68*(11), 1943–1947.

Arkes, J. (2010). Revisiting the hot hand theory with free throw data in a multivariate framework. *Journal of Quantitative Analysis in Sports, 6,* 1–12.

Arkes, J. (2011). Is controlling the rushing or passing game the key to NFL victories? *The Sport Journal, 14*(1), 1–5.

Arkes, J. (2012). How does youth cigarette use respond to weak economic periods? Implications for the current economic crisis. *Substance Use & Misuse, 47*(4), 375–382.

Arkes, J. (2013). Misses in "hot hand" research. *Journal of Sports Economics, 14*(4), 401–410.

Arkes, J., & Shen, Y. C. (2014). For better or for worse, but how about a recession? *Contemporary Economic Policy, 32*(2), 275–287.

Brooks, D. (2013). The philosophy of data. *New York Times,* February 4. Retrieved May 9, 2013, from http://www.nytimes.com/2013/02/05/opinion/brooks-the-philosophy-of-data.html, accessed July 10, 2018.

Carroll, R. J., Ruppert, D., Stefanski, L. A., & Crainiceanu, C. M. (2006). *Measurement error in nonlinear models: a modern perspective.* Boca Raton, FL: CRC Press.

Freedman, D. H. (2010). Lies, damned lies, and medical science. *The Atlantic*. November 2010 issue. http://www.theatlantic.com/magazine/archive/2010/11/lies-damned-lies-and-medical-science/308269/, accessed July 10, 2018.

Gibbons, C. E., Serrato, J. C. S., & Urbancic, M. B. (2019). Broken or fixed effects? *Journal of Econometric Methods*, *8*(1), 143.

Gilovich, T., Vallone, R., & Tversky, A. (1985). The hot hand in basketball: on the misperception of random sequences. *Cognitive Psychology*, *17*(3), 295–314.

Guolo, A. (2008). Robust techniques for measurement error correction: a review. *Statistical Methods in Medical Research*, *17*(6), 555–580.

Harder, V. S., Morral, A. R., & Arkes, J. (2006). Marijuana use and depression among adults: testing for causal associations. *Addiction*, *101*(10), 1463–1472.

Heckman, J. (1979). Sample selection as a specification error. *Econometrica*, *47*(1), 153–161.

Hosek, J. & Francisco M. (2009). *Military Reenlistment and Deployment During the War on Terrorism*. Santa Monica, CA: RAND Corporation.

Ioannidis, J. P. (2013). Implausible results in human nutrition research. *BMJ*, *347*, f6698.

Kennedy, S., & Ruggles, S. (2014). Breaking up is hard to count: the rise of divorce in the United States, 1980–2010. *Demography*, *51*, 587–598.

Messerli, F. H. (2012). Chocolate consumption, cognitive function, and nobel laureates. *New England Journal of Medicine*, *367*(16), 1562–1564.

Miller, J. B., & Sanjurjo, A. (2018). Surprised by the hot hand fallacy? A truth in the law of small numbers. *Econometrica*, *88*(6), 2019–2047.

Peck, T., Scharf, R. J., Conaway, M. R., & DeBoer, M. D. (2015). Viewing as little as 1 hour of TV daily is associated with higher change in BMI between kindergarten and first grade. *Obesity*, *23*(8), 1680–1686.

Schwingshackl, L., Balduzzi, S., Beyerbach, J., Bröckelmann, N., Werner, S. S., Zähringer, J., … Meerpohl, J. J. (2021). Evaluating agreement between bodies of evidence from randomised controlled trials and cohort studies in nutrition research: meta-epidemiological study. *British Medical Journal*, *374*, n1864.

Shen, Y. C., Arkes, J., & Pilgrim, J. (2009). The effects of deployment intensity on post-traumatic stress disorder: 2002–2006. *Military Medicine*, *174*(3), 217–223.

Stone, D. F. (2012). Measurement error and the hot hand. *The American Statistician*, *66*(1), 61–66.

7 | Strategies for other regression objectives

Recall from Section 2.2 that there are four main objectives of regression analysis. These are listed in Table 7.1, along with the main result(s) a researcher would hope to obtain from each type of regression.

Chapter 6 focused on the PITFALLS of modeling strategies for the first of these objectives, estimating causal effects. For the other objectives of regression analysis, the PITFALLS and modeling strategies are different, as the PITFALLS from Chapter 6 do not apply to each regression objective. (Things that could go wrong in regard to the standard errors and the validity of the sample apply to all four objectives.) This chapter offers general guidelines that will work most of the time when using regressions for objectives other than estimating the causal effects.

DOI: 10.4324/9781003285007-7

Table 7.1 Review of the four main objectives of regression analysis

Objective	Main result
Estimating causal effects	Estimated causal effect of a treatment on an outcome
Forecasting/predicting an outcome	Best guess (forecast) of the dependent variable for a single subject (e.g., GDP growth in the European Union) or for multiple subjects (prediction, such as the probability each Army soldier will not fulfill their initial contract)
Determining predictors of an outcome	Estimated amount that the dependent variable is higher or lower with a given one-unit higher value in the predicting variable, or the explanatory power of a given predicting variable
Adjusting outcomes for various factors	A value for each subject represented in the sample based on the dependent variable after factoring out contextual factors. This could be used to estimate "value-added" or to detect anomalies

In this chapter, you will learn:

- What the best strategy is for the regression objectives of forecasting/predicting an outcome, determining predictors, and gauging relative performance
- What PITFALLS apply to each objective
- When you don't want to control for demographic factors.

7.1 Strategies and PITFALLS for forecasting/predicting an outcome

7.1.1 What are the strategies?

Let us go back to the lemon-tree example from Section 4.5. To properly estimate the causal effect of water on the number of lemons, we decided that we did not want to control for the height of the tree, as this would be a mediating factor, and doing so would prevent us from estimating the full effect of watering. This would violate PITFALL #5 in Chapter 6.

But what if the farmer wanted to give a potential buyer an estimate of how many lemons she can produce each month? In this case, the farmer needs a forecast/prediction, not a causal effect. And so the objective of any regression analysis she would estimate would be to produce the best possible **forecast** or **prediction** for the number of lemons. Do not confuse this with the next regression objective of **determining predictors**, which is figuring out what factors are the best determinants of a dependent variable. Rather, for this regression objective, the goal is to get as accurate a prediction as possible of the dependent variable.

The height of the trees could provide important predictive power, and so estimating a regression with height as an explanatory variable would likely help generate a more accurate forecast of the number of lemons her trees will produce than a model that does not control for the height of the tree. It does not matter if one does not estimate the true causal effect of certain factors. This example demonstrates that the strategy for what control variables to include in the model depends on what the objective of the regression is.

There are many cases in which a forecast is needed. In logistics, parts suppliers may want to forecast the demand for various parts of a machine or vehicle that would be needed for repairs. Sports teams may want to forecast attendance for each game so they can set a more profitable ticket price or stock enough beer. Google may want to forecast how much space people will use on their Google Drive cloud space. Any business would want to forecast demand for their products to plan on production numbers. The U.S. Army may want to forecast how many soldiers will attrite in their first year of service. And an insurance company may want to predict the probability that a given customer will get in a car accident in a given year.

Some of these examples involve time-series variables, which we will see in Chapter 10. Other forecasts and predictions could be based on cross-sectional analyses, with multiple subjects and multiple explanatory variables.

This is how it would work for the insurance company. The insurance company would have some historical data on its customers that is something like the following:

- Y = whether the person got in an accident in a given year
- X_1 = number of accidents the person had in the last ten years
- X_2 = whether the person has a college degree
- X_3 = age
- X_4 = income
- X_5 = a dummy variable equal to 1 if the person had a white-collar job.

(A more developed model could use a set of dummy variables for many different types of jobs.)

Note that X_1 (the number of accidents in the last ten years) would likely be a statistically-significant determinant of having an accident, but I suspect it would still be a weak overall predictor in that it would not explain many accidents that occur. If the company were to estimate the causal effects of a college degree on the probability of an accident, then it would exclude X_4 and X_5 from the model, as these variables could be mediating factors for the effects of a college degree. That is, part of the reason why a college degree (likely) leads to a lower probability of an accident is that it increases a person's income and the probability that a person obtains a white-collar job (and perhaps increases the value of their car, which could affect how careful they are). Thus, including these variables in the model would prevent the estimation of the full effect of schooling on the likelihood of an accident.

But the causal effect of a college degree on the probability of an accident is not of concern to the insurance company. The company is only interested in the best guess for a customer's probability of getting into an accident. Thus, it would include X_4 and X_5 in the model.

The forecast, or predicted probability of an accident, for a particular person would be $\hat{Y}_i$, or what is obtained by multiplying the $\hat{\beta}'s$ by the value of the associated X variables and summing them together, as follows:

$$\hat{Y}_i = \hat{\beta}_0 + \hat{\beta}_1 X_{1i} + \hat{\beta}_2 X_{2i} + \hat{\beta}_3 X_{3i} + \hat{\beta}_4 X_{4i} + \hat{\beta}_5 X_{5i} \qquad (7.1)$$

7.1.2 What PITFALLS matter?

In forecasting/prediction, the objective is to obtain the most accurate prediction of $\hat{Y}$. Given that forecasting regressions are not concerned with estimating causal effects, most of the PITFALLS are not applicable. For example, the existence of omitted-factors bias (PITFALL #2) just means that an included observable variable is picking up part of the predictive power of some omitted factors on the outcome. It does not mean that the forecast would be biased in any way due to the unobserved variable.

Similarly, including mediating factors (such as the height of the lemon tree) for some key-explanatory variables can be good because they have potential explanatory power for the outcome. Again, it does not matter that the model would only be estimating the partial effect of another explanatory variable.

Generally, when forecasting is the goal of the regression analysis, throwing in the kitchen sink of explanatory variables is a good strategy to follow, with a few exceptions:

- If having continual forecasts is a goal, the variables should be easily obtainable for people to plug values of the variables into the model (multiplying them by the coefficient estimates) so that the outcome can be predicted in the future.
- Variables subject to reverse causality (PITFALL #1) should be avoided because it would then be forecasting the outcome with something that is a function of the outcome itself. Thus, it would be ideal that all variables are determined before the outcome. This implies that other outcomes should not be included as explanatory variables if they are concurrently determined or determined after the dependent variable is realized.

All of this means that there is no *bad variation* when using regression analysis to forecast/predict outcomes, with the exception of variation in an explanatory variable due to reverse causality.

These simple rules make forecasting an outcome one of the easiest in terms of avoiding biases. That said, recall the lesson from Section 2.12, that effects can change over time. That is, you must make a leap of faith that the determination of the outcome in the future will follow a similar set of rules as what happened in the past. Whereas lemon-tree production probably does not change how it follows the rules of nature, how GDP growth depends on various factors (such as gas prices) very well could structurally change with an economy that shifts its industrial make-up or that adds financial instruments that could reduce (or increase) instability.

Just to quickly review, here are how the PITFALLS play out for forecasting analyses:

- **Reverse causality**: This is the most important PITFALL that could be problematic for forecasting, giving a forecast with exaggerated accuracy.
- **Omitted-variables bias**: Not a problem. This can be good in that one factor captures the explanatory power of other factors.
- **Self-selection bias**: Not a problem. This also could help gain a more accurate forecast.
- **Measurement error**: For forecasting an outcome for a single subject, measurement error in a variable could lead to a less precise forecast of the outcome, but it should not lead to a biased forecast. Moreover, the forecast would likely be more accurate with the variable that is subject to measurement error included in the model than it would be without the variable. For predicting the outcome for multiple subjects, measurement error could lead to a systematic bias of those predictions.
- **Using mediating factors or outcomes as control variables**: Not a problem because the more variables included, the better the forecast will be, as long as the outcome-as-a-control-variable occurs before the dependent-variable outcome.
- **Improper reference group**: Not a problem ... just like it is not a problem for control variables when estimating causal effects.
- **Over-weighted groups**: It is rare that forecasting would involve separating a model into groups.

7.1.3 What variables should be excluded in a forecast/prediction?

In *Weapons of Math Destruction*, Cathy O'Neil (2016) describes an example of how race was used in the sentencing of a convicted Black man, with the argument that recidivism (committing another offense) was more likely among Black people, and so this person should not have the chance of parole. This example was probably one of many implicit or explicit "informal" uses of race to assess recidivism likelihood in sentencing. Courts have moved away from that practice, but now there is a formal-yet-indirect way that race/ethnicity is still used. O'Neil describes fancy recidivism models that do not include race/ethnicity but do incorporate factors such as how often they had been stopped by police and the criminal records of friends and relatives. We know that under-represented groups are more likely to be stopped by police due to their race or what neighborhood they are from or live in, with most stops not involving an arrest.

As another example, the military has been attempting to determine who is at risk of "attriting" in their first enlistment term, meaning leaving the military for some reason before he/she completes the initial obligated service. Attrition is costly due to the large upfront training costs, so the military explores whether it can identify who is at high risk of attriting, with the ultimate goal of not allowing high-attrition-risk individuals to enlist in the first place. Such factors could include whether the serviceperson has a high school degree and the AFQT (aptitude) score. Suppose that, in a model, they were to include racial/ethnic and gender variables, and they find that Black and female servicepersons are more likely to attrite. What could the military do with this information? Not much. It would be wrong (and illegal) to base their recruiting efforts and decisions on what recruits to accept based on race/ethnicity or gender.

These examples show that any prediction model should assess whether including certain demographic and socio-economic factors would treat people differently based on race/ethnicity, gender, and other groups that should not be treated differently based on being part of that group.

7.1.4 How accurate is the forecast/prediction?

I am certain that for over a century, researchers on the stock market have searched for predictors of stock-market performance. They often found legitimate results for what factors helped to forecast stock-market performance in whatever period they were examining. But that often does not translate into what subsequently happened in the stock market.

If one of these researchers includes enough variables, he/she will certainly find some things to have significant relationships with stock-market performance. Some of these relationships could be by chance (Type I errors); some could be real relationships that were specific for the period studied; and some could be real relationships that are persistent over time. To increase confidence for whether any significant relationship is real and persistent, they would need to test how well the model predicts the outcome with new data. Unfortunately, one has to wait for new data to emerge (more stock-market returns for a few years, perhaps), or one would need to do an **out-of-sample prediction** by leaving part of the sample out of the forecast model and then seeing how well the forecast model predicted stock-market performance in the out-of-sample data. Of course, in that situation, you'd need to hope that the relationship continues beyond the out-of-sample period and into the future.

Whether using in-sample data, out-of-sample data, or new data, one option to determine the accuracy of the forecast is to calculate the **average forecast error**, which is the average of the absolute values of the difference between the actual outcome and the forecasted/predicted outcome:

$$\text{Average forecast error} = \sum_{i=1}^{n} \left| Y_i - \widehat{Y}_i \right|$$

Another statistic is the **root mean square (forecast) error (RMSE or RMSFE)**, which penalizes a model more (in terms of greater error) for larger forecast misses. The statistic is simply:

$$\text{RMSFE} = \sqrt{\sum_{i=1}^{n} \left(Y_i - \widehat{Y}_i \right)^2}$$

In theory, these statistics might be used for model selection. Perhaps some variable contributes little to reducing RMSFE and so it may be dropped to help simplify the forecast model, or to reduce the costs of data collection.

7.1.5 Machine learning and AI

Forecasting is the objective underlying the fairly new data-analytics topic of machine learning, which falls under AI (artificial intelligence). The idea is for a statistical program to grind through gadzillions of ways that variables could be related to each other to find the best way that they fit together.

There has been some debate on the value of this method. One concern is that relationships change over time, so finding a highly-complex way that some variables are related could be a temporary relationship that would change with the inevitable change in environment the following year (or week). Furthermore, with greater complexity often comes greater uncertainty.

A recent machine-learning failure occurred with Zillow, the tech company that offers a database of home values and homes for sale. The company aimed to use machine-learning to profitably buy and sell homes based on believing they could better forecast true home values relative to other market participants. It was a huge failure, leading to a loss of $881 Million in 2021 (Parker, 2022). The problem might have been that bad data caused inaccurate forecasts from measurement error. In addition, it could have been that what determines home prices one month changes the following month, as other developments in the economy emerge.

I believe there is some value in machine learning, but I imagine that the popularity of machine learning (without full understanding of the PITFALLS) will be applied to many situations in which its value would be over-stated. This could lead to poor business decisions, such as what happened with Zillow.

7.2 Strategies and PITFALLS for determining predictors of an outcome

7.2.1 What are the best strategies?

Sometimes, a researcher may want to avoid a complex forecast model and simply want to know:

- Whether a certain factor predicts an outcome,
- How well a certain factor predicts an outcome,
- What the best predictors for an outcome would be.

My favorite example comes from a recent study that found that drivers of expensive cars were more likely to be jerks, as indicated by not stopping for pedestrians (Coughenour et al., 2020) – it was news agencies, such as CNN, and not the authors that used the term "jerks," but I like it (Pincheta, 2020). The researchers had hired pedestrians to attempt to cross a street at a crosswalk, and they noted the car and whether the driver yielded to the pedestrian. They then estimated the cost of the car from manufacturing websites and private sales. The researchers found that an extra $1,000 value of the car was associated with between 1% and 6% lower probability that the driver would stop for the pedestrian. They did hold the gender and race of the pedestrian constant. The experiment was conducted in Las Vegas, so I am not sure this is a representative sample of the drivers and car values in the rest of the country.

I do not believe that the researchers were interested in the causal effect of the cost of the car on the likelihood of stopping for the pedestrian. Rather, I believe they wanted to determine how well the cost of the car predicted whether the driver would stop.

Indeed, the pedestrian is concerned about:

- "how much higher the probability is that a car won't stop if it is an expensive car."

The pedestrian is *not* concerned with:

- "how much higher the probability is that a car won't stop if it is an expensive car, after adjusting for whether the driver is rude to his/her mother."
- "the causal effect of driving an expensive car on the probability the driver stops."

Whereas the pedestrian would like to know that information on whether the driver is rude to his/her mother, the only information the pedestrian would have would be some gauge on how expensive the car is. So the pedestrian wants to know how well the cost of the car *predicts* the likelihood that the driver stops.

As another example, with suicide being a major problem in the military, especially during the Global War on Terrorism, the military might want to know what factors predicted suicide attempts. If it were interested in whether "being fired upon" predicted suicide, the military may not want to hold other factors constant. It comes down to whether you are interested in:

- Does "being fired upon" predict the probability of a suicide attempt? or
- Does "being fired upon" predict the probability of a suicide attempt beyond any predictive power that seeking counseling (and other factors) have?

In my view, the first bullet would be more informative. This would mean that the best strategy would be to not hold any other factors constant. This wouldn't be as sexy as a regression with many controls, but it would be more useful for determining how well certain factors predicted suicide attempts.

To demonstrate the logic behind the best strategies for determining predictors, let's explore, with the NLSY, what factors predict "health status at age 50" for females (Bureau of Labor Statistics, 2014). When respondents reached ages 40 and 50 in the NLSY survey, they were asked to rate their health status on a 1–5 scale, with the choices being: poor (1), fair (2), good (3), very good (4), and excellent (5). In Table 7.2, I present the results from several regressions examining factors of "health status at age 50." (As will be described in Section 9.3, OLS may not be the appropriate method to use when the outcome is based on an ordered set of categories. Nevertheless, it helps to make the point here.) The

Table 7.2 Predicting health status at age 50 for females (n = 2849)

	(1)	(2)	(3)	(4)
Health status at age 40	0.537***	0.577***		
	(0.017)	(0.017)		
Black	−0.055		−0.299***	
	(0.038)		(0.043)	
AFQT	0.005***			0.010***
	(0.001)			(0.001)
Constant	1.234***	1.252***	3.422***	2.937***
	(0.065)	(0.062)	(0.024)	(0.032)
R-squared	0.317	0.300	0.017	0.077

Source: Bureau of Labor Statistics (2014).

Standard errors are in parentheses. Standard errors are corrected for heteroskedasticity.

***$p < 0.01$, **$p < 0.05$, *$p < 0.1$.

model in column (1) includes the full set of explanatory variables. Columns (2–4) then include just one of the explanatory variables at a time.

Let's address the issue of whether being Black is a significant predictor of health-at-50 (relative to the reference group of non-Blacks). In column (1), when all variables are included, being Black has an insignificant coefficient estimate. Thus, one may conclude that there is no evidence that race predicts health at age 50. But is this correct? In column (3), for which the variable for Black is the only explanatory variable, it has a strongly significant coefficient estimate. Note also that the AFQT score is a relatively stronger predictor when it is the only explanatory variable – in column (4) – than in the full model in column (1).

What is going on here? Why is being Black understated as a predictor in column (1)? And how would we answer the question of whether race significantly predicts health at age 50?

The basis for the answer comes from column (2). Note that the R^2 is 0.300 from just the one variable of health-at-40 as an explanatory variable, not much below the R^2 of 0.317 in column (1) when all variables are included. This means that this one variable, health-at-40, is sopping up a significant amount of variation in health-at-50, leaving less variation to be explained by the rest of the variables.

Deciding what variables should be included in the model when searching for predictors of an outcome should be based on whether one is interested in:

- How much a certain variable predicts the outcome, or
- How much a certain variable predicts the outcome, after adjusting for other factors.

We can make two statements regarding the relationship between being Black and health-at-50:

- Health-at-50 is significantly worse for Black females than non-Black females.
- There is no evidence that health-at-50 is significantly worse for Black females, once health-at-40 and the AFQT score are adjusted for.

Whether to control for other factors depends on which of these is more interesting. In most cases, the second statement (from both sets of bullets above) has little value.

When determining predictors of an outcome, most people in the research community would be more interested in the model that controls for everything. But this makes it a horserace with the odds favoring the variables that are less correlated with other variables. Thus, there could be one factor that is indeed the best predictor, but it is highly correlated with a few other factors, causing its predictive power to be spread out to those other variables. We would have the second-bulleted interpretation (from each set above) which is pretty nebulous, and we would be unable to determine how well it alone predicted the outcome.

Personally, for determining predictors of an outcome, I'm more inclined towards the models that keep it as simple as possible and include just:

- One explanatory variable at a time,
- One set of dummy variables representing one concept (e.g., racial/ethnic groups), or
- One interaction of explanatory variables (e.g., race/ethnicity interacted with gender).

Note that, if there were just a dummy variable as a potential predictor, this strategy would be equivalent to estimating a difference in the means for the groups (e.g., Black vs. non-Black). But the regression method offers a simpler and quicker method.

Note also that those who use such information (such as the military trying to determine which servicepersons were at risk for suicide attempts) may not have the capabilities and knowledge to run a regression or to combine the effects of multitudes of predictors. Thus, it would probably be best to know which factors acting *alone* are the best predictors of dropping out. Or perhaps they may want to know what combination of two factors were the best predictors.

How do you determine what the best predictor is? It is not just the variable with the largest-in-magnitude coefficient estimate for two reasons. First, the scale of the explanatory variable needs to be considered (see Section 3.4 on standardized effects). Second, the variation in the explanatory variable will determine how well the variable predicts the outcome. For example, if we were trying to find the best predictor for a teenager having a baby before age 18, one variable that probably has a high predictive ability for the outcome is a dummy variable for "having an older sister who had two babies before age 18." But this would apply to such a small percentage of the sample that it would not be effective for predicting whether the subject has a baby herself.

Perhaps the best indicators would be the R^2 and Root Mean Square Error (RMSE), as introduced in the prior section. Of course, to label one variable as the winner for being the best predictor, it would need to be well above others in R^2 or well below others in RMSE in order to take the prize. Small differences in R^2 could be from natural sampling variation rather than one predictor being stronger.

7.2.2 What PITFALLS matter?

Regarding the seven PITFALLS, they are not all-important for the objective of "determining predictors," largely because it is not important to estimate the true causal effect of any factor. The following is how they should be considered for analyses attempting to determine predictors:

- **Reverse causality:** This should be avoided because you would be predicting the outcome with itself (because the explanatory variable is a product of the outcome with reverse causality).

- **Omitted-factors bias:** Not a problem. In fact, you may want the predictor to capture unobservable factors, as it would give a variable greater predictive power.
- **Self-selection bias:** This is also okay, as with omitted-factors bias.
- **Measurement error:** This would be a problem because measurement error in an explanatory variable could lead to an understatement of how well the variable can predict the outcome. However, it does not mean that the variable should not be considered as a predictor.
- **Using mediating factors or outcomes as control variables:** This would be a problem because it would take away from the predictive power of the explanatory variable and goes against the idea of having a single factor in the model.
- **Improper reference group:** Not a problem, as it would not impact the predictive power of the factor.
- **Over-weighted groups:** This would rarely be applicable for this objective.

As with forecasting, one need not be concerned with *bad variation* other than reverse causality when using regression analysis to determine predictors.

7.3 Strategies and PITFALLS for adjusting outcomes for various factors and anomaly detection

The unadjusted life is not worth comparing.

–paraphrasing Socrates

7.3.1 Main approaches

When we want to determine how strong the performance was for sports teams, workers, businesses, etc., just comparing the outcome itself may be a flawed approach as subjects may have different conditions or environments that make success simpler or more difficult. The concept of *adjusting outcomes* involves factoring out influences that reflect determinants of performance other than the actions of the subjects being compared. This allows one to estimate how subjects performed relative to what would be expected, or what the **value-added** of the person or organization is.

This is the concept behind the new statistic used in basketball of "real-plus-minus," which is a player's average impact on net points per 100 offensive and defensive possessions. The "real" part is that it factors out the teammates and opponents who were on the court at the same time as the player (based on how many possessions they shared on the court with that player).

Falling within this realm of adjusting outcomes is **anomaly detection**, which is the process of finding outliers or abnormal observations. This might be useful to find the best and worst performers (such as teachers). In addition, it could be used to detect fraudulent credit-card use, if spending were anomalously high relative to normal for a person.

There are two main approaches to this regression objective:

1. Adjust for all factors in a model by simply using the residual.
2. Adjust for a subset of the factors in a model by subtracting out the influence of just that subset of factors. This would be done if the model necessitates extra variables.

The simpler approach, obviously, is the first one of using the residual. Relative performance (RP) would be:

$$RP_i = \hat{\varepsilon}_i = Y_i - E[Y \mid X_i] = Y_i - \hat{Y}_i \tag{7.2}$$

However, sometimes there are explanatory variables in the regression that should not be adjusted for. These variables may be in the model to help isolate the causal effect of some key variables that are being adjusted for. For example, suppose that Y is regressed on four variables, X_1 to X_4,

$$Y_i = \beta_0 + \beta_1 X_{1i} + \beta_2 X_{2i} + \beta_3 X_{3i} + \beta_4 X_{4i} + \varepsilon_i \tag{7.3}$$

but you want to condition on just two of the variables, X_1 and X_2. This could be the case if X_3 and X_4 were needed to help towards accurately estimating the causal effects of X_1 and X_2. Relative performance would be:

$$RP_i = Y_i - \left(\hat{\beta}_1 X_{1i} + \hat{\beta}_2 X_{2i} \right). \tag{7.4}$$

Let's consider a few examples.

7.3.2 Example 1: Payroll and wins in baseball

This example from earlier is based on the idea that simply comparing wins or championships for, say, the Oakland A's to that of the New York Yankees does not speak to which team was more effective because they are on completely different levels for payrolls. It must be much easier to win if you can spend the annual GDP of France in payroll every year, compared to other teams that, with payrolls closer to the revenue of a hot-dog vendor outside Yankee Stadium, have difficulty attracting good players to sign with the team. If we adjust for payroll, we can get a measure for relative performance (or payroll-adjusted performance). We may simply run a regression of the number of wins in a season on the payroll and use the residual. Thus, from the following regression from Section 2.7:

$$\widehat{wins} = 71.24 + 0.09 \times \left(\text{payroll in \$millions} \right) \tag{2.17}$$

we would calculate:

$$\begin{aligned} \text{Relative wins} = \hat{\varepsilon}_i &= Y_i - \hat{Y}_i \\ &= Y_i - \left[\hat{\beta}_0 + \hat{\beta}_1 \times \left(\text{payroll in \$millions} \right)_i \right] \\ &= Y_i - \left[71.24 + 0.09 \times \left(\text{payroll in \$millions} \right)_i \right] \end{aligned} \tag{7.5}$$

A nice feature of using the residual is that the average residual equals zero. Thus, a positive residual means that performance was better than expected.

Does this represent the true causal effect? Probably not, as payroll isn't exactly random. But this is a situation in which it may be okay, as it produces a payroll-adjusted number of wins.

7.3.3 Example 2: Evaluation of professors

University professors (and instructors) are typically evaluated on their teaching effectiveness based on student evaluations. But many argue that such evaluations are highly biased by grades and class size, among other things. This means that just using a professor's average evaluation by the students may not make for fair comparisons because of differences in these factors. Furthermore, a school might want to identify the best professors to determine what contributes to effectiveness. Just selecting the top professors based on evaluations might be taking those who were popular because they taught small classes, in contrast to others who teach classes with hundreds of students.

Schools can potentially adjust for these other factors. Let's take the example of class-size, as we have done with earlier examples. Unfortunately, we cannot just regress "average evaluation" in a class on class-size because there could be some omitted-factors bias occurring, as we established back in Chapters 4 and 6. To address this, we would need a bunch of dummy variables for the professors, making it so a professor's evaluations and class-size in a given class are being compared to his/her other classes, and not being compared to those of other professors. This would give us a better gauge of the true average causal effect of class-size on the average evaluation of a professor, which would then allow us to more accurately adjust performance based on class-size.

Unlike the baseball example above, with this method, we would not be able to use the residual to gauge relative performance. The residual would take out the professor effect, and so all professors would have the same average residual of zero – this will be explained in more detail in Section 8.1. And so the residual would make it seem like each professor is performing equally well. Instead of using the residual, we would just want to adjust based on the class-size, as follows:

$$Y_{ic} = X_{ic}\beta_1 + \beta_2 CS_{ic} + \varepsilon_{ic} \tag{7.6}$$

$$\text{Relative evaluation} = Y_{ic} - \left(\hat{\beta}_2 CS_{ic} \right) \tag{7.7}$$

where:
- Y_{ic} = average evaluation for professor i in class c
- CS = class-size
- X = a set of dummy variables for each professor.

Note that there would be multiple observations per professor, so each observation would indicate the professor's relative performance in a given class, after adjusting for average class-size. These relative-performance measures could then be averaged for each professor.

This is not a perfect method for a few reasons. First, the estimated effects of the class-size might be biased, perhaps from measurement error or from over-weighted groups (PITFALLS #4 and #7), which means the adjustment would be biased. Second, the class-size effect ($\hat{\beta}_2$) could differ by the professor. So the ideal approach would be to adjust each professor by his/her individual $\hat{\beta}_2$. But these would be imprecisely estimated, and so we are forced to adjust based on an estimated average $\hat{\beta}_2$ across all people. Despite these concerns, adjusting for the class-size would give a better gauge of a professor's effectiveness than just comparing unadjusted average evaluations. And it would help detect anomalies: which professors were especially effective (and ineffective), given their contextual factors.

7.3.4 Using dummy variables to gauge relative performance

A completely different method could be used if there were multiple observations per person (or team). In that case, a model could use dummy variables for each person and compare the values of the coefficient estimates on those dummy variables. For example, with the prior example, the coefficient estimate on each professor could be the indicator for the effectiveness of the professor relative to the reference-group professor. In such a model, it might be ideal to not use a constant term so that a professor does not need to be excluded as a reference group. The professors with the highest coefficient estimates would be the best guess for who the most effective professors were. Ideally, standard errors would be used for determining how strong the evidence is that one professor performed better than others.

This strategy does not work if there is only one observation for each subject because then the professor dummy variables would perfectly predict the outcome and there would be no variation left for the adjustment for class-size.

7.3.5 What variables probably should not be adjusted for

I have not come across any discussion of strategies for using regression analysis for this objective, so I'm not sure if there has been much written on the best strategies. But I could think of two types of factors that should not be adjusted for gauging relative performance or value-added or for anomaly detection:

• Those that represent other measures of performance (and perhaps health)
• Those that end up holding different groups to different standards.

Regarding the first one, think back to the baseball example. If we were to adjust the number of wins for not just payroll but also batting average or the number of home runs the team hit, then we would over-adjust. Some teams may use salary effectively for big home run hitters at a cheap price. This is part of a team's relative performance. These are statistics (or characteristics) of players that higher payrolls buy more of, which should lead to more wins. The issue comes down to how well the teams used money or managed their players to get more production (stats and wins) for given amounts of salary. In this case, these mediating factors should not be controlled for.

The other factor, mentioned above, to avoid adjusting for would be to make sure subjects are not held to different standards. Recruiters in the military are typically assigned to be a recruiter for 36 months. There is usually high pressure to recruit at least one person each month, and there are several awards based on how many people and how many "high-quality" people they recruit in certain periods of time, such as a 3-month period. One issue is that some unlucky recruiters are sent to Vermont or strong-economic areas (where recruiting is difficult), while others are sent to Dallas or weak-economic areas (where recruiting is easier). We cannot gauge the relative effectiveness of recruiters in these different types of areas just by comparing the number of recruits they sign. Rather, we would need to adjust the number of recruits based on the area and conditions the recruiters are given.

So we need to determine what factors should be in the regression model and what factors should be adjusted for when calculating relative performance. Obviously, geographical indicators and economic factors would be important. Including them in the model would mean that a recruiter would be judged relative to what would be expected for their location and economic conditions.

Should we also include the gender and race/ethnicity of the recruiter as explanatory variables? If we were to do so, we would be holding males and females to different standards, and we would be holding those of different races and ethnicities to different standards. For example, let's say that the dependent variable was the number of recruits signed in a year. And let's suppose that the coefficient estimate on the variable for "female recruiter" was 3, indicating that females signed an average of 3 more recruits per year than males, after adjusting for other factors. If we were to factor out the gender effect, this would mean that if a male and female who were observationally equivalent (i.e., same location, time period, and characteristics other than gender) and had the same number of recruits in a year, the female's predicted success would be 3 recruits greater than the male's. This would mean that the male recruiter would be considered to have performed better because his "adjusted outcome" would be higher than the female's adjusted score by 3 recruits.

To demonstrate this with an example, let's take that "female effect" of 3 and suppose that the *predicted values* for a female and male recruiter (Jane and John) who are observationally the same $\left(X = \tilde{X} \right)$ other than their gender are the following:

- Jane: $\hat{Y} = E(Y \mid \tilde{X}, \text{female}) = 15$
- John: $\hat{Y} = E(Y \mid \tilde{X}, \text{male}) = 12$.

And let's say that Jane does slightly better than John by signing 14 recruiters in a year, versus 13 for John. Their *relative performance* would be:

- Jane: $14 - 15 = -1$
- John: $13 - 12 = +1$

Even though Jane signed more recruits than John (14 to 13), according to the model, John's relative performance would be 2 recruits better than Jane's ($+1$ to -1). If, however, the relative performance were not conditioned or adjusted based on gender, then Jane would have performed one recruit better than John, given that their predicted values would be the same.

The lesson from this is that you want to adjust for only the factors that you would like success to be conditioned on or adjusted for. And gender, race/ethnicity, and other personal characteristics usually are not good factors to use for adjusting outcomes to gauge relative performance.

7.3.6 What PITFALLS matter?

If a causal effect were under-estimated or over-estimated, then it would not adjust enough or over-adjust for a given factor. Thus, in some cases, without an accurately- and precisely-estimated average causal effect, the comparisons become distorted. This means that, if causal effects are important, then all PITFALLS should be considered; but, as we saw with the professor example above, it does not mean that you condition on all variables used in the causal-effects model. One possible exception is mediating factors. This may not be important because, with mediating factors, the effect of the key-explanatory variable is still being captured by a combination of its own coefficient estimate and the coefficient estimate on its mediating factor. Thus, the effects of the key-explanatory variable would still be fully adjusted for. For example, when adjusting military recruiting success for the unemployment rate, we could also include a variable for the local wage rate, which some may say is a mediating factor for the unemployment rate. This is fine, as all that is important is that a recruiter's performance is adjusted for the unemployment rate and any effects of its mediating factors. We just do not want to control for mediating factors that are related to performance, such as with the mediating factor of home runs in the baseball example above.

One PITFALL to be especially concerned with would be measurement error. A good example comes from the aforementioned *Weapons of Math Destruction*, in which Cathy O'Neil describes the case of a highly-regarded middle-school teacher in the Washington, DC public school system. One year, she was in the bottom 5% of teachers in terms of value-added (effectively the change in achievement scores of her students from the prior to the current year), so she was fired as part of an effort to rid the school system of ineffective teachers. However, O'Neil described how there was some evidence suggesting that the prior year's scores for her students were artificially-inflated. The school district did not wish to allow exceptions to their strategy, and so the teacher's firing was upheld. The point is that if the conditioning variables are subject to error, then there will be a biased estimate of a subject's value-added, or relative performance.

7.4 Summary of the strategies and PITFALLS for each regression objective

Table 7.3 offers a summary of which PITFALLS could cause a problem and what the "General Strategy" should be for each objective. In the table, "Yes" indicates that the question does need to be asked, and that problems with the PITFALL need to be avoided. "No" indicates that the PITFALL is not a concern or issue for the regression objective.

Table 7.3 Strategies and which PITFALLS need to be asked for the regression objectives

PITFALLS	*Regression objective*			
	Estimating causal effects	*Forecasting the outcome*	*Determining predictors*	*Adjusting outcomes for certain factors and anomaly detection*
1. Reverse causality	Yes	Yes	Yes	Yes
2. Omitted-variables bias	Yes	No	No	Yes
3. Self-selection bias	Yes	No	No	Yes
4. Measurement error	Yes	No for single-subject forecasting; Yes for multiple-subject prediction	Yes	Yes
5. Using mediating factors and outcomes as control variables	Yes	No, provided it precedes the dependent variable	Yes	Depends
6. Improper reference group	Yes	No	No	Yes
7. Over-weighted groups	Yes	No	No	Yes

PITFALLS	Regression objective			
	Estimating causal effects	Forecasting the outcome	Determining predictors	Adjusting outcomes for certain factors and anomaly detection
General strategy	Avoid or address all 7 PIT-FALLS	Include the kitch-en sink of X vari-ables, except for factors that could result in treating protected groups differently	Include just one X variable, one set of categories (e.g., race), or one interacted set of categories per regression	Only control for factors that you want to adjust for, and be cautious of demo-graphic variables

The objectives of "Determining predictors" and "Forecasting the outcome" have fewer things that could go wrong (with more "No's") and are generally straightforward. "Adjusting outcomes," on the other hand, involves more thought as to what factors to condition on and what PITFALLS could apply.

Exercises

1. Identify the regression objective of the following research questions (from the four options of es-timating causal effects, forecasting/predicting an outcome, determining predictors of an outcome, and adjusting an outcome).
   a. Who was the most effective new-car salesman for Ford cars last year in the U.S., given the strength of the economy in their area?
   b. How does attending a charter school affect the test scores for inner-city members of under-represented groups
   c. How much is the amount of car sales in a local area impacted by advertising expenses?
   d. What is the best guess for how many emergency-room visits there will be from drug over-doses in each city this year?
   e. How much will the dollar value of U.S. imports be next year?
   f. What is the single best predictor of whether a female will give birth before age 18?
   g. How did the Clean Air Act affect the intelligence of people who grew up in large metropol-itan areas?
   h. How much does consistently reading chapters ahead of class affect your grade?
2. With the **democracy2** data set, determine what the best predictor is for life expectancy (*life_exp*) with 1985 data (based on a sample for which *condition1* = 1), among the variables: *democracy*, *avgeduc educgini*, and *urbanpct*. How did you arrive at your answer?
3. Repeat #2, but determine the best predictor for *democracy* among: *life_exp*, *avgeduc educgini*, and *urbanpct*.
4. Use the data set **lemon_tree**, which is similar to the lemon-tree example from Chapter 4, except lemons are now measured in weight (kilograms). The data set has the following variables:
   o *lemon5* = weight of lemons produced by the tree in year 5
   o *lemon4* = weight of lemons produced by the tree in year 4
   o *height* = height at start of year 5

o   *water* = amount of weekly water (randomly assigned)
o   *good* = dummy variable for being in the "good part of the yard"
o   *id* = tree ID number.

For each problem, explain why you did not control for any potential control variable not in the model (among *lemon4, height, water, good*).

a.   Design the best model to estimate the causal effect of *water* on the weight of lemons from a tree in year 5 (*lemon5*). Give the regression equation (with coefficient estimates). What is the main result?

b.   Suppose that trees 26–50 (based on *id*) were planted one year later so that you do not know, at the time of your analysis, what *lemon5* is for them. And, suppose that Trader Joe's wants to buy your year-5 lemons from trees 26–50. Design a model (with a sample of trees 1–25) to estimate the best prediction for *lemon5* for trees 26–30. What is the regression equation (with coefficient estimates)?

c.   Back with the full sample of 50 trees, is the height a statistically-significant predictor of the weight of the lemons produced by a tree in year 5? How did you determine this?

d.   Suppose that you marry a tree doctor, who says he/she will give you one free tree checkup (before charging you standard rates). What tree ID seems the least healthy, given the circumstances it was given? Be specific about the methods you used to arrive at your answer.

References

Bureau of Labor Statistics, U.S. Department of Labor. (2014). *National Longitudinal Survey of Youth 1979 cohort, 1979–2012 (rounds 1–25)*. Columbus, OH: Center for Human Resource Research, The Ohio State University.

Coughenour, C., Abelar, J., Pharr, J., Chien, L. C., & Singh, A. (2020). Estimated car cost as a predictor of driver yielding behaviors for pedestrians. *Journal of Transport & Health*, 16, 100831.

O'Neil, C. (2016). *Weapons of math destruction: How big data increases inequality and threatens democracy*. Portland, OR: Broadway Books.

Parker, W. (2022). Zillow's Shuttered Home-Flipping Business Lost $881 Million in 2021. *Wall Street Journal*. February 10, 2022. https://www.wsj.com/articles/zillows-shuttered-home-flipping-business-lost-881-million-in-2021-11644529656.

Pincheta, R. (2020). If you drive an expensive car you're probably a jerk, scientists say. CNN. February 26, 2020. https://www.cnn.com/2020/02/26/world/expensive-car-drivers-study-scli-scn-intl/index.html.

8 Methods to address biases

DOI: 10.4324/9781003285007-8

Quasi-experiments (like metaphysics) comprise a dark ocean without shores or lighthouses, strewn with many a philosophical and statistical wrecks. But, if you somehow make one work, it's wicked bitchin'.

              – Immanuel Kant

You know, Hobbes, some days even my lucky rocket ship underpants don't help.

             – Calvin (of Calvin and Hobbes)

Chapter 6 discussed many potential PITFALLS that arise when using regression analysis to estimate causal effects. Some of these PITFALLS are impossible to address. For example, if there is measurement error in the key-explanatory variable, then there may not be a correction. Other PITFALLS (improper reference groups or using mediating factors and outcomes as control variables) could often be addressed simply by changing the model. And then there are the PITFALLS of non-random explanatory variables. These are sometimes addressable if you are innovative and lucky enough to find good data.

As mentioned in Chapter 6, the ideal and cleanest method (albeit not always perfect) would be having random assignment to the treatment. But, in our observational (non-experimental) world, we often need to rely on other methods. In this chapter, I discuss methods of addressing problems associated with non-randomness of the key-explanatory variable – from reverse causality, omitted-factors bias, or self-selection bias. Recall that key-explanatory variables can have *good variation* and *bad variation*. One strategy for addressing potential *bad variation* and a bias in the coefficient estimate due to non-random factors determining the value of the key-X variable would be to convert the *bad variation* from being *operative* to being *held-constant*. This makes it so that the *operative variation* that goes into estimating how the key-X variable and the outcome are related to each other is based entirely on *good variation* – i.e., the variation that does not contribute to reverse causality, omitted-factors bias, and self-selection bias. Another strategy is to somehow rid the key-X variable of the *bad variation*. This is what I did in the rushing-vs.-passing example I gave in Box 6.2, in which my strategy was to attempt to strip the key-X variables (passing and rushing advantages of the home team) of the *bad-variation* component by just using first-half statistics. These are the two objectives of the methods of this chapter – isolate the *good variation* in the key-X variables by either holding constant the *bad variation* or somehow ridding the key-X variable of the *bad variation*.

Some studies use what are called **Natural Experiments**. They are actually (most of the time) human-made experiments. They are "natural" in that the researcher does not need to create an experiment, but rather uses an already-created source of randomness that was probably not designed as an experiment. For example, in a study I will describe in Chapter 11, on the topic of peer effects, researchers found that the Air Force Academy randomizes cadets to roommates and squadrons, which "naturally" creates a set of randomly-determined peers.

It remains a rare thing that one can use a Natural Experiment in a research study. It is for those who can search for randomness and create a research topic from that, and not for those who are assigned a topic and need to find a method to address potential biases. And so researchers often rely on **Quasi-Experimental Methods**. These are methods that do not have random assignment, but rather researchers design a model so that each observation is compared to other observations that are as similar as possible, except that they have different levels of exposure to the treatment. For example, with multiple observations per subject, it is possible to design a model so that a subject is compared to him-/her-/itself, pre-treatment to post-treatment (or for different levels of the treatment), which reduces much of the *bad variation*. This is what was done in the model estimating how class-size affects professor evaluations.

This chapter discusses several quasi-experimental methods. These methods are not perfect solutions, as they may have limitations for interpretation and may, at times, exacerbate other problems. Furthermore, just because one of these methods is applied does not mean that the researcher fully corrected for a given PITFALL. There are underlying conditions or assumptions that are needed, and so it is not always possible to validly apply these advanced methods to a particular empirical issue. But, if you were lucky and/or innovative enough to discover or create a valid quasi-experimental method, it would help towards ruling out explanations for empirical relationships that are alternative to the causal effect you are attempting to estimate.

In this chapter, you will learn:

- Various methods to address the PITFALLS of regression analysis, particularly to address the problem of non-random key-X variables
- The conditions necessary for such models
- The interpretations of the methods, along with detail on what part of the population the results would apply to (i.e., how widely the results can be extrapolated)
- That, sometimes, due to data or modeling limitations, a regression cannot address a research question, and you need to punt.

8.1 Fixed effects

This section presents a simple, albeit not always perfect, solution to address various biases from omitted-factors bias and, occasionally, reverse causality. A **fixed-effects model**, in most cases, is similar in nature to having a series of dummy variables representing the categories to be controlled for. In fact, other than a few situations (e.g., with heteroskedasticity corrections and non-linear models that you will see in Chapter 9), a fixed-effects model is the exact same as including a set of dummy variables. A few minor advantages of the fixed-effects model over merely including a set of dummy variables are that, if there are a large number of categories, you can avoid having to create all the variables (keeping the data set small) and avoid having many non-useful coefficient estimates from all those dummy variables (making the results easier to read).

Analyses using fixed effects can be of a few different types, based on the type of data and whether the key-explanatory variable is specific to a single subject (e.g., individuals) or applies to many subjects. Here are a few types of analyses that could use fixed effects, along with some examples:

1. Examining multiple subjects over time (panel data), with a subject-specific key-explanatory variable that could change over time:
   o How a person's oatmeal consumption affects their cholesterol.
   o How having an unemployed parent affects a teenager's drug use.
   o How state tax rates affect state-level economic growth.
   o How state-level drunk-driving laws affect the number of drunk-driving arrests in the state. (Even though the law applies to everyone in the state-year, the subject in this case is the state for a given year, and so the law is specific to the subject.)
2. Examining how a key-explanatory variable applying to many subjects affects those subjects:
   o How the state unemployment rate affects an individual teenager's drug use. (Note that the state unemployment rate applies to all teenagers in the state, as opposed to the example above in which having an unemployed parent is determined for each person.)
   o How a state-level drunk-driving law affects the probability that a person is arrested for driving drunk. (This is different from above because the subjects are individuals, not states.)

8.1.1 Setting up a model that could use fixed effects

Let's return to the topic from Chapters 4 and 6 on the issue: "How does class size affect student evaluations of professors?" A basic approach would be to estimate the following model:

$$E_{ipc} = \beta_1 CS_{ipc} + \varepsilon_{ipc} \tag{8.1}$$

where:
- E_{ipc} is the average evaluation for individual class i for professor p in course c
- CS_{ipc} is the class-size.

Compared to the earlier models that just had subscript i, we need the extra subscripts to incorporate the fixed effects. (Be mindful with the notation, as the subscript c refers to the course, and the subscript i refers to the individual class, which I did to be consistent with i representing an individual observation.)

We imagine that class-size could have a causal effect on the average evaluation of a professor, but could there be alternative reasons for why class-size and the evaluation of the professor would be associated with each other?

Yes! There are a few quite plausible alternative scenarios that could contribute to a relationship between class-size and the evaluation. Whereas these scenarios could be described in several ways, perhaps omitted-factors bias is the most fitting PITFALL. Higher quality for a professor would lead to higher evaluation scores and could lead to different class sizes: the high-quality professors would draw more students, they may get assigned to teach larger classes (perhaps the "intro" courses) to draw in more students to a major, or they might be rewarded by the department with smaller classes.

Likewise, there could be omitted-factors bias from the characteristics of a course. An interesting course (e.g., Regression Analysis) would tend to draw more students and would generally lead to higher evaluation scores regardless of the professor. In contrast, some courses would not be as interesting, drawing fewer students and causing all professors to have lower evaluation scores when teaching the course. Or it could be, by the nature of things or incidentally, that the larger intro courses (e.g., General Psychology) are less interesting than the smaller upper-level courses (e.g., Regression Methods in Psychology) ... or *vice versa*. In this case, inherent, unobservable differences in the courses (how interesting they are) could affect the evaluations as well as affect the class size. Again, we would have omitted-factors bias, and the direction of the bias could be positive or negative.

Given these possible sources of omitted-factors bias, before we claim that any relationship between class-size and evaluations is due to a causal effect of class-size, we need to rule out these alternative stories.

We probably cannot *fully* rule out alternative stories, but we can get closer to the true causal effect by including professor and course **fixed effects**. To understand how it works, let's rewrite equation (8.1) as follows:

$$E_{ipc} = \beta_1 CS_{ipc} + X_{ipc}\beta_2 + \left(\alpha_p + \alpha_c + e_{ipc} \right) \tag{8.2}$$

where, from equation (8.1), a set of control variables, X, is included, and the error term, ε, is separated into three parts:

- An average effect for the professor (α_p)
- An average effect for the course (α_c)
- The remaining error term (e_{ipc}) that could capture professor-specific effects for a given course or other reasons for higher or lower evaluations: (1) a professor may have a stronger or weaker-than-normal performance in a class for some reason; (2) due to natural variation or some meaningful trend, the students would be different in each class in terms of how well they receive or appreciate the material and teaching; and (3) other general sources of variation.

The problem, again, is omitted-factors bias in that factors that are part of the error term, (many of which would be captured in α_p or α_c) could be correlated with class-size, presumably not by class-size affecting these variables. This violates Assumption **A5** because the error term contains the effects of factors that are correlated with class-size – namely, the quality of the professor and the course. In plain English, this means that, by design, by the nature of things, or by an unplanned coincidence, the class-size is not random with respect to the average evaluation of the professor in the class because the class-size could be determined in some way that is related to the professor or the course, which have their own effects on the evaluations. Most of this would be *bad variation* in the class-size variable.

8.1.2 One-way fixed effects

To demonstrate what including fixed effects does in correcting for omitted-factors bias (and trying to convert *bad variation* from *operative* to *held-constant variation*), let's start by fixing the problem of differences in quality across professors. Applying professor fixed effects to the model would simply involve indicating in the statistical program that the model includes professor fixed effects. (The data do not need to be balanced in that all subjects have the same number of observations.)

This is almost equivalent to simply including a dummy variable for each professor, leaving one out as the reference category. For pure linear methods, such as OLS, these two methods are equivalent other than the standard errors when there is a correction for heteroskedasticity or for clustering. For non-linear methods (e.g., probit and logit models, which are used for dummy-variable outcomes and will be discussed in the next chapter), it is more complicated to use fixed effects – in fact, it cannot be used in probit models. Just using a set of dummy variables to represent the factor (each professor in this case) would be just as effective and would give a close-enough approximation to the interpretation that I would consider it equivalent enough. But the safer approach is to indicate fixed effects when doing heteroskedasticity or clustering corrections to the standard errors.

Applying a one-way-fixed-effects-method for the professor would estimate the mean value for the evaluation of each professor, conditional on CS and the variables in X. That is, the value of α_p for each professor in equation (8.2) is estimated (though not reported in results) and is usually denoted by μ_p, as follows:

$$E_{ipc} = \beta_1 CS_{ipc} + X_{ipc}\beta_2 + \mu_p + \left(\alpha_c + e_{ipc}\right) \tag{8.3}$$

Note that the convention is to use μ when describing a fixed effect and α when describing a component of an error term.

An important point to notice is that, in the error term in equation (8.3), α_c and ε_{ipc} no longer have the inherent differences across professors, α_p, as these differences are controlled for now. Thus, the error term should no longer be correlated with the class-size (CS) with respect to the quality of the professor. That is, as class-size varies in the model, the professor does not change because the professor is held constant. It is still possible that course-specific professor effects in the remaining error term, e_{ipc}, are correlated with class size. But this is almost certainly a smaller empirical association than that between professor quality and class-size.

What does adding fixed effects do to the model? It's the same as including a set of dummy variables to separate observations into the groups defined by the fixed effects. Recall from our example on this topic back in Section 4.3 that the coefficient estimate on the class-size variable represents the average of how the average evaluation tends to move with the class-size within each professor's set of classes, or the estimated effect for each professor. It is not an exact average of the coefficient estimates for the professors, but rather a weighted average. We then saw with PITFALL #7 in Chapter 6 that controlling for a categorization (which fixed effects do) could cause bias by over-weighting certain groups in the calculation of that average. I will describe this again in Section 8.1.7 and demonstrate how to address this bias in Section 8.2. For now, the important point is that, with the fixed effects, as class-size changes, the professor does not change; the professor is held constant.

In this case, the interpretation of β_1 in the fixed-effects model, equation (8.3), is how within-professor differences in class size (i.e., differences from the within-professor mean) are related to within-professor differences in the evaluations they receive, adjusting for the factors in X.

Another interpretation of fixed-effects models is that it transforms the data so that the professor's mean is subtracted from each variable. Thus, the estimates represent how divergences from the mean class size for a professor are related to divergences from the mean evaluation for the professor, adjusting for the other factors. Subtracting the professor's mean from the components in equation (8.2), we would have:

$$E_{ipc} - \bar{E}_p = \beta_1 \times \left(CS_{ipc} - \overline{CS}_p\right) + \left(X_{ipc} - \bar{X}_p\right)\beta_2 + \left(\tilde{\alpha}_c + e_{ipc}\right) \tag{8.4}$$

where the bars above the variables indicate the average for all observations for professor p. Note that α_p in equation (8.2) is no longer in the error term in equation (8.4) because it is a constant and becomes zero when subtracted by its average, and $\tilde{\alpha}_c$ is now the average effect for course c, factoring out the professor effect.

This one-way fixed effect (for professors) would rule out any explanation to the relationship between class-size and student evaluations of the professor (β_1) that is due to inherent differences across professors. It would move the variation in class-size due to the professor from *operative* to *held-constant variation*. This is a quasi-experimental method because a class for a given professor is being compared to a very similar set of observations – other classes for the same professor. However, we still have not addressed the potential omitted-factors bias from the course, which leads to …

8.1.3 Two-way fixed effects

Now, let's add a second set of fixed effects, for the course, to address omitted-factors bias due to "how interesting or demanding the course is" being related to class-size and affecting evaluations. The model (how it could be represented in an article or report) is the following:

$$E_{ipc} = \beta_1 CS_{ipc} + X_{ipc}\beta_2 + \mu_p + \mu_c + e_{ipc} \tag{8.5}$$

which adds μ_c, the fixed effect for each course.

This is now a two-way-fixed-effects model because two sets of categorizations are being controlled for. The equation says that the evaluation of the professor is determined by the class-size, a set of other factors (X), an effect particular to the professor, an effect particular to the class, and a random error component.

The interpretation of β_1 is now different. In equations (8.3) and (8.4), the estimate represented how within-professor differences in evaluations are related to within-professor differences in class size, adjusting for the variables in X. Now, with the two-way fixed effects in equation (8.5), the interpretation is:

How within-professor differences (deviations from the mean) in evaluations are related to within-professor differences in class size, adjusting for the course and the variables in X;
    or
How within-course differences in evaluations are related to within-course differences in class size, adjusting for the professor and the variables in X.

What this indicates is that two-way fixed effects is not as clean in terms of holding both factors constant. Only one factor (or categorization) can be held constant and have the estimated effect of the key-X variable be based on observations within each category or group of the categorization. The other factor is merely "adjusted for," meaning that the adjustment is subject to imprecision in the coefficient estimates. So, we either hold constant the professor and imperfectly factor out the course effects, or we hold constant the course and imperfectly factor out the professor effects. It turns out that, either way, it gives the same answer. And, even though it is not perfect, it is still better to use the fixed effects for both factors to minimize omitted-factors bias. That is, adjusting imperfectly for a factor is better than not adjusting at all.

We have now converted the *bad variation* in class-size (from both professor and course characteristics that affect both class-size and the evaluations) from *operative* to mostly *held-constant variation*. This, however, is not a perfect solution for three main reasons:

1. If a course were to change over time to be more or less appealing to students, in terms of how interesting or how demanding it is, there would be differences in course effects that are not controlled for with the course fixed effects. Similarly, if a professor were to change over time in his/her effectiveness, then fixed effects would not capture that.
2. Some professors might be better at teaching some classes than they are for other classes, leading to greater class-sizes and better evaluations.
3. As described above, one of the factors is imperfectly adjusted for and not held constant.

From any of these, there could still be omitted-factors bias, albeit much reduced from a model without the fixed effects.

8.1.4 Interacted fixed effects

Interacted fixed effects can address the just-stated second and third problems with two-way fixed effects. Instead of separate fixed effects for professor and course, this would involve interacted professor-course fixed effects as follows:

$$E_{ipc} = \beta_1 CS_{ipc} + X_{ipc}\beta_2 + \mu_{pc} + \varepsilon_{ipc} \tag{8.6}$$

In equation (8.6), the interacted fixed effects, μ_{pc} (having a double subscript and replacing the separate fixed effects, μ_p and μ_c) would effectively involve a separate fixed effect for each course that a professor teaches. For example, if there were 20 professors, 30 courses, and each professor taught four different courses, then:

*   Equation (8.5) would have 20 professor fixed effects and 30 course fixed effects
*   Equation (8.6) would have 80 (20 times 4) professor-course fixed effects.

The latter model would only work if professors had multiple segments of a given course so that there would be variation in class size within the 80 professor-course groups. The interpretation would become:

How differences in evaluations are related to differences in the class size in a given professor-course combination, adjusting for the factors in X.

This would make for even more similar comparison groups, and it would be back to the professor and course being fully held constant rather than one of them being imperfectly adjusted for. But, as mentioned above, changes in the quality of a professor or course over time can still lead to omitted-factors bias. Likewise, changes in a professor's quality/effectiveness for a given course could lead to omitted-factors bias. Still, this would be an improvement and help get an estimate closer to the true causal effect.

8.1.5 The trade-off of addressing bias vs. precision

The example above with the separate professor and course fixed effects vs. the professor-course-interacted fixed effects demonstrates the trade-off involved with using large sets of fixed-effects. Going from 20 professors and 30 course fixed effects in equation (8.5) to the 80 professor-course fixed effects in equation (8.6) has the following primary advantage and disadvantage:

- **Advantage**: It should reduce bias further, as identification of β_1 would come from how the evaluations of professors in a specific course change when the class-size changes in that course for that professor. This reduces any potential omitted-factors bias from some professors teaching certain classes better than others.
- **Disadvantage**: The greater number of fixed effects sops up a good portion of the variation, leaving less *operative variation* to get precise estimates. In other words, standard errors would likely be much larger and estimates would have less precision.

Researchers need to weigh the importance of further reducing *operative-bad variation* and the possibility of remaining omitted-factors bias versus improving the precision in the estimates when deciding how narrow they make the fixed effects. The larger sample a researcher has, the greater latitude there would be to add more fixed effects.

8.1.6 Can fixed effects address reverse causality and self-selection bias?

The fixed-effects method occasionally has the potential to address reverse causality. This would be the case in the rare circumstance that the reverse causality occurred across fixed-effects groups but not within the groups.

However, fixed effects do not address self-selection bias. A fixed-effects model essentially compares subjects before and after a treatment or at different levels of exposure to treatment. Consider the example from Section 6.6 on the effects of minimum-wage increases on employment. I suggested that the states and cities that would be less harmed from minimum-wage increases (in terms of potential employment loss) would be more likely to enact the increases. Thus, a fixed-effects model based on a panel data set that tracks states or cities over time would estimate the effects of minimum-wage increases more for those cities/states whose employment levels would likely be less harmed by such increases than for those whose employment would be affected. Thus, even with fixed effects, we'd still have a positive bias (in this case) from cities/states choosing whether to or how much to increase the minimum wage based on how it would affect them. The same argument could apply to estimating how state tax rates affect state economic growth. The states that chose to increase tax rates could be the states that expected, perhaps due to the strength of the state's economy, that it would have minimal impact on economic growth.

When there is self-selection bias, then a fixed-effects model does not estimate the Average Treatment Effect (ATE). Rather, it would be estimating what is called the **Average Treatment effect for the Treated** (ATT). This is what we would expect to be the experiences of those who chose to receive the treatment rather than an average effect for everyone (or a random subject). This is much less useful than the ATE, as it does not represent what the average effect would be nor what the expected effect would be for a random subject.

Whether there is self-selection bias in a fixed-effects estimate depends on whether the treatment involves a conscious choice by the subject (or by someone closely tied with the subject, like a parent) or is out of their control. For example, estimating how a divorce affects children, the parents have the choice to divorce, so there would likely be self-selection bias. Regarding aggregate data at the state level, estimating the effects of minimum-wage increases involves a choice by states, so there would likely be self-selection bias. In contrast, estimating the effect of the state unemployment rate on health outcomes would probably not involve self-selection bias because states do not choose their unemployment rate – perhaps states can slightly affect the unemployment rate with certain policies, but those would rarely be made based on how the unemployment rate affected health or similar outcomes.

8.1.7 Problem #1 from fixed effects: bias from over-weighted groups (PITFALL #7)

As discussed in Section 6.10, it turns out that not all groups that are controlled for with dummy variables or with fixed effects would contribute to the estimation of the causal effect, β_1, proportional to their sample size. Recall equation (4.5):

$$\hat{\beta}_1 = \sum_g \hat{\beta}_{1g} \times \left[\frac{N_g \times \text{var}(X_1 \mid g,\, X_2)}{Z} \right] \tag{4.5}$$

which states that the coefficient estimate represents the average of the within-group estimates, where the groups are defined by a set of dummy variables for a certain categorization. This bias was demonstrated in Table 6.12 in Section 6.10. The model naturally gives weights to groups that are disproportionate to their sample size, based on the variance of the key-X variable.

The notional example I created in Section 6.10 had different effects across professors and distinctly different variances of class-size. Thus, there was a sizable bias. A similar story, in a real-world situation, could be made on courses. Courses that are always around the same size would have a small contribution to the estimation of β_1, whereas courses with greater variation would contribute more to the estimate. And there could be different effects of class-size for different courses.

Without any correction for this problem that occurs with fixed effects (or merely using a dummy variable or set of dummy variables to separate a sample into categories), the estimated effect could be biased. If the coefficient estimate were to be compared before and after the correction with fixed effects, any change from reducing omitted-factors bias (or another bias) would be confounded with changes in the weighting of the groups. That is, all observations would be essentially weighted proportionately to their number of observations in the cross-sectional model, as each professor in my notional example effectively has 25% weight in the sample. But in the model controlling for the professor, the weights shift. In that example, Professor D has a much greater effective weight, while Professor A has a much smaller weight. Thus, fixed-effects-corrected estimated effects could be different from uncorrected estimates due to: (1) correcting for the bias; and (2) shifting weights across groups. Without a correction for shifting weights, a researcher cannot determine how much the coefficient estimate was biased in the uncorrected model. And the researcher could not estimate an unbiased effect. I present a correction for this bias in Section 8.2.

8.1.8 Problem #2 from fixed effects: greater bias from any measurement error

It was discussed back in Section 6.7, on PITFALL #4 on measurement error, that adding control variables could exacerbate any bias from measurement error. This is especially the case with fixed-effects, which switch all *operative variation* across fixed-effects groups to *held-constant variation*. With an analysis of class-size and student evaluations using actual data, measurement error (for the explanatory variable) could occur because there could be differences between the numbers of students enrolled, showing up for class, and filling out the student evaluation. Using fixed effects reduces *operative variation* in class-size but does not reduce variation from measurement error. Thus, variation from measurement error will constitute a higher share of the remaining *operative variation* in the class-size variable when fixed effects are applied. With the greater measurement-error-variation-as-a-percentage-of-*operative-variation*-in-the-key-X-variable, there would likely be greater attenuation bias in the estimates (i.e., a greater bias towards zero), as I demonstrated in Table 6.7 in Section 6.7.4.

Note that it is not the percentage of observations that have a mismeasured key-X variable that matters for the extent of bias from measurement error. Rather, the extent of bias depends on the percentage of the "*operative variation* in the key-X variable" that is due to error. When we control for certain factors, we have less *operative variation* that contributes to the coefficient estimate, which causes variation from measurement error to be a greater percentage of *operative variation*.

As with the bias from PITFALL #7, when comparing an estimated effect from before and after fixed effects, the correction from reducing other biases (such as omitted-factors bias) could be confounded with the increased bias from measurement error.

Thus, when using fixed effects, one needs to consider how much error there is in the key-explanatory variable. An insignificant estimate may be attributable to attenuation bias, and a significant estimate may be indicative of a larger effect that is dampened by the measurement-error bias.

Unlike the bias from over-weighted groups (PITFALL #7) that is introduced or exacerbated with fixed effects, there is no solution to the increased bias from measurement error with such models. The same concept will apply to first-difference (FD) methods, in Section 8.4, for which I will give an example that demonstrates how this problem could lead to ambiguous interpretations.

8.1.9 Problem #3 from fixed effects: bias from using lagged-dependent variables

A less-common problem could arise in fixed effects when there is a panel data set (i.e., multiple observations per subject) and you have a lagged-dependent variable as an explanatory variable. The problem is that, if the lagged-dependent variable is greater than the within-subject mean, then the current dependent variable is more likely to be less than the within-subject mean. This occurs because the fixed effects make it so a person (or entity) is just being compared to him/herself, so one observation being above the mean would necessitate that the other observations for that person would be, on average, below the mean. This would contribute a negative bias to the estimated relationship between the lagged and current dependent variables. Arellano and Bond (1991) developed an approach to address this problem, with what is called a Generalized Method of Moments model.[1] (See the Stata and R code on the book's website to correct for this problem.)

8.1.10 Application – an actual study on class-size and professor evaluation

Some researchers examined this issue at the University of California–Santa Barbara (Bedard and Kuhn, 2008). The authors have many sets of results, but Table 8.1 displays the results from their Appendix Table A.1 that are the most easily summarizable. The results provide an estimated average linear effect, whereas the author's preferred specifications, rightly, had non-linear effects with quadratic and higher-order polynomial functions of class-size or categories of class-size. Note that a single observation represents a given class; and, for that class, the dependent variable is the average evaluation score and the key-explanatory variable is the class-size.

This set of results presents an interesting case. In the "quasi-cross-sectional" model in which there were no controls for the professor or the course (the first column of results), the coefficient estimate on class-size is statistically insignificant, providing no evidence for any effect of class-size on professor evaluations. But this estimate could be affected by the various sources of omitted-factors bias. In order to rule out other explanations for how class-size and professor evaluations were related, they included professor and course fixed effects (in the second column of results). They did not estimate models with professor-course-interacted fixed effects, probably because there would not have been enough variation to do so precisely.

With the professor and course fixed effects, the estimate became negative and significant (-0.0011), as might be expected. One could argue that it is not that strong of an effect, given that a one-standard-deviation increase in the class size (of 108) would only be expected to decrease evaluations by 0.12, which is less than one-fifth of the standard deviation in evaluations (0.65). Furthermore, the lower bound of the 95% confidence interval on the estimated effect would be around -0.0003. Nevertheless, this provides some evidence for how other things besides professor effectiveness could impact evaluations. There was no correction for over-weighted groups, as this study was conducted before this bias was known.

8.1.11 Summary of fixed effects

Fixed-effects models can effectively address omitted-factors bias in some circumstances. It can not address any self-selection bias or, in most cases, reverse causality. There are some cases in which applying fixed effects creates more problems. If there were any measurement error in the key-X variable (or any other variable), any bias from that measurement error would be exacerbated with fixed effects (PITFALL #4). Any bias from measurement error cannot be detected, but we must use knowledge of how the key-X variable was created to gauge the existence and extent of measurement error. In addition, using fixed effects could over-weight some groups with larger variances in the key-X variable (PITFALL #7). This latter problem could be fixed by re-weighting observations, as will be done in

Table 8.1 The effects of class size on average professor evaluation from Bedard and Kuhn (2008)

	Dependent variable = average professor-evaluation score for the class	
	Quasi-cross-section (no fixed effects) (n = 655 classes)	Fixed effects for professor and course (n = 459 classes)
Class size	−0.0004	−0.0011**
	(0.0003)	(0.0004)

Other variables included in the model are the year and quarter variables. ** indicates $p < 0.05$.

the next section. In contrast, any bias from measurement error cannot be fixed. This does not mean that it is not worth applying fixed effects, as correcting for omitted-factors bias is essential, and the bias from measurement error usually causes a bias towards zero, meaning that it rarely would bias an estimate from being correctly insignificant to incorrectly significant. Generally, fixed-effects models work well if the key-X variable is not a choice and there is minimal measurement error.

Box 8.1   Do professional golfers behave badly (or, act irrationally) on the golf course?

Most economic theories rely on the assumption that people and firms always act in their best interest … you know the story … to maximize their utility or their profits. Well, Pope and Schweitzer (2011) uncovered some evidence that says professional golfers don't always act in their best interest. They investigated whether golfers act irrationally around the arbitrary reference point of par, which is the expected number of shots an expert golfer would take to complete a given hole. The idea is that golfers should try to complete a hole in as few shots as possible. And so, in most situations, effort and risk should be the same, regardless of how many shots they have taken for a given hole. But golfers may be subject to the concept of "loss aversion," which is that people tend to take costly measures to avoid a loss. In this situation, anything worse than par could be considered a "loss."

The authors aimed to compare whether golfers are more likely to make a putt for par than a putt for an eagle (two shots better than par), a birdie (one shot better than par), or a bogey (one shot worse than par. Missing the putt for par would result in a perceived "loss." The authors used a data set of over 2.5 million putts from men's professional tournaments, with information on the location of the ball relative to the hole. They could have just compared all putts for par versus putts for the other scores, controlling for the distance to the hole. But there could be omitted-factors bias in that better players may be more likely to have easier shots for birdie than weaker players. To address this, they included in the model *player fixed effects*. This means that comparisons of birdie-vs.-par-vs.-bogey putts were just being made for each player individually and then combined into average effects. This helps rule out this potential source of omitted-factors bias. There are other potential sources of omitted-factors bias that the authors attempt to rule out with other sets of fixed effects in some models, such as fixed effects for the particular tournament-hole-round. In addition, all models controlled for a 7th-order-polynomial for shot distance − i.e., distance, distance-squared, …, distance-to-the-7th-power. Here are the results, based on a linear probability model, with the dependent variable being whether the player made the putt (from column 4 in Table 3 of the article, with both the player and tournament-round-hole fixed effects).

(Dependent variable = whether the player made the putt)	
Variable	Coef. Est. (Std. Error)
Putt for eagle	−0.042 (0.002)***
Putt for birdie	−0.029 (0.001)***
Putt for par	Reference category
Putt for bogey	0.003 (0.001)***
Putt for double bogey	−0.003 (0.002)

*** indicates $p < 0.01$.

Note that three of these estimates are highly statistically significant, with narrow confidence intervals. So, compared to the par putt, players are an estimated 4.2-percentage-points [95% confidence interval of 3.8–4.6-percentage points] less likely to make a putt for birdie, holding the shot distance (and player) constant. The estimates are actually similar to those without player-fixed effects (column 1 in that table, which I do not report here). Nevertheless, it was worthwhile to use the fixed effects, just to make the analysis cleaner and minimize the risk of certain sources of omitted-factors bias.

One thing these results could signify is that players try their hardest when they face a potential loss (the putt for par) or greater loss (the putt for bogey). In addition, it could mean that a player's goal is shifted for the birdie (or eagle) putt from making the putt to making sure that he keeps himself in position to make the par putt (or birdie putt) if he misses.

Subsequent research (Stone and Arkes, 2016) found that players don't only bracket around the reference point of par on a single hole, but also on a rolling set of two holes and on a round (in contrast to the tournament). That is, if they are above par for the round of 18 holes (at least for Round 1 of a tournament), the evidence suggests that they try extra hard (or take a greater risk) to get a birdie on the current hole to make up for being behind for the round. And this comes at the cost of an increased chance of a bogey on the current hole as well.

8.2 Correcting for over-weighted groups (PITFALL #7) using fixed effects

With the bias from PITFALL #7 (Section 6.10 and reviewed above in Section 8.1.7), there needs to be a correction to properly use fixed effects when there are different causal effects and variances of the key-X (treatment) variable across groups. In the example I used in Chapter 6, there were negative class-size effects for Professors A and B, but the estimated effects for Professors C and D, both of which are close to zero, dominated the overall estimate in the fixed-effects model. The disproportionate weights for Professors C and D (relative to their sample size) caused the overall fixed-effect estimate to be weighted towards their near-zero estimated effects of class-size. Thus, varying weights due to different variances of the key-X variable could cause the fixed-effects estimate to be biased. The same bias occurs with a regular OLS model (without fixed effects) that has dummy variables classifying the sample into groups.

I mentioned back in Section 6.10 how Gibbons et al. (2019) formalize this bias. They also propose a change to the fixed-effects model by re-weighting observations by the inverse of the variance of the key-X variable within each fixed-effects group and conditional on the other X variables. This weight would be constant for each observation in a given fixed-effects group. They call this the **regression-weighted estimator**.

This correction should be applied not just to fixed-effects models, but to any model that uses dummy variables to categorize observations in a sample. This includes any categorization for states, and even something as simple as racial/ethnic indicators.

With the notional data I created back in Section 6.10 on how class-size affects professor evaluations, the correction is fairly simple, as there were not any other confounding factors other than the professor. The correction merely involves weighting each observation for a given professor by the inverse of the variance of class-size for that professor. Table 8.2 provides the new calculations that correspond

Table 8.2 Demonstrating the correction for over-weighted groups when using fixed effects (or a categorization with dummy variables)

(1) Prof.	(2) N_g	(2a) Weight = $1/var(CS)$ = $1 \div (5)$	(3) $N_g/var(CS)$ (2) × (2a)	(4) $\hat{\beta}_{1g}$	(5) var(CS)	(6) Weight numerator (3) × (5)	(7) Final weight	(8) $\hat{\beta}_{1g}$ × weight (4) × (7)
A	25	0.0126	0.3152	−0.0343	79.3100	25.0000	0.2500	−0.0086
B	25	0.0039	0.0970	−0.0120	257.6767	25.0000	0.2500	−0.0030
C	25	0.0023	0.0586	−0.0004	426.4601	25.0000	0.2500	−0.0001
D	25	0.0011	0.0274	0.0015	911.1898	25.0000	0.2500	0.0004
	100					100.0000	1.0000	**−0.0113**

Table 8.3 A comparison of a standard and regression-weighted fixed-effects model

All (course fixed effects)	Dependent variable = average evaluation from the class (n = 100)	
	Model from Section 6.10 no correction)	Correction with using the inverse of within-professor var(CS) as sample weights
Coefficient estimate (standard error) on class-size	−0.0027 (0.0037)	−0.0113 (0.0083)

The other three methods for fixed effects (in the Stata and R code guides to the text analyses, on the book's website) give lower standard errors for these two models. This only happens with corrections for heteroskedasticity.

to Table 6.13 in Section 6.10. The big difference from earlier is that the sampling weight is added in column (2a), which is the inverse of the variance in column (5). This weight then combines with the sample size for the group in column (3) and is then used for the weight numerator in column (6) and the final weight in column (7). Now, the weight for each group is even, which is in proportion to the sample size for each group. The overall estimate comes to −0.0113, which is much closer to the true Average Treatment Effect I had imposed of −0.0100 than the estimate without the correction of −0.0027.

Of course, the easier method (than doing all these calculations) is to simply estimate the regression with the sample weights shown in column (2a). The regression gives the standard error of the overall estimate. And so, in Table 8.3, I show the new regression compared to the one that was subject to the bias in Section 6.10. Now, the estimated effect of class-size on evaluations, −0.0113, is highly statistically significant and an unbiased estimate of the average effect I had imposed. If I were to re-randomize and re-estimate this an infinite number of times, the average estimated effect would be exactly −0.0100, which means that the estimate of −0.0113 is unbiased. Still, even though it is unbiased, it is off-target by 11.3%. This is the product of sampling variation, and it demonstrates even an accurate (unbiased) estimate might still be wrong due to imprecision.

The correction above was simple, as there were no other control variables to use in calculating the conditional variance of class-size for each professor and the subsequent weights. If there were other variables in the model, then those would need to be factored out before calculating the weights. The steps would be:

Step 1: Regress the key-X variable (CS) on the other explanatory variables and fixed effects.
Step 2: Calculate the residuals for each observation from that regression.

Step 3: Calculate the variance of the residual within each fixed-effects group.
Step 4: Estimate the fixed-effects model, using as sample weights the inverse of the variance of the residual for each fixed-effects group from Step 3.

An important consideration is that sometimes the weight of a fixed-effects group comes out to be extraordinarily large due to having hardly any variation in the key-X variable, particularly after adjustment for other explanatory variables. This could result in far too high a reliance or weight on an imprecise estimate. In turn, this could lead to higher standard errors and lead to estimates that are far off from the true causal effect. This is where some regression diagnostics might be useful. It could be worthwhile to check the weights and perhaps delete from the sample observations that have too high a weight. It is probably better to use some standard such as requiring a certain minimum variance or standard deviation in the original key-X variable or in the residual of that key-X variable after factoring out the other explanatory variables and fixed effects. Unfortunately, there is no standard for what is too high a weight. This is another reason why regression is an "art."

Another consideration is using the proper standard errors. Gibbons et al. (2019) provide a method to calculate the new standard errors. This requires some complicated matrix algebra. From a practical standpoint, the standard errors they propose should not be that different from what you would obtain naturally as you re-weight the observations, and it is debatable whether the change in standard errors you would get from that correction is worth the effort to obtain them, particularly with all the issues discussed in Chapter 5 on the problems with p-values and hypothesis tests. Perhaps the prudent thing to do is use a little lower p-value requirement to conclude that a hypothesis test provides evidence for an empirical relationship.

Finally, the method described here can address over-weighted groups for one categorization of fixed effects (or a set of dummy variables). However, if there were multiple categorizations (two-way or more fixed effects), then there is no easy solution. For example, there could be reasons why the effects of class-size on evaluations and the variance of class-size were different across courses so that some courses would get over-weighted. The best option, if feasible, is to do interacted fixed effects so that it is effectively one-way fixed effects. Another option is to do the correction for the categorization that has the greater differences across groups in the variance of the key-X, or the categorization that you would theoretically expect to have the greater differences across groups in the effects of the key-X variable on the outcome. However, the more conservative approach would be to perform this correction for each categorization to determine how similar or different the overall estimated effects were.

There is an exercise question for this chapter that takes an interesting article from the *American Economic Review* on how temperature affects GDP growth and applies the correction to give a different result from what the study found.

As a quick note similar to the one in Section 5.4.2, the two main statistical programs that I use (Stata and R) produce the same coefficient estimates but different standard errors for the fixed-effects models, particularly for the heteroskedasticity-corrected standard errors. I am providing the standard errors produced by Stata, as they are larger – i.e., more conservative.

8.3 Random effects

A **random-effects model** is an alternative to fixed effects that, in some cases, can produce smaller standard errors. The requirement for a random-effects model is that the variation in effects of the subjects (such as a professor effect or a course effect) is random with respect to the other explanatory variables. From our example, the professor and the course effects would be uncorrelated with the class size and other explanatory variables. That is, from a generic equation with a single-dimensional fixed effect of the individual, i:

$$Y_{it} = X_{it}\beta + (\alpha_i + e_{it})$$

(8.7)

the following conditions must hold: cov $(X, \alpha_i) = 0$.

If this were to hold, then applying a random-effects model would improve the efficiency of the estimates. Furthermore, random-effects models allow a researcher to estimate the effects of subject-specific traits that would be held constant in a fixed-effects model. For example, a model using fixed effects for professors could not estimate the effects of professor gender or race, but using random effects for professors would allow one to estimate the gender and race effects.

If the random effects were not random with respect to the other explanatory variables, then it leads to inconsistent estimates, meaning that as the sample size increases, the estimates do not converge to the true population coefficients.

Basically, using random effects is a way of getting more efficient estimates (with lower standard errors), which increases the likelihood that you achieve statistical significance and narrows confidence intervals. However, it comes at the cost of not being consistent if there is any non-zero covariance (or correlation) of the effects of certain subjects (e.g., the professor or the course) with the class size or other X variables.

One way to determine whether to use random effects is by conducting a **Hausman test**. The Hausman test has the following hypothesis test:

$$H_0 : \mathrm{cov}\left(X, \alpha_i\right) = 0$$
$$H_1 : \mathrm{cov}\left(X, \alpha_i\right) \neq 0$$

If there were a single X variable, then the Hausman test statistic would be:

$$H = \frac{\left(\hat{\beta}_{FE} - \hat{\beta}_{RE}\right)^2}{\left(\mathrm{var}\left(\hat{\beta}_{FE}\right) - \mathrm{var}\left(\hat{\beta}_{RE}\right)\right)}$$

(8.8)

where $\hat{\beta}_{FE}$ and $\hat{\beta}_{RE}$ are the coefficient estimates on the single X variable for the fixed-effects and the random-effects models. This test statistic, H, can be tested under a chi-squared distribution with one degree of freedom: $H \sim \chi(1)$. In the more likely situation in which there is more than one X variable, the Hausman test statistic relies on a Linear-Algebra calculation, with vectors of coefficient estimates and covariance matrices:

$$H = \left(\hat{\beta}_{FE} - \hat{\beta}_{RE}\right)' \left[var\left(\hat{\beta}_{FE}\right) - var\left(\hat{\beta}_{RE}\right)\right]^{-1}\left(\hat{\beta}_{FE} - \hat{\beta}_{RE}\right)$$

(8.9)

Luckily, this is easily computed in our various computer programs so we do not have to deal with the Linear Algebra.

The idea behind these test statistics is that, if the differences between the coefficient estimates in the random effects and the fixed-effects models were large relative to the efficiency gains (in terms of lower standard errors), it would suggest that the random-effects estimates would be inconsistent. Some argue that a researcher should go with fixed effects if the Hausman test statistic, H, is statistically significant. That said, one could argue that just because it is insignificant does not mean that the X variable and the subject-specific effects are uncorrelated. Thus, I would argue that the fixed-effects model is a more conservative approach. In addition, it has a nice interpretation of being based on within-subject effects.

As an example of an application of random effects, consider a study evaluating a new surgical procedure (the treatment) relative to a standard surgical procedure (the control).[2] The problem is that the effects of the surgical team could impact the estimated effectiveness of the new surgery relative to the standard surgery. Ideally, several surgical teams would be trained in performing both the standard and the new surgery.

If the surgical teams are then randomized for which surgery they perform, along with the patients being randomized to the surgery, then random effects can be applied as follows:

$$Y_{ij} = X_{ij}\beta_1 + \beta_2 T_{ij} + U_j + \varepsilon_{ij} \tag{8.10}$$

where:
- Y is the post-surgery outcome for patient i and surgical team j
- X is a set of control variables
- T is the treatment (if the patient received the new surgery)
- U_j is the random effect of the surgical team.

The idea here is that, by treating the surgical team as a random instead of a fixed factor, the results could be generalized to all potential surgical teams rather than just to the surgical teams involved in the study.

Again, using random effects relies on the assumption that the assignment of the individual factor (in our case, the surgical team) is random with respect to the other explanatory variables, including the treatment, T_{ij}. Unless you are certain that this is the case, then fixed effects is typically the more conservative approach.

8.4 First-differences

8.4.1 The concept of using first-differences

As with fixed effects, first-difference (FD) models are meant to address the problem of omitted-factors bias. The idea behind FD models is that, to eliminate an unobserved subject-specific factor that may be correlated with the key-explanatory variable, you examine a change over time rather than just the outcome at a single point in time. So you examine how the change in the outcome (Y) moves over a certain period with a given change in the key-X variable. However, there are also cases in which two observations that occur at the same time for the same subject are differenced, such as for different classes for a student, as is used in Box 8.2.

The concept behind FD models is applied by most school districts, often without a regression, in how they evaluate teachers. It is generally understood that we cannot compare the end-of-year achievement of one teacher's students to the students of other teachers because there could be large differences in the original preparation and background of the students that teachers have. These differences may be due to systematic patterns, as teachers in richer school districts will tend to get better-prepared students than those in lower-income districts. Natural variation (i.e., luck) could also cause variation in the preparedness of students a teacher gets in a given year.

To reduce the impact of differences in the preparedness of the students in the evaluation of teachers, most school districts use the average change in the students' achievement over the course of the year (or from one year to the next). This is often called the "value-added." This eliminates the influence of student-specific factors that stay constant over time. But there still could be students who naturally learn more easily than others. So there may still be student-specific factors, such as the ability to learn, that influence comparisons of teachers, but these should be much less than the overall differences across students.

FD models have the potential to address omitted-factors bias. However, as with fixed-effects models, they do not address self-selection bias (for the same reasons as for fixed effects). And so, as with fixed-effects models, in the presence of self-selection bias, the FD model would estimate the Average Treatment effect for the Treated (ATT), not the Average Treatment Effect (ATE).

8.4.2 First-difference example with aggregate data

Let's apply the FD approach to build on the model on the unemployment rate and teenage drug (marijuana) use from Sections 3.3 and 6.8. We will use aggregate rates of state-level teenage marijuana use rather than data on individuals, as in Section 6.8. We need to move the *bad variation* in the state unemployment rate due to state effects from *operative* to *held-constant variation.*

To examine this, I took one observation from each state for both the 2006–2007 period and the 2009–2010 period, averaging the youth marijuana use and the unemployment rate for the two years within each period. Two-year averages are used because that is how the youth marijuana use rates are reported to improve the precision of the estimated use rates for smaller states.[3]

The model for the cross-sectional model is simply:

$$MJ_{st} = \beta_0 + \beta_1 UR_{st} + \varepsilon_{st} \tag{8.11}$$

where
- MJ_{st} is the youth marijuana use rate in state s in period t
- UR_{st} is the average unemployment rate in state s in period t
- $\varepsilon_{st} = \alpha_s + \varepsilon_{st,}$ where α_s is the *unobserved state effect* for marijuana use, and ε_{st} is the random component of the error term.

To address any potential omitted-factors bias, we can estimate an FD model as follows:

$$\left(MJ_{s2} - MJ_{s1}\right) = \beta_0 + \beta_1 \times \left(UR_{s2} - UR_{s1}\right) + \left[\left(\alpha_s + e_{s1}\right) - \left(\alpha_s + e_{s2}\right)\right] \tag{8.12a}$$

or

$$\left(MJ_{s2} - MJ_{s1}\right) = \beta_0 + \beta_1 \times \left(UR_{s2} - UR_{s1}\right) + \left(e_{s2} - e_{s1}\right) \tag{8.12b}$$

where subscripts 1 and 2 on *MJ, UR,* and the error terms refer to period 1 (2006–2007) and period 2 (2009–2010). Note that equation (8.12b) is devoid of a state-specific effect (α_s), as they cancel each other out in the difference. The interpretation will simply be:

How the change in state teenage marijuana use rates from one period to the next is related to the change in state unemployment rate.

Of course, there still could be omitted-factors bias from incidental correlation. But this incidental correlation would likely be smaller than any omitted-factors bias from state effects that had been discussed earlier.

As demonstrated in Figure 8.1, this model mimics a cross-sectional model, as there is one observation per state. Every state had an increase in the unemployment rate over this time, as the latter period (2009–2010) was during the Financial Crisis. Most states also had an increase in teenage marijuana use over this period. But these two statistics, together, do not say that the unemployment rate increases led to increases in teenage marijuana use. Rather, a better test would be to examine whether those states with the larger increases in the unemployment rate tended to have larger increases in teenage marijuana use. Using a similar quadrant analysis as that from Figure 2.2 in Section 2.4, it looks like the points in the top-right and bottom-left quadrants dominate (with Arizona, AZ, being a large exception), although, given that I use sample weights of the square root of the 2010 state population, the observations would not be equally counted.

Table 8.4 shows the results of the models. Columns (1) and (2) have separate cross-sectional samples for the two periods – equation (8.11). And column (3) shows the FD estimate from equation (8.12b). Note that only the cross-sectional coefficient estimate on the unemployment rates for the 2006–2007 analysis is positive and significant, albeit not strongly significant, as the lower bound of the 95% confidence interval is only 0.047. But the estimate from the FD model is much lower than the other two estimates. This suggests that there was some omitted-factors bias affecting the cross-sectional estimates, as the FD estimates should be much more trustworthy. That said, measurement error could become a larger problem with FD models (just as with fixed-effects models), again because the measurement-error-as-a-percentage-of-operative-variation-in-the-key-X-variable is now higher. This would likely lead to a bias towards zero in the estimates. Thus, it cannot be determined whether the reduction in the coefficient estimates on the unemployment rate is from reducing omitted-factors bias or from increasing bias from measurement error. In the end, with these data, I

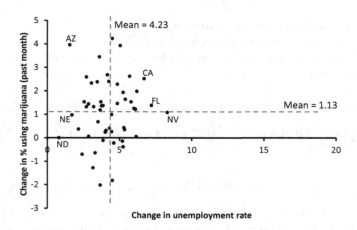

Figure 8.1 The first-difference model for the unemployment rate and teen marijuana use

Table 8.4 The effects of the unemployment rate on youth marijuana use (n = 51)

	(1) Cross section for 2006–2007 averages	(2) Cross section for 2009–2010 averages	(3) First-difference model
		Dependent variable	
	2006–2007 use rates	2009–2010 use rates	Change in use rate from 2006–2007 to 2009–2010
Unemployment rate (2006–2007)	0.524** (0.237) [0.047, 1.001]		
Unemployment rate (2009–2010)		0.244 (0.148) [−0.054, 0.542]	
Change in the unemployment rate			0.153 (0.106) [−0.061, 0.366]
Constant	7.638*** (1.065)	8.971*** (1.406)	0.480 (0.533)
R-squared	0.071	0.035	0.030

Sources: NSDUH (https://www.datafiles.samhsa.gov/dataset/national-survey-drug-use-and-health-2020-nsduh-2020-ds0001) for youth marijuana-use rates by state; and Bureau of Labor Statistics (https://www.bls.gov/web/laus/laumstrk.htm) for state unemployment rates.

Standard errors in parentheses. The standard errors are corrected for heteroskedasticity. The 95% confidence intervals are in brackets. The observations are weighted by the square root of the 2010 state population. $***p < 0.01, **p < 0.05, *p < 0.1$.

would conclude that there is no convincing evidence for an effect of the unemployment rate on state teenage-marijuana-use rates.

There is one other interesting thing to note here. The R^2 is lowest for the FD model, but it is the model we probably should place the most faith in. *This is a good example where the "goodness-of-fit" should not dictate the best model.*

Box 8.2 Are teacher qualifications important?

Who are the better teachers for our kids? How do we select the most qualified teachers? Dee and Cohodes (2008) examine how much subject-specific certifications and college majors are indicative of teacher quality (measured by student test scores). For example, a math teacher may be more effective if he/she has a math-teaching certificate or majored in math in college. The naïve approach to examine this would be to just do a comparison of average student scores for teachers who have subject-specific certifications and majors to student scores for teachers without such a credential or a major, but there could be differences in the quality of the students that a particular teacher may get.

To address this issue, Dee and Cohodes estimate a first-difference model for student achievement. They use data from the National Education Longitudinal Study of 1988, which matches standardized test scores for 8th-grade students with information on their teachers from two subjects: one from math or science, and one from reading or social studies. The regression model, slightly amended from their version, is the following:

$$\left(Y_{1ic} - Y_{2ic}\right) = \lambda\left(Z_{1ic} - Z_{2ic}\right) + \left(\varepsilon_{1ic} - \varepsilon_{2ic}\right)$$

where subscripts 1 and 2 are school subjects 1 and 2, i is the student, and c is the class. Y is the standardized test score (each point equals one standard deviation), and Z is the set of teacher-qualification variables. Note that the first-difference is for the student across classes. Furthermore, any student traits would fall out of the model with the first-difference, so no student variables are included. Here are their main results, from Table 2 of the article:

Dependent variable = standardized test score		
Variable	OLS, with school fixed effects	First-difference
Teacher certified in the subject	0.122 (0.026)***	0.042 (0.021)**
Teacher majored in the subject	0.055 (0.016)***	0.009 (0.013)

*** $p < 0.01$, ** $p < 0.05$, * $p < 0.1$.

Without the first-difference by the student, the OLS model suggests that both subject-specific teacher certifications and majors contribute to greater student learning. However, the FD model suggests the OLS model overstates those effects. There is no evidence that having a teacher majoring in the subject he/she teaches is associated with different test scores. In contrast, there is some evidence that having a teacher certified in the subject is associated with higher test scores, with the estimate being an effect of about 4% of a standard deviation. However, note that the lower bound of the 95% confidence interval is pretty close to zero. So the evidence may be suggestive of such an effect, but it is certainly not definitive.

Note that this is a case in which the data were not panel (multiple observations over time for a subject), but rather multiple observations per subject at the same time. The first-difference still works.

8.5 Difference-in-differences

8.5.1 The basic difference-in-difference (DD) model

Difference-in-difference (DD) models can be effective in addressing omitted-factors bias. While there are variants, the classic DD models involves:

- a treatment and control groups that can be compared over two different periods
- the treatment occurs that between periods.

The primary condition to make the DD model valid would be that the treatment and control groups are similar enough so that, without the treatment, both would have had the same average changes in the outcome between the two periods. If that condition is the case, then DD models estimate either:

- The Average Treatment Effect (ATE) if the control group would have had the same average change in the outcome from periods 1 to 2 as the treatment group did, had they received the treatment.
- The Average Treatment effect for the Treated (ATT) if the control group would have a different average change in the outcome (from the treatment group) had they had the treatment.

Any self-selection bias from a choice in whether to receive the treatment would cause the estimated effect to be the ATT rather than the more desired ATE. As stated earlier, the ATT tells us little about what the average effect in the population would be, or what a random subject might expect his/her individual effect to be. Whether it is the ATE or ATT typically comes down to whether the treatment was a conscious choice of the subject or just something out of the subject's control.

Let's consider a notional example of how participating in a meditation program affects the growth in math proficiency from 10th to 11th grade. A naïve approach would be to regress the math test score (Y) on whether the student participated in the meditation program (T). In this case, there would likely be omitted-factors bias. It may be the more open-minded (or hard-working and stressed) students who choose to participate in the meditation program, leading to perhaps a positive bias on the estimated effect. There is also a potential problem of self-selection bias. The ones who would participate in the meditation program would tend to be those who believe that they would benefit more from the program, which would also contribute to a positive bias. This will have implications for the interpretation below.

A DD model effectively compares the change in average student test scores, say from 10th to 11th grade (one "difference") for the treatment group and the control group (the other "difference"). Figure 8.2 shows graphically what the DD model is estimating. The DD model allows for initial differences between the treatment and the control group, indicated by the different average scores in 10th grade. But it assumes that the hypothetical average growth rate in the scores for the treatment group, had they not had the treatment, (indicated by the dashed line for the treatment group), would be the same as (parallel to) the actual average growth rate for the control group. This is something we can only theorize on rather than check, as we cannot observe the counterfactual. The difference

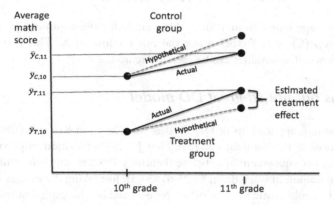

Figure 8.2 Difference-in-difference notional example

between the actual and hypothetical 11th-grade scores for the treatment group would be the estimated treatment effect, which is positive in Figure 8.2.

The assumed hypothetical line for the control group (their dashed line, representing the change in test scores for them if they had the treatment) would need to be parallel to the growth of the treatment group for the DD model to produce an estimated effect that represents the ATE. If this were not the case, then the model would only estimate the ATT. Because participating in the meditation program would be a conscious choice and could be more likely to be done by those who would benefit more from the program, it is likely that there would be self-selection bias, which would mean that the model would only estimate the ATT – the control group's hypothetical line would likely be flatter than the treatment group's actual line.

Operationally, the DD model would be the following:

$$Y_{ig} = X_{ig}\beta_1 + \beta_2 \times G11_{ig} + \beta_3 \times T_i + \beta_4 \times \left(T_i \times G11_{ig}\right) + \varepsilon_{ig} \tag{8.13}$$

where:
- Y_{ig} = the math score for student i in grade g
- X = a set of control variables
- $G11$ = an indicator for the post-treatment period (11th grade)
- T = an indicator for being in the treatment group; this variable gets a value of one for observations both in the pre- and post-treatment period, as it is meant to capture the 10th-grade average difference in achievement between the treatment and control groups.

The estimated treatment effect is $\hat{\beta}_4$, which is the coefficient estimate on the interaction of being in the treatment group (T) and being post-treatment in Grade 11 ($G11$). Let us call

$$\overline{y}_{j,g} = Y_{j,g} - E\left[Y_{j,g} \mid X_{j,g}\right],$$

where subscript j indicates the treatment (T) or control (C) group and subscript g is the grade (10 or 11). This is the average student GPA for each group after factoring out the variables in X. The estimated treatment effect is $\hat{\beta}_4$, which is:

$$\hat{\beta}_4 = \left(\overline{y}_{T,11} - \overline{y}_{T,10}\right) - \left(\overline{y}_{C,11} - \overline{y}_{C,10}\right) \tag{8.14}$$

or the change in average scores from 10th to 11th grade for the treatment group (T) minus that for the control group (C), after factoring out the other values in X. This is why it is called the difference-in-difference. These values can be seen in Figure 8.2.

8.5.2 A famous but not-so-great DD model

One of the most famous applications of DD models was Card and Krueger (1994), who examined the effect of an increase in the minimum wage in New Jersey on fast-food employment. The authors examined the change in employment from before (February 1992) to after (November 1992) the April 1992 increase in the minimum wage (from \$4.25 to \$5.05). Just taking the change in employment for New Jersey would be problematic because other things could be changing that could affect fast-food employment. They needed a control group that should have had a similar change in employment as New Jersey would have had without the treatment of the minimum-wage increase. They didn't

Table 8.5 Summarizing results from Card and Krueger's (1994) Table 3 (Numbers represent average FTE workers at fast-food establishments)

	Pre-increase (February 1992)	Post-increase (November 1992)	Difference
New Jersey (Treatment group)	20.44***	21.03***	0.59
	(0.51)	(0.52)	(0.54)
Pennsylvania (Control group)	23.33***	21.17***	−2.16*
	(1.35)	(0.94)	(1.25)
Difference	−2.89**	−0.14	2.76**
	(1.44)	(1.07)	(1.36)

Standard errors in parentheses. ***$p < 0.01$, **$p < 0.05$, *$p < 0.1$.

choose Texas or Montana (or Kazakhstan) as the control group. Rather they chose New Jersey's neighbor, Pennsylvania. And so they compared the change in employment for New Jersey to that of Pennsylvania, again relying on the assumption that the two states should have had similar changes in fast-food employment over this time period without the treatment for New Jersey.

Table 8.5 summarizes some key results, with the numbers representing average full-time equivalent (FTE) workers at fast-food establishments. New Jersey had some increase in employment per establishment (0.59 FTE), but the estimated treatment effect, the difference-in-difference estimate (in the lower right corner of the table) is much larger at 2.76. The problem with this estimate, however, is that it is mostly driven by a drop in employment for Pennsylvania, which largely reflects much higher employment in the pre-increase period for some reason. Thus, the 2.16 decrease for Pennsylvania may have been correcting for an abnormally high initial employment rate, which is something that New Jersey did not appear to experience. This could be problematic because the assumption that they would have changed at the same rate between periods had New Jersey not had the minimum-wage increase (see Figure 8.2 above) may not be valid. Thus, we may not be able to conclude that raising the minimum wage leads to a large increase in employment.

This is also a case in which there could be remaining self-selection bias. It probably was not random that New Jersey opted to increase the minimum wage and Pennsylvania did not. It may have been connected to how well New Jersey believed businesses could absorb the increase relative to Pennsylvania. Thus, as with the fixed-effects and the FD models, there is a strong potential for self-selection bias, meaning that what is estimated is not the Average Treatment Effect (ATE), but rather the Average Treatment Effect for the Treated (ATT).

8.5.3 A more-convincing DD model

Hoynes, Miller, and Simon (2015) examined the effects of an increase in payments in the Earned Income Tax Credit (EITC) program on mother/infant health. The EITC is a policy with the objective of fighting poverty while simultaneously incentivizing work. Hoynes et al. aimed to examine how a policy that increased credit payments in the EITC in 1993 impacted the probability of having low birth weight for a baby (a sign of poor health and nutrition for the mother). Because the 1993 change to the EITC program increased payments more so for mothers with one child and even more for mothers with two-or-more children, any impact on babies' health from improved health and nutrition of the mother would be greater for babies who were the mother's second (parity = 2) and third-or-more (parity = 3+). Thus, babies who were the mother's first (parity = 1) could be used as a control group, with the treatment groups (for receiving the greater increase in payments) being babies who were their mothers' second and higher.

They used aggregated data, with each observation being a group based on state, year, parity of mother, mother's education, mother's race and ethnicity, and mother's education. The authors focus on mothers who are most likely to be impacted by the EITC change: single mothers with no more than a high school diploma. For this sample, there were over 47,000 aggregated groups for the sample.

The dependent variables were: (1) the average birth weight for babies in the group; and (2) the percentage of babies with low birth weight (with 2,500 g, or 5.5 pounds) as the main marker for low birth weight. There are certain timing strategies for assigning babies to the relevant tax year that I will skip over so as not to get too much in the weeds.

Using "parity = 1" babies as the control group does not require that the probability of low birth weight is the same for those babies as higher-parity babies. Rather, the underlying assumption here is that, had there not been the treatment of the increase in EITC payments, the probability of being born with a low-birth-weight would *change*, from before to after 1993, at the same rate for "parity = 2" and "parity = 3+" babies as it would for "parity = 1" babies. This is the assumption that needs to be assessed when evaluating a DD model. In this case, the assumption seems quite reasonable.

Operationally, the DD model would be the following (rewriting the equation a bit to match the style I have been using):

$$Y_{pjst} = \beta_0 + \beta_1 \times \left[(after)_t \times (parity2plus)_p \right] + X_{st}\beta_2 + \mu_p + \mu_j + \mu_s + \mu_t + \varepsilon_{pjst} \qquad (8.15)$$

where:
- subscript p = parity group
- subscript j = demographic group
- subscript s = state
- subscript t = effective tax year
- Y = the average baby weight measure
- $[(after)_t \times (parity2plus)_p]$ = an interaction of the indicator for being after the 1993 payments increase and the baby being the mother's second-or-more baby
- μ = fixed effects for the parity group, the demographic group, the state, and the effective tax year.

Note that the typical variable for the post-treatment period is captured by the tax-year fixed effects, while the variables representing the control group are captured by the other three fixed effects. The DD coefficient of interest is the interaction between being post-policy (*after*) and being a higher parity (*parity-2-plus*). Table 8.6 provides my summary of what I consider to be the main results, coming from Tables 2 and 3 of the article. Note that I created the confidence intervals, as they were not reported.

Let's focus on the effects for Black single mothers, for whom the results are strongest. The increase in payments for mothers who had one child (so parity = 2 for the baby) were estimated to reduce the likelihood of the baby being low birthweight by between 0.03 and 0.59 percentage points (95% confidence interval). The effect was larger for mothers with at least two children, with the estimated effect ranging from −1.35 to −0.73 percentage points. For the latter, this ranges from about 5% to 9% of the mean percentage of low-birthweight babies for Black mothers (of 14.9%).

Generally, the effect of the increased payments on reducing the likelihood of having a low-birthweight baby was greater for "parity = 3-plus," as the increase in payments was even greater for these mothers.

Table 8.6 Main results from Hoynes et al. (2015) on how increased EITC payments affect the probability of a baby having a low birthweight

	Dependent variable = % of babies with low birthweight in the group			
	All	*White*	*Black*	*Hispanic*
[(*After*) × (*parity* = 2)]	−0.164**	−0.114*	−0.310**	−0.060
	(0.072)	(0.065)	(0.144)	(0.078)
	[−0.31, −0.02]	[−0.24, +0.01]	[−.059, −0.03]	[−0.21, +0.09]
[(*After*) × (*parity* = 3+)]	−0.529***	−0.151	−1.040***	−0.191**
	(0.091)	(0.093)	(0.160)	(0.087)
	[−0.71, −0.35]	[−0.33, +0.03]	[−1.35, −0.73]	[−0.36, −0.02]
Average rate (%)	10.2	8.2	14.9	6.8
Number of obs.	47,687	16,247	10,273	10,951

Standard errors in parentheses. The 95% confidence intervals are in brackets. The standard errors are corrected for heteroskedasticity. ***$p < 0.01$, **$p < 0.05$, *$p < 0.1$.

8.5.4 Other notes on DD models

Note that the treatment does not have to be a dummy variable, as it could be a continuous variable. However, the common application for the DD model is using a dummy variable as the treatment.

Also note that this model is similar in spirit to a model that has state and time-period fixed effects, such as the model from Section 6.8 that estimated how state tax rates affect state economic growth – state and year dummy variables were used, which is similar to fixed effects. In such a fixed-effects model, the interpretation of the main coefficient estimate would be how within-state variation (difference from the mean) in economic growth is related to within-state variation in tax rates, factoring out the year effects.

Keep in mind that the DD method sometimes works well, but the examples here point out that just because you use the DD method does not mean that you solve the self-selection bias, omitted-factors bias, or other empirical problems. The right conditions have to hold, as outlined above.

8.6 Two-stage least squares (instrumental-variables)

Imagine there is a rabid Los Angeles Angels (baseball) fan named Harvey who also happens to be a rare combination of superstitious and statistically-minded. Harvey notices a pattern in that Mike Trout, the Angels' star player, tends to do better when Harvey transforms his hat into a "rally cap" – turning the cap inside out. But, being statistical, he wonders whether there is omitted-factors bias in his informal analysis. Could it be that Harvey puts his rally cap on in situations in which Trout is more likely to get a hit? For example, it may be easier to get a hit when a pitcher is distracted by runners on base, and that is when Harvey likes to put his rally cap on. To test whether his rally cap is helping, hurting, or having no effect on Mike Trout's success at the plate, Harvey needs to create variation in wearing his rally cap that is random to the situation for Trout's plate appearance. One method could be to don the rally cap every other plate appearance. Another option could be to flip a coin to determine whether he puts on the rally cap. This method creates variation in "whether the rally cap is worn" that is random with respect to the game situation or who the pitcher might be. Using this *good variation* instead of the potentially *bad variation* (of putting the rally cap on when conditions are ripe for a hit) would help create an unbiased test for whether the rally cap works.

This is the concept behind the instrumental-variables (IV) regression: isolating the *operative variation* in the key-explanatory variable (wearing the rally cap) to be only the random variation (*good variation*) so that it does not move with other relevant yet unobservable/hard-to-quantify factors (the game situation) and is not subject to reverse causality.

8.6.1 The steps of the 2SLS method

The Two-Stage-Least-Squares (2SLS) method – the most common application of the IV regression – aims to eliminate non-randomness in the key-explanatory variable by using only a source of random variation in the variable. The method can address bias from all three PITFALLS related to non-random explanatory variables, in addition to any bias from measurement error. The steps are the following:

Step 1: Find a variable or set of variables, Z, that affects the non-random X variable (say, X_1) and only is related to the outcome (Y) through its effect on X_1. (This is much more difficult than meets the eye.)

Step 2: For the first-stage regression, regress X_1 on Z and any other control variables (X_2) determining Y.

Step 3: Calculate the predicted value of X_1 from that equation. Thus, variation in the predicted value of X_1 only comes from variation in Z and the explanatory variables that are controlled for (X_2) and not from the non-random components that created the *bad variation* in X_1. Unlike X_1, the predicted value $\hat{X}_1$ should have only *good variation* if Z has no independent effect on Y.

Step 4: For the second-stage regression, regress Y on the predicted value, $\hat{X}_1$, and X_2, excluding Z from the regression.

Step 5: Standard errors need to be adjusted because using a predicted value for a regressor causes bias in standard errors. Most statistical packages will automatically fix the standard errors.

Note that:

- More than one instrumental variable can be used for a given non-random key-X variable.
- If there are multiple non-random key-X variables, then there needs to be at least one separate instrumental variable for each non-random key-X variable.

The top panel of Figure 8.3 shows two PITFALLS in the pathways:

- Omitted-factors bias in that there is an omitted (unobservable) variable X_3 (thus, the circle) that affects both X_1 and Y, causing the coefficient estimate on X_1 to pick up the effect of X_3.
- Reverse causality in that Y affects X_1.

When both or one of these problems (or self-selection bias) exist, then the 2SLS method can potentially fix the problem. The bottom panel of Figure 8.3 demonstrates the 2SLS fix for this problem. The trick, again, is finding a variable, Z, that affects X_1 but has no effect on Y other than through its effect on X_1. A predicted value for X_1 is calculated, for which its effect on Y is estimated.

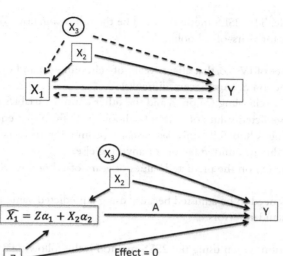

Figure 8.3 The two-stage-least-squares method

In contrast to the actual X_1 variable, the predicted variable, $\hat{X}_1$, would not be affected by the omitted factor, X_3, and should not be systematically correlated with X_3. And, addressing reverse causality, $\hat{X}_1$ would not be affected by the outcome, Y. Thus, all *operative variation* in X_1 is *good variation*. As mentioned earlier, this method would also address any bias from measurement error in X_1.

In the case of the fan's rally cap and Mike Trout's success at the plate, the instrumental variable(s), Z, would be whether the coin flip is heads or tails. Unlike most cases, the coin flip would perfectly predict the rally-cap variable.

The essential condition for this technique to be valid is that the "direct effect" of Z on Y needs to be zero. This would capture all the reasons why Z would affect Y, other than through X_1. It seems reasonable that the coin flip would not have any effect on the batting outcome for Mike Trout, other than possibly getting Harvey to wear his rally cap. If this were not the case, then the estimated causal effect of X_1 on Y would pick up that direct effect of Z on Y – there would be omitted-factors bias. This is because Z is excluded from the equation determining Y.

Unfortunately, it is actually quite rare to come up with a valid instrumental variable. The problem in most applications is that there is no way to prove that Z does not have an independent effect on Y. There are "overidentification tests" for whether Z does affect Y or is independently correlated with Y, but you cannot prove the null hypothesis that there is no effect or independent correlation. If Z does affect Y, then the model is not valid because $\hat{X}_1$ would be correlated with another omitted variable (Z) that affects Y, causing omitted-factors bias.

Let's repeat steps (1) to (5) from above with the classic example of the effects of years-of-schooling on income. The problems in estimating the effects of schooling on income with conventional methods are that: (1) the years-of-schooling variable is likely affected by other factors affecting income, such as aptitude and motivation (omitted-factors bias); (2) those expecting a greater return to schooling will self-select into higher levels of education (self-selection bias); (3) there is measurement error in the education variable. The 2SLS method would be the following, now for simplicity of notation, using S rather than *educ* for years-of-schooling:

Step 1: Find an IV or set of IVs, Z, that affects years-of-schooling (S) and only is related to income (Y) through its effect on S. (Again, very difficult.)

Step 2: Regress years-of-schooling (S) on Z and the other control variables (X).

Step 3: Calculate the predicted values of years-of-schooling ($\hat{S}$) from that equation. Thus, variation in years-of-schooling is hopefully only *good variation*, coming from variation in Z and X and not from the variation due to omitted factors or anything else.

Step 4: Regress income (Y) on the predicted values of years-of-schooling ($\hat{S}$) and the control variables (X).

Step 5: Standard errors need to be adjusted because using a predicted value for years-of-schooling causes bias in the standard errors.

The formal set of equations when using the 2SLS method is the following:

$$S_i = X_i\delta_1 + Z_i\delta_2 + \mu_i \tag{8.16a}$$

$$Y_i = X_i\beta_1 + \beta_2\hat{S}_i + \varepsilon_i \tag{8.16b}$$

The predicted value, $\hat{S}_i$, hopefully is not correlated with omitted factors, and $\text{cov}(\hat{S}, \varepsilon) = 0$. That predicted value would hopefully be based on factors that create *good variation* in years-of-schooling. Measurement error should also be less of a problem because the variable for years-of-schooling is a dependent variable (in equation 8.16a) when creating the predicted value of years-of-schooling – recall from Section 6.7 that measurement error in the dependent variable does not bias the coefficient estimate.

Let me put all of this in English based on one of the more intriguing applications of instrumental variables (that also serves as a great example for issues we discuss below). Angrist and Krueger (1991) used a subject's quarter of birth as an instrumental variable for years-of-schooling to estimate the effects of schooling on income. The argument is that, with compulsory-schooling laws, those born earlier in the year would be able to legally leave school earlier than those born later in the year, and that the quarter of birth should have no effect on income 20–40 years later, other than through the amount of schooling a person receives. While the quarter of birth would probably have little effect on years-of-schooling today, the subjects of their study were teenagers around the 1950s, which is a time period when more teenagers would quit school to work to help support their families. There was some critique of the quarter of birth as an IV (see Bound et al., 1995), but the study certainly was innovative.

8.6.2 The problem with weak instrumental variables

Sometimes, there are nice, powerful (sets of) instrumental variables that explain a significant part of the variation in the non-random key-X variable. Other times, the IVs are weak in that they have little explanatory power for the key-X variable. Having a weak IV or set of IVs could cause large standard errors on the predicted key-X variable and potentially non-normal error terms. The problem is that a weak IV would lead to a relatively small amount of variation in the predicted key-X variable. We learned back in Section 5.1 that less variation in an explanatory variable leads to larger standard errors. Furthermore, the lower amount of variation is similar to having a reduced sample size. This means that any problems from non-normal errors could result even though you have a sample size well above 200. We discussed the consequences of non-normal error terms in Section 5.6. It basically just means that you would need to require lower p-values to conclude that there is a real relationship with any certainty.

What determines whether an IV or set of IVs is sufficiently strong? Stock and Yogo (2002) suggest that the set of IVs should have a joint significance F-test value of at least 10 in the first stage. If there were only one IV, which is the situation most of the time, then an F-statistic of 10 would be the square of the equivalent t-stat on that variable, or 3.16.

In general, the stronger is the connection between the instrumental variable and the non-random key-X variable, the more precise will be the IV-estimated effect of the key-explanatory variable on the outcome.

A weak connection between the instrumental variable and the key-X variable also exacerbates any bias caused by any independent effects the instrumental variable may have on the outcome – i.e., effects not through the key-explanatory variable (see Bound et al., 1995).

8.6.3 The narrow ability to extrapolate from 2SLS models

Remember in Section 2.11, I said that the OLS method produces the average effect (or, average association) across all people. Well, the 2SLS method does not quite estimate the same average effect as OLS. *Rather, it estimates the effect for the (unidentifiable) group of people whose treatment exposure would be affected by the instrumental variable for the parts of the treatment exposure that would be affected by the instrumental variable.* For the education–income issue, it estimates the average effect of years-of-schooling on income for people whose years-of-schooling depends on the instrumental variable, Z, and for the levels of schooling that would be affected by Z (Card, 1999). This is known as the **Local Average Treatment Effect** (LATE).

Applying this concept to the Angrist and Krueger (1991) example, the estimated effect of schooling on income is based on those whose schooling depends on their quarter of birth and on the levels of schooling that are affected by the quarter of birth. Using OLS methods, there would be variation in years-of-schooling from the full distribution of schooling levels, with most variation occurring in the college years. In contrast, with the instrumental variable of the quarter of birth, the variation in schooling produced by the quarter of birth should mostly be in high-school years, perhaps with some people being induced to not just stay longer in high school by the compulsory-schooling laws, but also attend college.

Thus, the 2SLS method, in this case, produces more of an effect-of-high-school-years, whereas the OLS method produces more of an effect-of-general-schooling-years, weighted more by college years – see Figure 2.6 in Section 2.6.

Also, those whose number of years-of-schooling depends on the quarter of birth are people who tended to be only marginally attached to their schooling. They are likely different in this regard compared to the larger population of people contributing to the OLS estimate. To the extent that the returns to schooling are different for these "marginally attached students," the 2SLS/IV estimate may be different. I should note that those whose years-of-schooling depends on the quarter of birth are not identifiable – we cannot determine who dropped out due to an early-in-the-year quarter of birth (versus another reason) or who stayed due to a late quarter of birth.

8.6.4 A quick note on the math behind the general IV estimator

The IV estimate, provided the IV variable, Z, were valid, would be:

$$\beta_{IV} = \frac{\sum_{i=1}^{n}(Z_i - \bar{Z})(Y_i - \bar{Y})}{\sum_{i=1}^{n}(Z_i - \bar{Z})(X_i - \bar{X})} = \frac{\text{cov}(Z_i, Y_i)}{\text{cov}(Z_i, X_i)} \tag{8.17}$$

This is simpler than it looks. The numerator just measures how deviations from the mean for the instrumental variable (Z) and the dependent variable (Y) move together. The denominator indicates how deviations from the mean for Z and the key-explanatory variable, X, move together.

8.6.5 The current state of the 2SLS method

The 2SLS method was popular for many years, with journals publishing papers using the method, almost regardless of how valid the instrumental variable appeared to be. But the method has lost respect in recent years due to: (1) the unlikelihood of any instrumental variable being truly valid (i.e., having no independent correlation with the outcome, Y); and (2) the different interpretation 2SLS methods give, which is removed from what we normally want (the Average Treatment Effect, or the effects of a random change in X on the outcome, Y). The exception is for studies that combine the 2SLS methods with the regression–discontinuity approach, which we turn to in the next section.

Box 8.3   How much does school attendance affect student achievement?

Gottfried (2010) examines this issue for a sample of urban minority elementary- and middle-school students. This issue, if examined conventionally, certainly has potential PITFALLS. The author mentions the possibility of omitted-factors bias from student motivation, which could positively affect attendance and student achievement. And there could be other factors causing omitted-factors bias, such as the importance parents place on schooling. These omitted factors would likely contribute to a positive bias on the estimated effect of attendance on student achievement. Further positive bias could come from reverse causality. If a student is not doing well in school, he/she may be less motivated to attend school when not feeling well and deciding whether to attend. Alternatively, it is possible that not doing well in school could motivate some students (and maybe the parents) to not miss any more school – this would contribute to a negative bias on the estimated effect.

Gottfried addresses these issues by: (1) using a student fixed-effects model; and (2) using a 2SLS model. I will discuss the latter. He used as an IV the distance to school. The condition needed is that distance to school should affect attendance and have no effect on achievement beyond its effect on attendance. Is this reasonable? For an urban setting, I see no great reason to believe that this is not a reasonable condition. (If this IV were used for a sample of rural students, I would not be so certain that this would be a valid IV.)

He finds, in the first stage, that each mile away from school a student lived was associated with about one-half of a day that the student misses in a school year. In the second stage, the results are surprising (to me). The estimated positive effects of attendance on student achievement (e.g., GPA and achievement test scores) are larger with the 2SLS model than in the uncorrected model, with the estimates indicating that each day present at school increases one's GPA by around 0.02–0.03. (It is probably more easily-interpretable with the opposite effect: that *missing* 10 days versus 0 days leads to a reduced GPA of 0.2 to 0.3.) The larger estimates for the 2SLS model may be due to the LATE-nature of 2SLS estimates – e.g., the effect of attendance could be larger for the (unidentifiable) group of students whose attendance depends on the distance from school, compared to those who miss school for other reasons. Nevertheless, the results strongly suggest that attendance is important for academic success.

8.7 Regression discontinuities

The method of regression discontinuities (RD) is the current trendy approach to identifying causal effects. Many economists coming out of graduate school use this approach in their job-market papers. It involves using arbitrary threshold values that qualify someone/something for a certain treatment and uses any shift in the regression line for those beyond the threshold value to identify the impact of the treatment. Using this technique requires:

- A continuous eligibility index for a treatment (e.g., a test score)
- A defined cut-off value for eligibility.

8.7.1 The basic regression-discontinuity (RD) method

Suppose that there is a new advanced academic program for gifted elementary students. To get into the program, a student must score at least 80 on a beginning-of-the-year test (the pre-test) designed to identify gifted students. And suppose that the school administrators want to test whether the new program had a positive effect on the students. On the surface, we cannot just compare the results of those who are in the program vs. those not in the program, as better students will, on average, score higher and perhaps have stronger growth.

This is a perfect case for an RD method. The idea here is that students with a score of 80 (or a little higher) will tend to have better outcomes at the end of the year than students with a score of 79 (or a little lower) for two basic reasons:

- The students with an 80 are, on average, better students
- The students with an 80 had the treatment of the new academic program.

The RD technique attempts to distinguish these two effects from each other and to generalize to a *slightly-wider range* of test scores. The simple model with an RD method is the following:

$$Y_i = X_i\beta_1 + \beta_2 TS_i + \beta_3 D_i + \varepsilon_i \tag{8.18}$$

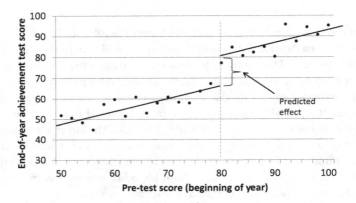

Figure 8.4 Graphical representation of a notional regression–discontinuity model

where:
- Y = the end-of-year achievement test score for student i
- X = a set of demographic or other observable factors that could affect achievement
- TS = the test score on the beginning-of-year pre-test determining acceptance into the new academic program
- D = 1 if $TS \geq 80$ (the threshold value); D = 0 otherwise.

So, in this model, the TS variable has a linear effect on the outcome, Y. The estimate for β_3 would then be based on the effect of meeting the threshold value beyond the linear effect of the test score (TS). That is, β_3 indicates the effect of participating in the new advanced academic program.

Graphically, Figure 8.4 is what this situation would look like. More advanced models could use a non-linear function to determine what the predicted scores would be without the treatment, such as:

- A spline function (see Section 3.2.3) separated at the threshold, typically modeled as two variables: (1) "score minus 80" just for values above 80; (2) "80 minus score" just for scores below 80.
- A quadratic function, from the threshold, with "distance-from-threshold" and "distance-squared" both below and above the threshold.

An example of this is in Box 8.4. See Lee and Lemieux (2010) for more details on the RD method.

8.7.2 Fuzzy regression-discontinuity method

There is a little more complexity when meeting the cut-off does not guarantee that the person obtains the treatment. This situation would call for an IV (or 2SLS) approach. This is sometimes called "Fuzzy RD," in contrast to the classic case of the threshold perfectly indicating who gets the treatment, or "Sharp RD."

A nice example comes from Ozier (2018), who estimates the causal effects of secondary schooling in Kenya on various outcomes. In a lesser-developed country such as Kenya, the self-selection bias and omitted-factors bias in this research question are likely major problems. Ozier noted that there was a cut-off score for the standardized 8th-grade examination (one close to the mean score) that gave a person an increased probability of being admitted to secondary school if surpassed. Ozier uses that cut-off as the source of a regression discontinuity to examine the effect of secondary schooling on the outcomes. The model is the following:

$$\text{Stage 1:} \quad S_i = X_i \beta_1 + \beta_2 TS_i + \beta_3 D_i + \varepsilon_i \tag{8.19}$$

$$\text{Stage 2:} \quad Y_i = \delta_{1i} \hat{S}_i + \delta_2 TS_i + \varepsilon_i \tag{8.20}$$

where
- S is a variable indicating whether the student attended and completed secondary school
- TS is the 8th-grade test score
- D is whether the student had at least the mean test score (TS)
- Y is one of the various outcomes (cognitive test performance, whether formally employed, and teen pregnancies).

The idea here is that meeting the threshold of the mean 8th-grade test score (beyond the linear effect of the 8th-grade test score on the outcomes) affects the outcomes only by affecting the likelihood of being admitted to secondary school.

In the first stage, he found that meeting the threshold was associated with a 16- and 13-percentage-points higher probability of completing secondary school for males and females, respectively, beyond the linear effect of the score on the probability of completing secondary school. Ozier noted that, for females, the IV of the regression discontinuity did not pass the Stock and Yogo (2002) F-test rule of thumb of 10. Among the statistically-significant estimates, the results suggest that secondary school completion increases cognitive-test performance for men and women, increases the probability of formal employment (vs. self-employment) for men, and reduces teen pregnancy for females. There were several insignificant estimates, which may have been due to high standard errors in the 2SLS/IV models. This echoes the story that standard errors get very large if the relationship between the IV and the treatment is not very strong.

8.7.3 Interpretations and limitations of the regression-discontinuity approach

The RD approach is considered to be pretty close to a true experiment, as it requires many fewer assumptions than other methods to address *bad variation*. This approach does have one major drawback that is similar to the drawback of 2SLS models, even the RD models not using 2SLS. Just as the 2SLS approach estimates the Local Average Treatment Effect (LATE) (the treatment effect for those on the margin of receiving the treatment), the RD method also estimates the LATE for those close to the eligibility threshold score. If the effect were systematically different for those far from the threshold, the estimated causal effect would be biased as an estimate of the Average Treatment Effect.

One situation where the RD approach would not work is if the subjects can manipulate, to some extent, the "score" determining the assignment. For example, if some parents knew that their child was close to the cut-off score, they may encourage the child to study more or to take the test more seriously in order to meet the threshold score. This would invalidate the use of the RD approach. What to look for is whether the distribution of the qualification variable has a kink around the threshold, in the form of fewer observations than there should be right below the threshold and more than there should be right above the threshold (or *vice versa* if the lower value indicates qualification status).

While the RD method is a well-respected and strong approach to addressing the problems of non-random explanatory variables, it is unfortunately a rare occurrence to have such an opportunity to use the method. There needs to be a threshold based on a continuous variable that determines whether a person receives a given treatment. The research using RD largely springs from a threshold being found in policy and creating a research question from that policy rather than searching for an RD threshold for an already-established research question.

Box 8.4   Is there an advantage to a halftime deficit in basketball?

This is something I long ago thought could be the case, but I did not have the data to examine it (nor the idea of using the RD method). Berger and Pope (2011) used data on about 12,000 NBA games and 29,000 college basketball games to test whether being slightly behind at halftime affects a team's chance of winning beyond what would be expected given the score. They estimate the model:

$$(\text{Win})_i = \beta_1 \times (\text{losing-at-halftime})_i + \beta_2 \times (\text{halftime-score-difference})_i + X_i \beta_3 + \varepsilon_i$$

They use the home team as the subject—i.e., the dependent variable was whether the home team won—but the results would tell the exact same story if the visiting team were the reference team. In the set of variables in X, they include the home-team and visiting-team winning percentages.

For the NBA, they find that losing-at-halftime was associated with an estimated increase in the probability of winning of 3–9 percentage points ($p < 0.01$), beyond any effects of the halftime-score-difference. Using a cubic representation of halftime-score-difference, the estimated effect of losing-at-halftime is estimated to increase by 4–12 percentage points. For the NCAA games, the estimates were smaller and statistically significant with the linear control for the halftime-score-difference but insignificant with the cubic control for halftime-score-difference.

Why would there be a relative advantage to losing at halftime (particularly in the NBA)? It could be that players exert extra effort if they are behind, or that coaches are more likely to think that they need to make adjustments to the game plan if they are losing.

So the idea here is that there should be a systematic relationship between the halftime-score-difference and the probability that a team wins, and after adjusting for that relationship, "losing" at halftime appears to have a positive effect on the probability of winning. The authors say that it is being "slightly behind" that can have a discontinuous effect on a team's chances of winning. This speaks to the nature of the RD estimates being Local Average Treatment Effects.

8.8 Knowing when to punt

Yogi Berra once said, "If you ask me anything I don't know, I'm not going to answer." This is relevant in statistical research because there will be times when there is no solution to a likely PITFALL, and it would be irresponsible to claim otherwise. In such cases, it is probably best to move on to a different topic or make it loud and clear in a report that the PITFALL could not be addressed.

Imagine this research question: "Does marijuana use affect grades?"

This would be a difficult topic to examine because marijuana use and grades conceivably could have common factors. Thus, we are left with just observational data, which have the problem that, with respect to grades, it may not be random as to who uses marijuana. ~~Unfortunately (again), no one funded my brilliant idea of randomizing the treatment (in this case, marijuana use) in the population so we can estimate these effects properly.~~

Theoretically, a model using 2SLS methods (Section 8.6) could be estimated. Practically, this would require having an instrumental variable that affects marijuana use, but has no direct effect on grades, other than through its effect on marijuana use. This would not be easy.

One theoretically-possible instrumental variable for this problem would be local marijuana prices, provided that the location of the youth is known. This would rest on the dubious assumption that changes in marijuana prices were purely supply-driven and not demand-driven (the latter of which would make marijuana prices a product of marijuana use). Regardless, there are just no decent data available for marijuana prices in more than a select few locations over time. Thus, this is a topic for which it is highly unlikely that a researcher would be able to identify the true causal effect.

There are many research topics for which the PITFALLS are too egregious and have no viable solution. Probably the best thing to do in such a situation (after letting it marinate for a while and not finding a solution) is to "punt," admit (to yourself) that there is hardly any way to identify the causal effect and go on to another research topic. Alternatively, you could call it an "association" and suggest that further research attempt to somehow isolate the causal effect.

8.9 Summary

In this chapter, I have introduced a few methods for addressing problems associated with non-random explanatory variables from Chapter 6 (mostly omitted-factors bias). These are considered quasi-experimental methods, as they are models designed so that subjects are compared to themselves or to a set of subjects that are very similar. Table 8.7 reviews the methods.

Table 8.7 A summary of the general idea and the limitations of various methods to address the PITFALLS

Method	General idea	Limitations
Fixed effects	Estimate within-group relationships between the treatment and outcome	Exacerbates bias from measurement error, does not correct for self-selection bias
First-difference	Estimate how a change in the Y variable moves with a change in the X variable	Same as for fixed effects
Difference-in-difference	Comparison of changes (typically over time) for treatment vs. control group	Same as for fixed effects
Two-stage least squares	Estimate how variation in the treatment variable (from an instrumental variable that affects treatment but not outcome) affects the outcome	Results only apply to the (unknown) subjects whose treatment is affected by the instrumental-variable; typically has imprecise estimates
Regression discontinuities	Use the jump at a discontinuity threshold relative to what would be expected from the increased value	Results only apply to those close to the threshold level

Remember that, just because a researcher uses one of these (or other) quasi-experimental methods does not mean that the model is producing an unbiased estimate of the causal effect. All of the methods require underlying conditions or assumptions to hold be valid.

In addition, such models have limitations. They often exacerbate other problems, such as measurement error and imprecision. And the 2SLS and RD methods estimate an effect for a narrow segment of the population, meaning that the results cannot be extrapolated to a wider population.

The best of these approaches (in terms of both effectiveness and practicality), from my experiences, are the fixed-effect, first-difference, and difference-in-difference techniques. While not perfect, when they can be applied, they often do a solid job to remove unobserved differences to address omitted-factors bias. As long as there is not non-trivial measurement error in the key-X variable and the key-X is not a choice (meaning there is no self-selection bias), then these simpler models have the greater potential to accurately and precisely estimate the Average Treatment Effect.

Exercises

1. Suppose that you were examining how state marijuana legalization has affected the number of car accidents in a state. Suppose that you had data over a 20-year period, during which 23 states had decriminalized marijuana. And suppose that you have the following data (and variable names):
    o   Year (Y)
    o   State (S)
    o   Accidents per capita in the state and year (A)
    o   A dummy variable for whether marijuana is decriminalized in a state in a given year (MJD)
    o   The population of the state in the year (P) for weighting the observations.
       a.   With a Simple Regression of $A_i = \beta_0 + \beta_1 \times (MJD)_i + \varepsilon_i$, why might there be omitted-factors bias?
       b.   Write an equation for a regression model with fixed effects that addresses potential omitted-factors bias.
       c.   Which states would be contributing to the estimated effect of decriminalization?
       d.   How would you interpret the coefficient estimate on MJD in (b), in light of the interpretations in Section 8.1?
2. Use the data set **temperature_gdp**.
       a.   Estimate the effects of temperature (*temp*) on GDP growth (*gdpgrowth*), using fixed effects for the country and interacted region-year (with the variable *ry* having a distinct value for each region-year), and correcting for any heteroskedasticity.
       b.   Assess, theoretically rather than with data, whether bias from over-weighted countries (PITFALL #7) could apply, using the criteria from Section 6.10.
       c.   Repeat (a), but correct for the over-weighting of countries by following these procedures:
           i.   Regress *temp* on the region-year dummy variables (it would be **i.ry** in Stata and **factor(ry) − 1** in R code).
           ii.   Calculate the residual.
           iii. Calculate the variance of the residual by country.
           iv.   Create a weight based on the inverse of that variance.
           v.   Apply the weights to the fixed-effects model in (a).
           How does the coefficient estimate on *temp* change from (a) with the weights?
       d.   Explain how the change in the coefficient estimate from (a) to (c) could occur.

3. Use the **cigsales** data set. This data set comes from David Simon and is part of a preliminary analysis in an examination of how childhood exposure to cigarette smoke affects various childhood outcomes (Simon, 2016)

   a. Estimate the effects of the cigarette-tax-rate-per-pack, in 2009 prices, (*tax09*), on cigarette-sales-per-capita (*cigsalepc*). Use state and year fixed effects. You may need to use fixed effects for either state or year and just a set of dummy variables for the other. Also, use robust standard errors clustered at the state level, and weight the model by the 2000 state population (*pop2000*). If using Stata, use the **areg** command, as **xtreg** will not allow different weights within a fixed-effect group. What is the 95% confidence interval for the coefficient estimate on *tax09*?

   b. Estimate the same model, but add control variables for the unemployment rate (*urate*), the beer tax (*beertax*), and whether smoking is allowed in bars (*bar*) and restaurants (*restaurant*). And, add the variables for the state trends (*statetrend1–statetrend51*). How does the estimated effect of the tax rate compare to that from (a)?

   c. From (b), what is the interpretation of the coefficient estimate on the tax rate, in terms of what observations are compared to what observations?

4. Use the **cig_1st_diff** data set. This is based on the changes from 1990 to 2000, and it is extracted from the data set used in Question #3. Estimate a first-difference model, as follows: regress *cigch* on *taxch*, *uratech*, and *beertaxch*. Weight the model by *pop2000*, and use robust standard errors. Interpret the estimate on *taxch*.

5. From the example in Section 8.5 from Card and Krueger (1994) on estimating the effects of minimum-wage increases on employment, write out the regression equation for the difference-in-difference model.

6. Use **notional_eitc_data**. This notional data set (that I created) is intended to examine the effect of a general change in the Earned Income Tax Credit program that gives greater incentives for single mothers to work. This is a simplified version of Meyer and Rosenbaum (2001). (There were several changes over the years to the EITC program to increase such an incentive for single mothers, but I am simplifying it to a one-time permanent change occurring in 1990.) The sample consists of 5,000 single women from before the change (1985) and 5,000 single women from after the change (1995). The variables are:

   o *employed* = dummy variable for being employed in the past week
   o *mother* = dummy variable for whether the single woman was a mother of a child under 18 years old
   o *d1995* = dummy variable for whether the observation was in 1995 (rather than 1985).

   (Note that the original Excel data set with my notional data creation is on the website, and the formulas can be adjusted to create different-sized effects.)

   a. Estimate a difference-in-difference model to identify the causal effect of the program change on the employment of single mothers, in which the comparison group consists of single women without children. Indicate what the estimated causal effect is, its significance level, and the 95% confidence interval. (Don't forget the correction for heteroskedasticity.)

   b. What underlying condition is necessary for this technique to be valid in estimating the causal effects of the EITC change on the probability of employment for a given week?

7. Use the **notional_summer_educ** data set.[4] The idea behind this exercise is that 3rd-grade students who are at a reading level under 85 (one standard deviation below the mean of 100) are

required to attend summer school. But some students below the threshold do not attend, while some students above the threshold choose to attend voluntarily. We want to estimate how summer school improves the reading test scores of the students. Given that the threshold does not automatically dictate summer-school attendance, this is a Fuzzy RD model. The variables are:

test3 = a test at the end of 3rd grade
test4 = a test at the end of 4th grade (the dependent variable)
summer = a dummy variable for whether the student went to summer school between the 3rd and 4th grades.

    a.   Estimate a Fuzzy RD model with an instrumental-variables model to estimate the effect of summer school (*summer*) on 4th-grade test performance (*test4*). Use just a linear model to capture the discontinuity in summer-school attendance from *test3*.

    b.   Estimate the same model, but use a quadratic function from both below and above the threshold of 85 for the effects of *test3* on *test4*.

    c.   From (b), what is the interpretation of the estimated effect of summer school, in consideration of the limitations of how results could be extrapolated?

8.   Use the data set **oecd_gas_demand**. From Question #7 in Chapter 3, add fixed effects for the country, along with a heteroskedasticity correction.

    a.   How does the coefficient estimate on *lrpmg* change from Question #7 in Chapter 3 with the fixed effects added?

    b.   How does this change which observations are compared to which observations?

9.   Return to the **tv-bmi-ecls** data set used for Exercise #5 in Chapter 6. From that exercise, along with other descriptions of the research issue, there is much potential omitted-factors bias.

    a.   Explore the data description and variable list (from the file "Exercises data set descriptions" on the book's website). Design a model to address the omitted-factors bias.

    b.   Are there any shortcomings to your approach?

10. How would using interacted fixed effects for two sets of fixed-effects groups (for two sets of factors) affect bias from measurement error, compared to using two-way (separate) fixed effects for the two sets of factors?

Notes

1 This model uses methods we have not covered yet, including using changes in the variables rather than actual levels and using lagged values as instrumental variables.

2 This example comes from www.ma.utexas.edu/users/mks/statmistakes/fixedvsrandom.html, accessed July 10, 2018.

3 These state marijuana use rates come from the National Survey on Drug Use and Health and refer to 12–17-year-olds. The state unemployment rates come from the Bureau of Labor Statistics.

4 This notional data is based off of the concept in Jacob and Lefgren (2004). The authors used confidential data, so I created simulated data.

References

Angrist, J. D., & Krueger, A. B. (1991). Does compulsory school attendance affect schooling and earnings? *The Quarterly Journal of Economics, 106*(4), 979–1014.

Arellano, M., & Bond, S. (1991). Some tests of specification for panel data: Monte Carlo evidence and an application to employment equations. *Review of Economic Studies, 58*(2), 277–297.

Bedard, K., & Kuhn, P. (2008). Where class size really matters: class size and student ratings of professor effectiveness. *Economics of Education Review, 27*(3), 253–265.

Berger, J., & Pope, D. (2011). Can losing lead to winning? *Management Science, 57*(5), 817–827.

Bound, J., Jaeger, D. A., & Baker, R. M. (1995). Problems with instrumental variables estimation when the correlation between the instruments and the endogenous explanatory variables is weak. *Journal of the American Statistical Association, 90*(430), 443–450.

Card, D. (1999). The causal effect of education on earnings. In *Handbook of labor economics* (Vol. *3A*), O. Ashenfelter, & D. Card, eds. Amsterdam: Elsevier Science and North-Holland, 63 p.

Card, D., & Krueger, A. B. (1994). Minimum wages and employment: a case study of the fast-food industry in New Jersey and Pennsylvania. *American Economic Review, 84*(4), 772–793.

Dee, T. S., & Cohodes, S. R. (2008). Out-of-field teachers and student achievement: evidence from matched-pairs comparisons. *Public Finance Review, 36*(1), 7–32.

Gibbons, C. E., Serrato, J. C. S., & Urbancic, M. B. (2019). Broken or fixed effects? *Journal of Econometric Methods, 8*(1), 1–12.

Gottfried, M. A. (2010). Evaluating the relationship between student attendance and achievement in urban elementary and middle schools: an instrumental variables approach. *American Educational Research Journal, 47*(2), 434–465.

Hoynes, H., Miller, D., & Simon, D. (2015). Income, the earned income tax credit, and infant health. *American Economic Journal: Economic Policy, 7*(1), 172–211.

Jacob, B. A., & Lefgren, L. (2004). Remedial education and student achievement: a regression-discontinuity analysis. *Review of Economics and Statistics, 86*(1), 226–244.

Lee, D. S., & Lemieux, T. (2010). Regression discontinuity designs in economics. *Journal of Economic Literature, 48*(2), 281–355.

Meyer, B. D., & Rosenbaum, D. T. (2001). Welfare, the earned income tax credit, and the labor supply of single mothers. *The Quarterly Journal of Economics, 116*(3), 1063–1114.

Ozier, O. (2018). The impact of secondary schooling in Kenya a regression discontinuity analysis. *Journal of Human Resources, 53*(1), 157–188.

Pope, D. G., & Schweitzer, M. E. (2011). Is Tiger Woods loss averse? Persistent bias in the face of experience, competition, and high stakes. *The American Economic Review, 101*(1), 129–157.

Simon, D. (2016). Does early life exposure to cigarette smoke permanently harm childhood welfare? Evidence from cigarette tax hikes. *American Economic Journal: Applied Economics, 8*(4), 128–159.

Stock, J. H., & Yogo, M. (2002). Testing for weak instruments in linear IV regression. (Available at http://scholar.harvard.edu/files/stock/files/testing_for_weak_instruments_in_linear_iv_regression.pdf, accessed July 10, 2018).

Stone, D. F., & Arkes, J. (2016). Reference points, prospect theory, and momentum on the PGA tour. *Journal of Sports Economics, 17*(5), 453–482.

9 Other methods besides Ordinary Least Squares

Box 9.1 Do the shoes matter?

"Wait! Why do we have a police escort to dinner?" I asked. I glanced down at my shoes and wondered if I'd gone a bit too far with my mantra I remember from something Norm Peterson (on *Cheers*) once said: "All great thinkers [e.g., Socrates, Jesus, Larry Bird, Tim Duncan] had comfortable shoes." When told seven minutes earlier on that evening in 1999, while sitting at the hotel pool, that we were about to leave for dinner and dancing, I raced to my room, got dressed, and laced up my basketball shoes in record time. Only in response to my query about the police escort was I told that we were going to the Presidential Mansion first.

DOI: 10.4324/9781003285007-9

We had earlier that day attended the inauguration of the new El Salvadoran President, Francisco Flores. And so here I was, a relative "nobody," sitting in the living room of the President's mansion, in the company of the new President, his wife and kids, Prince Albert of Monaco, Nat King Cole's twin daughters, and four others, and I had on my basketball shoes, not quite matching my dark suit and tie. As the night later turned to dancing at a nightclub, I was clearly outshined by everyone, particularly Prince Albert. The problem was no longer my shoes … but rather my dance moves (or lack thereof). In the end, wearing dress shoes would have been more appropriate for the occasion, but it wouldn't have solved the fundamental problem of the evening – my bad dancing.

This is what I think of when there is a non-standard dependent variable. The appropriate-for-the-occasion method would likely be some alternative to OLS. However, in the end, using any alternative method won't make a difference if there are any meaningful biases to the coefficient estimates from non-random explanatory variables or other fundamental issues that remain unaddressed.

In some analyses, the nature of the dependent variable or the nature of the effect one is attempting to capture may dictate using a non-linear method, or something other than OLS. In this chapter, you will learn:

- The different types of dependent variables and how those often warrant a different method (with the main focus on dependent variables that are dummy variables)
- The basics of those new methods and how to estimate them.

The estimation method used in most of the regressions discussed in this chapter is the Maximum Likelihood method. Recall from Section 2.5 that OLS aimed to minimize the sum of the squared residuals. The Maximum Likelihood method involves finding the set of coefficient estimates that maximize the likelihood of observing the given data.[1]

9.1 Types of outcome variables

Most of the examples considered in this book have involved outcome variables that are considered continuous, in that they can basically take on any value. This, of course, is not technically true, as, for example, there are no decimal places in the income variable. But we can innocuously assume that the variables are approximately continuous.

There are many instances in which researchers have outcomes that are not approximately continuous, but rather discrete, qualitative, or restricted in values.

- **Dichotomous (dummy) variables** take on just the values of 0 or 1. The 0-value category is typically for a "no" or for not meeting a threshold, while 1 typically indicates "yes" or meeting a threshold. Examples include: (1) whether a person uses marijuana; (2) whether a student is retained to repeat a grade; (3) whether a cancer patient survives for ten years; and (4) whether a basketball player makes a given shot.

- **Ordinal variables** have multiple categories for which the order or value has meaning. For example, the highest degree earned would be an ordinal variable with values, say, of:
  - 0 for no high-school diploma
  - 1 for a high-school diploma
  - 2 for an Associate's degree
  - 3 for a Bachelor's degree
  - 4 for a graduate degree.
- **Categorical variables** involve categories for which there is no obvious order. An example could be the type of car a person chooses to buy (SUV, sedan, hatchback, crossover). Other examples include the candidate a person votes for, the region of the country a person chooses to move to, and the type of college a person chooses to attend.
- **Censored variables** are (typically) approximately continuous variables for a certain set of values, but have an upper and/or lower bound for values. The censoring can occur due to limits imposed on a survey or just that values naturally do not go beyond a certain level. The income that respondents report in surveys can be censored in both directions. Surveys may have a top code for income of, say, $1 million. And income cannot go below zero (in most cases) for those who do not work.
- **Count variables** indicate the number of occurrences of some event. It has to be an integer. If the number of possible values gets large enough and has a relatively low amount of "low numbers" (i.e., not too much bunching at the bottom end), then one can just assume that it approximates a continuous distribution. For example, with years-of-schooling as a dependent variable, the OLS method is often used, as there is little bunching at low years-of-schooling. Examples of count variables for which the OLS method may not be appropriate include: (1) the number of migraine episodes per month; (2) the number of times a person has been arrested; and (3) the number of hospital visits a person has in a year. Note that the variables listed here would likely have a relatively high proportion of observations with a value of zero.

When the dependent variable comes in one of these non-approximately-continuous forms, then applying linear models (such as with the OLS method) may result in:

- Biased coefficient estimates
- Biased standard errors
- Misleading statistics related to the significance of estimates, hypothesis tests, and confidence intervals.

The correction to this problem is to use a method that is appropriate given the distribution of the dependent variable. This chapter provides basic descriptions of the various methods to use based on the type of dependent variable. While using the appropriate method is typically best, the biases and other problems stemming from not using OLS (in most cases) are relatively minor compared to the biases from the PITFALLS in Chapter 6.

9.2 Dichotomous outcomes

This is a common type of outcome, so I will discuss the methods used for dichotomous models with extra detail compared to the other methods. There are three basic options when the outcome is dichotomous: linear probability models, probit models, and logit models. I will introduce the three models in the next three sub-sections and then use all three models on the same data in sub-Section 9.2.4.

9.2.1 Linear probability models

A linear probability model (LPM) simply uses the OLS method to estimate how a set of explanatory variables determine the outcome. Operationally, the model is:

$$Y_i = X_i\beta + \varepsilon_i \tag{9.1}$$

where Y takes the values of 0 or 1. But, effectively, the model estimates:

$$\Pr(Y_i = 1) = X_i\beta + \varepsilon_i \tag{9.2}$$

This approach has the advantage that the estimates are more directly interpretable than with the probit and logit models, with a coefficient estimate on an X variable being the estimate for how much the probability of Y occurring increases with a one-unit increase in the value of the X variable. In addition, certain fixes for addressing non-random explanatory variables, such as fixed effects, are often easier in the LPM than in a probit or logit model.

However, there are problems with the LPM. These include:

- Sometimes, the predicted probability will be outside of the [0, 1] range. This is less likely to be a problem when there are more X variables and when the overall probability of the outcome in the sample is not close to zero or one. But this is one problem with LPM that should be avoided.
- Relatedly, the estimates may be biased and inconsistent due to predicted probabilities outside the [0, 1] range. However, the magnitude of this problem may be small, depending on the situation.
- The error terms may be non-normal, which violates Assumption **A3** in Section 2.10. This would be less of a problem with an adequate number of observations and explanatory variables. And a high level of significance would make this assumption violation meaningless. But it would be a concern if the level of significance was marginal, not just from reaching the typical threshold p-values, but taking into account the informal Bayes approach from Section 5.5. In such a situation, it may be worth conducting a test for the normality of the error terms.

9.2.2 Probit models

The probit model, one of the two non-linear probability models for using dichotomous outcomes, avoids the problem of predicted probabilities being outside the [0, 1] range and the problem of error terms being non-normal (provided there are at least 200 observations). The model for outcome Y and a set of explanatory variables, X, is the following:

$$\Pr(Y_i = 1 \mid X_i) = \Phi(X_i\beta) \tag{9.3}$$

where Φ is the cumulative density function of the standard normal distribution. That is, Φ is a function that produces a probability between 0 and 1, with the probability being higher for higher values of $X_i\beta$. In a statistical program, you would typically just indicate a "probit" model. But behind the curtains, the estimation involves a latent variable model as follows:

$$Y_i^* = X_i\beta + \varepsilon_i \tag{9.4}$$

where $\varepsilon \sim N(0,1)$ – i.e., the error term has a standard normal distribution.

The variable Y^*, representative of (but not equal to) the propensity for Y to equal 1, is latent and is represented in the data by:

$$
\begin{aligned}
Y &= 1 \quad \text{if} \quad Y^* > 0 \quad \text{or} - \varepsilon < X\beta \\
Y &= 0 \quad \text{otherwise}
\end{aligned}
\tag{9.5}
$$

Unfortunately, the estimates for β do not represent the marginal effects. A **marginal effect** is how the estimated probability of the outcome changes with a one-unit increase in the value of the X variable, which is what an LPM or any OLS model naturally estimates. These are not directly produced by the model, as the coefficient estimates represent how a one-unit change in a given X variable affects the latent outcome variable. Further program code is often necessary to determine the marginal effects. And the marginal effect of a given one-unit change in an explanatory variable, X_1, will vary depending on the values of the other explanatory variables (and thus, the predicted probability of the outcome). If the values of all variables put an observation at a 96% chance that the outcome will occur, there is little room for further increases in that predicted probability from a one-unit change in a variable, X_1.

Because the marginal effect for a variable depends on the values of the other variables, the common practice is to use the means of the X variables as the starting point to estimate the marginal effects of any variables. To calculate the marginal effect for an explanatory variable that is a dummy variable, you cannot start at the mean, but rather have the mean for all other variables and calculate what happens to the predicted probability going from 0 to 1 for the dummy variable.

9.2.3 Logit models

The **logit model** is another non-linear probability model that also restricts the predicted probability to be in the [0, 1] range and avoids the potential problem of non-normal error terms. Again, in most statistical packages, you just specify the logit model, but behind the curtains, the model first involves the logistic function for the probability that a variable Y takes on the value of 1:

$$\Pr(Y = 1) = \frac{1}{1 + e^{-(X\beta)}} \tag{9.6}$$

As with the probit model, for high values of $X\beta$, this function approaches one; and for low values of $X\beta$, the denominator increases, and the probability approaches zero.

Like the probit model, the logit model does not indicate the marginal effects. These marginal effects also depend on the values of the X variables. A nice feature of logit models is that they have an easy transformation of the coefficient estimates on the X variables to the **odds ratios**, which are the change in the relative odds of an outcome occurring given the exposure to some treatment relative to the baseline odds without exposure to that treatment. (The treatment could be an extra unit of an approximately continuous variable, such as the AFQT score.) The transformation is calculated simply by exponentiating a coefficient estimate. I will show this in the next sub-section.

9.2.4 Example using all probability models

Let's do an exploratory analysis to examine what factors predicted marijuana use among a sample of youth in the year 2000. For simplicity, rather than using separate models as would be suggested as a strategy for determining predictors of an outcome in Section 7.2, I include several explanatory variables in the model at once.

For this analysis, I use the younger cohort of the NLSY, which started with 12–17-year-olds in 1997 (Bureau of Labor Statistics, 2015). I use data from the fourth round of interviews for this cohort, conducted in 2000–2001. The dependent variable is whether the person used marijuana in the prior 30 days (coded as 1 if they had used marijuana and 0 otherwise).

Table 9.1 shows the results from using each type of probability model: LPM (using OLS) in column 1; probit model, with the coefficient estimates in column 2 and marginal effects in column 3; and logit model coefficient estimates in column 4 and marginal effects in column 5.

Table 9.1 Determinants of "whether the youth used marijuana in past 30 days (in years 2000–2001)," using three different probability models (n = 7995)

	(1)	(2)	(3)	(4)	(5)
		Probit model		Logit model	
	LPM (OLS)	Coefficient estimates	Marginal effects	Coefficient estimates	Marginal effects
Male	0.056***	0.219***	0.057***	0.390***	0.056***
	(0.009)	(0.033)	(0.009)	(0.059)	(0.009)
Age	0.009***	0.036***	0.009***	0.064***	0.009***
	(0.003)	(0.011)	(0.003)	(0.020)	(0.003)
Race/ethnicity (non-Hispanic Whites form the reference group)					
Non-Hispanic Black	−0.082***	−0.320***	−0.077***	−0.572***	−0.076***
	(0.010)	(0.042)	(0.009)	(0.077)	(0.009)
Hispanic	−0.047***	−0.178***	−0.044***	−0.319***	−0.043***
	(0.011)	(0.044)	(0.010)	(0.078)	(0.010)
Other race/ethnicity	−0.058**	−0.222**	−0.052***	−0.394**	−0.051***
	(0.022)	(0.093)	(0.019)	(0.169)	(0.019)
Parents lived with at age 12 (excluded category is both biological parents)					
One biological parent	0.042***	0.160***	0.042***	0.287***	0.042***
	(0.010)	(0.039)	(0.011)	(0.070)	(0.011)
One bio. and one other parent	0.088***	0.316***	0.093***	0.550***	0.093***
	(0.024)	(0.077)	(0.025)	(0.132)	(0.025)
Other situation	0.020	0.078	0.021	0.134	0.020
	(0.012)	(0.049)	(0.013)	(0.088)	(0.013)
Constant	−0.005	−1.649***		−2.816***	
	(0.052)	(0.206)		(0.363)	
R-squared	0.017				

Source: Bureau of Labor Statistics (2015).

Standard errors in parentheses. ***$p < 0.01$, **$p < 0.05$, *$p < 0.1$.

As discussed above, the marginal effects depend on the baseline values of the X variables. Think of it this way. Certain factors could make an outcome nearly a certainty. For example (if we had data), having an older brother use marijuana may be a very strong predictor of a person's marijuana use. For these people, the additional effects of further variables on the probability of using marijuana will probably not be as large as for other people, as there is less room for any increased probability. Typically, and in Table 9.1, the mean values of the X variables are assumed for these calculations. This is the obvious choice that would give average marginal effects for the explanatory variables.

The example in Table 9.1, not by design, turns out to be a case in which it really does not matter which model is used. The LPM results (column 1) are very similar to the marginal effects from the probit and logit models (columns 3 and 5). The largest determinant of using marijuana appears to be living with "one biological parent and one other parent" (relative to living with both biological parents), as it is associated with about an estimated 9-percentage-point higher probability of marijuana use in the past month. However, we need to be careful here in that there are alternative stories (to a causal effect) as to why those having such living arrangements have higher marijuana use.

What is important here is that the differences in estimates between the models are fairly small. In fact, they are probably much smaller than any bias on the causal effects from the explanatory variables being non-random, if causal effects were our objective.

As mentioned above, logit models have a special feature. With the results from a logit model, you can calculate **odds ratios:** the change in relative odds of the outcome being "yes" ($Y = 1$), for each one-unit change of the **X** variable. The relationship between the coefficient estimate and the odds ratio is the following:

- Variable is positively associated with the outcome, *ceteris paribus*

  ➔ odds ratio > 1

- Variable has zero association with the outcome, *ceteris paribus*

  ➔ odds ratio = 1

- Variable is negatively associated with the outcome, *ceteris paribus*

  ➔ odds ratio < 1.

Table 9.2 shows the results from the logit model from Table 9.1, with the coefficient estimates and associated marginal effects in columns (1) and (2) copying columns (4) and (5) from Table 9.1, and the associated odds ratios in column (3). All results come from the same logit model. As an example of interpreting the model, being male is associated with an estimated 5.6-percentage-points higher probability of using marijuana in the past month, or a 47.7% higher odds of using marijuana, *ceteris paribus*. (The 1.477 odds ratio comes from exponentiating the coefficient estimate: $e^{0.390} = 1.477$.) Being non-Hispanic Black is associated with an estimated 7.6-percentage-point or 43.5% (($1 - 0.565$) × 100) lower likelihood of using marijuana.

9.2.5 Which probability model is best?

There are different schools of thought on which probability model to use. Horace and Oaxaca (2006) show that the linear probability model is inconsistent and biased in most cases. Others argue that the

Table 9.2 Demonstration of odds ratios for the probability of marijuana use (n = 7995)

	Dependent variable = whether the youth used marijuana in the past 30 days		
	(1)	(2)	(3)
	Coefficient estimates	Marginal effects	Odds ratios
Male	0.390***	0.056***	1.477***
	(0.059)	(0.008)	(0.088)
Age	0.0638***	0.009***	1.066***
	(0.020)	(0.003)	(0.021)
Race/ethnicity (non-Hispanic Whites form the reference group)			
Non-Hispanic Black	−0.572***	−0.076***	0.565***
	(0.077)	(0.009)	(0.044)
Hispanic	−0.319***	−0.043***	0.727***
	(0.077)	(0.010)	(0.057)
Other race/ethnicity	−0.394**	−0.051***	0.674**
	(0.168)	(0.019)	(0.114)
Parents lived with at age 12 (excluded category is both biological parents)			
One biological parent	0.287***	0.042***	1.332***
	(0.069)	(0.010)	(0.093)
One bio. and one other parent	0.550***	0.093***	1.733***
	(0.131)	(0.025)	(0.228)
Other situation	0.134	0.020	1.143
	(0.088)	(0.013)	(0.101)
Constant	−2.816***		0.060
	(0.372)		(0.022)

Source: Bureau of Labor Statistics (2015).

Standard errors in parentheses. ***$p < 0.01$, **$p < 0.05$, *$p < 0.1$.

probit and logit models are likely mis-specified also, so they are no better than the LPM. (And it is rare that the probit and logit would give meaningfully different results.)

In the grand scheme of things, it probably does not matter in most cases. (How many planets are there, again, in just our universe?) That said, the probit and logit models are more accepted, as some people are flabbergasted that someone would use an LPM. If you have a good reason to use the LPM (such as needing to use fixed effects or estimating an instrumental-variables model), it is usually accepted. If you have other reasons for using the LPM, a good strategy is to also use a logit or probit model to examine whether the answer is the same and report this in the analysis.

9.2.6 Goodness-of-fit measures for probit and logit models

Because the probit and logit estimation methods are not linear, an R^2 cannot be calculated. The R^2 can, of course, be calculated with an LPM. An alternative measure for probit and logit methods is a measure of the percent correctly predicted by the model. Most statistical packages do not compute this, so it would have to be estimated with additional code. The calculation would be comparing the actual outcome with the predicted outcome based on the predicted probability from the model – a predicted probability >0.5 would indicate that the model predicts the event to occur for an observation.

The primary problem with this measure is that it only is useful for outcomes that have about a 50% overall chance of the event occurring – i.e., $\Pr(Y = 1)$ is close to 0.5. If it diverges much from 50% and if there are enough explanatory variables, then a likely scenario is that all predicted probabilities will be above or below 0.5, meaning that they would all be predicted to occur or all predicted not to occur.

There are no great options for goodness-of-fit measures for probit and logit models. This may give a good reason to use the LPM when a goodness-of-fit measure is needed.

9.3 Ordinal outcomes – ordered models

This is not that common of a regression model (and not my favorite). Let's take the example of an analysis on estimating the determinants of people's self-assessment of health at age 40, with data from the NLSY that we used in Table 7.1 (Bureau of Labor Statistics, 2014). In this case, we will use a sample of males and females, we'll change up the set of explanatory variables a bit, and we'll use the health outcome at age 40 instead of age 50. The choices for the outcome were (poor, fair, good, very good, and excellent), coded as values 1–5. OLS may not be appropriate because going from, say, *poor* to *fair* (1 to 2) is not necessarily similar to going from *very good* to *excellent* (4 to 5) or any other transition, even though a given X variable would be estimated to have the same effect on all single-step transitions (from *poor* to *fair* and from *very good* to *excellent*). An ordered model would allow for more flexibility for varying effects on different single-step transitions of the outcome.

The model would be:

$$Y_i^* = X_i\beta + \varepsilon_i \qquad (9.7)$$

where Y^* is a latent variable for general health. We do not observe Y^*, but rather we observe:

$$Y = \begin{cases} 0 & \text{if } Y^* < \mu_0 \\ 1 & \text{if } \mu_0 < Y^* < \mu_1 \\ 2 & \text{if } \mu_1 < Y^* < \mu_2 \\ 3 & \text{if } \mu_2 < Y^* < \mu_3 \\ 4 & \text{if } \mu_3 < Y^* < \mu_4 \end{cases} \qquad (9.8)$$

where the μ's are thresholds for the latent variable Y^* to be categorized into each level of health. The cut-off points between levels of Y^*, the μ's, are estimated by the model, and they contribute to predicting the probability of a given outcome. There are different lengths of the intervals between cut-off points, which allows the X variables to have varying marginal effects on moving from one level of Y to the next level of Y. Table 9.3 shows the main results, and Table 9.4 shows the varying marginal effects for different levels of Y.

Table 9.3 Ordered Probit results for "health at age 40" (n = 7705)

	Dependent variable = health status at age 40	
	Coef. Est.	Std. Error
Years-of-schooling	0.082***	(0.007)
AFQT	0.004***	(0.001)
Black	−0.067**	(0.032)
Hispanic	−0.052	(0.035)
Male	0.145***	(0.024)
/cut1	−0.780	(0.079)
/cut2	0.093	(0.076)
/cut3	1.037	(0.077)
/cut4	2.125	(0.078)

Source: Bureau of Labor Statistics (2014).

Standard errors in parentheses. ***$p < 0.01$, **$p < 0.05$, *$p < 0.1$.

Table 9.4 Marginal effects from Ordered Probit Model

	Poor	Fair	Good	Very good	Excellent
Years-of-schooling	−0.0039	−0.0122	−0.0155	0.0089	0.0227
AFQT	−0.0002	−0.0006	−0.0008	0.0005	0.0012
Black	0.0033	0.0102	0.0126	−0.0076	−0.0185
Hispanic	0.0025	0.0078	0.0097	−0.0059	−0.0142
Male	−0.0070	−0.0021	−0.0275	0.0157	0.0403

Source: Bureau of Labor Statistics (2014).

The other variables are as we have used them earlier, but with the variable for years-of-schooling being from 1996 (before everyone in the sample turns 40). We see that years-of-schooling, AFQT score, being Black, and being male have significant coefficient estimates. The "cut" variables at the bottom of Table 9.3 are the μ's from equation (9.8) above. These are estimated within the model. They help determine the marginal effects in Table 9.4.

As an example of interpreting the marginal effects in Table 9.4, one extra year of schooling is associated with lower probabilities of reporting health as *poor* (by 0.39 percentage points), fair (by 1.22 percentage points), and *good* (by 1.55 percentage points); an extra year of schooling is associated with a higher probability of reporting health as *very good* (by 0.89 percentage points) and *excellent* (by 2.27 percentage points). Note that the marginal effects sum up to 0 (across a row), other than some rounding errors.

In contrast to the results for schooling, being Black is associated with a higher probability of *poor*, *fair*, or *good* health and a lower probability of *very good* or *excellent* health. In general, note that the proportional effect of one variable relative to another stays constant across the outcomes – e.g., the marginal effects of being Hispanic are roughly three-quarters of that for the variable for Black.

As a side note, Ordered Logit Models are very similar in nature and interpretation to the Ordered Probit Model.

From my experience, the Ordered Probit/Logit Models are fairly shaky in that slight changes to the model can have disproportionate effects on the results. An alternative to ordered models is to do a series of probability models. For example, the ordered model can be broken down into probability models. For example, we could model:

- Pr(health is fair or worse)
- Pr(health is very good or worse)
- Pr(health is good or better)
- Pr(health is excellent or better).

These would be more flexible and easier to interpret, and they would be more stable models than the ordered models.

9.4 Categorical outcomes – Multinomial Logit Model

Multinomial Logit Models can be used when:

- The outcome is categorical in that the order does not mean anything
- The outcome is quantitative, but various factors can cause the outcome to move in opposite directions for various parts of the population as a result of a treatment; that is, the outcome may move away from or toward a central tendency.

I will present a theoretical example of using the model for categorical outcomes and an empirical example for capturing separate effects in opposite directions.

9.4.1 Using Multinomial Logit Models for categorical outcomes

Suppose that a political party is choosing among a field of four candidates to nominate for the presidency. The candidates and their characteristics are:

Candidate A: moderate, disagrees with the party platform on some issues
Candidate B: tough talker, wants to pre-emptively strike Greenland
Candidate C: always agrees with the party's platform, even if it runs counter to positions he has had in the past
Candidate D: smart person, has views mostly in line with the party, but got caught cheating on his wife five years ago.

Let's suppose that a campaign official for candidate A wants to know what causes a potential voter to prefer one of the other candidates over candidate A.

Unlike the dependent variable in the previous section that had a clear order (level of health), there is no ordering of the candidates that has any meaning. The preferred candidate for a voter is, thus, a *categorical variable*.

If there were two categories (e.g., yes or no on some issue, such as whether the citizen voted in the election), then a probit, logit, or linear probability model could be used. But it is more complicated in this case with multiple choices.

In the Multinomial Logit (MNL) model, one first chooses a baseline category, say candidate A, and then models the log odds of each choice relative to the baseline choice/outcome:

$$\ln\left(\frac{\Pr\left(y = \text{candidate B}\right)}{\Pr\left(y = \text{candidate A}\right)}\right) = \beta_0 + \beta_1 X_1 + \beta_2 X_2 + \cdots + \beta_K X_K + \varepsilon = X\beta + \varepsilon \tag{9.9}$$

To calculate the predicted probability of a choice, equation (9.9) would be transformed into:

$$\Pr\left(\text{candidate B}\right) = \frac{1}{\sum_{k \neq B} e^{-X\beta}} \tag{9.10}$$

where X includes a constant and X_1 to X_k. From this, "marginal effects" (which again are not necessarily causal effects) can be calculated, as shown in Section 9.2.4. The same MNL model would estimate marginal effects for each variable for candidates C and D, relative to candidate A.

9.4.2 Using Multinomial Logit Models for outcomes that can move in opposite directions

Let me refer back to Section 5.8, in which I argued that one reason why an estimate could be insignificant is that the positive and negative effects of the treatment are canceling each other out. This could only occur when there are plausible mechanisms that could cause some subjects to be positively affected by a treatment and others to be negatively affected.

A divorce could be such a treatment, as we saw in Section 3.2.1 on interaction effects. While the conventional wisdom is that a divorce would negatively affect children, there is the possibility that a divorce could help some children, particularly if it removes them from a high-conflict household. Thus, it is possible that divorces do positively affect some children, negatively affect other children, and yet the estimated average effect that is observed in a study is insignificant because the opposing effects cancel each other out.

In a study of mine (Arkes, 2016), I used data on children of the female respondents of the NLSY to estimate how a marital disruption (a divorce or separation) affects problem behavior among her children. I started with a first-difference model:

$$Y_{i2} - Y_{i1} = \beta_1 \times \left(A_{i2} - A_{i1}\right) + \beta_2 \times \left(D_{i2} - D_{i1}\right) + \varepsilon_i \tag{9.11}$$

where:
- Y_{i2} and Y_{i1} = Behavioral Problems Index (BPI), with a higher score indicating more problems, for periods 1 and 2; BPI is standardized to have a mean of 100 and a standard deviation of 15
- A = age in months
- D = an indicator variable for whether the mother was Divorced or Separated from her husband.

The samples are limited to children whose parents were still married as of period 1 and are based on the change over a two-year period. Thus, the quantity $(D_{i2} - D_{i1})$ can only take the value of 0 or

1. One sample has people aged 5 or 6 in the first period and aged 7 or 8 in the second period. The other two samples have similar two-year changes going forward to ages 9 or 10 and to ages 11 or 12. Note that it is not necessary to control for certain demographic information (e.g., gender and race/ethnicity) because they stay constant between the two periods.

Estimating equation (9.11) with OLS gives an overall, average estimated effect (using the continuous variable for actual score change) and may miss what is occurring for certain segments of the population. Using a MNL model may provide extra information, as it would examine effects in both directions.

For each sample, I estimated a MNL model based on the three outcomes that represent the change in BPI: a decrease of 5+ points, an increase of 5+ points, and a change of less than 5 points. The outcome is constructed as follows:

$$
\begin{aligned}
Y_i &= -1 && \text{if } \left(Y_{i2} - Y_{i1} \le -5\right) \\
Y_i &= 0 && \text{if } \left(-5 < Y_{i2} - Y_{i1} < 5\right) \\
Y_i &= 1 && \text{if } \left(Y_{i2} - Y_{i1} \ge 5\right)
\end{aligned}
$$

A separate outcome variable was constructed similarly but based on 10-point changes.

The Multinomial Logit equations are:

$$
\ln\left(\frac{\Pr\left(Y_i = 1\right)}{\Pr\left(Y_i = 0\right)}\right) = \beta_{0a} + \beta_{1a}\left(A_{i2} - A_{i1}\right) + \beta_{2a}\left(D_{i2} - D_{i1}\right) + \varepsilon_{ia} \tag{9.12a}
$$

$$
\ln\left(\frac{\Pr\left(Y_i = -1\right)}{\Pr\left(Y_i = 0\right)}\right) = \beta_{0b} + \beta_{1b}\left(A_{i2} - A_{i1}\right) + \beta_{2b}\left(D_{i2} - D_{i1}\right) + \varepsilon_{ib} \tag{9.12b}
$$

in which the main difference is in the numerator of the dependent variable.

Table 9.5 shows the results. For the second sample (going from ages 7–8 to 9–10), the model using the OLS method (the standard approach) shows no significant coefficient estimate. However, the MNL models, for both Models 2 and 3, show that there are significant coefficient estimates in both directions. Using the marginal effects (M.E.), experiencing a parental divorce/separation in those two years is associated with an estimated 5.5-percentage-point increase in the probability of a decrease in the BPI by 5+ points (improved behavior) and an estimated 8.3-percentage-point increase in the probability of having an increase in BPI by 5+ points (worsening behavior). Whereas I am hesitant to claim that I have validly estimated causal effects (due to various PITFALLS), *using the Multinomial Logit Model was able to uncover both positive and negative associations between parental divorce and behavioral problems that were masked by the models using the OLS method, which only measured an average association, in which positive and negative associations partly canceled each other out.*

For the younger sample, there were no significant coefficient estimates. For the older cohort, the standard estimated divorce effect (with OLS) is weakly significant, but it is more strongly significant when separately examining just increases in behavioral problems (for both 5-point and 10-point increases).

Table 9.5 Coefficient estimates of marital disruption on problem behavior

	Dependent variable = behavioral problems index		
	Sample		
	From 5–6 to 7–8 years old (n = 3144)	From 7–8 to 9–10 years old (n = 3332)	From 9–10 to 11–12 years old (n = 2781)
Dependent variable			
Model 1 (OLS)			
Change in scores	−0.584	1.262	2.722*
	(1.228)	(1.213)	(1.578)
Model 2 (MNL)			
Decrease of 5+ points	0.077	0.597***	0.389
	(0.203)	(0.228)	(0.250)
	M.E. = 0.040	M.E. = 0.055	M.E. = 0.011
Increase of 5+ points	−0.223	0.675***	0.629***
	(0.214)	(0.217)	(0.237)
	M.E. = −0.059	M.E. = 0.083	M.E. = 0.100
Model 3 (MNL)			
Decrease of 10+ points	0.065	0.407*	0.273
	(0.228)	(0.239)	(0.272)
	M.E. = 0.011	M.E. = 0.032	M.E. = 0.017
Increase of 10+ points	−0.080	0.661***	0.584**
	(0.240)	(0.213)	(0.246)
	M.E. = −0.015	M.E. = 0.098	M.E. = 0.089

Source: Bureau of Labor Statistics (2014).

Standard errors in parentheses ***$p < 0.01$, **$p < 0.05$, *$p < 0.1$.

9.5 Censored outcomes – Tobit models

In some cases, an outcome is censored at the bottom or top level of the distribution. For example, SAT scores are bottom- and top-coded at 200 and 800, so the scores are not able to distinguish between the abilities or aptitudes of those who score 800. As mentioned in the chapter introduction, another example is income, which is censored at 0 for those who do not work. This means that there is a relatively large percentage of observations with a value of 0, particularly for women, who historically have had lower labor force participation rates.[2] Furthermore, the income data we have used from the NLSY is top-coded for 3.9% of the sample.

One can imagine that some adults who have very low levels of education are less likely to work because their income would be too low, so they choose not to work or are unable to get a job. An extra year of schooling, which should make them more productive, can then have two effects:

1. increase the likelihood that the person works and earns income
2. increase income for those already working.

When there are these two separate effects, OLS is problematic because it results in inconsistent estimates. James Tobin developed a model to address this, which became known as the **Tobit model**. The model is:

$$Y_i^* = X_i\beta + \varepsilon_i \tag{9.13}$$

where Y_i^* is a latent variable that is observed for values of Y greater than zero (provided that 0 is the censor point):

$$Y = \begin{cases} Y^* & \text{if } Y^* > 0 \\ 0 & \text{if } Y^* \leq 0 \end{cases} \tag{9.14}$$

This model, also estimated by maximum likelihood, uses the assumption that the error terms are normally distributed. A problem with the Tobit model is the ambiguity of what expected value to use and, thus, what marginal effects to calculate. The coefficient estimates themselves are on the latent variable, Y^*, and so they are not interpretable themselves. The potential expected values could be:

- The expected value of the latent variable: $E[Y_i^*] = X_i\beta$, which comes straight from the reported output, but Y_i^* typically has no useful meaning
- The expected value of the outcome, conditional on X and being positive: $E[Y_i | Y_i > 0, X]$
- The expected value of Y is conditional on just X, $E[Y_i | X]$.

The latter two are more complicated to calculate, as they incorporate how the X variable affects the probability that the person has a positive income.

Given the ambiguity of the Tobit model, a common approach is to estimate two models that are more concrete:

- How the X variables affect the probability that the person has a positive value for the dependent variable
- How the X variables affect the dependent variable, conditional on the dependent variable being positive.

This would be more tractable, and it would have more straightforward interpretations. Remember that, often, simpler is better.

9.6 Count variables – Negative Binomial and Poisson models

As mentioned in the chapter introduction, most variables are not truly continuous (i.e., being able to take on any value), but can be approximated as continuous based on having an adequate amount of variation. Other variables, however, are clearly discrete, such as a "count" variable. Let's take the example of the number of children a teenage female desires to eventually have. This variable would be censored at zero, highly concentrated at low values, and highly skewed to the right.

Using OLS causes problems because: (1) the error terms are not normally distributed, violating Assumption **A3** for OLS; and (2) the model may give predictions that are less than zero, which cannot actually occur.

There are two models that are commonly used with count data: the Negative Binomial regression model and the Poisson regression model. Both have the general format of:

$$\log\left[E(Y \mid X)\right] = X\beta$$

or

(9.15)

$$E(Y \mid X) = e^{X\beta}$$

This means that the coefficient estimate indicates the percentage increase in the count outcome associated with a one-unit increase in X. This is not exactly a marginal effect, but rather a quasi-elasticity.

Behind the curtains, there are some extra details and differences between the Poisson and Negative Binomial models, but they are very math intensive, and presenting them would be contrary to the spirit of this book.

The Negative Binomial model is the more flexible of the models and should be used most of the time. Poisson is better when there is "under dispersion," meaning there is less variation in the model than expected – I know, a very abstract concept. You're safer sticking with the Negative Binomial model.

To demonstrate count models, I examine the issue of how much females' educational expectations determine their fertility outcomes. I take a sample of the 1331 16–17-year-old females from the initial NLSY round in 1979 who had not had any kids as of their initial 1979 interview and were still in the sample five years later. I then examine how various factors determine the number of kids they had by their interview about five years later, in 1984 (Bureau of Labor Statistics, 2014).

Figure 9.1 shows the histogram of the outcome. It obviously is not a continuous outcome, having only five different values. Plus, there is the bunching at zero. Thus, it is unlikely that the error terms would be normally distributed if OLS were used.

Table 9.6 shows a comparison of results from a Negative Binomial, Poisson, and linear model using the OLS method, along with marginal effects of the Negative Binomial and Poisson models. The primary explanatory variable of interest is expected years of education. For 16–17-year-old females, each expected year of schooling is associated with a centralized estimate of 14% fewer births over the next five years (from the primary Negative Binomial and Poisson models – columns 1 and 3), holding the other factors constant. These translate into a marginal effect of 0.051 fewer births – columns 2

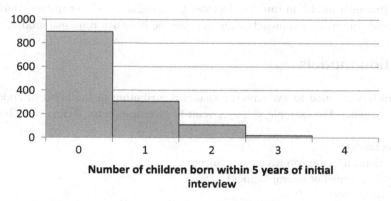

Figure 9.1 Frequency of the number of children born in the first 5 years of the NLSY survey

Table 9.6 Results from Negative Binomial, Poisson, and OLS (n = 1331)

	Dependent variable = number of births (in 5 years after first observed at age 16–17)				
	Negative Binomial model		Poisson model		Linear model using OLS
	(1)	*(2)*	*(3)*	*(4)*	*(5)*
	Estimates	*Marginal effects*	*Estimates*	*Marginal effects*	*Estimates / Marginal effects*
Expected years of schooling	−0.138***	−0.051***	−0.137***	−0.051***	−0.062***
	(0.024)	(0.009)	(0.024)	(0.009)	(0.010)
AFQT	−0.012***	−0.005***	−0.012***	−0.005***	−0.004***
	(0.003)	(0.001)	(0.003)	(0.001)	(0.001)
Race/ethnicity (non-Hispanic and non-Black is the reference group)					
Black	0.402***	0.165***	0.397***	0.163***	0.197***
	(0.108)	(0.050)	(0.108)	(0.050)	(0.053)
Hispanic	0.212*	0.0849	0.209*	0.083*	0.094*
	(0.121)	(0.052)	(0.120)	(0.051)	(0.055)
Constant	1.255***		1.245***		1.385***
	(0.275)		(0.276)		(0.131)
R-squared					0.113

Source: Bureau of Labor Statistics (2014).

Standard errors are in parentheses and are corrected for heteroskedasticity. ***$p < 0.01$, **$p < 0.05$, *$p < 0.10$.

and 4. The OLS estimate, also in terms of the change in the number of births, is 0.062 fewer births. Being Black is associated with about 40% (or 0.16) more births.

While OLS may sometimes give very similar results, in this case, the results are a bit different. I would trust the Negative Binomial and Poisson results more than OLS, given that the OLS estimates are probably inconsistent. One last note is that a Poisson model gives almost the exact same results as the Negative Binomial model, in this case. In most cases, it likely will not matter which model you use, but the more conservative approach, again, is using the Negative Binomial model.

9.7 Duration models

Duration models are used to examine the factors contributing to the event of ending time in a given state of existence. For example, one may want to investigate what factors contribute to:

- Businesses failing
- Cancer patients in remission having a recurrence
- People leaving a spell of unemployment
- A couple divorcing
- How long a machine lasts before malfunctioning.

Duration models are also called:

- Survival models (e.g., the machine surviving in the "working" state)
- Hazard models (the hazard of a machine malfunctioning).

The survival time is the amount of time that a subject remains in a certain state. That is, how long will a cancer patient remain in the state of "remission"? How long will the unemployed person remain in the state of "being unemployed"? The survival time may be censored in that not everyone will change states by the end of the study period. Also, it could be the case that not everyone is observed when first going into the initial state (e.g., remission). That is not ideal, but duration models can account for this.

The survival function, $S(t)$, represents the probability that a subject survives in a given state for t periods, and is represented as:

$$S(t) = \Pr(T > t) \tag{9.16}$$

where T is the actual survival time.

The hazard function, $h(t)$, would then be the probability that the subject changes to the other state in a given period t:

$$h(t) = \frac{f(t)}{S(t)} \tag{9.17}$$

where $f(t)$ is the value for a given t in the probability density function of the distribution of the survival time of T.

Choosing the correct probability density function $f(t)$ and hazard function $h(t)$ unfortunately presents a researcher with several options. The two choices that are most often used, based on the flexibility of the model, are:

- Using the Weibull distribution. This has flexibility over what the distribution of the survival time (T) is, but it requires the researcher to make assumptions on what that distribution looks like. It allows varying underlying hazard rates (probability of failure) as the survival time increases.
- Using the Cox proportional-hazards model. This does not require any prior knowledge of the hazard distribution. The downside is that it requires the underlying hazard rate (before the effects of other explanatory variables are accounted for) to be constant for each value of t, meaning, for example, that the underlying divorce rate would be constant at each year of marriage in the model if there were no influences from other factors. The basis of using the Cox proportional-hazards model is that the hazard (and survival) distribution is not known, so assigning an incorrect distribution causes more bias than assuming no distribution.

The safest approach typically is using the Cox proportional-hazards model. The model is:

$$h(t \mid X) = \Pr\left(\text{subject changes states in period } t\right) = h_0(t) \times e^{X\beta} \tag{9.18}$$

where $h_0(t)$ is the baseline hazard for a given period and X is the set of explanatory variables.

This means that the estimated effect of a one-unit change in an X variable on the probability of the person changing states (i.e., not surviving in the current state) is the exponential of the coefficient estimate on that X variable. Sounds strange, but it works well.

As mentioned above, the model can incorporate censored data – cases in which a person is first observed after the initial state has begun (e.g., unemployment) or before the initial state ended (finding a job). The censored points just need to be indicated in the statistical program.

As an example, a colleague and I examined how the strength of the economy, proxied by the state unemployment rate, affects the probability of divorce (Arkes and Shen, 2014). We examined the effect of the lagged unemployment rate (during the $(t-1)$th year of marriage) on the probability that the couple's marriage survives through year t. For example, how does the average state unemployment rate in the 3rd year of marriage determine whether the couple survives through the 4th year of marriage? We used the lagged unemployment rate because of the likelihood that divorces take time to be carried out.

Table 9.7 shows a summary of the two primary models, displaying the estimated hazard ratios and standard errors (as reported in the article), not the coefficient estimates. Each estimate represents the estimated change in the odds of a divorce, relative to the baseline odds, from a 1-percentage-point increase in the unemployment rate. Model (1) estimates the effects for all married couples, while model (2) estimates separate effects by the length of the marriage.

There is a weakly significant positive estimated effect of the unemployment rate on the probability of divorce. However, when estimating separate effects by the length of the marriage, the evidence is stronger that a higher state unemployment rate increases the probability of divorce for those in their 6th to 10th years of marriage. The point estimate (the best guess for the estimated effect of the unemployment rate) for this group says that a 1-percentage-point higher unemployment rate would lead to a 7.9% higher risk of divorce, relative to the baseline odds. There is no evidence that the unemployment rate affects the probability of divorce in those in other stages of marriage.

One factor to keep in mind is the point from earlier about the measurement error in the state unemployment rates. And these models had state and year controls, which is almost equivalent to fixed effects. This means that one reason why there were insignificant estimates of the unemployment rate might be that there was a large bias toward zero from measurement error.

Earlier, I argued against the use of national variables. For example, using national unemployment rates for estimating the effects of the economy on drug use or using national tax rates to estimate

Table 9.7 Cox proportional-hazards model for the effects of state unemployment rates on the probability of a couple divorcing ($n = 95,472$)

	Using state unemployment rates	
	(1)	(2)
Unemployment rate	1.034*	
	(0.021)	
(Unemployment rate) × (in years 1–5 of marriage)		1.014
		(0.030)
(Unemployment rate) × (in years 6–10 of marriage)		1.079***
		(0.029)
(Unemployment rate) × (in years 11+ of marriage)		1.004
		(0.036)

Source: Bureau of Labor Statistics (2014).

The models also control for demographic factors, religion, age of marriage for both spouses, 3-year-group indicators, and state indicators. ***$p < 0.01$, **$p < 0.05$, *$p < 0.10$.

the effects of tax rates on economic growth (Section 6.5) introduces a great potential for omitted-factors bias. With divorces, however, one could argue that national unemployment rates could be used because divorce rates do not change much at a national level within short periods of time other than due to the strength of the economy. (If we were wrong on this assumption, then our results when using the national unemployment rate should not be trusted.) Exceptions may include the September 11 attacks (which some argue brought families together more), a well-publicized domestic violence incident (which could encourage more women to leave marriages), and the effects of social-distancing and shutdown policies due to COVID on marriages.

By including 3-year-group controls (i.e., fixed effects), the effect of the national unemployment rate is identified by how within-3-year-period variation in the national unemployment rate is related to such variation in the probability of divorce. With the national unemployment rates, the results (not shown here) were much stronger: a higher national unemployment rate was estimated to lead to a higher probability of divorcing for those couples in their 6th to 10th year of marriage by 23.4%. Note that this does not mean that a 1-percentage-point increase in the unemployment rate leads to an increase in the probability of a couple divorcing (by 23.4 percentage points from 3.1% to 26.5%). Rather, it would be 23.4% on top of 3.1% (or 3.1% times 1.234), which would mean 3.8%.

All that said, in retrospect, we could have been more responsible in how we conducted and described this research. I will discuss what we could have done better in Chapter 13 on the ethics of regression analysis.

9.8 Summary

This chapter presented alternative methods to use in certain situations in which the dependent variable is not continuous or approximately continuous. As stated earlier, using OLS when the error terms are not normally distributed could cause:

- Inefficient estimates
- Biased estimates
- Misleading statistics related to the significance of estimates, hypothesis tests, and confidence intervals.

That said, sometimes using these models presents new problems or makes it impossible to apply a correction for non-random explanatory variables, creating even worse biases to the estimates. In general, the biases or inconsistency resulting from the improper model being used is much smaller than the biases associated with the PITFALLS from Chapter 6. The best approach is to use the appropriate model, as outlined in this chapter, unless it prevents the use of proper methods to address certain biases.

Exercises

1. With the data set, births18 (which comes from the NLSY cohort that started in 1997), use a probit, logit, and linear-probability model to regress birth18 (whether the female respondent gives birth before age 18) on black, hisp, mixed, momhs, momcoll, momeducmiss, dadhs, dadcoll, dadeducmiss, notbiomom, and notbiodad. Use the 7th round (2003) sample weight (wt2003). For two variables (black and momhs), compare the point estimates for the marginal effects on

the probit and logit models and from the linear-probability model (which naturally estimates a marginal effect).

2. What is the estimated odds ratio on momhs from the logit model? Interpret this odds ratio and the corresponding marginal effect for momhs from the logit model in #1.

3. Use the data set, **temperature_gdp**, to estimate how temperature affects the likelihood of negative GDP growth (using the dummy variable, *neg*, indicating negative GDP growth, as the dependent variable. Use both the standard fixed-effects model (repeating Question #2a from Chapter 8) and the correction for over-weighted groups (similar to Question #2c from Chapter 8). Interpret the result.

Notes

1 More specifically, the Maximum Likelihood method involves finding the set of coefficient estimates that give the highest likelihood of the data occurring as it did. That is, the likelihood function maximizes $\ln[\Pr(Y_1, Y_2, Y_3, ..., Y_n \mid X_1, X_2, X_3, ..., X_n)]$ for the n observations, with the X's representing all explanatory variables.

2 The same issues occur if the dependent variable is "truncated," meaning that only observations meeting a certain threshold for the dependent variable are included in the sample. Examples of this include restricting samples to: honor students with a GPA of 3.5 or better; low-income individuals who earn no more than the poverty level; people with a minimum of $10,000 of income.

References

Arkes, J. (2016). On the misinterpretation of insignificant coefficient estimates. SSRN Working Paper. (Available at http://papers.ssrn.com/sol3/papers.cfm?abstract_id=2821164, accessed July 10, 2018).

Arkes, J., & Shen, Y. C. (2014). For better or for worse, but how about a recession? *Contemporary Economic Policy, 32*(2), 275–287.

Bureau of Labor Statistics, U.S. Department of Labor. (2014). *National Longitudinal Survey of Youth 1979 cohort, 1979–2012 (rounds 1–25)*. Columbus, OH: Center for Human Resource Research, The Ohio State University.

Bureau of Labor Statistics, U.S. Department of Labor. (2015). *National Longitudinal Survey of Youth 1997 cohort, 1997–2013 (rounds 1–16)*. Columbus, OH: Center for Human Resource Research, The Ohio State University.

Horace, W., & Oaxaca, R. (2006). Results on the bias and inconsistency of ordinary least squares for the linear probability model. *Economics Letters, 90*(3), 321–327.

10 Time-series models

DOI: 10.4324/9781003285007-10

As Yogi Berra once said, "The future ain't what it used to be." The future ain't what it was, but "what it used to be" *might* help predict the future. **Time-series models** involve one entity or subject (e.g., a country or a business) that is followed over many periods. This contrasts with a cross-sectional model, which has many subjects in just one period. And time-series models are different from panel models, which have multiple subjects over multiple periods.

Time-series models can be categorized into two types:

- **Contemporaneous (static) models** that examine the contemporaneous (current) effects of an X variable on an outcome
- **Dynamic models** that examine how lagged values of an X variable and/or lagged values of an outcome determine the current value of the outcome.

These models are often for the purpose of forecasting the outcome and estimating the causal effects of various factors on the outcome. Either way, time-series models are useful when a dependent variable has inertia or some factor could have drawn-out effects over time. For example, an oil-price increase could cause airline ticket prices to increase, but the effect may not be immediate, as priorly-established contracts for jet fuel purchases could dictate current ticket prices.

Time-series models have so many subtleties that whole textbooks are written on the various types of time-series models for different situations. This chapter represents just an introduction to time-series models. In this chapter, you will learn:

- The basics of time-series models
- How to estimate common time-series models
- Some of the most common problems to be conscious of when conducting time-series analysis
- How to conduct basic forecasting and gauging the precision of forecasts.

10.1 The components of a time-series variable

A time-series variable can be decomposed into four basic components:

- A trend component – the value may tend to move over time
- A seasonal component – the value may tend to be different in certain periods, such as parts of the year
- A cyclical (often called "irregular") component – the value may go through cycles, such as macro-economic business cycles or drug epidemics
- A random-disturbance component – this is just due to the random things that happen in life.

Not all time-series variables will have all of these components. For example, whereas a quarterly unemployment rate would have a seasonal component (the rate is typically higher in the winter quarter), an annual unemployment rate would not have any seasonal component. In addition, many time-series variables will not have any trend, tending to return to a long-run average. For example, corporate profit margins, while currently maintaining a sustained higher-than-average rate, have historically returned to the long-run average.

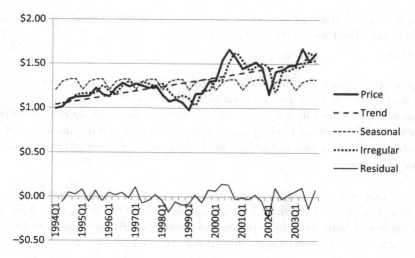

Figure 10.1 Decomposition of a time-series variable (quarterly gas prices)

Figure 10.1 demonstrates the different components of the time-series variable, the average U.S. gas price, based on the first Monday of each quarter. The lines are:

- Price = actual price for the given date
- Trend = linear trend from the model: $\left(\widehat{Price}\right)_t = 1.023 + 0.013 \times t$
- Seasonal = quarterly effects: $\left(\widehat{Price}\right)_t = 1.204 + 0.092 \times \left(spring\right)_t + 0.118 \times \left(summer\right)_t + 0.119 \times \left(fall\right)_t$
- Irregular: $\left(\widehat{Price}\right)_t = 0.202 + 0.854 \times \left(Price\right)_{t-1}$
- Random disturbance (residual) = the residual from including all other components in a joint model:

$$\hat{\varepsilon}_t = \left(Price\right)_t - \Big[0.213 + 0.004 \times t + 0.134 \times \left(spring\right)_t$$
$$+ 0.091 \times \left(summer\right)_t + 0.069 \times \left(fall\right)_t + 0.725 \times \left(Price\right)_{t-1}\Big]$$

Some of these components will be integral for subsequent lessons. For example, the irregular component will be the basis for autoregressive models in Section 10.3.

10.2 Autocorrelation

Consider three time-series variables:

- The winning percentage for your favorite sports team (I'll use mine, the San Antonio Spurs of the National Basketball Association, even though I have never been in Texas)
- The number of minutes a doctor spends with a patient
- The daily percentage change in the stock price of Google.

Think about how these variables might move over time. Specifically, think about how a given observation might be correlated with prior observations.

I would expect:

- The winning percentage for the Spurs to be positively related to recent, prior years, as most key players tend to stay the same from one year to the next
- The number of minutes a doctor spends with a patient to be negatively related to prior patients because more time spent with prior patients means the doctor will feel more rushed
- The daily percentage change in Google's stock price would not depend in any systematic way on prior daily changes.

These are indicators of the extent of **autocorrelation** (also called **serial correlation**) in a variable. Autocorrelation is a situation in which a variable is correlated with its lagged values. Technically, autocorrelation would come from the correlation of the errors. First-order autocorrelation would be the case in which, from a time-series regression with an error term of ε_i:

$$\varepsilon_t = \rho\varepsilon_{t-1} + \eta_t \tag{10.1}$$

$\rho \neq 0$. (The component of equation (10.1), η_t, is the part of the error term that is truly random and independent of any other error term and assumed to be normally distributed.) In the examples above, the estimate for ρ would likely be positive for the Spurs' winning percentage, negative for the number of minutes a doctor spends with a patient, and close to zero for the daily change in Google's stock price.

Any autocorrelation could be due to correlated period effects (such as having a star player for certain years) or due to some factor or event having lasting or drawn-out effects. For example, in an analysis of opioid overdoses, epidemics could cause higher-than-normal overdose rates for a few years, leading to a positive correlation of the error terms. And, with drawn-out effects, oil-price increases could have lagged effects on airline ticket prices, as contracts might have contracted jet fuel prices. Thus, the ticket prices might have effects from the higher oil prices that last long after the oil prices have returned to their normal price range.

The concept of autocorrelation is similar to that of **spatial correlation**, which is the case in which locations close to each other would have correlated values of a variable. In spatial correlation, the correlation is by geographical proximity, whereas autocorrelation is the correlation of observations that are in proximity by time.

To demonstrate what positive vs. negative correlation looks like, let's consider two different time-series variables for the Spurs:

- Their winning percentage each season
- The change in their winning percentage from the prior season.

Figure 10.2 shows the time series for these two variables for every year that the Spurs have been part of the National Basketball Association. As expected and discussed above, it appears that there is a positive correlation between successive values for the winning percentage. However, for the change in winning percentage, it appears that there is a negative correlation between values. That is, when one value is high (positive), the next value appears to decrease or be negative. And, when one value is low, the next value tends to be higher. This makes sense, as an increase in winning percentage in one year

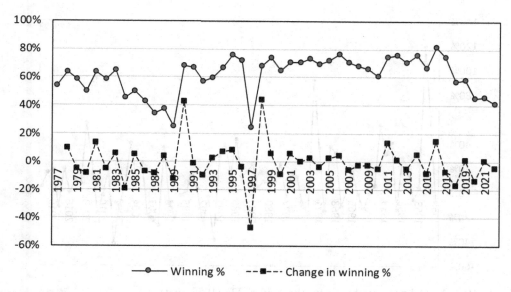

Figure 10.2 San Antonio Spurs winning percentage and change in winning percentage, by year

may partly be due to random luck in winning a few games, and reversion to the mean would then cause a tendency for the change to the next year to be negative. These, again, are cases of autocorrelation, positive in the first case and negative in the second case.

Autocorrelation creates problems if one is using time-series variables to analyze the relationship between different variables, particularly when there is a lagged-dependent variable. This partly occurs because the effective sample size decreases, as there are fewer independent observations when there is autocorrelation. There is also the possibility of biased coefficient estimates. I will discuss these problems in Section 10.5, but first I will introduce the autoregressive and distributed-lag models in the next few sections, with the autoregression in the next section being a way to model autocorrelation.

10.3 Autoregressive models

Autoregressive models represent a method of modeling (approximating) autocorrelation. They involve regressing a time-series variable on one or more lags of the variable.

Let's consider the annual returns on the Japanese stock market index, the Nikkei 225. Let's start with a visual examination in Figure 10.3. While there are occasional single-week dips and peaks, there does seem to be a pattern of the percent change being relatively high or relatively low (or negative) for a few years in a row. Of course, humans are imperfect for assessing patterns in data merely by visualization, so we could test how a single value is related to prior values. To formally test whether the percent change in the Nikkei 225 can be forecasted by that for recent years, we would estimate an **autoregression**, which is a regression of a time-series variable on some of its lagged values.

A first-order autoregressive model, AR(1), would be:

$$Y_t = \beta_0 + \beta_1 Y_{t-1} + \varepsilon_t \qquad (10.2)$$

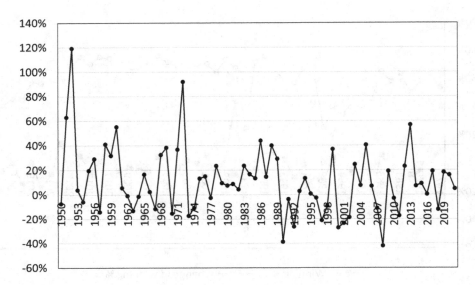

Figure 10.3 Annual percent change for the Nikkei 225 (1950–2021)

Source: https://www.macrotrends.net/2593/nikkei-225-index-historical-chart-data.

A jth-order autoregressive model, AR(j), would be:

$$Y_t = \beta_0 + \beta_1 Y_{t-1} + \beta_2 Y_{t-2} + \cdots + \beta_j Y_{t-j} + \varepsilon_t \tag{10.3}$$

There is a trade-off in that higher orders to the autoregressive model (i.e., adding more lags) may provide important information that can help forecast current values, but it also brings greater imprecision to the estimates of the coefficients on the existing lags. This occurs because there may be a high correlation between explanatory variables, which are all lags of each other.

How do you choose the optimal order (i.e., number of lags) to use for an autoregression? You may need to use BIC, AIC, and AICc (corrected AIC), which were briefly mentioned in Section 6.11. The idea behind them is to evaluate models based on how much additional variables contribute to the explanation of the data, while punishing the model, to some extent, for having to add more variables. The following is a brief description of each, with $\hat{L}$ being the maximum value of the model's likelihood function (see the endnote in the Introduction of Chapter 9), k being the number of parameters to estimate, and n being the sample size:

- $BIC = \ln(n) \times k - 2 \times \ln(\hat{L})$

- $AIC = 2k - 2 \times \ln(\hat{L})$

- $AICc = AIC + \dfrac{2k^2 + 2k}{n - k - 1}$

The lower the value, the better the model; even if the statistics are negative, the models with the more-negative criteria statistics are the better-fitting model. The AICc was created because BIC is considered by some to penalize added variables too much, and AIC does not penalize extra variables

Table 10.1 Autoregressive models for the Japanese annual unemployment rate (n = 57)

	Dependent variable = Japanese unemployment rate			
	AR(1)	AR(2)	AR(3)	AR(4)
Y_{t-1} (unemployment rate in the prior year)	0.955***	1.399***	1.482***	1.538***
	(0.031)	(0.124)	(0.177)	(0.151)
Y_{t-2}		−0.450***	−0.707**	−0.933***
		(0.114)	(0.300)	(0.242)
Y_{t-3}			0.180	0.642***
			(0.164)	(0.153)
Y_{t-4}				−0.301***
				(0.105)
Constant	0.159**	0.166**	0.150**	0.169**
	(0.0754)	(0.0720)	(0.0729)	(0.0709)
R-squared	0.943	0.955	0.956	0.960
BIC	30.2	20.9	23.2	22.1
AIC	25.9	14.4	14.5	11.3
AICc	26.1	14.9	15.3	12.4

Heteroskedasticity-corrected standard errors are in parentheses. ***$p < 0.01$, **$p < 0.05$, *$p < 0.10$.

enough, particularly for small samples. And so AIC is more likely to say that models with more variables are "better." The AICc statistic adds a little extra penalty for adding X variables.

In Table 10.1, I present the AR(1) to AR(4) models for a different outcome, the Japanese unemployment rate, along with the BIC, AIC, and AICc values.

The first lag, Y_{t-1}, has a statistically-significant positive coefficient estimate and is fairly high, suggesting a strong connection between the Japanese unemployment rate from one year to the next – not exactly a surprising result. (Note that the estimate on a lag would rarely be above 1.0.) As more lags are introduced, there seems to be an alternating positive-vs-negative coefficient estimate, and the coefficient estimate on the first lag goes beyond 1.0.

Which of these is the optimal model? The R^2, of course, is highest for the AR(4) model, but notice that it is already high in the AR(2) model. Also note that the standard error on the first lag is lower in the AR(1) model than in the AR(4) model. In addition, although the BIC is lowest in the AR(2) model, the AIC, and AICc both have the lowest values for the AR(4) model. This points to the optimal autoregressive model for the Japanese annual unemployment rate being four or more lags.

10.3.1 Lagged scatterplots

Sometimes, a basic autoregressive model may not represent well the actual extent of autocorrelation. A good check might come from using a **lagged scatterplot**, which is a scatterplot of a time-series variable with its lagged value. The lagged value could come from the prior period or from several periods ago.

What a lagged scatterplot could indicate is:

- Whether, despite insignificance in an AR model, there is a non-linear relationship between the lagged values and current values
- Whether there are any outliers that could be driving the autocorrelation.

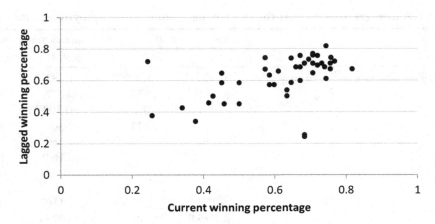

Figure 10.4a Scatterplot of current versus lagged winning percentage for the Spurs

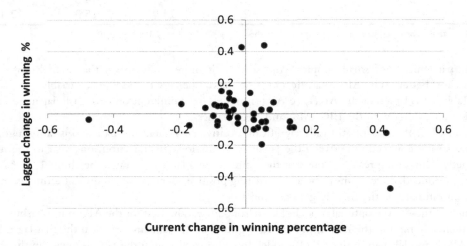

Figure 10.4b Scatterplot of current versus lagged change in winning percentage for the Spurs

Figures 10.4a and 10.4b show the lagged scatterplots for the Spurs' winning percentage and the change in winning percentage (corresponding to the lines in Figure 10.2). Figure 10.4a appears to show a clear positive correlation between the variables, and this is confirmed in Model (1) in Table 10.2. In contrast, Figure 10.4b shows a less certain relationship between the change-in-winning-percentage from one year to the next. There is a single outlier (the 1998 observation) that could be driving the negative autocorrelation. Indeed, as shown in Table 10.2, with an AR(1) model based on the change in winning percentage, the coefficient estimate on the lagged-winning-percentage is reduced in magnitude by a large amount when the 1998 observation is excluded (Model (3)), although the coefficient estimate on the lagged-change-in-winning-percentage is insignificant both with and without the 1998 observation.

Table 10.2 AR(1) model for the Spurs winning percentage and change in winning percentage (1978–2022)

	Dependent variable = winning percentage (Y)	Dependent variable = change in winning percentage (ΔY)	
	AR(1)	AR(1) (all obs.)	AR(1) (excludes 1998)
Y_{t-1} (winning % in prior season)	0.494** (0.198)		
ΔY_{t-1}		−0.353 (0.216)	−0.144 (0.149)
Constant	0.309** (0.130)	−0.006 (0.020)	−0.014 (0.020)

Note: Heteroskedasticity-corrected standard errors are in parentheses. *** $p < 0.01$, ** $p < 0.05$, * $p < 0.10$.

10.3.2 Autocorrelation functions (ACF) and partial autocorrelation functions (PACF)

The **autocorrelation function (ACF)** indicates how correlated different observations are based on how many periods away the observations are from each other. Typically, the further away two data points are, the closer to zero would be their correlation, but this is not always the case.

The **partial autocorrelation function (PACF)** is the same, but it factors out other variables. In particular, it typically just factors out the correlations of the other lags.

Figure 10.5a shows the ACF for the Japanese unemployment rate. The shaded area represents 95% confidence intervals. Anything beyond the shaded area would represent a statistically-significant correlation (at the 5% level). The confidence interval naturally gets wider at longer lags due to smaller sample sizes.

Even though no lagged-dependent variable beyond the first lag has a statistically-significant coefficient estimate (from Table 10.1), observations are still statistically significant at the 5% level up to six years away, although not quite significant for three and four years away. This could be because the cumulative set of autocorrelations from successive periods away makes the 6th lagged observation value correlated with the current value.

The correlations do approach zero as the lags increase, but they strangely start becoming more negative at the 17-year lag. That said, those long-lagged estimated correlations are statistically insignificant. The PACF, in Figure 10.5b, shows, for the first few lags, the alternating nature of the coefficient estimates between positive and negative.

The two-period lag (the second data point in these figures) provides a good demonstration of the difference between the ACF and the PACF. Observations from two years apart are positively correlated by a significant amount (as indicated by the point in the ACF being outside the shaded region representing the 95% confidence interval). But observations from two years apart are not significantly correlated with each other after factoring out the other correlations, particularly the one-year-apart correlations. This may suggest just an AR(1) process for the Japanese unemployment rate.

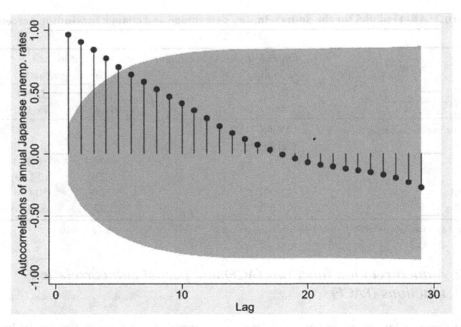

Figure 10.5a Autocorrelation function (ACF) of the annual Japanese unemployment rate

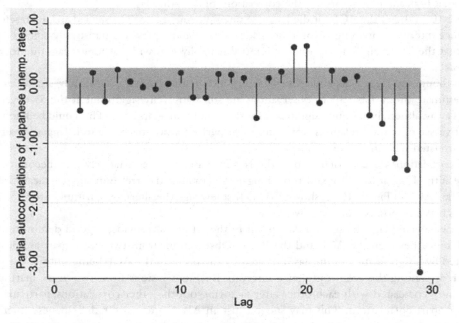

Figure 10.5b Partial autocorrelation function (PACF) of the annual Japanese unemployment rate

10.4 Distributed-lag models

10.4.1 The basic distributed-lag model

Sometimes, you may expect some factor to have an effect on an outcome that lasts for several periods. The classic example, from economics, is that an increase in a country's income could affect growth in consumption for several quarters or perhaps a few years after the income increase. In such a situation, the optimal model may be a distributed-lag model.

The distributed-lag model is of the form:

$$Y_t = \beta_0 + \delta_0 X_t + \delta_1 X_{t-1} + \delta_2 X_{t-2} + \cdots + \delta_p X_{t-p} + \varepsilon_t \tag{10.4}$$

Unfortunately, it is rare that any theory would dictate a certain number of lags, so the lags should often be determined empirically. Perhaps the information criterion (BIC, AIC, and AICc) would be useful measures rather than relying on the statistical significance of each lagged-X variable.

The distributed-lag model can be problematic because the lagged values of the X variable are often highly correlated with each other. This could cause:

- Large standard errors and greater imprecision of the estimates
- Challenges in interpreting the estimated contribution of a given lagged-X variable, while holding constant other lagged-X variables
- Coefficient estimates on successive lags that have sign-reversing or non-monotonic decreases in coefficient estimates as lags increase, which probably makes little theoretical sense – this occurs because the highly correlated lags often battle each other for explanatory power.

The easiest approach to address these problems is to estimate a model with the current X variable and a lagged Y variable as the explanatory variables:

$$Y_t = \alpha + \beta Y_{t-1} + \delta_0 X_t + \varepsilon_t \tag{10.5}$$

If you iteratively plug in the equivalent equation for Y_{t-1}, you get:

$$Y_t = \alpha + \beta \times \left(\beta Y_{t-2} + \delta_0 X_{t-1} + \varepsilon_{t-1} \right) + \delta_0 X_t + \varepsilon_t \tag{10.6}$$

And so the effect of X_{t-1} on Y_t is $\beta \times \delta_0$. In fact, the effects of lagged X variables are constrained to be smooth in this model, and the jth lag of X will have an effect on Y_t of $\beta^j \times \delta_0$.

Table 10.3 demonstrates the model with an analysis of how current and lagged values of the the percentage change in the Nikkei 225 index determine the Japanese unemployment rate. Models (1) to (4) are distributed-lag models, with up to four lags. Model (1) may not be ideal, as there are further lagged effects of the unemployment rate. Sure enough, according to the BIC, AIC, and AICc, the subsequent lagged models are better fits, and the optimal model of the four appears to be Model (4), with each lagged-unemployment-rate variable having a negative and statistically-significant coefficient estimate.

In some cases, the inclusion of multiple lags could cause the coefficient estimates on consecutive-lagged variables to jump around, alternating between positive and negative. In addition, with multiple

Table 10.3 The relationship between the annual Japanese unemployment rate and the percent change in the Nikkei 225 index

Dependent variable = Annual Japanese unemployment rate					
	(1)	*(2)*	*(3)*	*(4)*	*(5)*
Unemployment rate					
1–year–lagged					0.966***
					(0.031)
Nikkei 225 % change					
Current level					0.00002
					(0.00140)
1–year–lagged	−0.0128*	−0.0109*	−0.0131**	−0.0121**	
	(0.007)	(0.006)	(0.006)	(0.006)	
2–year–lagged		−0.0155**	−0.0139**	−0.0157***	
		(0.006)	(0.006)	(0.006)	
3–year–lagged			−0.0149**	−0.0133**	
			(0.006)	(0.005)	
4–year–lagged				−0.0143***	
				(0.005)	
Constant	2.900***	3.026***	3.158***	3.286***	0.114
	(0.180)	(0.188)	(0.196)	(0.198)	(0.075)
BIC	208.3	206.2	204.1	201.9	
AIC	204.0	199.8	195.6	191.2	
AICc	204.2	200.2	196.3	192.3	
Observations	62	62	62	62	61
R-squared	0.059	0.148	0.230	0.305	0.947

Robust standard errors in parentheses. *** $p < 0.01$, ** $p < 0.05$, * $p < 0.1$.

lags, the standard errors can get larger due to the lagged variables being highly correlated with each other. Neither of these is the case in our example.

However, if these problems did apply, the correction, as stated above, would be to use equation (10.5), which includes the lagged value for the unemployment rate and the current value of the stock-market change, as depicted in Model (5). Whereas Model (5) addresses the problems of the distributed-lag model, it has its own problems stemming from autocorrelation, as will be described in the next section.

10.4.1 Granger Causality tests

The Granger Causality test examines whether the lags of the X variables have significant coefficient estimates, but this would not necessarily be a true test of *causality*, as the name implies. Yes, any lagged values of the unemployment rate would certainly precede the stock-market performance in year *t* and thus avoid PITFALL #1 (reverse causality). But it could be subject to a few other PITFALLS. The most likely, perhaps, would be omitted-factors bias in that there could be common factors determining Japan's lagged unemployment rate and current stock-market performance. Furthermore, there

Table 10.4 Granger Causality model for the Japanese unemployment rate and Nikkei–225-index percent change (n = 61)

	(1)	(2)
	Granger Causality	*Granger Causality with Newey-West standard errors*
	Dependent variable = annual % change in Nikkei 225	
Y_{t-1} (% change in Nikkei 225 in the prior year)	0.06	0.06
	(0.13)	(0.09)
UR_{t-1} (lagged unemployment rate)	−1.77	−1.77
	(2.56)	(2.65)
Constant	12.03	12.03
	(7.52)	(7.95)
R-squared	0.014	---

Heteroskedasticity-corrected standard errors are in parentheses.

could be measurement error in the unemployment rate. This measurement error would likely be random with respect to stock-market performance, and therefore likely lead to a bias toward zero. So this would not be a true test for causality.

Nevertheless, the model for Granger Causality is based on an **autoregressive-distributed-lag model**, which would include both lagged values of the dependent variable and the explanatory variables, as follows:

$$Y_t = \beta_0 + \beta_1 Y_{t-1} + \delta_1 (UR)_{t-1} + \varepsilon_t \qquad (10.7)$$

This tests whether stock-market performance in year t (Y_t) moves with the unemployment rate from the prior year (UR_{t-1}). Table 10.4 presents the results in column (1). There is no evidence that the annual percent change in the Nikkei 225 tends to move with the lagged unemployment rate. I only use one lag, but such models could use multiple lags. (The second column for Table 10.4 will be referred to below.)

10.5 Consequences of and tests for autocorrelation

10.5.1 Consequences for models without lagged-dependent variables

Autocorrelation is a violation of Assumption **A2** from Section 2.10 – that the error terms are independent and identically distributed. This would mean that the OLS-estimated standard error would be biased, which implies that the hypothesis tests would be unreliable. This means that the OLS estimator would no longer produce the minimum-variance estimator of the coefficient estimate. The logic for why these problems occur, as with clustered standard errors (Section 5.4.3), is that having correlated observations means that there are fewer independent observations that create variation in the explanatory variable for more precise estimates. Thus, the effective sample size is lower, and the estimates should be less precise.

10.5.2 Consequences for models with lagged-dependent variables

When a model contains a lagged-dependent variable as an explanatory variable, then autocorrelation could also (in addition to biasing standard errors) cause *biased coefficient estimates*.

Combining the equations for the autocorrelation (equation 10.1) and the model to address problems with distributed-lags (equation 10.5),

$$\varepsilon_t = \rho\varepsilon_{t-1} + \eta_t \tag{10.1}$$

$$Y_t = \alpha + \beta Y_{t-1} + \delta_0 X_t + \varepsilon_t \tag{10.5}$$

we would have:

$$Y_t = \alpha + \beta Y_{t-1} + \delta_0 X_t + \rho\varepsilon_{t-1} + \eta_t \tag{10.8}$$

Because the lagged error and lagged-dependent variable (ε_{t-1} and Y_{t-1}) are positively correlated with each other, the current error and lagged-dependent variable (ε_t and Y_{t-1}) are correlated with each other in equation (10.5). This causes a violation of Assumption **A5**, and it comes in the form of omitted-factors bias. The likely outcome of this would be that the coefficient estimate $\hat{\beta}$, would be overstated (positively biased if $\rho > 0$ and $\beta > 0$). This would then bias, $\hat{\delta}_0$, the coefficient estimate on X_t.

Let's consider what's occurring operationally. If we were to estimate how opioid prices affect opioid overdoses, there could be positively-correlated errors (e.g., due to epidemics) that would lead to an overstated estimated effect of the prior periods' opioid overdoses on that for the current period. This leaves less variation in the number of opioid overdoses (Y) for the current price (X) to explain, leading to a downward-in-magnitude bias in $\hat{\delta}_0$. This is similar to PITFALL #5 on including outcomes as control variables. This bias occurs only if a lagged-dependent variable is used as an explanatory variable and there is autocorrelation.

10.5.3 Tests for autocorrelation

In models without a lagged-dependent variable, the test for autocorrelation has historically been the **Durbin-Watson test**. This can be used if the following conditions hold:

- The regression model includes an intercept term
- The error terms have a first-order structure ($\varepsilon_t = \rho\varepsilon_{t-1} + \eta_t$)
- (As stated above) there are no lagged-dependent variables
- The explanatory variables are purely exogenous (meaning that they have no sources of *bad variation*).

The test statistic is:

$$d = \frac{\sum_{t=2}^{T}\left(\hat{\varepsilon}_t - \hat{\varepsilon}_{t-1}\right)^2}{\sum_{t=1}^{T}\hat{\varepsilon}_t^2} \tag{10.9}$$

This test would produce:

- A value of 0 if there were perfectly positive autocorrelation, as the numerator would equal 0
- A value of 2 if there were no autocorrelation (this can be seen if the quantity in the numerator were expanded)
- A value of 4 if there were perfectly negative autocorrelation, as the numerator would equal $\sum \left(2\hat{\varepsilon}_t\right)^2$
- The critical values for the test statistic are a lower value (a δ_L that is less than 2) and an upper value (a δ_H that is greater than 2). One would conclude that there was autocorrelation if the test statistic, d, were less than δ_L (indicating positive autocorrelation) or greater than δ_H (indicating negative autocorrelation). The critical values are available on various websites.[1] Statistical packages will conduct the test and determine its significance for you.

The Durbin–Watson test is likely biased by the inclusion of lagged-dependent variables. In particular, there is a bias towards a test statistic of 2, which would indicate no autocorrelation. In addition, the Durbin–Watson test cannot test for autocorrelation beyond a one-period lag. In such cases (with lagged-dependent variables or autocorrelation beyond a one-period lag), the best test is the **Breusch-Godfrey test** (also known as the Lagrange Multiplier Serial Correlation test).

Step 1 of this test is, from equation (10.5), to estimate the residuals as:

$$\hat{\varepsilon}_t = Y_t - \left(\hat{\alpha} + \hat{\beta}Y_{t-1} + \hat{\delta}_0 X_t\right) \tag{10.10}$$

Step 2 is to regress the residuals on the same set of explanatory variables plus the lagged residual:

$$\hat{\varepsilon}_t = \beta_0 + \beta_1 Y_{t-1} + \beta_2 X_t + \beta_3 \hat{\varepsilon}_{t-1} + \eta_t \tag{10.11}$$

Step 3 is to calculate the test statistic of multiplying the sample size (n) by the R^2 for equation (10.11), which effectively tests whether $\beta_3 = 0$:

$$nR^2 \sim \chi^2(1).$$

The null hypothesis is that $\hat{\rho} = 0$ (from equation (10.8) above), meaning the error terms are not serially correlated. This chi-squared test has one degree of freedom because only one lagged residual is being tested. If one were to test for correlation with p lagged error terms, then there would be p degrees of freedom for the chi-squared test. Furthermore, the test can be conducted with other forms (e.g., with multiple lags of Y or X).

From Model (1) in Table 10.3, the Breusch-Godfrey test produces a $\chi^2(1)$ statistic of 0.488, which gives a p-value of 0.446. And a Breusch-Godfrey test for two lags of autocorrelation produces a $\chi^2(2)$ test statistic of 2.405 ($p = 0.300$). These show no evidence for autocorrelation.

Some would argue that the Breusch-Godfrey test should always be used rather than the Durbin–Watson test, given the restrictions and assumptions on the Durbin-Watson test. I would agree with this.

10.5.4 Can you correct for autocorrelation in models without lagged-dependent variables?

With the problem being biased standard errors in models without lagged-dependent variables, there are two potential methods to address the bias in the standard errors. First, there is what is called a Generalized Least Squares method, which typically requires a complicated two-step, iterative model, with the Cochrane-Orcutt and Prais-Winsten methods being perhaps the most commonly used approach (Cochrane and Orcutt, 1949; Prais and Winsten, 1954) – the latter is just an extension to save the very first observation, but that most likely does not matter in relatively large samples. In my view, for purposes other than forecasting, this is not worth the effort, in part because it produces a different set of estimates from what OLS produces. And so I will leave this for Section 10.8 below, on forecasting, for which the method would likely generate more accurate forecasts.

A simpler (albeit imperfect) solution, when forecasting is not the goal, is to use **Newey–West standard errors** (Newey and West, 1987). Again, it's a complicated calculation (behind the scenes), but the concept for calculating the Newey–West standard errors is similar in nature to the correction for heteroskedastic standard errors. The Newey–West standard errors are still biased, but they are typically more accurate than OLS standard errors in the presence of autocorrelation. The typical correction is that they would be larger than OLS standard errors, resulting in a lower likelihood of achieving statistical significance. Further caution should be used for formal hypothesis tests and assessing the strength of evidence for an analysis, given the remaining bias in these standard errors.

Model (2) from Table 10.4 above applies the Newey–West standard errors to the Granger Causality model. The standard error on the coefficient estimate on the lagged unemployment rate is slightly higher, producing a wider confidence interval.

10.5.5 Can you correct for bias in coefficient estimates from autocorrelation in models with lagged-dependent variables?

In most cases, there is no correction for the bias in coefficient estimates from autocorrelation in models with lagged-dependent variables. There is an approach using Generalized Least Squares, as just described a few paragraphs up, but that approach requires large samples and adjustments to the standard errors; furthermore, there are problems under various circumstances (Betancourt and Kelejian, 1981). Another approach is to use the instrumental-variables method (Section 8.6). Every so often, someone comes up with an innovative instrumental variable that affects the lagged-dependent variable, Y_t, and is uncorrelated with ε_t. But this is a rare event.

10.6 Stationarity

Perhaps one of the most important characteristics for a time-series variable to have is **stationarity**. A stationary time-series variable, X_t, has:

- A constant mean over time
- A constant variance over time
- A correlation coefficient between X_t and one of its lagged values, X_{t-j}, that depends solely on the length of the lag (and no other variable).

If any of these do not hold, then the time-series variable would be nonstationary. Nonstationarity can cause problems for time-series models, typically leading to biased estimates of the relationship between variables. This is often called a **spurious regression** because the key-explanatory variable and the outcome are related at least in part because they both are changing over time.

10.6.1 Examples based on autoregressive models

Let's consider an autoregressive model (without an intercept term):

$$Y_t = \beta Y_{t-1} + \varepsilon_i \tag{10.12}$$

with $\varepsilon_t \sim N(0, \sigma^2)$. And let's consider three cases of the actual values of β:

- $|\beta| < 1$: This means that $E(Y_t)$ will approach zero in the long run. Thus, while the mean value could be larger in magnitude as it takes the time to approach zero, the eventual mean should be stable around zero, with a constant variance. So such a time-series variable would be stationary.
- $|\beta| > 1$: The value of Y_t, in this case, would grow in magnitude over time. It is possible that a value of $\beta < -1$ could cause a mean to be steady around zero, but the variance would increase over time. Thus, this time-series variable would not be stationary.
- $|\beta| = 1$: This is a case called **unit root** or **random walk** ($Y_t = Y_{t-1} + \varepsilon_t$). This is also a case in which the time-series variable would not be stationary. One reason for this is that a random drift away from a temporary mean could persist.

What these examples demonstrate is that a time-series variable that is unit root or a value of $|\beta|$ that is greater than one will be nonstationary. Thus, time-series regressions using time-series variables with a unit root (or worse) would be subject to spurious regression. And so a test is often needed to ensure that a time-series variable is indeed stationary.

Spurious regression is not the only problem that results from unit roots. In an AR(1) model for a unit-root variable, in which the coefficient (b) should be one, there is a bias on $\hat{\beta}$ as $E(\hat{\beta}) = 1 - 5.3/T$, where T is the number of observations in the time series. This would affect forecasting if there were indeed a unit-root autoregression. Furthermore, the distribution for the t-statistics for the coefficient estimates would be non-normal, meaning that the t-tests and p-values would be incorrect.

10.6.2 Test for stationarity

An initial check for nonstationarity could come from a visual inspection of the variable over time. If it looks like the mean is changing or not converging, or if the variance of the variable appears to change over time, then there is likely nonstationarity.

The most common formal approach to testing for stationarity is the **Dickey-Fuller test** (Dickey and Fuller, 1979). This is a test to determine whether there is sufficient evidence to determine that $|\beta| < 1$ in equation (10.12), which would indicate that the time-series variable is stationary. From equation (10.12), Y_{t-1} is subtracted from both sides of the equation, which would give:

$$Y_t - Y_{t-1} = (\beta - 1)Y_{t-1} + \varepsilon_t \tag{10.13}$$

or

$$\Delta Y_t = \gamma Y_{t-1} + \varepsilon_t \tag{10.14}$$

where $\gamma = \beta - 1$.

Thus, the hypothesis test becomes:

$H_0: \gamma = 0$ (nonstationarity)
$H_1: \gamma < 0$ (stationarity).

Note that the default (null hypothesis) is nonstationarity, so the test is whether we can conclude that there is stationarity. This Dickey-Fuller test is based on the assumption that equation (10.12) is the correct model for Y_t. However, the model could also include a constant term or a trend.

With a constant, the model would be:

$$\Delta Y_t = \alpha + \gamma Y_{t-1} + \varepsilon_t \tag{10.15}$$

And, with a constant and a trend, the model would be:

$$\Delta Y_t = \alpha + \gamma Y_{t-1} + \delta \times t + \varepsilon_t \tag{10.16}$$

where the variable t is a trend, taking on the values, sequentially, of 1, 2, 3, ... T. Including a trend would capture natural "trends" over time in a variable. For example, we know that stock prices generally go up over time, and the coefficient estimate on the trend would capture that.

In addition, an **augmented Dickey-Fuller test** can be estimated for higher-order autoregressive models (i.e., with more than one lag). The model testing for stationarity based on an $AR(p)$ model would be:

$$\Delta Y_t = \alpha + \gamma Y_{t-1} + \lambda_1 \Delta Y_{t-1} + \lambda_2 \Delta Y_{t-2} + \cdots + \lambda_p \Delta Y_{t-p} + \varepsilon_t \tag{10.17}$$

Regardless of the model, the hypothesis test would be the same, as it would test whether the coefficient estimate on the lagged variable is less than zero – that is, $\gamma < 0$. The critical values do not follow the standard Student t-distribution table. However, most statistical packages will conduct the test and determine the level of significance and the p-value.

Tests for stationarity tend not to be very reliable, as they depend on the assumption of constant variance. Nevertheless, this may be the best test available. Not being able to conclude the stationarity of a time-series variable suggests that measures should be taken to address the nonstationarity.

10.6.3 Cointegration

As described above, one of the most harmful products of nonstationarity is spurious regression, in which two nonstationary time-series variables may have their estimated association with each other biased. The most likely cause of this is that both variables have changing means over time.

However, just because two time-series variables (a dependent variable and an X variable) are nonstationary does not necessarily mean that it causes a spurious regression. If the two variables have "matching" degrees of nonstationarity in that the residual from the regression is stationary, then the two variables are said to be **cointegrated**. This would mean that the model is not a spurious regression.

Any type of time-series model with two variables that we have seen so far could be tested for cointegration. From a model with a trend of:

$$Y_t = \beta_0 + \beta_1 X_t + \beta_2 t + \varepsilon_t \tag{10.18}$$

the test would involve first calculating the residual:

$$\hat{\varepsilon}_t = Y_t - \beta_0 - \beta_1 X_t - \beta_2 t \tag{10.19}$$

Next, a Dickey-Fuller test would be conducted on the residuals. In this case, while the standard Student-t distribution does not exactly apply, the adjusted critical values are not that different from the actual Student-t distribution.

If there were evidence for the residuals being stationary, then it would support the notion that X_t and Y_t are cointegrated. This means that the original model, (equation 10.18), could be used. On the other hand, if there were no (or weak) evidence for stationarity, then we have to assume there is nonstationarity and another approach is needed.

10.6.4 How to address nonstationarity

In the case in which stationarity between two variables cannot be concluded from a Dickey-Fuller test on each variable or from a Dickey-Fuller test on cointegration, then a simple correction for this problem may be to just take the first difference of the model. Thus, the model, from (10.18), would be:

$$Y_t - Y_{t-1} = \left(\beta_0 + \beta_1 X_t + \beta_2 t_t + \varepsilon_t \right) - \left(\beta_0 + \beta_1 X_{t-1} + \beta_2 t_{t-1} + \varepsilon_{t-1} \right) \tag{10.20a}$$

or

$$\Delta Y_t = \beta_1 \Delta X_t + \beta_2 + \varepsilon_t - \varepsilon_{t-1} \tag{10.20b}$$

This does not always fix the problem. If there is seasonality, then equation (10.20b) would be problematic because it confounds the relationship between lagged and current values of a time-series variable, and so a seasonal term would be needed in conjunction with any differencing. Also, it is possible that important information on the levels of X_t or Y_t would be lost with this approach. However, this is certainly not always the case, and it may be the only approach to address a spurious regression in the presence of nonstationarity.

10.6.5 Example with the price of oil and the stock market

Let's explore the relationship between the price of oil and the stock market. We will use as data:

- Price of oil: based on crude oil, West Texas Intermediate;[2]
- Stock market: S&P 500 index.

We will examine this relationship for two different five-year periods: 1990–1994 and 2010–2014. Let's first do a visual examination of the data. Figures 10.6a and 10.6b show these two variables for the two time periods, respectively.

From the figures, it looks like there could be trends in the data, some that are subtle. These trends could make it seem like the two variables were related, even if they were not. Table 10.5 shows the results of the Dickey-Fuller tests. Only in one of the four cases (oil price in the first period) is there

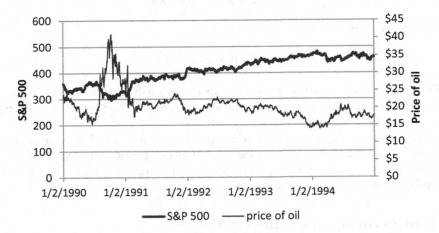

Figure 10.6a Daily prices for the S&P 500 and oil, 1990–1994

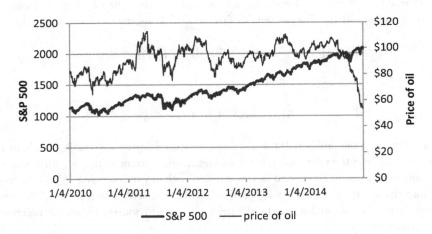

Figure 10.6b Daily prices for the S&P 500 and oil, 2010–2014

Table 10.5 Dickey-Fuller tests for stationarity

	1990–1994 (n = 1265)	2010–2014 (n = 1257)
S&P 500	−1.020 (p = 0.746)	−0.005 (p = 0.958)
Price of oil	−4.439 (p = 0.003)	−1.327 (p = 0.617)

Table 10.6 The relationship between oil prices and the S&P 500 index

	1990–1994		2010–2014	
	(1)	(2)	(3)	(4)
	S&P 500	Δ(S&P 500)	S&P 500	Δ(S&P 500)
1-day-lagged S&P 500	0.994***		0.999***	
	(0.002)		(0.002)	
Current oil price	−0.076**		0.063	
	(0.033)		(0.042)	
Δ(oil price)		−0.477***		3.732***
		(0.178)		(0.354)
Constant	4.212***	0.078	−3.932	0.820**
	(1.535)	(0.081)	(3.766)	(0.347)
Observations	1265	1265	1257	1257
R-squared	0.997	0.030	0.998	0.175

Robust standard errors in parentheses. Changes are one-day changes. *** $p < 0.01$, ** $p < 0.05$, * $p < 0.1$.

evidence of stationarity for the variable. This suggests that a regression using these two variables could result in biased estimates that largely would reflect how the trends of the variables move with each other, particularly for the later period.

In Table 10.6, for both time periods, I estimate the model as both a regular dynamic model and a model transformed to use changes in the variables to address the nonstationarity. There are a few interesting results here. First, the estimated effects of oil in the differenced models – Models (2) and (4) – are significantly different from their non-differenced corresponding estimates in Models (1) and (3). This is likely a result of the spurious (biased) regression resulting from the nonstationarity. The trends in the variables are dominating the actual effects of the variables. Second, practically speaking, oil-price increases appear to negatively affect the stock market in 1990–1994 but positively affect the stock market in 2010–2014. This could be due to the combination of reduced reliance on oil in the U.S. economy (partly from the shift away from manufacturing) and the increased production of oil products in the U.S. economy.

10.7 Vector Autoregression

The **Vector Autoregression (VAR) model** involves multiple time-series regressions that include the lagged values of each variable in the model. The individual equations within a VAR are estimated by OLS, although with an extra feature. The models allow the error terms to be correlated with each other. (This is similar to a Seemingly Unrelated Regression [SUR] model.) A model with two variables (X_t and Y_t), and p lags would be characterized as a VAR(p) model with the following two equations:

$$Y_t = \alpha_0 + \alpha_1 Y_{t-1} + \alpha_2 Y_{t-2} + \cdots + \alpha_p Y_{t-p} + \beta_1 X_{t-1} + \beta_2 X_{t-2} + \cdots + \beta_p X_{t-p} + u_t \quad (10.21)$$

$$X_t = \delta_0 + \delta_1 X_{t-1} + \delta_2 X_{t-2} + \cdots + \delta_p X_{t-p} + \lambda_1 Y_{t-1} + \lambda_2 Y_{t-2} + \cdots + \lambda_p Y_{t-p} + v_t \quad (10.22)$$

Table 10.7 Vector Autoregression (VAR) for Japanese stock-market performance and unemployment rates (n = 60)

	Change in %-change in Nikkei 225	Change in the unemployment rate
Lagged change in %-change in Nikkei 225	−0.383***	−0.0027**
	(0.125)	(0.0011)
Lagged change in the unemployment rate	9.818	0.542***
	(13.790)	(0.117)
Constant	−0.449	0.011
	(3.814)	(0.032)

Robust standard errors are in parentheses. The 95% confidence intervals are in brackets. *** $p < 0.01$, ** $p < 0.05$, * $p < 0.1$.

The VAR model can have more than two variables. Having five variables would mean five equations with p lags for each variable in each model. The optimal number of lags could be determined by BIC, AIC, or AICc, as described above in Section 10.3.

Alternatively, one could conduct an F-test for the joint significance of the lagged variables in the individual equations within a VAR. For example, we may want to test whether the last lag is jointly significant, making the null hypothesis:

$$H_0 : \alpha_p = 0, \beta_p = 0, \delta_p = 0, \lambda_p = 0.$$

VARs can be used for forecasting, as well as attempting to estimate causal relationships. In fact, the VAR is just an extended form of a Granger Causality model (from Section 10.4). Still, one must be cautious of all of the PITFALLS from Chapter 6, as well as any problems with nonstationarity, before concluding that relationships are causal.

I use a VAR model for the Japanese stock-market performance and the unemployment rate. Preliminary Dickey-Fuller tests for stationarity suggest stationarity for the percent change in the Nikkei 225 ($p = 0.000$), but not for the unemployment rate ($p = 0.702$). Thus, corrections are needed. Subsequent Dickey-Fuller tests for the change in the variables yield p-values of 0.000 for both variables. Thus, I use the "change" variables for the VAR model, which I show in Table 10.7. The bold coefficient estimates are the ones of interest. The −0.0027 coefficient estimate on the lagged change in the Nikkei 225 is weak evidence that increases in the Nikkei 225 lead to reductions in the unemployment rate. Going the other way, there is no evidence that lagged changes in the unemployment rate affect stock-market performance.

10.8 Forecasting with time series

Much of the prior examples in this chapter dealt at least implicitly with the objectives of estimating causal effects or determining predictors. As described in the introduction of this chapter, a common use of time-series models is to forecast an outcome. I discussed forecasting in Section 7.1, and how the optimal strategy was pretty much to throw in all variables you could, other than those that may result in reverse causality. The goal in Section 7.1 was more to predict values for a subject based on a set of known X values. For example, an insurance company may want to predict the likelihood that a potential customer would get in a car accident based on data on other people. Forecasting with time-series models involves trying to forecast/predict future values for a time-series variable based on the subject's prior values. This section discusses some of the issues involved with forecasting time-series variables.

All of the models used in this chapter could be used for forecasting, but the presence of nonstationarity or autocorrelation could cause problems. Stationarity might be fixable with a differenced model. With autocorrelation, the Generalized Least Squares method (the Cochrane-Orcutt or Prais-Winsten method) would likely improve the forecast.

10.8.1 Generalized Least Squares correction for autocorrelation

Recall that the problem with autocorrelation is that part of the error term would include a component of the error terms from prior observations. This would mean that the T observations in a time-series model are not independent, and the effective sample size is lower, as there are no T independent observations. While the correction can be done with practically any time-series model, let's take equation (10.18) and say we want to forecast the value of Y_{T+1}. We can combine equation (10.18) with the autocorrelation equation (10.1):

$$Y_t = \beta_0 + \beta_1 X_t + \beta_2 t_t + \varepsilon_t \tag{10.18}$$

$$\varepsilon_t = \rho \varepsilon_{t-1} + \eta_t \tag{10.1}$$

to get:

$$Y_t = \beta_0 + \beta_1 X_t + \beta_2 t_t + \rho \varepsilon_{t-1} + \eta_t \tag{10.23}$$

Addressing autocorrelation would involve removing ε_{t-1} from equation (10.23), by first lagging equation (10.18) and multiplying by ρ:

$$\rho Y_{t-1} = \rho \beta_0 + \rho \beta_1 X_{t-1} + \rho \beta_2 t_{t-1} + \rho \varepsilon_{t-1} \tag{10.24}$$

and subtracting that from equation (10.23):

$$Y_t - \rho Y_{t-1} = \beta_0 (1 - \rho) + \beta_1 (X_t - \rho X_{t-1}) + \beta_2 t_t - \rho \beta_2 t_{t-1} + \eta_t \tag{10.25}$$

Now, the model is free of any autocorrelation. Operationally, this is estimated by Generalized Least Squares. The method involves iteratively solving for $\hat{\rho}$ and the $\hat{\beta}$'s, all through OLS, until the estimate $\hat{\rho}$ converges to a steady value. From this, transformations can be made using equation (10.25) to generate forecasts of Y_{T+1}.

This method is easily done for you in Stata and in R – see the documents with code for the Prais-Winsten method on the book's website. As mentioned above, this method should produce more accurate forecasts.

10.8.2 The ARIMA model for forecasting

Perhaps the "it" thing now in forecasting is the **autoregressive-integrated-moving-average (ARIMA)** model or the **autoregressive-moving-average (ARMA)** model, which excludes any independent (X) variables. From a basic model with just an intercept and error term:

$$Y_t = \alpha_0 + \varepsilon_t \tag{10.26}$$

the ARMA model is:

$$Y_t = \alpha_0 + \underbrace{\lambda_1 Y_{t-1} + \lambda_2 Y_{t-2} + \cdots + \lambda_p Y_{t-p}}_{\text{Autoregressive part}} + \underbrace{\delta_1 \varepsilon_{t-1} + \delta_2 \varepsilon_{t-2} + \cdots + \delta_p \varepsilon_{t-p} + \varepsilon_t}_{\text{Moving-average}} \tag{10.27}$$

The autoregressive part is that Y_t depends on its prior values. The moving-average part is that Y_t depends on past random errors.

If Y_t were nonstationary, then we would need the ARIMA model, which uses ΔY_t. Basically, the differencing is the "integrated" part of ARIMA.

With the 2010–2014 data on the S&P 500 stock-market index, I used an ARIMA model, with one lag, two lags, and three lags. I present these in Table 10.8. The arguments for an ARIMA(a, b, c) model are that *a* is the number of lags for the autoregressive part of the model, *b* is the number of times the variable was differenced to address stationarity (typically just one), and *c* is the number of lags for the moving-average part of the model. These models will be used next for determining how accurate the forecast is.

10.8.3 Determining the accuracy of the forecast

Testing how accurate a forecast is requires some out-of-sample observations, which was mentioned in Section 7.1. Such observations could come from:

*   Observations that have yet to be realized (that you are forecasting), or
*   Observations at the end that you leave out of the sample.

For the latter, there is a trade-off: the more observations you leave out for testing the forecast accuracy, the stronger will be the test but the weaker will be the model (as it would have fewer observations).

With the ARIMA(1, 1, 1) model in Table 10.8, I used the first five trading days in 2015 as the out-of-sample prediction. Sometimes, the explanatory variables (in this case, the lagged dependent variables and residuals) would need to be forecasted as well. But in other cases, as I do here, the explanatory variables are available. From the forecasts, I calculate two common measures of forecast accuracy/error:

*   Mean absolute percent error (MAPE)
*   Root Mean Square Error (RMSE), which is the square root of the mean square error, from equation (2.16).

Table 10.8 ARIMA models for daily S&P 500, 2010–2014 (n = 1257)

	Dependent variable = daily S&P 500 index		
	ARIMA(1,1,1)	ARIMA(2,1,2)	ARIMA(3,1,3)
S&P 500 variables (Y_t)			
1-day-lagged	−0.847***	0.101	0.403
	(0.097)	(0.136)	(0.751)
2-day-lagged		0.820***	0.731***
		(0.106)	(0.203)
3-day-lagged			−0.229
			(0.572)
Residuals			
1-day-lagged	0.797***	−0.167	−0.450
	(0.107)	(0.132)	(0.757)
2-day-lagged		−0.792***	−0.678***
		(0.104)	(0.253)
3-day-lagged			0.186
			(0.548)
Constant	0.737**	0.746***	0.744***
	(0.370)	(0.205)	(0.231)
Standard error of the	13.47***	13.44***	13.43***
residual	(0.393)	(0.400)	(0.398)

Standard errors in parentheses.

*** $p < 0.01$, ** $p < 0.05$, * $p < 0.1$.

The first one, MAPE, is exactly what it sounds like. Table 10.9 shows the *absolute forecast error* for each of the first five observations of 2015, based on the ARIMA(1,1,1) model. From these five observations, the MAPE is the average of the absolute forecast error, which is 1.2%. The RMSE is then the square root of the average squared forecast error, which comes to 27.2:

$$\text{RMSFE} = \sqrt{\sum_{i=1}^{n}\left(Y_i - \widehat{Y_i}\right)^2} = \sqrt{(-2.4)^2 + (-37.6)^2 + (-21.2)^2 + (23.6)^2 + (35.8)^2} = 27.2$$

10.8.4 Forecast intervals

At home games for the New York Mets, at Citi Field, there is a sushi bar near the right-field corner, so I've been told. The Mets probably want a good forecast of how much sushi to stock for a given game. But the point forecast may not be enough information. If they order the point forecast for every game, they would not have enough sushi for about 50% of all games, causing them to miss out on selling something that probably has a nice profit margin. And they would have ordered too much on about 50% of the games, which means they would likely have to give the sushi away to staff, as sushi probably will not stay fresh for the next game.

Table 10.9 Forecasts and statistics for first five trading days of 2015 for the ARIMA(1,1,1) model

	S&P 500	Predicted value	Residual	Absolute percent forecast error (%)
1/2/2015	2058.2	2060.6	−2.4	0.1
1/5/2015	2020.6	2058.2	−37.6	1.9
1/6/2015	2002.6	2023.8	−21.2	1.1
1/7/2015	2025.9	2002.3	23.6	1.2
1/8/2015	2062.1	2026.3	35.8	1.7

In this situation, the Mets would probably want a confidence interval for the forecast or a **forecast interval**. The forecast interval for the next value from a forecast model (with T observations) of an outcome, Y_{T+1}, is:

$$Y_{T+1} \pm s_F \times t_c \tag{10.28}$$

where s_F is the standard error of the forecast and t_c is the critical t value for the given confidence interval.

The formula for s_F, in the case of there being one explanatory variable, X_t, is:

$$s_F = \sqrt{1 + \frac{1}{T} + \frac{\left(\hat{X}_{T+1} - \bar{X}\right)}{\sum_{t=1}^{T}\left(X_t - \bar{X}\right)^2}} \tag{10.29}$$

This is somewhat complicated, and you probably will not need to calculate this, as your statistical program will do so. But what's important is that the standard error of the forecast will be lower when:

- There are more observations in the forecast model (T);
- The value of $\hat{X}_{T+1}$ is closer to the mean value of X.

Let's suppose that:

- Y_t = the number of orders for sushi (assuming they count the people who ask for sushi after they run out);
- X_t = the average price of a bleacher (standardized) seat.

The average price of a bleacher seat may be a good composite indicator of the expected attendance and the willingness of the audience for a particular game to pay for the expensive sushi. The forecast interval would be narrower with more observations in the model and the closer is the value of X_t to its mean (or the internet average price for the game to the sample average price for a bleacher seat).

The formula for the standard error of the forecast would obviously be more complicated with more variables added. But the same concepts would apply in that the forecast would be more accurate (with a narrower forecast interval) with a larger model and with X values (or lagged-dependent variables) closer to their mean values.

10.9 Summary

This chapter introduced time-series models and noted some of the more common problems, most notably autocorrelation and nonstationarity. Keep in mind that, if the objective of the regression is causality (whether it be a contemporaneous model, a Granger Causality model, or a Vector Autoregression), all of the PITFALLS from Chapter 6 need to be checked before concluding causality. Corrections for nonstationarity (with using changes in the variables rather than actual values) may be one method of avoiding any biases associated with omitted-factors bias.

Exercises

1. Use the data set **ford_amazon_2017**, which has the 2017 daily change in stock prices (adjusted for splits and dividends) for Ford and Amazon.
   a. Estimate an AR(2) model for both Ford and Amazon stock-price changes, using robust standard errors. Conduct individual and joint tests of the significance of the lagged stock-price changes at the 5% significance level.
   b. Estimate an autoregressive-distributed-lag model by regressing the change in Ford's stock price on the lagged change in Ford's and Amazon's stock price, using robust standard errors. What can you conclude?

For Questions #2 through 6, use the data set **wine_beer**, which indicates the per-capita wine and beer consumption in the U.S. from 1934 to 2016.
2. Estimate AR(1) to AR(4) models for beer consumption per capita, using robust standard errors. Use BIC, AIC, and AICc to gauge which is the best model.
3. Test beer and wine consumption for stationarity using the Dickey-Fuller test, based on one lag. What can you conclude?
4. Estimate a Granger Causality model for how wine consumption affects beer consumption. Adjust the model as you see fit based on the results of the stationarity tests from Question #3. What does the model tell you?
5. From the model in Question #4, test for autocorrelation using the Breusch-Godfrey test. What does the test tell you?
6. Estimate a VAR model, with two lags, for wine and beer consumption. Adjust the model as you see fit based on the results of the stationarity tests from Question #3. What does the model tell you?

For Questions #7 through 9, use the observations for Chile from the data set, **democracy2**, for which there are non-missing values for *democracy* and *gdpgrowth*.
7. Test *democracy* and *gdpgrowth* for stationarity using the Dickey-Fuller test, based on one-year lags. What can you conclude?
8. Estimate a Granger Causality model for how the change in *democracy* affects the change in *gdpgrowth*. What does the model tell you?
9. Estimate a VAR model, with one lag, for the changes in *democracy* and *gdpgrowth*. What does the model tell you?

Notes

1 One website with a table of the critical values is: https://www3.nd.edu/~wevans1/econ30331/Durbin_Watson_tables.pdf, accessed July 10, 2018.
2 This oil-price data comes from https://fred.stlouisfed.org/series/DCOILWTICO.

References

Betancourt, R. & Kelejian, H. (1981). Lagged endogenous variables and the Cochrane-Orcutt procedure. *Econometrica*, *49*(4), 1073–1078.

Cochrane, D. & Orcutt, G. H. (1949). Application of least squares regression to relationships containing auto-correlated error terms. *Journal of the American Statistical Association*, *44*(245), 32–61.

Dickey, D. A. & Fuller, W. A. (1979). Distribution of the estimators for autoregressive time series with a unit root. *Journal of the American Statistical Association*, 74(366a), 427–431.

Newey, W. K. & West, K. D. (1987). A simple, positive semi-definite, heteroskedasticity and autocorrelation consistent covariance matrix. *Econometrica*, *55*(3), 703–708.

Prais, S. J. & Winsten, C. B. (1954). *Trend estimators and serial correlation* (Vol. *383*, pp. 1–26). Chicago, IL: Cowles Commission Discussion Paper.

11 Some really interesting research

11.1 Can discrimination be a self-fulfilling prophecy?
11.2 Does Medicaid participation improve health outcomes?
11.3 Estimating peer effects on academic outcomes
11.4 How much does a GED improve labor-market outcomes?
11.5 How female integration in the Norwegian military affects gender attitudes among males

In this chapter, I review a few articles that I found to be interesting and soundly conducted and that had multiple lessons using the concepts from this book. I must relate my experience in writing this chapter. I browsed through some of the top journals in economics, business, and the social sciences in order to find articles to discuss for this chapter, and there were hardly any articles that had insignificant estimates on the key-explanatory variables.

11.1 Can discrimination be a self-fulfilling prophecy?

The first article we will discuss is: "Discrimination as a Self-Fulfilling Prophecy: Evidence from French Grocery Stores," by Glover et al. (2017). The article examines whether minority cashiers at a grocery-store chain in France are less productive and more likely to be absent when they have a work shift under a manager with greater bias against minorities. (Please note that, in light of the negative connotations associated with the word "minority" that many have been concerned about, I prefer using the term "under-represented group." But, to keep consistent with this article and for ease of exposition, I will continue to use the term "minority.") I chose this article because it applies several important concepts from this book: interacted variables, fixed effects, difference-in-difference models, linear probability models, several potential PITFALLS, and a convincing method to address the primary PITFALLS. I briefly described this study back in Box 3.1. Here, I give a much fuller description, now that we have more skills to analyze the study. (Note that the term "bias" is used in two ways in this discussion: (1) the personal bias, or discrimination, of the manager against minorities; and (2) the bias related to the regression PITFALLS.)

DOI: 10.4324/9781003285007-11

Study questions

If you want to test your knowledge, you can read the article and consider these study questions before reading the description of the study I give below:

1. Why might there be reverse causality in this study?
2. What is the explanation the authors give for why there may not be reverse causality in their model?
3. Why could there be omitted-factors bias in a basic model on this topic (i.e., not with the methods this article uses)?
4. How do the authors address the main source of omitted-factors bias?
5. Why is there likely bias from measurement error for the key interacted explanatory variable? What is the likely implication for the results from any bias from measurement error?
6. With the combination of fixed effects for the cashiers, what is the source of *operative variation* for estimating, among minorities, the effect of working for more-biased managers?

Background

The entry-level cashiers at this grocery-store chain are new workers hired under a government-subsidized six-month contract. The authors chose these workers because, unlike the established workers, the new ones do not have any choice in their schedule. A computer program determines their schedule. The cashiers know their shift times and which manager will be on duty during their shifts several weeks in advance. These are large stores (30–80 registers in each store), as they typically have 100–250 cashiers and around five different managers for a given store.

Sample

Whereas data were obtained on 218 cashiers, only 204 are part of the sample because some had to be excluded due to there not being data on the bias of the manager for their shifts. For those 204 cashiers, there are a total of 4371 shifts as the primary sample. Of the 204 cashiers, 28% are classified as minorities. For a reason that you will see soon, the sample includes non-minorities as a control group for the difference-in-difference approach.

Outcomes

The government program is meant to give a trial work period to these young (often inexperienced) workers. The stores end up offering employment contracts to 30%–40% of them. To be able to make informed decisions, the chain keeps excellent records and has invested in creating some performance metrics. The productivity outcomes for the analysis are:

- Whether the cashier was absent on a given day
- Minutes worked in excess of schedule
- Articles scanned per minute
- Time between customers.

Key-explanatory variables

The key-explanatory variable is an interaction of two variables, both of which are likely measured with error:

- **Minority worker**: The race/ethnicity of workers is not allowed to be collected in France, but names are. The authors had experts in France give their best guess on the minority status of each cashier based on their name. Obviously, the experts may have made mistakes.
- **Manager bias (toward minorities)**: This is based on an Implicit Association Test (IAT) (Greenwald et al., 1998; Lane et al., 2007). The test is standardized so one unit is a standard deviation and a positive (negative) value indicates a bias against (in favor of) minorities. The average score among the managers was 1.35, meaning that the managers were, on average, 1.35 standard deviations away from neutrality/unbiasedness and towards bias against minorities. As with any test, there could be error in this variable. The IAT was taken, on average, 17 months after the data on cashier shifts were collected.

Potential sources of bias (PITFALLS)

Let's consider what potential biases could occur in a naïve model for worker performance:

$$Y_i = \beta_0 + \beta_1 \left(minority_i \times bias_i \right) + \varepsilon_i \tag{11.1}$$

where Y is the worker-productivity measure. So β_1 estimates the interacted effect of a minority worker and a manager's level of bias. The following are the potential sources of bias or other problems.

- **Reverse causality**: This could occur if poor performance of the cashier affected the manager's bias. The authors note that this is unlikely for a few reasons. First, 85% of the managers had worked there for more than ten years, so any bias would likely not be appreciably affected by a few recent minority cashiers. Second, the managers oversee 100–250 cashiers at a given time (not per shift), and so one less productive minority cashier should not affect them. Third, the Implicit Association Test (see the study for the description) uses male names, but over 90% of the cashiers are female.
- **Omitted-factors bias**: There are two main sources of omitted-factors bias. First, any manager bias could be correlated with other aspects of the manager that would make any cashier less productive. Second, the cashiers with the worse (or better) outcomes might be more likely to be assigned to the more-biased managers, just due to randomness (incidental correlation). I will explain how these were addressed when discussing the model below.
- **Self-selection bias**: The cashiers cannot select their schedule, so they cannot choose to work with a manager with low bias. Thus, this is not an issue.
- **Measurement error**: As mentioned above, this could occur due to mismeasurement of the minority status of the cashier (which again is done by experts analyzing the name of the cashier) and error in the Implicit Association Test in measuring the extent of any manager bias against minorities. Because these would likely be measurement error that were non-differential, the bias on the coefficient estimate for the interaction of "minority" and "manager-bias" should be in the direction of zero. If so, then the estimates may understate the relationship between manager bias and worker productivity.

- **Error terms may be correlated**: A given store may be very busy, and so there would be greater pressure for cashiers to work fast. Thus, the error terms for cashiers for a given store may be correlated with some of the performance metrics.

Overall, the major concern should be for omitted-factors bias and measurement error. Unfortunately, only omitted-factors bias can be addressed.

The model

Their model is the following:

$$Y_{ist} = \beta_0 + \beta_1 \left(minority_i \times bias_{ist} \right) + \beta_2 \left(bias_{ist} \right) + \delta_i + X_{ist}\beta_3 + \varepsilon_i \qquad (11.2)$$

where:
- Subscripts are for the cashier (i), the store (s), and the day (t);
- Y_{ist} = one of four dependent variables listed above (for cashier i on shift s in time period t);
- $minority_i$ = whether the cashier is believed to be a minority;
- $bias_{ist}$ = bias (measured by the "Implicit Association Test") for the shift manager assigned to cashier i's shift s in time period t;
- ($minority \times bias$) = interaction of the two variables;
- X = a set of other shift characteristics (which are not terribly important);
- δ_i cashier fixed effects.

This is actually both a fixed-effects and difference-in-difference model. The primary fixed effects are on the cashier, δ_i. Let's think about what this means for the *operative variation*. Now, the shifts for minority cashiers are being compared to their other shifts. That is, for each minority cashier, there is an estimate for how the cashier's performance changes with having a shift manager with a one-unit (i.e., one-standard-deviation) increase in bias against minorities. The estimate for β_1 would be the weighted average of each of these individual-cashier estimates. This avoids the possibility of omitted-factors bias from better- (or worse-) performing cashiers just happening (incidentally) to be assigned to shifts overseen by higher-bias managers. However, it does introduce the possibility of PITFALL #7 on over-weighted groups, as some cashiers, due to randomness, might experience greater variation in manager-bias than other cashiers.

The inclusion of the *bias* variable alone addresses the other potential source of omitted-factors bias that managers with greater bias (i.e., against minorities) might systematically (across all racial/ethnic groups of cashiers) encourage different worker productivity than managers with less bias.

This effectively makes the problem a difference-in-difference model with the following controls:

- Each cashier is controlled for with fixed effects, which effectively controls for *minority*.
- The variable *bias* is controlled for. (It typically is a dummy variable in a difference-in-difference model, but it is continuous in this case.)
- The interaction of *minority* × *bias* is then the key-explanatory variable.

Thus, the study examines within-cashier effects of manager-bias on productivity and averages them separately for whom they believe are non-minorities and for minorities. The coefficient estimate, $\hat{\beta}_1$,

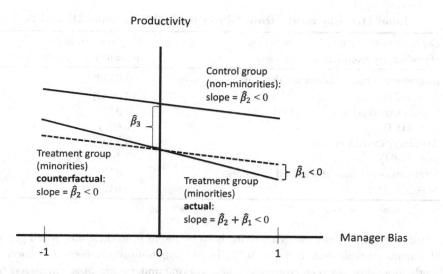

Figure 11.1 A graphical depiction of Glover et al.'s (2017) study on discrimination

indicates how minority cashiers respond to higher manager bias against minorities relative to how non-minority cashiers respond to the same higher bias (also against minorities).

To depict a simpler version of this in a chart similar to Figure 8.2 in Section 8.5.1 but consistent with Glover et al.'s (2017) equation, let's simplify the model to:

$$Y_{ist} = \beta_0 + \beta_1 \left(minority_i \times bias_{ist} \right) + \beta_2 \left(bias_{ist} \right) + \beta_3 \left(minority_i \right) + \varepsilon_i \tag{11.3}$$

Figure 11.1 shows this graphically. Unlike Figure 8.2, there are not just two values of the treatment variable (manager-bias) observed, but rather the treatment is a continuous variable. The coefficient, β_3, would be the difference in productivity at a manager-bias level of zero between the treatment group (minorities) and control group (non-minorities). I made it negative in the figure just because it was easier to draw the figure this way. The coefficient on manager-bias, $\hat{\beta}_2$, would be the slope for the control group, which also comes out negative. And $\hat{\beta}_1$ would be how the effect of manager bias is different for minorities from that for non-minorities. This is negative in Figure 11.1 because the slope for minorities is more negative than that for non-minorities, and it is also represented by the difference in productivity (at *bias* = 1 vs. *bias* = 0) in the actual value for the treatment group (the solid line) vs. the hypothetical value for the treatment group (the dashed line).

To address the potential for correlated error terms, the authors cluster at the store level. That is, they allow for a correlation of error terms for all observations from a given store. There is no reason to include store fixed effects because that is probably captured by the cashier fixed effects, assuming almost all cashiers only work at one store while in the sample.

Key results

Table 11.1 summarizes the estimated effects of the interaction of *minority* (cashier) and *bias* (from the manager) on four dependent variables, measuring some form of productivity. The first outcome

Table 11.1 Key results from Glover et al. (2017), Tables III and IV

Dependent variable measuring some form of productivity (positively or negatively)	Coefficient estimate on the interaction of minority $\times$ bias
Indicator for being absent for the shift	0.0177***
(n = 4371)	(0.0042)
Minutes worked in excess of schedule	−3.327*
(n = 4163)	(1.687)
Articles scanned per minute	−0.233**
(n = 3,601)	(0.108)
Inter-customer time (measured in seconds)	1.417**
(n = 3287)	(0.649)

Standard errors are in parentheses. *** $p < 0.01$, ** $p < 0.05$, * $p < 0.10$.

indicates that cashiers are significantly more likely to be absent from their shift when getting scheduled with a manager with more bias ($p < 0.01$). In addition, minority cashiers scan fewer items and allow slightly more time between customers when working under more-biased managers ($p < 0.05$). Of lower significance is that the minority cashiers work fewer minutes beyond their schedule with more-biased managers ($p < 0.10$). Despite the statistical significance of these estimates, note that the 95% confidence intervals for the interacted effects of *minority* and *bias* are fairly wide and include values that are near or below zero for three of the outcomes. Keep in mind that measurement error is likely biasing the estimated effects toward zero.

What are the mechanisms at play?

The authors conducted a survey of the cashiers, in which they asked about particular managers, which the authors then merged with the productivity data. Their more important findings were that:

- Interestingly, minority cashiers tended to rate the more-biased managers more positively and more enjoyable to work with, and that the cashiers had more confidence working with them, although all of these differences were statistically insignificant. Still, this is evidence against any animus by the more-biased managers leading to lower work performance.
- More-biased managers are less likely to ask minority cashiers to do the unpleasant task of closing their register and doing cleaning duties (at the end of the shift). This is consistent with the theory that more-biased managers interact less with minority cashiers.
- Workers had greater productivity working under managers whom they had more interactions with.

What this suggests, in the end, is that manager-worker interaction is the key ingredient that appears to lead to greater productivity of the workers. This is a lesson many of us could use.

General things I liked about this article

The authors were forthright about potential problems. They gave their honest take on whether each potential PITFALL could be a problem in the end. Furthermore, they used a quite straightforward approach with easy interpretations. They did not get unnecessarily complicated. If I would consider how interesting the results were for how much I like the article, then I would add that as another reason to like the article. But I won't do that, as we should focus on methods and soundness, both of which the authors do extremely well with.

11.2 Does Medicaid participation improve health outcomes?

Medicaid, a joint federal and state program, provides a low-cost form of health insurance to several disadvantaged groups, including those with low income, the disabled, and the elderly. In the last several years, some states have opted to expand Medicaid in an effort to improve health outcomes. But it was uncertain how much this would actually improve health.

How Medicaid participation affects health outcomes would normally be a difficult topic to examine because it is far from random who applies for Medicaid. The potential problems are the following:

- **Reverse causality**: This could work in two opposite ways. It could be the ones who are in need of health care who are more likely to apply for Medicaid. This could contribute to a negative bias on the causal effect of Medicaid participation on health. On the other hand, it may be the more health-conscious people who are interested in getting health insurance are the ones more likely to apply, which would contribute to a negative bias.
- **Omitted-factors bias**: There could be common factors for health and whether someone applies for Medicaid. Perhaps difficulty finding a job makes a person have health problems from stress and also makes the person apply for Medicaid, being in need of health insurance.
- **Self-selection bias**: It would likely be those who think they could benefit most from Medicaid (in terms of health-outcome improvement) who are more likely to apply for Medicaid.

Oregon made it simpler for researchers by instituting a lottery to determine eligibility for an expansion of its Medicaid program. The state randomly selected roughly 30,000 of 90,000 on the Medicaid waiting list. Those 30,000 were then offered Medicaid if they met the eligibility requirements.

Baicker et al. (2013) designed a study to examine the effects of this Medicaid expansion in Oregon. Their model involved a two-stage least squares (2SLS) approach, with the lottery as the instrumental variable determining Medicaid participation, and the predicted Medicaid participation was then included in a series of models to determine its effects on various health outcomes. Not everyone who won the Medicaid lottery ended up enrolling in Medicaid, as some became ineligible (e.g., due to income increasing) or may have chosen not to take it. The identification was based on the assumption that the lottery determining eligibility for Medicaid would not affect health other than affecting Medicaid participation. (One of the great features of this study is that the authors outlined their whole methods in a publication before they collected and compiled the final data for their analysis.)

While this study design is likely the best that could be done with available data, it is not perfect. There could be attenuation bias (toward zero) because those not on Medicaid could have a replacement action:

- People with low income might still receive treatment (perhaps paid for by the state) when needed;
- People might make an extra effort to get health insurance through a job if they were not selected in the random draw to become eligible for Medicaid.

The main results were:

- No statistically-significant effects of Medicaid participation on clinical outcomes (e.g., blood pressure and cholesterol), with the exception of increasing the likelihood of a diabetes diagnosis and using medication for diabetes.
- Significantly reduced risk of screening positive for depression, although the 95% confidence interval was quite wide and bordered near zero: (−16.7 to −1.6 percentage points).
- Significantly greater health-related quality-of-life, although also with a 95% confidence interval close to zero.
- Significantly reduced out-of-pocket expenses, and reduced risk of having medical debt or needing to borrow money to pay medical expenses.

The finding that there was no evidence for most clinical outcomes being affected by Medicaid coverage is quite interesting. However, we need to keep in mind that some of the insignificant estimates may be due to bias toward zero from measurement error.

Why I liked this article

One nice feature of this article is that, instead of the standard errors, they gave 95% confidence intervals and p-values. In some sense, these are more valuable than the standard error. Also, given that I had such a difficult time finding studies that had insignificant estimates on key-explanatory variables, I liked that many of the key estimates in this article were insignificant (for the clinical outcomes). It is also good that the authors published their methods before conducting the analysis. This held the authors to an implicit contract to follow these methods. This is a good practice to follow, to publish your methods online in a working paper before conducting the primary analyses.

11.3 Estimating peer effects on academic outcomes

Teenagers and young adults are an influential lot. They generally want to fit in, and so teenagers can be highly influenced by their peers in many regards. This could include academic success, as teens can learn study habits from their friends; or teens could get distracted from studying by friends (who may be less interested in academics) introducing them to other time-consuming or non-enriching ventures.

Examining peer effects on academic outcomes would typically involve a model as follows:

$$Y_i = \beta_0 + X_i\beta_1 + \beta_2\left(Y^P\right)_i + \varepsilon_i \tag{11.4}$$

where:
- Y is some measure of academic success for person i;
- Y^P is the measure of academic success or qualifications for person i's peers or friends;
- X is a set of demographic and contextual factors for person i.

Potential sources of bias

Figuring out the PITFALLS on this topic is like shooting fish in a barrel, as there are plenty of problems with the standard approach to estimating peer effects.

- **Reverse causality**: There are two types of reverse causality here. The direct type is that the youth's friends may be positively (or negatively) influenced in their academic outcomes as a result of the subject youth's academic success (or lack thereof). So cases in which the youth's level of academic success affects that of his/her friends would contribute to an upward bias for β_2. In some sense, any reverse causality would be evidence itself for peer effects, but it would upwardly bias any estimated effects of peers. The second type of reverse causality is that a teenager intent on doing well academically may seek out friends who are academically successful. Likewise, someone who has little interest in doing well would not choose friends based on their academic success. Thus, something closely tied with the dependent variable would determine the value of the key-explanatory variable. Some call this the "selection effect" in that you select your friends based partly on whether their own outcome is desirable. This could also be considered *self-selection bias* in that those who expect greater academic benefits from smart friends are more likely to choose smart friends.
- **Omitted-factors bias**: Just as with reverse causality, there are a few types of omitted-factors bias on this empirical issue. First, a youth and his/her friends may have common factors for academic success. This could include positive factors, such as the prevalence of a good role model among an older sibling for one of the friends or successful parents. It could also include negative factors, such as being from a neighborhood with a lot of violence and not having much peace to study well. In addition, the friendship may have been initially formed non-randomly. Perhaps the youth had formed these friendships long ago over factors that could contribute to better academic outcomes (e.g., playing computer games) or worse academic outcomes (e.g., interest in substance use). Thus, the level of academic success use for the subject and his/her friends would be positively correlated due to the reasons leading them to become friends in the first place. Again, this would contribute to a positive bias in the estimated peer effects.
- **Measurement error**: There could be measurement errors from the youth misrepresenting how academically successful their friends are. Also, it could result from the youth not listing his/her most academically influential peers. Perhaps the youth would have a few sets of friends – some that he identifies with academically and others he identifies with to activate his fun side. The youth may indicate the latter if they are responding to questions about friends, even though the academic friends are entirely different. These cases would not be random measurement error, so we cannot determine the direction of the bias on the estimate of β_2 from measurement error.

Let me note that the story on all of these biases would be similar if we were discussing peer effects of substance use.

Addressing the PITFALLS

Random assignment of peers or friends would be the optimal solution to be able to correctly estimate peer effects. Unfortunately, I don't think we can convince any youth, for the larger good of knowledge and some researcher getting a decent publication, to accept a situation in which he/she is randomly assigned friends. But a few researchers realized that some youth (college freshmen) are randomly assigned roommates. Few schools use random assignments, but when they do, this presents the opportunity for a Natural Experiment. And so these researchers examined how the pre-college traits of a college freshman's roommate and other randomly assigned peers affect the freshman's outcomes.

Perhaps the most notable study regarding peer effects on academic outcomes is by Carrell et al. (2009), who use roommate and squadron random assignments at the Air Force Academy (AFA) to examine the effects of SAT (a college entrance test) scores and other pre-college characteristics among a freshman's peers on the freshman's first-semester course grades. Cadets at the AFA are randomly assigned to their roommate and to one of 36 squadrons, each of which has 120 students (from Freshmen to Seniors), with about 33 per freshmen class. In addition, freshmen are not allowed to enter the premises of other squadrons for the first seven months, meaning that they have limited contact with those from other squadrons, other than in their classes. This suggests that the roommate and squadron may indeed be the relevant peers. Furthermore, the first-semester courses are standard for all freshmen, and they cannot choose their professors or sections. Thus, the courses and sections, usually around 20 students, are random (with just *good variation*) as well.

Carrell et al. (2009) estimate the following equation (changed somewhat from their version for the purpose of simplification):

$$\text{GPA}_{ics} = \beta_0 + X_{ics}\beta_1 + \left(X^P_{ics}\right)\beta_2 + \mu_{cs} + \varepsilon_{ics} \qquad (11.5)$$

where:
- i = the individual cadet
- c = the course
- s = the section
- GPA = the GPA of the cadet's grade in the given course
- X = the pre-AFA characteristics of the cadet
- X^P = the pre-AFA characteristics of the cadet's peers (the roommate(s) and the other squadron freshmen)
- μ_{cs} is the fixed effect for the course section (a class).

One aspect that is essential to their study, in order to avoid reverse causality, is that the measures of the quality of the peers (the variables in X^P) occur before the freshmen are exposed to each other. These measures of quality include verbal and math SAT scores, as well as academic and leadership scores (based on high-school experiences) and a fitness score (which also presumably occurs before exposure to each other in the squadrons).

The course-section (class) fixed effects mean that the relationship between the peer pre-AFA characteristics and the cadet's GPA in a given course (adjusting for the other factors) is estimated for each of the roughly 1000 sections (classes). The overall estimated effects, $\hat{\beta}_2$, are the weighted averages of the 1000-or-so $\hat{\beta}_2$'s for each course-section.

Table 11.2 summarizes the primary results, which come from the first two columns of Table 3 in the study. Interestingly, only one of the roommate pre-Air-Force characteristics had a statistically-significant coefficient estimate – that for leadership, although the lower bound of the 95% confidence interval is quite close to zero. The stronger results come from the characteristics of the other freshmen in the squadron, where two of the characteristics have significant estimates. The one for SAT verbal seems reasonable, as having squadron members who are better at verbal skills may help a given student do better in his/her classes. Also, freshmen with squadron members who had greater pre-Air-Force fitness scores also do better in their classes. While this empirical relationship is plausible, it is also possible that this may be a Type I error, as I am not aware of an obvious mechanism underlying this effect. Further results (not shown here) suggests that there is some evidence suggesting that this verbal-SAT effect is stronger for students whose own pre-AFA characteristics are weaker.

There have been a few studies using random college roommate assignments regarding substance use – e.g., Duncan et al. (2005) on marijuana use. The more interesting Kremer and Levy (2008),

Table 11.2 Summary of the main results from Carrell et al. (2009), Table 3

	Dependent variable = grade (GPA) in a given class	
	Model (1)	Model (2)
	Roommate	Other freshmen in squadron
SAT verbal	0.003	0.338***
	(0.019)	(0.107)
SAT math	0.005	0.119
	(0.021)	(0.097)
Academic composite	0.0004	0.018
	(0.005)	(0.032)
Fitness score	0.022	0.153**
	(0.013)	(0.064)
Leadership composite	0.012**	0.024
	(0.006)	(0.041)

Models also include the own characteristics for each subject, course-section fixed effects, and year fixed effects. Standard errors are in parentheses. *** $p < 0.01$, ** $p < 0.05$, * $p < 0.10$.

combining the concepts of substance use and academic outcomes, found that, for males, having a freshman roommate who drank in the year before college had a quarter-point lower grade point average (GPA). That said, I do wonder whether this study is useful. Whatever the findings could have been, I am not certain whether there would be anything actionable.

What I like about this study

The study takes advantage of randomness that someone else instituted. Overall, there is not overwhelming evidence for peer effects. That is okay. This is a well-executed and pretty clean study in terms of the lack of alternative stories that could explain the results.

11.4 How much does a GED improve labor-market outcomes?

Many Americans who choose not to (or are not allowed to) complete high-school attempt to earn a General Equivalency Diploma (GED). The GED is supposed to be an "equivalent" to a high-school diploma. Thus, a GED serves somewhat as a signal to employers that the GED holder may be a few steps ahead of other non-high-school-grads. And a GED is typically required for those wanting to further their education with college or other professional courses.

There have been many attempts to estimate how earning a GED affects one's labor-market outcomes. This topic could have the same empirical problems as one would have if they were estimating the effects of years-of-schooling on income. Just like it isn't random how many years-of-schooling a person would obtain, it wouldn't be random who (among those without a high-school diploma) would earn a GED.

Two of the most notable problems may be omitted-factors bias and self-selection bias. There could be omitted-factors bias because, among non-high-school-grads, those with higher motivation and intelligence would likely have a higher probability of taking and passing the GED and would, on average, do better in the labor market. Self-selection bias may occur because those who earn a GED may tend to be the ones who believe they can highly benefit from having one. Thus, they may be more motivated to earn one.

Jepsen et al. (2016) devise a regression-discontinuities model to estimate the effects of the GED on a few labor-market outcomes. The authors focus on roughly 44,000 males and 42,000 females who first took the GED test in Missouri between 1995 and 2005. Restricting the sample to those who took the GED reduces one source of omitted-factors bias – the motivation to take the GED – but, perhaps not the motivation to do well on the GED. The GED is a national test, although there have historically been small differences across states in what is required to pass. The requirements for passing in Missouri were scoring at least 400 on all five sub-tests and 2250 total (out of 4000). People were allowed to retake the test, and their sub-scores and the total score (and pass status) would be based on the highest of each of the five sub-test scores over the prior two years. The authors find high retake rates for those who score just under 2250, and (in their Figure 1) they find a discontinuity for the final score (after retakes), with a big jump right at the passing score of 2250. This demonstrates that few people stick with a score right below 2250 without retaking the test.

Given that 2250 does not necessarily dictate passing the GED (due to sub-scores potentially being too low), the situation calls for a *Fuzzy* RD model. But there is a problem with using the final total score. Recall back in Section 8.7, I said that an RD model will have problems if the subjects can manipulate the scores. That would be the situation in this case if the authors had used the final score, as subjects could conceivably keep taking the test until they passed and it wouldn't be random which subjects did so. Jepsen et al.'s solution is to use the first-test total score as the continuous variable underlying whether the person passes the GED. They demonstrate (in their Figure 3) that there does not appear to be a discontinuity for the first score, in contrast to the final score after retakes.

Their model involves:

- **Stage 1**: Regression of GED certification on a dummy variable for meeting the 2250 threshold on the first test and quadratic variables on total score below and above the threshold.
- **Stage 2**: Regression of the labor-market outcome on the predicted-GED probability from Stage 1 and the same quadratic variables below and above the threshold. The excluded variable is the dummy variable for meeting the 2,250 thresholds on the first test.

Let's recall that RD models produce local average treatment effects (LATE's), so what these authors estimate is the effect of a GED for those right by the threshold on the first test.

With the outcome of quarterly earnings, examined for each of the 30 quarters after the first test, the authors find mostly no significant effects for males and females, with a few exceptions for males. For males, for quarters 6–9 after the first test, the estimated effect of the GED was significant at the 5% level, with estimated point effects ranging from about $430 to $600 in quarterly earnings. Being only significant at the 5% but not the 1% level, the 95% confidence intervals included values not far off from zero.

For the outcome of whether the person was employed in a quarter (i.e., had positive income), there was only one of 60 estimated effects (30 quarters times 2 genders) that had a significant estimate. Thus, there is no evidence that having a GED affected a person's probability of employment.

There was one alternative story that could not be ruled out by the RD model. Earning a GED could increase one's probability of attending further schooling, which would then reduce earnings while in school. The authors do find evidence that the GED does indeed increase the probability that someone is enrolled in a post-secondary school. But they describe and show in an Appendix not included in the main article that restricting the sample to those not enrolled in school results in a similar set of results as described above.

What I like about this study

This is a sound study, for which I could not come up with any alternative stories that the authors had not considered. Again, I like the general finding of insignificant estimated effects, although in this case, the insignificant estimates make for quite an interesting result: there is little evidence that a GED improves labor-market outcomes, on average. That, of course, does not mean that this result is true for several reasons. First, insignificance does not prove there is no effect, as we learned in Section 5.8. Second, with RD models, the results apply just to those very close to the thresdhold. Thus, people well above (and perhaps well below) the threshold might have experienced much stronger effects. Third, the study was conducted in one state. Finally, earning a GED could have huge impacts for some people near the threshold, but based on the study, the effects were undetectable when averaged.

11.5 How female integration in the Norwegian military affects gender attitudes among males

For females to have a fair shot and maximize their contribution in the workplace, there need to be healthy and objective attitudes toward women among co-workers. Worldwide, females are becoming a larger share of the workforce.

This is especially true in militaries across the world, which are likely all male-dominated (other than Themyscira). The trend, at least in the developed world, is certainly to increase female integration into the military. Women are becoming increasingly eligible to serve in roles that used to be exclusively for men. For example, several NATO countries now allow females to serve on submarines. The ultimate success of females in male-dominated workplaces could depend on males' attitudes toward females.

An important issue that then arises is how greater gender integration affects males' attitudes. Without randomization, this would be a difficult topic to study. Figure 11.2 sets up the problem. The main potential PITFALLS are:

- **Reverse causality**: Perhaps more positive male attitudes toward females cause males to seek occupations with more females.
- **Omitted-factors bias**: Prior experiences working with females that were positive could contribute to more positive attitudes and a greater likelihood of choosing to work in occupations with more females. Furthermore, over time, there could be general trends in both female integration and male attitudes toward females that could get incorrectly credited to an impact of gender integration.

Dahl, Kotsadam, and Rooth (2021) devise a way to address these problems in a study of the historically male-dominated Norwegian military the military. Females have become an increasing part of the Norwegian military. In 2014, females comprised 13% of the military (compared to 15% in the United States). As of 2020, one-third of those completing basic training in Norway were female.

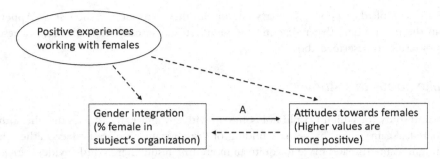

Figure 11.2 Flowchart for how female integration affects male gender attitudes

The Norwegian military has what is considered a selective compulsory military service. All 17-year-olds must register for the military draft and be screened for suitability. The first part of the screening process is an online questionnaire about the desire to serve, criminal record, and other matters. At the time of the analysis (2014), of about 60,000 filling out the forms, about one-third of them are selected for physical and cognitive screening at ages 18 and 19. Of those, the military would take around 8,000–10,000 recruits per year. At the time of the study, service would be compulsory for males if selected, but not for females. In 2015, it became compulsory for females as well, when Norway became the first NATO country to impose a draft on both males and females. This was part of a goal to increase female participation throughout the military.

Upon entering the military, recruits go through bootcamp for eight weeks. This involves classroom and field training. Most tasks are done in squads of five to seven people, in order to foster effective teamwork. A given squad not only works together but also lives together, sharing one big bedroom. After bootcamp, mandatory service lasts 10 months, at which point service-members make the decision of whether to stay in the military.

The assignment of females to squads was not random. And so, to accurately gauge the effects of female integration on male attitudes, Dahl et al. convinced three battalions in the Army's North Brigade to randomly assign female recruits to squads. Out of 156 squads that were part of the study, 96 had zero women, 11 had one, 38 had two, and 8 had three or four women.

Table 11.3 shows some key results, coming from Tables IV and VII of the article, based on the models with control variables. All dependent variables, noted at the top of each column, are defined so that a value of one (instead of 0) or a higher value for the non-dummy variables indicates more-positive attitudes toward females. The authors found that those who had a female were significantly more likely to:

- disagree that single-gender teams work better
- believe that it's important to share household work equally (among males and females)
- choose a military occupation that has more females in it.

Equally important findings come from a follow-up after six months of service when the soldiers have been in their post-initial-training work units and likely had a smaller share of females they worked with. There were no longer any significant estimated effects of having a female in one's bootcamp squad. This suggests that any improvement in attitudes toward females wanes over time, so there is still work to do.

Table 11.3 **Main results from Dahl et al. (2021) on gender integration**

	Disagree that same-gender teams perform better	Agree that it's important to share household work equally	% women in chosen military occupation	% women in chosen occupation
At end of bootcamp				
Whether had a female in bootcamp squad	0.133**	0.082**	0.022**	
	(0.053)	(0.041)	(0.007)	
# observations	522	526	657	
Six months into service				
Whether had a female in bootcamp squad	−0.012			0.025
	(0.058)			(0.023)
# observations	370			654

Standard errors are in parentheses. **p–value < 0.05. *p–value <0.10.

There are other outcomes regarding which gender the service-person believes makes up the best leaders. I hope this was not subconsciously ignoring insignificant estimates (on my part), but all estimates on the treatment variable (having a female in one's bootcamp squad) were statistically insignificant for these other outcomes.

There are ways, I believe, the authors could have improved the study. Just using a dummy variable for "whether there is was a female in the squad" misses the variation in the number of females. I do not believe the treatment variable should have been "the number of females," as there would likely be non-linearities. In Appendix Table A.7, the authors present results from separate variables for "one female" and "two-or-more females" in the squad. (I would have made the first variable "at least one female.") The problem was that there was great imprecision due to the sample size being fairly limited. This is likely why they used just an indicator for whether there were any females in the squad.

Why I like this study

This is an important topic, as there seems to be increasing integration of many under-represented groups into various occupations, particularly the military. It is a topic that almost certainly would require randomization. They realized that randomization would be simple and would not negatively impact the mission, so they convinced the Norwegian military to do so. In addition, the authors recognized that such effects could be temporary, and they tested for that to show evidence supporting the notion that any effects results were not sustained over time.

References

Baicker, K., Taubman, S. L., Allen, H. L., Bernstein, M., Gruber, J. H., Newhouse, J. P., ... Finkelstein, A. N. (2013). The Oregon experiment: effects of Medicaid on clinical outcomes. *New England Journal of Medicine*, *368*(18), 1713–1722.

Carrell, S. E., Fullerton, R. L., & West, J. E. (2009). Does your cohort matter? Measuring peer effects in college achievement. *Journal of Labor Economics*, *27*(3), 439–464.

Dahl, G. B., Kotsadam, A., & Rooth, D. O. (2021). Does integration change gender attitudes? The effect of randomly assigning women to traditionally male teams. *The Quarterly Journal of Economics*, *136*(2), 987–1030.

Duncan, G. J., Boisjoly, J., Kremer, M., Levy, D. M., & Eccles, J. (2005). Peer effects in drug use and sex among college students. *Journal of Abnormal Child Psychology*, *33*(3), 375–385.

Glover, D., Pallais, A., & Pariente, W. (2017). Discrimination as a self-fulfilling prophecy: evidence from French grocery stores. *The Quarterly Journal of Economics*, *132*(3), 1219–1260.

Greenwald, A. G., McGhee, D. E., & Schwartz, J. L. K. (1998). Measuring individual differences in implicit cognition: the implicit association test. *Journal of Personality and Social Psychology*, *74*(6), 1464–1480.

Jepsen, C., Mueser, P., & Troske, K. (2016). Labor market returns to the GED using regression discontinuity analysis. *Journal of Political Economy*, *124*(3), 621–649.

Kremer, M., & Levy, D. (2008). Peer effects and alcohol use among college students. *The Journal of Economic Perspectives*, *22*(3), 189–206.

Lane, K. A., Banaji, M. R., Nosek, B. A., & Greenwald, A. G. (2007). Understanding and using the implicit association test: IV. What we know (So Far) about the method. In *Measures of attitudes* (pp. 59–102), B. Wittenbrink, and N. Schwarz, eds. New York: Guilford Press.

12 How to conduct a research project

DOI: 10.4324/9781003285007-12

Box 12.1   Is it art?

"Boy, that went well," Calvin gloated, as he emerged from the Pentagon, having presented his Army reenlistment model to Defense officials who, in turn, would soon report his results to Congress.

"They believed you on everything," Hobbes replied, "even the part about being able to perfectly predict which Soldiers would reenlist."

"Yeah ....Was it hot in there or what?"

Hobbes paused a moment. "Yogi Berra once said, 'If you ask me anything I don't know, I'm not going to answer.'"

Calvin stopped in his tracks and turned to Hobbes. "Listen, you furry, omnivorous, baboon-posing-as-a-feline stuffed animal. My research is *art*! People always make the mistake of thinking art is created for them. But really, art is a private language for sophisticates to congratulate themselves on their superiority to the rest of the world. As my 'artist's statement' explains, my work is utterly incomprehensible and is therefore full of deep significance.[1]"

Bewildered, Hobbes replied, "I thought you were doing regression analysis."

In this chapter, I describe how to conduct a research project. You will learn about:

*   Strategies for choosing a topic
*   Fundamental processes for conducting the analysis
*   Strategies for writing a clear report that covers all the important information, without overburdening the reader.

12.1 Choosing a topic

There are four general approaches to choosing a topic that I will describe:

*   Searching data sets to come up with a topic
*   Choosing a topic and searching for data to address it
*   Finding better ways to approach an existing issue that others have examined
*   Being on the lookout for randomness and other things.

12.1.1 Searching data sets to come up with a topic

There are plenty of data sets available with rich data. Some data sets have individual-level information on academic achievement and social, behavioral, and economic outcomes. These include the NLSY, National Educational Longitudinal Survey (NELS), Early Childhood Longitudinal Survey (ECLS), National Survey on Drug Use and Health (NSDUH), Behavioral Risk Factors Surveillance Survey (BRFSS), and many more. There are many sources for economic data at the national and state/local level. There are data sets on business financial data, and more and more big data is becoming available on things such as sports and internet searches. Browsing through these data sets could be quite fruitful for finding interesting empirical relationships to explore and test, around which there might be an interesting theory you could develop.

12.1.2 Choosing a topic and searching for data to address it

Alternatively, you could choose a topic that interests you and try to find data for it. The topic could come from discussions with friends on human behavior. You might read about some topic in the news, and that could spark a thought on a tangential topic.

It is easier to write about a topic that you know something about. This could make it easier for understanding the mechanisms or theory underlying any empirical relationships you are testing for. Furthermore, having some knowledge about the topic could give some perspective on interpreting results – particularly, surprising results. We have seen the problems of Nobel Prize winners, who have probably never played basketball, incorrectly interpreting results on the hot hand in basketball. All that said, you would need to be careful about bringing preconceived notions to the project.

With your topic, you can search for data. If feasible, you could even create your own data by conducting a survey. This is easier said than done, as there is a science behind conducting surveys to obtain a high level of honesty in the responses and an adequate response rate. There are also strict rules on human-subject protections, with a review typically required by your organization's Institutional Review Board.

12.1.3 Finding better ways to approach an existing topic

Another method is to read through existing studies (browsing titles to start with) to find a topic that you believe could be examined in a better way. You may encounter a research finding that you find preposterous – e.g., the finding that "the hot hand in basketball is a myth." Think of ways you can develop a model that produces a more accurate test for the topic. Consider whether there are potential PITFALLS in the existing studies, evaluate how well the studies addressed them, and indicate whether you have a better approach. Or perhaps you could merely test for evidence of the bias you hypothesize, without necessarily claiming to validly estimate the true causal effect. (I did this in Arkes, 2018.)

12.1.4 Be on the lookout for randomness and other things

Think of the discrimination study we discussed in Section 11.1. I do not know how the authors came up with the idea. Perhaps one of the authors became aware of the great performance metrics that the grocery chain had been collecting and noted the possibility of issues regarding young, inexperienced, minority cashiers and managers who may have bias against minorities. Or the authors may have found out that the cashiers are randomly assigned to their shifts.

And think of the study by Carrell et al. (2009) on peer effects at the Air Force Academy (Section 11.3). They knew that the Air Force Academy assigned freshmen to roommates and squadrons pretty much randomly, making sure demographic groups were fairly evenly split. They were then able to create a study around that random (good) variation.

The bottom line is that you could be on the lookout for:

- Unique data
- Some random source of variation determining an endogenous treatment variable (such as a lottery for Medicaid)
- Thresholds dictating eligibility for treatment (for regression-discontinuity models)
- Panel data that track people over multiple time periods.

All of these could be the ingredients for a great research paper. However, make sure that the topic is important to people's lives, which (unfortunately) was not one of my great concerns when I chose topics.

12.2 Conducting the empirical part of the study

12.2.1 Gathering data

The empirical part of the study begins with collecting data. This may involve collecting multiple data sets and merging data. Perhaps there is geographical information (such as state unemployment rates) that can be merged with data that have the corresponding geographical information. And it may involve collecting your own data by a survey.

12.2.2 Creating the proper sample

With the data, one must choose the proper sample. The sample should be representative of the population for which you wish to make inferences. If the analysis is on people, then consider what age groups to use. Are there certain characteristics that make some observations less relevant? Studies that examine how state tax rates affect state economic growth often exclude Alaska and Hawaii, as capital and businesses are not easily moved to or from these states, as they would be for the 48 contiguous states. Thus, it is theorized that tax rates have less of an effect on these states. Is that a good reason to exclude them? I'll let you consider that. Also of consideration is how to keep observations with missing data, which I describe below.

12.2.3 Dependent variable

There may be one obvious dependent variable that you have in mind, but having multiple dependent variables can be helpful in painting a sharper picture of what outcomes the treatment may have an impact on and whether the treatment has a consistent impact on various outcomes. For example, the Oregon Health Study (Baicker et al. 2013), as described in Section 11.2, examined how Medicaid coverage affects a wide set of health-outcome measures. That said, including multiple outcomes is a method to p-hack (as I will describe in the next section). So it is not advisable (and even unethical) to keep adding outcomes until significance is found. It is optimal to describe why you chose certain outcomes, and all analyses with various outcomes should be reported.

12.2.4 Key-explanatory variable

The key-explanatory factor may be obvious, as it would likely be part of the initial choice of a topic. However, it is worthwhile to consider how to characterize the factor. If it is a yes/no treatment, then it is simple. For continuous variables, one could consider non-linear effects (Section 3.2). Furthermore, there could be interacted effects if the effect could vary across observations based on some factor. Do you want to estimate an overall effect or how the effect varies by group?

12.2.5 Designing the model (and choosing the optimal set of control variables)

The method (and sample) should be chosen and the models designed to minimize potential biases. If the objective is estimating causal effects, then the choice of control variables should be based on the guidelines presented in Section 6.11. For other objectives of regression analysis, Table 7.2 in Section 7.4 should be considered.

12.2.6 Check the data

Check the frequency of the values for each variable used in the regression. Sometimes, in survey data, missing values are coded as negative numbers, with codes for various reasons why the value is missing for the observation. If left as is, this could have a large impact on the regression results. It is also good to check for incomprehensible values of a variable. This can often be done by finding the minimum and maximum values of the variables. Be on the lookout for large outliers in either an explanatory variable or the dependent variable, as they could have significant impacts on the results. Such outliers should be assessed for how they impact the model and whether they are legitimate data versus potential mistakes.

12.2.7 Correcting for missing data

It is rare that data for regressions are perfect. There is often missing information. This may be due to coding errors, a respondent choosing not to answer a question, or the data just not being available. How missing data can be treated depends on what information is missing, and it may not be necessary to throw out an observation with missing data.

12.2.7.1 Missing data on the dependent variable

In this situation, there is nothing that can be done. The observation would need to be excluded from the regression. You may want to think about whether there is a pattern based on which types of observations have a missing dependent variable. Any pattern should be noted, as it speaks to one of the "things that could go wrong" in regression analysis, *non-representative samples* (Section 6.12).

12.2.7.2 Missing data on the key-explanatory variable

If the key-explanatory variable is missing, then this is another situation in which the observation should be dropped. To impute a number would introduce measurement error (PITFALL #4). Again, the data should be investigated for patterns in having the key-explanatory variable missing.

12.2.7.3 Missing data on other explanatory variables (the control variables)

This is the one case in which it may be best to keep the observation. Control variables, again, are ones that are included just to obtain more accurate estimates of the key-explanatory variables. The strategy for including the observation is to:

- Assign the same value to the missing variable for all observations missing that variable – the mean value is a good choice.
- Create a new dummy variable equaling one if the original value was missing on that variable and zero otherwise.

For example, with the NLSY data, the AFQT percentile score is missing for about 6% of the sample (Bureau of Labor Statistics, 2014; 2015). In the models in earlier chapters involving the AFQT score, I just excluded this 6% from the sample. But instead, I could have assigned 50 (the national median) to the AFQT score for these people (or the sample average of 43.8) and created a variable, *afqtmiss*, which equals one if the *AFQT* was originally missing and zero otherwise.

The idea here is that the observations have value in describing the relationship between the key-explanatory variable and the outcome. Excluding observations, because they have missing data on control variables, would cause us to lose any information the observations provide. So, we assign them a value near the middle of the distribution (so it has a minimal effect on the estimate on the AFQT score) and then have an extra variable in there to see if those with a missing AFQT score have systematically higher or lower outcomes than others, after adjusting for other factors. Generally, more observations produce more precise estimates, so saving observations from the chopping block can be a good thing if done correctly.

12.2.8 Extra analyses

There are various reasons to estimate variants of the primary model. Make sure you do not overdo it, but the following are some reasons that could justify estimating multiple models:

- Conduct a sensitivity analysis. This is meant to test whether the results are "sensitive" to alternative specifications or characterizations of the treatment. For example, the key-explanatory variable might be characterized as a spline or quadratic function. (Just because a model variant gives a better answer is not a reason to make it the main model and result.)
- Split by demographic group (or other segments of the sample) to see if there is a stronger/weaker empirical relationship for particular groups.
- Demonstrate the effects of a correction for a PITFALL. For example, you may want to show the results from what happened without and with fixed effects (to address omitted-factors bias). This could be indicative of how much of an omitted-factors-bias problem there was initially. At the same time, be aware of other explanations for the differences in results between uncorrected and corrected models. For example, with fixed effects, differences in results could be due to greater bias from measurement error and a re-weighting of groups of observations (PITFALLS #4 and #7).
- When there is an ambiguous modeling decision (e.g., whether to include a variable or whether to use OLS or probit), you could estimate the model both ways to determine whether the results are relatively stable or if they meaningfully change with different modeling decisions.

12.3 Writing the report

The main things I keep in mind as I write a paper or report is to: (1) keep the report as readable as possible; and (2) make it so someone could skim through the article and get the general gist within a few minutes. To this end, I attempt to avoid complicated language, and I try to make tables as clear as possible so that a reader does not have to check in the text to understand the table.

12.3.1 General components

The following is the general order of the components of a paper or article:

- Abstract
- Introduction
- Theoretical/Conceptual Framework
- Data
- Methods
- Results
- Conclusions/Discussion
- References.

Having these distinct sections improves the readability of the paper, as it makes it easier for a reader to find a particular point they are searching for and it just breaks up the paper. While some journals require a fixed format (that may not follow this exact ordering), often there is flexibility in some of the ordering and which components are necessary. Sometimes sections are too short to stand on their own, so it is better to incorporate them into other sections. For example, the conceptual framework (which discusses the mechanisms for why there should be the empirical relationship you are hypothesizing) could be quite simple and straightforward. Thus, it could be part of the Introduction or the Methods section. Likewise, the Data description may be small enough to be included in the Methods section. Sometimes more sections are needed. If there are multiple research questions or just a long set of results, it may be worthwhile to split the Results section into two or more sections. Finally, note that other names are often used to title a section. The same general concepts apply.

12.3.2 Abstract (or executive summary)

The Abstract should summarize most of the research project: the research question, data, methods, results, and conclusions (and maybe the contribution relative to prior studies, if space allows). How much detail you go into depends on how much space you have. For academic articles, you may be limited to 100 words, or sometimes you may be allowed as much as 250 words. And sometimes, the abstract is allowed to be free-flowing, and sometimes it needs to be structured into specific sections.

For non-academic reports (e.g., to sponsors), there is often an Executive Summary of a few pages instead of or in addition to an abstract. The "Executive" reading the "Summary" should be able to understand what was done in the report within a few pages. They can then refer to the body of the report for more detail.

12.3.3 Introduction

There is typically not any standard form for an Introduction. The Introduction should provide a concise description of the whole study. Some say that you should introduce your topic in the first paragraph. But, if the title of the paper is self-explanatory and you describe your topic in the abstract, then you should have a little "artistic license" for how to start your paper. Although few do so, starting the Introduction with some captivating story could draw in readers. Let me suggest that we start a trend of beginning a paper/

report with a short story that leads into the introduction of your topic. As an example, in my book, *Confessions of a Recovering Economist* (Arkes, 2022) describing the problems with economic research and how to fix the problems, I start with a two-page story on how economists, including the Nobel laureates, got it wrong on the basketball hot hand for decades and how that their research and interpretations contained most of the widespread problems in economics (that this book hopes to address). The story could be a quick, funny story from your life that has some meaning for the research topic. It could be a story you make up, such as the foul-shooting contest I had with LeBron James in my head. Alternatively (or, in addition to a story), you could include a relevant quote from one of the great philosophers: e.g., Socrates, Yogi Berra, Yogi Bear, Bob Dylan, Gregg Popovich, Chris Rock, Jules Winnfield, Andy Dufresne, Norm Peterson, Omar Little, Kim Kardashian, Calvin, and Hobbes. If you're not sure it works, take a chance. I'm sure I misfired on some of my stories in this book or quotes that I thought were funny, but I hope that a few worked. Remember, this is supposed to be fun … in addition to being informative, and there could be synergy between the fun and informative parts.

One important component of the Introduction is your empirical objective. Your topic should not just be exploring the relationship between two variables, but indicate whether your objective is to estimate a causal effect, determine the best predictors of some outcome, forecast the outcome, gauge relative performance, or some other purpose that guides your research.

Another important component of the Introduction is some discussion on why the topic is important. Why might the world (or some segment of the world) benefit from this research? Many economists overstate the importance of their study, as I had done often before I knew better. Be rational and honest about the implications.

The last part of the Introduction is often a brief map of the structure of the paper. This may not be necessary, as the structures of reports are fairly standard, and a reader could easily skim through the paper to see this.

In some academic fields, a new trend is to have a Positionality Statement included in the Introduction. (I was recently asked to do this for a journal article.) This is a statement that indicates how your world views or your experiences may have bearing on the research. It may include some statement on how you became interested in the research topic in the first place.

12.3.4 Literature review

This is the section in which you highlight how your research fits into the general literature on the research topic. This will indicate what your contribution will be. Sometimes, if brief, the Literature Review is folded into the Introduction. The topics to cover in this section include:

- What, if anything has been done on your specific topic?
- What has been done on related topics (if nothing has been studied specifically on your topic)? Generally, it is not necessary to discuss the methods of each article you describe. But it would be useful to do so for a few key articles that are closely aligned with your study.
- Is there a hole in the literature on this topic?
- Why have prior studies been inadequate in addressing the research question, or why is it worthwhile to do another study on the issue? This could be that prior studies used poor methods, had inadequate or old data, or had mixed evidence with no definitive or convincing answer. Or it could just be that there are few studies on an issue, and it merits another examination to provide further evidence.
- What will your contribution be? This could be a new question never examined before (to your knowledge). For topics that have been addressed, your contribution may be a new approach or method, better data, updated data, or merely another study to add to the existing studies.

12.3.5 Theoretical/conceptual framework

In this section, you indicate why there should be a relationship that you are hypothesizing. There are two general approaches:

1. You could extend an existing theory or develop a new theory. You would then make predictions or hypotheses about what behaviors, actions, or relationships should be observed based on that theory. You would then empirically test those predictions.
2. You start with a hypothesized empirical relationship, and you then use theory to explain why there could be such a relationship. Of course, the hypothesized empirical relationship might be based on some basic theory to start with (e.g., that basketball players can get into a higher level of play and have the hot hand), but the emphasis would be on the empirical relationship.

Some academic journals like to see a full theoretical model with utility or production functions (along with a little Calculus). Sometimes, such models may have some value. But often, just describing the mechanisms that could be at play should be adequate.

Sometimes, in the second approach above, the mechanisms are obvious enough that they could be described very briefly. In this situation, the options are:

- Just incorporate the theory into the Introduction.
- Combine the theory with the Literature Review, and call it a "Background" section.
- Put the theory in the Methods section.

The Theory or Conceptual Framework may require an extra review of the literature. That is, some mechanisms may have some literature supporting them as a mechanism, and that may give your theory more credibility.

This section could be placed before the Literature Review. Which ordering is better is situation-specific and depends on how you weave the story.

12.3.6 Data

This section could be combined with the Methods section (which comes next); it largely depends on whether one or both of these are long and complicated on their own, or if at least one of them could be described fairly briefly.

The descriptions for the data collection and creation of the sample should be detailed enough so that someone could easily replicate what you did in terms of compiling and preparing the data. The main components for describing the data include the following:

- Data source(s) and how the data were accessed
- Sample criteria, along with reasons for using non-obvious criteria
- Perhaps how various sample criteria affected the sample size
- The final sample size, or the range of sample sizes if the sample varies based on the dependent variable or the model used.

The variables used should be indicated. This could go under the Data or the Methods part of the description. They include indications of:

- The dependent variable(s) – i.e., outcome(s)
- The key-explanatory (or treatment) variables
- The control variables.

If it is not obvious, it is worthwhile to describe why you chose to characterize the variables as you did. In addition, it is helpful to describe why you chose the control variables, along with why you chose to exclude other potential control variables.

After describing these variables, it is conventional to present a table with some descriptive statistics, such as the mean and standard deviation of the variables. One practice that could help with clarity is to have separate panels in this table for the dependent variable(s), the key-explanatory variable(s), and the control variables.

12.3.7 Methods

The components of the Methods description should include:

- What challenges are involved with estimating the model (e.g., there is potential omitted-factors bias, and so you need to design the model to address that).
- What method is used (e.g., OLS, fixed effects, logit model, etc.).
- Why you chose that method if it is not obvious (e.g., how does it solve your research issue).
- What the different specifications you estimate are and why. For example, you may want to estimate a model with and without certain fixed effects to demonstrate what the "fix" you apply does to the estimated effects.
- Some want to see the formal hypotheses, but the mere topic (even from the title sometimes) should have enough information so that explicitly laying out the hypotheses would be unnecessary.
- The limitations of your analysis. Are there any PITFALLS that remain unaddressed? Often, it is uncertain but a possibility that there are remaining PITFALLS. You want to say that. Remember that our objective is the truth, and your job is to present evidence and not try to convince.

If the situation calls for Model Diagnostics, then it is typically a good idea to discuss in the Methods section if any change in method is required. For example, you could describe a heteroskedasticity test you conducted, and due to the results, you correct for heteroskedasticity – although, you really should almost always do this, as it is a costless fix. Another example is that, if the situation presents the possibility of non-normal errors (to be discussed in the Results sub-section that follows), it may dictate the use of a certain method (e.g., logit method instead of OLS for a dummy-variable dependent variable).

Recently, in my research articles, I have started to include a table at the end of the Methods section that summarizes the main points from the data and methods descriptions. This includes points such as the data source, the sample size, the dependent variable, the key-explanatory variable(s), the control variables, the method (e.g., OLS), any fixed effects used, and the relevant potential limitations. This is a general list; yours may not have all of these points and may include others. For most people who look through articles, they want to get the idea quickly (as they may have many articles they're sifting through). This is an easy reference for the readers to use to get the main gist of what you did. See Table 1 in Arkes (2017) for an example. (This is another trend I'd like to start.)

12.3.8 Results

This section is for presenting and interpreting the results of the quantitative analysis. (In Section 14.4 below, I summarize some of the main points from this book, including important points on interpretations.) You will present and describe table(s) of results. This description should include the interpretation in terms of what the magnitude of the estimates indicate and how statistically significant they are, taking into account the critiques of the p-value from Section 5.5. If the coefficient estimate on the key-explanatory variable is insignificant, consider the four reasons for insignificance. Is it possible that there are counteracting positive and negative effects? Is the confidence interval for the estimate narrow enough to conclude that there is no meaningful effect?

If you have a large set of explanatory variables, focus on the interpretations for the key-explanatory variables and perhaps a few notable control variables – maybe those control variables with surprising results or those that appear to have the highest levels of significance. Describing the estimates and significance for each variable would not be fun for the reader. They can see the results in the tables.

There may be extra models you want to estimate to test for the robustness or sensitivity of your results. These are, in one sense, beneficial for representing how "robust" or "shaky" any key result is. However, researchers have generally gone too far with these tests, which have increased the length of research articles in the last few decades, which I mention below in Section 14.3. Some semi-consequential sets of results can be described very briefly, but have the results in an Appendix, in an online version of the paper for anything published in an academic journal, or just made "available upon request."

Each table should be able to stand on its own and not require someone to read the text to understand it. Some people just look at the tables, and so you want them to see the table and understand the results. Here are a few presentation tips for tables to make it easier for the reader:

- Give the sample size and what each model does (e.g., what fixed effects are included).
- Clearly identify the dependent variable in either the table title or above all models (if it is the same for each model). If the dependent variable is different for each model, then identify it at the top of each column.
- Indicate what each explanatory variable is (use short variable descriptions if possible and not hard-to-decipher variable names).
- Present estimates on the key-explanatory variables first.
- Group categories together and indicate the reference group (see Table 9.1 as an example).
- While some present the t-stats under or next to the coefficient estimate (in parentheses), most people prefer to see the standard errors so readers can construct their own quick confidence intervals. Also useful would be the 95% confidence interval and indicators for meeting key p-value thresholds – or, the p-values themselves, as Baicker et al. (2013) present (see Section 11.2). But do not overstate the importance of the p-value, given our discussion on the drawbacks of the p-value from Section 5.5.
- Don't overdo the decimal places. Having 3 significant values is usually enough (which may mean zero decimal places), with 3 or 4 decimal places typically being the maximum it should ever be. Sometimes, more decimal places are needed, depending on the scaling, to give the reader a better gauge of the t-stats and confidence intervals.

12.3.9 Conclusions/discussion

This is where you draw everything together. You can briefly remind the reader what the objective of the analysis was and what the holes in the literature were. You then briefly discuss the important findings, regardless of whether they were statistically significant. Next, provide a discussion of what this means for the research question, in relation to the prior literature (if there is any). Beware of your preconceived notions and cognitive biases (see Section 14.1).

Be honest again about the study's limitations. Being frank, honest, and self-reflective impress me more in a researcher than significant estimates do. The limitations should include alternative stories that could explain your results – i.e., stories that are alternative to your hypothesized theory. Again, a researcher's job is to present evidence and give an objective interpretation. One can give their interpretation and opinion on the final result, but that should be backed up with evidence. If you need to make some leaps of faith, then you're trying to convince.

The Conclusions section should include a discussion on what the implications of the findings are for a policy or anything else – e.g., business strategy, health behaviors. In addition, if there were subsequent research topics that you could recommend, that would be a good point to end on … unless you have another great quote to sum up the paper.

12.3.10 References/bibliography

Provide a list of references at the end of the report or perhaps before any Tables and Appendices. The format will depend on your discipline or the requirements of the academic journal.

Note

1 From this story, only part of Calvin's last quote came from one of Bill Watterson's actual comic strips: "People always make … full of deep significance." The rest of the story was my *artistic* interpretation of the context. CALVIN AND HOBBES © Watterson. Reprinted with permission of ANDREWS MCMEEL SYNDICATION. All rights reserved.

References

Arkes, J. (2017). Separating the harmful versus beneficial effects of marital disruptions on children. *Journal of Divorce & Remarriage, 58*(7), 526–541.

Arkes, J. (2018). Empirical biases and some remedies in estimating the effects of selective reenlistment bonuses on reenlistment rates. *Defence and Peace Economics, 29*(5), 475–502.

Arkes, J. (2022). *Confessions of a Recovering Economist: How Economists Get Almost Everything Wrong.* (Self-published), https://www.amazon.com/dp/B0BLG2PFHF/.

Baicker, K., Taubman, S. L., Allen, H. L., Bernstein, M., Gruber, J. H., Newhouse, J. P., … Finkelstein, A. N. (2013). The Oregon experiment – effects of Medicaid on clinical outcomes. *New England Journal of Medicine, 368*(18), 1713–1722.

Bureau of Labor Statistics, U.S. Department of Labor. (2014). *National Longitudinal Survey of Youth 1979 cohort, 1979–2012 (rounds 1–25).* Columbus, OH: Center for Human Resource Research, The Ohio State University.

Bureau of Labor Statistics, U.S. Department of Labor. (2015). *National Longitudinal Survey of Youth 1997 cohort, 1997–2013 (rounds 1–16).* Columbus, OH: Center for Human Resource Research, The Ohio State University.

Carrell, S. E., Fullerton, R. L., & West, J. E. (2009). Does your cohort matter? Measuring peer effects in college achievement. *Journal of Labor Economics, 27*(3), 439–464.

13 The ethics of regression analysis

I have committed wrongs in my research life. I never manipulated numbers or knowingly neglected to mention certain limitations to a study, but I searched for significance – i.e., trusted a model more and reported it if it gave significant estimates. And I have sometimes been in the "convincing" mode rather than the mode of "these-possible-alternative-explanations-to-my-results-are-distinct-possibilities-and-should-not-be-discounted-as-being-remote-possibilities." I recognized my wrongs when I saw it in other articles, and it hit me that this ain't right. This doesn't contribute to public knowledge. I had to right my wrongs, and so I wrote this song on regression analysis.

To open Chapter 2 and as discussed briefly in Chapter 6, I referred to the old adage "with great power comes great responsibility." You have learned by now that knowing how to estimate a regression model, in a sense, gives a person great power in that they will report their results, and some might interpret the findings as a "fact" on how certain factors are related to each other or how one factor causes some outcome. In the process, many over-reaching conclusions make it to the public arena, without proper filtration along the way. The responsibility that should come with the know-how to estimate a regression model is to design a model to minimize biases and to make responsible conclusions. The objective should not be to get the most publishable or the most tantalizing results. This means that the researcher should be sure that the conclusions are not over-reaching and that the uncertainties – the imprecision of the estimate and potential alternative explanations – are made loud and clear.

Understanding the ethics of statistical analysis requires examples of unethical practices, along with the causes. Most of these have been covered throughout this book, so this is largely (but not fully) a summary.

I have noted in a few places that regression analysis is an art. This does not mean that you can have "artistic license" to choose the model that gives the best answer. Rather, it is an art to be creative to find solutions or find topics that can be studied with a reasonable amount of validity. And it is an art to assess the potential biases to minimize their influence as much as possible.

In this chapter, you will learn:

- What we hope to see in others' research
- How incentives affect research
- Various unethical practices (to avoid)
- Proper ethical principles and practices to guide your research.

13.1 What do we hope *to see* and *not to see* in others' research?

This is a very short section because the answer is quite simple. Yet, it is an important enough question to merit having a separate section.

Statistical research helps towards informing society on best practices. This could be on household and business behavior or government policy that promotes healthy behaviors, consumer welfare, profitability, economic growth, and more.

As we conduct our research, we should think of what we would want from others' research. What would help society the most would be to have research that aimed to estimate the best possible model, meaning the model that has the least possibility of biases that would invalidate the results. Also, ideally, the results would be fairly precise. We also want an objective assessment of the validity of the results, with a responsible account of how much we can trust the results.

What we do not hope to see in others' research is their attempt to attain statistical significance. That tells us nothing about causal effects or other empirical relationships we are interested in from regression analysis. Furthermore, we do not want a sales job for how the model and estimates are valid.

13.2 The incentives that could lead to unethical practices

Outside of working in for-profit corporations and in the federal and state governments, most researchers work in one of three types of establishments: academia as a professor/instructor, consulting firms, and think tanks. All three types of jobs involve incentives that could lead to unethical practices. (I have worked in all three types of jobs.)

In academia, whereas some are judged based on their teaching, most professors are judged much more on their publications, particularly their success in getting published in highly respected journals. Thus, publications are typically necessary to receive tenure (i.e., effectively a lifetime employment guarantee) and any further promotions. Publications are also what give academics more opportunities for moving to better jobs.

In the consulting world, the goal is to obtain funding from sponsors to do research. Obtaining a contract to do research for a sponsor typically requires that an individual researcher and/or the researcher's organization have a decent reputation for solid research. In addition, having pleased the client with prior projects could help as well.

For think-tankers, the objective is also to obtain funding, but the optimal source of funding they pursue is grants. Whereas contracts are for doing work specifically for the sponsor, grants are meant to do research for public welfare. Thus, in the United States, it is typically the National Institute of Health (in the U.S. Department of Health and Human Services) and philanthropic non-profit foundations that fund grants. Grants are partly given based on the proposed research, but often an important factor is the track record of the researchers and organization, which is based on having been well-published and sometimes having tantalizing research results related to the new issue being proposed for the grant. Thus, again, having a strong publication record helps someone be successful in the think-tank world.

(There is some overlap among these three types of jobs. For example, think-tankers sometimes attempt to obtain contracts, and academics sometimes get grants and contracts. In addition, many in the think-tank and consulting world hope to publish extensively to keep the door open for shifting to academia.)

One of the first lessons of introductory economics is that people respond to incentives. When there is an incentive to achieve a result, people are more likely to do that. With the incentive to publish, please the client, and find tantalizing results, it would not be surprising that researchers would sometimes artificially push their research in that direction.

The unfortunate thing in research is that there is often a gray area for what the best approach or model is. This gray area gives license to people to choose the approach that gives the best answer, whether it would please a client or make a paper more likely to be published. In addition, some researchers just believe that their research sponsors/funders wouldn't know any better if the researchers did not use the model that minimized the biases versus another model. Indeed, from my experience, sponsors and funders are often more concerned about the answer than the methods used to get that answer. Thus, these incentives sometimes lead to unethical practices. I will highlight in the next section what such practices could entail.

13.3 P-hacking and other unethical practices

This section lists and describes what I believe are the most common unethical practices. Some of this had been mentioned in earlier discussions. But I figure spelling these out as the main unethical practices could make the practices they should avoid more explicit to future researchers.

P-hacking. This is the product of making one's goal statistical significance or the most interesting result one could come up with. It involves trying to "hack" the p-value so that it comes under the typical thresholds that others see as making research worthy, which is typically 0.05 or 0.01. This would be for the purpose of attaining significance in order to make a paper more likely to be published or to be more pleasing to a sponsor. There are six main methods that people might use to p-hack:

1. Changing the model by adding or cutting control variables to get the desired result.
2. Trying new dependent variables.

3. Attempting various forms of the treatment or dependent variable. This could involve changing cut-off points that define an outcome or treatment, such as the amount of average daily wine consumption.
4. Changing the method. For example, if a probit model does not produce a significant coefficient estimate, then one might try a linear probability model to see if significance is attained.
5. Changing the sample criteria or expanding the sample.
6. Changing the comparison group.

With all of these options, a researcher has a significantly greater chance at finding significance. But all of this is antithetical to the concept that we should be attempting to produce the optimal model to answer a research question. We should not be reporting on our efforts to find statistical significance – yet, this is what many academics engage in. Similarly, and just a bit less egregious, one should not trust a model more because it gives a result more in line with your pre-conceived thoughts or what you hope to find, which is something I have been guilty of doing in the past.

Overstating the model's ability to hold factors constant. We saw in Chapter 4 that, with non-categorical variables, we can only adjust for the factors rather than fully hold the factors constant. Yet, researchers (including prior versions of myself) commonly say that they held certain factors constant. There is a huge difference between holding constant and merely adjusting for certain factors.

Failing to mention or downplaying potential PITFALLS. This is a common practice. What is often done by researchers is that either they do not recognize the PITFALLS or they hope the readers (referees at a journal, research sponsors, etc.) will not notice. Or researchers will acknowledge the possible bias to show journal referees that they are aware of the potential PITFALL, but then they would overstate a reason why the bias is unlikely to be meaningful. As mentioned in Chapter 6, biases can rarely be proven to exist. Rather, assessing the likelihood of any biases would require thinking about how factors are related to each other, how people and entities act, and how accurate the data are. Researchers often take advantage of this vagueness to downplay the PITFALLS/biases and hope no one notices. Sometimes researchers use highly-complex models that end up distracting from the fact that the greater complexity does nothing to address the inherent biases that could mar a study. This is the case with the Dynamic Retention Model (DRM), which is the U.S. Department of Defense's (DoD's) go-to model to estimate effects such as how the DoD's new military retirement system would affect reenlistment rates across the services or how much bonuses impact reenlistment rates. The DRM is so complex that it could not even be run by normal computers until about 15 years ago. The problem is that the DRM does nothing to address all the PITFALLS that have been discussed in this book.

Downplaying the imprecision. The typical practice is to focus the description of the results on the coefficient estimate on the key-X variable. But we learned back in Section 5.2 (Figure 5.2) that the coefficient estimate itself is only a central estimate, often with a low likelihood of the true coefficient (or true effect) being in a range close to that central estimate. Not discussing the imprecision of the estimated effects could mislead the readers. For example, assuming that there were no biases on the coefficient estimate, the 95% (better yet, 99%) confidence interval gives a reasonable range for likely values. If, despite the statistical significance, one endpoint of that interval is close to zero or would be a trivial effect if it were the true value, then that should be made clear so the reader can fully judge the research. Similarly, not taking into account the prior probabilities and the Bayesian critique of p-values would lead to overstating how certain the results were.

Overstating how applicable results are. As we saw in Chapter 8, many of the methods used to address potential biases end up having a result that applies to a narrow slice of the population. For example, with the "it" method of regression discontinuities, the results apply only to those very close to the discontinuity threshold. Yet, often, results are described as if they have captured the Average Treatment Effect by addressing the biases. Below, I will give an example of this practice from one of the top economic journals.

Over-reaching conclusions. In a fun study I conducted, I found that gamblers of NBA games over-compensate for the effects of team momentum, as indicated by betting point-spreads (which reflect bettor sentiment) moving in the direction of a team that has won a few games in a row or performed better than expected (Arkes, 2011). I found that the point-spreads move farther than they should have, given the information that the momentum has on performance in the next game. I then went on to claim that this has implications for other prediction markets that involve something with emotional stakes. The problem was that the study probably has zero implications for other prediction markets. This is one of several ways that studies over-reach with their conclusions. Someone could overstate the importance of the research by stating how the information could come in handy for households, businesses, or governments to make decisions. (I have been guilty of this in cases beyond the study just mentioned.) It also could involve overstating the validity of the research by ignoring/downplaying the potential biases or the narrow segment of the population to which the results would apply. The problem is that we all want to promote our research, for the glory, for the effects on our career, etc. But this leads to misinformation in the public domain, and it is unethical.

13.4 How to be ethical in your research

Because what we hope to see in others' research is the product of the optimal model they can develop and not the product of their efforts to find statistical significance, our goal in conducting research should be to develop the best model to answer a research question and to give a responsible assessment of that model. I will provide here a set of general principles to adhere to as one is conducting research and then give specific practices for different parts of the research process.

Spelling out these principles and best practices is important to foster more ethical research. A student relayed a story to me on the impact of these lessons. She had an insignificant estimate on her treatment variable in her thesis. Based on the lessons learned in her prior econometrics courses, she had the temptation to change the model to see if she could make it significant. But the simple discussion we had – that statistical significance is not the goal of research – helped her resist that temptation.

The problems from unethical practices lead to some of the reasons why the public is justified to question the usefulness of economic research. I discuss those reasons in the next chapter, some of which are closely related to what I discussed in this chapter.

13.4.1 Ethical principles

The overarching principles for conducting research are:

* The research should help promote finding the truth.
* Statistical significance is not the goal.

- Interpretations and conclusions should not over-reach what the regression tells us.
- There are human beings (or other living things) at the other end of our research, along with their livelihood and health. We have the responsibility to pursue honest and objective research.

13.4.2 Best ethical practices

For designing the methods and models:

- All decisions on the primary sample, estimation method, and model (i.e., set of control variables) should not be guided by which gives the best results; rather, the modeling decisions should be determined before conducting the regression. That should be your main regression and results.
- Take the most honest approach.
- Give arguments for why to include/exclude potential control variables.
- Be cognizant of cognitive biases, particularly confirmation bias (discussed in the next chapter). Do not change the model because it's not what you think (or hope) the result would be.
- Consider posting online the optimal research design before conducting the analyses.
- If plans change and additional models are added (or dropped), explain the rationale for doing so.
- When using regressions to predict an outcome (such as criminal recidivism) or to gauge relative performance or value-added, be cautious on whether using racial/ethnic and gender variables (or other factors that are closely tied with demographics) could lead to the judging of people differently based on these factors.

For interpreting the results, it is important to guide readers to properly synthesize the meaning and conclusions that can be drawn from a study, as follows:

- Be honest and objective over how well the model was able to hold constant vs. imperfectly adjust for certain factors.
- Fully disclose any potential PITFALLS (biases) that could not be sufficiently ruled out and do not try to convince readers otherwise. Most of the time, such biases cannot be proven to exist. What needs to be assessed is whether there is the potential for such biases, and that information would need to be discussed with honesty and forthrightness to make for a responsible research report or article.
- Discuss the prior probability that there would be a meaningful effect and discuss the Bayesian critique of p-values to properly synthesize results. Not doing so would likely overstate the likelihood that the result is legitimate.
- Make it clear what part of the population the results would apply to. If the method estimates an effect for just a narrow segment of the population, make that loud and clear.
- Don't over-reach on conclusions. Be honest about potential PITFALLS and the likelihood you were able to address them. Be honest about how widely results would apply to others.
- Do not overstate the importance of the research in how it could inform people on optimal behaviors and policy or how it would apply to other situations.

13.5 Examples of how studies could have been improved under the ethical guidelines I describe

I will not give examples of unethical practices. I have been guilty of some myself in the past before I knew better. And it is difficult to distinguish between purposeful vs. subconscious unethical practices. Instead, I will review a few articles and describe how they could have been improved in their interpretations based on the principles and best practices discussed in this chapter.

The first article is one of mine. The other article was highlighted by the American Economic Association (AEA) as one of the top contributions of 2020. For that article, part of what could have been done better was that the AEA's summary itself could have been more straightforward about the limitations of the study.

13.5.1 How unemployment rates affect the likelihood of a couple divorcing

This study (Arkes and Shen, 2014), described as an example of duration models in Section 9.7, was motivated by news stories during the 2008 Financial Crisis about how financial struggles were causing some married couples to divorce and simultaneously causing other couples to not be able to afford to divorce. The outcome of a divorce is only a possibility for couples who were married, and so what seemed most appropriate was a survival/hazard model, in which we tested how the state unemployment rate affected the hazard of ending the marriage (divorcing).

We started with the typical approach I had used in such studies examining how state unemployment rates affect various outcomes, as I described in Section 6.11. What we failed to recognize was that there is a great deal of measurement error in state unemployment rates, and controlling for the state exacerbates that bias, driving the estimates towards zero. (We should have recognized the bias from measurement error, but I'll give us a pass on how controlling for states exacerbates bias from measurement error, as neither of us was aware of this at the time.)

What occurred was that the standard approach I had used in prior studies produced an insignificant coefficient estimate on the state unemployment rate. This, of course, was unfortunate, given the effort that went into collecting and prepping the data for the analysis. There could have been off-setting positive and negative effects that caused the estimate to be insignificant. It might have been the bias towards zero from the measurement error.

Regardless, what we did next was to explore further to determine if we could find significance. We tried estimating separate effects based on what year of marriage the couple was in. We found a significant coefficient estimate on the state unemployment rate for those in years 6–10 of marriage, but not those couples in years 1–5 nor years 11-plus of marriage.

Due to the relatively weak results, we tried using the national unemployment rate instead of state unemployment rates. This produced larger coefficient estimates. Normally, national unemployment rates should not be used since trends in the outcome could be incidentally correlated with the national unemployment rate. But we figured it would not be so bad because divorce rates don't exactly move over time like drug use and other health outcomes do.

I am a bit torn on this. In some sense, it is okay to do exploratory analyses. But I believe that we had the responsibility to describe how we decided to try the various models, and we did not do so. We should have described why we examined national rates, which was that we found weak results with state unemployment rates.

Another way in which we could have been more responsible was by discussing the Bayesian critique of p-values. The prior probability that there could be an effect of the unemployment rate on the probability of divorce is not high, particularly because the effect could have gone either way. Thus, the significance of several coefficient estimates at the 5% (and not 1%) level for the couples in years 6–10 of marriage is weak evidence at best, especially given that there was no significant coefficient estimate for the other years-of-marriage groups.

13.5.2 Does attendance at a selective high school improve student outcomes?

Barrow et al. (2020) examine whether students attending one of 10 selective high schools in Chicago, particularly through a neighborhood-based-affirmative-action policy, benefits participating students. A conventional model to address this issue would be subject to omitted-factors bias and self-selection bias, as it certainly would not be random as to who would attend selective high schools.

To address these potential biases, the authors use a regression-discontinuity model. The discontinuity occurs at the cut-off point for the admittance test score. They found that students from low-SES neighborhoods attending the selective high school (compared to attending their local public high school):

- feel safer at school (weak evidence)
- have lower GPA (strong evidence)
- have a lower likelihood of enrolling in a selective college (squishy evidence).

There was no evidence that attending a selective high school increased standardized test scores.

Let's consider what could have been done a little better, in light of the guidance on ethics that I have described. First, in the abstract, the authors state: "[W]e find that these schools do not raise test scores overall." This would be an interesting result if true, but it is not technically correct. The relevant coefficient estimates were statistically insignificant. The proper interpretation should have been that they found no evidence that these schools raise scores. So, this was an over-reaching conclusion.

What would also be important for responsible conclusions would be to make it loud and clear in the abstract that the results apply to a select population: just those with an admittance-test score close to the cut-off. (That is the interpretation for regression-discontinuity models, as described in Section 8.7.) The results could be much different for those farther above and possibly those below the cut-off score. Furthermore, in the research summary given by the American Economic Association, the same caveat should have been given.

The study should also have considered the Bayesian critique of p-values. Perhaps the most important result, that those attending the selective high school have a lower chance of attending a selective college, has a p-value of about 0.016 (my calculation). Based on my own subjective probability, this is likely a toss-up (about a 50% chance of there being an effect). This would mean that the probability that the result is correct is only about 86%, which is by no means considered strong evidence, as portrayed by the article.

In the AEA description of the study, there are also apparently over-reaching conclusions, with my paraphrasing but keeping the gist of the statement: the results show that the elite schools do not improve students' academic outcomes relative to what they would have had in their neighborhood schools (Smith, 2020). The study had weak evidence to support this conclusion. My guess is that, with better data, they would find that the opposite were true, at least for some students. Furthermore, the study would probably be more valuable after a few more years of data, when they can examine whether these students graduated from college, provided that they continue to follow these students.

I consider this to be a valid and innovative study. But conclusions could have been a bit more accurate. I don't blame the authors, as I had made similar mistakes in the past (before I knew better). Yet, this top economics journal should have known better. This is the product of the conventional method of teaching econometrics, and it highlights how emphasis should be shifted from high-level math to being able to more accurately interpret regression results, along with the ethics of regression analysis.

13.6 Summary

The world of research should not act like the sales industry. Researchers should be guided by finding the truth. Unfortunately, it is inevitable that researchers want to promote themselves to help their careers, as I did. To the extent that researchers act like salespersons, the whole industry of research loses credibility, as the resulting incentives can lead to unethical research practices.

What would happen if everyone conducting research engaged in the unethical practices I highlighted? There would be no value at all to research. Immanuel Kant argued that we are morally obliged to individually act in a way that we need everyone to act.

Ideally, researchers would adhere to the basic principle of attempting to find the truth rather than be guided by finding statistical significance. And, hopefully, researchers would objectively assess their research and fully disclose their study's limitations in validity, precision, and applicability.

References

Arkes, J. (2011). Do gamblers correctly price momentum in NBA betting markets? (July 15, 2011). *Journal of Prediction Markets, 5*(1), 31–50. Available at SSRN: https://ssrn.com/abstract=1886655.

Arkes, J., & Shen, Y. C. (2014). For better or for worse, but how about a recession? *Contemporary Economic Policy, 32*(2), 275–287.

Barrow, L., Sartain, L., & de la Torre, M. (2020). Increasing access to selective high schools through place-based affirmative action: Unintended consequences. *American Economic Journal: Applied Economics, 12*(4), 135–163.

Smith, T. (2020). Elite education and affirmative action: Do selective high schools help students with disadvantaged backgrounds get into better colleges? American Economic Association. https://www.aeaweb.org/research/affirmative-action-unintended-consequences-chicago?T=AU.

14 Summarizing thoughts

You had me at "holding other factors constant."

                – Anonymous

14.1 Be aware of your cognitive biases

I've got plenty of common sense … I just choose to ignore it.

          – Calvin (from Calvin and Hobbes)

DOI: 10.4324/9781003285007-14

All researchers and their readers are subject to cognitive biases, probably more so than other members of the animal kingdom. Sometimes, a cognitive bias is the result of hubris, but often it is an innocent subconscious thought process. Regardless, it could cause misguided research strategies, improper interpretations of research, and unjustified acceptance/rejection of others' research. Being conscious of your cognitive biases could help your research.

One important cognitive bias is **confirmation bias**, which is a situation in which people have prior beliefs on some issue, and they reject any new information that is contrary to their beliefs or what they want to hear, and they accept/absorb any new information that is consistent with their beliefs. Confirmation bias can cause great harm, as that was an ingredient in some people's assessment of the COVID-19 vaccine. Despite overwhelming evidence on how the vaccine massively reduced the chance of severe illness from COVID and death, many were distrustful of the vaccines due to disregarding this scientific-based evidence and instead absorbing non-scientific stories (mostly from dubious sources) that the vaccines were non-beneficial and even dangerous.

Evidence of how prevalent confirmation bias is in society comes from the correlation of viewpoints on some political issues. I imagine that there is a strong correlation of viewpoints between: (1) whether humans are contributing to global warming; (2) whether gay marriage should be allowed and recognized; (3) whether tax rates should be lower; (4) whether there should be more stringent guns laws; (5) whether the U.S. should have invaded Iraq; and (6) whether marijuana should be legalized. Yet, these are independent issues that, I believe, should have no common factor other than how consistent a given viewpoint is with a political party's platform. Thus, followers of one political party will want to listen to what their party leaders have to say, form their initial opinions, and then discount any opposing evidence or arguments.

I mention confirmation bias because it could have a huge impact on research. A researcher may estimate a model and obtain some result that is contrary to what he believes to be the case. He may then change the model (for the worse) until he obtains a statistical relationship that is more in line with what he believes or what he wants to be the case. The model would be designed based on the pursuit of a result, not based on what would be the ideal design.

A peer reviewer subject to confirmation bias could recommend that a paper does not get published if the paper has findings that are contrary to his/her prior belief on the topic. Likewise, a peer reviewer may be too quick to accept research with questionable methods if it produces a result consistent with his/her prior views. Avoiding confirmation bias is important when reading and properly assessing research.

Learning the proper methods, PITFALLS, and interpretations of regression analysis should reduce the leeway researchers have to be subject to confirmation bias and to "regression fish" for good results. And it should reduce the leeway that consumers of research have in letting their cognitive bias get in their way of gaining knowledge.

How else would you avoid confirmation bias? A simple lesson may come from the famous British philosopher and intellectual, Bertrand Russell. A *New York Post* writer, Leonard Lyons, discussed Russell in a 1964 story.[1] Lyons recounted how he had once asked Russell whether he would die for his beliefs. Russell replied that he would not given that he might be wrong. The lesson is that the key to avoiding confirmation bias is to know that you *may* be wrong on a long-standing belief you have.

So one of the most important things to do when conducting or reading research is to have an open mind. You can have strong pre-conceived notions of the answer to the research question. But you will give a more thorough and objective assessment of the research if you at least entertain the notion that the issue is not settled and your pre-conceived notion, even if it is based on prior research, may be wrong. This strategy could help to offset any confirmation bias you may have on the topic.

Another important bias that is quite prevalent in many quantitative research studies is the **Dunning-Kruger effect**. This bias is that, when people gain just a small amount of information on a topic, they believe they are much greater experts than they actually are – they are ignorant of their ignorance. The more they learn on the topic, the more they realize how little they actually understand the topic.

Researchers are highly subject to this, as they believe that if they can estimate a regression model with data on the topic, they can understand the topic well, particularly if they found a statistically-significant coefficient estimate.

As I describe in Arkes (2022), the Dunning-Kruger effect was likely at play with the initial basketball-hot-hand researchers and the Nobel laureates writing about the hot hand. They believed they could understand whether there could be a hot-hand effect because they had data and could estimate a regression or conduct some other statistical test. But, beyond their errors in logic and modeling, they did not understand that the hot hand is much more intricate than simply whether a player makes a prior shot. In addition, what they found in experimental settings has hardly any bearing on what would happen in the heat of a game.

I believe the Dunning-Kruger effect applies to econometrics or regression analysis, in general. Merely knowing how to estimate a regression seems to give people a false sense of how well they understand regression analysis. But, as I attempt to convey in this book, there is so much more to understand on the PITFALLS and proper interpretations than most practitioners are aware of. That is a large part on why I wrote this book.

Besides confirmation bias and the Dunning-Krueger effect, there are a few other cognitive biases that you should be aware of to avoid succumbing to them. Here are a few.

- **Anchor-point bias.** This is closely tied to confirmation bias. It occurs when someone observes an initial estimate on a statistical relationship (e.g., increasing the minimum wage by 10% reduces employment by 2%) and discounts any study that finds anything far off from 2%. The 2% estimate was their "anchor."
- **Exception fallacy.** This is a case in which a person discounts a research finding because he/she knows an exception to the finding. For example, there may be a study that demonstrates a positive association between marijuana use and depression. Someone may respond that he has a friend who smokes pounds of marijuana and is the happiest person he knows, and so the finding can't be true. Other than in the hard sciences, there are few deterministic relationships in the world. Just because marijuana use and depression may be positively related does not mean that everyone who uses marijuana is depressed and everyone who doesn't use marijuana is not depressed. Remember, regressions indicate how two variables move together, on average. They typically do not indicate a singular effect/association that fits everyone.
- **Ecological fallacy.** This is almost a reverse of "exception fallacy." It occurs when someone takes a general research finding and makes conclusions about an individual. Using the example above, based on the positive association between marijuana use and depression, assuming someone who is depressed is using marijuana (or *vice versa*) would be committing the ecological fallacy.

14.2 What betrays trust in published studies

Most published studies, I believe, are based on objective, well-intentioned analyses. However, strong incentives researchers face could affect the quality of some of the studies that become disseminated. Furthermore, the peer-review process is not as strong as one might think.

I discuss these issues to make you aware of further incentives (for researchers and reviewers) that could affect the quality of research. And this highlights that a research article should not be trusted just because it is published in a respectable journal.

14.2.1 Funded research and incentives for researchers

I discussed in the prior chapter the various incentives that researchers have and how that could influence research. Perhaps the worst offender among those incentives is when someone is doing research for an organization that would profit from a particular finding. This issue makes me think of a movie I once saw on a criminal trial (but I can't think of the name of the movie). I probably have some details wrong, but I believe someone was on trial for murder, and the prosecution brought in a psychologist as an expert witness. Here is my recollection of the defense lawyer questioning the psychologist:

Psychologist: "The defendant is mentally fit, and was not insane when he committed this crime."
Defense lawyer: "How many trials have you been an expert witness for?"
Psychologist: "About 160."
Defense lawyer: "How many of those 160 cases have you found the defendant to not be mentally fit?"
Psychologist: (sheepishly) "None."

The problem, as you have probably figured out, is that the psychologist is being paid by the prosecutor to give certain testimony. The psychologist had been a reliable witness for the prosecutor, always giving the answer consistent with their story, and so the psychologist kept getting hired for his expert testimony. The same holds for any type of expert witness in a criminal or civil trial.

There is a similar problem with funded research. If researchers are being paid by oil companies to investigate whether humans' use of fossil fuels is contributing to global warming, it is unlikely that the researcher will produce and disseminate any research finding that human activity is actually contributing to global warming. Three reasons for this are:

- The sponsors would likely search for researchers who have shown sympathy to their argument that humans are not causing global warming
- The sponsors would not release a study contrary to their viewpoint
- The researcher would have the incentive to find that humans are not contributing to global warming if they hope to get funded by these sponsors again.

Anyone reading research should be aware of the incentives researchers (and their sponsors) have. Academic journals typically require authors to disclose who funded the research, and that is typically reported in the article. But, when research is cited or is discussed on the news, there is rarely a mention of who the funder of the research was. Yet, this is critical information.

Trust research more if it isn't funded by organizations with vested interests, such as the oil industry and pharmaceutical companies – not to say that ALL research funded by these types of organizations is biased.

Similar problems occur when research is conducted for government agencies, particularly the military. Sponsors of the research might be hoping for a particular result or at least some significant results. If a researcher were to present inconclusive results (due to insignificance or potential biases that could not be addressed), then the sponsor might not be happy with the researchers and might not turn to them next time. Thus, there is an incentive for researchers to come up with something conclusive, which may not be from the model design that minimizes any potential biases.

Yet, beyond such studies funded generously by those with vested interests or expectations for something conclusive, researchers have the incentive to find interesting, tantalizing, and statistically-significant results, as described in the prior chapter.

14.2.2 Publication bias

In a 2010 article in *The Atlantic*, David Freedman (2010) had his readers imagine a scenario in which five research teams conducted analyses to test a medical theory. In his scenario, four of the research teams conduct the research responsibly and correctly find no evidence to support the theory. The fifth team isn't so careful and due to mistakes, luck, and changing the sample until they find a good result, they end up finding evidence for this theory. Freedman then asked us to guess which of the five studies our doctor is more likely to read about and that we are more likely to see in the news.

It is natural that people tend to find statistically-significant estimates more interesting than insignificant estimates. So, as journals compete for readers, they tend to be hesitant to publish a finding of "no evidence of an effect" as readers would be less interested in it and would be less likely to build further research off of such a finding. That would mean fewer citations and a lower ranking for the journal.

What I have described here is called **publication bias**, which is the tendency for journals to publish results that have significant results. The bias would be in the direction of larger and significant effects, as the smaller, insignificant results are less likely to be published. In Freedman's example above, if just the first study was published and no journal would accept the other four studies, then 100% of the studies (1 of 1 study) on this topic find the theory to be true. But the reality is that only 20% (1 of 5 studies) found evidence supporting the theory to be true.

The bias doesn't stop at the journal, as it has secondary effects on some researchers, who strategize their behavior given the biases by journals. I can think of two reactions, one of which is understandable and the other one not okay. Both contribute to publication bias. The first reaction – the understandable one – is that, if they do research and find a non-interesting result, researchers may choose to shift their focus away from that research and towards some topic that has better prospects (for journal quality and the probability of getting published). So these presumably valid results would never be known to the research community.

The less understandable reaction is p-hacking (described in the prior chapter), when researchers change the model until the results are statistically significant. This leads to misinformation for the public and is antithetical to the ideal general objective of research. We rather see the best model than someone's attempt to achieve statistical significance. It is possible that p-hacking is due to the authors having a certain belief about what an effect could be, and so they change the model until they get the effect they think it should be. But it could also be that the authors are just trying to get results that could be published. The result of p-hacking would be a disproportionately large share of p-values just below key significance values (particularly, 0.05) and a smaller-than-expected share of p-values just over the key significance values. Some evidence for p-hacking can be seen in Head et al. (2015), which demonstrates the distribution of p-values to have a disproportionate concentration of values just below the key significance level of 0.05. That said, the study also finds no evidence that p-hacking is a widespread-enough phenomenon that it would meaningfully affect any general consensus on research findings. But the lack of evidence does not prove it does not exist, and I have clearly seen it in my career.

Some academic journals are realizing the problems such practices cause and are reported to be more receptive to "no effect" findings. For example, the well-regarded *American Journal of Public Health* has a stated policy that "Studies with negative results, or those challenging previously published work or widely held beliefs, receive equal consideration." There are even new journals in a few fields that focus on publishing "negative results," called *All Results Journals*.

Along the same lines as publication bias, among the 80-plus job-market candidates (coming out of graduate school) I have seen over the years at my organizations, I cannot remember one who had insignificant primary results. The problem is that dissertations are tomes that typically involve developing a theory and testing it empirically. If there were an insignificant result, some people assessing the candidate may take it as a signal that the candidate developed a theory that is not supported by data. Thus, there is an incentive for the job-market candidates to produce a dissertation with significant estimates. As with publication bias, this could collectively be the product of some candidates finagling the model until something significant comes up, or it may be due to candidates switching topics if they do not find anything significant.

Personally, I would really appreciate a candidate who had insignificant results because it would be a good signal that they didn't keep playing with the model to find something significant. One of the candidates I was impressed by had a nice significant result but said that she tried everything she could to "kill the effect" (i.e., make it insignificant) and was unable to do so.

Hopefully, readers will be mindful of publication bias (and these incentives) and use the PITFALLS in Chapter 6 to guide them to develop the best possible model, regardless of the result.

14.2.3 *The not-so-great scientific-review process*

The scientific/peer-review process is what determines which studies receive funding and which studies get published. Researchers choose a journal to submit a paper to. An editor of the journal then decides whether the journal would be interested in the research, and if so, sends the paper to a few referees for a peer review. These referees are typically not known to the researcher, and often, the author is not officially known to the referees, although they might have seen the paper online or presented at a conference. The referees critique the study and make recommendations to the journal's editor on whether to reject the paper, offer the authors the opportunity to revise and resubmit the paper or accept the article for publication. Regardless of the editor's decision, the authors typically receive a set of comments by the referees.

Most researchers would agree that the peer-review process is highly random, and many consider it extremely flawed. From my personal experience, I will share a few stories. There is one journal to which I have sent four different articles for publication. The only one they accepted was the least informative and least innovative of the four. In another case, a colleague of mine tells a story of how she and co-authors submitted an article to a high-quality journal, got rejected, subsequently submitted the paper to six other lower-quality journals, and continued getting rejected. They then submitted it again to the original high-quality journal (forgetting they had already done so), and it got accepted for publication!

These are two of numerous anecdotes that researchers can tell. More formal tests of the peer-review process, as discussed in Section 1.3, demonstrate the random nature of the process. There are also conflicts of interest for referees, who are often people who have researched the issue before. Thus, if the results are contrary to what the referees had found, they may be (perhaps subconsciously) more critical of the paper.

I likely experienced this with my basketball-hot-hand research. In Arkes (2010), my evidence for a hot hand in basketball was contrary to the existing literature that claimed that the hot hand in basketball does not exist. In the first journal to which I sent my article, the referee recommended rejecting the paper because my results had to be wrong because it had been "proven" that the hot hand does not exist. This may have been one of the prior authors. Regardless, it was "confirmation bias" in that the referee discounted my research, not based on the methods, but based on the fact that the findings were different from past research.

Referees of papers in which they are cited may have the incentive to get the paper published, as it would provide a citation for their own research, which boosts their count on "Google Scholar Citations Index" or other such citation counts. And referees are not always well-conversed in the PITFALLS of regression analysis.

The bottom line is that the media and other consumers of research should not rely on the peer-review process and where the article is published to determine the quality of a research study. Judge articles on your own. Plenty of invalid studies are in top journals.

14.2.4 The wide range of results on the same topic

Neumark and Shirley (2021) assess 69 studies on the effects of minimum-wage increases on employment. They find that the results of the studies lean towards negative effects, but there are many studies with positive effects of minimum-wage increases on employment. Neumark and Shirley do not assess the validity of the studies. Economists have taken the various studies and have given testimony to congress about what the effects of raising the existing minimum wage (perhaps to $15) would do to employment. In testimony a few years ago, one economist argued that the preponderance of evidence says a minimum-wage increase would lead to a large decrease in employment, while another economist at the same hearing argued that the studies with the most valid research designs indicate that there would be minimal employment loss from a minimum-wage increase. Which do we believe?

The important point is this: if the effects of minimum-wage increases could be tested rigorously, we should have a consistent answer coming from these studies. But we don't. There are many reasons for the wide range of estimated effects, with the main ones being:

- Various PITFALLS are biasing the estimated effects to different degrees. (These may come from omitted-factors bias or self-selection bias.)
- The effect depends on the circumstance.

Regarding the second bullet, the effects of a minimum-wage increase would depend on the current economic conditions in a given location, the size of the increase, and where the new minimum wage sits relative to the market low-skill wage. To the best of my knowledge, San Francisco and Seattle had a minimal-to-no decrease in employment resulting from their gradual increase in the minimum wage to above $15/hour, likely due to strong economies and already high existing wages. However, if other cities or states (or the federal government) were to implement a $15/hour minimum-wage there would likely be large employment losses.

This is just one of many topics in which statistical studies find quite different results on the same topic. There have been problems replicating economic studies with randomized control trials, although the replication problem in economics is not nearly as bad as it is in psychology (Bohannon,

2016). These naturally make a person wonder why they should trust one study over another. And so what often happens is that people take the studies (and testimony) that best suit their political beliefs. This is what happened with studies and guidance on wearing a mask and social-distancing policies during the COVID pandemic.

14.2.5 Unrecognized biases

This is perhaps an issue that causes distrust more so for those well-versed in regression analysis and the inherent problems. I'm still shocked that Nobel prize winners in economics did not recognize the inherent bias from measurement error in the basketball-hot-hand studies. Heck, I'm shocked that I didn't recognize the bias either (despite arriving at the correct conclusion on the hot hand). I've discussed a few cases of some of my own studies being subject to biases that I did not recognize. It is a widespread occurrence of researchers not recognizing biases. Furthermore, PITFALL #7 in Chapter 6, on over-weighting of some groups, is a new major source of bias that was just recently recognized after over half a century of researchers having no clue on the matter ... and I have yet to see it addressed in anyone's research. All of this makes *me* not trust much economic research. (This is why I wrote this song on regression analysis.)

14.3 How to do a referee report responsibly

The average article in the top economic journals is three times lengthier than it was in the 1970s (Card and DellaVigna, 2013). Are these articles anywhere close to three times as informative? Heck no! And they are about 5.2 times more painful to read ... on average.

The likely cause of the increase in article length is greater demands for revisions by referees. Yes, the refereeing process has run amok! Referees demand many checks on the results to make sure they stand up to different specifications. While such checks can be useful at times, they need to be applied more judiciously.

In a recent article in *Journal of Economic Perspectives*, Berk, Harvey, and Hirshleifer (2017) give several much-needed recommendations on how to conduct a responsible referee report, which should help towards improving the scientific-review process. These recommendations include the following:

- Decline performing the review if you have conflicts of interest.
- Weigh the importance/relevance/contribution of the research along with how sound it is. That is, be prudently more forgiving of flaws for more important research, as hardly any research is perfect. (Of course, make sure that the authors acknowledge those flaws.)
- Be clear on what comments are necessary for the author to address and what comments are just suggestions for improving the paper.
- The comments that you deem to be necessary to be addressed need to be scientifically justified.
- Be properly skeptical of evidence for an effect that has low prior probabilities, particularly if the p-value is not sufficiently small. Consider the informal Bayesian approach (Section 5.5).
- Be courteous and impartial.
- Generally, use the criterion of whether you would have been proud to have written the paper.

14.4 Summary of the most important points and interpretations

The effects of all of the problems mentioned so far in this chapter (cognitive biases, incentives for researchers, publication bias, and the poor refereeing process) could be largely mitigated if the research community and consumers of research had a better understanding of regression analysis and the right questions to ask when assessing research. The better scrutiny would, hopefully, force researchers to put forth more solid research. This section summarizes the main lessons to assess research, whether it's your own or someone else's research. In addition, it provides key interpretations that are often misunderstood.

14.4.1 The various objectives of regression analysis

Regression analysis is mostly used to estimate the causal effects of some factor(s) on an outcome, but there are other uses of regressions. Regressions can forecast or make a prediction for an outcome. They can determine the strongest predictors of some outcome. And regressions can be used to adjust outcomes to eliminate the influences of factors unrelated to the performance so that the outcomes can be compared across subjects – e.g., how strong an instructor's evaluations are, adjusting for the difficulty of the class taught and the class size. Keep in mind that the strategies for properly estimating regression analyses differ based on the objective.

14.4.2 Everyone (or every subject) has their own effect

With most economic and social phenomena, there is not a universal effect. Rather, everyone or every entity (such as a state, a country, or a state/country in a given time period) would react differently to certain treatments. A coefficient estimate (or its associated marginal effect for certain models) represents how two variables move together, on average, in the sample. If the model is free from biases, then the model validly tests for the *average effect*. There may be some subjects (such as individuals or states) that are affected more by the treatment than others; and there may be some that are not affected at all. Also, what appears to be a small effect may be a rather large effect for some combined with a zero effect for others. For example, parental divorce may harm 30% of children experiencing one, while the rest of the children may be unaffected by parental divorce. There could even be some who are positively affected and others who are negatively affected by a treatment (such as a divorce). Combining them, the average effect may be negligible. In this case, the conclusion that a divorce does not affect children would be incorrect.

14.4.3 The limitations of "holding other factors constant"

One of the most beautiful aspects of regressions is that one can design a model to adjust for certain factors that might confound a cause-effect relationship. However, this can only be cleanly executed (so that you "hold the factor constant") when the confounding factor can be fully characterized by a set of dummy variables. In other cases, the best one can do is imperfectly adjust for the factor. When the treatment is a conscious choice, it is a rare circumstance that using control variables addresses any omitted-factors bias or self-selection bias. Controlling for variables is more effective at addressing potential biases if the treatment is outside the control of the subject and it is merely incidental correlation that is being adjusted for.

14.4.4 Assessing research for biased estimates

Research can be, in some ways, open to interpretation and at times ambiguous. Researchers may find a given empirical result that is "consistent with a given theory," and from that, they may conclude that the theory is true. But there may be stories that can give alternative explanations to the empirical result. These sprout from the limitations of a model in controlling for certain factors.

Remember that a regression just indicates how two variables move together, after adjusting for other factors. Any conclusion of causality (if that is the objective) must rely on how well the researchers were able to rule out any alternative explanations for the variables moving (or not moving) together. This typically comes down to whether the PITFALLS are addressed. These PITFALLS, applying to the objective of estimating causal effects, are:

1. Reverse causality
2. Omitted-factors bias
3. Self-selection bias
4. Measurement error
5. Using mediating factors or outcomes as control variables
6. Improper reference groups
7. Over-weighted groups (when using fixed effects or dummy variables)

These are the PITFALLS that need to be considered regardless of whether the results indicate a real empirical relationship between two variables or no evidence for such a relationship. If there are alternative stories and the researchers did not take measures to correct for the PITFALLS, then any conclusion on the existence or magnitude of the causal effect has to be questioned. At the same time, the severity of the PITFALLS needs to be considered.

14.4.5 Fancy methods to address PITFALLS often create new problems or have a limited ability to apply to new situations

In some cases, the advanced methods can be effective in addressing the PITFALLS. However, in many situations, they exacerbate existing problems. The most-glaring example, which I did not learn until late in my career, was that the methods of fixed effects, first-difference, and difference-in-difference all can exacerbate any bias from measurement error. Furthermore, any self-selection bias typically remains a problem with these methods, meaning that, if the treatment involved a conscious choice or was the result of personal actions, the results would apply only to those subjects/entities that chose to receive the treatment (or implement a policy). In addition, a few fancy methods (instrumental variables and regression discontinuity) have narrow segments of the population that any estimated effects would apply to, making them potentially useless.

14.4.6 P-values are not what they seem to be

The p-value is the primary measure that most researchers use to gauge how strong the evidence is for the empirical relationship they are testing. However, the p-value, by itself, has little meaning. It needs to be combined with the before-the-fact likelihood that there would be a relationship. Results that are more surprising (i.e., against the nature of how we understand how factors are related) would need greater levels of significance (lower p-values) to be considered strong evidence. Truly assessing a result should also take into account other considerations, such as the economic significance of the magnitude of the range of values in a confidence interval and how likely it is that any PITFALLS could be ruled out.

14.4.7 Statistical significance is not our goal

Our goal is to advance knowledge. Our goal is *not* to find a statistically-significant coefficient estimate. Our goal is *not* to come up with some amazing result that will wow people. Well, that would be nice, but it should come within the parameters of honest and objective research.

14.4.8 What does an insignificant estimate mean?

An "insignificant coefficient estimate" could be the result of:

1. There actually being no effect of the explanatory variable on the outcome;
2. A modeling problem causing a bias;
3. Inadequate power to detect an effect; and
4. Varying and counteracting effects in the population.

Thus, whereas an insignificant estimate is often referred to as evidence of "no effect" or "no relationship" between the variables, the proper interpretation of an insignificant estimate is that "there is no evidence of a significant relationship." If, on the other hand, the confidence interval (95% or greater) is narrow and near zero on both ends, then you could conclude that there is not any meaningful relationship between the variables. Remember, there is no evidence that there is other intelligent life in the universe … nor is there evidence that we are alone!

14.5 Final words of wisdom (and one final Yogi quote)

For those who have read this far (rather than waiting for the motion picture to come out), let me end with a few thoughts and one last Yogi quote.

One of my greatest revelations in life came to me in 2015: that officials in the Department of Defense (DoD), for which I did much of my career work, tend to put more faith in research and models that are more complicated and that they understand the least. These DoD officials are not the only ones who do so. But, based on my experience, the simpler and more direct models tend to be the more robust and reliable models. From Chapter 8, the better methods to address non-random explanatory variables are the simpler ones: first-differences, and fixed effects. More complex methods, such as instrumental variables, are typically less stable, highly dependent on questionable assumptions, and representative of an effect for a smaller segment of the population.

Summing up the past 362 pages, remember when you conduct and read/assess research:

- Have an open mind.
- Entertain the notion that your preconceived notions on the topic may be wrong.
- Understand that a more complex model does not mean it's producing a result that is any closer to the truth.
- Assess whether other possible explanations can be ruled out.
- Be honest about the limitations of your models.

Understanding this will keep the researchers (or yourself) honest and make them do strong, sound research. If we do this, we will have the potential to make better decisions for ourselves and for society. And maybe someday some visitor from another planet will find, on this planet, "intelligent" life, along with "intelligent" policies and practices based on high-quality research. All that said, to quote Yogi Berra one last time, "I never said most of the things I said."

Note

1   1964 June 23, *New York Post*, Section: Post Daily Magazine, The Lyons Den by Leonard Lyons, Quote Page 27 (Magazine Page 3), Column 3, New York.

References

Arkes, J. (2010). Revisiting the hot hand theory with free throw data in a multivariate framework. *Journal of Quantitative Analysis in Sports*, 6(1).

Arkes, J. (2022). *Confessions of a Recovering Economist: How Economists Get Almost Everything Wrong.* (Self-published), https://www.amazon.com/dp/B0BLG2PFHF/.

Berk, J., Harvey, C. R., & Hirshleifer, D. A. (2017). How to write an effective referee report and improve the scientific review process. *Journal of Economic Perspectives*, 31(1), 231–244.

Bohannon, J. (2016). About 40% of economics experiments fail replication survey. *Science*, 3.

Card, D., & DellaVigna, S. (2013). Nine facts about top journals in economics. *Journal of Economic Literature*, 51(1), 144–161.

Freedman, D. H. (2010). Lies, damned lies, and medical science. *The Atlantic*. November 2010 issue. (Available at www.theatlantic.com/magazine/archive/2010/11/lies-damned-lies-and-medical-science/308269/, accessed July 10, 2018).

Head, M. L., Holman, L., Lanfear, R., Kahn, A. T., & Jennions, M. D. (2015). The extent and consequences of p-hacking in science. *PLoS Biology*, 13(3), e1002106.

Neumark, D., & Shirley, P. (2021). *Myth or measurement: What does the new minimum wage research say about minimum wages and job loss in the United States?* (No. w28388). National Bureau of Economic Research.

Appendix of background statistical tools

This chapter reviews some statistical tools that will serve as building blocks to the concepts covered in this book. There will not be any Calculus (other than in two endnotes); the Calculus just isn't necessary for understanding regression analysis (despite what others say).

Before beginning, we need to understand these two terms:

- A parameter is a number that describes a population, such as a mean.
- A statistic is a number describing a sample from the population.

We calculate statistics from samples to estimate what the population parameters are.

A.1 Random variables and probability distributions

Random variables are variables that quantify the product of a random process. This could be something from a known probability distribution, such as rolling a die. Or it could be something that has a prior unknown probability distribution, such as the annual number of Nicolas Cage movies.

Random variables typically are represented by a capital letter, with Y being a common variable name for an outcome and X being a common variable name for a factor that predicts the outcome.

Just because we call them random variables does not mean that the variables are completely random. Obviously, certain events can contribute to more Nicolas Cage movies in some years and less in others.

There are two types of random variables:

- **Discrete random variables** have a set number of possible values, such as rolling a die, which has only six possible values.
- **Continuous random variables** have an infinite number of possible values. This would include any variable measuring time, weight, height, volume, etc. Also, some variables that are discrete but have many possible outcomes are often approximated as continuous.

Continuous random variables will be more relevant to regression analysis, but understanding discrete random variables helps towards understanding the theory behind continuous random variables.

Discrete random variables have probability distributions, as depicted in Figure A.1 on rolling a 6-sided die. The value of the random variable, we'll call X, takes on the value of the die roll. Each possible value has a probability of 1/6, or 0.167.

Note that the sum of the probabilities equals one. With the probability distribution, we can calculate the probability of various events occurring. For example, $\Pr(X \geq 5) = \Pr(X = 5) + \Pr(X = 6) = 1/6 + 1/6 = 1/3$.

As you can imagine, the probability distribution is more complicated for a continuous random variable, as there is an infinite number of possible values. Thus, what is used is a **probability density function** (PDF). Let's consider the easiest PDF possible in the top chart in Figure A.2: a uniform distribution between 0 and 5, with a height of 0.2. Note that, analogous to the probability distribution for the die roll above, the area under the density function equals 1.0 (5×0.2).

The probability of a range of values for the random variable will now be the area under the probability density function between the two values. For example, $\Pr(1 < X < 3) = 2 \times 0.2 = 0.4$. This is the base times the height of the area between 1 and 3. What this also means is that the probability of any one value is equal to 0. This is true for all continuous distributions.

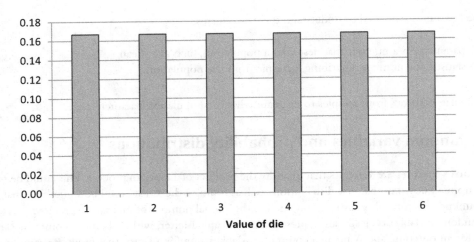

Figure A.1 Probability distribution for the value of a roll of a die

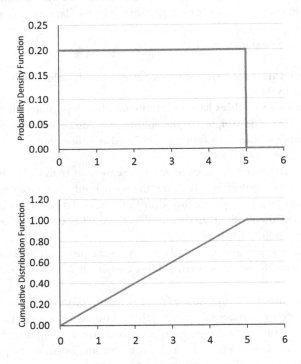

Figure A.2 Probability density function and cumulative distribution function of a (continuous) uniform distribution

Another important function is the **cumulative distribution function (CDF)**, which indicates the probability that the random variable will have a value less than or equal to a given value. The bottom chart in Figure A.2 shows the CDF corresponding to the uniform distribution in the top chart. It increases by 0.2 for each unit and reaches 1 at a value of 5, which is the right end of the uniform distribution.

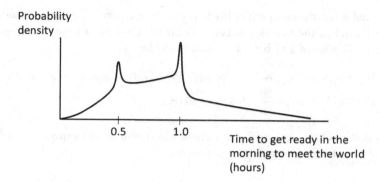

Figure A.3 A non-standard continuous distribution

The continuous distribution that is most commonly used is the normal distribution, which is the bell-shaped, symmetrical curve that many of us are familiar with. We will discuss that in the next section. Note that not all continuous distributions are smooth and symmetrical as that for the uniform or normal distribution. Imagine the distribution for how long it takes people to get ready in the morning to meet the world. My notional example is in Figure A.3. This distribution has two spikes, for those who set their alarm exactly 30 minutes and 60 minutes before they need to leave their home. Also, the distribution would be considered skewed to the right in that there are many people in the right tail of the distribution. In other words, from the mean value (maybe somewhere around 0.8 hours), the values range much farther above than below the mean.

A.1.1 Expected values and means

There are various measures of the central tendency of a variable. There is the median (the middle value), the mode (the most common value), and the mean (the average). With regression analysis, we are mostly concerned with the mean, or **expected value**, of a variable or distribution.

The expected value of a discrete random variable will be the probability-weighted average of the values. With the random variable of the value of a die roll, the expected value, $E(X)$, would be:

$$E(X) = \mu_X = \left(\frac{1}{6} \times 1\right) + \left(\frac{1}{6} \times 2\right) + \left(\frac{1}{6} \times 3\right) + \left(\frac{1}{6} \times 4\right) + \left(\frac{1}{6} \times 5\right) + \left(\frac{1}{6} \times 6\right) = 3.5 \qquad (A.1)$$

This would be the mean value, μ_X, of an infinite number of rolls of the die.

For the expected value of a continuous random variable, it is based on the same concept in that it is the average of the range of values, weighted by the probability of each small range of values. To keep my promise of avoiding Calculus, I will relegate the formal definition to this endnote.[1] For a symmetrical PDF, the expected value will be the median value. For our continuous uniform PDF in Figure A.2, there is no singular mode, but the expected value is the median, or 2.5.

Perhaps a useful application of expected value is for a bet on a roulette wheel. A roulette wheel has 38 slots:

- 18 numbers between 1 and 36 that are *red*
- 18 numbers between 1 and 36 that are *black*
- 2 numbers that are *green* (usually 0 and 00).

A typical bet would be on the color red or black. If you get it correct, you win the amount you bet. If you get it wrong, you lose the money you bet. Let's call the random variable, X, the amount that you win. So the expected value of a \$1 bet on, say red, would be:

$$E(X) = \Pr(red) \times (gain \; or \; loss \; if \; red) + \Pr(not \; red) \times (gain \; or \; loss \; if \; not \; red)$$

$$E(X) = \frac{18}{38} \times (\$1) + \frac{20}{38} \times (-\$1) = -\$0.053 \tag{A.2}$$

Thus, for every dollar bet on a color for the roulette wheel, you should expect to lose 5.3 cents, provided that you do not have any secrets to the universe.

A.1.2 Variances and standard deviations

Whereas the expected value indicates the central tendency of a random variable, the variance and standard deviation indicate how spread out the values of the random variable are. This is known as a "measure of dispersion." Recall from basic statistics that the variance of a set of observations in a sample is:

$$s^2 = \frac{\sum_{i=1}^{n} (x_i - \bar{X})^2}{n-1} \tag{A.3}$$

That is, the variance is the sum of the squared differences of the value for each observation from the mean, divided by the sample size minus one. The standard deviation of the set of values would then be the square root of the variance.

The same concept applies for random variables with a fixed probability distribution, but it is weighted by the probability of each value (or a small range of values) so that there is no need to divide by the sample size. The calculations for variance and standard deviation of the random variable of the value of the die roll are:

$$V(X) = \sigma_X^2 = \left(\frac{1}{6} \times (1-3.5)^2\right) + \left(\frac{1}{6} \times (2-3.5)^2\right) + \left(\frac{1}{6} \times (3-3.5)^2\right) + \left(\frac{1}{6} \times (4-3.5)^2\right)$$

$$+ \left(\frac{1}{6} \times (5-3.5)^2\right) + \left(\frac{1}{6} \times (6-3.5)^2\right) = 2.917 \tag{A.4}$$

And the standard deviation of $X = \sigma_X = \sqrt{\sigma_X^2} = 1.708$.

Note that the Greek letter, σ, is used when the standard deviation and variance are known, whereas "s" is used when they are calculated from a sample from an unknown distribution. Again, the formula for a continuous distribution is relegated to a footnote.[2]

A.1.3 Joint distributions of two random variables

Table A.1 shows a **joint probability distribution** of two variables: age group (random variable X) and whether the teenager uses Facebook (random variable Y). This distribution indicates the probability that certain values of the two variables occur jointly. The sum of the probabilities equals one,

Table A.1 Example of a joint probability distribution

	Does not use Facebook	Uses Facebook
	$Y = 0$	$Y = 1$
Age 15–17 ($X = 0$)	0.5	0.1
Age 18–19 ($X = 1$)	0.1	0.3

just as with a probability distribution or probability density function for a single random variable. From the joint probability distribution, we can calculate several important probabilities and statistics.

A.1.4 Unconditional (marginal probability)

This is just the probability of the value of one particular variable. For example, $\Pr(X = 0) = 0.6$ (which is the sum of all the probabilities in the "$X = 0$" row, 0.5 and 0.1).

A.1.5 Conditional probability

This is the probability of the value of one random variable, given a certain value for the other random variable. The formula is:

$$\Pr(Y = 1 \mid X = 0) = \frac{\Pr(Y = 1, X = 0)}{\Pr(X = 0)} = \frac{0.1}{0.6} = 0.1667 \tag{A.5}$$

A good way to think of conditional probability is with poker. From the cards you observe in your hand and on the table, you may be able to figure out the probability that a player has a certain card or set of cards that can beat you. But, conditional on the other player betting large, the conditional probability that they have that winning card would be higher (depending on how often that player bluffs).

A.1.6 Conditional expectation

This is the expected value of one variable, given a certain value of another variable. This normally would involve variables with a larger range of values than just the two values Y has, but the idea is the same. The formula, for a case with j different values of the Y variable:

$$E(Y \mid X = x) = \sum_{i=1}^{j} y_i \times \Pr(Y = y_i \mid X = x_i)$$
$$E(Y \mid X = 1) = (0 \times 0.25) + (1 \times 0.75) = 0.75 \tag{A.6}$$

The conditional expectation will be seen in Chapter 2, with the predicted value of the outcome (Y), given value(s) of the predicting variables (Xs). For example, from a regression, we can estimate the predicted income for someone with 11 years-of-schooling (and perhaps other predicting variables). One other important statistic is the *conditional variance*, $V(Y \mid X = x)$.

A.1.7 Covariance

This measures how two random variables tend to move with each other. The calculation for the covariance is:

$$cov(X,Y) = \sigma_{XY} = E\left[\left(X - \mu_X\right)\left(Y - \mu_Y\right)\right]$$

$$= \sum_{i=1}^{a} \sum_{j=1}^{b} \left(x_i - \mu_X\right)\left(y_i - \mu_Y\right) \Pr\left(X = x_i, Y = y_j\right) \tag{A.7}$$

where a and b are the number of values for variables X and Y.

If a covariance is positive, it means that when one variable is above its mean, the other variable tends to be above its mean. In contrast, a negative covariance indicates the opposite in that when one variable is above the mean, the other variable tends to be below the mean.

Other than the sign (positive vs. negative), the covariance has no meaning by itself, as it needs to be considered in light of how much variation there is in one of the variables. For example, if the X variable measured the weight of something, the covariance would have quite different values based on whether the weight is measured in grams, pounds, kilograms, or manatees.

When the covariance is combined with the variation in the explanatory variable, we will find out how much one variable (an outcome) tends to move with a one-unit change in the other variable (the explanatory factor).

A.1.8 Correlation

Unlike the covariance, the correlation has a bounded range of -1 to 1 by dividing the covariance by the variance of the two variables, thereby making it independent of any unit. The formula is:

$$corr(X,Y) = \frac{cov(X,Y)}{\sqrt{V(X)V(Y)}} = \frac{\sigma_{XY}}{\sigma_X \sigma_Y} \tag{A.8}$$

A positive correlation means that X and Y tend to move in the same direction, while a negative correlation indicates that X and Y tend to move in opposite directions. The sample correlation between X and Y is indicated as: $r_{X,Y}$.

A.1.9 Independence

Two variables are said to be independent if the value of one variable has no bearing on the value of another variable. This would mean that:

- $COV(X,Y) = 0$
- $corr(X,Y) = 0$
- $E(Y \mid X) = E(Y) = \mu_Y$

A.1.10 *Linear functions of random variables*

To later understand the distribution of combinations of variables, it is important to learn how the expected value and variance of transformations of random variables are calculated. Consider the case of the two random variables, X and Y:

$$Y = a + bX$$

Or, with our die example, let's say that Y depends on the die roll as follows:

$$Y = 3 + 2X$$

The mean, variance, and standard deviation of a random variable, Y, would be:

- $E(Y) = E(a + bX) = a + b \times E(X)$
- $V(Y) = V(a + bX) = b^2 \times V(X)$
- Standard-deviation $(Y) = b \times \sqrt{V(X)}$

With the die example:

- $E(Y) = \mu_Y = E(3 + 2X) = 3 + 2 \times E(X) = 3 + 2 \times 3.5 = 10$
- $V(Y) = \sigma_Y^2 = V(3 + 2X) = 2^2 V(X) = 4 \times 2.917 = 11.667$
- Standard-deviation $(Y) = \sigma_Y^2 = \sqrt{11.667} = 2 \times \sqrt{2.917} = 3.416$

Note that the constant, a, has no bearing on the variance. It merely shifts the distribution and does not affect how spread out the data are.

Other calculations that will come in handy deal with combinations of multiple random variables. The formulas are:

$$E(X + Y) = E(X) + E(Y) \tag{A.9}$$

$$V(X + Y) = V(X) + V(Y) + 2\,COV(X, Y) \tag{A.10}$$

A.2 The normal distribution and other important distributions

A.2.1 *The normal and standard normal distributions*

Perhaps the most important distribution in statistics is the normal distribution. This is the bell-shaped distribution that can describe many things in life – e.g., intelligence, motivation, height, weight, grumpiness in the morning, and more.

The normal distribution is denoted as $N(\mu, \sigma^2)$, with μ being the mean and σ^2 the variance. This distribution has several nice properties:

- It is symmetrical, so the median, mode, and mean are all in the middle of the distribution.
- 68.3% of all observations are within one standard deviation of the mean.

- 95.4% of all observations are within two standard deviations of the mean.
- 95% of all observations are within 1.96 standard deviations of the mean.

Given these features, to the extent that we can use normal distributions, our interpretations will be much easier.

Any normal distribution can easily be transformed into a **standard normal distribution**, which has a mean of zero and a standard deviation of one: N(0,1). The transformation for a value from the distribution simply involves subtracting the mean (μ) from a normal variable and dividing by the standard deviation (σ) as follows:

$$Z = \frac{X - \mu}{\sigma} \qquad (A.11)$$

The resulting value of the standard normal variable, commonly denoted as Z, has the nice property that it represents the number of standard deviations below or above the mean.

Furthermore, the standard normal distribution has a known PDF and CDF that allow one to easily calculate the probability of various values. The cumulative probability for a given value can be calculated in Excel (NORM.S.DIST function, with the Z value as the first argument and "true" as the second argument).

Let's take the simple case of IQ, which has a population mean of 100 and a standard deviation of 15. You are probably thinking that IQ is usually reported as a discrete variable, but it is often approximated as a continuous variable, given the fairly large number of possible values. The probability calculations require a transformation of the random variable to the standard normal (Z) distribution by subtracting the mean and dividing by the standard deviation.

The probability that a random person has an IQ above 115 is:

$$Pr(IQ > 115) = Pr\left(\frac{IQ - \mu}{\sigma} > \frac{115 - 100}{15}\right) = Pr(Z > 1) = 1 - Pr(Z < 1) = 1 - 0.8413$$
$$= 0.1587 \qquad (A.12)$$

Note that on both sides of the inequality, I subtracted the mean and divided by the standard deviation – the symbols (μ and σ) on the left side to transform the random variable to Z, and the actual population parameters (100 and 15) on the right side to determine the Z value we are using in the calculation. Furthermore, the probability usually given is from the CDF for the Z distribution. That is why I transformed [$Pr(Z > 1)$] to [$1 - Pr(Z < 1)$].

The probability that the IQ of a random person is less than 105 is:

$$Pr(IQ < 105) = Pr\left(\frac{IQ - \mu}{\sigma} < \frac{105 - 100}{15}\right) = Pr(Z < 0.3333) = 0.6305 \qquad (A.13)$$

The probability that the IQ of a random person is between 97 and 106 is:

$$Pr(97 < IQ < 106) = Pr(-0.2 < Z < 0.4) = Pr(Z < 0.4) - Pr(Z < -0.2)$$
$$= 0.6554 - 0.4207 = 0.2347 \qquad (A.14)$$

While most calculations for hypothesis testing and similar statistical applications will rely on the Student's t-distribution (briefly described next), the same concepts as those in the standard normal distribution will apply.

A.2.2 The Student's t-Distribution

The **Student's *t*-distribution** is a normal distribution that is used for hypothesis tests and confidence intervals of coefficient estimates in regression analysis. In regression analysis (and other types of hypothesis tests using distribution statistics based on samples), the standard deviation of the population parameter is unknown, which creates another source of uncertainty. Thus, the distribution will be wider than the standard normal distribution, which is associated with a known population variance and standard deviation. With a wider distribution than a standard normal distribution, hypothesis tests and confidence intervals (which you'll learn about in Chapter 5) will be more conservative. The Student's *t*-distribution approaches the standard normal distribution as the sample size increases, and with a sample of around 100 or more, the Student's *t*-distribution is pretty close to the standard normal distribution.

A.2.3 The chi-squared distribution

The chi-squared distribution with k degrees of freedom, $\chi(k)$, represents the distribution for the sum of k standard normal variables that are independent of each other. This distribution will be used for tests for heteroskedasticity (Section 5.4.2).

A.2.4 The F-distribution

The *F*-distribution is based on the ratio of two chi-squared distributions. This means that two separate degrees of freedom are needed. The most common uses of the *F*-distribution are to test whether all or some of the coefficient estimates in a regression are jointly statistically significant in a hypothesis test, which comes from Chapter 5.

A.3 Sampling distributions

When there is polling for, say, an upcoming presidential election, one random sample from the population would likely be different from another random sample from the population. If a sample is drawn randomly from the population, then the values of variables from those observations in the sample would be a random variable. It follows that the sample statistics resulting from the random draw from the population, particularly the sample mean, are themselves random variables. And these random variables often have features that, again, make life easier for us.

From our samples, we are using statistics to make inferences on parameters for the population. When doing so, we want to know how confident we can be about the value of the population parameter or the likely range of values that the population parameter falls in. The larger is our sample, the closer the statistics will be to the population parameters.

The key sampling distribution is that for the sample mean. If we were to roll 3 dice (or roll the single die 3 times), giving you values (x_1, x_2, x_3), we would get a certain sample average, $\bar{X}$. The next sample of 3 dice will likely give you a different $\bar{X}$. Those $\bar{X}$'s, if calculated an infinite number of times, would have a certain probability distribution. As long as each observation is independent and identically distributed (meaning they come from the same possible distribution), then the sample-mean random variable will have the following properties:

- $E(\bar{X}) = \mu_{\bar{X}} = \frac{1}{n}\sum_{i=1}^{n} E(X_i) = \frac{1}{n}\left(E(X_1) + E(X_2) + E(X_3)\right) = \frac{1}{3}(3.5 + 3.5 + 3.5) = 3.5.$

- $V(\bar{X}) = \sigma_{\bar{X}}^2 = \frac{1}{n^2}\sum_{i=1}^{n} V(X_i) + \frac{1}{n}\sum_{i=1}^{n}\sum_{j=1,\,j\neq 1,}^{n} cov(X_i, X_j) = \frac{\sigma_X^2}{n} = \frac{2.917}{3} = 0.972.$

  (The covariance between any two observations equals zero if all observations are independent of each other.)

- *Standard deviation* $(\bar{X}) = \frac{\sigma_X}{\sqrt{n}}.$

So the expected value of a sample mean is equal to the population mean. And the variance of the sample mean is equal to the population variance of the random variable divided by the sample size.

Note that when we know the population variance, we use the term *standard deviation of the sample mean*. However, if we do not know the population variance, the estimator for the standard deviation of a population mean is called the *standard error of the population mean*. In regression analysis, we will use the term *standard error* for the standard deviation of the estimated relationships between variables (coefficient estimates) because we will not know the underlying population variance for those relationships.

Are the dice-roll observations independently and identically distributed? Yes, because the value of a die roll does not depend on the value of another die roll, and the distribution of possible values is the same. Sometimes, in regressions, this condition is violated. There could be siblings in a sample with correlated outcomes (due to correlated factors). Or, in an analysis of stock-market returns, companies from the same industry may have correlated observations. In these situations in a regression, there is a simple correction for this, which is described in Chapter 5.

Recall the nice properties that normal distributions have. If we can somehow get a normal distribution to work with, we can finish our work earlier and go have some other form of fun. With the sampling distribution of the mean, if the underlying population were normal, such as for IQ, then the sampling distribution of the mean would be automatically normal, regardless of the size of the samples taken. However, for other types of distributions that are not normal, the sampling distribution of the mean is *not necessarily* normal, but it will be with a large enough sample. This leads us to the Central Limit Theorem.

A.3.1 The Central Limit Theorem

The **Central Limit Theorem** says that the sampling distribution for a sample mean, if the sample size is sufficiently large, will be approximately normal. The term that is often used is that the distribution is **asymptotically normal**. So what is a sufficient sample size to get the sample mean being approximately normal? It depends on how approximately normal you want to be and how skewed the underlying distribution of the random variable is. For an even distribution such as dice rolls, getting to around a sample size of 30 would normally be adequate. For a more skewed distribution, it may take a bit more.

Figure A.4 demonstrates the Central Limit Theorem with some notional data on the distribution of years-of-schooling in the population. The first panel is the underlying distribution in the

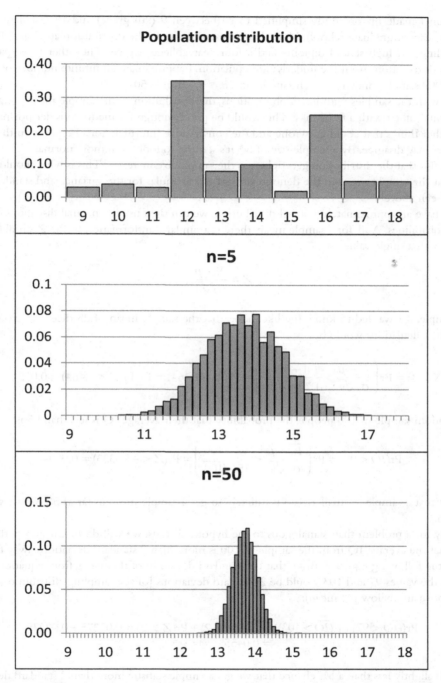

Figure A.4 Sampling distributions of the sample mean for various sample sizes (for the Central Limit Theorem)

population I made up, obviously simplified to be between 9 (9th grade) and 18 (a college degree plus two years of graduate school). Note that I created spikes in the distribution at 12 and 16 years-of-schooling – a high-school diploma and a four-year college degree. The other three panels are sampling distributions from the underlying population. I approximate an infinite number of samples with 10,000 samples drawn for each sample size: n = 5, and n = 50.

Even with the samples with just 5 observations, the distribution of the sample mean is starting to look normal, albeit with a few kinks. This would be good enough for me to consider normal (given all the other things that could go wrong and the conservative interpretations I espouse in this book), but others may disagree. By a sample size of 50, it's starting to look even more normal.

Note also that the distribution gets tighter as the sample size increases. This is what should happen given that the sample size is in the denominator of the formulas for the variance and standard deviation, as seen above.

If we have an approximately normal distribution, we can then use the normal distribution to calculate probabilities. And, for a sample mean, there is a similar transformation to the Z variable as was the case with a single value:

$$Z = \frac{\bar{X} - \mu}{\sigma/\sqrt{n}} \tag{A.15}$$

For example, if I wanted to know the likelihood that the sample mean of 25 dice rolls would be at least 4, the calculations would be:

$$\Pr(\bar{X} > 4) = \Pr\left(\frac{\bar{X} - \mu}{\sigma/\sqrt{n}} > \frac{4 - 3.5}{1.708/\sqrt{25}}\right) = \Pr(Z > 1.464) = 1 - \Pr(Z < 1.464) = 0.072 \tag{A.16}$$

For a random sample of 100 people, the probability that their average IQ is less than 95 is:

$$\Pr(\overline{IQ} < 95) = \Pr\left(\frac{\overline{IQ} - \mu}{\sigma/\sqrt{n}} < \frac{95 - 100}{15/\sqrt{100}}\right) = \Pr(Z < -3.3333) = 0.0004 \tag{A.17}$$

This says that a sample as small as 100 is unlikely to get a sample mean as far as 5 points away from the mean.

Finally, for a problem that is analogous to the hypothesis tests, we will do in Chapter 5, the probability that the average IQ from the sample of 100 is more than 2 standard deviations away from the mean is the following equation (note that the standard deviation of the mean, from equation (A.17), is 1.5, so the values 97 and 103 would be 2 standard deviations [of the sampling-distribution-of-the-mean] above and below the mean):

$$\Pr((\overline{IQ} < 97) \text{ or } (\overline{IQ} > 103)) = \Pr(Z < -2) + \Pr(Z > 2) = 0.02275 + 0.02275 \tag{A.18}$$
$$= 0.0455$$

Thus, it is slightly less than a 5% chance that we get a sample statistic more than 2 standard deviations away from the population mean.

A.4 Desired properties of estimators

When drawing samples of observations that are independent and identically distributed, then we can say that the estimators (namely, the sample mean, variance, and standard deviation) are *unbiased* and *consistent*. Here is what they mean:

- An estimator is **unbiased** if its expected value is the true value of the coefficient being estimated.
- An estimator is **consistent** if the estimator converges to the true estimate as the sample size increases.

This is what we will eventually desire in our regression models – unbiased and consistent estimators of the population parameters for how variables are related to each other. But this does not always occur. For the purpose of understanding these concepts better, I give two examples where one of these properties holds and the other does not.

A.4.1 Example of an estimator being unbiased (which is good) but inconsistent (bad)

From a sample of n independent observations of some variable X, $\{x_1, x_2, x_3, \ldots x_n\}$, say the true (and unknown) mean is μ. Consider the following estimator for the mean:

$$F(X) = x_1 \qquad\qquad (A.19)$$

That is, the estimator of the mean is just the first observation.

This is *unbiased* because $E(x_1) = \mu_x$.

However, it is *inconsistent* because as the sample increases (say, going from a sample of 5 to a sample of 1000), just taking the first observation will not get you any closer to the true mean of μ_x. In contrast, using the sample mean of 1000 observations versus 5 observations would get you closer to the true mean.

A.4.2 Example of an estimator being consistent (good) but biased (bad)

From a given sample, suppose that your estimate for the mean was:

$$F(X) = \frac{1}{n}\sum_{i=1}^{n} x_i + \frac{1}{n} \qquad\qquad (A.20)$$

The first component is the sample mean, which is an *unbiased* estimator for the true mean. Thus, adding the second component, $1/n$, causes the estimator to be biased. However, it is a *consistent estimator* because as n increases, then the second component will go to zero, and the estimator will converge to the true sample mean.

A.4.3 Applications to regression analysis

When evaluating whether a regression model is producing the correct estimates, researchers often use these terms – biased-vs.-unbiased and consistent-vs.-inconsistent. The more important property, for your sake, is "unbiasedness," as the most common pitfalls to regression analysis will center on whether the estimate is biased due to misspecification. In fact, almost anything that is biased will be inconsistent too. But "consistency" will also pop up a few times.

Notes

1 The expected value for a continuous random variable is: $E(X) = \int_{-\infty}^{\infty} x f(x)\, dx$, where f(x) is the height of the probability density function for a given value, x, of the random variable X.

2 The variance for a continuous random variable with a known probability distribution is: $V(X) = \int_{-\infty}^{\infty} (x - \mu_X)^2 f(x)\, dx$, with the standard deviation being the square root of that.

Glossary

Adjusted R-squared: A version of R^2 (see below) that is adjusted for the number of explanatory variables in the model.

Akaike Information Criterion (AIC) and corrected (AICc): Estimators of the relative quality of a regression model, in terms of being able to explain data.

Anchor-point bias: A situation in which someone observes an initial number or statistic and relies too heavily on that number/statistic when making decisions or drawing inferences on a population.

Anomaly detection: The process of finding outliers or abnormal observations, usually by analyzing residuals.

Attenuation bias: A bias in a coefficient estimate towards zero.

Attrition bias: A situation in which those who stay in a longitudinal sample are different from those who leave or stop responding to a survey.

Autocorrelation (serial correlation): A situation in which a variable is correlated with its lagged values.

Autocorrelation function (ACF): A function indicating how correlated different observations are based on how many periods away the observations are from each other.

Autoregression: A regression of a time-series variable on some of its lagged values.

Autoregressive-integrated-moving-average (ARIMA) model: A model that regresses a time-series variable on the lagged values of that variable and lagged values of the random error from its mean value, with "integrated" referring to having the variable differenced to avoid problems from potential nonstationarity.

Average forecast error: The average of the absolute values of the difference between the actual outcome and the forecasted/predicted outcome.

Average Treatment Effect (ATE): The average effect of the treatment in the population; or, if the treatment were assigned to everyone, how would a given outcome change, on average.

Average Treatment effect for the Treated (ATT): The average effect of the treatment on an outcome, for those subjects receiving the treatment (as opposed to the whole population).

Bad variation: Variation in the key-X variable due to factors that could be correlated with the dependent variable beyond through the key-X variable.

Bayesian critique of p-values: The p-value is not indicative of the probability that the regression result is wrong, but rather that probability also depends on the before-the-fact likelihood that there is a relationship.

Bayesian Information Criterion (BIC): One of a few estimators of the relative quality of a regression model, in terms of being able to explain data.

Bias: A property of an estimator in which it is off-target for some reason other than imprecision (i.e., some reason other than randomness in sampling or in how the outcome is determined).

Binary variable: See dummy variable.

Breusch–Godfrey test (also known as the Lagrange Multiplier Serial Correlation test): A test for autocorrelation, which is often used in the presence of second-or-higher-order autocorrelation or in models with lagged dependent variables.

Breusch–Pagan test: A test for heteroskedasticity.

Categorical variable: A variable whose values are based on some qualitative feature, and the order of the values has no meaning.

Causal effect: The effect that one variable has on another variable.

Causation: A situation in which one variable has an effect on another variable.

Censored variable: A variable whose value is only partially known, often due to there being an upper and/or lower bound for values.

Central Limit Theorem: The sampling distribution for a sample mean will be approximately normal if the sample size is sufficiently large.

Ceteris paribus: Holding other factors constant; Latin, meaning "all other things equal," and French, meaning "Don't put all of those damn things in my coffee at once so that I know what ingredients make it perfect."

Clustering: A correction to standard errors based on allowing certain observations to be correlated with each other in a model.

Coefficient estimate: An estimate for how much higher or lower a dependent variable (Y) is, on average, with one extra unit of an explanatory variable (X), after holding constant or adjusting for other factors.

Cognitive bias: A systematic error in thinking that causes someone to not be rational and objective in interpreting information, in decision-making, or in forming an opinion.

Cointegration: A situation in which two time-series variables that are nonstationary become stationary when considering a linear combination of the two variables.

Conditional probability: The probability of an event occurring, given that another event has occurred.

Confidence interval: A specified interval in which there is a certain probability that the true population coefficient lies within it.

Confirmation bias: The tendency to take evidence in favor of one's prior views as being confirmatory of his/her views and to discount any evidence contrary to one's prior views.

Consistent: A property of an estimator that involves the estimator converging towards the true population parameter as the sample size increases.

Constant term (intercept): In a regression, the expected value of the dependent variable (Y) when all of the explanatory variables equal zero.

Control variable: The set of variables included in the model to help identify the causal effects of the key-X variable(s).

Correlation: The extent to which one variable moves with another variable, standardized on a −1 to 1 scale.

Count variable: A variable that can only take on only non-negative integer values representing the count of some event occurring.

Covariance: A measure of how two random variables tend to move with each other; the value depends on the scales of the variables. More technically, the mean value of the product of diversions from the mean for two variables divided by the sample size minus one.

Cross-sectional data: A set of data with one observation per entity (e.g., person), typically at a particular point in time.

Cumulative distribution function (CDF): A function whose value is the probability that a variable will take on values less than or equal to a given argument of the function.

Degrees of freedom: The number of values that are free to estimate the parameters, which is the sample size minus the constraints (parameters to be estimated).

Dependent variable: (Also called the *outcome, response variable, regressand*, or Y *variable*), the variable that is being explained in a regression model by explanatory (X) variables.

Dichotomous variable: See dummy variable.

Dickey-Fuller test: A test for unit root, which indicates nonstationarity.

Difference-in-Difference (DD) model: A model in which a treatment and control group are compared from a period after the treatment to a period before the treatment.

Differential measurement error: A case in which the measurement error in a given X variable is related to the value of the outcome or any X variable.

Dummy (dichotomous/binary) variable: A variable that just takes on a value of 0 or 1 (typically to indicate whether a certain condition is true or not).

Dunning-Kruger effect: A cognitive bias in which, after gaining just a small amount of information on a topic, people believe they are much greater experts than they actually are. The more they learn on the topic, the more they realize how little they actually understand the topic.

Duration model: A model that examines the factors explaining the event of ending time in a given state of existence or how long it takes for an event to occur.

Durbin-Watson test: A test for autocorrelation that requires, among other things, the error terms to have a first-order lag structure, the model not having dependent variables, and the X variables being purely random with respect to the outcome.

Dynamic model: In a time-series model, an examination of how lagged values of the X and/or Y variables determine the current Y variable.

Ecological fallacy. A cognitive bias in which someone takes a general research finding and makes conclusions about a person or subject based on that finding (under the presumption that the general finding applies to all subjects).

Endogenous variable: A variable that is determined by factors within the model, with the variation in the variable being related to the dependent variable.

Error term: The difference between the actual value of the dependent variable and the expected value from the true regression model. (The actual observed error term is the *residual*.)

Exception fallacy: A cognitive bias in which a person discounts a research finding because he knows an exception to the finding.

Expected value: In general statistics, a predicted value of a variable based on the possible values and the probability of them occurring. In regression analysis, the predicted value of the dependent variable based on certain values of the explanatory variables.

Exogenous variable: A variable that derives its variation from outside the model and not anything related to the dependent variable.

Explained Sum of Squares (ExSS): Total variation in the dependent variable explained by the regression model.

Explanatory variable (or, X variable): A variable that is used to explain the dependent variable.

False negative: A test result that says the null hypothesis (e.g., the coefficient is zero) is not rejected even though the alternative hypothesis is true (and the null hypothesis is false).

False positive: A test result that says the null hypothesis (e.g., the coefficient is zero) is rejected even though the null hypothesis is true.

First-difference (FD) model: A model, with one observation per subject, in which observations are typically based on the change from one period to another period.

Fixed effects (FE) model: A model that separates subjects into certain groups, making it so subjects are only compared to other subjects in the same group.

Forecast interval: A confidence interval for the forecasted value of a particular observation.

Fuzzy regression discontinuities: A regression-discontinuities model in which the threshold value does not perfectly predict the likelihood that the subject receives the treatment.

Good variation: Variation in the key-X variable due to factors that are not correlated with the dependent variable, other than through the key-X variable.

Goodness-of-fit: The extent to which the observed data can be explained by the regression model.

Hausman test: A (not-so-great) test to determine whether to use a random- or fixed-effects model.

Hazard function: In a duration model, the probability that the subject changes to another state in a given period t.

Hazard model: See duration model.

Hazard ratio: In a duration model, the ratio of the risk of leaving a given state for two different values of an explanatory variable (e.g., when a treatment is applied vs. when the treatment is not applied).

Held-constant variation: Variation in the key-X variable that is "held constant" and does not go into determining how the variable is related to the dependent variable.

Heteroskedasticity: A violation of the condition for homoskedasticity, which leads to biased standard errors

Homoskedasticity: The variance of the error term, ε, is uncorrelated with the values of the explanatory variables, or $var(\varepsilon \mid X) = var(\varepsilon)$.

Hot hand (in basketball): A situation in which a player has a period (often within a single game) with a systematically higher probability of making shots (holding the difficulty of the shot constant) than the player normally would have.

Imprecision: The uncertainty in an estimator due to the randomness of sampling from a population or the randomness in how the outcome is determined.

Inaccuracy: See bias.

Incidental correlation: A situation in which two variables are correlated with each other by coincidence and not by any deterministic or systematic relationship.

Inconsistent: The estimator does not converge to the true coefficient as the sample size increases.

Independence: The characterization of two variables if the value of one variable has no bearing on the value of another variable.

Independent variable: (A bad) term to use for the explanatory (X) variable.

Interaction effect: The coefficient estimate on a variable that represents the product of two or more separate variables.

Intercept: See constant term.

Instrumental variable: A variable used in a Two-Stage-Least-Squares model that is assumed to affect a non-random key-explanatory variable but has no effect on the dependent variable other than by affecting the key-explanatory variable.

Invalidity: See bias.

Joint probability distribution: A set of probabilities for all possible joint values of two or more variables.

Key-explanatory (key-X) variable(s): (For regressions with the objective of estimating causal effects), the variable or set of variables for which you are trying to identify its causal effect on the outcome; (for regressions with other objectives), the more important variables used for determining predictors, forecasting the outcome, or adjusting outcomes.

Lagged scatterplot: A scatterplot of a time-series variable with its lagged value.

Lagged variable: A time-series variable that is a set number of periods before the current value for a given observation.

Linear-log model: A model with a dependent variable in original form and an explanatory (X) variable that is measured as a natural logarithm.

Linear probability model: A model that uses Ordinary Least Squares for a dichotomous dependent variable.

Logit model: A non-linear model used to explain a dependent variable that is dichotomous (a dummy variable).

Log-linear model: A model with a dependent variable measured as a natural logarithm and an explanatory (X) variable that is measured in its original form.

Log-log model: A model with both the dependent and explanatory variables measured as natural logarithms.

Longitudinal data: A data set in which subjects are tracked over several periods.

Marginal effect: How the outcome (or the estimated probability of the outcome for probability models) changes with a one-unit increase in the value of the X variable.

Mean square error: The average of the squares of the residuals from a regression.

Measurement error: A situation in which a variable (typically an explanatory variable) is measured with error or does not represent well the concept the variable is meant to capture.

Mechanism: A full reason why a change in a key-X variable would cause a change in the Y variable, with the pathways and at least one mediating factor.

Mediating factor: A factor through which the key-explanatory variable affects the dependent variable.

Model selection: The process of choosing the optimal set of control variables.

Moderating factor: A variable for which different values of it are associated with different values of a coefficient estimate on another variable.

Multicollinearity: A situation in which having explanatory variables that are highly correlated with each other causes the coefficient estimates to have inflated standard errors.

Multiple Regression Model: A regression model with more than one explanatory variable.

Natural experiment: A model in which the variation in the key-X variable is random due to natural processes or a policy or system that was designed to be random for other purposes.

Negative results: Results that are not statistically significant.

Newey-West standard errors: Standard errors that are imperfectly corrected for autocorrelation. (They are considered an efficient way to address autocorrelation, despite being imperfect.)

Non-differential measurement error: A situation in which any measurement error in a given X variable is independent of the values of any variable in the model.

Non-random explanatory variable: An explanatory variable that has *bad variation*, causing reverse causality, omitted-factors bias, or self-selection bias if not addressed.

Nonstationarity: A property of a time-series variable that has a mean or variance that changes over time.

Normal distribution: A continuous, bell-shaped probability distribution that has the same mean, median, and mode and has a standard percentage of observations falling within a given number of standard deviations from the mean.

Odds ratio: The odds of an outcome occurring given the exposure to some treatment (which could be one extra unit of an explanatory variable) relative to the baseline odds without exposure to that treatment (or without the additional exposure).

Omitted-factors bias: A situation in which the coefficient on one X variable is capturing the effects of another factor that is not fully held constant.

Operative variation: Variation in the key-X variable that is used to determine how the key-X variable is related to the dependent variable.

Ordinal variable: A categorical variable with the values having no meaning other than the order.

Ordinary Least Square: A method to estimate a regression model that determines the coefficient estimates that minimize the sum of the squared residuals.

Out-of-sample prediction: A predicted value for an observation that is left out of the sample, based on the coefficient estimates of a regression model with a given sample.

p-hacking: A situation in which researchers change the set of control variables, the dependent variable, the characterization of the variables, the method, the sample requirements, the comparison group, or some other part of a model to generate a more interesting result, which usually involves a lower p-value, typically in attempts to get below key threshold p-values of 0.10, 0.05, and 0.01.

p-value: The likelihood that, if the null hypothesis were true, random processes (i.e., randomness from sampling or from how the outcome is determined) would generate a statistic as far from the null hypothesis value as it is.

Panel data: A set of data that follows multiple subjects over time.

Parameter: A number that describes a population, such as a mean.

Partial autocorrelation function (PACF): The same as the autocorrelation function, but it factors out other factors.

Partial effect: (In this book), an estimated effect that is missing part of the full effect of a key-explanatory variable on a dependent variable due to having mediating factors or other outcomes as control variables in a model.

Perfect multicollinearity: A situation in which one X variable is an exact linear transformation of another X variable or set of X variables.

Power: (Generally) the ability of a model to detect a significant relationship if one exists; (technically) the probability that a model would reject a null hypothesis if it were false, given a coefficient estimate of a certain size.

Practical significance: The coefficient estimate has a value that would suggest a meaningful relationship between the X and Y variable.

Predicted value: What we would expect the value of the dependent variable would be, given the coefficient estimates from the regression and a given set of values of the explanatory variables.

Prior probability: (In regression analysis), a subjective probability that there is a relationship between two variables, before any formal test for a relationship.

Probability density function (PDF): A function of a random variable that indicates the relative likelihood of the variable taking on certain values.

Probit model: A non-linear model used to explain a dependent variable that is a dummy variable.

Publication bias: A bias towards a higher proportion of studies with statistically-significant primary results stemming, theoretically, from journals being more likely to publish significant results and researchers being more likely to try to publish research with significant results.

Quadratic model: A regression model that has both an X variable and its square as explanatory variables.

Quasi-experiment: A model that does not have random assignment in the key-X variable, but rather has a research design that makes each observation (some with and some without the treatment) be compared to other observations that are as similar as possible.

R-squared (R^2): The proportion of the variation in the dependent variable that is explained by the X variable(s).

Random-effects model: An alternative to fixed-effects models that requires that the variation in effects of the subjects (such as an instructor effect) is random with respect to the other explanatory variables.

Random explanatory variable: A variable that is random with respect to the dependent variable (having only *good variation*).

Random variable: A variable that quantifies the product of a random or uncertain process.

Random walk: The property of a time-series variable in which the value of the variable equals the prior value plus a random error term and perhaps a drift or trend.

Reference group: in characterizing a categorization, this is the group that does not have a dummy variable in the model so that any coefficient estimates are considered in reference to this group.

Regression model: An equation that represents how a set of factors explains an outcome and how the outcome moves with each factor (not necessarily causally), after holding constant or adjusting for other factors.

Regression discontinuity model: A regression method that uses a threshold value of some variable (Z) that determines whether someone receives a treatment and, essentially, compares the outcomes for people right above and below the threshold to estimate the causal effect of the treatment.

Regression–weighted estimator: A new estimator, for models with fixed effects or with dummy variables categorizing the sample into groups, that weights observations within a group by the inverse of the conditional variance of the key-X variable.

Rejection region: The part(s) of the sampling distribution for an estimator that indicates that a null hypothesis should be rejected.

Residual: The difference between the actual dependent variable (Y) value and the predicted Y value based on the regression equation; this is the predicted error term.

Residual Sum of Squares (RSS): The total variation in the dependent variable that remains unexplained by the regression model.

Reverse causality: A situation in which the dependent variable (Y) affects an explanatory variable (X).

Robust standard errors: Standard errors that are corrected for any bias from heteroskedasticity.

Root mean square error (RMSE): The square root of the mean squared error; also equal to the standard error of the regression.

Sample-selection bias: A situation in which the sample is non-random due to subjects (observations) being selected for the sample based on some factor related to the outcome.

Sampling distribution: A probability distribution for a statistic based on an ample number of samples drawn from a population.

Sampling error: A deviation of a sample statistic from a true population parameter just due to the sample being non-representative of the population; this can occur from random sampling from a population due to natural variation.

Self-selection bias: (Based on my definition), a situation in which the subject chooses the value of an explanatory (X) variable based on the perceived effects of the X variable on the outcome.

Serial correlation: See autocorrelation.

Significance level: For a hypothesis test, the probability that randomness in sampling or in how the outcome is determined would cause a true null hypothesis to be rejected (a Type I error, or false positive).

Simple Regression Model: A regression model with just one explanatory variable; also called a bivariate regression model).

Sources of variation (in the key-X or treatment variable): The reasons why the key-X variable has high values for some observations and low values for other observations, or why some receive the treatment and others do not.

Spline function: A regression that allows for different coefficient (slope) estimates at different values of the explanatory variable.

Spurious correlation: A situation in which two variables were correlated with each other, at least in part due to having a common factor.

Standard error (of a coefficient estimate): The standard deviation of a sampling distribution for the coefficient estimate.

Standard error of the forecast: The standard deviation of the forecasted value of an observation.

Standard normal distribution: A normal distribution with a mean of zero and a standard deviation of one. Each unit of the distribution represents one standard deviation.

Standardized effect: Based on the coefficient estimate on an X variable, how many standard deviations higher or lower the Y variable tend to be with a one-standard-deviation increase in the X variable.

Stationarity: The property of a time-series variable that the variable has a constant mean, variance, and covariance with its lagged value over time.

Statistic: A number describing a sample from the population.

Statistical bias: See bias.

Statistical significance: A status for a coefficient estimate (or a set of coefficient estimates) attained when it is far enough from the null hypothesis value that makes it unlikely (i.e., below a given significance level) to have occurred by chance.

Subject: A person or entity that is being examined in a statistical analysis.

Survival function: A function representing the probability that a subject survives in a given state for t periods.

Survival model: See duration model.

t-statistic: In regression analysis, the coefficient estimate divided by the standard error.

Time-series data: A set of data that follows one entity/subject (e.g., a country) over time.

Total Sum of Squares: The total variation in the dependent variable, measured as the sum (across the observations) of the squared deviations from the mean.

Treatment: The catalyzing factor for which one aims to estimate the causal effects of the dependent variable. This is typically the key-explanatory variable. It can be a dichotomous variable for yes/no on having received the treatment, or it can be a variable measuring different levels of the treatment.

Trend: A component of a time-series variable or a panel model that shows a general movement over time.

Two-stage least squares: A regression method that involves a first stage of predicting a key-explanatory variable that is likely non-random and a second stage of regressing the dependent variable on the predicted value of the non-random key-explanatory variable. This method requires an instrumental variable for the first stage.

Type I error (false positive): The null hypothesis is true, but it is rejected by the hypothesis test.

Type II error (false negative): The null hypothesis is false, but the hypothesis test fails to reject the null hypothesis

Unit of observation: What an observation represents in a regression model.

Unit root: (See random walk.) The property of a time-series variable in which the value of the variable equals the prior value plus a random error term and perhaps a drift or trend.

Unobserved heterogeneity: See omitted-factors bias.

Vector Autoregression Model (VAR): Multiple time-series regressions that include the lagged values of each variable in the model and allow the error terms of each regression to be correlated with each other.

Weighted Least Squares: A regression model in which different observations have different weights (i.e., importance/contribution) in the model.

X variable: See **explanatory variable**.

Index

Note: **Bold** page numbers refer to tables and *italic* page numbers refer to figures.

Printed in the United States
by Baker & Taylor Publisher Services